NEW FACES
in a **CHANGING**
AMERICA

NEW FACES
in a **CHANGING**
AMERICA
Multiracial Identity in the 21st Century

Loretta I. Winters
California State University, Northridge

Herman L. DeBose
California State University, Northridge

SAGE Publications
International Educational and Professional Publisher
Thousand Oaks ▪ London ▪ New Delhi

For information:

Sage Publications, Inc.
2455 Teller Road
Thousand Oaks, California 91320
E-mail: order@sagepub.com

Sage Publications Ltd.
6 Bonhill Street
London EC2A 4PU
United Kingdom

Sage Publications India Pvt. Ltd.
B-42 Panchsheel Enclave
Post Box 4109
New Delhi 110 017 India

Printed in the United States of America

Library of Congress Cataloging-in-Publication Data

New faces in a changing America: Multiracial identity in the 21st century / edited by
Loretta I. Winters and Herman L. DeBose.
    p. cm.
Includes bibliographical references and index.
ISBN 0-7619-2300-4 (Paper)
  1. Racially mixed people—Race identity—United States. 2. Racially mixed people—
United States—Social conditions. 3. United States—Race relations. 4. United States—Ethnic
relations. 5. United States—Social conditions—1980- I. Winters, Loretta I. II. DeBose, Herman L.
E184.A1 N379 2003
305.8′04073—dc21

2002014396

This book is printed on acid-free paper.

02 03 04 05 10 9 8 7 6 5 4 3 2 1

Acquisitions Editor:	James Brace-Thompson
Editorial Assistant:	Karen Ehrmann
Typesetter:	C&M Digitals (P) Ltd
Indexer:	Teri Greenberg
Cover Designer:	Michelle Lee

Contents

Part III Racial/Ethnic Groups in America and Beyond 125

Part IV Race, Gender, And Hierarchy 287

Part V Special Topics 333

Acknowledgments

We give a special thanks to William Flores, our former dean of the School of Social and Behavioral Sciences, California State University, Northridge (CSUN), who encouraged us to take on this project. It was through his suggestion and support that this book got off the ground and became a reality. The Sociology Department at CSUN provided travel resources to present materials and to attend different conferences to find other individuals interested in this topic, several of whom are contributors to the book. We express our gratitude to all contributing authors who had enough faith and trust in us to be willing to participate in this project. Thank you to our Sage editor, Jim Brace Thompson; his assistant, Karen Ehrmann; our production editor, Denise Santoyo; and our copyeditors, Linda Gray and Marzie McCoy, for all of their hard work. A special thanks goes to all those multiracial people who were willing to share information about their personal and family situations.

On a more personal note, Herman dedicates this book to and gives special thanks to his family, especially his wife, Maureen, and their four multiracial children, Renee Aketch, Monique Atieno, Genevieve Achieng, and Armand Lusiola, for their unselfish support and tremendous encouragement to complete this project. He also gives a special thanks to his parents, Mr. Theodore DeBose and Mrs. Lauretta Spain DeBose, who did not live long enough to see this project completed, and his brother, Theodore A. DeBose, who always encouraged and supported him in all his endeavors and when he did things differently.

Loretta dedicates this book to her rainbow children, Leah and Megan, and her rainbow grandchildren, Jayah, Dommonic, and Dylan, and those rainbow grandchildren and great grandchildren not yet born and ask that they all be the canaries that sing unfettered in an increasingly nonracist, non-race-centered society. She also dedicates this book to her husband, Daniel, whose support has been invaluable.

Introduction

HERMAN L. DEBOSE

"Who are you, what are you, where are you from, no, where are you really from, where are your parents from, are your grandparents American? Are you from here, what's your background, what's your nationality, where do you live? Are you black, are you white, do you speak Spanish? Are you really white, are you really black? Are you Puerto Rican, are you half and half, are you biracial, multiracial, interracial, transracial, racially unknown, race neutral, colorless, color-blind, down with the rat race or the human race? Who are you? Where are you coming from? Who are your people?"

— Jones (1994, pp. 53-66)

These questions are asked of the ever-increasing multiracial population in American society. This book is written to provide information about the increasing number of multiracial people in the United States and issues that confront them and America. The U.S. Census Bureau also recognized the increasing numbers of this population, resulting in a change on the 2000 Census form. This change allowed multiracial people to identify themselves as they see themselves through the creation of a new racial category: "two or more races." The new category will officially be required for all federal statistical forms starting in 2003. The term two or more races, according to the U.S. Census Bureau, refers to people who choose more than one of the six race categories (white, black or African American, American Indian and Alaska Native, Asian, Native Hawaiian and other, and some other race). The data gathered by the U.S. Census Bureau from Census 2000 present one of the first clear pictures (self-identifying) of this population in America.

The 2000 Census reported that the total population of the United States was 281,421,906, with 6,826,228, or 2.4 %, identifying as being of two or more races (Jones & Smith, 2001). In a Census 2000 brief (2001), "The Two or More Races Population: 2000" by Jones and Smith, several key facts were presented regarding individuals who checked the new category. The racial groups that reported the highest percentages of more than one race were the American Indian and Alaskan Native and the Native Hawaiian and other Pacific Islander populations. Whites and blacks had the lowest percentages of people reporting more than one race.

Forty percent of this population lived in the West, 27% in the South, 18% in the Northeast, and 15% in the Midwest. California, New York, Texas, Florida, Hawai'i, Illinois, New Jersey, Washington, Michigan, and Ohio were the primary residences of two thirds of this population. Alabama, Maine, Mississippi, South Carolina, and West Virginia represented less than 1% of this population. New York, Los Angeles, Chicago, Houston, and Philadelphia contained the largest numbers of this population.

The number of multiracial people, whose biological parents are from different racial groups, is increasing at a rapid rate, and this is changing the face and attitudes toward race in America. The number of multiracial people has increased as a result of the rise in interracial relationships and marriages. According to the U.S. Census Bureau, there were 149,000 interracial marriages in 1960 compared with 964,000 in 1990 and 1,264,000 in 1997.

No exact number of multiracial children in America has been recorded; however, the U.S. Census Bureau maintains statistics on children who have one or both parents of a different race, including children who are adopted. There were fewer than 500,000 children in this category in 1960 compared with 1,937,496 in 1990 according to the U.S. Census Bureau. In the United States, children's racial identity is significant and determines American societal benefits' distribution and people's response individually, culturally, socially, and collectively. How multiracial people identify themselves may have major consequences on their positions in their families, communities, and society. The number of multiracial people is growing because these individuals are presented with the opportunity to self-identify. With this growth comes a new voice in the political, social, and economic arenas and challenges to preconceived notions of racial identity.

This book addresses the issues that the multiracial population has and will encounter as their numbers grow. Additionally, it is an attempt to analyze the past, present, and future issues relating to this growing population. The book includes an examination of some of the most recent research and political activities in the area of multiraciality. It embodies the latest trends, placing them in historical context and discussing their impact on the future. The book is comprehensive in that it includes a discussion of identified prominent racial/ethnic groups in the United States and provides a different picture of multiraciality depending on minority group membership. It addresses issues in the United States, including the special case of Hawai'i as well as some other locations around the world.

The book is written primarily for an undergraduate college course but may be used as a supplement text for graduate courses. It is written for classes on multiracial identity issues and may be used as a reference for professionals who serves a large multiracial population (e.g., school personnel, therapists, human resource specialists, government agents). As the American population changes and becomes more diverse in organizations, corporations, and educational institutions, a book of this nature will provide the foundation to educate and train those who come into contact with this growing population.

Since the notion of multiraciality has come to the forefront, many stereotypes and misunderstandings of multiracial people have surfaced. The current literature does not provide a clear picture of the issues and desires of multiracial people. This book intends to fill a portion of that gap. It consists of five sections with a total of 18 chapters, a glossary of terms, and an appendix.

In Part I, Race as a Social Construction, two dynamic chapters address the issue of whether race is a social or biological construct. This question continues to be raised as American society faces a growing multiracial population, which is forcing society to address the issue of race differently. These individuals always been a part of the American mosaic but have never truly been given the opportunity to self-identify. Today a significant cohort of this population with political, social, and economic clout is willing and able to raise the issue of race as it pertains to them. Two authors, Maria P. P. Root and Mary Thierry Texeira, present different points of view on the discussion of race. Their arguments set forth the tone for the overall discussion of the remaining chapters in the book.

In Chapter 1, "Five Mixed-Race Identities: From Relic to Revolution," Maria P. P. Root focuses on the concept of race used as a social construct and its economic, political, and social implications. She introduces the reader to additional material for the discussion of multiracial identity, which suggests "that race as we know it may become a relic." Race, aided by modern science through The Human Genome Project, will be seen as a social rather than a biological construct. Also, this current multiracial population is not the product of rape or slavery but of meaningful relationships. These and many other factors have led this group to seek their identity as multiracial and challenge the idea of race as a biological construct. Root introduces the reader to a new model of identity and clearly describes the derivation of five identities for mixed-race people.

Chapter 2 by Mary Texeira, "The New Multiracialism: An Affirmation of or an End to Race as We Know It?" focuses on race as a social construct and the possibility of discarding all racial categories. Texeira suggests that we are all descendents of "strangers from different shores" who occupy the same space and even intermarry; and we must respect each other "or perish." She discusses and illustrates the issues of race, racism, and the movement for a multiracial classification and how race is defined by those in power. The author interprets the multiracial classification as a divisive tool in the fight to end racism and discrimination against those who are oppressed, especially African Americans. Texeira argues that the creation of this new classification promotes and perpetuates white supremacy and maintains the white power structure. She illustrates the divisiveness that this classification may bring based on issues within her own family as it deals with the issues of color and race.

Part II, The Multiracial Movement, contains five chapters that collectively present a history of the presence of multiracial people and their political activities, including the emergence of the multiracial movement, multiracial organizations, and activities that led to the current categorization of racial categories on the census. Chapter 3 by Ann Morning, "New Faces, Old Faces: Counting the Multiracial Population Past and Present," delivers a historical and current population count of the number of multiracial people in America and their characteristics. In anecdotes about the earliest official mulattoes' record, history reminds us that multiracial attitudes were embedded in complex webs of social, political, economic, and cultural premises and objectives. The true multiracial population dimensions have long presented challenges to researchers because of a lack of official statistics and definitions. Who can be considered multiracial? Biracial? The government has at times recorded mulatto and quadroon populations and kept records of blood quanta in the American Indian population. Although the introduction of the multiracial category on the 2000 Census is often depicted as an entirely new innovation, multiracial response categories were a common, although sporadic, feature on 19th-century censuses. Morning describes historical practices for counting the mixed-race population and links them with the racial ideologies that motivated and shaped them. Although the focus is on national census enumeration, past scientific efforts to enumerate multiracial populations through estimates are linked to the same racial preconceptions of their contemporary census officials. Historical and contemporary socioeconomic characteristics of the multiracial population are compared, suggesting that past weighted factors are still discernible today. The chapter places contemporary developments in multiracial reporting in a sociohistorical perspective, suggesting that white social, economic, and political interests are still relevant to the evolution of the national census.

In Chapter 4, "Multiracial Identity: From Personal Problem to Public Issue," Kimberly McClain DaCosta focuses on the emergence of the multiracial movement and explores the social conditions that led to the movement as well as the social changes activists have sought and accomplished. To further her research, DaCosta asks the question, "What changed to make the public claiming of multiracial identity very much the question in the 1990s?" She then proceeds to tackle two misleading tendencies: "Some activists and scholars treat multiracials as though they are a group constituted as such: conscious of itself, unified, but one that has not received social recognition. . . . The other tendency treats multiracials as though they are not a group at all—a statistical population, completely individualized and unaware of itself—and thus not worthy of social classification." She uses these issues to provide information on how the establishment of a multiracial category on the U.S. Census became reality. The chapter concludes by summarizing the steps that brought about the multiracial movement.

In Chapter 5, "From Civil Rights to the Multiracial Movement," Kim M. Williams argues that the multiracial movement would not have occurred had it not been for the civil rights movement. Williams develops a line of reasoning showing that the overall outcomes of the civil rights movement were imprinted on the multiracial movement in several areas. Additionally, she sets out to make three basic points. "Racial categorization is not only imposed . . . by the state [but] it is also appropriated from" groups that benefit from categorization of racial groups. Second, trends over the past 30 to 40 years have challenged the definition of race as established by the 1977 Office of Management and Budget (OMB) Directive 15. Third, Williams discusses why multiraciality became a social movement at this particular time and its relationship to other social movements during the last 40 years of American society.

Chapter 6 by Rainier Spencer, "Census 2000: Assessments in Significance," focuses on the discussions and debates regarding the introduction of the "two or more race" category on the 2000 Census by OMB Directive 15. Four primary stakeholders, the federal government, multiracial activists, African American organizations, and the American political right, are identified and their concerns regarding the introduction of this new category presented. The stakeholders' positions on racism and discrimination pertaining to this new category are also addressed. Arguments that multiracial movement political manipulation is being used to weaken federal government methods to monitor racial discrimination are presented. Spencer concludes that, regardless of the many myths that may surface concerning Census 2000, one can be sure that race, racism, and the need to be ever more vigilant concerning racial discrimination "have not changed one bit in the United States."

Chapter 7 by Nancy G. Brown and Ramona E. Douglass, "The Evolution of Multiracial Organizations: Where We Have Been and Where We Are Going," discusses the early years of multiracial organizing. The authors describe the formation and development of grass roots' organizations and their role in the 2000 Census "mixed-race people" category. It also highlights the experiences of six local/national multiracial organizations: Interracial/ Intercultural Pride (San Francisco, CA); Biracial Family Network (Chicago IL); Interracial Family Circle (Washington, D.C.); Multiracial Americans of Southern California (Los Angeles, CA); Project Race (Roswell, GA); and The Association of MultiEthnic Americans (San Francisco, CA). Each president of these organizations was surveyed regarding their views on the mission of their organizations, maintaining a multicultural organization, and their members' reaction to the "two or more" category on government forms. The results of the survey are discussed and analyzed. In addition, Brown and Douglass present other areas that have had an impact on multiracial organizations such as collaboration and conflict, crossroads in the movement, a house divided on nomenclature, new faces and emerging organizations, and building viable nonprofits.

Part III, Racial/ Ethnic Groups in America and Beyond, examines minority communities in the United States and how they respond to members who are of more than one race. It also explores the special case of Hawai'i and then examines multiracialism in a global perspective. In Chapter 8, "The Dilemma of Biracial People of African American Descent," Herman L. DeBose and Loretta I. Winters discuss the association between racial identity selection and the history of the relationship between African Americans and European Americans in the United States. Additionally, the history of African Americans, from slavery to affirmative action, is presented along with its impact on multiracial people of African descent. The historical analysis reveals that conflict continues to exist for these two groups. Additionally, a theoretical discussion of assimilation is presented that illustrates some of the dilemmas African Americans face that impact their offspring. Biracial people face identity issues such as "Where do I fit, which parent do I identify with, and what behavior is appropriate for me?" The authors discuss the results of a research project on identity of biracial people in terms of self-proclaimed identity, feeling of belonging, sense of value, and manner of living. DeBose and Winters argue that biracial people of African American and European American descent are different from biracial people of African American and non-European American descent in the way they identify, behave, and believe. This difference reflects the hierarchical arrangements that still exist between whites and people of color in the United States.

Chapter 9 by Teresa Williams-León, "Check All That Apply: Trends and Prospectives Among Asian-Descent Multiracials," focuses on multiracial identity among Asian Americans. Issues and writings of race and mixed race have been framed within black/white paradigms, although Asian Americans are perhaps the fastest outmarrying group of color since the post-1967 biracial baby boom era. The chapter examines the changing face of Asian America as intermarriage rates impact racial and ethnic dynamics of Asian America. Because the "one-drop rule" imposes definitions of blackness on multiracial African Americans, the authors ask, "Who is Asian American?"

In Chapter 10, "Beyond *Mestizaje*: The Future of Race in America," Gregory Velazco y Trianosky presents the Latino/a notion of *mestizaje,* or mixed race, as a model for the future of race in the United States. It presents the central racial reality of Latino life: Everyone is *mestizo, or mixed,* not the rigid *black-and-white* conception that predominates the United States. The chapter argues that social and political race constructions risk being lost through immigrant group socialization into the American bipolar black/white ideology and absorption into the white population. The author maintains that strategies must be found to maintain a critical cultural distance that may ultimately give us the vision required to dismantle the barriers of race that separate Americans.

Karren Baird-Olson in Chapter 11—"Colonization, Cultural Imperialism, and the Social Construction of American Indian Mixed-Blood Identity"— focuses on the mixed-race experience of American Indians She addresses the historical as well as contemporary political, economic, and cultural factors that have played a role in Indian identity categorization and the implications of determination for future individual well-being and Indian nation survival. Various schemata used to classify Indian identification and the social construction of race are discussed. The African American one-drop rule versus phenotypical appearance is compared and contrasted with American Indian federal blood quantum requirements. A call is made to replace the colonizized definition of American Indian with traditionally rooted criteria of group membership. The author concludes that European American internal colonization life has created the irrationality of the social construction of race in Indian categorization.

Chapter 12 by Laura Desfor Edles, "'Race,' 'Ethnicity,' and 'Culture' in Hawai'i: The Myth of the 'Model Minority' State," focuses on the unique issues that face Hawai'i concerning the topic of multiracial identity. Hawai'i's geographic isolation, external historical instructions, and its speed and quantity of change have had a profound effect on the development of race and ethnic identity on the island. The consequences of these issues are discussed in detail. High rates of intergroup contact and marriage make Hawai'i a mythical multiracial paradise, a model minority state. Significant historical, theoretical, and empirical problems with this myth are presented. Hawai'i's violent colonial history, overindividualization of race, and impact of interracial marriage are used to illustrate this myth. The chapter makes the argument for the role of culture in the complex process of racialization and identity formation.

G. Reginald Daniel in Chapter 13, "Multiracial Identity in Global Perspective: The United States, Brazil, and South Africa," outlines the similarities and differences in the origins, statuses, identities, and experiences of various global multiracial populations as a result of encounters between Europeans and non-Europeans beginning with the 15th century. Some of the salient characteristics that potentially differentiate and distinguish multiracial populations are displayed based on seven basic racial rules. The chapter provides a framework for understanding racial order in the United States, where racial categories and boundaries have historically been constructed to view racial groups and identities as mutually exclusive and as monoracial categories of experience. The rule of hypodescent, the one-drop rule, and its historical origins and relation to racial categories and identities are discussed. The recent movement in the United States toward recognizing a multiracial identity has been the impetus for this comparative historical examination of multiracial populations in a global perspective to help elucidate the extent to which multiracial populations differ in terms of the seven basic rules.

Part IV, Race, Gender, and Hierarchy, presents three chapters examining how other social characteristics interact with multiracialism, including race, in a narrow sense: sex and gender. In Chapter 14, "Does Multiraciality Lighten? Me-Too Ethnicity and the Whiteness Trap," Paul Spickard discusses the concept of "Whiteness" in the context of hierarchy or class privilege and it implications for those who are multiracial. Spickard discusses the increase in the number of books, university courses, and writings regarding multiraciality and Whiteness. He raises the issue that both may be focusing on Whiteness and possibly forgetting about the injustices to communities of color. Critics of multiracial advocacy state individuals are encouraged to flee identification with communities of color and seek a middle social position, lightened by recognition of their ancestral multiplicity. Critics of Whiteness state that white people are placed at the center, displacing people of color, resulting in "me-too" ethnic absorption. Spickard explores the extent of each of these criticisms and the connections between them. He also examines the lives of several prominent Americans who acknowledged their multiracial ancestry, including Alice Dunbar-Nelson, Mary Church Terrell, W. E. B. Du Bois, Wallace D. Fard, Jean Toomer, Walter White, Malcolm X, and Adam Clayton Powell, Jr., among others. They describe their lives and the impact of their multiracial understanding on their connections with the communities of color with which they are identified. The author concludes that the criticisms have theoretical validity in the multiracial and Whiteness studies movements. However, recognition of multiraciality does not mean that multiracial people fall into the Whiteness trap.

Caroline A. Streeter in Chapter 15, "The Hazards of Visibility: 'Biracial Women,' Media Images, and Narratives of Identity," focuses on biracial women through writings on identity and popular cultural imagery in selected examples from print advertisement and television. The first portion of the chapter explores texts that address a dominant tendency among biracial women who write to identify as women of color rather than as mixed race or biracial. Streeter argues that this phenomenon reflects the way that race has been conceived in North America as well as how identity is deployed as a strategic political tool. However, those identifying as biracial or multiracial rather than locating one's identity in an ethnic minority group have been characterized as assimilationists. The different strategies of identification deployed by biracial women in their writing and formation of communities are considered. In addition, the author considers popular cultural representations of biracial women in selected examples from print advertising and television. Contrasting messages of multiculturalism and miscegenation point to the tension invoked by permeable boundaries. Destabilization of the racial concept in recent decades has led to renewed fascination with the concept of borders and boundaries. Rejection of the melting pot notion, or cultural assimilation, by many academics has been replaced by the "morphed" American identity notion, which argues that the parameters of national, racial, ethnic, gender, and sexual identity are permeable and ever shifting. In conclusion, the chapter examines identity and representation in context through analysis of the publication, *Mavin,* a quarterly publication celebrating the mixed-race experience.

Darby Li Po Price's Chapter 16, "Masculine Multiracial Comedians," identifies the issues related to multiracial men as depicted in comedy. A theoretical overview of masculinity, mixed race, and ethnic comedy is provided. The author then examines how expressions of masculinity and racial multiplicity among comedians challenge dominant models of masculinity and mixed race. Price focuses on comic expression and subjectivity among comedy performers and writers of mixed Native American, African American, Chicano/Latino, Asian American, and Pacific Islander descent. Comic literature, film, television, performance, and stand-up from the 19th century to the present are examined using extensive ethnographic research methods. The author argues that meanings and cultural productions of mixed race are shaped by ethnic-specific identity politics that vary according to gender, race, ethnicity, and location.

Part V, Special Topics, composed of two final chapters, focuses on work in the area of multiracialism. Chapter 17, by Patricia O'Donnell Brummett and Loretta I. Winters—"Gang Affiliation and Self-Esteem: The Effects of a Mixed-Heritage Identity"—compares biracial and monoracial gang members and nongang members with the issue of self-esteem. The comparison assesses whether or not the effect of being multiracial (compared with monoracial) has an impact on the relationship between gang membership and self-esteem. Current discussion recognizes that juveniles engage in delinquent and gang behavior because they have low self-esteem and that gangs provide a sense of self-esteem and identity that cannot be obtained in legitimate ways. Race affects an individual's exposure to cultural norms and perception of fit into society and its subcultures. The authors explore the race role in mediating the relationship between gang membership and self-esteem. They conclude that biracial identity issues compound the typical monoracial identity issues encountered in adolescent years.

In Chapter 18, "Black/White Interracial Couples and the Beliefs That Help Them to Bridge the Racial Divide," Kristyan M. Kouri discusses the meanings that black/white couples assign to their marriages and families. The chapter uncovers the strategies mothers and fathers use to enable their children to develop an identity and to cope with racism. Overcoming social barriers that impede black/white interracial marriages are explored. Couples tend to develop an "everyone is equal" philosophy or to connect with people from different racial and ethnic backgrounds in integrated settings. Kouri concludes that couples use these same ideologies to help their children develop biracial identities and multiculturalism.

In the epilogue, "The Multiracial Movement: Harmony and Discord," Loretta I. Winters indicates that three models emerge from the material and literature presented by the contributing authors on the topic of multiracial identity. The models are: 1) Multiracial Movement (MM), 2) Counter Multiracial Movement (CMM), and 3) Ethnic Movement (EM). The MM primarily focuses on the individual level where multiracial people attempt to embrace all their backgrounds or ethnic heritage without any need for justification and in a comfortable manner. The CMM focuses on some members of minority communities believe that proliferating the current list of racial categories will only impede the dissolution of the harmful construct of race. The EM focuses on eliminating race in favor of ethnicity. Winters discusses all of these models and compares and contrasts them. She states that the three models may be seen "as paths to the demise of racialization in American society."

This book is the culmination of a significant amount of energy and work by all contributing authors. As the multiracial population continues to grow and influence change in American race discussion, additional knowledge and appropriate tools will be needed to address their issues. This book is an attempt to add to that needed body of knowledge regarding this increasing population of multiracial people.

REFERENCE

Jones, L. (1994). Is biracial enough? or, what's this about a multiracial category on the census?: A conversation. *Bulletproof diva: Tales of race, sex, and hair*. New York: Anchor.

Smith, A. S., & Jones, N. A. (2001, October). *I wanna be like Mike Tiger Woods! Exploratory analysis of race reporting for children in interracial households in Census 2000*. Paper presented at the Southern Demographic Association, Miami, FL.

U.S. Census Bureau. (2001). The two or more races population: 2000. *Census 2000 brief, November 2001*. Washington, DC: Author.

Part I

RACE AS A SOCIAL CONSTRUCTION

CHAPTER 1

Five Mixed-Race Identities

From Relic to Revolution

MARIA P. P. ROOT

The public use of a mixed-race identity parallels the growth of interracial unions and the children of these unions. In March 2001, the U.S. Bureau of the Census released race and ethnicity data showing that 2.4% of the population older than 18 years identified themselves as multiracial and, overwhelmingly, biracial (93%), but even more people younger than 18 years (4%) identified themselves as multiracial ("Poll," 2001). These figures were in line with census expectations. Demographers predict that by 2050 those identifying themselves as multiracial will account for 21% of the American population. Although there is a difference in the proportion of persons of Asian, Hispanic, African, and American Indian descent exercising their option to check more than one race in the 2000 census, 5% of those who checked the African American or black box, the political group

most opposed to this change in census accounting, also checked a second box ("Poll," 2001). Having been intimately involved in studying the trends in population demography, two former directors of the U.S. Bureau of the Census affirm that these changes are significant. Richie, director from 1994 to 1998, reflected "that this is the beginning of the end of the overwhelming role of race in our public life" (Kasindorf & El Nasser, 2001, p. 2A). Prewitt predicted that "as the classification system gets fuzzier and blurrier, we're going to have to recreate ourselves as a society without using a set of social policies which are based on race" (Kasindorf & El Nasser, 2001, p. 2A). Is it possible for race as we know it to become a relic?

The emerging public dialogue about mixed-race identity reflects more than a quarter century of psychological and demographic change since the Supreme Court repeal of

AUTHOR'S NOTE: This chapter was written in respectful and loving memory of Dr. Jan Robyn Weisman (April 29, 1959-January 31, 2001).

antimiscegenation laws in 1967. This provides a very different historical context for young persons coming of age in the next decade who will live with public acknowledgment of mixed race. They come of age when race is defined less by biology than by social construction. They come of age on the eve of completion of the human genome project declaring that there are no genes for race as a biological fact or construct. They come of age as beneficiaries of the civil rights movement and legislation to protect civil rights and legally end Jim Crow segregation through desegregation of educational settings and workplaces, voting rights acts, fair housing laws, and equal employment opportunity commissions. They come of age at a time when women have more rights and freedom to choose their partners than ever before. They come of age after the racial and ethnic pride movements have left a lasting swell of pride in heritage. They come of age when most first-generation mixed-race persons have not been a product of rape, war, or slavery and have a visible cohort of mixed-race peers and role models in the media. They come of age amid a cohort that has not sustained the trauma of racism to the same degree and frequency as their parents and grandparents.

Many foundational aspects that have supported the racial system as we know it have changed. Thus, the context into which people are born racially mixed and in which they establish personal versus public identities takes place in an ecological context that is multilayered. The opposition to different types of mixed-race identity may rest in all the ways this country has pretended that race mixing does not occur, is aberrant, or is not significant. Protests by some black civil rights organizations contend that the mixed-race option on census surveys as well as mixed-race consciousness will lead to a "dilution of membership, political clout and anti-discrimination enforcement efforts in employment, mortgage lending and other areas" (Kasindorf & El Nasser, 2001, p. 2A). Alongside these concerns are fears that the mixed-race consciousness will reinforce the divide between African Americans and the rest of America. I contend that with the trend toward race mixing, in 20 years, a significant number of Americans will have a relative or in-law who is of a different race, including African American. This firsthand experience of connection, even of love, challenges the stereotype that there is something inherent in racial or cultural differences that prevents meaningful interracial and cross-cultural connections. The dialogues about mixed-race identity reflecting pathology, self-hatred, and "passing" are relics of an era of history that is gone. Nevertheless, the identities and status of mixed-race persons continue to be used as pawns in race politics. Our voices have often been eliminated from direct representation as we have been infantilized, assumed to be ignorant and naive about race.

A multitude of factors converge at this time to transform race from caste to class. The permeability of boundaries when race is a class rather than caste marker cannot be underestimated. This is the source of fear, that a new class position or berth in the racial hierarchy will be created by mixed-race people. However, the emergence of mixed-race people across all the traditional different racialized groups, simultaneous with the decrease in daily trauma around race, changes the meaning and consequence of mixed-race identities. Although such an identity has always had a subversive framework (Daniel, 1992), these contemporary subversive declarations have shifted from a goal and consequence of creating a superior group of persons and elite type of "person of color" to a refusal to continue with racial rules as generations of us have learned. In her novel *Caucasia*, Senna (1998) illustrates these concepts in an African American father's theory about the role of mixed-race black/white persons to his mixed-race daughter:

On the chart, my father had handwritten our name, Birdie and Cole Lee, beside our birth dates. For Cole, 1964; for me, 1967. . . .

He explained to me his theory—that the mulatto in America functions as a canary in the coal mine. The canaries, he said, were used by coal miners to gauge how poisonous the air underground was. They would bring a canary in with them, and if it grew sick and died, they knew the air was bad and that eventually everyone else would be poisoned by the fumes. My father said that likewise, mulattos had historically been the gauge of how poisonous American race relations were. The fate of the mulatto in history and in literature, he said, will manifest the symptoms that will eventually infect the rest of the nation.

He pointed to the chart. "See, my guess is that you're the first generation of canaries to survive, a little injured, perhaps, but alive." (pp. 335-336)

We now have almost two full generations of racially mixed persons born since this fictional depiction. And history has marched on.

DECIPHERING THE AGENDAS FOR RACIAL LABELS

The historical context within which multiraced identities are declared must be attended to. Although more labels might be perceived to weaken the structural solidarity of a racially disenfranchised group, this outcome is yet to be seen. The U.S. Bureau of the Census ran field tests to determine where to place the race question and how to word it so as not to disenfranchise the traditional protected categories of racial minorities (U.S. Bureau of the Census telephonic briefing held February 16, 2001). The question regarding Hispanic origin was placed before the race question. Now it remains to be seen if indeed the results obtained in the field tests bear out in the actual decennial 2000 census.

However, whereas race is not a natural construct but a politically and economically motivated colonial one (Young, 1995), the process of categorization is natural. The issue is determining which dimensions become relevant for categorization and what purpose they serve. Ironically, because of our nation's brainwashing to notions of racial purity, many people have a hard time believing and understanding that someone can belong in several categories simultaneously. This is a cognitive task that we expect children in the early grades to have achieved; that is, an object can be both red and round. Artists learn to see that violet is the reflection of red and blue of various shades; they can see the blended color, but they can see the individual contributions of red and blue. Not only do we have a hard time doing this, but we have a hard time believing it can be done. At more of an extreme, some people refuse to try.

Certainly one of the social political advocacy groups, the Association for MultiEthnic Americans (AMEA), was very concerned when a conservative politician, Newt Gingrich, supported a single multiracial label advocated by Project Race. The concern was regarding the political agenda and how that label would be used rather than the accuracy of the label. Was this a move toward a colorblind policy that would undo the civil rights progress of the last quarter century? Or would this be a progressive move? Was this a visionary move that was beyond the dialogue that the American public was ready to participate in? Or was this a reflection of white naiveté about how race still operates in this country? We will not know the answers to these questions for at least a decade. Whereas the dialogue must change around race to include multiraced persons (i.e., persons born to parents who have had racial assignments to parents of different groups), it must occur within historical perspective. At this time, a single multiethnic or multiracial label cannot support the political tracking necessary to protect civil rights. Consequently, AMEA endorsed a more-than-one-race check-off format because it allowed for continued tracking of civil rights under the Office of Management and Budget Directive 15 from 1978 (Fernandez, 1995). Root (1996) suggested that a multiple check-off would allow the nation to continue to protect civil rights while reflecting a historical demographic change that will only increase. She also noted that rather than forcing people to identify themselves by hypodescent, which was created to protect whiteness, a multiple check-off forces the government's hand to discuss more openly race—past, present, and future—and not in the limited way that the Clinton task force on race tackled the subject without much attention to the very real issue of racial mixing and demographic complexity. The statisticians and decision makers still have the data available to apply hypodescent rules openly: That is, multiraced persons of African heritage can be collapsed back into the black/African American category, and persons of Asian descent can be collapsed back into the Asian American category. However, we also have the data to reflect on very real changes in race relations existing side by side with racial divides and hostilities. Some of these changes are driven by familiar patterns associated with increased intermarriage with each successive generation since immigration (Alba & Golden, 1986). For example, the census found that third-generation Asians and Latinos were marrying persons of different races more than 50% of the time ("Poll," 2001).

Of the 2.4% of people who checked more than one box on the census race question, 32.3% were of European ancestry, 15.9% were of white and American Indian/Alaska native ancestry, 12.7% were of white and Asian ancestry, and 11.5% were of white and black ancestry. Of persons indicating they were of Hispanic origin, a question placed before the race question in this census ("Poll," 2001), only 6.3% indicated that they were of two races. More telling about a different model of race already evident among Hispanics is that 42.2% said they were of some other race

(Kasindorf & El Nasser, 2001, p. 2A). This is no surprise to cultural interpreters of race from a Latin or Hispanic or multiracial perspective (e.g., Fernandez, 1992; Rodriguez, 1994).

FROM CASTE TO CLASS

Several obstacles emerge in discussing mixed race. First, it has been depicted as a movement, when in fact multiple voices are represented (e.g., Fernandez, 1995; Graham, 1995; Byrd, 2002). Second, dialogues on mixed race are no longer cast only in black and white; the proliferation of other racialized ethnic groups informs this discussion along with different histories. Third, the voice of mixed-race adults is often absent or dismissed in public debate.

Although these various groups of mixed-race voices may actually be savvy to the interplay of social forces opposing their "choice," public discussions about mixed race that do not include mixed-race persons are often unsophisticated because they adhere to inflexible models of identity, racial performance, and race relations and essentialized notions of race. That is, race is analyzed apart from gender, class, and sexuality. As Sanjek (1994) asserts, "Race, sex, and power remain the essential ingredients of the continuing 'American dilemma' of the United States. Race, sex, and power head the agenda of the country's social and political unfinished business" (p. 103). Discussion of the purpose of antimiscegenation laws to specifically protect whiteness is not always made clear. These laws existed not only between whites and blacks but between whites and every other racialized ethnic group that threatened white sovereignty and ownership of white women: Chinese, Japanese, Filipinos, Hindus, Mexicans, and Indians. In fact, in the internment of Japanese Americans, a significant number of mixed-race persons of Japanese descent were interned by these rules (Spickard, 1989).

Race, a construct in the service of colonial expansion and greed, necessarily had caste connotations across racial groups. Caste refers to the impermeability of boundaries. Removing the last antimiscegenation laws, repealing the last Jim Crow laws, and adding civil rights protections at the federal level promoted a transformation of race from caste to class. However, not all racial groups have achieved equal class status, but all groups show evidence of a transformation in process. Root (2001) suggests that the remnants of caste status remain most attached to people of observed or imagined African descent because we have not resolved our nation's racially traumatic past. White men continue to ignore the agency of white women in choosing to intermarry with black men. The caste remnant of status attached to blackness as it interacts with gender continues to explain why all groups' rates of intermarriage are higher than either African American men or women's rates of intermarriage (Zack, 1997). That African American men's rates of intermarriage departed from women's rates in the 1960s correlates with the repeal of antimiscegenation laws and the continued gender privilege of men to choose their wives and women hoping to be chosen.

Gender has largely been ignored as a significant piece of the dialogue on mixed race, except for the allegations that the mixed-race movement is somehow a white woman's movement. Gender, as with race, also has a class status, with privileges, having originally been justified based on biology and inherent in that morality. Unfortunately, gender and race analyses of social interaction tend to be mutually exclusive, obscuring a complex and very real dynamic (Collins, 1998; Hurtado, 1996; Zack, 1997). It seems important to examine how the juxtaposition of female gender, white race, and willingness to embrace blackness, but not shun whiteness, may be interpreted and misinterpreted. Heretofore, we have been taught that these social positions are mutually exclusive.

Why are men of any racial group not criticized as harshly as the women? Opponents from black civil rights groups have criticized white mothers. Why haven't they similarly criticized the black fathers? I do wonder, with evidence of the significant increase in African American women who are intermarrying (Root, 2001), what shape this dialogue and its attendant accusations will take. Similarly, the various Asian American communities and civil rights groups publicly and repeatedly castigated Asian women in the 1990s for intermarriage with white men. However, as the rates of intermarriage for Asian American men increase, will they be criticized as sharply? Why have white men not been criticized for intermarriage?

Root (2001) suggests that when the reproduction of race is a commodity, families protest intermarriage and will subsequently protest mixed-race identities. The production of children forever changes the racial authenticity of white families in communities or reference groups to whom race matters this much. Clinging to a mixed-race identity in racialized ethnic groups, particularly if the other race is European derived, challenges the foundation on which perceived solidarity was constructed. In contrast to a prior period of history, white parents, mothers and fathers, are overtly claiming their mixed-race children. The ability of women, particularly white women, to stand independently from their families does seem to make a difference.

Collins (1998) discusses the juxtaposition of gender/race/nation to understand the layers of power as they add to the dialogue in defining race. The United States, despite origins otherwise, has historically viewed itself as a white nation governed by men. When white men marry women of color, the opposition is not as great in the white community. The woman, because of both her gendered status and color status and usually country of origin status, is triply secondary in status and thus a less visible threat to the identity of the nation through the progeny; the progeny carry a European origin named. If white women are marrying nonwhite men, rules of patriarchy largely founded in the intersection of heterosexuality, race, and gender castigate these women for forsaking "their own" (Ferber, 1998; Young, 1995). The trends of intermarriage between blacks and whites follow rules of supply and demand. In essence, when a marriage cohort has a disproportionate number of one gender, some advantages are obtained for the sex in shorter supply. However, Guttentag and Secord (1983) observed the gender double standard that operates also in the public criticism noted previously. Thus, when men are in short supply, they can stay single longer, have multiple partners, and have their pick of partners, including going outside of the group. In contrast, when women are in short supply, they can have their pick of partners, but their ability to go outside the group to choose a partner or have multiple partners has been rigorously guarded. However, even this dynamic is changing, because the rate of intermarriage and interracial dating for African American women has soared.

Understanding this power matrix and its continued transformation is illustrated by contrasting patterns for Asian American intermarriage (Kitano, Fujino, & Sato, 1998; Lee & Yamanaka, 1990). For most Asian American immigrants, intermarriage for women increases first. The class transformation of Asians occurs in part through white male privilege, which has stereotyped Asian Americans as feminine, thereby emasculating men of Asian descent, making the latter less threatening (Root, 2001). Significant opposition was mounted with the intermarriage of Filipino men with white American women in the 1930s and 1940s (Cordova, 1983), which resulted in them being specifically added to the list of persons forbidden to intermarry with whites (Root, 2001). Contextually, the first significant waves of white-Asian intermarriages occurred as a result of marriageable age men being stationed in Asian countries during our various wars starting with World War II. The marriage

to women fit themes of rescue to justify U.S. military occupation and residence in these host countries (Root, 2001).

Yet a different pattern is observed for intermarriage with persons of Mexican descent. Because Mexican women could own property, white men's interest in them was justified. Potential economic gain transforms the attractiveness of the women but does not change the caste status of Mexican-descent persons immediately; it does, however, slowly erode the boundary. A history of intermarriage combined with very different notions of race further complicates the positioning of Hispanics in the national conversation on mixed race (Fernandez, 1992).

Last, the role of intermarriage in Indian communities is complex. Initially, British colonists regarded persons of African and Indian descent similarly but different from whites. Thus, intermarriage of whites with either group emerged in the 17th century (Tenzer, 1990). Indians were taken for slaves and sent to the West Indies. Hiding from capture or hostage, Africans and Indians aligned and naturally intermarried (Katz, 1986). Indians hid runaway slaves. Communities evolved in which Africans were assimilated into tribal life. Eventually, a sizable "free" nonwhite population emerged. The actual and potential economic competition resulted in attempts to deter African Indian alliances (Forbes, 1988). Intermarriage has been seen as a natural result of a variety of causes, ranging from proximity to access to resources to a replenishing of numbers for the survival of some tribes (Daniel, 1992). Traumatized by genocide, disease, and the bankruptcy of resources, Indian people have not been treated as a perceived economic threat by whites.

RACE AND TRAUMA

Racial identity theories started first with attention to African American identity. These theories began to emerge mostly in the 1970s and 1980s (Cross, 1991; Helms, 1990; Parham & Helms, 1985), at the same time as Ramirez's (1983) work on Chicano identity, and a mestizo psychology was introduced. Ramirez's work was followed by Anzaldua's (1987) subsequent feminist work intertwining ethnicity and gender and Collins's (1990), Hurtado's (1996), and Ferber's (1998) even more critical analyses of this intersection. However, these latter works have not had the same impact on racial identity constructions. Why? This relative invisibility may rest in this country's fixed hold on racial divides, particularly between black and white, cultural and gendered methods of protest, and the complex analysis undertaken that would force discussion of interracial sexuality. Likewise, important work on biculturalism and American Indian identity (LaFromboise, Coleman, & Gerton, 1993; Trimble, 1999) remained largely invisible to much of the dialogue. The presence of Asian Americans grew substantially after immigration laws changed in 1964 and 1965. The discussion on identity includes pan-Asian identity (Kitano, 1989; see Sue, Mak, & Sue, 1998). Domestically, general ethnic identity theories have attempted to accommodate the process of identity formation for Asian Americans who continue to be foreigners even after many generations. Regardless of the visibility of the racial identity theories, each of these broad groups has experienced severe trauma at the behest of the U.S. government. The theories reflect the transformation of traumatic experiences through political consciousness to reestablish pride by reframing the survival of certain experiences and providing corrective history about protests that were made (Omi & Winant, 1986; Takaki, 1993).

From a theoretical perspective of trauma, one's sense of a "just world" (McCann & Pearlman, 1990) is confronted and the individual is left with "shattered assumptions" (Janoff-Bulman, 1992) and even proof that evil exists (Staub, 1989; Thomas, 1993). The result of trauma is a hypervigilance to cues that may signal danger. However, this hypervigilance increases the likelihood of false positives (i.e., falsely interpreting a cue as a danger signal). In order for this vigilance to decrease, healing must occur, which requires a sense of spiritual transformation through either repeated kind acts that defy racist explanation or an existential understanding of one's experience such as with holocaust survival (Frankl, 1984); and some people never heal. In the case of racial trauma, the healing is offered through small progress that becomes evident with each successive generation and continued anti-oppression efforts. Within previous generations, a significant majority of people needed to seek refuge in their ethnic community of origin to establish a positive attachment and pride of their identity.

The role of hypervigilance as a trauma response provides some explanation for generational and regional differences toward persons who declare mixed-race identities. In the past, mixed race identities or moving between communities such as in passing (for white) had a fairly singular explanation and a very high price, further fracturing family ties, cutting off relatives, and establishing an elite type of black person (Daniel, 1992; Haizlip, 1994). Because this nation has not healed the wounds of racism, vigilance remains as a protective stance.

Part of establishing a positive racial identity required a refuge in the minority community of origin and a rejection of values and markers of mainstream European American culture. This insulation provides protection from further trauma and a way of integrating experiences and transforming them such that one feels less angry, more resilient, and ready to integrate with the general population. For people not particularly familiar with the details of the stage theories of identity, the end stages of some of the most widely used theories suggest a continued pride in one's heritage but with the ability to support human rights for everyone, to love beyond racial borders, and to associate with people of other races. The outcome of achieving this type of identity opens the door to intermarriage.

What has changed for many young people of color results from the benefits of those who have come previously to fight for civil rights. Many young people are not acquainted with the experiences of daily racism; they are less wounded. They are not traumatized to the extent their parents may have been. They have friends of different races. They believe there are not inherent differences of intellect based on race. They may even believe that this is a just world and that they will and should be judged for their actions. In addition, it has been a more just world than the one in which their parents and grandparents came of age. They do not necessarily need to isolate and retreat to the community of origin to feel racial or ethnic pride.

Although persons of mixed-race descent have been accused of not knowing their minority group(s) history or of being politically disengaged, they seem to be held more accountable than their monoracially identified brothers and sisters, who may similarly be disengaged from the political process to fight oppression. When persons of mixed heritage are charged with shirking the call to do antiracist work, we may be dealing more with a generational phenomenon than something unique to mixed-race people. I see young Asian Americans, African Americans, and Latinos caught by surprise when they encounter racially hostile work environments. They are outraged and not resigned to put up with it; they also do not necessarily recognize some of the subtle warning signs because they are not vigilant; they have not been traumatized. Their identity processes are more varied. They grow up in the midst of a "biracial baby boom."

Ironically, although sanctuary in the group of origin may intensify racial and ethnic pride by monoracially and monoethnically derived models, many mixed-race persons are traumatized by these experiences. To prove they belong, they may be required to endorse racist stereotypes against their parents, relatives, and friends. Questioning or challenging this rejection and denigration is threatening. Without an acknowledgment of how the multiracial person understands and negotiates their world, their authenticity is questioned. This process can be traumatic and ironically, because of exclusionary rules, can drive a process toward multiple group membership to meet needs. Although some persons of mixed heritage are quite protected and perhaps naive to how race is transacted, others are quite subversive. In Erdrich and Dorris's 1991 novel, *The Crown of Columbus*, the character of Vivian, an Ivy League American Indian professor, stated it eloquently:

I belong to the lost tribe of mixed bloods, that hodgepodge amalgam of hue and cry that defies easy placement. . . .

There are advantages to not being this or that. You have a million stories, one for every occasion, and in a way they're all lies and in another way they're all true. When Indians say to me, "What are you?" I know exactly what they're asking, and answer Coeur d'Alene. I don't add, "Between a quarter and a half," because that's information they don't require, first off—though it may come later if I screw up and they're looking for reasons why. If one of my Dartmouth colleagues wonders, "Where did you study?" I pick the best place, the hardest one to get into, in order to establish that I belong.

There are times when I control who I'll be, and times when I let other people decide. I'm not all anything, but I'm a little bit of a lot. My roots spread in every direction, and if I water one set of them more often than other, it's because they need it more. (pp. 166-167)

AN ECOLOGICAL FRAMEWORK OF RACIAL IDENTITY FORMATION

Various researchers over several decades have attempted to make the case for situational identity driven by the multiple identities each of us transacts in relationship to people who surround and reflect us from home, work, and religious communities (Miller, 1992; Stephan, 1992; Ramirez, 1983; Trimble, 1999). Cornell (2000) states that "ethnic identities are not given, fixed, or unchanging, but are continually evolving products of material and social circumstances and of the actions of groups themselves, wrestling with, interpreting, and responding to those circumstances, building or transforming identities in the process" (p. 42). When the ecological models incorporate historical, geographical, and gender lenses, identity, both racial and ethnic, will always be in flux because they are dynamic. The ecological framework for identity development not only explains the different ways in which people come to identify themselves but allows for understanding the environments and experiences that shape conventional monoracial identities, racially simultaneous identities, or multiracial identities (Root, 1999; Figure 1.1).

One must consider the geographical history of race, gender, family influences, individual "personality," community, and generation. Without taking the diversity apparent within these broad categories of influence, even among siblings, the attempts to discuss identity choices stay at a very unsophisticated level.

Geographical Historical Race and Ethnic Relations and Racial Demographics. Mixed-race people are neither evenly distributed nor represented by the same mixtures throughout this country. Demographers report that the trend toward an increase in the mixed-race populations is evident already in Arizona, California, Hawaii, south Florida, New Mexico, New York City, and Texas ("Poll," 2001). One of the explanations for the presence of mixing must be attributed to more opportunities for interracial contact that come through assimilation and immigration in a post-civil rights era. Although we see the greatest numbers of mixed-race persons in very large metropolitan areas, the size of a population in ratio to surrounding populations influences the process (Miller, 1992).

Generation. The generational lens, which understood mixed race as self-loathing or attempts at denegrification, does not work well in this period in history. I think this is a significant part of the divided attitudes on this topic. A generation still lives that has experienced first-hand Jim Crow segregation, anti-Asian sentiments, and denigration of persons of Mexican and Indian heritage. However, the latest census figures support generational differences. For example, whereas 64% of the nation felt favorably toward the multiracial trend revealed in the census, with only 24% opposed, the figures were even more telling about our future when 18- to 29-year-olds were surveyed in a *USA Today*/CNN/Gallup Poll ("Poll," 2001). Three quarters of this sector felt positive about a multiracial future for this country with no statistically significant difference between white and black attitudes. The pollsters suggested that older persons, particularly those older than 65 years, held unfavorable attitudes.

Family Influences. Family influences result from socialization, ethnic markers, and biology. They range from a parent's nativity that affected particular generations of mixed-race Asians (e.g., Korean War era and Vietnam War era), given names, languages spoken in the home, phenotype, sexual orientation, and so on. Generational history, regional influences, and a community also shape family influences. Despite the anecdotal information that phenotype has much to do with racial identity, some of the best-controlled research in early contemporary time did not bear this out (Hall, 1980, 1992). Root (1998) conducted a study of biracial siblings ranging in age from 18 to 55 years and found that perceptions of phenotype even between siblings seemed to be influenced by factors that are not observable and did not appear to have a high correlation with racial identity

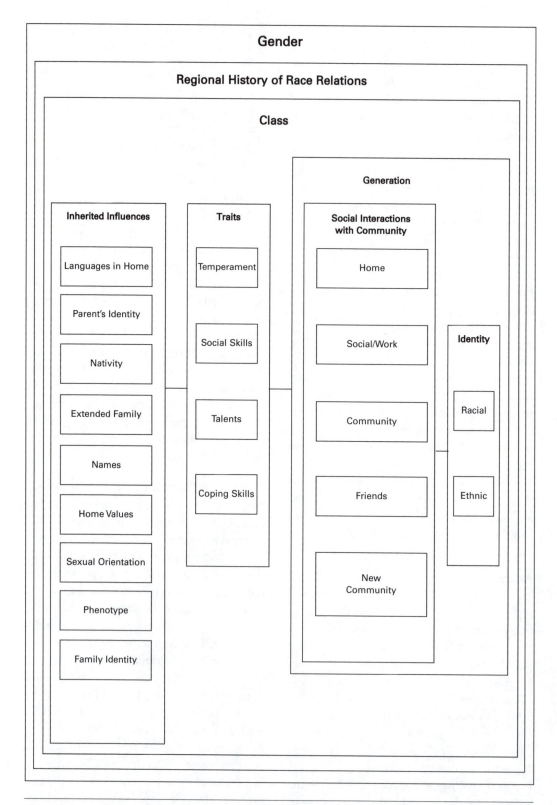

Figure 1.1   Ecological Framework for Understanding Identity Development

choices. Members of some of the collegiate mixed-race organizations confirm this, as we see a first generation of blond-haired people of declared and prideful African, Asian, Hawaiian, and American Indian descent.

Gender. Women have been given the assignment to pass on culture. Mixed-race women's presumed racial identity is derived more frequently than men's racial identity by their romantic or marriage partners. Twine (1996) discussed the research on strategic choices of mixed-race black/white women to partner with black men identified as African American. Guttentag and Secord (1983) provided statistical analysis indicating the double standard that exists when sex ratios are uneven. Power matrices in discussions of race must consider the intersection of gender to have more explanatory power (Root, 2001; Zack, 1997).

Community. The community in which one grows up reflects to varying degrees values, expectations, and a home. These can be one's actual home, neighborhood, school, workplace, place of worship, and places of recreation. Usually parents and older siblings negotiate a child's identity with each of these communities. Two predictable, difficult experiences that the mixed-race person may encounter illustrate the role of community, dating, and moving. In dating, the community will have some influence on the degree to which interracial dating is accepted and which groups are viable partners. Polls in the 1990s suggest that even these community restrictions are loosening, have less influence, or both (Root, 2001). The second potentially difficult transition point comes when mixed-race people leave their home communities and need to renegotiate their identity on their own.

Personality. The degree to which one has outstanding talents or social skills affects how he or she negotiates identity in the presence of opposition or authenticity testing. For example, if one is an outstanding athlete, musician, or student, he or she may belong to a subculture or group based on these skills. Race may often have background salience. If one is very "thin skinned," he or she may be acutely sensitive to slights. Race may be foreground.

These contextual influences contribute in various proportions to identity formation and different identity formation within the same families (Root, 1998). Thus, parents who raise their mixed-race children to identify as minorities are not guaranteed that this is how their children will identify. Likewise, those who raise their children to have mixed-race identities are not guaranteed this outcome. Phenotype and gender do not predict identification in contemporary times.

UNDERSTANDING THE DERIVATION OF FIVE IDENTITIES FOR MIXED-RACE PEOPLE

Root described five identity choices and the influence of the various variables described previously. The first four choices were apparent by the late 1980s (Root, 1990). There are clearly generational differences because the fifth identity choice did not appear with good adjustment in published research before the Biracial Sibling Project study (Root, 1998). Each of these identities is described next along with the social and political dynamics governing them.

1. *Accept the identity society assigns.* The hypodescent, or "one-drop," rule governs this identity. It was the only viable option available until the last quarter century. To have identified differently, until most recently in history, had a high price and many obstacles. At a fundamental level, there is a belief that one is born into an identity. This rule has been internalized so that all groups now have been co-opted to protect "whiteness" in the guise of solidarity. With

contemporary notions of choice, refusal to accept the identity society assigns is misinterpreted as disloyal, self-hating, or confused rather than, ironically, a reflection of duality or multiplicity into which one has been born. Nevertheless, at this point in history, uncritically accepting this identity perpetuates the myth of race and racial purity.

2. *Choose a single identity.* This identity choice is perceived as solidarity according to different national and community ethnic and racial groups amid a notion that "choice" exists. An active choice of a single racial identity, and one that often has the same resulting identity as hypodescent, involves an active process requiring varying degrees of critical thinking. It does not mean that a person believes in race but rather acknowledges that race matters. It may reflect the way one was raised, but not necessarily. It may be a political declaration. It may reflect an assessment of the social and psychological repercussions of a mixed-race identity. Most often, it reflects some of these processes convergent with a phenomenological experience of congruence with a single identity. Nevertheless, actively choosing a monoracial or monoethnic identity does not guarantee that one will be spared racial authenticity tests or "hazing" when one enters new communities in which he or she has to declare or negotiate an identity. Ironically, since the ethnic and racial pride movements of the 1960 and 1970s, individuals who are very European featured (in conventional racial assignments) or very African featured (in some Asian communities) may have perennial problems with this identity choice from members of their reference group. The process works differently with different combinations.

Sometimes the active choice of a single identity of a minority group reflected family dysfunction. For example, if a white parent had never been present, that side of the family was usually not present. More obvious

dysfunction by a white parent, such as domestic violence, child abuse, sexual abuse, alcohol and drug addiction, bigotry, and general irresponsibility, was color coded as white. An individual's active identity resolution as monoracial reflected an attempt to disavow attachment, relatedness, or need for this parent (Root, 1998).

3. *Choose a mixed identity.* We are developing into a polyracial nation, a process that started hundreds of years ago; the evidence is much more pronounced as time elapses since the repeal of the antimiscegenation laws. This is always an active identity choice beyond the early years of grade school years, when the label may be supplied by parents. The challenges to this identity are formidable, posed by strangers, the media, and family members. Thus, this is rarely a naive choice past midadolescence.

A mixed-race identity appears to be a possible choice for the first time in history for several reasons. First, there is a visible cohort of multiracial people within all racially identified ethnic groups. In some metropolitan areas, the proportions can be significant. Second, there are many popular television, movie, and music celebrities who not only acknowledge their mixed heritage but are matter-of-fact about this natural aspect of themselves despite being told it is an unnatural choice; they are public role models for this transformation. Third, as the stronghold of blatant, bigoted attitudes by people of European descent decreases as each generation's mortality claims it toll, many persons of mixed-race descent are loved by people on both sides of the family. They see themselves reflected in different colored and featured faces. They understand that solidarity and connection can transcend color and that support for social justice can come in all colors.

For children of immigrant parents, American nationality or citizenship is a source of their racial identity, particularly in the case of Asians of mixed descent. The children are often told they are not really Korean, Japanese, and so on. However, at a young age, children are not able to distinguish when this is a nation/culture declaration versus a race/culture explanation. For persons with African immigrant parents, the emphasis is on nation, as in "my children are American," while they are quickly learning about the racism of daily American life and, like many of their Asian counterparts, are not equipped to teach their children, initially, about American racism. Some of these experiences within the family or in the community have increased the attractiveness of a mixed-race identity.

Unfortunately, the hazing and authenticity tests that are applied to persons who appear phenotypically ambiguous or mixed may interact with individual personality and resources. The rejections hurt and may make it difficult to feel safe or believe that there is refuge in a single community of origin (Root, 1990). The mixed-race identity is often mistakenly interpreted to mean a lack of identification with the social and political realities of race. A mixed-race identity is not mutually exclusive of racial solidarity unless that solidarity is at a stage of racial identifications that requires denouncement or uncritical suspiciousness of all different persons and cultures, particularly if they are white.

4. *Choose a new race identity.* This identity choice comes in declarations of a blended identity, whether it is multiracial or simply mixed without the mixture signified. This identity choice is subversive, although not always intended as such. The motivations for this identity choice, a refusal to fractionate or double, are rarely understood because of the rigidity of our racial system. They are almost always pathologized as naive, reflecting shame of affiliation (particularly with blackness) or an attempt to recreate another tier on the racial hierarchy. This latter accusation and interpretation almost always invoke reference to slavery and privileges associated

with light skin. Nevertheless, this is a strategy that avoids fractionations (e.g., half Japanese, half black, or multiplication, e.g., both black and white). The identification of 42.2% of Hispanics as some "other" race other than one of the singular categories or a combination suggests a different model of race that is a blending ("Poll," 2001). Fernandez (1992) writes of La Raza and the celebration in some parts of Latin America of El Dia de la Raza (the Day of the [New Mixed] Race) (p. 127). Rodriguez (1994) writes of a paradigmatic shift in understanding and enacting race when it is perceived on a continuum informed by variables other than genealogy, such as class and education.

An example of how Identity Choices 1, 2, 3, and 4 can be transacted occurred when accompanying a recently deceased friend's 80-year-old mother and the mother's two 60-year-old nieces to the funeral home. For the purpose of completing the death certificate, the funeral director asked her mother "What race?" This is an extended family that has considered itself black despite some of the critical conversations my friend had had with family members over the years. I gave the funeral director credit that he asked the family her race. Both of the nieces replied, "Black" (Identity Choice 1 or 2). Her mother replied mixed (Identity Choice 3 or 4). I asked her if she wanted it listed as mixed or black/white (Identity Choice 4 or 3). The mother, who surprised me in her first response, reflected in her reply that she had been able to follow her daughter's identity choice outside of the frame of reference into which she was born. That frame would have only allowed her daughter Identity Choice 1 or 2. She did not pause to think further and assuredly said, "Just mixed" (Identity Choice 4). My friend would have wanted to be listed the way her mother did. Why? My friend had actively worked on racial and social justice and felt that this was her way of making a small contribution to challenging how we think, talk, and perform race. According to contemporary models of nigrescence, or black identity, she had actualized the final stage of racial identity. She was no stranger to racism from both sides. She could support social justice for African Americans and did, but was not willing to pay the price that solidarity compelled from her as a mixed-race woman.

5. *Choose a white identity.* I "discovered" this additional identity with a few of my respondents in the Biracial Sibling Project (Root, 1998). I saw it with persons of both mixed Asian and mixed African heritages. Other researchers are finding this in their research as well. Anecdotally, in previous unpublished research, those persons who declared a white identity did seem to exhibit more psychological distress on adjustment scales (Field, 1996). Not having interviewed many people who made this identity choice 10 or 15 years ago, I cannot offer a detached explanation for their choices in that period of history. I can be fairly certain that this choice 10 or 15 years ago may have still had the stress that a mixed-race identity choice would have had 20 to 30 years ago or more and reflected some psychic pain to distance from the other group or because of confrontation of this identity. Much psychic energy would have had to be spent living an identity that so few people would affirm or leave unchallenged.

In contrast, my research demonstrated two divergent explanations for white identity in persons of mixed heritage. I saw this choice with persons of African and white, Mexican and white, Asian and white, and Indian and white heritage. Several well-adjusted persons who made this choice reflected on their isolation from both ethnic family members and racially identified ethnic communities. In this case, there clearly was no disdain for their heritage, but there was no emotional attachment to it either. This aspect of their racial or ethnic self was symbolic. Having lost an ethnic identification, their default identification

was white, connoting a lifestyle derived from and reflected by the family and community surrounding them on a daily basis. Any mention of ethnic or racial identity was symbolic in the way that Waters (1990) spoke to symbolic ethnicity for many persons of European ancestry.

Family dysfunction emerged as the second source of explanation. If the parent of color had been mean, mentally ill, absent, irresponsible, or drug or alcohol addicted, some participants in their childhood coded this parent's behavior racially. Stereotypes and family disapproval of an interracial marriage or family bigotry supported this irrational coding (Root, 1998). White identity derived in this way for a participant correlated with adjustment problems and identity confusion in relationships as they attempted to "split" off this part of themselves to disavow this parent.

SUMMARY

Identity is dynamic and informed by one's life experiences in a historical context. My ecological framework of identity development (Root, 1999) suggests that the complexity of variables from family to community influences interacts within the framework of a generation, a geographic region's racial conflict history, gender, community, and personality. The civil rights legislation of the last quarter century provides the foundation for these variables to combine in such a way that we must expect that more complex racial identities are likely to stay and become part of the next stage of our racial discussion. This discussion must understand the implications of signification and consequence of identities in context. From both a social constructivistic and symbolic interactionist perspective, mixed race by fractions, multiplication, or blending provides a vehicle to examine where we are at this point in history. Shifting identities occur within contexts. Many of these maneuvers are natural and functional. I again call upon the words of Erdrich and Dorris's (1991) Vivian, a mixed-blood Indian character:

> I've read learned anthropological papers written about people like me. We're called marginal, as if we exist anywhere but on the center of the page. Our territory is the place for asides, for explanatory notes, for editorial notation. We're parked on the bleachers looking into the arena, never the main players, but there are bonuses to peripheral vision. Out beyond the normal bounds, you at least know where you're not. You escape the claustrophobia of belonging, and what you lack in security you gain by realizing— as those insiders never do—that security is an illusion. We're jealous of innocence, I'll admit that, but as the hooks and eyes that connect one core to the other we have our roles to play. (p. 167)

Eliminating race as a concept is not possible at this point in history. Although it is a social construct rather than a biological fact, racism does exist. We need to use the language we have for race to engage more evolved discussions that may further our healing. Ironically, the language of mixed race, rather than recreating the mixed-race societies of the 19th century, may at this point be used to dismantle the racial system, while acknowledging race-based oppression to be delusional at all times when it occurs.

To keep the racial categories exactly as they have been for decades continues to construct mixed-race people and their various identities, other than monoracial, as either illegitimate or pathological. It continues to deny the reality of our demographic change. Acknowledging that the U.S. population has been mixing with greater frequency and fewer obstacles makes understanding race more complex. The complexity may eventually render it a useless construct. However, just because we may reach a point at which the racial categorization of this country becomes unwieldy, we may need to

refocus how we acknowledge and think about sources of oppression and disenfranchisement. I do think the vestiges of racism will continue with African and Asian features ("featurism"), dark skin ("colorism"), non-European surnames, and non-European accents as sources of unconscious, if not conscious, discrimination for some time. I am, however, optimistic that each generation will erode these bases of bias as evidenced by work across racial combinations (Gaskins, 1999).

Mixed-race identity and intermarriage are not the solution to this country's traumatic racial history. We do need to continue to work toward social justice, acknowledgment, and reparations for the traumas that have forever changed the course of history for racialized ethnic groups in this country. I do believe we are in the midst of a constructive and revolutionary ideological transformation that forces us to examine race more critically. This systemic change, I predict, is consistent with the generational systemic change usually seen in family functioning; succeeding generations tend to be kinder and more open minded; the family system is characterized by less rigidity. This was repeatedly demonstrated in my study of intermarriage (Root, 2001) and reported in the initial analyses of the census ("Poll," 2001). There was a generation gap in the pervasiveness of racism and the degree to which race was the most special commodity in a family. This revolutionary transformation is fueled as much by love as by politics. Love is seldom acknowledged as a source of this transformation of race (Root, 2001).

Love is a formidable opponent in the issue of identities: children raised by parents who love them, received by both sides of the family; children taught to believe that all people are of equal worth; children raised with friends of different backgrounds so they can challenge stereotypes. The value of children in part rests in the fact that they eventually replace an older generation of adults who are bigoted, traumatized, full of hate, or unable to trust. The transformation of identity and even this decennial census should not be misattributed to the "white mother." It infantilizes and obscures the agency of mixed-race adults. Instead, the transformation should be attributed to a few successive cohorts of mixed-race adults who have survived the racial politics of this country and are speaking up.

Many persons of mixed-race descent are well acquainted with racism. We are privy to and recipients of the irrationalities and wounds inflicted by race from all groups and on our parents and grandparents. Nevertheless, many mixed-race people provide us an optimism that eventually race may be a relic. If a person can find a way to resolve racial identity at a microlevel, might we have a chance as a nation to continue to make progress at the macrolevel? I believe the hope rests in the effort to understand the processes that have conspired at this juncture to make mixed-race identity natural and revolutionary rather than the harbinger of an elitism.

REFERENCES

Alba, R. D., & Golden, R. M. (1986). Patterns of ethnic marriage in the United States. *Social Forces, 65,* 202-223.

Anzaldua, G. (1987). *Borderlands/la frontera: The new mestiza.* San Francisco: Spinsters/Aunt Lute Foundation.

Byrd, C. M. (2002). *Beyond race: The Bhagavad-gita in Black and White.* Self-published mansucript.

Collins, P. H. (1990). *Black feminist thought: Knowledge, consciousness, and the politics of empowerment.* New York: Routledge.

Collins, P. H. (1998). It's all in the family: Intersections of gender, race, and nation. *Hypatia, 13*(3), 62-82.

Cordova, F. (1983). *Filipinos: Forgotten Asian Americans.* Dubuque, IA: Kendall/Hunt.

Cornell, S. (2000). That's the story of our life. In P. Spickard & W. Jeffrey Burroughs (Eds.), *We are a people: Narrative and multiplicity in constructing ethnic identity* (pp. 41-53). Philadelphia, PA: Temple University Press.

Cross, W. (1991). *Shades of black: Diversity in African American identity.* Philadelphia, PA: Temple University Press.

Daniel, G. R. (1992). Passers and pluralists: Subverting the racial divide. In M. P. P. Root (Ed.), *Racially mixed people in America* (pp. 91-107). Newbury Park, CA: Sage.

Erdrich, L., & Dorris, M. (1991). *The crown of Columbus.* New York: HarperCollins.

Ferber, A. L. (1998). *White man falling: Race, gender, and white supremacy.* Lanham, MD: Rowman & Littlefield.

Fernandez, C. A. (1992). La Raza and the melting pot: A comparative look at multiethnicity. In M. P. P. Root (Ed.), *Racially mixed people in America* (pp. 126-143). Newbury Park, CA: Sage.

Fernandez, C. A. (1995). Testimony of the Association of MultiEthnic Americans. In N. Zack (Ed.), *American mixed race: The culture of microdiversity* (pp. 191-210). Lanham, MD: Rowman & Littlefield.

Field, L. D. (1996). Piecing together the puzzle: Self-concept and group identity in biracial black/white youth. In M. P. P. Root (Ed.), *Racially mixed people in America* (pp. 211-226). Thousand Oaks, CA: Sage.

Forbes, J. D. (1988). *Black Africans and Native Americans.* New York: Basil Blackwell.

Frankl, V. E. (1984). *Man's search for meaning: An introduction to logotherapy.* New York: Simon & Schuster.

Gaskins, P. F. (1999). *What are you? Voices of mixed-race young people.* New York: Henry Holt.

Graham, S. R. (1995). Grassroots advocacy. In N. Zack (Ed.), *American mixed race: The culture of microdiversity* (pp. 185-190). Lanham, MD: Rowman & Littlefield.

Guttentag, M., & Secord, P. F. (1983). *Too many women? The sex ratio question.* Beverly Hills, CA: Sage.

Haizlip, S. T. (1994). *The sweeter the juice: A family memoir in black and white.* New York: Simon & Schuster.

Hall, C. I. I. (1980). *The ethnic identity of racially mixed people: A study of Black-Japanese.* Doctoral dissertation, University of California, Los Angeles.

Hall, C. I. I. (1992). Please choose one: Ethnic identity choices for biracial individuals. In M. P. P. Root (Ed.), *Racially mixed people in America* (pp. 250-264). Newbury Park, CA: Sage.

Helms, J. E. (Ed.). (1990). *Black and white racial identity: Theory, research, and practice.* New York: Greenwood Press.

Hurtado, A. (1996). *The color of privilege: Three blasphemies on race and feminism.* Ann Arbor: University of Michigan Press.

Janoff-Bulman, R. (1992). *Shattered assumptions: Towards a new psychology of trauma.* New York: Free Press.

Kasindorf, M., & El Nasser, H. (2001, March 13). Impact of census' race data debated. *USA Today,* pp. 1A-2A.

Katz, W. L. (1986). *Black Indians: A hidden heritage.* New York: Atheneum.

Kitano, H. L. (1989). A model for counseling Asian Americans. In P. B. Pedersen, J. G. Draguns, W. J. Lonner, & J. E. Trimble (Eds.), *Counseling across cultures* (3rd ed., pp. 139-151). Honolulu: University of Hawaii Press.

Kitano, H. L., Fujino, D., & Sato, J. T. (1998). Interracial marriages: Where are the Asian Americans and where are they going? In L. C. Lee & N. W. Zane (Eds.), *Handbook of Asian American psychology* (pp. 233-260). Thousand Oaks, CA: Sage.

LaFromboise, T., Coleman, H. L. K., & Gerton, J. (1993). Psychological impact of biculturalism: Evidence and theory. *Psychological Bulletin, 114,* 395-412.

Lee, S. M., & Yamanaka, K. (1990). Patterns of Asian American intermarriage and marital assimilation. *Journal of Comparative Family Studies, 21*(2), 287-305.

McCann, I. L., & Pearlman, L. A. (1990). *Psychological trauma and the adult survivor: Theory, therapy, and transformation.* New York: Brunner/Mazel.

Miller, R. L. (1992). The human ecology of multiracial identity. In M. P. P. Root (Ed.), *Racially mixed people in America* (pp. 24-36). Newbury Park, CA: Sage.

Omi, M., & Winant, H. (1986). *Racial formation in the United States from the 1960s to the 1980s.* New York: Routledge & Kegan Paul.

Parham, T. A., & Helms, J. E. (1985). Relation of racial identity attitudes to self-actualization and affective states of black students. *Journal of Counseling Psychology, 32*(2), 431-440.

Poll. (2001, March 9). *USA Today,* p. 2A.

Ramirez, M., III (1983). *Psychology of the Americas: Mestizo perspectives on personality and mental health.* New York: Pergamon Press.

Rodriguez, C. E. (1994). Challenging racial hegemony: Puerto Ricans in the United States. In S. Gregory & R. Sanjek (Eds.), *Race* (pp. 131-145). New Brunswick, NJ: Rutgers University Press.

Root, M. P. P. (1990). Resolving "other" status: Identity development of biracial individuals. In L. E. Brown & M. P. P. Root (Eds.), *Complexity and diversity in feminist therapy* (pp. 185-205). New York: Haworth Press.

Root, M. P. P. (1996). The multiracial experience: Racial borders as a significant frontier in race relations. In M. P. P. Root (Ed.), *The multiracial experience: Racial borders as the new frontier* (pp. xiii-xxvii). Thousand Oaks, CA: Sage.

Root, M. P. P. (1998). Experiences and processes affecting racial identity development: Preliminary results from the biracial sibling project. *Cultural Diversity and Mental Health, 4,* 2237-2247.

Root, M. P. P. (1999). The biracial baby boom: Understanding ecological constructions of racial identity in the 21st century. In R. H. Sheets & E. Hollins (Eds.), *Racial and ethnic identity in school practices: Aspects of human development* (pp. 67-90). Hillsdale, NJ: Erlbaum.

Root, M. P. P. (2001). *Love's revolution: Interracial marriage.* Philadelphia, PA: Temple University Press.

Sanjek, R. (1994). Intermarriage and the future of races in the United States. In S. Gregory & R. Sanjek (Eds.), *Race* (pp. 103-130). New Brunswick, NJ: Rutgers University Press.

Senna, D. (1998). *Caucasia.* New York: Penguin Books.

Spickard, P. R. (1989). Injustice compounded: Amerasians and non-Japanese Americans in World War II concentration camps. *Journal of Ethnic History, 5*(2), 5-22.

Staub, E. (1989). *The roots of evil: The origins of genocide and other group violence.* Cambridge, England: Cambridge University Press.

Stephan, C. W. (1992). Mixed-heritage individuals: Ethnic identity and trait characteristics. In M. P. P. Root (Ed.), *Racially mixed people in America* (pp. 50-63). Newbury Park, CA: Sage.

Sue, D., Mak, W. S., & Sue, D. W. (1998). Ethnic identity. In L. C. Lee & N. W. S. Zane (Eds.), *Handbook of Asian American psychology* (pp. 289-324). Thousand Oaks, CA: Sage.

Takaki, R. (1993). *A different mirror: A history of multicultural America.* Boston: Back Bay Books.

Tenzer, L. R. (1990). *A completely new look at interracial sexuality: Public opinion and select commentaries.* Manahawkin, NJ: Scholars' Publishing House.

Thomas, L. M. (1993). *Vessels of evil: American slavery and the holocaust.* Philadelphia, PA: Temple University Press.

Trimble, J. E. (1999). Social psychological perspectives on changing self-identification among American Indian and Alaska Natives. In R. H. Dana (Ed.), *Handbook of cross-cultural/multicultural personality assessment.* Hillsdale, NJ: Erlbaum.

Twine, F. W. (1996). Heterosexual alliances: The romantic management of racial identity. In M. P. P. Root (Ed.), *The multiracial experience: Racial borders as the new frontier* (pp. 291-304). Thousand Oaks, CA: Sage.

Waters, M. C. (1990). *Ethnic options: Choosing identities in America.* Berkeley: University of California Press.

Young, R. J. C. (1995). *Colonial desire: Hybridity in theory, culture, and race.* New York: Routledge.

Zack, N. (1997). *Race/sex: Their sameness, difference, and interplay.* New York: Routledge.

CHAPTER 2

The New Multiracialism

An Affirmation of or an End to Race as We Know It?

MARY THIERRY TEXEIRA

California State University, San Bernardino

I want people to think I'm more than a ghetto girl. . . . I want to walk into dance halls and feel like a movie star, a white one.

— Serge F. Kovaleski (1999)[1]

Consider the following scenarios:

1. In the 19th century, with slavery of Africans in full bloom and antimiscegenation laws rabidly enforced, New Orleans' wealthiest white men gather for their annual quadroon ball. Amid a climate of the strictest separation of the races, they each choose a concubine from among a bevy of young women of color, all of whose ancestors include slaves.

2. The late tennis player Arthur Ashe, a black North American, is asked to play a tennis match in South Africa during the apartheid era, a time when the Japanese were designated "white" and the Chinese "colored." Ashe has some misgivings because, as a black man, he fears he will be subject to the rules of racial separation. South African officials devise a solution that will presumably make everyone happy. For purposes of his tour, Ashe is designated an "honorary white."

AUTHOR'S NOTE: I dedicate this chapter with love to my brother Aaron, whose light, like that of so many others', has been dimmed by the specter of race.

3. A young, dark-skinned woman from the Middle East immigrates to the United States. Upon completing her U.S. census form for the first time, she discovers to her amazement that she must designate her "race" as white. Until then, she had always considered herself Libyan.

These situations illustrate the way that race, as we have come to understand it in the Western world, is always in flux, changing over space and time and filled with historical, political, social, and psychological meanings. They also show how race is complicated and blurred, suited to each particular time and place in history and defined by the group in power.

Montagu (1942/1974) called race "man's most dangerous myth." His observation speaks to the seriousness and complexity of the conundrum of race. What the state calls a person or what that person calls himself or herself has vast and, as Montagu suggested, "dangerous" sociopolitical reverberations. Groups and individuals have either embraced or rejected various racial labels in part because of the privileges or penalties connected with those labels.

This chapter is an exploration of race, racism, and the movement calling for an official, government-sanctioned designation of "mixed race," "multiracial," or "biracial." I argue that this movement is another chapter in the divisiveness and counterproductiveness of racialization,[2] as much as or more than the situations involving the quadroon balls, Arthur Ashe, and the Middle Easterner. Moreover, we cannot understand the movement unless it is placed in the context of white supremacy.[3] White supremacy informs us that divisions, including racial labels and categories among people of color in the United States, have always benefited a white power structure that has often endorsed attempts to disunite nonwhites.

A few points of clarification are necessary. This critique of an officially sanctioned mixed-race category focuses on the African American experience for several reasons. First, in the perverse racial hierarchy that has been created in Western culture, black and white have always been in a stratified binary opposition. Our laws and customs have uniformly been about the business of protecting whiteness from blackness and gradations of blackness. People of African descent, as this chapter's epigraph sadly suggests, have been vilified because of their appearance that is linked to all that is dysfunctional and abnormal. Therefore, particular attention to "blackness" in this context is most appropriate and necessary. Second, as someone who identifies strongly with the African American community but who has been racially ambiguous outside of my own community, I am informed by the racial complexities that particularly befall African Americans and the need to find one's place in the world. Finally, much of the literature on multiracialism comes out of the African American experience because most African Americans are racially mixed. Yet African Americans have been the only group that has historically not had the freedom to acknowledge their full ethnic heritage (Jones, 1994). Indeed, although many in the multiracial movement are a variety of "mixes," those who are at the forefront of the movement are themselves or have children who are descended from Africans. It, therefore, is illuminating to deconstruct the socially constructed new category of mixed race from the African American perspective.

RACE: A SOCIAL CONSTRUCT; RACISM: A REALITY

Individuals and organizations that study race, including the American Anthropological Association and most multiracialists, agree that race is a social construct, founded not so much on biology as on the economic and social climates of the particular time and place. However, given the widely accepted belief that race is real, it is difficult, if not impossible, to discuss it as a construct. For example, discussions of the relationship between numerical intelligence (itself a social construct)[4] and race inevitably lead to the popular perception that intelligence is genetically determined and that race is one of its determinants (Gould, 1996). This perception has been supported by government policies such as "the one-drop rule" and antimiscegenation laws that were in effect for most of the 20th century. In addition, the popularity of the book *The Bell Curve* (Hernstein & Murray, 1994) and the resurgent efforts to link genetics to social problems such as crime point to the willingness of the public, government officials, and some scholars to embrace race as a scientific, biological phenomenon. Therefore, it is necessary to examine the historical evolution of the term *race* from a way of simply identifying travelers from other countries—as in "He is of the Hittite race"— to race as the subject of scientific investigation, categorization, and ranking. Concomitant with the "science" of race came its attendant meanings, stereotypes, and hierarchical ratings along various stages of the evolutionary continuum that ironically emerged during the so-called Age of Enlightenment.

Racism as we experience it today first appeared in 18th-century Europe (Mosse, 1999, p. 40). As its explorers went in search of untold wealth throughout the world, European scientists became obsessed with classifying all things in nature and determining what place humans had in the mix. As more colonies were established and more people enslaved, it was necessary to devise "proof" of the inferiority of non-Europeans. Comte Arthur de Gobineau has been called the "father of modern racism" (Bulmer & Solomos, 1999, p. 19) because it was he who first methodically classified and ranked the world's races, all in the context of European expansionism. Theories were developed to support the inferiority of the nonwhite races of the world (Biddiss, 1999). For example, one theory held that the skull so depressed "the anterior and superior positions of the [small] brain" that it rendered the African (who always seemed to have the smaller brain) less intelligent (Horsman, 1999, p. 47).

Race in the United States

Western racist ideology, science, and practice led Europeans to believe in their innate superiority and also found its way to their descendants in the colonies. The science of the superiority of the northern Europeans among all men was no less vigorous in the United States. Although southern and eastern Europeans, like the Irish and Jews, were the subjects of scientific racism when they first arrived in the United States, Africans were especially targeted for the new science that proved their inferiority. The scientific proof of the inferiority of the African was embraced by slave owners because it fit their worldview and allowed them to fill their coffers on the backs of "inferior stock" with little or no remorse. In turn, they devised methods to convince the slaves of their own inferiority. These methods included forbidding them to speak their own languages, taking away their religion and names, and convincing the lighter-skinned slaves that they were superior to the darker-skinned slaves.

Central to the hierarchy of race, and to controlling African Americans, were new classifications within the category "Negro" that ranked slaves and free people of color and pitted them against one another. Mixed-race African Americans were labeled Creole (in Louisiana), mulatto, quadroon, and octoroon depending on their degree of blackness. Those who were not considered "pure" African by the dominant society were given not only new designations but privileges, even if those privileges were, for the slave, just working in "the big house." Whether these privileges were granted because of the designee's nearness to the white ideal, because the white plantation owners or their sons were the fathers of these slaves, or because it was a way to disunify the slaves, the point is that the slave owner made light skin a status symbol (Graham, 1999; Russell, Wilson, & Hall, 1992). It was once a prevailing doctrine that the closer an individual was to white phenotype, the more intelligent and attractive he or she was, thus allowing the individual entrée where a pure African could not go. Indeed, many African American leaders such as Frederick Douglass, Booker T. Washington, and W. E. B. Du Bois were themselves light-skinned as a result of white or near-white parentage (Davis, 1991, p. 5). It is difficult to say with any degree of certainty how much their appearance helped them succeed in white society, but it undoubtedly did not hurt them. Accepting these historical facts, it is not difficult to understand how some even today would seek other status markers such as official racial designations that remove them from the taint of blackness (Russell et al., 1992). In the past, whites imposed labels such as mulatto, quadroon, and octoroon on subordinates. That mainly nonwhites, or whites acting in the behest of nonwhites, call for new designations makes little difference in the resultant divisiveness. The one-drop rule was developed not to give privilege to people of color but to preserve whiteness.

A Return to Yesteryear? Here I argue that the mixed-blood category under discussion is merely the mulatto, quadroon, octoroon, mestizo, and so on in a new guise. Whites created the color continuum by creating these various classes. Sociologist Edward Byron Reuter (cited in R. Spencer, 1999), in his 1918 book *The Mulatto in the United States: Including a Study of the Role of Mixed-Blood Races Throughout the World,* explained the new races and how they got that way:

> Lower culture of the Negro peoples is of course a simple observational fact and is to be accepted as such. To question it is to deny the obvious. . . . The intermixture of the races everywhere has gone on to the extent of the white man's wishes. The Negro woman has never objected to, and

has generally courted, the relationship. It was never at any time a matter of compulsion; on the contrary it was a matter of being honored by a man of a superior race. Speaking generally, the amount of intermixture is limited only by the self-respect of the white man and the compelling strength of the community sentiment. (p. 103)

Reuter argued that the offspring of this "mixture" sought the supposedly superior culture of white America. He patronizingly concluded that "there is not intention here to criticize the mulattoes or other men of mixed blood; quite the contrary. To recognize their desire to be white, their ambition to associate themselves through marriage or otherwise with the white race, is but to recognize their ability to appreciate the superior culture of the white group" (cited in R. Spencer, 1999, p. 106).

Some privilege was attached to the new racial designations. In the quadroon balls, a woman not "mixed" would not have been invited to participate except to serve cocktails and hors d'oeuvres, even though her daughter might be one of the attendees. The young quadroons were able to enjoy a middle-class status because their "exoticism" made them desirable to the white bourgeois men of New Orleans. In white supremacist societies, individuals in these categories have historically enjoyed more privileges than, for example, so-called pure Africans or indigenes. These divisions became a worldwide phenomenon under European colonialism and neocolonialism and aided and abetted these systems:

> To this day, in many countries, mixed-race individuals became a proxy for Europeans. They perfected the manner of their European masters, and control much of the economy of those countries. They were treated with great respect simply because of their skin color, and were always given preference over the darker-skinned Africans. (Millar, 1993, p. 12)

No other place best exemplifies the struggle with racial categorization more than the state of Louisiana.

Louisiana: A Case Study. The racialization of the people of Louisiana is a microcosm of racial classification in the United States and underscores the notion that nothing about race and racial classification is natural. Dominguez (1986) gives special attention to Louisiana because it typifies "the conscious manipulation" (p. xiv) of racial classification as she chronicles the inordinate amount of time, resources, and energy that local, state, and federal agencies have spent on race in the state.

In Louisiana, many French and Spanish colonizers took slave women as concubines and created an in-between class: neither white nor black. These were the *gens de couleur libre* (free people of color, or Creoles), many of whom were freed as a result of their relationship with whites. Most blacks were slaves. Nevertheless, as is the case today, the true fixations were white and not white and the necessity of keeping the two groups officially separated, the quadroon balls notwithstanding. State and local legislators developed capricious antimiscegenation statutes that would ensure white racial purity. For example, because so many female descendants of slaves were indistinguishable from white women, a local statute declared that the former had to wear *tignons*, a head wrap, to set them apart them from the latter (Dominguez, 1986, p. 25). Regarding themselves as occupying a step above the African, the *gens de couleur libre* devised ways to separate their group from the darker-skinned nonwhites. These included the paper bag tests, in which if one's skin was darker than a brown paper bag one could be denied admission to an event such as a dance or religious affair (Bates, 1993; McNeill, 1994; Russell et al., 1992, p. 30).[5]

For most of its history, Louisiana, like the rest of the United States and, indeed, the Western world, has been obsessed with racial designation, often resorting to the most convoluted arguments. The case of *State v. Treadaway,* in which a white man is accused of marrying a so-called octoroon, is illustrative:

> The Louisiana Supreme Court's case rested on the distinction between the terms *negro* and *person of color*. It argued that a negro is necessarily a person of color, but a person of color is not necessarily a negro. There are no negroes who are not persons of color; but there are persons of color who are not negroes. (Dominguez, 1986, p. 30)

The *Treadaway* case underscores the arbitrary, confusing, and contradictory ways in which race has been historically defined in the United States. As late as 1970, after passage of the Voting Rights Act and the official end of Jim Crow segregation, Louisiana included a racial formulation statute. The statute, one of many defining the one-drop rule, declared that a Negro was defined as anyone with at least 1/32 "Negro blood" (Dominguez, 1986, p. 2), thus clarifying the line between black and white, which was becoming, in the state's mind, dangerously blurred. The statute was used to decide, among others, the now-famous 1983 case of Suzie Guillory Phipps (*Jane Doe v. State of Louisiana*), a woman who, by all appearances, was white but whose birth certificate said that she was Negro. Phipps had an 18th-century relative who was a black slave. She attempted to get the designation of Negro removed from her birth certificate and replaced with white. Phipps lost the case; the court declared that a child, despite her appearance, could not change the parents' race that had been recorded on a birth certificate. "That appellants might today describe themselves as white does not prove error in a document that which designates their parents as colored" (Davis, 1991, p. 10). However, as Dominguez (1986), noted, the civil rights movement was fought over the issue of "rights *to* blacks, not the granting of rights *to be* white or black" [italics added] (p. 5).

Dominguez cited other cases in which the courts attended to racial designations in answer to individuals, like Phipps, who sought a white racial identity. Most plaintiffs were unsuccessful based on the traceability to "black blood." According to the courts, these cases were decided "in the public interest" (Dominguez, 1986, p. 43). The cost to the state is evident when one considers that in 1976 the City of New Orleans Department of Vital Statistics employees spent more than 600 hours deciding cases of racial identity alone (p. 45).

My own family's experiences illustrate how Louisiana's racial designation plays itself out in families both generationally and geographically. My Louisiana-born mother and father resembled one another, having light skin, curly hair, and fewer phenotypic African facial features than most African Americans. My siblings and I grew up listening to our grandparents speak the Creole version of French and watching them practice many Afro-French-Caribbean customs. It was not unusual for us to refer to aunts as *tante* or to be affectionately called *cher* by our parents and others. In another place and time, my siblings and I might have chosen to call ourselves "Creole" like many in our extended family. However, we moved to Watts, California, in the 1960s and, with one exception, have rejected every label except black or African American based on our belief that the term *Creole* would set us apart from other African Americans in our circle. However, some in my immediate and extended family do not wish to be associated with either term, including my own brother, who is phenotypically white. He moved back to Louisiana in his teenage years and is completely white identified, maintaining, like others in the family, minimal contact with the black and even Creole branches of his family. Dominguez (1986) described the sly maneuvering and anguish families endure when this occurs:

Many colored Creoles protect others who are trying to pass, to the point of feigning ignorance of certain branches of their families. Elicited genealogies often seem strangely skewed. In the case of one very good informant, a year passed before he confided in me that his own mother's sister and her children had passed into the white community. With tears in his eyes, he described the painful experience of learning about his aunt's death on the obituary page of the *New Orleans Times-Picayune*. His cousins failed to inform the abandoned side of the family of the death, for fear that they might show up at the wake or the funeral and thereby destroy the image of whiteness. Total separation was necessary for secrecy. (p. 51)

Race in other places both within and outside the United States in many ways mirrors race in Louisiana.

South Africa and Brazil

Marx (1998) compared attitudes about race in three distinct societies: South Africa, Brazil, and the United States. He noted that, like the United States, South Africa and Brazil were also built on the institution of slavery and racial separation and explored, post slavery, how they have addressed (or failed to address) their "race problem." He found that, even though Brazil and South Africa had somewhat dissimilar beginnings (although all within the context of European colonialism), they have both struggled with the race problem.

Here we need not review the appalling, violent history of apartheid in South Africa, but it is important to understand the extent to which the state went to enforce its racist ideology. Like the United States, South Africa had various labels for racial categorization, including white, colored, and black. The coloreds of South Africa were an intermediary group that included mixed-race, Chinese, Indians, Malays, Khoi, San, and Griqua (Pollard, 1997, p. 2). Although also suffering under the brutal system of apartheid, these groups nevertheless had more privileges than blacks. Notably, since the official end of apartheid, most coloreds have sided politically with whites (James, 1994).

Brazil was the largest slave-holding colony in the world (Marx, 1998); yet like other countries in South America, it continues to embrace the colonial and neocolonial notion of the superiority of the European. It did not codify race in the same way as South Africa and the United States; yet like the latter, it used the mixed-race individual as a buffer, serving an economic role between black slaves and their white masters (Marx, 1998). Although there are clearly racial distinctions in this former Portuguese colony, race takes a somewhat different form than in the United States and South Africa. Much more important to Brazilian society is class, but race is never far behind. Fredrickson (1999) described the salience of class and its relationship to race in Brazil:

> The Brazilian phrase, "money whitens," sums up the values of a society for which race is far from irrelevant as a basis of social classification but which nevertheless does not draw a rigid color line or sanction behavior that could be justified *only* on the ground that blacks or mulattos are innately inferior to whites. (p. 71)

Class distinctions notwithstanding, Brazil, like many parts of Central and South America and the Caribbean, still divides along the color line (Byrne, Harris, Consorte, & Lang, 1995). Indeed, one is hard-pressed to think of a place in the Western world where political, economic, social, and educational institutions are not dominated by those who are more European in appearance than the black and indigenous masses they rule.

BACK TO THE FUTURE OF RACIAL TAXONOMY? THE MULTIRACIAL MOVEMENT

A search of the Web pages of various groups that advocate a mixed or multiracial category

reveals that they or their children, or both, must also be included in racial categorization for purposes of self-esteem and medical information and to present their special issues. These groups include, but are not limited to, Multiracial Americans of Southern California, Association of Multiethnic Americans, and Project RACE.[6] One of the most vocal among the advocates of a multiracial designation is Susan Graham, a white woman whose children have a black father. She was horrified to find that the 1990 census form had no designation for her children; nor was there a satisfactory racial choice when she enrolled her son in kindergarten (Wright, 1994). Therefore, Graham and others argue, they must be recognized as an official racial group (Root, 1996; Wright, 1994). They rightly challenge the one-drop rule that creates an either/or dichotomy, especially in the case of whites and blacks.

Multiracialist groups came into prominence in the debate over the 2000 census as Graham and others petitioned the government to add a multiracial box to the existing categories (Wright, 1994). This set into motion a series of conferences and public meetings, culminating in the U.S. Census Bureau's decision in 1997 to reject a mixed-race category on the 2000 census form. The bureau's concession was that, for the first time, it would allow persons to designate more than one race by adding a "check all that apply" box to the current form. For purposes of civil rights data collection, the individual would be counted in the "minority" group, something that people in the movement say does not go far enough because, according to Graham, it still "relegates" her son and others to the black category (R. Spencer, 1999).[7]

The movement is made up of more than grassroots activists like Graham. As readers of this volume will discover, the academics at the forefront of the movement include G. Reginald Daniel and Maria Root as well as the philosopher Naomi Zack. These scholars have devoted much of their professional energy to addressing the special issues of persons who consider themselves mixed race. Zack (1993) perhaps gives the best summation of the goals of those like herself who are involved in this movement. She holds that "the American biracial system does not permit the identification of individuals, in the third person, as mixed race. If individuals cannot be identified, in the third person, as mixed race, then it is impossible for them to have mixed-race identities, in the first person" (p. 4). Here Zack argues that the mixed-race individual cannot self-actualize if the government does not first recognize them.

Zack wonders, for example, given writer and anthropologist Zora Neale Hurston's acknowledgment of her white, Indian, and African ancestry, why Hurston continued to call herself a Negro. She laments,

> Hurston does not explain how, if she sees herself as mixed race, she can *logically* identify herself as a Negro. . . . Hurston illustrates all too well how *morally good* [italics added] American identities of mixed race collapse into black racial identities. Such black identities may be admirable, but they are not logical or in fact identities of mixed race. (p. 147)

This passage reveals how much of the argument for a multiracial category is ahistorical. Zack writes as if (a) Hurston had any agency over her own official racial designation in the 1930s; (b) she did not grow up in a nurturing all-black town with which she strongly identified; and (c) all the "ingredients" of her racial heritage were placed on equal standing during that period. Hurston was simply doing what millions of blacks had been doing for hundreds of years: identifying with a community that raised, nurtured, and accepted them regardless of their genetic markers. Moreover, the racial climate did not give Hurston the luxury to choose her racial identity. People having African ancestry have been placed in boxes for hundreds of years in the United States, being told that they were not welcome in any other

communities. When finally accepting and even loving this place, they are blamed for not "choosing" to remove themselves from it (Jones, 1994).

Zack and other multiracialists do not (or cannot?) provide empirical evidence that supports their belief that individual self-esteem is in any way connected to official government racial labels. Helms (1990) asserted that one's racial identity is not the same as racial categorization. Rather, it is "a sense of group or collective identity based on one's *perception* that he or she shares a common racial heritage with a particular racial group" (p. 3). Children do not need an official racial category in order for them to have a sense of group identity. Indeed, entire groups of people, like the Creoles of Louisiana, have managed to maintain a separate group identity without official government sanction. Spencer (1997) described how he, like most of us, experienced a great deal of personal identity angst just growing up:

> Nearly all my friends had some aspect of identity that was in conflict with some imagined standard and therefore subject to teasing. Some were adopted, some were fostered; some were very poor, others were rather well-off; some were unhip, some had physical deformities, some were retarded mentally; some were ugly, some were gay, while some had seemingly nothing *wrong* with them and were teased precisely because of it. I had an entire neighborhood of friends who treated me as well and as poorly as any other kid we knew. If one of them called me an Oreo or Frankenstein, I likely responded by insulting his mother, and then we'd probably go over to my house or his to play Monopoly, chess, Sorry, or slot cars. (pp. 129-130)

Here Spencer does not wish to downplay childhood self-esteem crises; rather, he is illustrating that most children suffer some form of childhood teasing that may or may not lead to self-esteem problems.

Some multiracialists also argue that unless they embrace this category they are rejecting their white parent's culture, ignoring the fact that European Americans and African Americans have cultures that are so blended as to be, at times, indistinguishable. Smedley (cited in R. Spencer, 1999) counters:

> In American ideology, a black parent presumably has "black" culture, and the white parent has "white" culture, with the unstated understanding that these are incompatible ways of life. Aside from the fact that this idea is nonsense, it continues to feed the psychic stress of a few individuals who have the feeling that they do not know who they are. (p. 119)

Smedley is suggesting that another troubling aspect of the multiracial movement is that its proponents do not seem to mind painting their children as a group of neurotic "tragic mulattoes" (Sollors, 1986), like psychologists Ruth McElroy and Edith Freeman do:

> For children to view their mixed-racial background positively, the family must nurture both parts of the background by providing the child with both black and white role models and by exposing the child to black as well as white peers in the community and in school. In this process, the child is able to acquire more realistic attitudes and perceptions about his or her racial background. Mixed-race adolescents who are unable to reconcile their mixed cultural background into a personal and socially acceptable coalescence will not resolve this developmental stage. Thus, the individual may exhibit neurotic behavior. (cited in R. Spencer, 1999, p. 110)

R. Spencer (1996) noted that

> by accepting race construct as normative, these [multiracialist] researchers fail to consider the possibility that not everyone is as frantically affected by race as their studies presume. They also fail to consider that some persons may reject race while still acknowledging the *cultural* differences of their parents as well as the racism of much of society. (p. 110)

Multiracialists also believe that rather than hurt the cause of racial justice, their new designation could help to improve race relations. Professor Orlando Patterson, himself the father of mixed-race children, contends that "mixing is the best thing that could happen because by means of such a middle group people feel an investment on both sides" (Gross, 1996, p. A16). Professor Patterson offers an ideal scenario but fails to demonstrate exactly how increased empathy within families is supposed to promote an antiracist agenda, because as the histories of the United States, Brazil, South Africa, and the Caribbean suggest, "middle races" have always identified more with the dominant group.

Besides the self-identity concerns, individuals and groups in the movement focus on medical issues, arguing that physicians must know the entire background of the individual to make a well-informed diagnosis. This is the least persuasive argument because if multiracialists agree that race is not a biological concept (most acknowledge this), then how can they base one of their concerns on biology? Blacks in the United States have long been concerned about medical issues, less because of biological reasons than an equal medical care system that affects treatment and the tracking of disease. On this issue, R. Spencer (1999) quoted participants at a conference on race and ethnicity in public health surveillance:

> We focus on differences in skin color, not because the genes linked to skin color have been shown to be critical determinants of disease patterns, but in our society skin color (race), is a centrally determining characteristic of social identity and obligations, as well as a key determinant of access to desirable resources. (p. 158)

Thus, the medical basis of multiracialism cannot be sustained.

The Politics of Multiracialism

George Washington University Professor Amitai Etzioni (2000) concedes that the new multiracial categories could water down civil rights efforts. However, he believes that there is a more important issue at stake: "The social costs of the *political gimmick* of assigning people to a racial category that they seek to avoid are considerable" [italics added]. He argues that personal identity is more important than civil rights. According to Etzioni (2000),

> The new census [multiracial] category *may* go a long way toward softening sharply delineated racial lines and foster a society where differences are blurred. It will make it much more likely that the census of, say, 2030 will be more like Hawai'i where races mix rather freely, and less like India, with its castes [italics added]. (p. 19)

Etzioni is not completely forthcoming about Hawai'i, a state that had the highest proportion of its population that marked more than one racial category on the 2000 census. A former colony of the United States, Hawai'i is no bastion of liberal race relations, having a long and cruel history of exploitation based on race and ethnicity. Native Hawaiians, like other indigenous populations, succumbed to European diseases and violence, prompting much in-migration from various places like Japan, the Philippines and the mainland to work the plantations of wealthy North Americans. Yet the islands continue to struggle with racial issues with whites and, to a lesser extent, Japanese Americans, still in charge while Native Hawaiians experience myriad social ills (Takaki, 1993, pp. 251-266). Native Hawai'ians are currently involved in a fight for recognition and sovereignty much like the Native Americans on the mainland and Alaska (Kitano, 1997, p. 302). To outside observers, differences may be "blurred" but like the rest of the country, the difference that continues to be clear is that between whites on

one side and nonwhites on the other (Schaefer, 1998, pp. 307-311).

Although the leaders of the multiracial movement insist that theirs is a progressive movement, its supporters do not project a progressive worldview on other issues. They often push for their goals to the peril of broader, more progressive principles such as antiracism. Reactionary politicians like former Republican Speaker of the House Newt Gingrich (R. Spencer, 1999, p. 181) and conservative bellwether states like Georgia (Etzioni, 2000) that passed the most "progressive" multiracial statute (Williamson, 1995) are supportive of a multiracial category. This should give us cause for concern and speaks to the possibility that this is indeed a movement that is not progressive in regard to antiracist activism. Gurza (1999, p. B1) illuminated conservative supporters' thinking in one of their imagined statements: "We've had enough of those pesky racial statistics that document discrimination and [that] prompt the government to do something about social disparities." Gurza highlighted the possibility that this category will do away with tracking racial inequality. Others, like Gordon (1995, p. 393) indicated that some conservatives who support this movement have a desire for black people to simply disappear, in the process of what Fanon (1967) called "denegrification" (p. 111).

On the other side of the argument, civil rights organizations, including the NAACP, National Urban League, National Council of La Raza, Lawyers' Committee for Civil Rights Under Law, and National Congress of Indian Americans, have denounced an official mixed-race category (R. Spencer, 1999, p. 144). Although these groups, as I, would deny no one the right to call themselves what they wish to be called, they argue that there unfortunately continues to be a need to track racial injustice based on existing categories. According to Hilary Shelton, director of the NAACP's Washington bureau (cited in Lindsey, 2000),

The fundamental fear is that you're going to have people who look African-American, who have grown up in communities that are African-American, who are going to experience the discrimination that African-Americans have historically experienced, but not have even the existing civil rights protections because they're being identified now in this census in a way that's inconsistent with how it's been monitored in the past and how law enforcement is tooled to enforce it now. The numbers aren't important. The enforcement of civil rights are. No matter what you're calling yourself, we want to make sure you don't get lost or left on the periphery of civil rights protection. (p. 7)

Maslow's theory of hierarchical needs suggests that self-actualization is the last struggle for the indi]vidual. However, before group self-actualization, we must attend to the very basic needs that many in our society do not yet have. Although race may be a social construct, racism itself is very real. There is a vast ocean of humanity known as "the urban poor" or, more popularly, "the underclass" (Gans, 1999; Lemann, 1999; Massey & Denton, 1999), whose inferior education (Kozol, 1992), joblessness and abject poverty (Hartman, 1996; Wilson, 1987), and victimization by the criminal justice system (Texeira, 1995; Walker, Spohn, & Delone, 1999), all leading to a profound sense of hopelessness and nihilism (West, 1993), make them vulnerable to the vilest forms of racism in a country that has not granted them equal access to democratic rights and freedoms. Although middle-class African Americans may avoid some of the pitfalls of racism, their class position does not totally protect them (Cose, 1993). Indeed, the multiracialists may be sacrificing an urgent, as-yet-unresolved antiracist agenda at the altar of a movement whose main goal is self-actualization.

I believe that the call for the addition of new racial categories and the struggle to free all people of racial oppression are antithetical.

We must challenge race, not continue to reify it by the addition of more "racial" categories. Within the context of white supremacy, what one chooses to call oneself is not merely a matter of personal choice (although in an ideal world it would be). In this case, a personal choice has political ramifications ranging from making it difficult to track civil rights abuses and health issues to the formulation of voting blocs in congressional redistricting.

Divisions among people whose ancestry lies completely or partly in Africa, regardless of color and of what they call themselves, has profound significance, which, according to Howard Winant (1998)

is complex, even contradictory. On the one hand, the emergence of diverse and even conflicting voices in the black community is welcome, for it reflects real changes in the direction of mobility and democratization. On the other hand, the persistence of glaring racial inequality—that is, of an ongoing dimension of white supremacy and racism that pervades the entire society—demands a level of concerted action that division and discord tend to preclude. (p. 100)

Winant believes, as do I, that the addition of more voices in the black community can be healthy. He nevertheless contends that those who make up the African diaspora, like slaves on the plantation, can ill afford to present anything but a united front in the face of white supremacy. Another danger, according to Todd Gitlin (cited in Gross, 1996), is that the multiracialists "could become a tribe themselves and become captivated by exactly what they oppose" (p. A16).

Multiracialists sometimes miss the larger issue as the following example illustrates. In the *Montgomery Advertiser*, Major Cox (1996) recounted the story of Bethany Godby, whose father is white and mother is black. Bethany's newly integrated southern high school attempted to solve its racial integration "problem" by having two homecoming courts: one white, one black. Bethany found that she could not run for homecoming queen as white or black because she is neither. As the author explained,

> Children in Bethany's racial category will and should continue to speak out against a government racial classification system that compels them to deny their heritage. These children want their government to assign to them a racial category that represents their individual reality. Children born of both black and white parents want to be classified in that manner. And for Bethany Godby. . . . a Biracial category will be just fine (p. 2).

Here the focus is on Bethany's lack of qualifications to be homecoming queen from either group. With a biracial category, there would presumably be the creation of *another* category for which Bethany, and children like her, would be qualified. The author provided little critique of a racist system whose officials dare to allow even *two* homecoming courts that have undoubtedly caused divisions among the student body. He, instead, chose to discuss multiracialism.

Like the situation at Bethany's high school, racial divisions have proven very useful in U.S. history. Placing the science of race in a political, economic, and social context, Marable (1991) observed that

> race is . . . rooted in the structures of exploitation, power, and privilege. "Race" . . . was deliberately imposed on various subordinated groups of people at the outset of the expansion of European capitalism into the Western Hemisphere five centuries ago. The "racial" consciousness and discourse of the West [were] forged above the bowels of slave ships, as they carted their human cargoes into the slave depots of the Caribbean and the Americas. The search for agricultural commodities and profits from the extreme exploitation of involuntary workers deemed less than human gave birth to the notion of racial inequality.
>
> In the United States, a race is frequently defined as a group of individuals who share

certain physical or biological traits, particularly phenotype (skin color), body structure, and facial features. But race has no scientific validity as a meaningful biological or genetic concept. Beyond this, the meaning of race shifts according to the power relations between the racial groups. (p. 179)

Marable is suggesting that race and racism are the mother's milk of U.S. capitalism that could not (and cannot) survive without either. Neither race nor racism will die precisely because of their power to uphold the capitalist state by the creation of false divisions among citizens of the state.[8]

The more divided the population, the more labels that exist and the stronger is the state power (Marable, 1991). For example, in the racialized United States, European immigrants found it advantageous to relinquish labels like Irish, Swedish, and Italian (except on special occasions) for the more salient label of white. Labeling, as South Africa's President Verwoerd understood, can be a powerful weapon. When white unity was threatened in the country, he replaced the term "Afrikaner Republicans" with "white Republicans." This one act unified white South Africans of both British and Dutch origin. Meanwhile, the white Republicans disunified the nonwhite population by herding them into bantustans and by imposing labels such as black and colored (Marx, 1998, p. 107). Whites clearly understand and history demonstrates that at no time has there been a positive outcome (for subordinate groups) of separation of nonwhite groups. This can only lead to more, not less, conflict.

CONCLUSION

As I have attempted to demonstrate, racial designation and identity, whether imposed from the outside or chosen as an identity, are not *natural*. They are complicated, ever-changing, manipulated, contrived, and controlled designations that have been used to dole out "goodies" and to separate populations for more than 500 years. Racial designations are based on the mistaken notion of racial "purity" and simplicity, and the multiracialist approach suggests that humans can be cross-pollinated like oranges or roses. The movement seems to present itself as the last battle of the antiracist struggle. However, conservative support of the movement begs the question: Is this movement a throwback to a time when African Americans were routinely labeled by masters depending on the amount of their "white blood"?

Racism, although perhaps not natural, is nevertheless a fact of life in the United States. Race is irretrievably linked to racism. Race will not go away until racism goes away. The multiracialists, despite Etzioni's and others' heartfelt hopes, have failed to demonstrate how adding one or multiple race categories will lead to the beginning of the end of racism. We can choose to advance hypotheses about what might be, or we can, as I have attempted to do, examine how this categorization has played itself out in our past. As the experiences of Brazil, South Africa, and the United States show us, states have gotten involved in racial taxonomy at their most divided and racially oppressive times. Although our democratic ideals say we are equal under the law, history and contemporary observations tell a different story.

Although it is understandable that children and others of mixed marriages would be confused in this racialized society, there is little evidence to suggest that biracial children suffer any more than children whose parents are of one heritage. Many would agree that simply to be nonwhite in a white society is cause for considerable angst and suffering. Adding more categories to the official government race roster is not likely to ease the mixed child's anxieties about his or her identity. Rather, it is conceivable that concerns about *culture, heritage, and ethnicity*

(not race) might be better addressed by the child's parents who must convey to the child that race and skin color are individual genetic variables, not group markers in need of official government imprimatur.

Textbooks (including this volume) and newspaper articles may add different racial voices to the mix; but this movement is really about who is white(r) and who is not white. Of the Louisiana court cases that Dominguez cited, none were of individuals petitioning to change their racial designation from white to black, and none were of any person of European extraction wishing to remove the white designation from the records and add Swedish or Irish. Indeed, why, as J. Spencer (1997) asked, "can blacks be mixed but whites can't?" (p. 133). The racialized history of the United States informs us that mixed persons of African descent have had more privileges than darker-skinned persons, slave or free.

Another of my deepest fears is that the "multiracial agenda" will come to dominate racial discourse and research in the not too distant future. I believe this fear is well founded because of the growing numbers of racially mixed and European American researchers whose mostly middle-class backgrounds give them greater voice and whose work may be more acceptable because this discourse is less likely to challenge institutional racism and its most harmful effects. This is a kind of "racism light," a scholarship that takes little note of structural power (other than the government census), but that offers as the most profound effects of racism the lack of "a place for them."

Those of us who are involved in antiracist battles should step up efforts to track racism while allowing individuals to choose whatever personal designation they wish. As well, we need to imagine nothing less than a society free of the encumbrances of race and racialization, one in which every individual is free to call himself or herself nothing, everything, or something in between. Rather than calling for additional racial categories, would we not do better by placing all our energy and efforts into ridding our country of what Penn (1997) called "the skewer of race" (p. 7) and racialization that does immeasurable harm to communities and individuals? Do we want our children to be self-actualized at the expense of those who suffer and who are voiceless? Racism in its various manifestations persists because it is useful to the power structure. As descendants of strangers from different shores like Africa, Europe, Asia and Latin America, we occupy the same space and even intermarry. We must respect each others' cultural mix, and we must all eventually get along—or perish. The end of racism, although perhaps a utopian dream, promises us the right and comfort to check all that apply, to transcend race, and to have a genuinely color-blind society.

NOTES

1. Quoting a Caribbean woman on the phenomenon known as "the brownin," in which black women apply bleaching cream to their skin in dangerously high quantities to make themselves more socially appealing.

2. Throughout this chapter, I use this term, like Miles (1989, p. 75), to refer to racial classification, "defining an Other," and the notion that physical differences have structured human relationships in untold ways in Western society.

3. This term is popularly understood to refer to the Ku Klux Klan, skinheads, and other such groups. Here, however, I use it in the way that Hooks and West (1991) and others have: the institutionalization of wealth, power, and privilege based on the notion that to be white is to be superior to all others. Under such a divisive system, it follows that the more attractive, able, and intelligent individual, for example, is closest to the white ideal.

4. The reification of measured intelligence has been roundly criticized based, in part, on the narrow definition applied to intelligence and on the cultural loading of tests used to measure it. For a concise critique of this process, see Howard Gardner's "Cracking Open the IQ Box" (2000).

5. Sybil Klein's edited *Creole* (2000) provides, to date, the most extensive scholarly examination of the nonwhite Creoles of Louisiana. Also, E. Franklin Frazier (1957) and Lawrence Otis Graham (1999) provide fascinating and, some would say, voyeuristic insight into the world of the so-called black bourgeoisie (including Louisiana's Creoles), the class that beginning in the slave era was composed mainly of the lightest-skinned blacks.

6. Some of the more interesting websites include Project RACE (www.projectrace.com/director.html); Association of Multiracial People at the University of Wisconsin-Eau Claire (www.dc01.uwec.edu/orgs/display.asp?id=77); Multiracial Activist (www.multiracial.com/); and the online journal INTERRACE (www.hypatiatrust.com/interrace.html).

7. It is important to note that the U.S. census was never meant to be a heritage checklist. Its main purpose is to determine political representation and federal funding and to ensure compliance with civil rights legislation.

8. For a succinct and powerfully convincing discussion of how racism benefits the capitalist power structure, see Gans (1999).

REFERENCES

Bates, K. G. (1993, May 23). Shades of black: As U.S. blacks embrace a crazy quilt of backgrounds, their deepest roots lie in culture, not color. *Los Angeles Times Magazine*, p. 23.

Biddiss, M. (1999). Gobineau and the origins of European racism. In M. Bulmer & J. Solomos (Eds.), *Racism* (pp. 49-51). Oxford, UK: Oxford University Press.

Bulmer, M., & Solomos, J. (Eds.). (1999). *Racism*. Oxford, UK: Oxford University Press.

Byrne, B., Harris, M., Consorte, J. G., & Lang, J. (1995). What's in a name? The consequences of violating Brazilian emic color-race categories in estimates of social well-being. *Journal of Anthropological Research, 51*(4), 389-397.

Cose, E. (1993). *The rage of the privileged class*. New York: HarperCollins.

Cox, M. (1996, November 6). What's wrong with biracial label? *Montgomery Advertiser*. Available at www.majorcox.com/columns/godby.htm

Davis, J. (1991). *Who is black? One nation's definition*. University Park: Pennsylvania State University Press.

Dominguez, V. (1986). *White by definition: Social classification in Creole Louisiana*. New Brunswick, NJ: Rutgers University Press.

Etzioni, A. (2000). *A new American race*. Available at www.multiracial.com/readers/etzioni.html

Fanon, F. (1967). *Black skins, white masks* (C. L. Markham, Trans). New York: Monthly Review Press.

Frazier, E. F. (1957). *Black bourgeoisie*. New York: Collier.

Fredrickson, G. (1999). Social origins of American racism. In M. Bulmer & J. Solomos (Eds.), *Racism* (pp. 70-82). Oxford, UK: Oxford University Press.

Gans, H. (1999). Positive functions of the undeserving poor: Uses of the underclass in America. In C. A. Gallagher (Ed.), *Rethinking the color line: Readings in race and ethnicity* (pp. 154-166). Mountain View, CA: Mayfield.

Gardner, H. (2000). Cracking open the IQ box. In H. L. Tischler (Ed.), *Debating points: Race and ethnic relations* (pp. 37-44). Englewood Cliffs, NJ: Prentice Hall.

Gordon, L. R. (1995). Critical "mixed race"? *Social Identities, 1*(2), 381-396.

Gould, S. J. (1996). *The mismeasure of man*. New York: W. W. Norton. (Original work published 1981)

Graham, L. O. (1999). *Our kind of people: Inside America's black upper class*. New York: HarperCollins.

Gross, J. (1996, January 14). Diversity: Growing mixed race population seeks recognition and a more inclusive way to define ourselves. *Los Angeles Times*, p. A16.

Gurza, A. (1999, July 6). In search of a census pigeonhole. *Los Angeles Times*, p. B1.

Hartman, C. (Ed.). (1996). *Double exposure: Poverty and race in America*. Armonk, NY: M. E. Sharpe.

Helms, J. (Ed.). (1990). *Black and white racial identity: Theory, research, and practice*. New York: Greenwood Press.

Hernstein, R., & Murray, C. (1994). *The bell curve: Intelligence and class structure in American life*. New York: Free Press.

Hooks, B., & West, C. (1991). *Breaking bread: Insurgent black intellectual life*. Boston: South End Press.

Horsman, R. (1999). Superior and inferior races. In M. Bulmer & J. Solomos (Eds.), *Racism* (pp. 45-48). Oxford, UK: Oxford University Press.

James, W. (1994, July). *Racism, xenophobia and the extension of citizenship in South Africa*. Paper presented at the meeting of the International Sociological Association, Bielefeld, Germany.

Jones, R. (1994). The end of Africanity? The bi-racial assault on blackness. *Western Journal of Black Studies, 18*, 201-210.

Kitano, H. L. (1997). *Race relations* (5th ed.). Englewood Cliffs, NJ: Prentice Hall.

Klein, S. (Ed.). (2000). *Creole: The history and legacy of Louisiana's free people of color*. Baton Rouge: Louisiana State University Press.

Kovaleski, S. F. (1999, August 5). Shades of an identity crisis. *Washington Post*, p. A15.

Kozol, J. (1992). *Savage inequalities: Children in America's schools*. New York: Trumpet Club.

Lemann, N. (1999). The other underclass. In C. A. Gallagher (Ed.), *Rethinking the color line: Readings in race and ethnicity* (pp. 437-449). Mountain View, CA: Mayfield.

Lindsey, D. (2000, February 16). The stakes are a bit higher for us. *Salon Magazine*. Retrieved from nx5.salon.com/news/feature/2000/02/16/naacp/index.html.

Marable, M. (1991). Blacks should emphasize their ethnicity. In D. L. Bender & B. Leone (Eds.), *Racism in America: Opposing viewpoints* (pp. 175-183). San Diego: Greenhaven Press.

Marx, A. W. (1998). *Making race and nation: A comparison of the United States, South Africa, and Brazil*. Cambridge, UK: Cambridge University Press.

Massey, D. S., & Denton, N. (1999). American apartheid: The perpetuation of the underclass. In C. A. Gallagher (Ed.), *Rethinking the color line: Readings in race and ethnicity* (pp. 316-335). Mountain View, CA: Mayfield.

McNeill, T. (1994). *The politics of identity and race in the colored Creole community: The gens de couleur libre in Creole New Orleans, 1800-1860*. Retrieved from www-mcnair.berkeley.edu/UGA/OSL/McNair/94BerkeleyMcNairJournal/02_McNeill.html

Miles, R. (1989). *Racism*. London: Routledge.

Millar, H. (1993). *Towards a stronger African community in the diaspora*. Available at www.husky1.stmarys.ca/~hmillar/Unity.htm

Montagu, A. (1974). *Man's most dangerous myth*. New York: Oxford University Press. (Original work published 1942)

Mosse, G. (1999). Eighteenth-century foundations. In M. Bulmer & J. Solomos (Eds.), *Racism*. Oxford, UK: Oxford University Press.

Penn, W. (Ed.). (1997). *As we are now: Mixblood essays on race and identity*. Berkeley: University of California Press.

Pollard, A. B. III. (1997, March). *Color-consciousness in South Africa and the United States: A brief comparison*. Paper presented at the annual conference of the Society for the Study of Black Religion.

Root, M. (Ed.). (1992). *Racially mixed people in America*. Newbury Park, CA: Sage.

Root, M. (Ed.). (1996). *The multiracial experience: Racial borders as the new frontier*. Thousand Oaks, CA: Sage.

Russell, K., Wilson, M., & Hall, R. (1992). *The color complex: The politics of skin color among African Americans*. New York: Harcourt Brace Jovanovich.

Schaefer, R. T. (1998). *Racial and ethnic groups* (7th ed.). New York: Longman.

Sollors, W. (1986). "Never was born": The mulatto, an American tragedy? *Massachusetts Review, ENG, 27*(2), 293-316.

Spencer, J. M. (1997). *The new colored people: The mixed-race movement in America*. New York: New York University Press.

Spencer, R. (1997). Race and mixed race: A personal tour. In W. S. Penn (Ed.), *As we are now: Mixblood essays on race and identity* (pp. 126-139). Berkeley: University of California Press.

Spencer, R. (1999). *Spurious issues: Race and multiracial identity politics in the United States*. Boulder, CO: Westview Press.

Takaki, R. (1993). *A different mirror: A history of multicultural America*. Boston: Back Bay Books.

Texeira, M. (1995). Policing the internally colonized: Slavery, Rodney King, Mark Fuhrman and beyond. *Western Journal of Black Studies, 19*(4), 235-243.

Walker, S., Spohn, C., & Delone, M. (1999). *The color of justice: Race, ethnicity, and crime in America* (2nd ed.). New York: Wadsworth.

West, C. (1993). *Race matters.* Boston: Beacon Press.

Williamson, J. (1995). *New people: Miscegenation and mulattoes in the United States.* Baton Rouge: Louisiana State University Press.

Wilson, W. J. (1987). *The truly disadvantaged: The inner city, the underclass, and public policy.* Chicago: University of Chicago Press.

Winant, H. (1998). Racial dualism at century's end. In W. Lubiano (Ed.), *The house that race built* (pp. 87-115). New York: Vintage Books.

Wright, L. (1994). One drop of blood. In C. A. Gallagher (Ed.), *Rethinking the color line: Readings in race and ethnicity* (pp. 46-56). Mountain View, CA: Mayfield.

Zack, N. (1993). *Race and mixed race.* Philadelphia: Temple University Press.

Part II

THE MULTIRACIAL MOVEMENT

CHAPTER 3

New Faces, Old Faces

Counting the Multiracial Population Past and Present

ANN MORNING

Princeton University

Multiracial Americans have often been heralded as "new people" and in fact have been rediscovered as such more than once in the last century. Charles Chesnutt's 1899 novel *The House Behind the Cedars* features a mulatto character who uses the phrase to describe himself and others like him; in the Harlem Renaissance of the 1920s, "the new Negro" described a people that was "neither African nor European, but both" (Williamson, 1980, p. 3). More recently, Forbes (1993) has used the term "Neo-Americans" to denote populations combining African, European, and American Indian roots, and a century after Chesnutt's work appeared, numerous articles and books—including this volume—convey the sense of multiraciality's newness in titles such as "Brave New Faces" (Alaya, 2001) or "The New Face of Race" (Meacham, 2000).

Yet having populated North America for nearly four centuries, mixed-race people are far from being a recent phenomenon in the United States. Their early presence has been recorded to greater and lesser degrees in legal records, literature, and historical documentation. As far back as the 1630s and 1640s, colonial records attest to the punishment of interracial sexual unions and the regulation of mulattoes' slave status (Williamson, 1980). Dictionaries chart 16th-century English usage of the word *mulatow* (Sollors, 2000), although the meaning of this term has varied over time (Forbes, 1993). Finally, mixed-race people have long populated American literature, particularly since the early 19th century (Sollors, 2000). In sum, the multiracial community is not a new, 20th-century phenomenon but rather a long-standing element of American society.

By obscuring the historic dimensions of American multiraciality—emphasizing its newness but not its oldness—we may run the risk of ignoring lessons that past racial stratification offers for understanding today's outcomes. For one thing, older social norms still make themselves felt in contemporary discussion of mixed-race identity (Davis, 1991; Waters, 1991; Wilson, 1992). In addition, history reminds us that these attitudes toward multiraciality were embedded in complex webs of social, political, economic, and cultural premises and objectives, thereby suggesting that the same holds true today. Finally, turning to the past highlights how malleable racial concepts have proved to be over time despite the permanence and universality we often ascribe to them. Given the United States' history, the extent to which public attitudes toward mixed-race unions and ancestry have changed is remarkable. Perhaps the real new people today are not just those of multiracial heritage but also Americans in general who now conceptualize, tolerate, or embrace multiple-race identities in ways that were unacceptable in the past.

The history of census enumeration and scientific estimation of the multiracial population in the United States offers an illuminating window onto older conceptions of mixed-race status and a thought-provoking opportunity to compare past treatment of this community with its contemporary reflection. Although the introduction of multiple-race self-description on the 2000 census is often depicted as an entirely new innovation—much as multiracial people themselves are considered to be a new group (Nobles, 2000)—it was not in fact the first time that mixed-race origins have been recorded on the U.S. census. In the 19th century, multiracial response categories were a common, if sporadic, feature of decennial censuses whose appearance and disappearance can be traced to the social, political, and economic outlooks of the nation's white citizenry at the time. Accordingly, this chapter seeks both to describe historical practices for counting the mixed-race population and to link them with the racial ideologies that motivated and shaped them. Although the focus is on national census enumeration, I also study the efforts of scientists who sought for over a century to estimate the size of the multiracial population and

who tended to share the same preoccupations and preconceptions about race as the census officials of their day. Finally, I consider possible implications of the historical record for our understanding of the introduction of multiple-race classification on the 2000 census, suggesting that factors similar to those that weighed in the past are still discernible today.

DEFINITION

Before embarking on the stated inquiry, it is crucial to elaborate on the usage of terms such as *multiracial* and *mixed-race*. I use these adjectives interchangeably to denote people whose genealogical ancestry was understood in their day as combining distinct races regardless of whether this mixture stemmed from their parents' generation or farther back. This definition underscores the notion that who we consider to be mixed-race depends at any given time on what we consider to be races in the first place (Morning, 2000). As well, Americans' catalogue of races has varied over time, as the changing racial categories on the U.S. census suggest (Bennett, 2000; Lee, 1993). In 1790, the first national census featured only one racial label—"white"—although the accompanying "slave" category was understood to denote blackness. In contrast, the 2000 census offered six main racial categories that could be combined to yield 57 possible multiple-race identities (U.S. Office of Management and Budget [OMB], 2000a). However, even in what may seem like a contemporary plethora of choice, certain kinds of ancestry cannot be registered as multiracial in the current federal statistical system. Notably, the fact that *Hispanic* does not appear as a response option to the census race question— instead it is treated as a category on a separate ethnicity question—makes it difficult to express white and Hispanic identity, for example, as a multiracial one.

However we may conceive of mixed-race identity today, the following discussion is limited to the types of identity that census enumerators and other government officials and researchers understood to represent racial mixture in the terms of their time. In this account, there is no true demographic distribution of racial identities against which historic census takers' efforts can be measured. Instead, the historical record teaches us that race is and has been simply what we make of it.

MULTIRACIAL ENUMERATION ON THE U.S. CENSUS, 1790-1990

Approaches to counting mixed-race Americans have varied significantly over time. Although race has always figured on the U.S. census, the terms used, the definitions proposed, and the instructions designed for census takers and respondents have been so frequently altered that virtually no two census schedules are alike. Still, important continuities exist, notably in the differential attention to and statistical treatment of different combinations of racial ancestry.

Multiracial Census Categories and Counts

Before the year 2000, the U.S. census registered only two types of multiracial ancestry: the combination of black and white (generally referred to as *mulatto*) and American Indian race in combination with others (usually labeled *mixed blood*).[1] Moreover, it recorded these mixed ancestries somewhat sporadically.

Mulattoes. The first explicitly mixed-race category to make its way onto an American general population census schedule appeared in 1850 in the form of the mulatto option. Before then, the only racial terms used on the census had been *white, Indians (not taxed)* (and

thus excluded from enumeration), and *colored,* the latter not necessarily requiring African ancestry (Forbes, 1993). The mulatto category was used in census enumeration through 1920, with a brief disappearance from the 1900 census. However, this hiatus was preceded by an elaboration of taxonomy for black/white mixture in 1890, when *quadroon* and *octoroon* designations were added to the census.

Over the 70-year period in which they were enumerated, the proportion of mulattoes ranged from a low of 1.5% of the total population in 1870 to a high of 2.2% in 1910. As Table 3.1 shows, their share of the total black population (meaning both blacks and mulattoes) never fell below 11%, and it surpassed 20% in 1910. However, as the Census Bureau itself admitted in a 1918 report,

> It is probably true that a much greater population than 20.9 per cent of the Negro population in 1910 were of mixed parentage. The proportion more or less affected by the dissemination has been estimated as high as three-fourths, and although no adequate data are available to substantiate such an estimate, the estimate is not in itself improbable. (p. 209)

Despite this acknowledgment of the widespread applicability of the mulatto category, however, it would soon be removed from the U.S. census.

Mixed Bloods. Long viewed as members of foreign nations, American Indians were not recorded independently on the general census until 1860, and then "Indians Not Taxed" were excluded from the count. Census officials did not attempt to enumerate the entire American Indian population, taxed and untaxed, until 1890, 100 years after the first U.S. census. However, what would prove to be a long tradition of enumerating American Indians apart from other members of the population had already begun with a "special Indian census" in 1850 (Nobles, 2000).

Table 3.1   Census Enumeration of Mulattoes, 1850-1920

| | Mulatto Population | | | Total Black Population | | |
Year	Total	% of Total Black Population	% of Total U.S. Population	Total	% of Total U.S. Population	Total U.S. Population
1850	405,751	11.15	1.75	3,638,808	15.69	23,191,876
1860	588,363	13.25	1.87	4,441,830	14.13	31,443,321
1870[a]	584,049	11.97	1.51	4,880,009	12.66	38,558,371
1880[b]	NA	NA	NA	6,580,793	13.12	50,155,783
1890	1,132,060	15.12	1.80	7,488,676	11.90	62,947,714
1900[c]	NA	NA	NA	8,833,994	11.62	75,994,575
1910	2,050,686	20.87	2.23	9,827,763	10.69	91,972,266
1920	1,660,554	15.87	1.57	10,463,131	9.90	105,710,620

SOURCE: U.S. Census Bureau (1923) *Abstract of the Fourteenth Census of the United States 1920*, Table 20.

[a]1870 figures as enumerated, not as later adjusted.
[b]Published figures not available for 1880.
[c]Mulattoes were not enumerated separately in 1900.

In 1880, "Indian Division" schedules recorded whether respondents were "of full-blood" or whether they embodied "mixture" with whites, blacks, mulattoes, or another tribe (U.S. Census Bureau, 1973). Questions about the blood "quantum" (i.e., fraction) of individuals identified as American Indian remained on the census—on general, supplemental or special schedules—through 1910 and later reappeared in 1930 and 1950.

In contrast to its admitted undercount of mixed ancestry among blacks, the U.S. Census Bureau was more satisfied with its estimates of the degree of mixed blood among American Indians, which fell between 35% and 45% (Table 3.2). In a comparison of the Indian census results of 1910 and 1930, the U.S. Census Bureau maintained that "both censuses were reasonably accurate and comparable with each other" (U.S. Census Bureau, 1937). One caveat emerged, however: "In North Carolina, and also in many other areas, the proportion of Indians shown in the census of 1930 as of full blood is much too high. This is particularly true of those tribes in which there is a large Negro admixture." As review of the enumeration instructions will demonstrate, census officials at the time were loath to classify individuals with any African ancestry as American Indians.

Census Instructions for Racial Enumeration

The historical series of official instructions for enumerators reveals a great deal more preoccupation with mixed-race people than the limited range of multiracial census categories suggests. Even when multiracial categories were not included, directions for the census takers routinely took up the issue of classifying mixed-race people in the single-race categories available. Through 1960, when the U.S. Census Bureau switched from sending enumerators out to take the census in favor of mailing out questionnaires, the varying directions given to census takers offered powerful testimony to the ideological currents of their day.

Defining Mixed-Race Groups. One striking aspect of the enumerators' instructions is the

Table 3.2 Census Enumeration of Mixed Bloods, 1910-1950

Year	Mixed-Blood Population			Total American Indian Population			
	Total	% of Tot. Indian Population	% of Tot U.S. Population	Total	% of Total U.S. Population	Total U.S. Population
1910[a,b]	93,423	35.16	0.10	265,683	0.29	91,972,266
1920[d]	NA	NA	NA	244,437	0.23	105,710,620
1930[b]	141,101	42.45	0.11	332,397	0.27	122,775,046
1940[d]	NA	NA	NA	333,969	0.25	131,669,275
1950[c]	136,677	39.8	0.09	343,410	0.23	150,697,361

SOURCES: U.S. Census Bureau (1915) *Indian Population in the United States and Alaska 1910*, Table 12; U.S. Census Bureau (1937) *Indian Population of the United States and Alaska 1930*, Table 12; U.S. Census Bureau (1964) *U.S. Census of Population: 1960.* Vol. I, Characteristics of the Population, Part 1, United States Summary, Table 44; U.S. Congress, Office of Technology Assessment (1986) *Indian Health Care*, p. 76.

[a] 1910 Indian count does not include Alaska population.
[b] In 1910 and 1930, American Indians whose blood quantum is not reported are grouped with full bloods.
[c] 1950 figures use Office of Technology Assessment (1986) estimate of mixed-blood share, based on 1950 census returns.
[d] Blood quantum not recorded in 1920 and 1940.

variation in the ways the same terms were defined in different census years. In 1850, when the mulatto category was introduced on the census schedule, enumerators were not given any direction concerning who should be considered mulatto. It is likely that census officials felt the designation to be self-evident, especially in light of Forbes's (1993) contention that in the United States the word *mulatto* originally denoted all people of mixed-race ancestry, not just those with white and black origins. If this was still true to some extent in the mid-19th century (as Forbes claims), 1850 census takers might have assigned people to this all-purpose category without being overly concerned about precisely what type of mixture they represented. However, with time, definitions of who was mulatto appeared and for a while grew increasingly detailed. In 1870, enumerators were told that "the class *Mulatto*" included "quadroons, octoroons, and all persons having any perceptible trace of African blood" (quoted in

Nobles, 2000, p. 187). When those categories were themselves listed on the 1890 census schedule, the definitions of black/white ancestry became even more detailed, drawing on notions of blood proportions, or quanta, that had already been widely applied to American Indian mixed bloods (Nobles, 2000):

> The word "black" should be used to describe those persons who have three-fourths or more black blood; "mulatto," those persons who have from three-eighths to five-eighths black blood; "quadroon," those persons who have one-fourth black blood; and "octoroons," those persons who have one-eighth or any trace of black blood. (p. 188)

After 1890, however, degrees of black and white ancestry would never again be delineated as carefully. Mulattoes did not figure on the 1900 census at all, and when this category returned in 1910 and 1920 only, it would be defined simply as including "all persons having some proportion or perceptible trace of Negro blood" (Nobles, 2000, p. 188). In sum, over time the mulatto grouping was concretized, elaborately defined, simply defined, and then erased.

Census definitions of American Indian mixed bloods, on the other hand, endured until the advent of self-enumeration and generally grew more complex over time. When first mentioned in 1870, "half-breeds" were simply defined as "persons with any perceptible trace of Indian blood, whether mixed with white or with Negro stock" (U.S. Census Office, 1872, p. xiii), echoing the contemporaneous formula for identifying mulattoes. On the 1880 Indian Division schedules, mixture with mulattoes was added as another possible characteristic of mixed-blood status. In 1900, fractions or quanta of blood were introduced (down to one eighth), and interestingly enough, it was "white blood" and not Indian that was to be measured. In 1910, fractions of Indian, white, and Negro blood were recorded. In addition, although census takers reverted to a simple full-blood/mixed-blood dichotomy in 1930, the 1950 census reintroduced the blood quantum construct with the category "degree of Indian blood" and its response options: "full blood," "half to full," "quarter to half," and "less than ¼" (U.S. Census Bureau, 1973).

Census officials' definitions of mixed-race people of American Indian origin also differed from those concerning mulattoes in that they drew on a range of social, cultural, situational, and behavioral factors. The 1870 census report discussed the question of classifying American Indian half-breeds at length, concluding,

> Where persons reported as "half-breeds" are found residing with whites, adopting their habits of life and methods of industry, such persons are to be treated as belonging to the white population. Where, on the other hand, they are found in communities composed wholly or mainly of Indians, the opposite construction is taken. In a word, in

the equilibrium produced by the equal division of blood, the habits, tastes, and associations of the half-breed are allowed to determine his gravitation to the one class or the other. (U.S. Census Office, 1872, p. xiii)

Thus, the assignment of mixed bloods to one race or another did not depend entirely on their perceived genealogy but instead took into account their occupation, place of residence, social ties, and behavior. Although Indian blood quantum would later be carefully noted beginning with the 1880 census, the social status of the individual in question remained salient, as powerfully evinced by the 1930 census introduction of the idea of identifying Indians as those who were "accepted in the community" as such (U.S. Census Bureau, 1937, p. 1). This phrasing, which remained on the census through 1960, sanctioned the exceptional cases in which people of mixed-race ancestry could be assigned to the higher rather than the lower status of the two racial groups with which they were identified. That is, individuals of white and Indian origin could be designated as white if their communities recognized them as such, and those of Indian and black origin could be recorded as Indian. In contrast, mulattoes were afforded no such option; no amount of community recognition could legitimate the transformation from black to white.[2]

Enumerator Instructions in the Absence of Multiracial Categories. In most years in which multiracial categories were not used on census forms, enumerators received detailed directions about how to assign mixed-race people to single-race categories. Careful instructions regarding the proper classification of Indian half-breeds appeared in the 1870 census even though this category would not actually be enumerated until 1880. In 1940 and 1960, census takers were told how to treat "persons of mixed white and Indian blood" even though they could not be recorded as multiracial in those years.

Similarly, persons "of mixed white and Negro blood" still haunted the directions to enumerators 40 years after the removal of the mulatto category.

Moreover, the instructions for classifying multiracial groups often covered an even wider spectrum of racial mixtures than had ever been formalized in previous census race categories. In 1930, the mulatto category was absent and American Indians were recognized as full or mixed bloods only on a supplemental Indian schedule. Nevertheless, the enumeration instructions for the general population schedule took up the treatment of individuals of: black/white ancestry (to be designated as Negro); black/Indian ancestry (also to be returned as Negro in most cases); white/Indian mixture (usually to be labeled Indian); Mexican origin ("of a racial mixture difficult to classify," to be listed as Mexican), and other "mixed races." The directions for the last group were that "any mixture of white and nonwhite should be reported according to the nonwhite parent. Mixtures of colored races should be reported according to the race of the father, except Negro-Indian" (Nobles, 2000, p. 189). Thus, in a decennial census year in which essentially only one type of multiracial identity would be officially recorded (i.e., Indian mixed-blood status), a proliferation of directions was needed to channel all possible racial combinations into single-race groups. These extensive 1930 racial classification directions appeared through the 1960 census—the last to use enumerators' observations to a significant extent—and in fact they grew even more detailed during this period. The instructions on the 1950 census identified a little-known segment of the population to be specially counted: the eastern triracial isolate communities of white, black, and American Indian ancestry (Berry, 1963). Enumerators were instructed to record such individuals "in terms of the name by which they are locally known," such as "Siouian," "Croatan,"

"Moor," or "Tunica" (U.S. Census Bureau, 1953, p. 3B-5). In 1960, instructions about multiracial individuals were joined by directions concerning the racial classification of ostensibly ambiguous groups such as Italians, Puerto Ricans, and Syrians. Although these groups were not recognized as distinct races requiring independent census categories, their proper racial identification was deemed challenging enough—and important enough—to warrant special mention.

Investigation of historical U.S. enumeration reveals that although the range of racial categories used in any given census year was often limited, census officials were aware of and interested in a much wider range of racial configurations. Although only irregularly recorded as such, mixed-race people consistently figured in the Census Bureau's instructions to its enumerators. Despite the ways in which multiracial enumeration varied from census to census, certain facets were fairly stable, notably the asymmetric treatment of black and American Indian ancestry and the overriding focus on the classification of mixed-race people with white ancestry. Together they paint a picture of a system of racial stratification in which some boundaries were more permeable than others.

MULTIRACIAL CENSUS ENUMERATION IN HISTORIC CONTEXT

How can we explain the particular forms that multiracial census enumeration took on at different times in the past? Answers lie less with the nation's demographic profile than in the historical cultural beliefs, social structure, and political and economic interests of the white population. As the dominant racial group in the United States—indeed, virtually its only citizens when the first census was taken—the concerns, beliefs, and objectives of whites have informed every aspect of American census taking.

Demographic Shifts and the Perception of Racial Boundaries

A striking conclusion to be drawn from the historical record is that the presence or absence of multiracial census categories usually has not reflected the actual size of the American mixed-race population, even when contemporary bounds on what was considered multiracial are taken into account. This disconnect is demonstrated by the lack of attention to extensive black/Indian mixture (Forbes, 1993; Wilson, 1992) and by the removal of the mulatto category shortly after the Census Bureau itself put the mulatto share of the negro population at three quarters (U.S. Census Bureau, 1918). Similarly, interracial mixture involving Asians did not figure in any national census before 2000,[3] despite the presence of turn-of-the-century immigrant communities whose highly skewed sex ratios favored interracial unions (Barringer, Garner, & Levin, 1993; La Brack, 1999; Leonard, 1997), the interaction of thousands of white and black soldiers with Asian women during World War II and after (Spickard, 1989), and relatively high Asian outmarriage rates in recent years (Pollard & O'Hare, 1999).

It is tempting to attribute the introduction of multiple-race reporting on the 2000 census simply to significant growth in the American mixed-race population. In the wake of the Immigration Act of 1965, which ushered in a new wave of diverse non-European immigration, the 1967 U.S. Supreme Court *Loving v. Virginia* decision to invalidate state bans against interracial marriage, and the civil rights movement more generally, the number of U.S. married couples that involved either spouses of different races or Hispanics married to non-Hispanics more than quadrupled from 1970 to 1998, reaching 1.4 million couples, or 5%, of all married couples. Similarly, the annual share of multiracial births has grown from less than 2% of all births in 1977 to about 5% in 1997; in California that year, mixed-race infants made up the third-largest

group of births behind Hispanics and whites (Pollard & O'Hare, 1999). Clearly, a considerable increment is being added to the existing multiracial population of the United States.

However, such demographic shifts might well have gone unrecognized—as previous racial intermixture often had—had they not been accompanied by changing perceptions of multiraciality. Children in California that we now think of as mixed-race could instead have been described simply as monoracial, as has often occurred in both the past and present, especially with respect to black ancestry (Davis, 1991). To conclude, then, that multiple-race enumeration in 2000 was a "natural" reflection of the nation's demographic trends is to ignore two important attitudinal prerequisites. First, multiracial people had to be recognized as a distinct group (e.g., as mulattoes were once distinguished from blacks) before their separate enumeration could take place. Such perceptions cannot be taken for granted because they reflect particular judgments of which groups constitute distinct races and which people belong to them. Second, the introduction of multiple-race identification on the 2000 census also required a change of attitude about whether perceived interracial mixture should be officially acknowledged. Judging from the historical record, census recognition of multiraciality cannot be said to be an automatic response to the perception of racial intermixture: Recall that the same people who were understood to be mulatto on the 1920 census were collapsed into the "Negro" category in 1930. In other words, our approaches to recording racial mixture have been anchored less in the nation's demography than in our perspectives on racial variety and the desirability of its measurement.

Focus on Mixed-Race Groups With White Ancestry

An important question raised by review of U.S. enumeration practices is why only two types of multiracial heritage have consistently preoccupied American census takers: white/ black people and white/Indian people. One obvious reason is simple ethnocentrism on the part of whites, described by Wilson (1992) as the "underlying assumption of the greater importance of White-colored mixtures over colored-colored" (p. 110). However, Lee's (1993) statement that "race in the United States hinges most fundamentally on the colour line dividing White and Other (non-White) Americans" (p. 91) reminds us that the mixed-race people who inhabit the borderlands around the national color line play a unique part in our system of racial stratification. Sixty years ago, Kingsley Davis (1941) wrote that "the racial integrity of the upper caste is to be strictly maintained, to the degree that all persons of mixed racial qualities shall be placed unequivocally in the lower of the two castes" (p. 389). In other words, the classification of intermediate groups is instrumental for marking the boundaries and status of higher castes. Here Davis described a social structure characterized by hypodescent (i.e., the association of intermediate groups with lower-status rather than higher-status groups) as in the "one-drop" rule for blackness (Harris, 1964), but as F. James Davis (1991) noted, other social patterns have existed in different times and in different places. In early America, the social definition of individuals who descended both from whites and from blacks or American Indians—the two largest nonwhite groups— would certainly have commanded the attention of those who were concerned with preserving or reinforcing whiteness. This "gate-keeping" social function of mixed-race groups helps explain both the consistent interest of white Americans in people of mixed white and other ancestry (as opposed to, for example, black/American Indian background) and the variation in the degree of importance attached to, as well as the ways of classifying, multiracial groups. At different points in American history, it has been more

or less important to define and unify the white population (Jacobson, 1998).

The career of the mulatto census category exemplifies the relationship between multiracial enumeration and concerns about the nature of whiteness. As Nobles (2000) demonstrates, this racial category was first introduced on the 1850 census in response to scientists' calls for data they believed would help settle important questions about the biological consequences of hybridity. Comparison of the fertility and mortality rates of mulattoes, blacks, and whites would eventually be of great interest to scientists wishing to test theories of "survival of the fittest" and to assess the supposed benefits of slavery and later racial segregation. Hence, enumerators from 1850 to 1890 were admonished to use "particular care" with the increasingly complex mulatto category; as the 1870 census instructions elaborated, "Important scientific results depend upon the correct determination of this class" (Nobles, 2000, p. 187). However, in the Reconstruction aftermath of the Civil War, southern whites' fears for their political, economic, and social status led to widespread preoccupation with holding the line against black encroachment; these apprehensions were vividly symbolized by passionate antimiscegenation sentiment (Davis, 1991; Rosen, 1999; Williamson, 1980). In the same period, northern whites had to contend with the unsettling questions about just who was white that were raised by the great influx of new European immigrants, then viewed as members of distinct "races" such as Celtic or Slavic. Other rifts among whites—between North and South, elites and workers—also threatened the nation's social fabric. In these cases and others, anxiety about the status and unity of whiteness would be resolved by reinforcing boundaries between whites and people of color, particularly blacks (Jacobson, 1998; Marx, 1998). As Warren and Twine (1997), Bashi and McDaniel (1997), Gans (1999), and others have argued, blackness is the measure par excellence against which whiteness has traditionally been defined in the United States. Thus, a turn-of-the-century backlash against Reconstruction policies manifested itself in hardening Jim Crow segregation, antiblack violence, and a wave of state statutes outlawing black/white marriage. In implementing such bans, many states adopted racial definitions that instituted one drop of black blood as the determinant of blackness, signaling that no midway ground was possible between the poles of white and black (Davis, 1991). In this climate, the mulatto category was effectively rendered obsolete and removed from the census after 1920.

Just as mixed-race status marked social boundaries, it also played an instrumental role in the negotiation of access to political and economic resources. From the United States' earliest beginnings, race has governed fundamental aspects of life such as slavery and freedom, citizenship, enfranchisement, and property rights. Thus, multiracial people's intermediate social role also had material implications in a society in which, to white eyes, blacks represented a wealth of labor and Indians a wealth of land. How mixed-race individuals of European, African, and American Indian ancestry were defined could at times make all the difference between being property and owning it.

The experience of American Indian mixed bloods illustrates the importance of multiracial designation in regulating access to material resources. In the 18th and 19th centuries, mixed bloods received preferential treatment in many instances both from the white missionaries among them and from the U.S. government in the treaties it signed with American Indian nations (Churchill, 1999). The resulting privileges might take the form of special goods or services or extra or more preferable land parcels. Churchill (1999) argues that in this manner, whites sought to use mixed bloods as a "wedge" to curry favor or gain a foothold within tribal communities. The distinction between full and mixed bloods, however, was

more comprehensively entrenched in the land allotment process mandated by the Dawes Act of 1887. Not only did the allotment rolls identifying American Indians to receive land tracts take note of full- versus mixed-blood status, but later policy used blood quantum to determine the type of property title to be granted the new landowners (Prucha, 1984). Individuals with less than half Indian blood quantum were generally free to dispose of their land as they wished, whereas those with greater Indian ancestry were deemed less competent and the land assigned them was administered on their behalf by the U.S. government for several years. Giving free land title to mixed bloods had the ultimate effect of releasing this land to whites, for the allottees sold off their property in large numbers. Unrau (1989) concludes that over time, mixed bloods "played a pervasive role in the diminution of the Indian land base in the United States" (p. ix). By treating mixed bloods as a distinct faction of the American Indian community—and one more amenable to their goals—some whites hoped to gain access to resources that were otherwise off limits.

Different Measures for Mixed Bloods and Mulattoes

As we have seen, mulattoes and mixed bloods tended to be enumerated in very different ways on the U.S. census. First, the mulatto category was for the most part a 19th-century phenomenon, whereas the mixed-blood label lasted well into the 20th century and is still commonly used within and outside the American Indian community (Nagel, 1996; Wilson, 1992). Second, the mathematical accounting of blood quantum so pervasively applied to Indians was only rarely used to describe black/white mixture. Third, although the proper racial adjudication of individuals of white and Indian ancestry could draw on their social and occupational characteristics, the correct labeling of people with black and white ancestry was never more than a matter of their genealogy. Finally, whereas mixed bloods could occasionally be enumerated as white, this was never an option for mulattoes. Moreover, when it came to the blending of black and Indian blood, blackness was presumed dominant. Together these observations raise the question of why diverse types of racial mixture were enumerated so differently.

To some extent, the different implications of black and American Indian racial status for political, social, and economic outcomes explain why U.S. censuses enumerated mulattoes versus mixed bloods in very different ways. The economics of slavery (and later a nominally free but segregated work force) favored a one-drop system, which assigned mulattoes to the black population, thus augmenting the subjugated labor force available. This structure militated against the appearance of a mulatto census category at all, and in the period in which it was used its purpose was primarily to provide scientific ammunition in support of the indiscriminate enslavement or segregation of both blacks and mulattoes. American Indians, in contrast, were not sought as a labor force in early America (despite initial English attempts at their enslavement; see Smedley, 1999); rather whites coveted relations with them as a conduit to land acquisition. Thus, a one-drop rule for Indian identity had less immediate appeal from the perspective of whites; indeed, the contrary held for several purposes. First, beginning early in the 19th century, the U.S. government undertook a program of educating and "civilizing" Indians whose costs could be minimized the fewer the number of Indians for whom the government claimed responsibility. Such fiscal calculations remain relevant today: In 1986, the Congressional Office of Technology Assessment (OTA) estimated the current and future blood quantum composition of the American Indian population to project expected cost burdens on the Indian Health Service and to explore the possible impact of tightened blood quantum eligibility

requirements (U.S. Congress, OTA, 1986). Second, classifying American Indians of mixed-race ancestry as white (or black) eliminated potential Indian land claims based on treaties or federal law (Churchill, 1999). Finally, recognizing mixed-blood status served as a "divide-and-conquer" strategy with tangible benefits for land-hungry white settlers. In sum, a variety of structural factors have favored a more enduring and liberal use of the mixed-blood concept compared with the relatively brief life span of the mulatto category.

However, the contours of multiracial enumeration in the United States cannot be attributed solely to economic and political rationales, because the cultural mythology of race shared by early European Americans also exercised a powerful influence on the conceptualization and measurement of racial mixture. To the extent that whites viewed different nonwhite races in distinct ways, usually as embodying distinctly particular flaws, it is not surprising that their presumptions about different multiracial groups varied as well. According to Berkhofer (1978), American Indians were generally not considered "as low in the hierarchy of races as the Blacks" (p. 34). For example, President Thomas Jefferson made known his belief that unlike blacks, Indians were "in body and mind equal to the white man" (Wallace, 1999), and Prucha (1981) argues that this view of the Indian as "barbaric but redeemable" was shared by other major architects of federal Indian policy such as Secretary of War Lewis Cass and President Andrew Jackson. Indeed, Prucha contends that this belief was an essential ingredient of the federal government's persistent attempts to educate and civilize the Indian population in a period when education was forbidden to black slaves. However, the fact that the civilizing mission often served to herd Indians off lands that whites coveted (Tyler, 1973) is a reminder that racial ideologies combine material interests with cultural representations in ways that are difficult to disentangle.

Stereotypes that whites held helped both to initially introduce certain policies toward blacks and Indians and later to justify these modes of treatment. Thus, images of belligerent and uncivilized Indians justified their displacement and extermination, whereas supposedly childlike but hardy blacks were best off under the paternal care of slave masters (Berkhofer, 1978; Bieder, 1986; Nobles, 2000; Smedley, 1999; Williamson, 1980).[4]

The similarity or distance that white Americans calculated between themselves and other races had striking implications for their predictions concerning the nation's racial destiny. The fundamental humanity ascribed to American Indians gave rise to hopes for their eventual "amalgamation" (as it was frequently called) with the white population (Prucha, 1981; Tyler, 1973), whereas the irreducible inferiority of blacks made their "miscegenation" with whites an end to be avoided at all costs (Davis, 1991). Like Thomas Jefferson (Prucha, 1981), prominent early anthropologist Lewis Henry Morgan condoned Indian/white amalgamation; in the 1860s he wrote that the American Indian "must become a farmer and make money and throw off the Indian past. Those alone who do this will be able to save themselves and ultimately will be absorbed in our race" (cited in Bieder, 1986, p. 221). The alternative to Indians' amalgamation with whites, however, was widely claimed to be their extinction (Horsman, 1975; Tyler, 1973; Wallace, 1999). In Thomas Jefferson's *Notes on the State of Virginia* (1800), his picture of the vanishing Indian speaks to what Wallace (1999, p. 79) calls a "mordant fascination" with an increasingly widespread image of American Indians as "a conquered and dying race." The popular diagnosis—namely that Indians could not withstand contact with white civilization—gained even greater currency in the wake of Darwin's 1859 *On the Origin of Species*. The presumed imminent extinction of American Indians was then recast as a matter of the survival of the fittest, so that an 1865 congressional resolution would declare the decline of the Indian population to be the result of "the irrepressible conflict between a superior and an inferior race when brought in presence of each other" (Tyler, 1973, p. 76).

Given the diverse outlooks that whites held about the future of blacks and American Indians, the figures of the mulatto and the mixed blood were also imagined as having very different characteristics and destinies. Consistent with the mythology of an Indian race whose only salvation lay in amalgamation with whites, the mixed blood represented a marked improvement over the full-blooded American Indian (Bieder, 1986; Horsman, 1975), for whom he might serve as a role model (Unrau, 1989). In marked contrast, the mulatto represented no such step up the evolutionary scale: Instead, he was a debilitated figure—physically weak, high strung, and sterile—who represented the deterioration of both black and white stock (Williamson, 1980). Like the full-blooded Indian, the mixed-race mulatto was expected to eventually die out, especially once the abolition of slavery put an end to white/black miscegenation, leaving behind completely and appropriately separate black and white populations. Also like the full blood, the mulatto had an escape route open to him via amalgamation, but it involved absorption by the black rather than the white population (Williamson, 1980). Although American Indians could gradually be assimilated by the white population, this avenue was closed to those with black blood, ensuring that whiteness would continue to be defined as the absence of blackness. By virtue of their predicted demise, multiracial people served as bridges to the racial future envisioned by whites.

The mirror contrast between mixed bloods' predicted absorption by whites and mulattoes' absorption by blacks was closely linked to the amount of attention paid by enumerators to the details of their hybridity. Simply, the belief that American Indians could eventually become white justified a careful accounting of their proximity to or distance from whiteness: hence fractions of blood quantum. The meaningfulness of such calculation is apparent in Morgan's reckoning about white/Indian mixture (Bieder, 1986):

> The second cross, giving three-quarters Indian, is an advance upon the native; and giving three fourths white is still a greater advance. . . . With the white carried still further, full equality is reached, tending to show that Indian blood can be taken up without physical or intellectual detriment. (p. 231)

Because black blood, on the other hand, could never be washed away—not even the proverbial single drop—the exact quantity of white blood that mulattoes had was irrelevant.

The logic of tracking hybridity en route to eventual whiteness—a kind of alchemy[5]—is found throughout the Americas. Its apogee materialized in the 18th-century series of colonial Mexican paintings known as *las castas* or *los cuadros del mestizaje*, which depict couples of diverse races and racial mixtures in their characteristic dress and surroundings. Spurred on by Linnaeus's 1735 systematization of taxonomy, the *castas* portraits also present the progeny of dozens of distinct racial mixtures and name each one. These names, in turn, frequently refer to the distance or proximity of the mixture from whiteness: A child who was *salta atrás* was a "jump back," like a *torna atrás* (Nash, 1995). The colonial calculus of hybridity was also furthered by the development of special mathematical notation akin to the later U.S. measurement of blood quantum (Moreno Navarro, 1973). Yet the notion that racial impurity of any color could eventually be diluted to the point of disappearance, which appeared throughout the Western Hemisphere in the 18th and 19th centuries, made little headway against North American thinking about blacks.

Belief in the indelibility of blackness was one of the most striking cultural constructions to characterize 19th- and 20th-century census taking. Along with evaluations of the diverse qualities of multiracial people and predictions about the future of the American racial landscape, it formed a kind of racial cosmology that ordered the races, explained that ordering, and pointed the way toward its eventual resolution. At the same time, this cultural complex of beliefs, values, and symbols was interwoven with mixed-race people's structural position in a society in which race implied different relations to land and labor and delineated political and social communities. As a result, census enumeration of multiracial people reflected both the cultural meanings and material importance ascribed to them.

SCIENCE ESTIMATES THE MIXED-RACE POPULATION, 1920-1990

Motivated by many of the same concerns and perspectives on race as census officials, American scientists have demonstrated a long-standing interest in the mixed-race population. In the 19th century, they pressed for census enumeration of mulattoes and other mixed-race people in the belief that it would help address important scientific and policy questions. After the Census Bureau's early 20th-century termination of mulatto enumeration, social and natural scientists launched their own data collection efforts focusing on interracial mixture. Using both quantitative and qualitative methods, scientists developed a variety of techniques for assessing just how racially mixed the American population had become, with a steady focus on the blending of black and white. It was already widely presumed and accepted that the American Indian population would be absorbed into the white, but whether "black blood" could similarly be assimilated was a much more controversial and troubling prospect.

Anthropometry, Genealogy, and Survey Research in the Social Sciences

In his review of early 20th-century scientific thought regarding mulattoes, Williamson (1980) concludes that "social scientists took over the study of miscegenation and mulattoes where the census left off" (p. 115). Nobles (2000) also posits an alternating relationship between census enumeration and scientific theorizing on race when she writes that the census "has been most closely involved in developing ideas about race when (social) scientific thinking on race itself has been most unstable" (p. 26). Consistent with these views, certain academic research agendas on interracial mixture gained momentum once the Census Bureau permanently removed the mulatto category after 1920.

Anthropologists and sociologists in the first half of the 20th century were particularly interested in measuring the extent to which blacks had nonblack ancestry and the degree to which blacks had "passed" or were passing undetected into the white population. In other words, they sought to measure both past interracial mixture stemming from illicit unions and contemporary interracial mixture that occurred without being recognized. At times, their work countered beliefs that interracial sex had been minimal in the antebellum past, thus threatening cherished notions of white purity. In a period when white fear of "mongrelization" was rife—fueled not just by blacks, Indians, or Asians, but also by the new southern and eastern European immigrants (Kevles, 1985)—their work touched on the sensitive issue of "white blood" among blacks and, worse yet, "black blood" flowing in white veins.

One of the earliest examples of this work was sociologist Edward B. Reuter's (1918) *The Mulatto in the United States: Including a Study of the Role of Mixed-Blood Races throughout the World*. In the same year, Caroline Bond Day began her research on racially mixed families, tracing their genealogy, physical appearance, and attitudes toward interracial unions (Day, 1932). Melville J. Herskovits also linked anthropometry (the measurement of physiognomy) to genealogy. In his 1928 work, *The American Negro: A Study in Racial Crossing*, Herskovits reported that 78% of his black respondents claimed to have white and/or American Indian ancestry. In 1947, anthropologist Ralph Linton revised this estimate upward to 90% (Williamson, 1980, p. 118). As for passing, sociologist Charles S. Johnson believed that 10,000 to 20,000 mulattoes had disappeared into the white population each year from 1900 to 1920; in 1946 another sociologist, John Burma, guessed that 110,000 mulattoes were living as whites in the United States (Williamson, 1980, pp.103, 119).

Probing Genes, Blood, and Skin Color in the Natural Sciences

The long-standing equation of race with physical characteristics that had originally led researchers to study the anthropometry of mixed-race people was further invigorated when the science of genetics began to develop rapidly in the mid-20th century. Older understandings of "mixed blood" metamorphosed into new models of mixed genes for which new theories, measurement techniques, and instruments were developed. In a period of activity marked by Crick and Watson's 1953 discovery of the double-helix structure of DNA, biological researchers believed that genetic science would provide the precise answers about American multiracial ancestry that had eluded social scientists. At the same time, the study of mixed-race people promised to add to genetic knowledge, as attested by reports such as "Genetics of Interracial Crosses in Hawaii" (Morton, 1962) or "American Triracial Isolates: Their Status and Pertinence to Genetic Research" (Beale, 1957). Ironically, new insights into the human genome later challenged the long-standing belief that races were physically distinct groups (Marks, 1995).

An early but meaningful example of scientists' genetic analysis of the multiracial population comes from biologists Glass and Li's (1953) use of allele (gene variant) frequencies to study "the dynamics of the process of 'racial' or population intermixture." Specifically, they compared the frequency of a particular blood type in the black U.S. population to its frequencies in the white population and in some black African populations to estimate the "rate of gene flow from the U.S. White into the U.S. Negro population." In conclusion, they put "the accumulated amount of white admixture" at 31% of the black population.

The Glass and Li (1953) study illustrates how widely held presumptions about the workings of race informed ostensibly objective scientific inquiry. First, it announces that genes can be used to ascertain information about racial mixture (i.e., race is a matter of biology and not social science). In a haughty jibe, the authors write that "very much speculation has been indulged in on this subject by sociologists and others, but apparently without any serious, objective grounds for their opinions" (p. 14). However, although Glass and Li maintain that the new science of genetics can furnish answers never before possible, their focus on blood type actually harkens back to old beliefs in blood as the repository of racial difference (as seen in census categories measuring "Indian blood" or "white blood"). Second, the article posits gene flow as a one-way street whereby the black population is the receptacle for white genes. There is no flow of black genes into the white population, which remains pure of any nonwhite genes. Third, the study is also blind to the presence of any groups other than white and black:

> The simplest situation to analyze would obviously exist where only two base populations were intermixing, a situation such as occurs in North America, where the American Negro population has been formed largely by the intermixture of a pure

Negro population and a European white population. (p. 1)

Finally, Glass and Li's research is motivated by the prospect of the eventual assimilation of the black population by the white, the timeline for which they put at a comfortable distance of about 39 generations, or 10 to 11 centuries, in the future.

Later studies echoed the major themes sounded in Glass and Li (1953). In 1969, zoologist T. Edward Reed used a similar technique, proposing a particular blood type as the best example of a "Caucasian gene" with which to estimate the percentage of blacks' genes that derive from white ancestors. Sociologist Robert Stuckert (1958) undertook an opposite strategy by considering the extent of African ancestry among whites. In his updated estimates, he put the share of whites with some African ancestry at 24% in 1970 and the share of blacks with some non-African ancestry at 81% (Stuckert, 1976). In a related area of scientific study of multiracial people, skin color was measured to pinpoint the genetic distance between races. From the 1950s through the 1970s, physical anthropologists analyzed the reflection of light from African, Caribbean, Brazilian, and mulatto people's skin (see, e.g., Barnicot, 1958; Mazess, 1967). In one example, Wienker (1979) compared the "reflectometry curve" of a sample of black American men to a West African group, determining that this sample of Americans was "relatively more 'African' genetically" than previously studied mulattoes due to "the long-standing isolation of the caste from which they are derived." As with the measure of blood, new scientific techniques were brought in to quantify very old ideas of skin color as an indicator of racial heritage.

Over the course of the 20th century, techniques based on anthropometry and genetics were assumed to provide more reliable estimates of the extent of American multiracial ancestry than qualitative inquiries into individual genealogies. These new approaches would presumably ferret out the truth about interracial mixture from human bodies without having to rely on the dubious accuracy of personal accounts. To do so, however, racial evidence had to be found inscribed in the human body. When the idea that race was in fact a social construct and not a biological characteristic began to disseminate widely among academics in the late 20th century (although anthropologists such as Franz Boas and Ashley Montagu had proposed it in the 1930s and 1940s), these attempts to measure interracial mixture through physiology fell out of favor.[6]

CENSUS 2000 AND BEYOND

At the same time that the idea of race as physically measurable faced serious challenge in academia, the U.S. Census Bureau was also confronted with new data suggesting that racial classification was anything but a straightforward and self-evident matter. In 1960, the Bureau began to gather its information by having Americans complete mailed questionnaires instead of being enumerated and described by visiting census takers. As a result, millions of individuals were suddenly confronted with the complexity of pegging all racial identities into a few boxes, a challenge that had previously been apparent in instructions to enumerators. Although the Bureau provided some direction on its questionnaires, large numbers of Americans remained either confused about how they should choose a race (only one selection was permitted) or antagonized by the options they were given. In ensuing years, the assumption that racial identities corresponded to evident, fixed, and mutually exclusive categories would come under increasing attack; one response to this was the 1997 revision of the federal government's racial classification guidelines to permit multiple-race identification (U.S. OMB,

1997). However, without a clear consensus on what race is and how it is best measured, it is difficult to gauge the accuracy of this new approach to multiracial enumeration.

Challenges for Racial Classification

One of the earliest signs that traditional census classification overlooked significant dimensions of racial identity was the puzzling post-1960 growth in the American Indian population that could not be explained by fertility and mortality factors alone. Instead, demographers discovered that part of the increase was due to the inclusion of "new Indians," people who had previously identified themselves or been identified as belonging to another race (usually white) but switched to identification as Indian (Eschbach, 1993; Passel, 1976; Passel & Berman, 1986; Snipp, 1997). In addition, Snipp (1986) found that although 1.5 million people identified their race as American Indian on the 1980 census, more than four times as many claimed some Indian ancestry (pp. 47-48). Such findings coincided with studies characterizing whites' ethnic self-concepts as extremely subjective, mutable, optional, and indeed symbolic (Alba, 1990; Gans, 1979; Waters, 1990). These ideas about the fluidity and malleability of ethnic and racial identities ran counter to the system of racial classification used on the census, which assumed that individuals' identities were fixed and easily described by a handful of categories. The inadequacy of such an approach would also be highlighted by the reactions of Hispanics to the census questionnaire: From 1980 through 2000, nearly half eschewed the available racial categories and marked "other race" instead (Rodríguez, 2000; U.S. Census Bureau, 2001a). Research by the Census Bureau has since demonstrated that racial self-description is affected by the design of surveys—for example, question placement, phrasing, and mode of delivery (Gerber, De la Puente, & Levin, n.d.; Martin, Demaio, & Campanelli, 1990)—and other social scientists have explored how the expression of racial identity, and especially multiracial identity, is affected by such factors as setting, genealogy, type of racial mixture, definition of multiraciality, appearance, and socioeconomic status (Harris, 2000; Rockquemore, 1999; Root, 1992, 1996; Waters, 1991; Wijeyesinghe, 1992; Xie & Goyette, 1997). However, the definition of race had already been challenged enough by the mid-1970s that when the OMB promulgated its original racial classification standards in 1977, it cautioned, "These classifications should not be interpreted as being scientific or anthropological in nature" (cited in Edmonston, Goldstein, & Lott, 1996, p. 36). As Edmonston et al. (1996) point out, "The directive is clear about what it is not" (p. 36) but is inconclusive about what the basis of racial classification is or should be.

In this climate of uncertainty over the meaning of racial categories, a determined segment of the mixed-race community became the catalyst for a significant overhaul of the federal government's approach to racial classification in 1997 (Nobles, 2000). Largely at the impetus of the multiracial movement, in which interracial couples and their children figure prominently, the OMB revised its 1977 Directive 15 to permit multiple-race responses in the data collection efforts of all federal agencies (OMB, 1997). Although this change was implemented fairly quickly in some instances—for example, the 1999 American Community Survey fielded by the Census Bureau used the new race question format (Del Pinal, Taguba, Cresce, & Morning, 2001)—the 2000 U.S. census represented most Americans' first exposure to the "mark one or more races" approach.

The Multiracial Census Count in 2000

The 2000 census enumerated 6.8 million people, or 2.4% of the total U.S. population, as having marked more than one race (Grieco & Cassidy, 2001). This outcome was consistent both with preceding analyses that estimated the proportion of multiracial Americans to be in the low single digits[7] and with the early 20th-century estimates of mulattoes and mixed bloods added together, even though the new multiple-race format allowed for a much wider range of multiracial combinations than had ever appeared on the U.S. census before.

As stated earlier, the fact that Hispanics are not considered a racial group according to the federal standards for racial classification means that "Hispanic" could not be selected in conjunction with other races to form a multiple-race response on the 2000 census. Yet people who identified as Hispanic on the census's separate ethnicity question figured prominently in the enumerated multiracial population, contributing one third of all multiple-race responses even though they made up only 12.5% of the total national population (see Table 1 in U.S. Census Bureau, 2001b). This outcome is due to the number of Hispanics who chose to combine one of the five main races listed (i.e., white, black, American Indian or Alaska Native, Asian, and Native Hawaiian or other Pacific Islander[8]) with the sixth, "some other race" option. Just as Hispanics overwhelmingly constituted the some other race single-race category, contributing 97% of that category's responses, they made up two thirds of the white/some other race combined response, which was by far the most frequent multiple-race response on the 2000 census.[9] As Table 3.3 shows, the second-largest dual-race combination was white/American Indian and Alaska Native followed by the white/Asian pairing and the white/black group.

Table 3.3   Racial Composition of the United States According to the 2000 Census

Race	Number	% of Total Population
Single Race Only	274,595,678	97.57
White	211,460,626	75.14
Black or African American	34,652,190	12.32
American Indian and Alaska Native	2,475,956	0.88
Asian	10,242,998	3.64
Native Hawaiian and Other Pacific Islander	398,835	0.14
Some other race	15,359,073	5.46
Two Races	6,368,075	2.26
White and black	784,764	0.28
White and American Indian	1,082,683	0.38
White and Asian	868,395	0.31
White and Native American	112,964	0.04
White and some other race	2,206,251	0.78
Black and American Indian	182,494	0.06
Black and Asian	106,782	0.04
Black and Native American	29,786	0.01
Black and some other race	417,249	0.15
American Indian and Asian	52,429	0.02
American Indian and Native Hawaiian	7,328	0.00
American Indian and some other race	93,842	0.03
Asian and Native Hawaiian	138,802	0.05
Asian and some other race	249,108	0.09
Native Hawaiian and some other race	35,108	0.01
Three or More Races	458,153	0.16
Total	281,421,906	100.00

SOURCE: U.S. Census Bureau (2001). *Population by race and Hispanic or Latino origin for the United States: 1990 and 2000 (PHC-T-1).* Tables 1 and 2.

The 2000 census results also show a geographic pattern to multiracial identification, with multiple-race reporting being by far most prevalent in Hawaii, where more than 20% of the population selected two or more races (U.S. Census Bureau, 2001a). In general, rates of multiple-race reporting were highest in the west, often but not always in states with relatively large Hispanic populations (Figure 3.1). In contrast, the southeastern states recorded the lowest rates of multiple-race response.

Finally, multiracial identification on the 2000 census was also skewed toward younger ages. Whereas only 1.9% of adults 18 years of age and older chose more than one race to describe themselves, nearly 4% of people younger than 18 were described by two or more races. As a result, people younger than 18 years contributed 42% of all multiple-race responses even though they made up only 26% of the U.S. population (U.S. Census Bureau, 2001b). This pattern alone—without even taking rising interracial marriage rates into account—may portend higher rates of multiple-race reporting on future censuses.

Although the recent census opens a much more detailed window onto the American multiracial population than has previously been available, the 2.4% mixed-race population share it recorded could be interpreted as a serious undercount. When we consider the large degree of mixed ancestry likely embodied in the nonwhite population alone and recall that this segment now constitutes 25% to

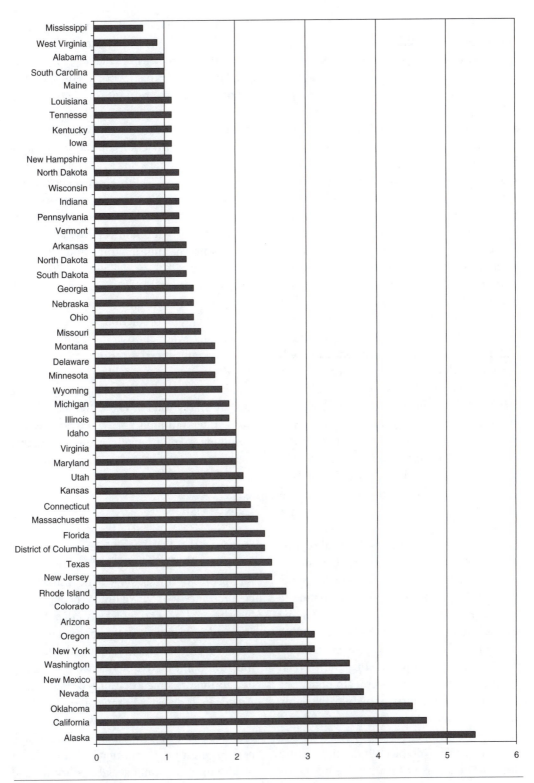

Figure 3.1 Percentage of State Population Reporting More Than One Race (Excluding Hawai'i), 2000

SOURCE: U.S. Census Bureau. (2001). Census 2000 redistricting data (public law 94-171). Summary file.

31% of Americans (depending on how Hispanics are classified; see U.S. Census Bureau, 2001b), a percentage 10 times the 2000 census estimate of the multiracial population share seems at least as plausible (Morning, 2000). As Forbes (1993) explains, a great deal of the complexity of modern Americans' ancestry has been obscured by long-standing practices forcing them "into arbitrary categories which tend to render their ethnic heritage simple rather than complex" (p. 271). The gulf between the size of the multiracial population counted in 2000 through self-identification and the much larger size we might expect from full genealogical data is probably due to a combination of factors including individuals' lack of knowledge about their ancestry, reservations about disclosing what they do know, and belief that multiple-race identity only applies to those with parents of different races (Goldstein & Morning, 2000). As Harris (2000) demonstrates, our count of mixed-race people has everything to do with how we define and measure multiraciality.

It is possible that contemporary multiple-race reporting is being driven by the "biracial" offspring of mixed marriages as opposed to the large number of people whose mixed ancestry derives from antebellum unions. As we have seen, multiracial reports on the 2000 census were disproportionately a youth phenomenon. Moreover, some state-level classification systems define a multiracial person solely as one "having parents of different races" (Nobles, 2000, p. 139). Such a bias toward recent rather than genealogically distant multiracial heritage could have several implications (Morning, 2000). First, it would probably affect the relative weights of the types of ancestry described (e.g., favoring Asian/white identity over black/Indian), because different racial groups have made up different proportions of the population and interacted at varying rates over time. Today American Indians and Asians are much more likely to marry partners of another race than are either blacks or whites (Pollard & O'Hare, 1999), yet black/white unions were an important source of interracial mixture in the past. A skew toward a particular segment of the mixed-race population could also color our assessment of multiracial people's socioeconomic characteristics (Harris, 2000). Finally, such a bias would necessarily affect projections of future population composition. For example, estimates by Edmonston, Lee and Passel (2000) put the multiple-race and -ethnicity population at 8% of the total in 2000 and project it forward to 34% in 2100. Although the latter figure may well prove to be an accurate prediction of the share of Americans who choose to identify themselves as multiracial a century from now, it could also be a reasonable guess about the number of mixed-race people living in the United States today. The difference lies in our understandings of whether we are becoming a multiracial nation or whether we have always been one.

CONCLUSION

Study of the U.S. census reveals that the nation has held a sustained interest in mixed-race people over the course of its history. The circumstances of mixed-race people have been treated as a sort of bellwether for the eventual outcomes of the nonwhite races from which they descend; thus, the fates of mulattoes and mixed bloods were integrally tied to the presumed destinies of blacks and American Indians. Multiracial people have also served as a bridge for white access to resources held by communities of color and, perhaps most important of all, as a yardstick of distance marking social, political, and economic boundaries between whites and others. From their presumed characteristics to their imagined futures, mixed-race Americans have been central to whites' understanding and definition of themselves.

Many aspects of older conceptualizations of multiracial status are still with us. For example, the divergent treatment and recognition of different types of mixed-race ancestry seems to persist. Xie and Goyette's (1997) study of biracial children of Asian ancestry found that more than 40% of the children of white/Asian marriages were identified by their parents as Asian, whereas less than 33% of black/Asian children were labeled that way. Rather than a 50-50 chance of being classified with one race or the other, social conventions still appear to influence which multiracial combinations are linked to which single races, with such rules remaining stronger with respect to black ancestry (Davis, 1991).

Given the extent to which mixed-race status has reflected societal beliefs and concerns in both the past and the present, it is worth trying to place contemporary developments in multiracial reporting in sociohistorical perspective. More specifically, we might ask why it is now possible for mixed-race people to identify themselves and be identified as such both on the census and to some degree in everyday life. In the past, the appearance and removal of multiracial census categories have been tightly linked to whites' political imperatives, economic objectives, social agendas, and beliefs concerning nonwhite peoples. Do the same factors shed any light on the introduction of multiple-race census reporting in 2000?

Of course, racial enumeration takes place today in a political and social context very different from the one that prevailed when the mulatto or mixed-blood census categories were introduced. First and foremost, it is anachronistic to presume that differentials in political power remain as lopsided in the wake of the civil rights movement. On a simple level, Census Bureau and other federal officials are no longer uniformly white, but, more importantly, American perspectives on race

and equality changed dramatically in the 20th century, if in theory more than in practice (Schuman, Steeh, Bobo, & Krysan, 1997). The civil rights struggle also led to another development with even more direct bearing on racial statistics: the series of legal prescriptions for combating discrimination embodied in the Civil Rights Act of 1964, the Voting Rights Act of 1965, and their amendments and extensions. Today the collection of data on race is motivated in large part by the need to monitor compliance with the requirements of these statutes regarding, for example, employment discrimination or congressional redistricting (Edmonston & Schultze, 1995). As a result, racial counts are now more likely to benefit minority groups than they were in the past. Finally, changing American attitudes about race following the civil rights movement surely have a great deal to do with new openness toward multiraciality; the Supreme Court's 1967 decision to strike down state laws that banned interracial marriage is an important instance of such transformation.

Yet the fact that racial stratification is still clearly an entrenched feature of American life (Smelser, Wilson, & Mitchell, 2001) suggests that the historical factors of whites' social, economic, and political interests are still relevant to the evolution of the national census. In particular, I suggest three developments that may have had some bearing on the recent introduction of multiple-race census classification. First, the contemporary (if diminishing) use of minority racial identity to determine access to special protections or programs may have made one-drop assignment of mixed-race people to beneficiary nonwhite groups less palatable to whites than it was in the past. This parallels the ongoing distinct recognition of mixed-blood American Indians in a context in which access to certain resources depends on Indian identification: When there are benefits to be gained from minority racial status, one-drop treatment of mixed-race people is less attractive to the majority.

Second, racial inequality today may be perpetuated through mechanisms that do not require the heavy-handed institutional practices of yesteryear, such as rigid, official racial classification schemes. Instead of the old Jim Crow racism that was extensively supported by state-sponsored segregation and other *de jure* racist practices, Bobo, Kluegel, and Smith (1997) argue that a new "laissez-faire racism" has taken hold in the United States, one that "relies on the market and informal racial bias to re-create, and in some instances sharply worsen, structured racial inequality" (p. 17). According to this perspective, "extant patterns of black-white socioeconomic inequality and residential segregation [are viewed]. . . . as outcomes of a free-market, race-neutral state apparatus" (p. 38). In such a climate, formal and overt racial classification standards may no longer be necessary for boundary marking and the allocation of rights and resources, and individuals' self-identification as multiracial may be permissible because it is materially inconsequential.

Finally, the growing awareness that whites are predicted to lose their numerical majority in the 21st century may favor shifts in racial boundaries that help shore up the white population count. Here Kingsley Davis's (1941) hypothesis about the boundary-marking role of mixed-race people remains especially relevant because it suggests that the new willingness to acknowledge multiracial identities—rather than following the hypodescent rule of treating them simply as members of lower-status monoracial groups—represents a softening in the dominant racial group's policing of its exclusionary boundaries. In a poignant reversal, 19th-century predictions of American Indian extinction now seem to be giving way to fears for the decline of the white population (Patterson, 2001; Warren & Twine, 1997). As in the past, "amalgamation" with other races may seem the only way out. The scenario of a future "beige majority" formed by the union of whites with Hispanics, Asians, and mixed-race people has been raised by writers who argue that the United States is moving from a system of racial stratification based on the distinction between whites and nonwhites to one in which a black versus nonblack dichotomy prevails (Gans, 1999; Lind, 1998; Sanjek, 1994). In such a shift, mixed-race Americans would be decoupled from the communities of color to which one-drop thinking has frequently assigned them in much the same manner as many people of American Indian ancestry have already come to be understood as white (Snipp, 1986). In their article "White Americans, the New Minority? Non-Blacks and the Ever-Expanding Boundaries of Whiteness," Warren and Twine (1997) point out that the perception that the nation is becoming less white depends crucially on who counts as white, and new recruits are always possible. Should efforts to limit admission to the white category be relaxed, as they were for new European immigrants nearly a century ago, American concepts of multiracial identity will surely be further transformed.

NOTES

1. The category "part Hawaiian" appeared in 1960 (Bennett, 2000), but this need not denote a mixed-race ancestry, depending on whether other components of the respondent's ancestry are considered to be racially distinct from a Hawaiian identity.

2.   Of course, mulattoes "passing" for white involved "community recognition" of sorts. However, although it relied on acquaintances' accepting the passer as white, it brooked no hint that he or she had any black ancestry. What is striking about the 1930 census instructions is that an individual known by the enumerator to be mixed blood could legitimately be recorded as white.

3.   However, the 1950 census of Hawai'i introduced a multiracial question that showed approximately 4% of its population to be of mixed race other than partial Hawaiian (U.S. Census Bureau, 1963, p. xi).

4.   See the equation of Indian "preservation and civilization" with removal and the reservation system in Tyler (1973, pp. 55, 80). Note also white settlers' quasi-religious belief in their right to take possession of lands not properly cultivated by American Indians, prefiguring the notion of manifest destiny (Prucha, 1981; Smedley, 1999; Tyler, 1973).

5.   This metaphor, equating the achievement of whiteness with the mysterious production of gold, appears elsewhere; see, for example, Jacobson's (1998) *Whiteness of a Different Color: European Immigrants and the Alchemy of Race*.

6.   However, some argue that biological concepts of race still structure scientific thought today; see Duster (1999), Harrison (1999), Keita and Kittles (1997), and Lieberman (1997).

7.   See Goldstein and Morning (2000), D. R. Harris (2000), OMB (2000b), Tucker et al. (1996), and U.S. Census Bureau (1996, 1997, 1999, 2000).

8.   Although these are the main racial groups into which the Census Bureau groups 2000 data, the Asian category is actually represented on the census form by several subcategories (e.g., "Asian Indian," "Chinese"), which are later aggregated for tabulation.

9.   Author's calculations based on the Census Bureau's 2000 Redistricting Data (Public Law 94-171) Summary File (U.S. Census Bureau, 2001a).

REFERENCES

Alaya, A. M. (2001, May 27). Brave new faces: The changing image of New Jersey: Multiraciality gaining prominence, acceptance. *Sunday Star-Ledger*, pp. 1, 8.

Alba, R. (1990). *Ethnic identity: The transformation of ethnicity in the lives of Americans of European ancestry*. New Haven, CT: Yale University Press.

Barnicot, N. (1958). Reflectometry of the skin in Southern Nigerians and in some mulattoes. *Human Biology, 30,* 21-31.

Barringer, H. R., Garner, R. W., & Levin, M. J. (1993). *Asians and Pacific Islanders in the United States*. New York: Russell Sage Foundation.

Bashi, V., & McDaniel, A. (1997). A theory of immigration and racial stratification. *Journal of Black Studies, 27*(5), 668-682.

Beale, C. L. (1957). American triracial isolates: Their status and pertinence to genetic research. *Eugenics Quarterly, 4*(4), 187-196.

Bennett, C. (2000). Racial categories used in the decennial censuses, 1790 to the present. *Government Information Quarterly, 17*(2), 161-180.

Berkhofer, R. F., Jr. (1978). *The white man's Indian: Images of the American Indian from Columbus to the present*. New York: Alfred A. Knopf.

Berry, B. (1963). *Almost white*. New York: Macmillan.

Bieder, R. E. (1986). *Science encounters the Indian, 1820-1880: The early years of American ethnology*. Norman: University of Oklahoma Press.

Bobo, L., Kluegel, J. R., & Smith, R.A. (1997). Laissez-faire racism: The crystallization of a kinder, gentler, antiblack ideology. In S. A. Tuch & J. K. Martin (Eds.), *Racial attitudes in the 1990s: Continuity and change* (pp. 15-42). Westport, CT: Praeger.

Chesnutt, C. W. (1899). *The house behind the cedars*. New York: Page, Doubleday.

Churchill, W. (1999). The crucible of American Indian identity: Native tradition versus colonial imposition in postconquest North America. In D. Champagne (Ed.), *Contemporary Native American cultural issues* (pp. 39-67). Walnut Creek, CA: Altamira Press.

Darwin, C. (1859). *On the origin of species by means of natural selection, or, the preservation of favoured races in the struggle for life*. London: J. Murray.

Davis, F. J. (1991). *Who is black? One nation's definition*. University Park: Pennsylvania State University Press.

Davis, K. (1941). Intermarriage in caste society. *American Anthropologist, 43*, 376-395.

Day, C. B. (1932). *A study of some negro-white families in the United States*. Cambridge, MA: Peabody Museum of Harvard University.

Del Pinal, J., Taguba, L. M., Cresce, A. R., & Morning, A. J. (2001). *Reporting of two or more races in the 1999 American Community Survey*. Annandale-on-Hudson, NY: Jerome Levy Economics Institute of Bard College.

Duster, T. (1999). *Buried alive: The concept of race in science*. Unpublished manuscript, New York University.

Edmonston, B., Goldstein, J., & Lott, J. T. (1996). *Spotlight on heterogeneity: The federal standards for racial and ethnic classification*. Washington, DC: Committee on National Statistics, Commission on Behavioral and Social Sciences and Education, National Research Council.

Edmonston, B., Lee, S. M., & Passel, J. S. (2000, September). *Recent trends in intermarriage and immigration and their effects on the future racial composition of the U.S. population*. Paper presented at the "Multiraciality: How Will the New Census Data Be Used?" symposium, Jerome Levy Economics Institute of Bard College, Annandale-on-Hudson, NY.

Edmonston, B., & Schultze, C. (1995). *Modernizing the U.S. census*. Washington, DC: National Academy Press.

Eschbach, K. (1993). Changing identification among American Indians and Alaska Natives. *Demography, 30*(4), 635-652.

Forbes, J. D. (1993). *Africans and Native Americans: The language of race and the evolution of red-black peoples* (2nd ed.). Urbana: University of Illinois Press.

Gans, H. (1979). Symbolic ethnicity: The future of ethnic groups and cultures in America. *Ethnic and Racial Studies, 2*(1), 1-19.

Gans, H. J. (1999). The possibility of a new racial hierarchy in the 21st century United States. In M. Lamont (Ed.), *The cultural territories of race: Black and white boundaries* (pp. 371-390). Chicago: University of Chicago Press and Russell Sage Foundation.

Gerber, E., De la Puente, M., & Levin, M. (n.d.). *Race, identity and new question options: Final report of cognitive research on race and ethnicity*. Washington, DC: U.S. Census Bureau.

Glass, B., & Li, C. C. (1953). The dynamics of racial intermixture: An analysis based on the American negro. *American Journal of Human Genetics, 5*(1), 1-20.

Goldstein, J. R., & Morning, A. J. (2000). The multiple-race population of the United States: Issues and estimates. *Proceedings of the National Academy of Sciences, 97*(11), 6230-6235.

Grieco, E. M., & Cassidy, R. C. (2001). *Overview of race and Hispanic origin*. Washington, DC: U.S. Department of Commerce.

Harris, D. R. (2000, September). *Does it matter how we measure? Implications of definitions of race on the characteristics of mixed-race youth*. Paper presented at the "Multiraciality: How Will the New Census Data Be Used?" symposium, Jerome Levy Economics Institute of Bard College, Annandale-on-Hudson, NY.

Harris, M. (1964). *Patterns of race in the Americas*. Westport, CT: Greenwood Press.

Harrison, F. V. (1999). Introduction: Expanding the discourse on "race." *American Anthropologist, 100*(3), 609-631.

Herskovits, M. J. (1928). *The American negro: A study in racial crossing*. New York: Alfred A. Knopf.

Horsman, R. (1975). Scientific racism and the American Indian in the mid-nineteenth century. *American Quarterly, 27*(2), 152-168.

Jacobson, M. F. (1998). *Whiteness of a different color: European immigrants and the alchemy of race*. Cambridge, MA: Harvard University Press.

Jefferson, T. (1800). *Notes on the state of Virginia*. Baltimore: W. Pechin.

Keita, S. O. Y., & Kittles, R. A. (1997). The persistence of racial thinking and the myth of racial divergence. *American Anthropologist, 99*(3), 534-544.

Kevles, D. J. (1985). *In the name of eugenics: Genetics and the uses of human heredity*. Cambridge, MA: Harvard University Press.

La Brack, B. (1999). South Asians. In E. R. Barkan (Ed.), *A nation of peoples: A sourcebook on America's multicultural heritage* (pp. 482-504). Westport, CT: Greenwood Press.

Lee, S. M. (1993). Racial classification in the U.S. Census: 1890-1990. *Ethnic and Racial Studies, 16*, 75-94.

Leonard, K. I. (1997). *The South Asian Americans*. Westport, CT: Greenwood Press.

Lieberman, L. (1997). Gender and the deconstruction of the race concept. *American Anthropologist, 99*(3), 545-558.

Lind, M. (1998, August 16). The beige and the black. *New York Times Magazine*, pp. 38-39.

Marks, J. (1995). *Human biodiversity: Genes, race, and history*. New York: Aldine de Gruyter.

Martin, E., Demaio, T. J., & Campanelli, P. C. (1990). Context effects for census measures of race and Hispanic origin. *Public Opinion Quarterly, 54*(4), 551-566.

Marx, A. W. (1998). *Making race and nation: A comparison of South Africa, the United States, and Brazil*. Cambridge, UK: Cambridge University Press.

Mazess, R. B. (1967). Skin color in Bahamian negroes. *Human Biology, 39*, 145-154.

Meacham, J. (2000, September 18). The new face of race. *Newsweek*, pp. 38-41.

Moreno Navarro, I. (1973). *Los "Cuadros del Mestizaje Americano": Estudio Antropológico del Mestizaje*. Madrid: Ediciones Jose Porrua Turanzas.

Morning, A. (2000). Who is multiracial? Definitions and decisions. *Sociological Imagination, 37*(4), 209-229.

Morton, N. E. (1962). Genetics of interracial crosses in Hawaii. *Eugenics Quarterly, 9*(1), 23-24.

Nagel, J. (1996). *American Indian ethnic renewal: Red power and the resurgence of identity and culture*. New York: Oxford University Press.

Nash, G. B. (1995). The hidden history of mestizo America. *Journal of American History, 82*, 941-962.

Nobles, M. (2000). *Shades of citizenship: Race and the census in modern politics*. Stanford, CA: Stanford University Press.

Passel, J. S. (1976). Provisional evaluation of 1970 census data for American Indians. *Demography, 13*, 397-409.

Passel, J. S., & Berman, P. A. (1986). Quality of 1980 census data for American Indians. *Social Biology, 33*, 163-182.

Patterson, O. (2001, May 8). Race by the numbers [Electronic version]. *New York Times*.

Pollard, K. M., & O'Hare, W. P. (1999). America's racial and ethnic minorities. *Population Bulletin, 54*(3).

Prucha, F. P. (1981). *Indian policy in the United States: Historical essays*. Lincoln: University of Nebraska Press.

Prucha, F. P. (1984). *The great father: The United States government and the American Indians* (Vol. 2). Lincoln: University of Nebraska Press.

Reuter, E. B. (1918). *The mulatto in the United States: Including a study of the role of mixed-blood races throughout the world*. Boston: Richard G. Badger.

Rockquemore, K. A. (1999). *Race and identity: Exploring the biracial experience.* Unpublished doctoral dissertation, University of Notre Dame.

Rodríguez, C. E. (2000). *Changing race: Latinos, the census, and the history of ethnicity in the United States.* New York: New York University Press.

Root, M. P. P. (Ed.). (1992). *Racially mixed people in America.* Newbury Park, CA: Sage.

Root, M. P. P. (Ed.). (1996). *The multiracial experience: Racial borders as the new frontier.* Thousand Oaks, CA: Sage.

Rosen, H. (1999). *The gender of reconstruction: Rape, race, and citizenship in the post-emancipation south.* Unpublished doctoral dissertation, University of Chicago.

Sanjek, R. (1994). Intermarriage and the future of races in the United States. In S. Gregory & R. Sanjek (Eds.), *Race* (pp. 103-130). New Brunswick, NJ: Rutgers University Press.

Schuman, H., Steeh, C., Bobo, L., & Krysan, M. (1997). *Racial attitudes in America: Trends and interpretations* (2nd ed.). Cambridge, MA: Harvard University Press.

Smedley, A. (1999). *Race in North America: Origin and evolution of a world view* (2nd ed.). Boulder, CO: Westview Press.

Smelser, N. J., Wilson, W. J., & Mitchell, F. (Eds.). (2001). *America becoming: Racial trends and their consequences.* Washington, DC: National Academy Press.

Snipp, C. M. (1986). Who are American Indians? Some observations about the perils and pitfalls of data for race and ethnicity. *Population Research and Policy Review, 5,* 237-252.

Snipp, C. M. (1997). Some observations about racial boundaries and the experiences of American Indians. *Ethnic and Racial Studies, 20*(4), 667-689.

Snipp, M. (1989). *American Indians: The first of this land.* New York: Russell Sage Foundation.

Sollors, W. (Ed.). (2000). *Interracialism: Black-white intermarriage in American history, literature, and law*: Oxford, UK: Oxford University Press.

Spickard, P. R. (1989). *Mixed blood: Intermarriage and ethnic identity in twentieth-century America.* Madison: University of Wisconsin Press.

Stuckert, R. P. (1958). African ancestry of the white American population. *Ohio Journal of Science, 58*(3), 155-160.

Stuckert, R. P. (1976). "Race" mixture: The black ancestry of white Americans. In P. B. Hammond (Ed.), *Physical anthropology and archaeology: Introductory readings* (2nd ed., pp. 135-139). New York: Macmillan.

Tucker, C., McKay, R., Kojetin, B., Harrison, R., de la Puente, M., Stinson, L., & Robinson, E. (1996). *Testing methods of collecting racial and ethnic information: Results of the current population survey supplement on race and ethnicity.* Statistical Note 40. Washington, DC: U.S. Bureau of Labor Statistics.

Tyler, S. L. (1973). *A history of Indian policy.* Washington, DC: U.S. Department of the Interior, Bureau of Indian Affairs.

Unrau, W. E. (1989). *Mixed-bloods and tribal dissolution: Charles Curtis and the quest for Indian identity.* Lawrence: University Press of Kansas.

U.S. Census Bureau. (1915). *Indian population in the United States and Alaska 1910.* Washington, DC: Government Printing Office.

U.S. Census Bureau. (1918). *Negro population 1790-1915.* Washington, DC: U.S. Government Printing Office.

U.S. Census Bureau. (1923). *Abstract of the fourteenth census of the United States 1920.* Washington, DC: Government Printing Office.

U.S. Census Bureau. (1937). *The Indian population of the United States and Alaska 1930.* Washington, DC: U.S. Government Printing Office.

U.S. Census Bureau. (1953). *U.S. Census of Population: 1950.* Washington, DC: U.S. Government Printing Office.

U.S. Census Bureau. (1963). *Nonwhite population by race*. Washington, DC: U.S. Government Printing Office.

U.S. Census Bureau. (1964). *U.S. Census of Population: 1960*. Washington, DC: Government Printing Office.

U.S. Census Bureau. (1973). *Population and housing inquiries in U.S. decennial censuses, 1790-1970*. Washington, DC: U.S. Government Printing Office.

U.S. Census Bureau. (1996). *Findings on questions on race and Hispanic origin tested in the 1996 National Content Survey*. Washington, DC: U.S. Government Printing Office.

U.S. Census Bureau. (1997). *Results of the 1996 Race and Ethnic Targeted Test*. Washington, DC: U.S. Government Printing Office.

U.S. Census Bureau. (1999, April 20). *Census 2000 dress rehearsal shows undercount persists; scientific methods correct race and ethnic differential*. Retrieved from: www.census.gov/Press-Release/www/1999/cb99-cn16.html, December 10, 2000

U.S. Census Bureau. (2000, July 28). *Data released from census bureau survey that may replace next census long form*. Retrieved from: www.census.gov/Press-Release/www/2000/cb00cn49.html, December 10, 2000

U.S. Census Bureau. (2001a). *Census 2000 redistricting data (public law 94-171) summary file*. Washington, DC: Author.

U.S. Census Bureau. (2001b). *Population by Race and Hispanic or Latino Origin for the United States: 1990 and 2000*. Washington, DC: U.S. Census Bureau.

U.S. Census Office. (1872). *The statistics of the population of the United States*. Washington, DC: U.S. Government Printing Office.

U.S. Congress, Office of Technology Assessment. (1986). *Indian health care*. Washington, DC: U.S. Government Printing Office.

U.S. Office of Management and Budget. (1997). *Revisions to the standards for the classification of federal data on race and ethnicity*. Washington, DC: Author.

U.S. Office of Management and Budget. (2000a, March 9). *Guidance on aggregation and allocation of data on race for use in civil rights monitoring and enforcement* (Bulletin 00-02). Retrieved from: www.white-house.gov/omb/bulletins/b00-02.html

U.S. Office of Management and Budget. (2000b). *Provisional guidance on the implementation of the 1997 standards for the collection of federal data on race and ethnicity*. Washington, DC: Author.

Wallace, A. (1999). *Jefferson and the Indians: The tragic fate of the first Americans*. Cambridge, MA: Belknap Press of Harvard University Press.

Warren, J. W., & Twine, F. W. (1997). White Americans, the new minority? Non-blacks and the ever-expanding boundaries of whiteness. *Journal of Black Studies, 28*(2), 200-218.

Waters, M. (1990). *Ethnic options: Choosing identities in America*. Berkeley: University of California Press.

Waters, M. C. (1991). The role of lineage in identity formation among black Americans. *Qualitative Sociology, 14*(1), 57-76.

Wienker, C. W. (1979). Skin color in a group of black Americans. *Human Biology, 51*(1), 1-9.

Wijeyesinghe, C. (1992). *Towards an understanding of the racial identity of bi-racial people: The experience of racial self-identification of African-American/Euro-American adults and the factors affecting their choices of racial identity*. Unpublished doctoral dissertation, University of Massachusetts.

Williamson, J. (1980). *New people: Miscegenation and mulattoes in the United States*. New York: Free Press.

Wilson, T. P. (1992). Blood quantum: Native American mixed bloods. In M. P. P. Root (Ed.), *Racially mixed people in America* (pp. 108-125). Newbury Park, CA: Sage.

Xie, Y., & Goyette, K. (1997). The racial identification of biracial children with one Asian parent: Evidence from the 1990 Census. *Social Forces, 76*(2), 547-570.

CHAPTER 4

Multiracial Identity

From Personal Problem to Public Issue

KIMBERLY MCCLAIN DACOSTA

Harvard University

> *Struggles over ethnic or regional identity. . . . are a particular case of the different struggles over classifications, struggles over the monopoly of the power to make people see and believe, to get them to know and recognize, to impose the legitimate definition of the divisions of the social world and, thereby, to make and unmake groups.*
>
> — Pierre Bourdieu (1991)

If for much of the 20th century claiming a "mixed" racial identity and having it recognized publicly was very much out of the question,[1] what changed to make the public claiming of a multiracial identity very much the question in the 1990s? This chapter explores the political, organizational, and cultural factors that lead to the reemergence of the problem of racial mixedness in the United States. I consider how "multiracials" emerged as a self-conscious interest group, how they came to resuscitate the issue of racial categorization and identification as a topic of public discussion, and why this happened

when it did. To explain this development requires a discussion of the most obviously public manifestation of this shift: the challenge to official racial classification. However, it requires moving beyond that event to show the relationship of this movement to broader social and cultural developments. In so doing, I seek to correct two misleading tendencies in treatments of collective organization of mixed-descent persons in the United States. On the one hand, some activists and scholars treat multiracials[2] as though they are a group constituted as such: conscious of itself, unified, but one that has not received social recognition (Association of Multiethnic Americans [AMEA], 1993; Omi & Espiritu, 2000). The other tendency treats multiracials as though they are not a group at all—a statistical population, completely individualized and unaware of itself—and thus not worthy of social classification (Spencer, 1997). What both evaluations obscure is that struggles over public recognition, of which the battle over official classification is a prime example, are fundamental means through which groups make themselves—by getting the state, that ultimate symbolic authority, to recognize and, in so doing help to create, its existence. Situating such struggles in social context allows us to understand what leads these actors to seek such recognition in the first place.[3]

THE MAKING OF A CATEGORY

The appearance in 1993 by multiracial activists at federal hearings assessing the U.S. government's policy on racial classification represented a significant shift in adjudications over racial categories. Multiracial activists argued for a new category that acknowledged multiple ancestry: either a stand-alone "multiracial" box to check or the possibility of checking multiple racial categories. Unlike other groups requesting a shuffling of their placement within the existing racial framework, self-identified multiracials claimed to be a formerly unrecognized group challenging the framework itself.

At these hearings, multiracial activists represented themselves in a national political arena as a unified collective. As such, it was the first time that a national audience heard from this putative community. Although at various times in U.S. history persons of multiple ancestry have been classified as such (e.g., "mulattoes," "quadroons") and socially organized around that principle (e.g., Louisiana Creoles, Lumbee Indians), this articulation of mixedness was different in that the groups

challenging the state's classifications included people of a variety of ethnoracial "mixtures" (e.g., Asian/white, black/Asian, black/white).[4]

The swiftness with which multiracial activists were able to respond to the solicitation for public comment on revisions to the state's racial and ethnic categories suggested a preexisting level of organization and collective consciousness among self-identified multiracial people that had been largely invisible to the broader public. Scholars as well had overlooked this development, perhaps best exemplified in F. James Davis' contention, as late as 1991, in the only extended study of hypodescent that the "one-drop rule" would remain unchallenged for the foreseeable future (see Davis, 1991, chapter 8). Despite such predictions, the one-drop rule has been challenged, resulting in the Census Bureau's decision in 1997 to allow individuals to check "one or more" racial categories.

The "Right" to Racial Classification

During the struggle over state racial classifications, a group of parents of multiracial children and multiracial adults claimed that because the state collected racial data, it had an obligation to "accurately" count an individual's race, which to them meant that the state would have to in some way count *multi*-raciality. In this they were like many others who have come to see the state's racial categories as opportunities to declare personal identity (Cornell, 1996; Nagel, 1995; Waters, 1990). What was different about multiracial activists' claims was the contention that ethnoracial self-identification was a person's right. They used the codes of liberal individualism, which constructs persons as choice-making selves who ought to be treated with dignity and respect.

The contention that racial classification is a right is a relatively recent understanding of racial classification. Before the 1960s, racial classification had largely been considered an objective characteristic of persons that the state merely labeled. As such, racial classification per se did not need to be claimed as a right. Racial struggles generally centered on the rights accruing to one classified in a particular way or one's categorization within a given set of categories. Multiracial activists claimed that the individual, rather than the state, should decide how one is racially classified. They pointed out that despite a Census policy of racial self-enumeration in place since 1960, the limits placed on the number of categories one could choose effectively took away a multiracial person's ability to self-designate race. Moreover, they argued that the interests of other parties (be they the state, institutions like schools, or other officially recognized ethnoracial groups) were secondary to those of the individual checking the box. Finally, activists situated the right to classification as one pertaining not merely to the individuals that the classifications were meant to identify but to those individuals' parents. Racial classification, according to activists, was an important means by which parents could lay claim to their children and through which children might signal their affiliation with and relation to their parents.

Multiracial activists' arguments cast racial classification in very individualistic terms. In calling for the option of checking multiple racial categories, they treated the state's racial classifications as a menu of options that could and should be customized to fit each unique individual rather than a set of mutually exclusive categories into which individuals must fit themselves. To advance this individualistic agenda, however, they had to argue on behalf of a group. Multiracial activists argued that the right to such a classification was essential to safeguard mixed-descent persons' equal protection under the law. In doing so, they began to talk about multiracial people as a distinct class, equivalent to any other ethnic group protected by civil rights legislation. Carlos Fernandez (1994), legal adviser to and past president of the AMEA, tried to make the case that the Revonda Bowens incident in Alabama could be a test case for gaining recognition of multiracial/ethnic people "as a distinct class by an agency of government."

The reactions of other contenders in the debate to the claims of multiracial activists were almost uniformly negative and challenged multiracials' claims to group status. Although these civil rights organizations focused on the possible harm of such a change in the system of racial classification on the monitoring of compliance with civil rights legislation and the likelihood that such a change would diminish the population size of established ethnoracial groups, they justified their opposition by challenging the assertion that multiracials shared sufficient commonalities as a group to warrant such protected status. The National Coalition for an Accurate Count of Asians and Pacific Islanders, for example, questioned "the salience of biraciality or multiraciality in relationship to the specific provisions and intended benefits" of civil rights programs (see Omi & Espiritu, 2000) because

> what can be stated about common experiences shared by biracial or multiracial persons? . . . Biracial or multiracial persons have the burden to document what distinct experiences or disadvantagement, in contrast to persons of protected single race backgrounds, they have because of their biraciality or multiraciality before the decision to establish a multiracial or biracial category would be appropriate. (p. 82)

The basis of the disagreement between opponents and proponents of multiracial classification lies in the way each camp interpreted the meaning and purpose of state racial classification. Opponents of multiracial classification were essentially arguing that decisions about changes to Directive 15 should be guided by the purposes for which the directive was originally created: as a means by which to track the effects of racial domination. For them, the question of how to classify persons was settled. What mattered to them was how the data gleaned from the given classifications were used. Multiracials, they argued, could not demonstrate that they had been unfairly treated because of their multiracial status and thus did not warrant the recognition as a group that state classification confers. To multiracial activists, on the other hand, the question of classification was far from settled and mattered to them because they understood classification as symbolic of their personal identity, which they had the right to choose for themselves.

Creating a New Constituency

Despite these competing interests, multiracial activists gained a measure of success in changing the way in which racial classification was enumerated.[5] Although the stand-alone multiracial category that some activists wanted was not approved, and multiple responses to the race question most likely will be disaggregated into the six race categories, beginning with the 2000 Census individuals are now instructed that they may check multiple responses to the race question.[6] That they achieved this success is particularly interesting when one realizes how few multiracial activists were involved in the negotiations at the state and federal levels. The most active lobbying groups, Project RACE and AMEA, were represented at these official events by only a handful of individuals. Yet they presented themselves as representatives of an already-existing community that was unified in its support for multiracial classification. Project RACE claimed to be a "national organization,"[7] whereas AMEA stressed its role as an umbrella organization representing numerous local multiracial organizations.

The swiftness with which multiracial coalitions were able to respond to the call to revise the racial and ethnic standards suggests a pre-existing level of collective consciousness and

organization among multiracial people that had been largely invisible to the broader public. Indeed this is true. Both AMEA and Project RACE drew personnel and resources from existing multiracial organizations. I-Pride, Biracial Family Network, and Multiracial Americans of Southern California, for example, are signatories on AMEA's charter.

Although it is true that AMEA and Project RACE draw support from various organizations, the impression put forth by activists that they represent the community of multiracials differs somewhat from the reality. The most visible representative of Project RACE was its founder, Susan Graham. Because membership lists of the organization are not made readily available, it is difficult to assess the extent of its support or the social position of its members. AMEA's organizational structure more closely reflects a representative body. Its leadership, for example, is elected by the membership of its signatory organizations. Even still, it is difficult to say that AMEA represents multiracials as such. Although long-standing networks have developed among various groups, and those groups have contributed resources to the lobbying effort put forth by AMEA, these ties exist for only a fraction of the universe of multiracial organizations. Although no official tally exists, based on advertisements published in multiracial organizational newsletters and media accounts, more than 60 such organizations in all parts of the country have formed in the last 20 years. Of those, 13 were signatories of AMEA's charter during the census debates of the 1990s. Thus, although multiracial organizations are forming in all parts of the country, and many are at least nominally involved in the classification debate, most are not. Moreover, these connections between groups are more accurately described as connections between individuals, typically the nominal leaders of the organizations, wherein the rank and file of these organizations are relatively uninvolved or uninterested in the debate over state classification. One local organizational leader recalled being "pressed into service" at the last minute for the 1996 Multiracial Solidarity March, with virtually no advance knowledge of either the event or the issues at stake.

The question of what community multiracial spokespersons represent is even more complicated when we note that many of the multiracial organizations that formed in the last 20 years no longer exist. Many organizations that existed in the early 1990s are no longer meeting regularly, if at all. Several of the past coordinators of these groups said their groups fizzled out because the participants' children "outgrew" the group. Others pointed to the difficulties of coordinating busy schedules. The temporary nature of many organizations suggests that the multiracial community as such is only loosely organized.

The point here is not that the goals of multiracial activists are entirely divorced from any constituency. Rather, it is to point out that gaining state recognition of social identities requires that activists make their claims on behalf of a putative group to create a constituency. Activists' references to a multiracial community were, in part, rhetorical devices self-consciously used to bolster claims that they represented a constituency. As one activist put it, "we made it seem like we were a massive force to be dealt with." This illustrates a fundamental feature of struggles over social classifications. It is not unusual for activists to claim to represent a community of shared interests that in reality does not exist as such, wherein the presumed members of the community are relatively uncommitted to the goals that motivate spokespersons of that community. Activists must make the community appear to exist in order to bring it into existence (Bourdieu, 1991b).

Although multiracial activists' ability to present themselves as representative of a community was key to their effectiveness, they also had to present that community as being unified over the issue of classification, even though there were significant differences in philosophy within the coalition of activists organized around classification. Susan Graham of Project RACE was deeply committed to getting a separate multiracial category on the census, whereas AMEA backed a category that allowed for specific ancestry responses. In June 1997, just before the Office of Management and Budget (OMB) was to make its final decision, Project RACE had agreed to support the multiple check-off option in conjunction with AMEA; however, that coalition broke down shortly after, with Project RACE ultimately supporting a stand-alone multiracial category. In the end, OMB adopted a version that more closely resembled the one backed by AMEA.

Key to AMEA's effectiveness was its ability to forge coalitions with strategically placed individuals and organizations. First, they drew on the symbolic capital of academics, several of whom either sat on their board or provided advice. Moreover, the messages in some of the writings by these academics, most of whom identify as mixed race or are themselves intermarried, are indistinguishable from those of activists. The Bill of Rights for Racially Mixed People, written by psychologist Maria Root (1996), illustrates the extent of this parity.[8] Academics lend legitimacy to the notion of organizing along the principle of multiraciality. Their work (creating courses on multiraciality, writing anthologies, memoirs) serves a powerful legitimating function because prestigious and seemingly neutral institutions such as universities and publishing houses support it. Moreover, the simultaneity of these messages alongside populist appeals makes the phenomenon of multiracial collective organization appear more coherent and widespread than it in fact may be.

Perhaps more important than the support AMEA garnered from academics is the coalition they formed with persons of partial Asian descent, represented by Hapa Issues Forum (HIF). Before 1997, HIF had not been active in the classification debate. As Greg Mayeda (personal communication, December 1997), one of its founders, noted, "The classification issue seemed less urgent than building relations with the Japanese American community." As the OMB decision deadline approached, however, Ramona Douglass of AMEA made a concerted effort to bring HIF into the debates over racial classification and succeeded in getting representatives of HIF to join the lobbying effort. The presence of HIF was important primarily because it strengthened the contention that multiracial activists' support was broadly based. In particular, the support of Asian multiracials eased the suspicion of some that those in favor of multiracial classification were actually interested in being a little less black. In another attempt to counter such accusations, multiracial activists stressed that the multiracial community contained within it persons who were "double minorities"—not part white—who, therefore, could not be accused of trying to gain white privilege.

Making the Acceptable Problematic

Although relatively few people, representing relatively few organizations, were actively involved in the classification debate, these organizations were quite important in facilitating the reemergence of questions of mixed racial identity. Multiracial activists were able to testify at public hearings because they were already organized in local groups that developed in the 1980s for social and supportive purposes. Those organizations, such as Multiracial Americans of Southern California, I-Pride in Berkeley, California, and Biracial Family Network in Chicago, served as networks in which grievances incubated and which lead to the more public and political expressions of identity. Carlos Fernandez, one of the original members of both I-Pride and AMEA, described such a transition. While in I-Pride, he noted that

we were spending a lot of time talking about cosmic questions and it began to get a little tiresome so we decided we've got to have a national organization so we can really do something about this instead of wasting our time talking about it. And that's how AMEA got started. (Personal communication, 1992)

Most of the membership of these organizations was uninvolved in the campaign to change racial classifications. What they were concerned with was destigmatizing the idea of a multiracial identity and multiracial families. "Talking about cosmic questions" is part of coming to understand what experiences and troubles one shares with others and lead to the politicizing of those concerns. It is through the organizations, formed for reasons other than changing official classification, that the challenge to state classifications emerges.

Multiracial organizations bring similarly situated persons into close, sustained contact with each other, providing a forum in which to begin to understand their commonalities. This is particularly salient because it allows us to understand why it is that an issue that has formerly been considered personal and private has become the focus of group mobilization. Many adult multiracials have grown up not knowing personally other mixed persons, which breeds the perception that they are alone in their circumstances. Under conditions of social isolation, people are more likely to commit the "fundamental attribution error": to explain their situation as a function of individual deficiencies rather than features of a system. Moreover, during the 1980s and 1990s, these organizations began to communicate with each other through newsletters and conferences.

The OMB's solicitation for public comment on revising Directive 15 provided a political opportunity for AMEA and Project RACE to challenge how racial data were collected and to present themselves as an already-existing ethnic community. Because the format of the hearings allows interested parties to prepare testimony and deliver it publicly, AMEA and Project RACE produced detailed testimony in which they questioned the legitimacy of the current system of racial classification.

The political opportunity to testify in a national forum allowed both groups to convey their messages to a much wider audience than they could have reached on their own. The public exposure given these hearings led to new opportunities for multiracial groups to frame their issues and disseminate their messages. In the 1990s, activists like Carlos Fernandez, Susan Graham, and Ramona Douglass appeared on several local and national broadcasts because of their exposure at the hearings, thus introducing their issues to a much larger audience.

Collective organization around the principle of multiraciality created new understandings of what it means to be mixed and facilitated the political mobilization of activists. That mobilization in pursuit of multiracial classification in turn strengthens the impetus for further organization around the principle of multiraciality. In 1994, in the thick of the classification lobbying effort, Carlos Fernandez of AMEA offered this:

> We don't really have a sense of (who we are) as a community yet. We can't really talk about a multiracial multiethnic community yet. That sense of community is not there. *That's precisely why we have our organizations.* It's because there is not a place for us... This community did not exist in the past to respond specifically to our issues. Now we do exist, in whatever form we are, however flimsy and fragile, we do exist. We have our *concept*, we have our name, and we have our *groups. And we need to build that.* And in fact the theme coming out of our meeting in Pittsburgh just last year was that *building a sense of community* is our next task. We're on the map. Our first five years were to establish the issue, publicize the issue, create it in a sense... But now the task

is to develop a sense of community, an idea that we have something in common. (You) may not necessarily as a black/white couple have something in common with someone who's Asian/Latino but you do have that— your interracialness—in common [italics added]. (Personal communication, 1994)

Perhaps more than he realized, Fernandez's comment illustrates the process of group making. Building organizations and developing shared understandings of their situation encourage multiracial activists to construct a community.

The public nature of struggles over social classification makes possible the irony that even if census officials had opted not to enumerate multiraciality, the very process of adjudicating state classification aids in the construction of multiracials as a group. The process of state classification requires that claims be made on behalf of a group and, therefore, encourages the construction of group organization and identification to reach such recognition. Moreover, the process gives a public presence to identities once considered personal, such that it gets others to know and recognize such an identity. "Categorical identities," Craig Calhoun (1994) argues, "can be invoked and given public definition by individuals or groups even when they are not embodied in concrete networks of direct interpersonal relationships. Indeed, they are quintessentially objects of such public address" (p. 26).

The multiracial community on behalf of whom activists claim to speak does not capture the universe of mixed-descent persons organized according to a sense of shared identity, but neither is it completely unorganized or lacking a common set of unifying experiences. In mobilizing around multiracial classification, activists named what they believed those unifying experiences to be, providing for those persons who are unconnected to multiracial organizations a vocabulary with which to describe themselves, with a new sense that such an identity has a community to support it.

ENABLING CONDITIONS

The (ongoing) construction of a notion of multiracial community was facilitated by the classification debate. Knowing the strategies and organizational resources multiracial activists used to challenge state racial classifications in the 1990s shows the immediate causes of the most public example of the reemergence of mixedness as a civic issue. Yet knowing these causes leaves unanswered why they deemed racial classification a significant issue and why framing the issue in terms of rights and personal identity made sense to them. Moreover, it begs the question of why multiracial organizations were forming in the first place.

It is tempting to conclude that collective activity around multiracial identity is a logical outcome of demography: There are simply more "mixed" people now, products of the "biracial baby boom" begun in the 1960s, entering adulthood, meeting each other, comparing experiences and grievances, and acting collectively to address those grievances.[9] Yet even if the majority of births were to parents of different racial categories, the mere quantity of mixed-descent persons cannot explain (a) why such people are organizing as multiracial, (b) why being mixed matters to them, and (c) why a political dimension to that activity centered on obtaining an official designation emerged. The inadequacies of demographic explanations are highlighted when we historicize the issue. According to conventional definitions of race, mixed-descent people have existed in American society since its inception, yet their multiplicity is not recognized by the state and has not served as a basis for collective action. So why has multiraciality come to be seen as an important idea around which to organize?

There have been several interlocking reasons why these people came to redefine their experiences in a way that made public recognition of a multiracial identity in the form of official classification seem obvious to them. First, changes in racial policy brought ever more frequent encounters with the task of describing one's racial classification and strengthened the social importance of ethnoracial identification and affiliation. Second, multiracial activists responded to changes in the ideological consensus on the meaning of racial identity. Finally, the social location of multiracial activists, particularly their education and family profiles, made them especially susceptible to the questioning of dominant methods of racial categorization, and encouraged the creation of multiracial organizational networks of which multiracial activists then took advantage. The cause lies not in the fact of classification itself. If it did, then this challenge might have emerged earlier. Rather, it is the new experiences around classification, which stem from changes in broader demographic, political, and social context, that facilitate the reemergence of this issue.

Changes in State Racial Policy

For most of its history, state racial classification has arguably served no other purpose than to define persons in categories so as determine who to exclude and exploit from the full benefits of citizenship and who to entitle. In the 1960s, however, with the passage of civil rights legislation[10] such as the Civil Rights Act of 1964, the Voting Rights Act of 1965, and the Housing Act of 1968, racial classification became an increasingly important tool for redressing the effects of racial domination. Although the intent of the landmark legislation of the 1960s may have been to achieve a color-blind standard, implementing it required race consciousness. Because legislative victories on these issues did not translate into actual achievements of equal access to public accommodations, schools, and employment, state officials instituted administrative systems to monitor compliance with the law. Although affirmative action in education and employment was guided by the principle of equal opportunity, the efficacy of such programs was measured by the numbers of persons from underrepresented groups they served and how those numbers compared with the overall size of each group. As such, the size of ethnic groups took on new significance (Graham, 1990; Skrentny, 1996). Moreover, the addition of ethnic groups to the list of protected categories and the public attention given to whether or not institutions were in compliance with federal standards gave previously private groupings a new public identity.

These programs provided a renewed purpose for collecting data on racial groups (for the purposes of redressing discrimination against racial minorities) and an increased reliance on such statistics for compliance purposes. It is precisely the government's need for "accurate" data on racial and ethnic groups that led to the hearings to revise Directive 15, providing an opportunity for multiracial activists to present their grievances—grievances that were themselves generated out of the state's insistence on categorizing people by race. Race-based policy to redress discrimination has brought with it a need to know one's race. It is this need that has galvanized many mixed-race activists, encompassed in the dilemma of "which box to check" that has served as a rallying point for multiracial people:

> Each and every time we confront one of these forms, we are faced yet again with the awkward, irrational and for many of us the offensive task of selecting a race or ethnicity which does not truthfully identify us and has the further result of failing to count our community. (AMEA testimony, June 1993)

The proliferation of efforts to collect racial data coincided with a new practice of recording racial data. Since 1960, the U.S. census has allowed respondents to self-enumerate their race. Before this time, a census taker, on visual inspection, enumerated an individual's race. Self-enumeration of race on the census gave control over categorization to the individual, albeit within the limits of the categories offered. The practice of self-enumeration lent support to the idea that the person being classified has the right to choose her classification. Moreover, it provided the conditions whereby individuals were obliged to wrestle with the choice of categories on their own rather than have an outside agent determine that choice for them. In so doing, it fostered the sense that the purpose of state racial categories was to record the individual's self-identity, something that only the individual could determine.

The precedent for self-enumeration made those situations in which respondents had a racial category assigned to them by someone else appear arbitrary and anachronistic. This is important because in administrative settings, such as schools and medical facilities, someone other than the person being classified often records race. Multiracial activists explicitly objected to this practice, which they dubbed "eyeballing" because it violated the ethos that individuals should determine their own identity.

The ever more frequent encounters with racial classification and the structure of "the box" such that a decision must be made about which racial category to check are important reasons why state racial policy matters so much for multiracial mobilization. However, these beg the question of why the categories themselves are considered meaningful. The decision of which box to check only becomes a dilemma when one has knowledge of and feels that there are equally valid alternatives, one or more of which will necessarily be left out if only one box is checked. However, the conditions under which one comes to see these options as equally relevant are related to the social context in which individuals find themselves.

Particularly important here is the family context of mixed-descent persons. Unlike in previous generations when children born of cross-category unions were often conceived in coercive conditions, today such children are most often born in the context of legal marriage. Many of these children share a household with both parents. Moreover, many respondents grew up having regular and intimate personal contact with relatives from both sides of their extended families, distinguishing their experience from previous generations and from "generationally mixed" persons.[11] Both activists and rank-and-file members of organizations described the fact that they are born of differently classified parents as unique and significant in shaping their experiences and their actions around multiraciality.

So significant are questions of kinship that they are the foundation on which multiracial organizations, whose formation preceded the challenge to state classification, rest. Interracial couples comprised most of the membership of the more than 60 local community groups formed in the last 20 years in order for multiracial people to meet others like themselves and share experiences. Through the formation of groups and the attempt to name one's experience ("multiracial"), interracial families try to make visible and normalize that which is conventionally invisible and pathologized (given that the family is usually thought of as a monoracial institution and interracial sex is taboo). The attempt to create a new multiracial label is also an attempt to make visible relationships that are often not assumed by others: that between parents and children who appear "racially different."

The Rise of Identity Politics

Throughout the struggle over state classification, multiracial activists likened their struggle to the civil rights movement of the 1960s, whose values of interracialism they admired and believed they were advancing. Yet although the civil rights revolution serves as inspiration for these activists, the more proximate ideology shaping their concerns are nationalistic movements such as "black power" that made explicit claims about the importance of culture and identity. During the 1960s, the assimilation paradigm to which many ethnic groups aspired and that had dominated much of social science writing on ethnicity gave way to an era in which consciousness and celebration of ethnic difference dominated. At this same time, a national black identity, as opposed to regional identities based on a North/South dichotomy, was emerging among African Americans, shaped by and fueling black protest in the 1960s. By the 1970s, pan-ethnic coalitions between Asian American ethnic groups began to form to combat anti-Asian prejudice, discrimination, and violence and, in so doing, to consolidate the sense of a shared identity across ethnicities (Espiritu 1992).[12]

In the mid- to late 1960s, the rhetoric of black power put questions of racial identity and solidarity at center stage, emphasizing black unity despite differences in skin tone and ancestry, and it discouraged, if not suppressed, the exploration of multiplicity in racial identity. Black power activists articulated a rationale for the importance of asserting one's racial identity and feeling positively about it. Second, they reversed from positive to negative the valuations African Americans had long attached to light skin and mixed ancestry. Moreover, they equated such actions as indicative of the psychological and social health of black people.

Pan-ethnic formation among Asian Americans, Native Americans, and Latinos heightened group consciousness, emphasizing common experiences borne of the tendency of others to lump persons from distinct cultural and national groups together as one racialized group while de-emphasizing class, language, and historical differences among such ethnic groups. As with African Americans, these groups have experienced similar phenomena in their processes of ethnoracial group making, in which individuals were encouraged to declare their affiliation with the racialized group not only through declarations of racial identity but through signs like language and dress that signal knowledge of one's culture and history. Such declarations were interpreted as a sign of loyalty to the group (Espiritu, 1992; Nagel, 1995; Oboler, 1995). Racial identity, in other words, came to be understood as indicative of one's political beliefs and group loyalty and fostered the development of essentialist views among groups of color over how to authentically "be" a member of the group.

Ironically, the reframing of the meaning of racial identity and its importance for group cohesion and collective advancement among groups of color helped create the conditions that led to the fragmentation of monoracial identities. Just as essentialized and highly politicized understandings of racial identity were taking hold in the 1960s through the 1980s, the cohort of mixed-descent persons challenging state classifications was growing up. Moreover, many of those involved in multiracial organizations were being raised in contexts that made it difficult for them to display their cultural credentials at a time in their lives when it mattered most, namely when they entered the highly politicized and racially polarized environment of the college campus.[13]

The sense of racial inauthenticity that many multiracials express feeling (or are aware that others attribute to them) in monoracial settings[14] arises not necessarily because they disagree with the political goals of such groups. Rather, they feel inauthentic because demonstrating ethnic loyalty usually requires one to demonstrate one's ethnic "credentials": a variety of dispositional characteristics (e.g., accent, language proficiency, dress, hairstyle), physical attributes (e.g., skin color, hair texture), class (particularly personal experience with poverty), and other criteria (such as being the victim of discrimination) that serve as emblems of authenticity.[15] Raised with limited contact

to the communities to which they are presumed to belong (by virtue of their physical appearance or ancestry), many mixed-descent persons do not possess the appropriate dispositions and cultural knowledge to secure their authenticity. Their sense of being inauthentic, then, comes not by virtue of having mixed ancestry but because key aspects of their biographies do not fit with the conventional definitions of racial membership.

Multiracial activists constructed their positions in opposition to black power ideology. By the 1980s, multiracial activists began to challenge the logic of the one-drop rule that they believe black power endorsed and that had become largely accepted in nonwhite communities. Although the one-drop rule was developed with specific reference to blacks and has not been applied to other groups with any consistency, and multiracials of non-African ancestry have been accepted as whites[16], it is still an important factor shaping nonblack respondents' understandings of their situation. The logic of hypodescent underlies the belief, currently fashionable in many ethnoracial communities, that individuals can and should only have one racial identity or affiliation. Respondents of Asian ancestry often located their grievances in Asian American notions of race that locked them out of authentic membership in Asian American communities because of their mixed status.

Most often respondents cited experiences with persons of color, not whites, as important for shaping their grievances over how multiracial people and identity are perceived. Thus, although the broader ideological force against which multiracial activists struggle is the logic of hypodescent, the more proximate ideological antecedent of multiracial activism is the rise of identity politics, a by-product of the work of the one-drop rule.

However, even as identity politics waged by ethnoracial groups helped spur challenges to the claims of such movements, these movements provided a model along which demands for multiracial identity would be couched almost 25 years later. On the one hand, they use the logic of the importance of taking pride and declaring one's racial identity that black power activists put forth so compellingly, arguing that the psychological health of multiracial people ("self-esteem") is at stake (Root, 1992, 1996). Yet at the same time, multiracial activists justify their positions using the values used to substantiate black power ideology in the first place. Arguing that they are entitled to determine their own identity for themselves, they fight for "choice" in racial identity rather than determination by the logic of hypodescent. Rejecting the idea that a monoracial identity could accurately reflect their racial identity, multiracial activists do not reject the idea of racial authenticity itself. Rather, they argued that one-drop ideology forced them into racial categories that cannot describe their authentic inner self.

Bodies in Search of Identities

In mobilizing around census classification, multiracial activists needed to present their desire to have their identity recognized on behalf of a putative group. The identity "multiracial" was, to quote Melissa Nobles's (2000) apt characterization, "in search of bodies"; however, why, we should ask, are these bodies in search of identities to begin with?

In part, multiracial activists' conceptualization of multiracial identity and their justification of official recognition in the terms of liberal individualism echo earlier social movements predicated on identity, such as gay liberation and women's movements. These movements reflect a "turn toward the self," truth, and authenticity that characterizes late 20th-century American culture (Bellah, Madsen, Sullivan, Swidler, & Tipton, 1996; Giddens, 1991). Concerns with self-actualization predominate in the stories of participants in multiracial organizations who conceptualize their public claiming of a mixed identity as

more truthful and accurate and that provides them with a sense of wholeness. By the 1990s, many multiracials sought to make their public identities consistent with their private feelings about identity. For them, concerns over self-realization had replaced preoccupations with political allegiance to monoracial groups in shaping expressions of identity for people of mixed ancestry.

However, the question remains as to why multiracial activists felt that a monoracial identity could not convey their identities truthfully and why racial identity came to be seen as crucial in conveying self-identity. Here again, the ethnic social movements of the 1960s are especially relevant. The political movements of established ethnoracial groups of the 1960s provided new ways of understanding race that inform contemporary multiracial politics. In showing the fundamental ways in which race mattered for determining who got what in American society, and revaluing upward subordinated racial positions in an effort to challenge racial inequality, they popularized the belief that persons should declare and feel good about their racial identity and renewed the emphasis on race as a fundamental axis of self-knowledge and definition in American life. Black power's emphasis on taking pride in, declaring, and expressing racial identity and the interpretation of such actions as indicative of the psychological and social health of black people revealed how important ethnic group honor is for granting social honor to individuals in American life. The urge to essentialize ethnic membership that develops out of it and other such movements was an attempt to mark the group as distinct and special, to shore up a degraded social position.[17]

Multiracial activists borrow many of the same ideas in their struggle for recognition. Through ethnic recognition, they argued, individuals of multiple ancestry would gain respect, and such respect would confirm the essential humanity of multiracials. This understanding is entirely in keeping with American understandings of race. Multiracials lack a specific ethnic honor in an age when social organization on the basis of race proliferates and tremendous importance is placed on ethnic identity, not only in various institutions of social life (e.g., educational occupational, governmental) but in the very ways in which one is said to exist socially. To exist in American society is to possess an ethnoracial identity, one that is recognized by the state and treated with dignity and equality. Moreover, in the United States, to know oneself is to know one's ethnoracial identity. In such a context, to possess a stigmatized ethnic membership is to have a tainted existence. To possess no ethnic identity at all is to be socially nonexistent.[18] Because the category multiracial does not exist as such, people who claim a multiracial identity have no specific ethnic honor to claim that fits with their understanding of themselves, so to recoup their social honor in an age when race is a primary means with which to communicate it, they must create a state category (the most powerful means through which social identities are granted recognition and legitimacy) and revalue upward stigmatized meanings of mixed identity.

A THEORY OF MULTIRACIAL MOBILIZATION

The emergence of multiracial activism was facilitated by a combination of factors. Since the 1960s, new policies of racial self-enumeration by institutions collecting racial data, the proliferation of efforts to collect such data in virtually all institutions of social life, the expansion of ethnic-specific social programs, and the increasing institutionalization of ethnic organizations heightened the imperative of knowing one's racial membership, creating new experiences wherein multiracial individuals were constantly called on to choose among

ethnoracial affiliations. At the same time, multiracial individuals were living in contexts that made this imperative to choose one racial affiliation feel artificial. In contrast to previous periods in U.S. history, this cohort of multiracial people had largely been raised with intimate connections to both sides of their families and cultural heritage. Raised in such a context, multiracial adults came to consider the state's policy of "check one only" racial category as forcing them to choose between their parents and communities. These experiences led multiracials to create their own organizations in an effort to diminish their own sense of isolation and stigmatization.

Activists in favor of multiracial classification drew on already-existing social networks of multiracial people and families. A few committed and well-placed members of these organizations took up the challenge to racial classifications—the most visible symbolic manifestation of those grievances—taking advantage of the opportunity to publicly comment on changes to Directive 15. Presenting themselves as representatives of the multiracial community, they succeeded in getting the state to change its policy on racial classification to allow and count multiple responses to the race question beginning with the 2000 Census.

Through this process, the idea of a multiracial community is given a social and cultural presence, even if most of the individuals who might be granted membership in such a community because they are of mixed descent are currently not organized with others so situated. Since the struggle over the census, references to the multiracial community have begun to appear in popular press, while public figures like Tiger Woods and Mariah Carey, known for holding a mixed racial identity, put a face on multiracials. Academics have begun to take notice of multiracial politics, even when their work is not necessarily about those politics suggesting that the phenomenon has come to be of interest beyond the predominantly multiracial activist/scholar community that was writing about it 5 years ago (Root, 1992, 1996).

Yet it remains to be seen whether or not multiracials will strengthen or create interests, institutions, and culture—elements that define ethnic affiliations (Cornell, 1996). Will they continue to express a shared interest in social recognition of multiracial families and multiracial identity? Probably. Will they continue to create organizations to explore multiracial identity and family issues? Most likely. Will political organization on the basis of "pan" multiracial identity develop further, where multiracials coalesce as have blacks, Asians, and Latinos? Much will depend on whether or not activists renew their fight for a stand-alone category, what academics, journalists, and institutions do with the census data emerging from the Census 2000 (whether or not they treat what is now a statistically observable population as a group defined against the currently recognized ethnoracial groups), and how persons of mixed descent interpret such changes. What is certain is that future changes in America's racial landscape will not be determined by the intent of multiracial actors alone. With the changes in the collection of racial data by the state, the genie is out of the bottle. No longer are persons of mixed descent as statistically invisible as they have been in the past, nor are they socially invisible. With such changes, it will be much more difficult to maintain the individualized sense of multiracial identity, one that resides at intersection of categories, in whose name multiracial actors waged their struggle.

NOTES

1. For most of the 20th century, the federal government had resolved the question of how to racially classify persons of mixed descent. By 1930, classifications of mixed descent persons had disappeared from official state counts of race (Davis, 1991; Nobles, 2000). The clear state consensus was that individuals would be counted in one racial group only according to the rule of hypodescent, one largely agreed on by state institutions and the people they classified. During this period, cases in which individuals or groups disagreed with how they were racially classified were privatized, dealt with on an ad hoc basis, sometimes adjudicated by the state but most often settled in everyday interpersonal interactions.

2. I use the term multiracial to refer to both persons of mixed descent and their parents involved in this movement. I use that term interchangeably with others like "persons of mixed descent" and "mixed race." This is in part to signal a distance between my analysis and the language movement participants use to advance their cause. The adoption of multiracial by activists is itself an identity-building device, a new term activists selected to distance their rendering of mixed identity from previous terms for racial mixedness (e.g., *mulatto*) that they deem derogatory and part of an attempt to persuade others that the group exists as in the way activists describe. My use of multiple terms is an attempt to avoid the fixity of group formation that any one term implies because my intent is to discuss a process of group formation rather than assume its result.

3. This analysis is drawn from DaCosta (2000), an interview-based study of the organizations developed by and for persons of mixed descent and their families and the actors involved in such organizations.

4.   The potential pool of multiracials is virtually unlimited, depending on how people understand themselves and definitions of race. Even if we use ancestry—the dominant principle underlying racial classification in the United States—to think more concretely about which populations might potentially understand themselves to be multiracial, this potential pool is certainly not limited to people in interracial unions and their children. This potential pool might include, for example, the estimated 70% to 98% of African Americans with multiple ancestry and a growing Latino population that understands itself to be a mestizo population. Yet clearly these populations do not think of themselves as multiracial in the same sense that current discourse of multiraciality describes, identifying themselves as members of the officially recognized racial categories and noticeably absent from the collective organizations formed for multiracials.

5.   Clearly this result comes not only because of the efforts of multiracial activists. Other interest groups and institutions such as the state, statisticians, academics, civil rights organizations, and politicians all played a role in the process (see Anderson & Fienberg, 1999, for details). My purpose is not to show that process in its entirety but to demonstrate how one such contender waged its struggle.

6.   Instructions for the race question in Census 2000 read, "What is Person 1's race? Mark one or more races to indicate what this person considers himself/herself to be." The categories "white," "black, African American, or Negro," and "American Indian or Alaska Native" appear as discrete categories, whereas several Asian national categories are listed separately, as are "Native Hawaiian," "other Pacific Islander," and "some other race." Despite the separation of these categories, promotional material published by the Census Bureau indicates that answers to the race question will be collapsed "into the six race groups needed by the federal government." These include "white," "black or African American," "American Indian and Alaska Native," "Asian," "Native Hawaiian and other Pacific Islander," and "other."

7.   Graham says of Project RACE's beginnings, "It's a grass roots movement and literally, overnight we became a national organization."

8.   Root (1996) writes, "I have the right to identify differently in different situations—and know I am not mixed up, disloyal, or weak; I have the right to change my identity over my lifetime—and more than once if need be" (p. 7). Root's Bill of Rights is a manifesto of sorts. It details some of the shared grievances of multiracial people, no matter their ancestry, as it creates a common sense of struggle. In earlier, unpublished versions of the Bill, Root used the pronoun 'we." This usage, along with the language of "rights," reflects a sense that multiracial people are a community, heretofore invisible, that is asserting its unacknowledged but nevertheless inherent right to identity. The language of rights emerges also in AMEA's official testimony at the federal hearings for multiracial classification.

9.   According to the U.S. Census, the number of intermarried couples increased by almost 10 times between 1960 and 1990, whereas the number of children from these unions quadrupled. Census figures counted approximately 157,000 intermarried couples in 1960. By 1990, that figure had risen to almost 1.5 million. In 1970, the total number of children from interracial unions was recorded at approximately 460,000. By 1990, that figure reached 1.9 million. These figures count only those children younger than 18 years, and so do not account for children born in earlier years who have reached adulthood. Nor do they count those individuals of multiple ancestry who have parents with the same racial designations. As such, they undercount the potential pool of persons who may hold a mixed identity.

10.   The Civil Rights Act of 1964 outlawed discrimination in public accommodations and employment. The Voting Rights Act of 1965 was aimed at reducing barriers to political participation on the basis of race. Racial discrimination in housing was banned through the Housing Act of 1968, while Federal Executive order 11246 put in place procedures to ensure that federal contractors comply with fair employment practices (McAdam, 1982; Morris, 1984).

11.   "Generationally mixed" is a term some multiracials have begun using to refer to people with ancestors from multiple ethnoracial categories but whose parents primarily identified with one (and the same) racial group. Their "mixture," in this formulation, originates in generations before the parental generation.

12.   Partly in response to increased ethnic cohesion and vociferousness of nonwhite groups, whites also experienced a resurgence in ethnic identification, manifest in increased efforts by third-generation descendants of immigrants to revive or invent traditions of their immigrant ancestors (Waters, 1990).

13.   It is not surprising then that many multiracial organizations are formed on college campuses.

14.   This sense of inauthenticity is revealed in many respondents' likening of publicly declaring their multiracial identity as "coming out" ("It felt like we were coming out of the closet," "You would have thought we were gay"), suggesting that before their true self was hidden behind a façade. Many multiracials involved in organizations say that what they considered their racial identity to be was often at odds with what they thought they were supposed to declare publicly. This fostered in many of them a sense that they had a personal private identity and a different public one.

15.   See Yanagisako (1995) for an analysis of the use of working class histories in Asian American studies classes as a means through which academics foster (intentionally and unintentionally) a pan-Asian ethnic identity.

16.   Davis (1991) argues that "racially mixed persons in the United States, except for those with black ancestry, generally have been treated as assimilating Americans after the first generation of miscegenation." Multiracials of one-fourth or less Asian or Mexican (Indian) ancestry are "most likely to be accepted the same way an assimilating immigrant from Europe is . . . They do not have to hide their racial minority background if it is one-fourth or less, so there is no need to pass as white" (p.118).

17.   Weber (1978) describes ethnic honor as part of a belief in common ethnicity in which members of a group believe they share a specific honor that outsiders do not. This sense of ethnic honor is manifest in rituals and customs that mark a group as distinct and sustained by "the conviction of the excellence of one's own customs and the inferiority of alien ones" (pp. 390-391).

18.   This social fact underlies what many mixed-descent persons define as a quintessential "mixed" experience, namely repeated and often unsuccessful attempts by others to place them in racial categories. These "what are you" encounters (Williams, 1996) reflect the importance Americans place on knowing another's racial position so as to know how to interact with another.

REFERENCES

Anderson, M., & Fienberg, S. (1999). *Who counts? The politics of census-taking in contemporary America.* New York: Russell Sage.

Association of MultiEthnic Americans. (1993). [Prepared statement before the Subcommittee on Census, Statistics and Postal Personnel of the House Committee on Government Reform and Oversight.]

Bellah, R. N., Madsen, R., Sullivan, W. M., Swidler, A., & Tipton, S. M. (1996). *Habits of the heart: Individualism and commitment in American life* (Updated ed.). Los Angeles: University of California Press.

Bourdieu, P. (1991). Social space and the genesis of classes. In J. B. Thompson (Ed.), *Language and symbolic power* (p. 248). Cambridge, MA: Harvard University Press. (Original work published 1982)

Calhoun, C. (1994). Social theory and politics of identity. In C. Calhoun (Ed.), *Social theory and the politics of identity* (pp. 10-36). Cambridge, MA: Blackwell.

Cornell, S. (1996). The variable ties that bind: Content and circumstances in ethnic processes. *Ethnic and Racial Studies, 19*(2), 265-289.

Davis, F. J. (1991). *Who is black: One nation's rule.* University Park: Pennsylvania State Press.

Espiritu, Y. L. (1992). *Asian American panethnicity: Bridging institutions and identities.* Philadelphia: Temple University Press.

Fernandez, C. (1994, October). Keynote address. Annual Multiracial Americans of Southern California Kaleidoscope conference, Los Angeles, CA.

Giddens, A. (1991). *Modernity and self-identity: Self and society in the late modern age.* Stanford, CA: Stanford University Press.

Graham, H. D. (1990). *The civil rights era: Origin and development of national policy, 1960–1972.* New York: Oxford University Press.

McAdam, D. (1982). *Political process and the development of black insurgency.* Chicago: University of Chicago Press.

Morris, A. (1984). *The origins of the civil rights movement.* New York: Free Press.

Nagel, J. (1995). Politics and the resurgence of American Indian ethnic identity. *American Sociological Review, 60*(6), 947-965.

Nobles, M. (2000). *Shades of citizenship: Race and the census in modern politics.* Stanford, CA: Stanford University Press.

Oboler, S. (1995). *Ethnic labels, Latino lives: Identity and the politics of (re)presentation in the United States.* Minneapolis: University of Minnesota Press.

Omi, & Espiritu. (2000). "Who are you calling Asian?": Racial classification and the census. In *State of Asian Pacific America: Transforming race relations, a public policy report.* Los Angeles: UCLA Press.

Root, M. P. P. (Ed.). (1992). *Racially mixed people in America.* Newbury Park, CA: Sage.

Root, M. P. P. (1996). *The multiracial experience: Racial borders as the new frontier.* Thousand Oaks, CA: Sage.

Skrentny, J. P. (1996). *The ironies of affirmative action: Politics, culture, and justice in America.* Chicago: University of Chicago Press.

Spencer, J. M. (1997). *The new colored people: The mixed-race movement in America.* New York: New York University Press.

Waters, M. (1990). *Ethnic options: Choosing ethnic identities in America.* Berkeley: University of California Press.

Weber, M. (1978). Ethnic groups. In G. Roth & C. Wittich (Eds.), *Economy and society* (pp. 385-398). Berkeley: University of California Press. (Original work published 1918–1920)

Williams, G. H. (1996). *Life on the color line: The true story of a white boy who discovered he was black.* New York: Penguin Books.

Yanagisako, S. (1995). Transforming Orientalism: Gender, nationality, and class in Asian American studies. In S. Yanagisako & C. Delaney (Eds.), *Naturalizing power: Essays in feminist cultural analysis* (pp. 275-298). New York: Routledge.

CHAPTER 5

From Civil Rights to the Multiracial Movement

KIM M. WILLIAMS

Harvard University

This chapter makes three primary claims. The most fundamental is that the multiracial movement could not have happened, nor could it have taken the forms it has, had it not been for both successes and failures of the civil rights movement. At first glance, the trajectory of largely acrimonious relations between the multiracialists and civil rights advocates over the past 10 years or so might seem to render this claim implausible. Yet this chapter demonstrates that outcomes of the civil rights movement are imprinted on the multiracial movement: they explain important aspects of the timing, characteristics, and even the goals of of the latter. To advance these arguments, I draw upon a number of social movement concepts to make clear the ways in which the civil rights successes helped to set in place a working definition of race that is currently under considerable strain.

The response of the civil rights establishment, most prominently the National Association for the Advancement of Colored People (NAACP), the National Urban League (NUL), and the National Council of La Raza (NCLR), to the multiracialists' demands for multiracial recognition was overwhelmingly negative. Although conceding that there are no pure races in a biological sense, civil rights groups nevertheless registered staunch opposition to the multiracialists' appeals at most every opportunity. The crux of their objection centered on the belief that the addition of a multiracial category on the census would "dilute" the traditional minority count in that substantial numbers of people who are now counted as "black," for example, would choose "multiracial" if given the option. Not only would this undercut the efficacy of the Voting Rights Act, they argued, but it would also undermine various state and federal programs aimed at minorities, such as minority business development programs and some affirmative action plans.

Civil rights groups have perceived the contemporary assertion of multiracial identity as a threat because it disrupts a logic of race in which such organizations have become increasingly invested over time. Racial statistics began to hold new political potential for disadvantaged minority groups in the 1960s and 1970s, which explains why civil rights organizations have been so adamant in their efforts to maintain or buttress the minority count since then.

NEGLECTED OUTCOMES OF THE CIVIL RIGHTS MOVEMENT: THE POLITICS OF RACIAL NUMBERS

Only a small number of groups, defined in specific ways, are accepted as legitimate cate-gories in politics, law, and official statistics. Official classifications raise problems of political decision. States must categorize, but the categories adopted for these institutional purposes do not float above society in thin air. They are entrenched in the structure of institutions. Through its practices of social classification, the state defines groups with common interests (Alonso & Starr, 1987).

Analyzing the ways in which working definitions of race are established and maintained in the United States and elsewhere requires attention to state practices. How are race-ethnic groups formally defined by the state and what are the benefits and risks of being classified in specific ways? What are the links between race-ethnic definitions and institutional developments? What is the relationship between such institutional developments and mobilization along race-ethnic lines? These are some of the broad questions that should be asked in any examination of race-ethnic mobilization. I elaborate on these inquiries in the context

of the racial landscape of the United States over the past 40 years.

It should be noted at the outset that present-day civil rights groups are not primarily responsible for our contemporary working definition of race; it has only been in the latter part of this century that such organizations have been able to exert any leverage whatsoever over the matter. Most of the history of the United States attests to the fact that racial designations have been used by the state as a tool of dominance, serving to separate and penalize those not defined as white (see, e.g., Lee, 1993). However, a crucially important shift began to emerge around 1970. Vital to recognize for our purposes, yet largely neglected in most assessments of the civil rights successes, is the fact that the civil rights movement marked the first time that minorities, through the political leadership of civil rights organizations, were able to materially use racial counts to their advantage. In the 1960s, the "very classifications that had previously been employed [to deny] civil rights now became useful in enforcing and monitoring these same civil rights" (Fernandez, 1996, p. 24). As a result of a number of civil rights successes (i.e., the outcomes of the civil rights movement), racial statistics became valuable to U.S. minority groups in new ways.

The Outcomes of Social Movements: Theoretical Referents

Although the social movement literature has traditionally focused much less on movement outcomes than on the emergence of movements and other aspects of social movement phenomena,[1] the small body of existing work in this area directs attention to two areas of concern: how to define outcomes and how to establish causality. Regarding the first issue, existing studies have largely focused on outcomes in terms of policy results. I consider the major legislative/policy outcomes of the civil rights movement to include the Civil Rights Act of 1964, the Voting Rights Act of 1965, and the Great Society programs associated with Lyndon B. Johnson's presidency. A related concern in the outcomes literature involves the fact that just as legislative and policy outcomes are obviously critical, we cannot regard outcomes solely in legal or policy terms. We cannot discount the fact that the civil rights movement marked a profound cultural shift in terms of the ways in which racial identity has since been both expressed and understood. For our purposes, probably the most important cultural outcome of the civil rights movement is that the movement helped to redefine "the political" toward a wider range of claims, including assertions of difference, identity, and language rights. These issues are discussed later.

The second persistent theme in the literature on outcomes concerns the problem of establishing causality. It cannot be asserted with absolute certainty that the civil rights movement was the cause of the aforementioned policy developments. However, given that the civil rights movement is one of the most thoroughly documented social movements of the 20th century, I sidestep this debate. Both the amount and the quality of research available on these issues justify the assumption that these major policy and legislative decisions were strongly related to the efforts of civil rights organizations pushing for such changes.

The remainder of this chapter deals with two questions: (a) What legal, political, and cultural outcomes of the U.S. civil rights movement prompted the establishment of a "working definition" of race in the United States over the past 30 to 40 years; and (b) how and why is this working definition changing? Without paying full attention to the complexity of the argument, much of what follows could be mistaken as a slight on the remarkable gains realized by the civil rights movement. The ways in which that movement created both the political and social space for many black Americans (and also served as a model for other disenfranchised sectors of American society) to prosper and advance simply cannot be overemphasized. As a result of the civil rights movement, the black middle class has vastly expanded, the number of black elected officials increased by over fivefold between 1969 and the present, and by most indicators of betterment (e.g., infant mortality rates, educational attainment), many black Americans are more prosperous than ever before. Much of that improvement is attributable to the fact that the civil rights movement ushered in the glaringly overdue process of further democratizing the United States.

Forty years later, however, we must face some difficult facts: The promise and optimism ushered in by the civil rights movement have all but evaporated. A sampling of current book titles dealing with various aspects of the post-civil rights era suggests as much: for example, *We Have No Leaders*; *The Dream Deferred*; *Faded Dreams*; and so on. Looking beyond the titles of these books to consider their substantive content, four principal themes emerge: (a) increasing skepticism as to whether the mere visibility of blacks in positions of power (e.g., as elected officials or business leaders) can in fact alter power relations; (b) criticism of the civil rights organizations that spearheaded the struggles of the 1950s and 1960s for evolving into co-opted and institutionalized entities in the 1980s and 1990s; (c) concern over what has been termed the essentialism of civil rights groups, for example, in terms of insensitivity to gender dynamics and intolerance of homosexuality; and (d) the widening socioeconomic gap between middle-class and poor blacks. Progressive academics and activists should not shy away from productively engaging the civil rights establishment in discussions about new problems and circumstances.

RACIAL UNDERSTANDINGS
AND CIVIL RIGHTS LEGISLATION

The Voting Rights and Civil Rights Acts, as well as the programs associated with the Great Society, spurred the reallocation of millions of dollars and some redistribution of political power. First, I review the ways in which racial data took on new importance as a result of these policy outcomes. Next, I will turn to the problematic definition of race on which these outcomes were conceptually based.

The Civil Rights and Voting Rights Acts of 1964 and 1965 dismantled the most egregious of discriminatory mechanisms: black disenfranchisement in the South and various types of public and private discrimination throughout the United States. The new laws required the collection of racial and ethnic data to monitor legislative compliance and the delivery of new social services and programs. For example, to implement and regulate the Civil Rights Act, racial data became important in order to identify the numbers of minorities employed in firms and the racial composition of schools. Similarly, for the purposes of redistricting and the creation of "majority-minority" electoral districts, enforcement of the Voting Rights Act required population tabulations by race at the level of city blocks. The War on Poverty and the Great Society programs initiated by the Johnson administration in the mid-1960s can be viewed in the same vein. Specifically intended to address problems faced by groups and to improve living conditions in cities, several of the social welfare programs of the Great Society distributed funds by means of statistically driven grant-in-aid formulas. By 1978, more than 100 such programs had been developed, using some measure of population to allocate funds for programs from preschool education to urban mass transportation (Choldin, 1994).

With funding and redistricting driven by federal census counts, it is no surprise that "across the country, communities and minorities began to examine closely their population numbers" (Choldin, 1994, p. 41). As a result, the operating procedures used to collect these data took on a greater significance. Perhaps most politically consequential for census taking in the post-civil rights era was Statistical Directive No. 15, issued by the Office of Management and Budget (OMB) in 1977. Known as OMB 15, this directive mandated the use of four standard racial categories (in addition to one ethnic category, Hispanic) to be used in the official collection and reporting of racial data in the United States:

- American Indian or Alaskan Native: a person having origins in any of the original peoples of North America and who maintains cultural identification through tribal affiliations or community recognition.
- Asian or Pacific Islander: a person having origins in any of the original peoples of the Far East, Southeast Asia, the Indian subcontinent, or the Pacific Islands. This area includes, for example, China, India, Japan, Korea, the Philippine Islands, and Samoa.
- Black: a person having origins in any of the black racial groups of Africa.
- Hispanic: a person of Mexican, Puerto Rican, Cuban, Central or South American, or other Spanish culture or origin regardless of race.
- White: a person having origins in any of the original peoples of Europe, North Africa, or the Middle East.

Instituted for the purposes of civil rights enforcement, Directive 15 specifically cautioned that the mandated categories "should not be interpreted as being scientific or anthropological in nature"; rather, they were developed to meet expressed congressional and executive needs for "compatible, non-duplicated, exchangeable" racial and ethnic data.[2] Gone was any reference to a purportedly scientific basis of race; these categories were intended as political instruments. Accordingly, they have been treated as such by elected officials, the Census Bureau, and various lobbying groups endeavoring to protect, change, or add categories. For example, Mexican American groups successfully lobbied to add the "Hispanic origins question" to the 1980 census, and several Asian categories were added to the 1980 and 1990 censuses in response to pressure exerted by Asian American organizations. At the other end of the spectrum, the Arab American Institute has worked (in vain) to reassign persons of Middle Eastern origin from "white" to a new "Middle Eastern" category. Meanwhile and from a different angle, other groups (Celtic Coalition, Society for German American Studies) have also been trying to disaggregate the white category (see, e.g., Espiritu, 1992).

A wide array of lobbying groups and other interested parties questioned the conceptual foundations behind the basic categories reported in Directive 15, and in response the OMB began a comprehensive review of the directive in 1994. This review culminated in a number of changes that were implemented in the 2000 Census. However, for 20 years (1977–1997), and thus until very recently, the directive mandated the use of official racial categories by the federal government, even as the definitions used in the directive became increasingly anachronistic. For instance, reflective of Census Bureau data from the 1960s to the early 1970s, the 1977 directive used terms such as "majority race" and "principal minority race" to refer to whites and blacks respectively. (Census Bureau data from that period indicated that blacks constituted 96% of the minority population [Ramirez, 1996]; in 2000, the bureau estimated that blacks constituted about 50% of the population of people of color). To be sure, these sorts of demographic changes have created problems not only for Directive 15 but also for the view of race

relations advanced in the Civil Rights and Voting Rights Acts. For instance, references to race relations in the Voting Rights Act are unmistakably bipolar in their orientation: The act treats race as if it is an exclusively black and white issue. Yet a number of court cases have challenged the Voting Rights Act in this assumption (*Johnson v. DeGrandy*, 1994; *Vera v. Bush*, 1996), raising the issue of how to construct districts where no one racial group comprises a majority of the voting age population (McManus & Morehouse, 1997).

In summary, the policy outcomes associated with the civil rights movement focused exclusively on racism, discrimination, and equality, leaving aside (a) the question of race itself and (b) the possibility of ongoing and considerable changes in racial demographics. Since the mid-1960s, racial statistics have provided a powerful means for civil rights organizations to make claims on the state and its services. However, such statistics are themselves characterized by both inconsistencies and anachronistic assum-ptions. In short, although the civil rights successes certainly created opportunities, this new fusion of statistics and politics would also usher in an attendant set of problems.

UNDOING THE "WORKING DEFINITION"

The racial assumptions on which the civil rights movement was predicated are showing perceptible signs of strain. In fact, it is arguable that the developments discussed next "combine to render the concept of race less powerful than it has ever been at any time in American history" (Payne, 1998, p. 169). This is not at all to suggest that racism does not still pervade American institutions or that race does not continue to have a strong grip on the American psyche. Rather, my claim is that a number of contemporary dynamics are seriously disrupting the logic of race as it was legally and socially understood and instituted only 30 to 40 years ago. Three factors have upended the dominant concept of race in recent years: (a) rapidly changing demographics, in particular, new immigration trends, and an exponential increase in interracial marriages and births; (b) a weakening sense of black unity; and (c) the publicizing of these developments.

Demographics. The current racial landscape of the United States looks radically different than it did 40 years ago. The civil rights movement occurred at a time when blacks were by far the largest minority group in the country and whites were by far the majority. If current demographic trends persist, within the next 50 years, as everyone is currently categorized, whites will no longer make up a majority of the U.S. population. Again, depending on how one counts, data from the U.S. census indicate that Latinos are now the majority-minority in the U.S. While almost all of the discussion of race in the civil rights era focused upon the nation's discrimination against blacks, racial debates in the post-civil rights era are more multidimensional. The point is this: Demographic shifts are blurring existing racial landmarks. Immigration and intermarriage trends represent two of the most notable causes in this regard.

Immigration. Over the past 30 years, an increasing number of immigrants have come to the United States from areas other than Europe, largely because of a 1965 change in immigration laws. Immigration from Latin America, the Caribbean, and Asia added some 18 million people to the U.S. population between 1965 and 1990; by 1994, 8.7% of the total U.S. population was foreign born, nearly double the percentage in 1970. By 2000, 10.4% of the U.S. population was foreign born and 76.5% of the foreign-born population came to the United States from Latin America, the Caribbean, or Asia.[4] A number of implications can be drawn from these developments, but most relevant for our purposes is that increasing numbers of Americans do not perceive race in the terms dictated by the U.S. Census Bureau. The most obvious evidence along these lines comes from the Census Bureau itself. Unable to find a box that applied to themselves, more than 7 million people marked "other" on the 1980 census race question, and close to 10 million did so in 1990. In 2000, over 15 million Americans selected "Some Other Race." Many of these people clearly did not understand the Census Bureau's mandates. Furthermore, it is comparably evident that the Census Bureau has found it difficult to categorize them. Take an example from 1990:

> For the 1990 Census, people who wrote that they were "multi-racial" or "bi-racial" were left in the "Other" race classification. Respondents who wrote "Black-White" were counted as Blacks; those who wrote "White-Black" were counted as Whites. Finally, imputation processes . . . are used to assign a standard race to more complicated cases. This usually involves checking the racial responses of other people in the same household or similar households in the neighborhood. (Lee, 1993, p. 83)

To summarize, immigration has amplified an already growing awareness that racial categorization and coexisting understandings about race are not immutable, universal facts. The Census Bureau's obvious confusion in this regard seems to support this conclusion. Millions of immigrants who have come to this country have had no prior experience with formal racial categorization (about half of the countries in the world do not collect racial data in their censuses; Edmonston & Schultze, 1995), and many of these people evidently do not relate to the Census Bureau's mandates in this regard.

Interracial Marriages and Births. Intensifying the effects of changing immigration patterns, there has also been a meteoric rise in the number of interracial marriages in the United States over the past 30 years. Such marriages grew from about 150,000 interracially married couples in 1960 (when antimiscegenation laws were still in effect in a number of states) to 1.4 million in 2000[5]; these numbers continue to grow. A word of caution: A logic whereby we can identify a subset of marriages as "interracial" implies that all other marriages are between two people of the same (pure) race. This type of reasoning poses an unresolved dilemma for multiracial movement advocates, to which I return later. Nevertheless, popular ideas of race (i.e., race as biological fact) are certainly challenged when we hear that between 25% and 33% of all marriages involving Japanese Americans are now out-group marriages, that more indigenous people marry outside the indigenous population than marry within it, and that marriages between blacks and whites have increased by 300% since 1970 (Hollinger, 1995). Like it or not, a society long hostile to acknowledging racial mixture will have to somehow come to terms with a rapidly increasing population of multiracial families and individuals.

Perhaps such acknowledgment is taking place more rapidly than one might otherwise suspect. Scholarly work demonstrates that even though interracial marriage rates are still relatively low, kinship ties multiply their effect dramatically. Defining kin as those related by blood or marriage, a study conducted at Princeton University found that interracial kin relations are so plentiful that "one in seven whites, one in three blacks, four in five Asians, and more than 19 in 20 Native Americans are closely related to someone of a different racial group" (Goldstein, 1999, p. 399). Although those related by blood or marriage do not inevitably form close emotional bonds, kinship ties increase the possibility of such attachments among individuals who might otherwise have little to do with one another. In this way, intermarriage patterns can potentially be viewed as an engine of social change, not just as an indication of social distance (Lieberson & Waters, 1988).

Weakening Black Unity. Numerous studies have documented the fact that racial identity and solidarity were powerfully cohesive forces in creating the culture of protest on which the civil rights struggles were launched and sustained. Although black unity and assumptions of black homogeneity underpinned the civil rights movement, this can be at least in part attributed to the brutality of white racism. In 1965, Jim Crow laws were just being lifted and interracial marriage was still illegal in 16 states. Institutional racism certainly helped to ensconce race as an objective fact, but it also had the "unintended consequence of defining, legitimating and provoking group identity and mobilization" (Marx, 1995, p. 159). So in part as a result of the successes of the civil rights movement, black solidarity has subsequently weakened. In effect, the civil rights movement helped to create the legal and social space for new possibilities and differentiations within "the black community" to emerge that were not previously possible.

For example, the civil rights movement is rightly attributed as the catalyst for the dramatic expansion of the black middle class over the past 30 to 40 years. While this is certainly a positive development, numerous studies have also documented that the civil rights movement marked the beginning of a profound (and still growing) class cleavage between middle-class and poor blacks (see, e.g., Wilson, 1987). In a similar vein, the civil rights movement also helped to create the social space for other disenfranchised groups within the black community to assert themselves politically. We usually think of this as an external process: The civil rights movement became a model for other socially and politically excluded populations (e.g., women and gays) to assert what they perceived as their rights as women and gays. It is in this sense that the civil rights movement is referred to as an "initiator" movement in the social movement literature. Such movements "signal or otherwise set in motion an identifiable protest cycle" (McAdam, 1995, p. 219), whereas "spin-off" movements, to varying degrees, model themselves after the initiator movement. However, for example, there were women and gays within the black community who began to recast the ideological and organizational lessons learned from the civil rights struggles toward other ends, namely to critique sexism and homophobia in black communities. In this way, although the civil rights movement was itself a largely Southern, church-based movement that did not exemplify much in the way of a progressive attitude toward the rights of black women or black gays, its example nevertheless gave rise to broader assertions of difference within black communities (see, e.g., Collins, 2000; Hooks, 1992).

Recall that the social movement literature on outcomes would have us look at the effects of the civil rights movement not only in policy terms but also in regard to its cultural manifestations and impacts. The civil rights movement certainly marked a profound cultural shift in how racial identity has since been expressed and understood both within the black community and beyond it. Although the civil rights movement is not often characterized as marking the beginning of the end of ostensibly uncomplicated notions of race in this country, that is precisely what I am asserting here. That is not to say that the meaning of blackness was not questioned or disputed before or even during the civil rights era (see, e.g., Smith, 1996), but that such debates were fewer, much more contained, and generally less conceivable for both the general American public and American elites (e.g., politicians,

educators, artists) than they are now. In the civil rights era, both analysts and activists could refer to blackness and evoke the same idea. When the civil rights era ended, so did this common understanding. Black unity can no longer be taken for granted as a given; ironically, this can be partially attributed to outcomes of the civil rights movement.

Publicizing These Developments. If racial lines, as we have generally tended to conceive of them in this country over the past 40 years, are rapidly eroding, this is largely because discussions in this regard have extended well beyond the walls of academia. The concept of race is currently considered, debated, and increasingly refuted in an unprecedented array of popularized arenas, such as television talk shows and weekly news magazines. From the ivory tower to Oprah, the mid-1960s concept of race has begun to fracture and fade.

FROM CIVIL RIGHTS TO THE MULTIRACIAL MOVEMENT

In spite of all the evidence just presented, the undoing of a working definition of race does not a social movement make. Clearly, the structural circumstances outlined previously greatly facilitate the possibility for a movement to challenge entrenched ideas about race to arise. But, racial understandings are always problematic and disputable, and it is only in recent years that they have become widely problematized and disputed in the United States. Thus, a number of questions remain. Obviously important queries about the timing, characteristics, and even the goals of the multiracial movement can be examined by considering the ways in which, ironically, it is part of a larger cycle of protest initiated by the civil rights movement.

"Cycles of protest" refers to the idea that different social movements are in fact connected. The concept helps us address questions of how one movement might be said to create the political or social space in which a later one can emerge, a similarity in the tactics or appeals through which movement leaders foster an insurgent consciousness, and the ways in which different movements can be said to respond to each other ideologically. Protest cycles were previously discussed briefly in relation to the concept of initiator and spin-off movements. I argue that the multiracial movement is a spin-off movement of the civil rights movement. More strongly stated, the multiracial movement could not have happened, nor would it have taken the forms it has, had it not been for both the successes and failures of the civil rights movement. At first glance, this is perhaps counterintuitive. The friction and hostility that have persisted over the past 10 years between civil rights and multiracial groups might compel an observer to conclude that they must necessarily have sharply divergent profiles. But the multiracial movement has not reinvented the wheel of protest. Rather, it has creatively adapted, reinterpreted, and built on tactics, ideologies, and legal outcomes established through the civil rights struggles. A closer look at the timing, characteristics, and goals of the multiracial movement should drive this point home.

Timing of the Multiracial Movement in Relation to Civil Rights

Broad structural processes such as immigration and the increase in multiracial births and marriages have been so habitually pointed to by the activists and scholars currently writing on multiracial issues that an analyst could comfortably conclude that these developments inevitably led to the rise of the movement. I want to dispel this notion by providing an alternative and more analytical account. To explain the rise of multiracial activism in the 1970s, as well as many of its successful campaigns in the 1990s, one must look at specific ways in which (from the 1960s onward) the political climate became less hostile and eventually, even favorable to the politicized concept of multiracial identity. To this end, we need to make a distinction between broad structural processes and specific "dimensions of the political environment that provide incentives for people to undertake collective action by affecting their expectations for success or failure" (Tarrow, 1994, p. 85). Such changes in the political environment are called "political opportunities" in the social movement literature, and a concept that especially helpful in answering the "why now?" question regarding the timing of a social movement. For our purposes, political opportunities can be understood as changes in the legal or institutional structure that grant more formal political access to challenging groups (McAdam, 1996).

Legal/institutional changes brought about by civil rights struggles were critical for the development of multiracial activism: until anti-segregation laws were implemented, and until anti-miscegenation laws were fully repealed in the United States, the possibility for a multiracial movement to materialize and prosper was remote. The legal system went from one that was overtly hostile toward interracial contact and unions in the early 1960s to one in which such contact was at least not regarded as criminal activity by the end of that decade. Thus, it is no surprise then that the first contemporary multiracial organizations began to form in the 1970s. Since 1979, approximately 80 multiracial organizations have formed across the United States. Many of these groups have since disbanded, but I have been able to establish the existence of 40 currently active multiracial groups across the country. These groups, to varying degrees, form the organizational base of the multiracial movement (Williams, 2001). In other words, the civil rights movement helped to remove fundamental barriers that in turn produced the legal and political space for multiracial organizations to form across the country in the 1970s and 1980s. Carlos Fernandez, the first president of the Association of MultiEthnic Americans (AMEA), now the largest multiracial umbrella group in the United States, seems to concur; he identifies the people who have created and joined these organizations over the past 20 years to be the "generation literally born from the successes of the civil rights movement" (Fernandez, 1996, p. 23).

Characteristics of the Multiracial Movement in Relation to Civil Rights

Any number of factors involved in the rise of a movement and the chances of its success are obviously beyond the direct control of the activists involved. Movements can ride the wave of political opportunities, and they can benefit from broader structural circumstances such as demographic shifts, but they cannot be said to ordain the terms of such things. Here, I am addressing the aspects of a movement that are more purposely coordinated by the activists involved. The influence (and example) of the civil rights movement is also apparent when looking at key characteristics of the multiracial movement that its leaders have had some control over, including ideological framing and the tactics used to draw attention to the cause.

Ideological Framing. Given the rigid definition of race that has been characteristic of American institutions and social attitudes, the multiracial movement has certainly brought challenging ideas about race to the fore. However, through key documents and statements made by leading multiracial activists involved in the movement over time, we can see that this has been achieved largely through the adept and creative recasting of

appeals made popular by the civil rights struggles. This is most obvious in the fact that multiracial activists routinely insist on framing multiracialism as a civil right. By arguing that the recognition of multiracial people is the "next logical step in civil rights" (R. Douglass, personal communication, June 14, 1998) multiracial activists have shrewdly drawn on the symbolism of the civil rights movement, yet in the process, cast themselves as more progressive than the so-called progressives (i.e., the civil rights lobby).

Take, for example, the multiracialists' innovative approach to the Voting Rights Act. The definition of race or color was left implicit in the law; in practice it meant "black" and "white" or "white" and "nonwhite." To this, multiracial activists have astutely responded that

> it is the biological aspect of race and racial mixture that is essential to racist thinking ... this attitude finds expression in the *failure of our society and its institutions to officially acknowledge racial mixture*, potentially the basis for a unifying national identity and a crucial step for breaking down traditional lines of social separation. (Fernandez, 1992, p. 133)

In personal interviews that I conducted with the major leaders of the multiracial movement, each made some reference to the effect that they see the multiracial movement (or their personal involvement in it) related to, but somehow a step beyond the civil rights movement. Ramona Douglass (personal communication, June 14, 1998), past president of AMEA, said that she has "been a part of the civil rights movement since the early 1970s and marched in the South with the Ku Klux Klan dancing in my face ... we [multiracial activists] are changing race as we know it." Susan Graham (personal communication, April 16, 1998), president of Project RACE (Reclassify All Children Equally), said, "Our objective is civil rights and equality for all" and so on. My point is that the multiracial movement has not so much created an ideological schema itself as it has creatively and effectively adapted an ideological framework that was readily available from the example of the civil rights movement.

Tactics. Another aspect of the movement's characteristics on concerns its tactics. Again, this is an element of movement activity that is more purposely directed than the sort of structural processes previously discussed. Over the past 10 years, a number of the 40 active multiracial organizations across the country have joined forces at various times and in diverse venues to stage marches, write and deliver position papers, organize forums, events, and symbolic commemorations, and plan street boycotts. Although sharp disagreements sometimes surfaced over some of these strategies,[6] the movement nevertheless used a repertoire of actions that clearly found inspiration in the civil rights struggles. The most conspicuous connection in this regard can be seen in the fact that a number of multiracial groups have come together in recent years to stage two "multiracial solidarity marches," one in Washington, D.C., in 1996, the other in Los Angeles in 1997. The 1996 march was even called a "March on Washington," an apt appropriation of terminology that is widely associated with civil rights efforts.

Goals of the Multiracial Movement in Relation to Civil Rights

In AMEA's mission statement, the objectives are normative and philosophical: Multiracial people should have a right to claim or incorporate their entire heritage, and embrace their total identity. AMEA says its "primary goal is education: to promote a positive awareness of interracial and multiethnic identity, for ourselves and for society as a whole." For Project RACE, the "major, overall objective is to mandate a multiracial

category on all forms requiring racial data," so that multiracial children do not have to suffer the adverse consequences of being regarded as "other." A Place For Us (APFU), primarily a religious organization, views the "support and encourage[ment] of interaction between anyone involved with interracial relationships" to be their purpose. APFU has engaged in extensive political activity to realize this aim: Its founders, Ruth and Steve White, delivered speeches at both multiracial solidarity marches (APFU sponsored the Los Angeles march). Moreover, APFU was heavily involved in the (failed) effort to add a multiracial category to California state forms in 1996–1997 (Williams, forthcoming). Perhaps the most extensively reproduced statement exemplifying the movement's broad goals can be found in Maria Root's (1996) Bill of Rights for Racially Mixed People, which has become something of a charter statement within the activist multiracial community. Some of the rights that Root identifies include "the right not to keep the races separate within me; the right to not be responsible for people's discomfort with my physical ambiguity; the right to not be forced to justify my ethnic legitimacy; the right to change my identity over my lifetime—and more than once" (p. 7). The themes of rights, recognition, and identity tie all of these statements together conceptually. The multiracial movement's philosophical grounding is remarkably consonant with Charles Taylor's (1992) understanding of the politics of recognition:

> The thesis is that our identity is partly shaped by recognition or its absence, often by the misrecognition of others, and so a person or group of people can suffer real damage, real distortion, if the people or society around them mirror back to them a confining or demeaning or contemptible picture of themselves. Nonrecognition or misrecognition can inflict harm, can be a form of oppression, imprisoning someone in a false, distorted, and reduced mode of being. (p. 25)

The politicization of these normative and philosophical objectives denotes a strong conceptual link between the outcomes of the civil rights movement and the goals of multiracial advocacy. It is one thing to assert that a group deserves acknowledgment and recognition; it is yet another matter altogether to look to the state for that endorsement. In considering the trajectory of the multiracial movement, we can see that even from very early on (i.e., efforts to get the Berkeley, California, school district to add a multiracial category in the late 1970s) a primary goal has been recognition in one form or another from the local, state, or federal government.

In thinking about how, in general, claims for the recognition of a group's existence and its identity became viewed as a matter for the state to address, we must again look to the cycle of protest set in motion by the civil rights movement. If "the appearance of a highly visible initiator movement significantly changes the dynamics of emergence for all groups who mobilize as part of the broader protest cycle" (McAdam, 1995, p. 219), then we can certainly see how the civil rights movement facilitated the entry of not only blacks but later of Latinos, Asian Americans, Native Americans, and women into the political process. Their entry not only transformed the dynamics of racial politics but also acted as a catalyst in the transformation of identity, difference, language, and "the personal" into political issues (Winant, 1994). In other words, the very definition of what is legitimately regarded as "political" can be said to have shifted as a result of this cycle of protest. (The OMB's 1977 decision to recognize the importance of self-naming on subsequent censuses can be identified as one of the state's tangible responses to these kinds of claims.) It is in this context that we should place the stated goals of the multiracial movement, which had the benefit of witnessing these prior struggles and of learning from their example.

All of this is not to suggest that the multiracial movement has nothing new to tell us; however, it does indicate that the movement could not have happened had it not been for both the premises on which the civil rights project relied, and for a number of key legal, political, and social outcomes of that movement.

SUMMARY

This chapter has aimed to make three closely related main points. Racial categorization is not only imposed from "above" (i.e., by the state); it is also appropriated from below. In other words, categorizing by race can result in consequences that the state did not bargain for, particularly when those who are subordinated are able to adopt the terms of their definition as the basis for mobilization (Marx, 1995). This is how we can make sense of the apparent irony that racial categories in this country were originally used to keep track of and augment the number of slaves, yet current day civil rights groups defend the practice and logic of racial categorization. In the hands of the socially or politically disenfranchised, numbers can provide a powerful means for race-ethnic groups to make themselves visible, articulate their differences, and make claims on the state and its services. As a result of the civil rights successes, racial counts provided new political potential for disenfranchised groups, which their leaders earnestly seized.

The second point asserted in this chapter is that while the civil rights movement left us with a working definition of race, inscribed both in law and in cultural practice, various trends over the past 30 to 40 years have combined to radically undermine this set of understandings about "what race is." These trends, which include rapidly changing demographics, rising immigration rates, increasing interracial marriages and births, and widening divisions within "traditionally defined" minority groups, make it difficult to refer to race in the sense in which it was understood only a generation ago. Indicative of this, the U.S. Census Bureau, the source of the most authoritative data available about the U.S. population, itself admits that it has become increasingly ineffectual in terms of its ability to reflect the racial complexity of the United States.

The third contention of this chapter is that broad-scale structural changes do not in and of themselves adequately explain much about the timing and other dynamics related to the multiracial movement. To this end, I have introduced key social movement concepts in order to grant us more analytic leverage on questions regarding aspects of the multiracial movement that its leaders have purposely generated (such as tactics, ideological framing, and goals) as well as aspects that are beyond their direct control (such as the repeal of antimiscegenation laws). In both cases, evidence is marshaled to demonstrate that the multiracial movement is in fact a part of a larger cycle of protest, initiated by the civil rights movement.

NOTES

1. Recent work, however, has begun to more systematically address the ways in which social protest impacts policy and, more broadly, how protest affects social change.

2. Before the directive, federal agencies used their own categorization policies, leading to recognition by several agencies of the need for a uniform set of race and ethnicity categories.

3. Because the 2000 census allowed respondents to mark more than one race, the size of racial groups was reported from minimum to maximum counts. Thus, depending on how one counts, blacks constituted either 49.5% or 50.7% of the minority population in 2000.

4. U. S. Bureau of the Census (2001, December). "Profile of the Foreign-Born Population in the United States: 2000," Current Population Reports. Series P-20-206.

5. U.S. Bureau of the Census (2000, March). "America's Families and Living Arrangements: March 2000," and earlier reports. Current Population Reports. Series P-20-537.

6. Regarding the solidarity marches, Ramona Douglass (1995) went on record with a posting to the (now defunct) saying: "I believe the pen is mightier than the picket line. . . . my demonstration days are numbered. . . . the board room is where lasting decisions can be made—not in the streets. This isn't Selma in the sixties." Nevertheless, she attended both marches and spoke energetically on behalf of AMEA; for tactical reasons, she felt obliged to attend and participate.

REFERENCES

Alonso, W., & Starr, P. (Eds.). (1987). *The politics of numbers.* New York: Russell Sage.

Choldin, H. (1994). *Looking for the last percent: The controversy over census undercounts.* New Brunswick, NJ: Rutgers University Press.

Collins, P. H. (2000). *Black feminist thought: Knowledge, consciousness and the politics of empowerment.* New York: Routledge.

Douglass, R. (1995, July 25). Message posted to interracial individuals discussion list, archived at http://soyokaze.biosci.ohio-state.edu/~jei/ii

Edmonston, B., & Schultze, C. (Eds.). (1995). *Modernizing the U.S. census.* Washington, DC: National Academy Press.

Espiritu, Y. (1992). *Asian American panethnicity: Bridging institutions and identities.* Philadelphia: Temple University Press.

Fernandez, C. (1992). La raza and the melting pot: A comparative look at multiethnicity. In M. P. P. Root (Ed.), *Racially mixed people in America.* Newbury Park, CA: Sage.

Fernandez, C. (1996). Government classification of multiracial/multiethnic people. In M. P. P. Root (Ed.), *The multiracial experience: Racial borders as the new frontier.* Thousand Oaks, CA: Sage.

Goldstein, J. R. (1999). Kinship networks that cross racial lines: The exception or the rule. *Demography, 36*(3), 399-407.

Hollinger, D. (1995). *Postethnic America.* New York: Basic Books.

Hooks, B. (1992). *Black looks: Race and representation.* Boston: South End Press.

Lee, S. (1993). Racial classifications in the US census: 1890-1990. *Ethnic and Racial Studies, 16,* 238-242.

Lieberson, S., & Waters, M. (1988). *From many strands: Ethnic and racial groups in America.* New York: Russell Sage.

Marx, A. (1995). Contested citizenship: The dynamics of racial identity and social movements. *International Review of Social History, 40,* 159-183.

McAdam, D. (1995). Initiator and spin-off movements. In M. Traugott (Ed.), *Repertoires and cycles of collective action.* Durham, NC: Duke University Press.

McAdam, D. (1996). Conceptual origins, problems, future directions. In D. McAdam, J. McCarthy, & M. Zald (Eds.), *Comparative perspectives on social movements: Political opportunities, mobilizing structures, and cultural framing.* New York: Cambridge University Press.

McManus, S., & Morehouse, L. (1997). Redistricting in the multiracial twenty-first century. In G. A. Persons (Ed.), *Race and representation.* New Brunswick, NJ: Transaction.

Payne, R. J. (1998). *Getting beyond race: The changing American culture.* Boulder, CO: Westview Press.

Ramirez, D. (1996). Multiracial identity in a color-conscious world. In M. P. P. Root (Ed.), *The multiracial experience: Racial borders as the new frontier.* Thousand Oaks, CA: Sage.

Root, M. P. P. (1996). A bill of rights for racially mixed people. In M. P. P. Root (Ed.), *The multiracial experience: Racial borders as the new frontier.* Thousand Oaks, CA: Sage.

Smith, R. C. (1996). *We have no leaders: African-Americans in the post-civil rights era.* Albany: State University of New York Press.

Starr, P. (1992). Social categories and claims in the Liberal State. *Social Research, 59,* 263-295.

Tarrow, S. (1994). *Power in movement.* New York: Cambridge University Press.

Taylor, C. (1992). *Multiculturalism and the politics of recognition.* Princeton, NJ: Princeton University Press.

Wilson, W. J. (1987). *The declining significance of race: Blacks and changing American institutions.* Chicago: University of Chicago Press.

Winant, H. (1994). *Racial conditions: Politics, theory, comparisons.* Minneapolis: University of Minnesota Press.

Williams, K. (2001). *Boxed in: The U.S. multiracial movement.* Ph.D. dissertation, Cornell University.

Williams, K. (forthcoming). Parties, movements, and constituencies in categorizing race: State-level outcomes of multiracial category legislation. In J. Goldstone (Ed.), *States, parties, and social movements: Pushing the boundaries of institutionalized politics.* Cambridge: Cambridge University Press.

CHAPTER 6

Census 2000

Assessments in Significance

RAINIER SPENCER

University of Nevada, Las Vegas

For 9½ years of every decade, most Americans forget completely about the census, but Census 2000 might prove to be an exception. When people years from now sit down to contemplate Census 2000, several questions might possibly come to mind. What was Census 2000? Was it an answer? A question? Was it perhaps both or, possibly, neither? What was the significance (or what were the multiple significances) of Census 2000 for that nebulous, amorphous, coalition of organizations purporting to constitute the "multiracial movement"? Why were Afro-American organizations and activists opposed to the goals of multiracial organizations and activists? Did partisan party politics have any connection to the debate over Census 2000? These are a few of the questions I address in this chapter, questions that usually are not asked because, frankly, commentators are typically so busy constructing their own particular myths of Census 2000 that they never get around to considering the real issues.

Even after Census 2000 had come and gone, participants on all sides were still at work on their various mystification projects, crafting elaborate fictions they in some cases actually believed to be true. It might do, therefore, before the mythology hardens completely, to have a serious and objective look at Census 2000, in particular that aspect of it that is being hailed in some quarters as the most progressive government statement regarding race in centuries, namely the change from an instruction to mark one race only to an instruction to mark as many races as apply on forms requesting racial identification.

That simple change is the essence of Census 2000 for many people. It represents, for some, everything they fought for and gained and, for others, everything they fought for and lost. Significant expenditures of time, energy, and rhetoric went into the battle that ended in the October 1997 decision of the Office of Management and Budget (OMB) to allow respondents for the first time ever to "mark all that apply" (MATA). Of course, heartfelt dedication to a particular position hardly implies that one's position is reasonable or that it even makes sense. Much of the intense and sometimes ugly sparring that took place during the census controversy can be traced to advocates on all sides internalizing their ideological positions to the extent that they could no longer entertain even a semblance of hypothetical objectivity. At best, the various sides were simply talking past each other; at worst, well, it certainly wasn't pretty. Part of what I intend to accomplish in this chapter is a brief mapping out of the basic positions of the key interests involved, which will allow me to frame the debate over Census 2000 in a way that brings its full implications to light, less the excessive emotion that marred the actual debate itself.

To recap briefly the major aspects of the census controversy, multiracial activists petitioned the federal government to add either a stand-alone multiracial category or a multiracial header with racial sublistings to the federal racial classifications already in use. The principal organizations involved were the Association of Multiethnic Americans (AMEA) and Project RACE (Reclassify All Children Equally). OMB agreed to consider such a move, thereby initiating a years-long, comprehensive study that included a public comment period, several congressional hearings, and a number of statistical surveys. Opponents of the multiracial category proposal, largely Afro-American organizations and other civil rights groups, engaged the multiracial advocates in a pitched battle for the ear of OMB. Ultimately, OMB rejected the idea of a federal multiracial category in either format, opting instead to allow respondents to mark any of the existing racial categories they felt applied. Thus, for better or worse, the age of MATA was ushered in, to be effective for Census 2000, and for all government agencies by January 1, 2003 (U.S. Executive Office of the President, 1997).[1]

Many commentators were quick to acclaim the MATA decision as heralding a sea change in the way that race is understood in the United States. It was immediately taken to represent no less than the dawn of a new era in terms of simultaneously fracturing the race concept and providing the means for those so inclined to proclaim their multiraciality. Levonne Gaddy, president of AMEA, exemplified this trend in announcing that "this is the beginning of our having to redefine this social myth that we call race and to look at it in a different way than we have in the past" (Schmitt, 2001, p. A14). However, in fact, such pronouncements were overstated by a significant degree. For one thing, from the very beginning OMB curtailed the most radical tendency of the new rules by amending them so as to require the statistical aggregation of certain multiple responses (U.S. Executive Office of the President, 2000). For example, black/white multiple responses would be counted as black for purposes of civil rights compliance monitoring.

This was not, as the conspiracy theorist wing of the multiracial movement charged, some sort of clandestine maneuver but was instead the only way yet determined for OMB to allow multiple responses while ensuring that civil rights compliance monitoring (the primary purpose of federal racial statistics) was not degraded in any appreciable degree. Nonetheless, from the perspective of someone wedded to the notion of a multiple response being counted exclusively as a singular statistical entity, OMB's aggregation and allocation policy must have been disappointing to say the least.

ON COUNTING AND BEING COUNTED

However, before becoming involved in questions of aggregation and allocation, let us first be clear on exactly what this discussion is about. Simple though it might seem, the issue of federal racial counting is far more complex than most have assumed. The central question here is one that has, for the most part, gone unasked and undebated. Precisely what kind of counting was it that multiracial activists actually wanted?[2] In what sense did they envision multiracially identifying respondents being counted? This is far from an idle question because there are a variety of ways one might conceive of racial counting taking place, although only one of those ways is correct.

What we need to be concerned with in this discussion is the sense of being counted in terms of the way the system of civil rights compliance monitoring was designed, which is to say being available to be counted whenever a data processor compiles a set of statistics. It is worth going into some detail with this because this is one of the most egregiously misunderstood aspects of the entire multiracial category debate. Hardly anyone outside of the federal government, multiracial activists included, understands precisely how federal racial statistics are used or, particularly, how an individual respondent is counted.

People are under the misperception that when one marks a checkbox on this or that form one has been counted definitively as if there exists some great racial registry containing precisely one line for each American citizen. Much of the more strident rhetoric of multiracial advocates has centered on this mistake. People assume, erroneously, that having marked a checkbox (or boxes), whether under the old "mark one only" system or the new MATA approach, one's personal racial identity has now been updated on some central racial data base. Nothing could be farther from the truth, however; a truth that several examples will serve to make clear.

For instance, let us imagine a female respondent who checks both "white" and "black" on an employment application. How may this person be counted? The answer is that irrespective of the respondent's personal ideology, how she is counted is for the most part determined by whomever is processing the data. Whether she sees herself as black, multiracial, or white, she has no control over how she is counted in many cases. To see why this is so, let us use our applicant in the following example. An analyst with the Small Business Administration might require that certain businesses in a particular city, county, or state submit the racial statistics they maintain on their employees. Our hypothetical respondent would, of course, be included in this data. First, the analyst might decide to run a statistic on the number of people who marked black to compare the result to the total employee population. That represents one way our respondent might be counted.

Next, our analyst might want to see how many people there are in the sample who checked off "white" and who are also female. Again, our respondent would be counted. However, if the desired result was to see how many people marked only white and who are female, our respondent would not be counted. Going on, we might find a statistical series designed to count the total number of respondents who marked something other than white, even if they marked white as well or, alternatively, those who only marked something other than white. Also, of course, our busy analyst might want to count the number of people who marked both the "white" and the "black" boxes only. It should be clear that there are numerous ways for multiple responses to be counted, and that celebrations over MATA allowing people to "be counted definitively as multiracial" indicate, quite frankly, a gross lack of understanding both as to why federal racial statistics are collected as well as to how they are in fact used.[3]

The point, the goal, of all those many, many racial checkboxes on those many, many forms is quite singular: to collect statistics that will allow the federal government to check for indications of possible covert and institutional discrimination. A particular suspicious statistic, whether in elementary school ability tracking or in mortgage-lending approval rates, does not by itself indicate the operation of racist practices but nonetheless may bear closer examination. It may well be that there is a perfectly justifiable rationale for what on the surface appears to be a case of institutional racism. It may well be that deeper examination reveals the suspicious statistic to be mere coincidence. On the other hand, closer investigation may demonstrate that racist practices are indeed at work. The point is that without the collection of racial statistics none of this kind of analysis is possible.

With racial statistics, it is possible to know that (although not necessarily to know why) Afro-American children in a particular school district are ability tracked at twice the rate of white children. With racial statistics, it is possible to know that (although not necessarily to know why) a particular mortgage lender rejects loan applications from Native Americans but approves loan applications from whites with similar financial portfolios. With racial statistics, one can at least launch a reasonable inquiry into such suspicious phenomena.

Without racial statistics, however, one could not know that these questionable irregularities even existed. Therefore, when during the census debate certain multiracial activists suggested that potential respondents undermine the federal statistics-keeping effort (see later discussion), I often wondered where their politics actually lay. Indeed, the distinct lack of any engagement with substantive social justice issues remains one of the most compelling criticisms of the multiracial movement. For instance, Heather Dalmage (2000) finds that "without an antiracism agenda, multiracial organizations seem to be distancing themselves socially and politically from blacks, creating one more layer in the racial hierarchy in which whites remain privileged, blacks disadvantaged, and multiracials somewhere in the middle" (p. 139).

An example of this that also serves as one of the more interesting ironies of the census debate involves the act of marking multiple responses. During the debate period (and thus before final acceptance of the MATA option), some multiracial leaders advised their "constituencies" to do whatever they could to inhibit, degrade, or otherwise damage the government's civil rights compliance monitoring effort by checking all the boxes on forms. In an editorial on the 2000 census, Charles Byrd (1998), maintainer of *Interracial Voice*, a Web site that fancies itself the philosophical voice of conscience of the global multiracial movement, frantically advised his readers that in support of a stand-alone multiracial category, they should "Check White!, Check Anything But Black!, Check Every Box on the Form!, Don't Return a Census Form At All!, Check Hispanic!, Check American Indian!"

The apparent logic was that such actions would render the respondent's results indecipherable and thereby undermine the government's racial statistics collection endeavor. In fact, Byrd's frenzied bloviations only serve to make Dalmage's point that "instead of challenging essentialism and racism. . . . many multiracial family members demand government protection of their individual right to create the racial identities they desire" (Dalmage, 2000, p. 173). Presumably, the cost to others is irrelevant, as in this case the reliability of statistics on a chronically oppressed group such as Native Americans was deemed less important than Byrd's immature temper tantrum.

What we see in this example is an interesting intersection of competing social justice claims; however, the respective claims are not equivalent. Charles Byrd wanted (and indeed still desperately wants) a separate multiracial category, presumably so that people who identify as multiracial may be recognized as such in terms of civil rights compliance monitoring.[4] Yet Byrd also proposed quite plainly that the civil rights compliance monitoring effort on behalf of other groups be sabotaged unless he got his way, which raises an intriguing question. Does the multiracial movement locate itself in a position that is supportive of anti-racist efforts, or is it concerned exclusively with achieving the self-interested goal of a federal multiracial category, even to the extent of explicitly advocating the harming of oppressed groups, as Byrd's editorial so strongly and unquestionably urged? If the material found on Byrd's site actually represents the global conscience of the multiracial movement, we had perhaps all better watch our collective back.[5]

The irony, then, is the fact that after OMB's MATA decision, multiracial advocates are once again advising that people should check as many of the boxes as they can; only this time rather than sabotaging the federal racial statistics-keeping effort via such instructions, the intent is to take advantage of it. So I wonder what the reaction of these activists would be to the hypothetical call of some newly dissatisfied group for respondents to somehow undermine federal racial statistics. Would multiracial advocates adopt a position of solidarity, or would they now complain that it would be blindly hurtful to tamper with the very important apparatus of civil rights compliance monitoring?

Imagine that Arab-Americans, who tried and failed during the Census 2000 debate to have their own federal racial category established, suggested in protest that people purposely undermine the federal statistics-keeping effort by always marking every box, no matter how many racial categories they personally identified with or that actually made up their ancestry. Under such a scenario, the accuracy of the numbers of "real" multiracial people would be degraded by every respondent who joined the protest. Would Charles Byrd be willing to support such a protest effort, one that undermined the very numbers he seeks to build? If not, we should ask why, because in this hypothetical case the protesters would be advocating precisely the same harm to other groups that Byrd proposed in his editorial.

For multiracial advocates, then—whether they favored a fully separate multiracial category or the header/subcategory option—OMB's decision on Census 2000 represented more of a moral victory than a clear accomplishment of primary goals. Because of the way that federal racial statistics actually work, the MATA format allows multiracially identifying persons to assert their multiraciality only in the most narrowly solipsistic way. Whether or not a multiple MATA response is counted exclusively as multiracial is completely out of the hands of the respondent. This fact suggests that there will likely be increased agitation for a federal multiracial category the next time America wakes up to an impending census.

THE AFRO-AMERICAN APPROACH TO CENSUS 2000

The general Afro-American response to Census 2000 was, not surprisingly, quite different from that of multiracial activists. One way of viewing the debate over Census 2000 is to see it as a battle between multiracial activists on one side and Afro-Americans on the other.[6] This is not to say that all Afro-Americans were opposed to the establishment of a multiracial category or that all Americans who identify as multiracial aligned themselves with the multiracial activist camp. Nonetheless, the loudest public voices in the debate came from two primary sources: (a) multiracial advocacy groups favoring some sort of federal multiracial category and (b) Afro-American organizations arguing that the establishment of such a category would prove disastrous to Afro-American interests. As a compromise, the MATA decision would prove wholly acceptable to neither side.

Throughout the course of the debate period, Afro-American politicians, public figures, and celebrities argued in tune with articles in Afro-American-oriented magazines that blackness requires ideological unity no matter the actual diversity of one's ancestry. Advised racially mixed rock artist Lenny Kravitz,

> You don't have to deny the White side of you if you're mixed. Accept the blessing of having the advantage of two cultures, but understand that you are Black. In this world, if you have one spot of Black blood, you are *Black*. So get over it. (Norment, 1995, p. 112)

In line with this kind of thinking, Census 2000 was seen by many Afro-Americans as yet another last stand against yet another assault on Afro-American rights and progress. The first priority was to absolutely stop any attempt to add a stand-alone multiracial classification to the federal racial categories. As a result of this stance, Afro-American rhetoric took on a self-defensive orientation that would linger well beyond the final decision.

The second priority was to criticize any other potential alterations to the federal race categories, such as the MATA option, for instance. The likely effect of MATA and other alternatives was less easy to gauge than was the potential effect of a stand-alone multiracial category, however. Therefore, arguments against the several alternative options usually revolved around the unknown damage that would accrue should this or that change to the federal categories be undertaken. The comments of U.S. Representative Carrie Meek in regard to the MATA proposal are typical:

> I applaud the Office of Management and Budget for its hard work. It gets an "A" for effort. But we cannot yet give it *any* grade for accomplishment. That is because the proposed regulation does not answer in detail a critical question—how will the data be tabulated and presented if individuals are instructed that they can check several racial categories on the census form. . . . I

applaud OMB's decision to not create a multiracial category. But I am very troubled by OMB's alternative of letting people check as many racial categories as they desire. I understand that this alternative allows the children of racially-mixed marriages to avoid choosing between their parents when answering the census questions. But we must remember that the primary purpose of the racial questions on the census is to permit enforcement of both the equal protection provision of the 14th amendment of the Constitution and the anti-discrimination laws that past Congresses have enacted. (Federal Measures of Race and Ethnicity, 1997)

Meek's concern reflects the general distaste Afro-Americans demonstrated for accommodating the self-esteem of multiracially identifying persons at the expense of civil rights compliance monitoring. This is a legitimate concern, because the potential of a multiracial category to disrupt the government's ability to track discrimination is tremendous. As real as this concern is, however, it was not the primary apprehension expressed by Afro-American voices that were arrayed against a multiracial category. That more prevalent concern is what I like to refer to as the *numbers* argument, illustrating yet another misunderstanding involving racial statistics.

On this view, the gravest danger posed by a stand-alone multiracial category—indeed, even by the MATA option—would be a loss of Afro-American numbers via a defection of mixed-race Afro-Americans from the ranks of the Afro-American statistical population. While testifying before Congress in 1993 on the undesirability of a federal multiracial category, then chair of the U.S. Commission on Civil Rights, Arthur Fletcher—himself Afro-American—put it this way:

> I can see a whole host of light-skinned Black Americans running for the door the minute they have another choice. And it won't

necessarily be because their immediate parents are Black, White, or whatever, but all of a sudden they have a way of saying, "I am something other than Black." Now, what kind of problem that will produce I don't know, but I am ready to bet that if that [multiracial] category were added you would see a significant diminution in the number of Black Americans who under the present set of circumstances are identified as Black. (Federal Measurements of Race and Ethnicity, 1993)

Fletcher's warning became the unifying call of Afro-Americans opposed to the idea of a federal multiracial category. It is worth taking a moment to question his ominous prediction, however, because Fletcher, a brown-skinned man, may have merely been projecting his own feelings about light-skinned Afro-Americans as opposed to providing any kind of intelligent analysis of the issue. Indeed, statistical surveys before Census 2000 as well as the actual results of Census 2000 show Fletcher's divination of a mass exodus to have been not only inaccurate but dead wrong. Obviously, he did not know light-skinned Afro-Americans as well as he thought he did.

We may still discover something of value in that wildly false prediction, however, for we see in Fletcher's words the primary misunderstanding with which most Afro-American opponents of a multiracial category involved themselves. People failed to recognize that what they dreaded most was not any real loss of numbers but rather a feeling of rejection. As a result, the numbers argument remained center stage, while more legitimate concerns about civil rights compliance monitoring remained for the most part unarticulated.[7] We may note that Representative Meek's previously mentioned discomfort with the MATA proposal came only after that particular option was recommended by the interagency committee OMB had established for reviewing racial and ethnic standards. The threat of a stand-alone category was perceived to be so

great that it literally obliterated all other possibilities until OMB's October 1997 decision that (at least for the moment) killed the federal multi-racial category and simultaneously brought MATA to life.

After OMB's unveiling of the MATA decision, the focus of Afro-American opposition shifted to cataloguing the problems and the dangers inherent in tabulating multiple responses. This is the anxiety expressed in Representative Meek's comments and echoed by many others as the census itself came nearer and nearer. I can recall one such example in March 2000. While attending an academic conference in San Diego, I heard a radio advertisement advising Afro-Americans to mark only the black box on their census forms regardless of whether they had white or other ancestry of which they were aware or otherwise recognized. It was the Kravitz principle, broadcast to an entire city. This bizarre exercise, although unnecessary, was nonetheless perfectly compatible with the general Afro-American response to Census 2000.

The perceived threat to Afro-American numbers, even with the rejection of a federal multiracial category, had become such an obsession that Afro-American leaders took the extraordinary step of suggesting that Afro-Americans refrain from expressing their full heritages on forms allowing them to. The condescension inherent in this advice was palpable, and I ultimately found the advertisement to be extremely offensive, a patronizing example of racial politics at their very lowest. Through this embarrassing performance, Afro-American leaders had at the very least demonstrated that Charles Byrd held no monopoly on poor taste when it came to suggestions for Census 2000.

THE POLITICAL RIGHT

In terms of the American political landscape, the overwhelming support for a federal multiracial category as well as an accompanying hostility to the tracking of racial discrimination came (and continues to come) from the far right, and it certainly is legitimate to question why this is the case. The two most notable figures have been former Speaker of the House Newt Gingrich and University of California Regent Ward Connerly, two men whose influence divides neatly into the pre-decision and postdecision periods. Gingrich was just beginning to become a factor in the multiracial picture near the time of OMB's decision, but he faded from that scene when he abruptly vacated the national political arena. Connerly, although he may have been active before the MATA decision, has been more publicly prominent since that time, consistently voicing opposition to the use of racial statistics in nearly any way.

During the public debate period, Gingrich voiced strong support for a federal multiracial category and was embraced especially closely by Project RACE, a multiracial advocacy organization that remains dedicated to establishing a federal multiracial category solely for self-esteem purposes. Susan Graham, executive director of Project RACE, took special pains to court Gingrich during the same time that he had become the unquestioned champion of American neoconservatism and was, through his politics, reawakening the hopes of many a white supremacist group throughout the nation. However, why would a demagogue such as Newt Gingrich align himself with the aspirations of multiracial advocates? Do we really suppose he felt sympathy for multiracial children—seeing them caught betwixt and between the races—and that he therefore dedicated himself to easing their pain? No; quite frankly, we do not.

What motivated Gingrich and others like him to support a federal multiracial category was the negative impact such a classification would have on the system of civil rights compliance monitoring. The historical continuity of civil rights data sets would become immediately unstable throughout the federal government with the advent of a multiracial category. Moreover, racist employers could ambiguously classify their employees as multiracial, as opposed to black or Native American, and in so doing mask the practice of covert and institutional discrimination. Completely unrelated groupings of people (black/white, Asian/Native American, white/Asian) would all be compiled under a singular multiracial category, thereby producing statistical data that would be completely meaningless in terms of tracking discrimination.

Neoconservative support for such a troubling scenario is not difficult to understand. What is less easy to understand is the willing embrace of neoconservatives by multiracial leaders such as Charles Byrd (see later discussion) and Susan Graham.[8] The extent to which these two, at least, have been willing to sacrifice the well-being of other groups is more than a bit unnerving. In fact, one of the more peculiar spectacles of the multiracial category debate was the consistent longing of Graham—the multiracial movement's quintessential white mother—for Newt Gingrich. Lamented Graham in a Project RACE Web site editorial: "He was on our side. The Speaker of the House, Newt Gingrich, was in our corner. Now he has resigned" (Graham, 2001). Incredibly, continuing to ignore reality, Graham went on in her editorial to blame Gingrich's national downfall on his having "surrounded himself with the wrong people" (Graham, 2001). Ultimately, the growing entwinement of Gingrich and Project RACE finally precipitated a bitter split among the major multiracial organizations and led to the further isolation of Project RACE on the movement's fringes (Spencer, 1999).

Ward Connerly, on the other hand, has been the special showpiece of Charles Byrd's *Interracial Voice*, having been extended the privilege of writing several guest editorials in recent years. Connerly's general stance, which has found a receptive home at *Interrracial Voice*, is that the practice of maintaining federal racial statistics should cease immediately without regard to the resultant impact on civil rights compliance monitoring:

> Eliminating the race boxes from American public life has many advantages. It gets government out of the business of defining races, a task. . . . for which government is wholly unsuited. . . . Eliminating these boxes from our government forms also allows Americans to protect their racial privacy. Perhaps most importantly, eliminating the race boxes allows Americans to clear the final hurdle in our journey to fulfill the democratic dreams of our greatest statesmen. This is the next step in America's quest to eradicate race from our national psyche. Until the race boxes are gone, we will continue to damn generations of black people. (Connerly, 2001)

Not much in the way of critical thought is required to see that Connerly is involved in a maneuver of massive burden shifting here. Although I would be the first to agree that race is a biological fiction and that we must work to move away from federal racial classification, the fact is that until we find a way to do so without compromising civil rights compliance monitoring, we simply cannot eliminate it summarily. To do so would be a benefit only to those interested in engaging in covert and institutional discrimination.

Contrary to Connerly's assertions, Afro-Americans are not damned by racial check boxes. They are damned by racists whose actions those racial check boxes are our best means of uncovering and counteracting. Without the check boxes, racists need fear neither detection nor prosecution for their discriminatory activities. That Connerly's harmful views are given a preferred airing via *Interracial Voice* reinforces Heather Dalmage's earlier contention that the multiracial movement expresses little interest in antiracist projects, appearing instead to be far more interested in focusing on its own narrow goals regardless of the negative impact on other groups.

We may also note two other conservatives who were figures in the multiracial category debate. Although not members of Newt Gingrich's hardcore neoconservative cadre, Representative Stephen Horn, who chaired the 1997 congressional hearings, and Representative Thomas Petri, author of the unsuccessful H.R. 830 (his patronizingly named "Tiger Woods Bill"), were Republicans who offered support for a federal multiracial category.[9] Generally speaking, Republicans favored a multiracial category while Democrats did not, which is consistent with the tendency of conservatives and especially neoconservatives to pretend that racism is not a significant issue in the United States and that it, therefore, deserves fewer, not more, resources devoted to uncovering and combating it.

In this way, the multiracial movement was—and some would argue, is still being—appropriated by political manipulators whose end goal is to weaken the federal government's best means of monitoring racial discrimination. If Horn and Petri do not themselves go quite this far, Gingrich and Connerly more than certainly do. That Charles Byrd and Susan Graham apparently have no problem being complicit with this manipulation (and that other multiracial leaders and organizations are mostly silent about it) points again to the hard reality of the multiracial movement's problematic position vis-à-vis antiracist efforts. The one notable exception to that silence was the previously mentioned split between Project RACE and a large portion of the multiracial movement. Aside from that episode, however, there has been little in the way of any self-reflective critique concerning the ways that the movement has been appropriated by conservatives, some of whom are quite open regarding their hostility toward civil rights compliance monitoring. This appropriation began during the debate period, has continued beyond Census 2000, and will likely end only if multiracial movement leaders themselves act firmly to reject it.

CONCLUDING ASSESSMENTS

The four main stake holders considered in this chapter are the federal government, multiracial activists, Afro-American organizations, and the American political right. Who won and who lost in terms of Census 2000? We might not be surprised to learn that the federal government, if it lost at all, lost the least of the four. Although the MATA decision meant an exponential jump in the number of potential racial designations (up to 63 when all combinations are considered) and, therefore, presented a problem in comparing new statistics with historical data sets, OMB's aggregation and allocation policy works to lower those possibilities back down to manageable levels (U.S. Executive Office of the President, 2000).

The MATA decision also avoided what OMB wanted most of all not to happen: the establishment of a federal multiracial category either as a stand-alone box or as a header with subcategories. In addition to maintaining its authority in these matters, OMB was able to ensure the maintenance of civil rights compliance monitoring via federal racial statistics. Although it will take some time to verify for certain that MATA has no long-term damaging effect on compliance monitoring, the federal government appears to have lost little in the transition to "marking all that apply."

The same might be said for Afro-American interests in the multiracial category question. The greatest damage on the Afro-American account was to the collective ego of those persons and organizations that desired to see no change at all to the federal racial classification scheme. To this group, even the MATA option represented a dangerous path down which to tread. Unwilling to accept anything other than a singular category for Afro-Americans to mark, MATA was bound to be seen as a

disappointment in this corner. However, as we have seen, this fear was misplaced. Given the federal government's interest in continuing to aggressively counter covert and institutional racial discrimination, OMB's decision on the Census 2000 question and its aggregation and allocation policy were victories for Afro-Americans as well. Unfounded and irrational fantasies concerning large numbers of light-skinned Afro-Americans leaving the black category notwithstanding, MATA appears at least to do no harm to Afro-American interests.

One certain loser in this debate was the political far right, which favored a stand-alone multiracial category that would serve to disrupt the federal government's ability to track racial discrimination. Because MATA, along with OMB's aggregation and allocation policy, preserves the federal government's ability to uncover and investigate suspicious patterns in any area in which racial statistics are compiled, it serves to frustrate neoconservative efforts to undermine civil rights compliance monitoring. For the far right, victory could only be achieved via a stand-alone multiracial category that would aid racists by masking covert and institutional discrimination.

We are left, then, with the multiracial movement. Did it win or did it lose once the dust from Census 2000 had finally cleared? Clearly, OMB's rejection of a federal multiracial category was a major loss, although one that some organizations (such as AMEA) were able to handle and adjust to more effectively than were some others (such as Project RACE). Once it became clear that MATA was the format OMB was going to favor, AMEA quickly moved to a position of support for that particular option. Possessed of leaders who were a good bit more astute politically than those of either Project RACE or *Interracial Voice*, AMEA quite intelligently worked to support the best option it could get, while the former two settled for a rather typical round of temper tantrums and generalized pouting.

I would be remiss, though, not to mention the way that the multiracial movement benefited to some degree from the MATA decision. In a sense, multiracial advocates are tormented by a gremlin similar to that of Afro-American activists in this matter. Afro-Americans are plagued by a misguided fear of a phantom "loss of numbers," whereas multiracial activists are plagued by a misguided need to "identify expressly as multiracial."[10] Even though multiple responses under MATA are counted in the way the particular tabulator ultimately chooses, multiracially identifying individuals may nonetheless believe they are making some kind of personal identity statement, even though no one but themselves might see it that way. So this would have to be counted as a victory of sorts.

Until such time as a federal multiracial category is actually established, however, celebrations over people finally being able to proclaim their multiraciality are simply premature. At present, OMB's preference for facilitating civil rights compliance monitoring holds sway over calls for federal validation of personal self-esteem. Whether it will continue to do so for Census 2010, however, remains to be seen. Until then, and regardless of the many myths and mystifications that may surface concerning Census 2000, we may be certain that race, racism, and the need to be ever more vigilant concerning racial discrimination have not changed one bit in the United States.

NOTES

1. This was the recommendation of OMB's interagency committee. OMB's decision to accept most of the committee's recommendations came on October 30, 1997.

2. I say multiracial activists here, rather than multiracial persons, because more than a few white parents of multiracial children continue to conceive of themselves as members of a purported multiracial community. Although not the subject of this chapter, the prominence and the actions of white parents in the multiracial movement have, on occasion, proven to be something of an embarrassment.

3. Although OMB's allocation policy directs the aggregation of particular racial combinations for civil rights reporting purposes, the specifics of how this is to be done remain vague. The same set of statistics might in one case be deemed civil rights related and in another case not. Again, the point is that how one is counted depends on who does the counting.

4. In fact, I offer this generous interpretation purely for purposes of argument. The evidence suggests overwhelmingly that the primary goal of the most vocal of multiracial activists—such as Byrd, for example—is establishment of a stand-alone multiracial category purely for the enhancement of self-esteem.

5. There are, of course, varying currents within the multiracial movement, not all of which are supportive of Byrd's rhetoric. Nonetheless, the consistent silence of those other factions in refusing to speak out and explicitly repudiate Byrd's stance is truly deafening.

6. In fact, Afro-Americans were actually on both sides because many multiracially identifying persons are themselves Afro-American.

7. I make a distinction between the crude numbers argument described previously and the more complicated considerations of compliance monitoring. The former is concerned with the illusory defection or migration of persons, whereas the latter is concerned with the ability to track discrimination whether the numbers in question are reduced or not.

8.   To those who would object that neither Byrd nor Graham represent the mainstream multiracial advocacy position, I respond that the lack of anything resembling a critical internal dialogue within the multiracial movement tends to grant legitimacy to the voices that are the loudest, not necessarily those that are the most cogent.

9.   Petri's H.R. 830 never received floor action in the House and was not passed before the end of the 105th Congress. The identical fate had previously befallen the same bill, which he introduced as H.R. 3920 (albeit without the fulsome appellation) in the 104th Congress.

10.   This need is misguided because race (and multirace as well) does not exist.

REFERENCES

Byrd, C. (1998, January 7). Census 2000 protest: Check American Indian! *Interracial Voice*. Retrieved from www.webcom.com/~intvoice/editor.html

Connerly, W. (2001, November 27). Towards a twenty-first century vision of race: Why we should get rid of the race boxes altogether. *Interracial Voice*. Retrieved from www.webcom.com/~intvoice/connerly3.html

Dalmage, H. M. (2000). *Tripping on the color line: Black-white multiracial families in a racially divided world*. New Brunswick, NJ: Rutgers University Press.

Federal measures of race and ethnicity and the implications for the 2000 Census: Hearings before the Subcommittee on Government Management, Information, and Technology, of the House Committee on Government Reform and Oversight, 105th Cong., 1 (1997) (testimony of Carrie Meek).

Federal measurements of race and ethnicity: Hearings before the Subcommittee on Census, Statistics, and Postal Personnel, of the House Committee on Post Office and Civil Service, 103rd Cong., 1 (1993) (testimony of Arthur A. Fletcher).

Graham, S. (2001, November 27). Multiracial life After Newt. *Project RACE: From the Director*. Retrieved from www.projectrace.com/fromthedirector/archive/fromthedirector-110998.php

Norment, L. (1995, August). Am I white, black, or in between? *Ebony*, pp. 108-112.

Schmitt, E. (2001, March 13). For 7 million people in census, one race category isn't enough. *New York Times*, pp. A1, A14.

Spencer, R. (1999). *Spurious issues: Race and multiracial identity politics in the United States*. Boulder, CO: Westview Press.

U.S. Executive Office of the President, Office of Management and Budget recommendations.

CHAPTER 7

Evolution of Multiracial Organizations
Where We Have Been and Where We Are Going

NANCY G. BROWN

Association of MultiEthnic Americans

Kaiser Department of Psychiatry

RAMONA E. DOUGLASS

Association of MultiEthnic Americans

Precision Dynamics Corporation

The first multiracial groups in the United States, formed during the late 1970s to 1980s were largely grass roots. They provided a safe place to talk, dispelled stereotypes regarding interracial marriage, allowed multiracial children to claim their full identity, and provided a forum for multiracial adults to share their life experiences with each other and new interracial couples with children. They also opened the doors for people of any sexual preference and families who adopted transracially to be part of an accepting, diverse group. The focus of the groups tended to be educational, recreational, and social, usually led by socially/politically conscious and passionate people concerned with justice and racial harmony.

In 1995, multiracial organizations finally had a voice in Washington, D.C., to articulate the needs of multiracial individuals and families. Two separate national organizations were at the forefront of this discussion: the Association of MultiEthnic Americans (AMEA) and Project RACE. AMEA ultimately was granted a seat on the 2000 Census Advisory Committee and Ramona Douglass, president of AMEA at the time, accepted this challenge. Before this time, multiple state groups whose activities were largely grass roots and provided services for their local populations were carrying out the multiracial movement. The authors had cowritten a chapter for Maria P. P. Root's (1996) anthology *The Multiracial Experience: Racial Borders as the New Frontier*, which detailed the emergence of the multiracial movement in this country. Several key organizations were showcased. In this chapter, our goal is to show how these organizations evolved since 1995, and we approach the material in four sections. We first summarize the early years of multiracial organizing from 1979 to 1995 and highlight the formation of six local/national groups. We also examine the original missions and visions of these groups before 1995 and factors that altered their perspectives after 1995. Second, we discuss collaboration and conflict in the multiracial movement and detail the launching of the National Multiracial Bone Marrow Donor Drive by AMEA and Project RACE at the first multiracial solidarity march on Washington, D.C., dated July 20, 1996. We then outline the strategic conflict between showcasing "health and well-being issues" versus fighting for a separate multiracial identifier. Next we discuss the challenges, conflicts, and outcomes of the June 1997 Multiracial Leadership Summit in Oakland, California, and how this gathering put the multiracial community at a crossroads with itself creating a house divided over nomenclature. Specifically, AMEA and its cross-cultural support for a "check one or more" box format are contrasted with Project RACE and A Place for Us/*Interracial Voice* commitment to a "multiracial stand-alone" identifier. Finally, we delve into maintaining a viable multiracial organization in the 21st century, detailing what it takes to run a successful nonprofit multiracial organization and give a summary on (a) grants, (b) work partnerships, and (c) national conferences. We close with a discussion of future projections on our community ideals and what it will take to enroll a new generation of multiracial individuals in community advocacy work.

METHODS

Several organizations were selected and interviewed because of their longevity and level of activity in the nation. The purpose of this exploration is to offer a brief history of (a) how grass-roots multiracial organizations were formed, (b) how they developed over time, and (c) how they related to the changes posed by the revisions in the racial and ethnic standards that allowed a check one or more box option on the 2000 Census race question. The president of each of the organizations was asked to answer the following questions: What is the current mission and activities of the group? How has the group gone about achieving their mission? What has been learned in the past 5 years about maintaining a multiracial organization that had not been known previously? What changes, if any, have there been in organizational structure or leadership? What has been your membership's reaction to the check one or more format for the census versus a stand alone multiracial category? Their answers are discussed after each organization is briefly summarized.

Several multiracial organizations have distinguished themselves over a long period of time or are notable because of their impact on the movement:

I-Pride (Interracial/Intercultural Pride; San Francisco, CA)

The Biracial Family Network (BFN; Chicago, IL)

The Interracial Family Circle (IFC; Washington, DC)

Multiracial Americans of Southern California (MASC; Los Angeles, CA)

Project RACE (Roswell, GA)

Association of MultiEthnic Americans (AMEA; Tucson, AZ)

EARLY YEARS OF
MULTIRACIAL ORGANIZING

The original missions of the first four of these groups are presented briefly followed by a current review of their organizational development and major foci. The last two, Project RACE and AMEA, developed separate national platforms around the questions of racial identity and recognition of multiracial people on all government forms requiring racial data. The divergence of Project RACE and AMEA, what caused it, and the end results are discussed in depth later in this chapter.

I-Pride

Formed in 1979 and incorporated in 1982, this is the oldest multiracial organization in the country. Their original mission was to establish a multiracial category on school forms in the Berkeley, California, public school district, which in the early 1980s was still a very new concept. They were successful. Its second and longest-term president, Carlos Fernandez, also became a major catalyst for the formation of AMEA.

Responses to the survey indicate that I-Pride has maintained a focus on education for all people with a special interest in fighting prejudice around interracialism. It attempts to unify the local multiracial community for mutual support and public recognition, which furthers its educational goals. They achieve their mission by providing meetings, support groups, recreational events, and a newsletter. A lack of volunteers is a challenge for the organization, and the respondent to the survey wondered whether the community feels less of a need for I-Pride than in previous years. One year ago, I-Pride was able to hire an executive director, who is the organization's first paid staff member, along with a subcontractor, who assists with the newsletter production. As previously stated, I-Pride was the first organization in the country to ask for a multiracial category on school forms. The survey respondent reported that most members are happy with the check one or more format, although it was difficult to poll every member and no formal tool was used for this. There was a consensus of concern as to how the census results would be tallied. I-Pride is a founding chapter and affiliate of AMEA and has been in full support of AMEA activities since the organization began. They continue to contribute to the multiracial movement by their active status as an organization, the services they provide to their local population, and their representation as an AMEA affiliate each year at the AMEA annual meeting.

BFN

Formed in 1980 and incorporated in 1986, BFN began when Irene Carr, a European American mother of a multiracial son, contacted I-Pride to obtain information on how to start a multiracial group. With the guidance she received, she developed a parent's support group that began with six mothers of multiracial children. This grew to four affiliate organizations that encompassed a spectrum of activities for interracial couples, families, and children. BFN's original goal of promoting integration had expanded to combating racism. In 1989, two multiracial adults produced a 1-hr documentary on the organization: jazz stylist Paul Serrano, and then publicity chair Ramona Douglass. In 1992, an anthology on multiracial identity titled *Interracial Identity: Celebration, Conflict or Choice?* was completed as an attempt to share positive examples of multiracial families for future generations. It was in its third printing as of 1994. Irene Carr is past treasurer of AMEA and current president of BFN.

BFN has been a consistently active organization, a founding member and affiliate of

AMEA. Their goals have been to establish comfortable spaces for families to dialogue and work against racism and discrimination and to educate people and communities about multiracial experiences. They have meetings with speakers on multiracial themes approximately 10 times per year, potlucks and picnics, parenting groups, and adult social groups. They distribute a bimonthly newsletter, and in September 2000 a college scholarship fund for multiracial youth was established. As with other organizations, volunteer recruitment is a challenge as is member attendance at events, geographic spread, and the ability to obtain funding through grants. BFN reports a relatively stable organizational structure since 1985 with annual elections. The memberships' response to the check more than one format was of great interest at a meeting held between the group and a Chicago census official. Overall, President Carr reports that most members keep their self-identification to themselves (personal communication, Jan 3, 2001). Ms. Carr feels a multiracial classification would be the simplest and best identifier for multiracial individuals. President Carr has also been an AMEA board treasurer. It was also from BFN that Ramona Douglass emerged and achieved further prominence in the multiracial community through her board and executive positions with AMEA.

IFC

Formed in 1984, the IFC was conceived as an antidote to the sense of isolation that many interracial couples experience. Six interracial families came together for socialization, the sharing of common goals and concerns, and to provide support to one another. They met in Washington, D.C., northern Virginia, and Maryland. Later the membership expanded to singles, couples with or without children, and transracial adoptive families. The IFC is also noted for hosting the first national conference celebrating the 25th anniversary of the Loving Decision, which dismantled the miscegenation laws by its 1967 Supreme Court ruling. Of great significance were the keynote speakers Bernard Cohen and Philip Hirschopf, attorneys for Mildred Loving (also in attendance) and her deceased spouse, Richard Perry Loving. The conference was held in 1992 under the leadership of Edwin Darden, who now sits on the AMEA Board as director of Law and Civil Rights.

The IFC reported that since 1995 they have continued their trend to commemorate important historical figures. They have sponsored two celebrations for Dr. Martin Luther King, Jr., that were profiled by the media as well as a panel on interracial issues, which was open to the public. They have a variety of groups for families with children and singles, adult discussion groups, picnics, seasonal events, ladies day-out lunches, and events at local attractions. Also a founding member of AMEA, the IFC achieves its mission by the provision of their activities, attempts at gaining publicity, and participation in AMEA. Managing a large geographic area and recruiting enough volunteers are the organization's obstacles. Some board members' duties are rotated between those available because of this shortage, and the position of recording secretary has been temporarily eliminated. IFC reports a positive response to the check more than one format, with members supporting AMEA in their quest for the census change.

MASC

Formed in 1987 and incorporated in 1989, MASC was cofounded by Nancy G. Brown, a partner in an interracial marriage, and Levonne Gaddy, a multiracial adult. The varied life experiences of the initial core group helped to establish the organization's mission: to meet the educational, cultural, and social needs of racially and culturally blended couples, families, and individuals. Major goals were to raise the public's consciousness of the right of multiracial adults and children to embrace their total identity, eradicate stereotypes, and celebrate unions based on love and mutual respect. MASC is noted for being the one organization in the country that hosted an annual conference on multiracial issues called Kaleidoscope beginning in 1987. Many keynote speakers and workshop leaders from around the country received their start from MASC. They have gone on to teach courses at universities, do research, and publish books that for the first time in history, portray multiracial individuals positively instead of as the tragic mulatto. MASC has also been widely used as a resource for the media, the organization, and members, having been mentioned or seen numerous times on television or radio and in magazines and newspapers.

MASC's original mission has not changed much since its inception. It seeks to enrich the lives of multiracial individuals, interracial couples with or without children, and families who have adopted transracially. This has been accomplished through a variety of social and educational activities such as evening gatherings for adults, a quarterly multiracial adult book study group, monthly children's group, periodically a teen group, and quarterly newsletter. MASC continues to appear in the media; members speak at colleges or in the workplace whenever asked. After 9 years of hosting the annual Kaleidoscope conference, MASC has diversified its annual event to include a 10th anniversary celebration dinner dance and a multiracial film festival the following year. MASC was host to the annual AMEA meeting in October 2000.

MASC has achieved its mission by providing the events and activities just described. More recently MASC is working to increase its board of directors, has done an extensive membership survey, and has collaborated with a variety of community, college campuses, and city organizations to market the organization. MASC held an organizational retreat in February 2001 to reevaluate its mission, goals, and activities. Organizational challenges include maintaining an adequate volunteer base to run programs, planning events that will appeal to the entire membership, obtaining funding, and marketing the organization to a very large geographical area.

There have not been significant changes in the leadership structure, although a number of seasoned board members have had to move on to other commitments, creating a need for new board members who are willing to give the time and dedication necessary. The MASC board meets monthly and has four executive board positions as well as general board of director positions. President Thomas Lopez and current President Eamon Buehning have played an active role in promoting MASC through their participation in other community and civic organizations, such as the Los Angeles Media Image Coalition, which seeks to review how people of color are portrayed in the media and entertainment industry (personal communication, Dec 24, 2000). A major development has been the building of a MASC Web site (www.multiculti.org), which will be used to help market MASC further. MASC is also a founding chapter and affiliate of AMEA.

MASC's member reaction to the check one or more format has been difficult to ascertain individually and geographically. MASC partnered with a local census partnership specialist and tried, with little success, to get them to educate the public adequately regarding the new option in answering the race question. The membership has been most concerned with understanding how the census data will be tabulated and used.

Project RACE

Project RACE was founded in 1991 by Susan Graham and Chris Ashe. The main goal, as stated by Ms. Graham (personal communication, 1994), was to achieve "a multiracial classification on school, employment, state, federal, census, and medical forms requiring racial data." Project RACE is noted for its many legislative accomplishments between 1992 and 1994. Multiracial categories were achieved for school districts in Ohio and Illinois. In 1994, legislation was passed in Georgia to include a multiracial classification on school forms and state agency forms, including employment forms and applications. Project RACE testified before the Congressional Subcommittee on the Census in June 1993. Susan Graham remains this organization's executive director and is a partner in an interracial marriage with two multiracial children.

Between 1995 and April 2000, Project RACE had as its primary mission the inclusion of a separate and distinct "multiracial category" on the U.S. census and all other forms requiring racial identification. Executive director Susan Graham testified at three congressional hearings on the census and racial classification between June 1993 and July 1997. When the U.S. Office of Management and Budget decided that a check one or more box format rather than a multiracial category would be added to the 2000 Census race question, Project RACE spearheaded the protest that admonished the government for not recognizing multiracial people as a distinct racial group. It was the belief of this organization and others that the check one or more format did not adequately identify multiracial people as having their own community interests with issues impacting education, health, and personal self-esteem. Since then, it has become unclear to those who are not a part of its membership or organizational leadership what new goals have launched Project RACE into the 21st century. Will the changing face and aspirations of multiracial people cause this organization to reassess its mission and vision? Only time will tell what path will be taken and what results can be expected.

A number of characteristics unite Project RACE and the other four organizations just discussed. Most were formed within the same decade and were in communication with each other regarding that process. Their overall missions were similar in that they sought to raise America's consciousness regarding the existence and validity of a multiracial heritage and the right of individuals to celebrate their interracial/intercultural unions. Each organization has had several noteworthy, passionate, and committed individuals who have taken on major leadership roles in both the local and national arenas of the multiracial movement. The challenges for these organizations are also similar (with the exception of Project RACE) in that they continue to struggle with maintaining an adequate volunteer base, attracting participants for their activities, and marketing their organizations without the benefit of paid staff or obtaining funds through grants.

AMEA

By 1988, a sixth organization came into being, out of its commitment to giving interracial families and multiracial people a national voice. The AMEA held its founding meeting on November 12, 1988 in Berkeley, California. Fourteen charter member organizations from across America elected AMEA's first executive committee: President, Carlos Fernandez (I-Pride); Vice President, Ramona Douglass (BFN); Secretary, Reginald Daniel (MASC); and Treasurer, Sarah Ross, Honor Our New Ethnic Youth (HONEY). Thus, the first national multiracial federation was born. Those original networking organizations included

Interracial Family Alliance (Atlanta, GA)

Interracial Club of Buffalo (NY)

Biracial Family Network of Chicago (IL)

HONEY (Eugene, OR)

A Place for Us Ministry (Gardena, CA)

Interracial Family Alliance (Houston, TX)

MASC (Los Angeles, CA)

Interracial Connection (Norfolk, VA)

Parents of Interracial Children (Omaha, NE)

Interracial Families, Inc. (Pittsburgh, PA)

IMAGE (San/Diego, CA)

I-Pride (San Francisco, CA)

Interracial Network (Seattle, WA)

Interracial Family Circle (Washington, DC)

In the early years of its development between 1988 and 1993, AMEA perceived itself as a newly emerging business venture, and its executive committee drafted what constituted a 2-year and a 5-year plan. Within the first 2 years, AMEA determined its strengths and weaknesses. It gauged what role it would be able to play on a national scale based on the commitment of its member organizations and the skill sets of its executive committee. It published a national newsletter that was targeted to have quarterly issues. A basic statement of purpose was drafted, which defined AMEA as an educational organization that "promoted a positive awareness of interracial and multiethnic people and families" (Fernandez, 1990). Within the 5-year framework, AMEA hoped to launch an education and legal defense fund. It envisioned the possibility of a multicultural resource center, and it was committed to staffing a political action committee that would lobby for changing official forms to include a multiracial category with the ability to check all that applied.

Although its 5-year plan was ambitious, based on limited funds and even more limiting human resources, AMEA did accomplish some amazing results by September 1994. It had incorporated in the state of California with 501c3 (nonprofit) status pending and established a national 800 telephone number. Members of its Political Action Committee (PAC) had testified before Congress on the necessity for inclusion of a multiracial/multiethnic category on all federal forms requiring racial/ethnic data. Through its far-reaching ties to prestigious institutes of learning across the country, AMEA created an educational and legal advisory board. Out of its commitment to forming alliances with other national advocacy groups such as Project RACE, AMEA also took on the monitoring of local state and federal activities affecting our interracial communities (Douglass, 1995).

The most important boost and shift in AMEA's capability and focus came in December 1995, when its president, Ramona E. Douglass, was appointed to a post on the federal 2000 Census Advisory Committee in Washington, D.C. Douglass, a multiracial adult of Italian, Native American/Lakota, and mixed African-American ancestry, had been a part of AMEA's Executive Board since its inception in the late 1980s. Her personal testimony on behalf of multiracial people had been read into the *Congressional Record* in June 1993 when AMEA appeared before a congressional subcommittee that was charged with reviewing racial and ethnic standards for the Office of Management and Budget as well as the U.S. Census. Before then, much of the emphasis and strategic outcomes of the multiracial movement were focused on local state issues, centered in cities where AMEA affiliates or active Project RACE members resided. The successful push for the inclusion of a separate multiracial category in the states of Georgia, Illinois and Ohio before 1995 put the multiracial community issues on the map.

However, it was only after AMEA was treated as a stakeholder in the national conversations on race and the census that it truly had a real say in the matter of who we were and how we wished to be identified.

Ramona Douglass remained AMEA's president through the summer 1999. She subsequently retained a board position as director of Media and Public Relations and continued to serve on the federal Decennial Census Advisory Committee in Washington, D.C. Since then, AMEA has had two new presidents, who incidentally were the cofounders of MASC in 1987. Levonne Gaddy was elected president in September 1999 followed by Nancy G. Brown in July 2001. Both these women had strong grassroots backgrounds as part of the multiracial movement and leadership. By the time Ms. Gaddy became AMEA's president, she had already formed a second local organization between 1996 and 1997 called Multiethnics of Southern Arizona in Celebration (MOSAIC) with the aid of M. Craig, another multiracial adult in the Tucson area. MOSAIC later joined AMEA as an affiliate. Nancy G. Brown was AMEA's vice president for the duration of the Douglass administration and remained in this position throughout Ms. Gaddy's presidency.

The most significant change that took place for AMEA between 1999 and 2001 was its shift from a grassroots operational model to a professional and national resource model. Thanks to Gaddy's organizational skills and the amazing national accomplishment records of its former presidents Douglass and Fernandez, AMEA was awarded its first grant in the year 2000. This funding, provided by a private foundation, enabled AMEA to hire two directors of development who were charged with promoting and marketing AMEA on a national scale.

In May 2001, for personal and professional reasons, Ms. Gaddy stepped down from her post as AMEA's president. Vice President

Nancy G. Brown then assumed the role as acting president and was formally elected to the post on July 22, 2001, at a conference planning retreat in Los Angeles. Major outcomes of this retreat included the following:

- The creation of a detailed plan for a national conference entitled: "The Multiracial Child: What Professionals, Families and Communities Need to Know"
- A commitment to the annual celebration of the anniversary of the Loving Decision
- The inclusion of multiracial young adults on the Board of Directors
- The institution of an annual volunteer and affiliate of the year awards

COLLABORATION AND CONFLICT IN THE MULTIRACIAL MOVEMENT

To understand the rise of the multiracial movement to a level of national significance, it is essential to understand the relationship between two national advocacy groups: AMEA and Project RACE. Other entities such as Charles Byrd's *Interracial Voice* Internet Web site as well as AMEA's former charter affiliate *A Place for Us Ministry* (now known as A Place for Us-National) had their own unique platforms and supporters. However, when it came to battling with the federal bureaucratic processes, AMEA and Project RACE were consistently called on to represent multiracial issues at the highest levels of government.

Between 1995 and 1997, AMEA was bombarded with media exposure, local affiliate requests, and national campaigns centering on the issues of racial identity and the impact of any category changes on health, education, and social welfare both within and outside the multiracial community. At that time AMEA viewed Project RACE as a fellow traveler on the road to multiracial recognition.

It was during this period of heightened public exposure that the presidents of both AMEA and Project RACE chose to join forces to accelerate community awareness on the medical issues facing multiracial people. Research uncovered on this subject made it imperative for those of multiple racial/ethnic descent to be distinguished in such a way that the diseases that impacted them, the diagnoses that eluded them, and the treatments that had been denied to them would finally be uncovered. Susan Graham, executive director of Project RACE, and Ramona Douglass, president of AMEA in 1996 decided that the launching of the National Multiracial Bone Marrow Donor Drive at the first multiracial solidarity march on Washington, D.C., would be a good beginning. This drive served three strategic purposes: (a) It created useful alliances and conserved valuable resources to get the right message on medical issues to key people across the country; (b) it improved relations and clarified issues with different factions within the multiracial community; and (c) it gained needed public recognition and support from such prestigious organizations as the National Institutes of Health (NIH), and a number of bone marrow donor registries across the nation. The multiracial solidarity march itself, sponsored by Charles Byrd, founder and editor of the *Interracial Voice,* drew fewer than 500 participants. However, national and local media coverage and subsequent pledges for multiracial donor drives in California, Texas, Florida, and so on made it clear that the needs of multiracial people and interracial families were not acceptable losses to be incurred simply to assuage the special interests or fears of those who opposed multiracial recognition.

Ramona Douglass, speaking on behalf of both AMEA and the interests of Project RACE for the national donor drive, stated at the Washington, D.C. rally:

We are—as an untapped minority—not among those who are counted by local, regional or federal-level agencies that gather racial/ethnic data for medical research purposes and other health-related matters. We are virtually invisible to the medical community statistically, and unless we take this issue to our legislators, the mailbox, and the ballot box, the Census Bureau, the State Capitol and to all the healthcare providers in the country—we will remain at risk and the last to receive accurate, adequate, or equitable medical treatment. (Douglass, 1996)

As a result of that speech and the emphasis that AMEA and Project RACE placed on the medical imperatives of multiracial recognition, a distinct, clearly defined line was drawn between two factions in the multiracial movement. The first faction represented those who favored a multiracial category as an inalienable right to self-identification. The second faction saw the life-and-death clinical issues posed by continuing to ignore the distinctions between multiracial/multiethnic heritage and presumed monoracial heritage. Those who championed the medical initiatives won great support from other ethnic communities and medical/professional entities. These cross-cultural and professional supporters recognized the importance of clear, complete medical data for research purposes as well as better patient care regardless of ethnic/racial background. It was the strategy of sound science and a willingness to collaborate with other like-minded forces that gave the multiracial movement, AMEA and Project RACE in particular, a much-needed entrée to the U.S. congressional hearings held on May 22, 1997 and again on July 25, 1997. It should be noted that what was being emphasized for congressional consideration were (a) the dispelling of myths related to blood and race; (b) the distinctions between infant mortality, birth weight, gestation duration, and race; and (c) the impact of ethnic differences on reaction rates and medication. The following is text excerpted from Douglass's May 1997 testimony on the lack of multiracial research.

> The blood running through the veins of black children cannot be distinguished from the blood running through the veins of other children no matter what color they are or what culture they eventually embrace. All blood is red. Rather than continue to obsess over "who's black and who's not," we will better serve all communities medically if we concentrate on what impact, if any, ethnicity (rather than race) has on genetic frequency and disease. Tay Sachs, Sickle Cell Anemia and Cystic Fibrosis are diseases. . . . linked to genetic frequency, not race as we rigidly define it today. (Polednak, 1989, pp. 3-4, 78-81, 90, 295)
>
> Flagging multiracial/multiethnic individuals would at least prompt healthcare professionals to look beyond surface appearances and ask more detailed questions on ethnic origin and medical history. (Douglass, 1997)

Regarding issues of infant mortality, birth weight, gestation duration, and "race," the following information is food for thought. Every obstetrical professional in the country knows that black infants have a higher mortality rate and lower mean birth weights than white infants. (This is attributed to environmental conditions for the most part and not genetics.) However, who is tracking the birth weights and mortality rates of multiracial/ multiethnic children? Only a handful of studies have been done on multiracial infants (see Collins & David, 1993; "Gestational Duration and Birth Weight," 1991). Without the ability to count or monitor multiracial infants, research on our community will not be forthcoming, and our children will remain at risk. This inequity and oversight cannot continue.

There is an ongoing debate within the pharmaceutical industry concerning medications, reaction rates, and ethnic differences. Extensive research has been done by the pharmaceutical industry linking race and ethnic origin to differences in response rates and side effects associated with antidepressants, analgesics, alcohol, and other controlled substances. In 1993 the National Pharmaceutical Council determined that Hispanic and Chinese respondents require lower doses of antidepressants, but the side effects were greater in Hispanics. In addition, Asians were found to be more sensitive to the adverse effects of alcohol and American Indians were said to have faster metabolic rates.

Looking at these and other related conclusions regarding medication, reaction rates and ethnic variations, it logically follows that multiracial/multiethnic response rates would have distinctions of their own. We as a community found our greatest champion for the cause of greater medical awareness when the American Medical Association (AMA) endorsed the need for more detailed data in tracking racially/ethnically linked diseases.

Critical support for the multiracial movement and the medical imperative for distinguishing people of multiple racial and ethnic backgrounds came when the AMA endorsed the "check one or more box" format for the 2000 Census race question. On August 1, 1997, the AMA officially endorsed the recommendation of the federal Interagency Committee for the Review of the Racial and Ethnic Standards to change Office of Management and Budget (OMB) Statistical Directive 15. This shift in policy allowed respondents to check one or more boxes when answering the race/ethnicity questions on the 2000 Census and other future government forms. In a letter to Katherine K. Wallman, chief statistician at the Office of Information and Regulatory Affairs of the OMB, the AMA stated that "permitting multiple self-designation allows health service researchers to differentiate more accurately among different subgroups of research participants" (Wooton, 1997). AMA President Percy Wooton, MD, emphasized that "the alarming lack of sufficient bone marrow donors for multiracial/ multiethnic cancer patients. . . . can be linked, in part, to an inability to better classify their genetic, racial and ethnic backgrounds." He also noted that "clinical research trials and epidemiological research will benefit from more detail about racial and ethnic backgrounds of research participants" (Wooton, 1997).

By the time the AMA had handed the OMB its endorsement of the check one or more box format for the 2000 Census race question, there had already occurred a crossroads in the multiracial movement. The heart of the community efforts had become a house divided by nomenclature. The struggle between conflicting ideologies and unfortunate petty rivalries among national multiracial organizations surfaced with a vengeance after the close of the Third Multiracial Leadership Summit (Oakland, CA) and hosted by AMEA affiliate I-Pride on June 7, 1997. This meeting was supposed to solidify the prominent multiracial organizations on the issue of a multiracial identifier and the ability to check all the races that applied. AMEA affiliates were there to participate in an annual board meeting. They were joined by guest organizations Project RACE, HAPA Issues Forum, and Unity: A Multiracial Social Group (Jacksonville, FL) as well as distinguished academic advisors Maria P. P. Root, PhD, and Reginald Daniel, PhD. Henry Der, a member of the federal 2000 Census Advisory Committee, was also present to give an opposing perspective on the inclusion of a multiracial category for 2000 Census. What transpired at that meeting was next to miraculous: choosing to let go of the special interests of a few to embrace the multifaceted/ diverse interests of the many.

It was determined that the multiracial community leadership may have been disappointed in the lack of support coming from traditional civil rights organizations on the question of multiracial recognition. However, there was far more trust in the possibility of enrolling those factions in the equity and integrity of our struggle than faith in embarking on an unholy alliance with the right-wing factions of the Republican Party. Especially unacceptable at the time was having our community aligned with then house speaker Newt Gingrich. When Project RACE attempted to serve up the multiracial/Gingrich alliance at the multiracial summit, there were no other takers. In fact, one of our guests, a multiracial psychologist from Los Angeles, abruptly left the conference, not really sure who was in charge: the multiracial adult leaders or one interracially married parent of a multiracial child trying to define multiracial identity for everyone according to personal bias. Despite that communication breakdown, the final result was a multiracial summit statement, which unknowingly mirrored the decision made by the Interagency Committees for the Review of Race and Ethnic Standards to endorse a check one or more format on the Census race question.

- We the undersigned organizations represent the intersection of traditional racial communities comprised of individuals and families who identify with more than one racial background.
- We advocate a "check one or more" box format for the collection of racial data which will not adversely affect existing civil rights protections. We do not advocate a stand-alone multiracial category on the federal level.
- A "check one or more" format will enable all Americans to respond truthfully on the Census and other forms that collect racial data.
- A "check one or more" box format will ensure the identification of all Americans who may be at risk for life-threatening diseases for which genetic information is critical.

This statement was embraced by all the participants in the multiracial summit except Project RACE, which revoked its initial endorsement within 24 hours. It is a statement that broke the alliance between AMEA and Project RACE. A positive outcome of this split was that it forged a stronger, healthier, and more inclusive alliance between AMEA and the leadership of many other academic, community, medical, political, and scientific entities. This included (a) Japanese American Citizens League (JACL); (b) Asian American Donor Program; (c) National Association for the Advancement of Colored People (NAACP; Mid-Peninsula, CA); (d) Professor Ronald Takaki, Asian American Studies Department, University of California at Berkeley; and (e) AMA.

AMEA and its allied groups, which had long advocated changing OMB Directive 15, promptly expressed support for the recommendations of the Interagency Committee. This policy shift was considered a tremendous breakthrough for multiracial, multiethnic people who, under the check-one-box-only rule of the existing Directive 15 (adopted in 1977), had been unable to accurately identify their mixed ancestry. AMEA conveyed its support for the recommendations at a July 25, 1997, hearing of the House Subcommittee on Government Management, Information, and Technology. Carlos Fernandez, former AMEA president and director of Law and Civil Rights, testified on AMEA's behalf. At the same hearing, the NAACP and members of the Congressional Black Caucus also expressed their support for the Interagency Committee's recommendations.

Project RACE, on the other hand, began working with Charles Byrd of *Interracial Voice* and some of the members of A Place For Us–National. They continued to advocate a multiracial identifier with or without the ability to "check all the boxes that applied." Of the two collaborative ventures (AMEA or Project RACE), history will decide which was the most beneficial or the most detrimental to the multiracial community and its long-term objectives.

MAINTAINING A VIABLE MULTIRACIAL ORGANIZATION IN THE 21ST CENTURY

For state-of-the-art information regarding the elements necessary to maintain a viable multiracial organization, we turned to AMEA's directors of development for their input. Ms. Diana Sheldon, the southern regional director in Arizona, highlighted three areas: (a) development, (b) recruitment, and (c) vision and mission. Development necessitates funding in the form of planned giving through vehicles such as estates, trusts, stock gifts, and major monetary gifts. The latter involves developing a relationship with an individual (donor) over time who will get to know the organization and who believes in its mission. Major gifts start at $10,000 and can be pledged over a period of 3 to 5 years. Recruitment is necessary to ensure ongoing organizational leadership and participation. It should take the form of a structured nominating process in which organizational needs are matched with the skills of potential board members. This is in contrast to the manner in which many of the state groups operate in that they have often used board members based on the person's interest and availability only. According to Sheldon, a nonprofit needs to structure its vision like a corporation. The organization should keep its mission close but must never lose sight that it is a business and profits are included in the pie. Without funds the organization cannot further its mission despite the impact it may have on the community as a whole. The mission of the organization should be reviewed at least every other year to determine whether the direction should remain the same or be altered.

Ms. Patricia Dawson, AMEA's former northwest regional director in Oregon, developed a comprehensive needs assessment tool that included all pertinent areas for an organization to use for their organizational development. The following may be applied to any state or national organization:

I. Existing Programs/Activities
   A. Assessing our internal capacity
      1. What purpose do we serve?
      2. What do we believe in?
      3. What are the current state of skills, knowledge, and abilities of our board of directors and consultant?
      4. What critical job tasks/standards are necessary to accomplish the goals and objectives of our mission?
      5. Are there internal problems such as new processes and equipment, changes in staffing, and outside issues that must be addressed?
      6. Who is our target population?
      7. Whom do we serve?
      8. Which of their needs do we meet?
      9. What are the priority items for funding that move us toward our stated mission?
      10. What resources are available to us?
      11. Is there a funding plan in place?

   B. Assessing the external environment.
      1. What is the correct terminology for the people we serve?
      2. What are the demographics of the communities we serve today?
      3. Are the demographics changing?
      4. What are the implications of today's trends for the future of those we serve?
      5. What other agencies (for profit or nonprofit) currently provide the same or similar services as our organization and can be recruited to collaborate with or join our organization?
      6. How do we communicate with other similar organizations and dissimilar organizations?
      7. What unmet needs exist today and may exist tomorrow that our organization can fulfill?

II. Current/Future Needs and Gaps
   A. Identify the current and future human service organizational needs.
   B. Identify where gaps exist in service/programs/activities and for which groups these gaps exist.
   C. Identify where gaps exist in physical space requirements for additional/modified services/ programs/activities.

III. Strategies to Overcome These Needs and Gaps
   A. Make recommendations on how to improve delivery of existing services, how to fill gaps in services, how to form partnerships to better deliver services, and how to plan for future needs.
   B. Make recommendations on what physical facilities are needed (e.g., office space, meeting space), timing for adding facilities, and possible funding sources for the construction, operation, and maintenance of these facilities.

GENERATING MISSION VISION AND VALUES IN THE NEW MILLENNIUM

What does a national organization seeking to represent diverse interests and cultural blends need to assess and generate for today's Internet-savvy young adult multiracial community? Matt Kelley, AMEA's Vice-President, is also the founder/editor-in-chief of *MAVIN Magazine* and the MAVIN Foundation, a nonprofit organization. Matt, a proud HAPA (mixed-race Asian) of Korean and European American descent, believes that standing for something that engages youth, excites them, and calls them to action are essential elements in any national network claiming to speak for their interests. Transracially adoptive families, single parents of multiracial children, multigenerational multiracial adults, and interracial families all have expectations they may seek to fulfill through a national or local community advocacy group.

AMEA, which has been discussed at length in this chapter, represents one possible model for a 21st-century multiracial organization. Can any single organization in existence today meet all the needs of the multiracial community? It is highly unlikely. What is more realistic is an organization choosing to focus on two or three key goals or projects and then enrolling the human and financial resources to fulfill those goals. It is important to reassess any organization's mission and vision periodically to ensure that they remain in step with the current leadership, members, and circumstances which that particular organization is facing. For example, in January 2001 AMEA took a long, hard look at its mission and stated goals and saw a need to update its commitments for now and the future. A new mission statement was drafted, as follows:

> To educate and advocate on behalf of multiethnic individuals and families by collaborating with others to eradicate all forms of discrimination. We are also bound by the values of listening to one another, treating each other with honor and respect, conducting our transactions with integrity, actively engaging with one another and striving to be accepting, inclusive role models for ourselves and others.

Living up to these values and fulfilling its mission will require AMEA to envision a world in which it can make a difference through the programs it generates via education, advocacy, and collaboration with others who are committed to similar goals. Organizations that hope to capture the spirit of the multiracial movement in its current form must be willing to accept that the community itself is forever changing, expanding, and redefining itself, its needs, and its future.

REFERENCES

Brown, N. G., & Douglass, R. E. (1996). Making the invisible visible: The growth of community network organizations. In M. P. P. Root (Ed.), *The multiracial experience: Racial borders as the new frontier* (pp. 323-340). Thousand Oaks, CA: Sage.

Collins, J. W., & David, R. J. (1993). Race and birth weight in biracial infants. *American Journal of Public Health, 83*(8), 1125-1129.

Douglass, R. E. (1995). *Personal journal of AMEA history.* Unpublished manuscript.

Douglass, R. E. (1996, July 20). *A call for community action and vision for America's future.* Presented at the multiracial solidarity march of the Association of MultiEthnic Americans, Washington DC.

Douglass, R. E. (1997). Congressional testimony. Retrieved from www.ameasite.org/classification/test597.asp

Fernandez, C. (1990). *AMEA mission statement.* Tucson, AZ: Association of MultiEthnic Americans.

Gestational duration and birth weight in white, black and mixed-race babies. (1991). *Pediatric and Prenatal Epidemiology.*

Polednak, A. P. (1989). *Racial and ethnic differences in disease.* Oxford, UK: Oxford University Press.

Root, M. P. P. (Ed.). (1996). *The multiracial experience: Racial borders as the new frontiers.* Thousand Oaks, CA: Sage.

PART III

RACIAL/ETHNIC GROUPS IN AMERICA AND BEYOND

CHAPTER 8

The Dilemma of Biracial People of African American Descent

HERMAN L. DEBOSE
LORETTA I. WINTERS

California State University, Northridge

Many outsiders think of the United States as a country ridden with tension between African Americans and European Americans.[1] The history of slavery, segregation, and race riots, in particular, has bred this perception. The highly publicized 1965 Watts riot developed primarily in response to police brutality. The even more publicized 1992 Los Angeles riot was a response to the justice system's minor reprimands of the police officers responsible for the beating of Rodney King in 1991. Rodney King's question of "Why can't we all just get along?" has been widely quoted and depicts the frustration common to many Americans. Public disagreement on the innocence or guilt of O. J. Simpson further indicates the black/white conflict. The dragging death of James Byrd in Texas in 1999 and the shooting (41 times) of Amadou Diallo in New York in 1999 are other recent examples.

This skewed image of the United States does not capture the cooperation that has existed for centuries between some African Americans and European Americans and whose relationships have resulted in biracial children. This chapter focuses on biracial people in the context of this conflict between African Americans and European Americans. The interest was prompted by the biracial[2] "baby boom" that has occurred since 1967 when the U.S. Supreme Court overturned antimiscegenation laws in 16 states, most of them in the south.

The landmark ruling responsible for eliminating antimiscegenation laws was the outgrowth of a case in which an interracial married couple was convicted of a felony under the Virginia antimiscegenation law in 1958. They were exiled from their home state of Virginia for 25 years. The couple appealed their case to the U.S. Supreme

Court, which eventually overturned the Virginia law and similar antimiscegenation laws of 15 other states. This case exemplifies the fact that some African American and European American people consciously choose to marry in spite of social and legal pressures to the contrary.

In 1960 there were 157,000 interracial marriages compared with 1,161,000 in 1992 (U.S. Bureau of the Census, 1998a). Between 1980 and 1992, the number of African American marriages involving a white spouse increased dramatically. There were 121,000 black/white couples married in 1980 and 246,000 in 1992 (U.S. Bureau of the Census, 1998b). As we enter the 21st century, inter-racial marriages are continuing to increase. According to the U.S. Census Bureau, there were 149,000 interracial marriages in 1960 compared with 964,000 in 1990 and 1,264,000 in 1997.

The growth in the numbers of multiracial[3] people has also been striking. Although no exact numbers of multiracial children exist, the U.S. Bureau of the Census keeps statistics on children who have one or both parents of a different race. Some of these children may be adopted, but many are expected to be multi-racial children. In 1960 in the United States, fewer than 500,000 children had one or both parents of a different race compared with 1,937,496 in 1990 (U.S. Bureau of the Census, 1998). Although all data from the 2000 census are not available, of the 281,421,906 people recorded in the census, 6,826,228, or 2.4%, reported they were members of the new census category: two or more races. This percentage of the national population indicates that the numbers of multiracial people are growing and with this growth comes a new voice in the political arena.

Until recently, identity choice for biracial people of African American descent has not been a reality. The rule of hypodescent or the "one-drop rule" legally used for centuries had enforced choice of an African American identity. The rule indicated that one drop of black blood makes one black. It emerged in the 1600s to ensure that mixed-raced persons remained in slavery. When the one-drop rule lessened as an important legal distinction (postslavery), it continued to be used in a social context. That is, any individual with nonwhite blood was considered to be non-white. Racial identity has historically been extremely important in the United States, determining how society's benefits are assigned and how people are responded to individually and collectively. Because racial identity can influence how one is received or how rewards are distributed, group member-ship becomes especially important for bira-cial people and society itself. A European American identity provides privilege. If biracial persons of African American and European American descent were to "pass" as white, they would fit into the dominant group, securing all the advantages that accompany that group.

Alongside the civil rights movement, another reason for identifying as African American rather than European American arose. Because African Americans have been underrepresented in institutions of higher learning and in professional occupational positions that have been predominantly white, the Nixon administration (1968–1974) created affirmative action policies. These policies established nonwhite goals in employment as well as federal entitlements to schools for educational purposes. Although the original intention of this policy was to compensate for a history of discrimination, regardless of numbers, affirmative action has more recently been justified or attacked based on numbers and issues of diversity and inclusiveness. In the United States, the African American community has been underrepresented politically, socially, econo-mically, and educationally compared with whites as long as it has existed. Because numbers have always been connected to political clout, African Americans have always been disadvantaged when attempting to make their voices heard in the political arena.

The idea of a multiracial identity has created some bitterness in the African American community. Many African Americans point out that such a choice is not without consequences. Portions of the African American community believe that for a biracial person of African American and European American descent to select any designation other than African American amounts not to wanting to embrace a dual heritage but rather to removing themselves from a perceived inferior race to reap societal benefits. On the other hand, this is the first step in forcing society to allow multiracial people to make their own identity choices.

The U.S. Census Bureau reported the following figures for the African American population: 22,580,289 (11.1%) in 1970; 26,295,025 (11.7%) in 1980; 29,986,060 (12.1%) in 1990; and 34,658,190 (12.3%) in 2000. In comparison, the figures for the European American population were as follows: 177,748,975 (87.5%) in 1970; 188,371,622 (83.2%) in 1980; 199,686,070 (80.3%); and 211,460,626 (75.1%) in 2000. This comparison indicates an increase in the overall African American population and an overall decrease in the European American population. African Americans need these numbers to increase even more to gain the kind of political leverage that European Americans possess. Therefore, biracial people of African American descent identifying with a group other than African American would decrease the numbers used to determine where various resources are directed and where political clout can be mustered.

Regardless of political pressure to the contrary and in response to the new growth of multiracial people, the 1990s brought a different view of identity for individuals of mixed race: identification with more than one racial group. Some multiracial people and their parents started to voice their dismay toward coercion to eliminate part of who they are in the construction of their identity. In standing up as a block, multiracial people and their parents put pressure on society and the government to acknowledge a multiracial identity. The Clinton administration proposed changes in the racial categories on the census forms to reflect a multiracial identity. Starting with the 2000 census, the U.S. Census Bureau allowed citizens with multiracial backgrounds to check "two or more races." This government decision added controversy to the already difficult struggle regarding race. As interracial relationships and marriages increase along with the social issues that accompany this phenomenon, the perspectives of multiracial people take on different complexions.

Before continuing with a discussion of the identity choices for mixed-race people of African American descent, a historical and theoretical context is provided. Two areas of African American history have helped shape the contemporary African American family: (a) the history of slavery, prejudice, and discrimination; and (b) assimilation to European American society.

A BRIEF HISTORY OF THE AFRICAN AMERICAN IN THE UNITED STATES

Several historians and scholars have researched and written extensively on the experience of African Americans in the United States. They include, but are not limited to, Kelley and Lewis (2000), Franklin and Moss (2000), Marable (2000), Hill (1999), and Levine (1996). They all indicate that slavery, reconstruction, Civil War, and Jim Crow laws have had a major impact on the African American and the African American family. The overall impact has left a negative impact on the perception of the entire African American community.

Because African Americans have been perceived as different and unequal biological beings compared with European Americans, they have experienced a bleak and troublesome existence in America. The founding fathers of America believed in freedom, dignity, equality, and human rights; however, discussion of freedom and rights was originally meant only for European American men with property. These white men's need for an ample cheap labor supply for a developing agricultural economy was a major impetus for the inception of slavery. Racism was part of the justification of slavery, and prejudice and discrimination were a manifestation of racism. The economy and the economic survival of white America before the Civil War, in particular, depended on the free labor of African Americans.

The institution of slavery and the issues surrounding it have left a lasting legacy of shame on the United States of America and hardship on the African American community. The African American arising from slavery, reconstruction, and de facto as well as de jure segregation had few educational opportunities, political rights, and occupational choices and even fewer ways of expressing their grievances. Along with attempts to erase African culture, the lives of slaves were very harsh and difficult. Slaves were considered chattel that could be bought and sold at the discretion of their owners. They were not considered to be human beings and worked long, hard days in the fields without any rewards. The profits derived from slave labor went directly to the owners, who used harsh punishment to maintain control over the slave population.

Slavery first created the pattern where it became common for African American women to be single parents. Initially, men were seen as those who could handle the heavy labor required and, therefore, women were not seen as valuable. However, when they were imported as regularly as men, Franklin and Moss (2000) say that "the vulnerability of slave women to sexual abuse by masters and male slaves, plus their ability to produce and nurture children, brought a distinctiveness to their experiences as slaves" (p. 67). Female slaves were accorded the responsibility of their children until they were of working age. Male slaves were separated from their families to a great extent; Marable (2000) states, "Even the most humane master, when confronted with the inevitable economic declines that are a permanent feature of capitalism, would disrupt Black families by selling off a spouse or several children" (p. 71). Men were no longer accorded the status of a traditional man providing for their families. Slavery emasculated African American men, and its legacy continues to affect some African American men today. However, the African American family is experiencing changes in several areas (i.e., marriage patterns, income, and educational attainment). Although patterns developed during slavery led to lower rates of formal marriages to signify family, the African American community responded to the somewhat improved social circumstances after slavery and began forming traditional families, (e.g., families with mother, father, and children). The extended family of African culture, however, continued to take precedence.

Slavery certainly could have been ended on moral grounds alone, but politics was the element that brought its demise. The westward expansion of the United States during the middle and early 1800s brought about important political events. Northerners feared that the Southerners would obtain control of Congress if the new western territories entered the Union as slave states. The attempts of northern whites to exclude slavery from the new western territories angered Southerners, which, in turn, helped bring on the Civil War in 1861. This war was the beginning of the end of slavery. Few northern whites expressed concern over the human rights and dignity of the slaves. Abraham Lincoln, for one, believed African Americans were inferior to whites and showed little concern over their enslavement from a human rights perspective. However, by late summer of 1862, Lincoln became convinced that the time was right to change the nation's policy toward slavery. Therefore, on January 1, 1863, he issued the Emancipation Proclamation, which some believed freed the slaves. Levine (1996) states, "When Lincoln signed the Emancipation Proclamation . . . he justified it as a military necessity, not as an act of liberation" (p. 85). In reality, the Emancipation Proclamation freed no slaves because it applied only to the Confederate states, where it could not be enforced. It did, however, lead to the Thirteenth Amendment to the Constitution, adopted in December 1865, which ended slavery in the United States. Lincoln's primary motive in this process was to preserve and save the Union, not to free the slaves.

Following the Civil War was the Reconstruction (1865–1877), another period in American history that had a tremendous impact on African Americans. During Reconstruction, the United States was restored to a Union and the rebuilding of the South was started. Reconstruction failed to solve the educational, economic, and political problems of African Americans. At the end of Reconstruction, African Americans gradually lost the rights they had gained (e.g., voting). By the early 1900s, the majority of southern states had passed Jim Crow laws, making it more difficult for blacks to vote. Additional laws were

eventually passed to ensure that other rights were not exercised. In 1896, the U.S. Supreme Court *Plessey v. Ferguson* decision required racial separation in schools and public places. Soon the dictates of these laws became the norm in the free African American community.

World War II brought about new opportunities in education, employment, and economic development for African Americans. These opportunities provided an avenue for some African Americans to achieve middle-class status, and many began to migrate from the south to the north. The war afforded many African Americans mobility and the opportunity to travel and have different experiences through military service. Despite obtaining a higher class status and serving their country, black military personnel were kept in separate and segregated facilities from whites by the government. Returning African American soldiers began to protest their segregated treatment in the military. Because of this action and other pressures, desegregation of the armed forces began on a trial basis before the end of World War II. Desegregation of the military was finally implemented soon after President Harry Truman issued a 1948 executive order calling for the equal treatment of all persons in the armed forces.

Another significant point in history for African Americans was when the U.S. Supreme Court ruled that racial segregation in public schools was unconstitutional (*Brown v. Board of Education,* 1954). Since the Supreme Court ruling, efforts have been organized to acquire equal rights and opportunities for all Americans. In the 1960s the focus of the struggle shifted to additional civil rights in the public sector. Under the leadership of President Lyndon B. Johnson, Congress passed the Civil Rights Act of 1964. In recent years, the focus of the civil rights movement has shifted toward economic equality through the attainment of higher education. More African Americans are enrolling in institutions of higher learning as well. The premiere issue of *Just the Facts* (1998) reported that in 1996 more African Americans were pursuing a college education than ever before. In 1990, African Americans represented only 9.6% of all college undergraduates, whereas in 1996 they represented 11%. In addition, between 1990 and 1996 the percentage of African American undergraduates increased by 18%, whereas that of European American undergraduates decreased by 6%. African American enrollment in graduate schools increased by 50% between 1990 and 1996. They represented 7.2% of all graduate students in 1996 and only 5.3% in 1990. In a competitive capitalist society that demands an informed populace and a highly skilled work force, educational achievement is becoming increasingly important for those who wish to actively participate in and achieve economic success. Bowen and Bok (1998) show the impact of a college education on blacks in their study, *The Shape of the River: Long-Term Consequences of Considering Race in College and University Admissions*. They reviewed data from 45,000 students of all racial backgrounds who entered the top 28 universities and colleges in America over a 20-year period. Bowen and Bok evaluated them from a variety of areas, including test scores, grades in college, graduation rates, careers, and overall attitude toward the college experience. Their research found that (a) blacks admitted to the 28 institutions had high Scholastic Aptitude Test scores for college applicants but these scores were lower than those of their white counterparts, (b) the more prestigious the institution the more likely it was that the black student would graduate, (c) black graduates were just as likely as their white counterparts to pursue and earn professional degrees in business, medicine, or law, (d) the black graduate, on entering the work force, strengthened the position of the black middle class and was most actively engaged in civil activities with their white classmates, and

(e) the majority of these black graduates indicated that they had an overall positive experience at the predominantly white institution. African Americans have made tremendous strides in education and economic development over the last 30 years, and the results are seen in an expanding middle class. Integration is expected to be a result of the expanding African American middle class. The focus of the discussion now shifts to the different theories that attempt to explain how minority people, including multiracial people, adjust and identify themselves while becoming a part of the American mosaic.

THEORETICAL FRAMEWORKS

Because biracial identity development is influenced by the social context, a discussion of assimilation is important. The foundation of American society has its roots embedded in the contributions of all racial/ethnic groups. Assimilate comes from the Latin word "assimilare," which means to make similar. The idea of assimilation, as applied to racial and ethnic relations, comes from biological assimilation, wherein foreign objects, such as food, become a part of a larger organism. Food, during the process of digestion, is reassembled in cellular structure before it is allowed into the system of the host organism. In this same manner, foreign groups of people are thought to be assimilated into the dominant group. Assimilation is a process that can occur after the initial contact of two or more groups of different people distinguished by race or ethnicity, whereby the minority group adopts the customs, values, and so on of the host or dominant group.

Park and Burgess (1921) gave what Gordon (1964) called an early and influential definition of assimilation.

> Assimilation is a process of interpenetration and fusion in which persons and groups

acquire the memories, sentiments, and attitudes of other persons or groups, and, by sharing their experience and history, are incorporated with them in a common cultural life. (p. 735)

The assimilation model proposes that members of American society who start out disadvantaged can pull themselves up by their bootstraps by taking advantage of the educational and economic opportunities in American society, resulting in even more successful assimilation. Assimilation is considered to be inevitable and desirable. In the case of biracial people of African American and European American descent, those who embrace the benefits that hypothetically come with assimilation would be accepted by mainstream European Americans.

Interracial marriages and biracial children can be placed in the context of Gordon's (1964) seven subprocesses of assimilation:

1. Cultural or behavioral assimilation (acculturation): "change of cultural patterns to those of the host society"

2. Structural assimilation: "large-scale entrance into the cliques, clubs, and institutions of the host society on the primary group level"

3. Marital assimilation (amalgamation): "large-scale intermarriage"

4. Identificational assimilation: "the development of a sense of peoplehood based exclusively on the host society"

5. Attitude receptional assimilation: "the absence of prejudice"

6. Behavior receptional assimilation: "the absence of discrimination"

7. Civic assimilation: "the absence of value and power conflict" (p. 71)

Assimilation is a process that according to Gordon, takes place over generations. Gordon believes that this process is impossible for the first generation and may be a conscious choice for the second generation. By the time people of different racial groups marry in mass, they have already assimilated to a certain extent by "changing their cultural patterns to those of the host society" and by entering into "the cliques, clubs, and institutions of the host society on the primary group level." Thus, Gordon feels that assimilation proceeds in a particular order. However, though a firm believer in and supporter of assimilation, Gordon acknowledges that the assimilation process may be decelerated. The process may even stop at cultural assimilation. He pinpoints two ways in which cultural assimilation is delayed indefinitely: (a) if a minority group is spatially isolated and segregated in a rural area; and (b) if discrimination occurs to such an extent as to keep large numbers of the minority group deprived of educational and occupational opportunities, thus forcing a lower socioeconomic status. Structural assimilation is thought to be the most powerful aspect of the whole process of assimilation. When structural assimilation occurs, all the other types will simultaneously or subsequently follow. Gordon asks the question whether attitude receptional and behavior receptional assimilation can even occur without structural assimilation.

Gordon has some definite ideas of how African Americans fit into this scheme of assimilation. Cultural assimilation has occurred for African Americans but more so for the middle class than for the lower class. He points out how African American and European American middle-class families are more alike than African American middle-class and African American lower-class families are. Even though this may be true, he does not

claim that the acculturation process has proceeded so far that all differences in values and norms between the middle classes, for instance, of all minority ethnic groups and the white Protestant middle class have disappeared. For one thing, the psychological and sociological experiences of belonging to a minority group must inevitably affect one's way of looking at the world, even apart from the effect of the specific content of the minority group's cultural heritage. (Gordon, 1964, p. 172)

He concludes his discussion of African American class structure by stating that "the subculture of the Negro lower-class testifies eloquently to the power of prejudice and discrimination to retard the acculturation process both in external behavior and internal values" (Gordon, 1964, p. 173).

Structural assimilation explains the process by which social institutional barriers are placed before African Americans. African Americans, although acculturating, have experienced prejudice and discrimination. They have not been welcome to the cliques, clubs, and other social networks of the host society on the primary group level. Gordon sees the formation of an African American "social world" or "network of organizations and institutions" as a response to this barrier. Gordon indicates that Jim Crow laws have contributed to this state; however, he is unhappy with the lack of integration of African Americans after legal barriers of Jim Crow and antimiscegenation laws have been eliminated. Glazer (1997), like Gordon, points out that despite efforts to the contrary, in the form of equal rights and affirmative action, African Americans are separated as no other nonwhite group. This separation, he refers to as "apartness."

Marital assimilation, Gordon's third stage, is when people of different racial groups marry and produce biracial children. He points to incidents of de facto segregation and the low rates of black/white intermarriage, which he considers to be an index of "communal separation." According to Gordon, while some states still had antimiscegenation laws on the books, low rates of intermarriage existed in states in which no such laws were enforced. Although marriage rates have increased since Gordon's analysis, the

proportions are still small. Because African Americans are hindered from structural assimilation and Gordon's stages are expected to occur in sequence, marital assimilation would not be expected in large numbers. The stages following marital assimilation are identificational assimilation, attitude receptional assimilation, and behavior receptional assimilation. Therefore, African Americans, because they are blocked from structurally assimilating, form their own cliques, clubs, and institutions; identify with a black or African American subculture; continue to experience prejudice and discrimination; and continue to experience value and power conflicts in American society. These social reactions are consistent with Gordon's (1964) analysis of how assimilation proceeds.

Gordon points out that structural barriers exist that prevent African Americans from assimilating. Structural assimilation is so important that the other subprocesses will inevitably follow. If African Americans have not, on the whole, embraced identificational assimilation, it is for one of two reasons: (a) failure on the part of American society to allow African Americans into the cliques, clubs, and institutions of the host society or (b) despite efforts on the part of the dominant society to clear the way for structural assimilation, some African Americans have chosen to live alongside European Americans in a pluralistic way. When African Americans make the attempt to embrace American society and culture, they are many times rejected. However, Gordon makes the point that structural assimilation must precede identificational assimilation. If African Americans are to develop a sense of peoplehood based exclusively on the host society, they need to be structurally assimilated. Gordon recognizes that a certain retention of cultural practices and attachment is real, but the stronger allegiance should be to the host society; that is, to what Americans have in common that cross lines of religion, race, and ethnicity. This is where assimilationists criticize African Americans for not embracing what it means to be American. First, because many African Americans focus on their color, they are separated from mainstream society. Second, because some African Americans embrace a history that is connected to another part of the world as African Americans, rather than as simply Americans, they are again separated. So if African Americans would direct their attention to being human rather than black and to mainstream American history rather than African American history, they would become full-fledged Americans, and prejudice would disappear followed by the demise of discrimination.

To continue a discussion of assimilation and to understand how other leading scholars differ from Gordon, it is important to outline the "three central ideological tendencies" of assimilation (Gordon, 1964, p. 85). Gordon acknowledges that different versions of the assimilation model exists. Gordon proposes the Anglo conformity model and considers this to be the dominant, implicit theory of assimilation in America. According to this version of assimilation theory, all ethnic or racial minorities are encouraged to imitate or emulate the dominant Anglo-Saxon Protestant value system. A process that demands the "complete renunciation of the immigrant's ancestral culture in favor of the behavior and values of the Anglo-Saxon core group" (p. 85). Gordon feels that this model has only occurred as far as his stage of cultural assimilation. Salins (1997) and Glazer (1997), with more optimistic appraisals of group assimilation, agree that African Americans have not assimilated.

The melting pot version of assimilation views ethnic minorities as all contributing to the formation of a hybrid society in which many sets of values contribute to the societal consensus. Gordon feels that the melting pot

version of assimilation also falls short of reality in describing American culture. He believes the ideal applies only to the early process of nation making in America, the result being what is considered the Anglo culture. This process would have to occur for Gordon with the absence of prejudice. Any melting that exists for Gordon is melting into the host group. Later research (Hirschman, 1983) confirms Gordon's conclusion regarding the melting pot version of assimilation theory.

Cultural pluralism is a more recent view than Anglo conformity. Horace Kallen (1924) developed the concept of cultural pluralism. He felt that individuals were related to ethnic groups involuntarily. He also felt that his ideas were in harmony with the traditional ideas of American political and social life and that attempts to impose Anglo conformity is a violation of American ideals. In addition, he believed that the existence of various ethnic cultures within the framework of a democratic society was a positive force for the nation and that cultural pluralism is more an ideal rather than a reality. William Newman (1973) suggested that assimilation may be described as $A + B + C = A$, where A equals the dominant group. Also, he suggested that assimilation may be described as $A + B + C = D$, a situation in which cultural, structural, and marital assimilation occur. Cultural pluralism may be described as $A + B + C = A + B + C$, in which groups coexist. Cultural pluralism is the most tolerant form of assimilation. According to this view, ethnic minorities are able to identify with and to take pride in their unique cultural heritage while being integrated into the dominant political and economic systems. Gordon feels that structural rather than cultural pluralism exists. Relevant here is the competition between the two prominent models today. During the time that Gordon (1964) wrote the book *Assimilation in American Life*, cultural pluralism had not taken hold in the same way it has today. Most African Americans, in the spirit of Dr. Martin Luther King, Jr., were hoping to become fully integrated members of American society. Although Gordon acknowledged the necessity of an ethnic community, he did not promote the kind of emphasis placed on ethnic identity today. He ended his book on assimilation with the following observation:

> In sum, the basic long-range goal for Americans, with regard to ethnic communality, is fluidity and moderation within the context of equal civic rights for all, regardless of race, religion, or national background, and the option of democratic free choice for both groups and individuals. Ethnic communality will not disappear in the foreseeable future and its legitimacy and rationale should be recognized and respected. By the same token, the bonds that bind human beings together across the lines of ethnicity and the pathways on which people of diverse ethnic origin meet and mingle should be cherished and strengthened. In the last analysis, what is gravely required is a society in which one may say with equal pride and without internal disquietude at the juxtaposition: "I am a Jew, or a Catholic, or a Protestant, or a Negro, or an Indian, or an Oriental, or a Puerto Rican;" "I am an American;" and "I am a man." (Gordon, 1964, p. 265)

Even Peter Salins, a strong supporter of assimilation and a child of immigrants himself, acknowledges ethnic communities. He challenges the notion that assimilation entails the complete renunciation of the immigrant's ancestral culture in favor of those of the dominant group. He argues that immigrants are "free to be as ethnic as they pleased" (Salins, 1997, p. 7) but preferred that this expression of ethnicity be restricted to more private spheres like home and local communities. Salins's model of assimilation or "assimilation, American style" approximates the Anglo conformity model. Rather than focusing on an Anglo base, however, he stresses three cultural

unifiers: language, democracy, and a mass popular culture. Key to Salins's (1997) model is that "American culture is not static, but a work in progress, continuously transformed by influences imported through immigrants and other external sources" (p. 86). Although Salins sees American culture as multicultural, where immigrants can conform to it in any degree, his model is not cultural pluralism. He strongly emphasizes unity and commonality. A cultural pluralistic model, he believes, is divisive. Assimilation diffuses ethnic conflict and cultural pluralism fuels it. His model of assimilation is not about "people of different racial, religious, linguistic, or cultural backgrounds becoming alike; it is about people of different racial, religious, linguistic, or cultural backgrounds believing they are irrevocably part of the same national family" (Salins, 1997, p. 17). Salins focuses on what Gordon calls identification assimilation as the key to assimilation. This is prevented by the promotion of cultural pluralism.

Glazer (1997) also sees multiculturalism, what he calls the modern version of cultural pluralism, in the public school as the challenge to assimilation. His version of multiculturalism is different than the multiculturalism that Salins speaks of because it is not restricted to the private sphere. Multiculturalism, for Glazer, changes the common understanding of American history. He calls the African American variant of multiculturalism Afrocentrism. He points out that African Americans were not considered a part of the assimilation paradigm until the 1960s. Today, whatever the causes of apartness of African Americans, it is apartness that feeds multiculturalism. The policies in schooling and residential location address apartness, but "despite good intentions and substantial efforts, these efforts to overcome the separation of most blacks from the American mainstream have not been successful" (Glazer, 1997, p. 121). Again, African American identity is not encouraged.

Gordon and Glazer have five things in common: They both (a) view assimilation as the solution to ethnic conflict in American, (b) strongly emphasize the voluntary nature of assimilation, (c) deplore governmental intervention as reflected in policies like affirmative action, (d) agree that African Americans have not assimilated, and (e) offer no solutions to foster the integration of African Americans in this society. Implicit in Gordon's work and explicit in Glazer's work is their distaste for cultural pluralism. Built into the assimilation model is the assumption that all minority groups have the opportunity to be equal members alongside the majority group. This model underestimates the power of the ideology that accompanies the one-drop rule that African Americans are inherently inferior to European Americans. This belief operates at a personal level and systematically places barriers to equal access at the institutional level, making it difficult to identify the exact mechanism by which opportunities are blocked.

In the late 1960s and early 1970s, several criticisms were aimed at the assimilation model's approach to race relations, and are useful for assessing its adequacy in dealing with race relations. A major criticism was that hierarchy or stratification except in the early stages of assimilation was not acknowledged. Marxist models, which focus on economics, and power/conflict models, which are broader by nature, better address these issues. The internal colonialism model deals with specific limitations of assimilation theory. According to this model, racial groups rather than being gradually integrated into society, as the assimilation model would predict, are subordinated by the dominant group, which benefits from their subordinate status. This subordination is economic, political, and cultural.

Robert Blauner, in his 1972 book *Racial Oppression in America*, challenges assimilation theory in a four ways. He challenges (a) the view that racial and ethnic groups are neither central nor persistent elements of modern societies, (b) the idea that racism and racial oppression are not independent forces but ultimately reducible to economic or psychological forces, (c) that the most important aspects of racism are the attitudes and prejudices of white Americans, and (d) the notion that there are no essential long-term differences between the racial minorities and the European groups in relation to the larger society. To sum, Blauner's internal colonialism provides a model in which racial division and conflict are basic elements rather than phenomena to be explained in terms of other forces and determinants. His focus on colonialism attempts to integrate race and racial oppression into a larger view of American social structure. He recognized that the ideas of white superiority have a powerful impact but does not see prejudicial attitudes as the most important component of racism. The important issue for Blauner is the existence of domination and hierarchy of the social structure that institutionalizes the nature of racism and the processes that maintain domination.

For Blauner, inequities resulting from privilege (unfair advantage in terms of money, power, position, or learning) become systematic and fall most heavily on people who differ in color or national origin. So for Blauner, race and ethnicity are primary principles on which people are excluded or blocked in the pursuit of their goals. Labor and its exploitation are viewed as the first cause of modern race relations, although he believes that racial privilege extends to all institutions.

Internal colonialism emphasizes the historical and sociopolitical context in which racial oppression is imbedded. This theory has strength in that it deals with racial prejudice, culture, mode of entry, and the special relationship to government bureaucracies or the legal order. This theory explains the different role that applies to racial groups other than Asians. Scholars have used internal colonialism as describing the conditions under which blacks, Hispanics, and American Indians have a relationship with mainstream America. Some discussion does exist regarding the extent to which the internal colonial model applies to the United States; however, Doob (1999), drawing from Blauner (1972), identifies four conditions of the internal colonial model that are present in American society:

(1) control over a minority group's governance, (2) restriction of its freedom of movement, (3) the colonial labor principle, and (4) belief in the inferiority of racial minorities' culture and social organization. (p. 12)

Doob relates the first condition to the differential treatment neighborhoods receive with respect to government services. This applies to how neighborhoods that are composed of a large proportion of African Americans receive fewer services. The second condition is reflected in the way African Americans are more likely to be stopped, searched, and interrogated by police than are European Americans. The third condition described how African Americans are channeled into jobs and occupations that tend to serve white interests and needs, and the fourth condition reflects the history of racism both covert and overt in the United States. This condition is particularly important to the dilemma that presents to biracial children when they explore identity as a product of two hierarchically arranged heritages.

So assimilation is not the answer for all ethnic and racial minorities. It is an adequate model for ethnic minorities who have come to the United States voluntarily and with the intent on improving their lot in life. However, it fails to be an adequate explanation of why some minorities have fared badly. Although a number of explanations have come forth to refine or elaborate on the ideas set forth in the assimilationist and internal colonial models, the major distinctions tend to be between the focus on cooperation versus conflict. The assimilationist model was prominent in the 1950s

and 1960s and, although challenged by more radical models, it has by no means been erased from the minds of many social scientists and policymakers (Glazer, 1997; Salins, 1997).

Some theoretical models that deal with the identity of mixed-race people respond to macro assimilationist models. Daniel (1996) sees black and white identities as lying on a continuum between pluralism (which affirms differences) and integration (which nurtures commonalities). He describes a pluralistic identity as one most common to multigenerational people who have not had the experience of two different parental backgrounds in the home or through extended family as have first-generation children of interracial couples. The integrative identity is common to first-generation children. Both the integrative identities and pluralistic identities may be synthesized (equal amounts of identification or commitment to black and white communities) or functional (various amounts of identification or commitment to black and white communities). Daniel describes these new identity models as affirming the "complementary and simultaneous nature of pluralistic and integrative dynamics" while challenging the "inegalitarian modalities of both pluralism and integration" that turn "differences into inequalities" (p. 139). What is important to note about Daniel's typology is that multiracial people are rejecting the rule of hypodescent and "unsevering the ties" that bind them to European American family members while maintaining ties to the African American community.

Reynolds and Pope (1991) sought to explore how a group of multiracial individuals choose to identify and ascertain some of the factors that may influence that choice. They call the option of assimilation passive when society or one's community or family determines one's primary group. The assimilation model would encourage multiracial people to identify with one aspect of self, that aspect that is most closely connected with the dominant society. They also allow for a conscious identification with one aspect of self. However, as long a racial identity determines how one receives treatment at the social political levels, one might question whether identification with one aspect of self could be truly conscious. The social forces emanating from the structures of the dominant white society as well as from the civil rights movement are readily at work to force that choice.

The multidimensional identity proposed by Reynolds and Pope (1991), "identity with multiple aspects of self," could take two different forms: one in which multiracial individuals will choose to "embrace all aspects of their identities by living in separate and sometimes unconnected worlds" (p. 179) and the other—one that is considered beneficial to self-esteem and pride—that identifies as a new group, one that focuses on the intersection of one's identities. This is an integrative model. If multiracial people were to adopt this model, they would embrace all racial groups that come with their heritage. Assimilation appears to be an important element of theoretical explanations for the identity development of mixed-race people. Because the middle class is where assimilation has taken place among African Americans to the greatest degree, it is the African American middle class that we now turn.

THE AFRICAN AMERICAN MIDDLE CLASS

The African American middle class has existed since the demise of slavery. It is important to understand how the contemporary African American middle class varies depending on the time considered. Landry (1987) examines the position of the African American middle class in contemporary society by placing it in a historical context. He does so by examining three phases of the African American middle class: (a) the period of the old mulatto elite, which highlights the period of emancipation to 1915; (b) the period from 1915 to 1960 in which the old black middle class dominates; and (c) the period of the new black middle class, which reflects the period from about 1960 to the 1980s. Landry's typology of the black middle class is useful for identifying the different environments that African Americans face and the advances that they have made in relation to history. An accurate assessment of the improvement can only be made relative to past achievements of the black middle class and to those achievements of whites.

The old mulatto elite, or what Frasier (1962) called the "black bourgeoisie," reflects the era in which the black middle class was imbedded in "separate but equal" facilities.[4] The old mulatto elite were identified by their association with the white aristocracy as descendants of white slave owners as indicated by their light black skin. In an attempt to be whiter, the black elite mimicked white society in every possible way. This group was different from the new black middle class in that it reflected or rather copied the white upper crust in terms of behavior and social institutions and discriminated against darker blacks.[5] The old mulatto elite started to lose their stronghold in terms of both networks with the old white aristocracy and the monopoly they had on the occupational sector that serviced whites. That is, their eager attempts to assimilate failed as a result of prejudice and discrimination. Their belief in having an easier time assimilating than dark-skinned blacks, because of their fair skin, was inaccurate. To regain the prestige they formerly had, the black mulatto elite started mixing with the old black middle class. So rather than becoming part of the dominant society, they were forced to associate and identify with the minority group over the majority group. This old black middle class held positions of a professional nature (e.g., doctor, lawyer), which were unlike the service occupations of the old mulatto elite. The era of the old black middle class, although not subject to the "separate but equal" laws, embraced another "separate but equal" phenomenon. With few exceptions, more covert forms of prejudice forced black professionals to practice in black neighborhoods, generally servicing only minorities. Different from the old mulatto elite, the old black middle class felt allegiance to blacks and, in many cases, felt obligated to serve poor persons.

The new black middle class that evolved since 1960 reflects not only conditions of economic prosperity but also a new antidiscrimination practice arising in response to the civil rights movement. This black middle class differed from the old black middle class in that it moved into mainstream white America. Desegregation of housing and better occupational positions for the black middle class was an outcome of this period. Important to note is that the new black middle class arose in an age in which covert forms of racism were controlled legally by antidiscrimination laws and socially by the idea that racism was no longer socially acceptable.

The increasing levels of education obtained by African Americans since the 1960s has helped fuel the development and continuing growth of the African American middle class and their exodus from the urban center. The white flight from major cities that followed school integration in the 1970s has been much discussed and documented in the literature. Less discussed and documented has been the flight of middle-class black families. Since the 1970s, middle-class black families have poured out of the cities in an unprecedented exodus. In 1992, 56% of all African Americans lived in central cities compared with 26% of European Americans, yet 29% of African Americans also lived in suburbs compared with 51% of European Americans

(U.S. Bureau of the Census, 1994). In the wake of their departure came a doubling of the crime rate, a drop in overall school performance, and a depletion of the middle-class stability that anchors most African American communities. A significant number of black middle-class families left the city or urban center seeking good schools, affordable housing, a safe community, convenience to shopping, and an easy commute to their places of employment. Their list of desires was no different than that of any other middle-class family moving from the city.

Jaynes and Williams (1989) compared the economic advancement of African Americans with that of Europeans Americans. They found that African American family incomes have increased during the 1950s and 1960s; however, the increases became stagnant during the recession of the 1970s and 1980s. That is, the "economic fortunes" (as Jaynes and Williams called them) of African Americans have been found to be tied to a strong economy along with strongly enforced policies against discrimination. This economic increase for African Americans is related to their educational attainment and has contributed to the growth of the African American middle-class. Earl Graves (1998), editor of *Black Enterprise* magazine, stated the following regarding blacks' economic success in America:

> When one looks at how far we've come during this century, it is reasonable to believe that our best days are ahead of us. We've gone from being all but excluded from American industry, to owning nearly a million companies, doing business not just nationally, but globally. The 270 companies featured on this year's BLACK ENTERPRISE 100s listings, the centerpiece of our 26th Annual Report on Black Business, generated in excess of $14 billion in business and employed more than 60,000 people in 1997. We've also made great strides in increasing our income and building our consumer power. Our total

money income is projected to exceed $459 billion in 1998. (p. 17)

In the 30 years following the start of the civil rights movement, a tremendous growth of the African American middle class has occurred. Even though the majority of studies on African Americans focused on issues concerning the lives and conditions of poor African Americans, the majority of African Americans are not poor, and their experience remains untold and unexplored (Billingsley, 1992). Even though there has been a tremendous growth in the African American middle class, Hacker (1992) points out that African Americans live in a different America than European Americans. African Americans must endure a segregation that is far from freely chosen. Cose (1993), in his book *The Rage of a Privileged Class*, asks the questions: Why are middle-class blacks angry? Why should America care? The 1990 U.S. Census data discussed earlier provide an understanding of this rage. If the assimilation model were truly operating, African Americans would gain parity with European Americans.

Some African Americans who have successfully achieved middle-class status and are living in predominantly white neighborhoods may also experience rage. A study of African American families in predominately European American communities (Tatum, 1987) supplements Gordon's discussion regarding the integration of African Americans into American society. According to Tatum, as African American families move from urban centers to the suburbs, economic success and an improved lifestyle create stress. Stress is found in their work environment, in their neighborhoods, and in their children's schools. This stress is a result of hidden racism. Tatum's analysis shows that although some African Americans have entered the middle class, they still experience the apartness of which Glazer

(1997) speaks. To deal with this feeling of apartness, McCoy (2000) states that some middle-class blacks are choosing to live in predominantly black communities. In her study *Black Picket Fences: Privilege and Peril Among the Black Middle Class*, McCoy found that not all middle-class blacks are moving to white suburban communities. She found that a significant number of blacks employed in middle-class occupations who can afford to move to white suburban communities are remaining in multigenerational black neighborhoods with strong family ties that include all socioeconomic classes, somewhat similar to days of segregation. So, as recently as 2000, integration is not realized.

In the area of employment, African Americans in predominantly white work environments feel that they have to outperform everyone else just to be accepted and judged competent. Living in suburbia limits the sources of support available to this group. To maintain the lifestyle that they now enjoy, they (both husband and wife in most cases) have to work long hours, leaving what little free time they have for their children. Little time is left for getting together with family or friends who live in the old neighborhood and making new friends in the new neighborhood. Although family (nuclear and extended), friends, and the church are relied on a great deal for support, it takes great effort to use those social supports. Friendships in these communities also tend to be somewhat limited to other African Americans and not European Americans.

The hidden racism experienced by black middle-class children is the most painful and disheartening for their parents. Marger (1994) discusses the economic status of blacks in *Race and Ethnic Relations, American and Global Perspectives* and elaborates on the hidden racism related to income and wealth, occupations, education, political power, and housing. Hidden racism may also occur are in the health care system and the criminal justice system.

One issue that parents had to confront was the impact of the new social environment on the development of their black children's self-esteem. In the past, the black church and the extended family mediated negative messages from white society about blacks. When these two protections are not readily available to black children, their response to negative messages received about the black community may be problematic and hinder development of a sense of self. Schools located in these neighborhoods also create an arena in which self-esteem may be challenged. Hidden racism is enacted when the contributions of African Americans are not included in the school curriculum and by the school system not expressing concern over their children's specific needs (i.e., being one of the few African Americans in a predominant European American environment).

The majority of middle-class African Americans in Tatum's (1987) study experienced hidden racism with their European American neighbors and did not rely on them for support. Their homes within the white neighborhood were seen as a safe environment after leaving a hostile one. It was also seen as a place where one could receive respect and love. Outside one's home was another matter. African Americans reported that their European American neighbors do not understand the issues they have to confront. Some European Americans assume that if you are an African American living in a middle-class neighborhood, you have a good paying job, live in a good and safe white neighborhood, and cannot possibly have any problems related to being black. In other words, you have achieved the American dream. Some of this lack of understanding may be related to differences in certain behaviors (e.g. child rearing) among them, which hinder friendship development.

These families generally existed in two distinct mutually exclusive categories: (a) very race conscious and (b) very class conscious. The group that was very class conscious was more likely to develop friendships with their white neighbors. Tatum's discussion of these families is relevant to Gordon's discussion of how middle-class families are more similar than they are different. This group of African Americans expressed similar views and behaviors as their white neighbors. In McCoy's (2000) study, middle-class blacks, with the economic resources, chose to remain in a predominantly black community because they felt comfortable and secure among their own. This adds evidence to the fact they were not fully accepted or allowed to assimilate into the white suburban community.

The black middle class, in many respects, is no different from any other middle-class family. They are ambitious, make an above-average income, and are well educated. They expect and demand the same for their children and share the same concerns as their white counterparts: to build wealth, educate their children, and prepare for their retirement. Common outlooks on life make it easier for the members of the middle-class to mingle and form bonds regardless of race. Here is an opportunity for contemporary biracial people that the old mulatto elite did not have. Our focus now turns to contemporary biracial people.

AFRICAN AMERICAN INTERRACIAL MARRIAGE AND BIRACIAL CHILDREN

Interracial marriages have increased as a result of desegregation, greater interracial contact, and educational and economic development for African Americans. At the turn of the 20th century, W. E. B. DuBois said that the problem of the century would be the problem of the color line. Indeed, that has been true and is manifested when individuals of different racial groups marry. With the demise of antimiscegenation laws and laws against segregation, along with efforts to desegregate, middle-class African Americans began moving into more racially diverse areas.

Johnson and Campbell (1981) indicated that migration for African Americans must be viewed as an ongoing and continuing phenomenon. Despite the constraints of slavery and discrimination since the arrival of the first Africans in America, there always has been African American mobility. The Civil War, World Wars I and II, and the Civil Rights Laws of 1965 were significant periods that brought numerous changes. Between the two world wars, the largest mass migration in the history of the United States brought more than 500,000 African Americans out of the rural south into the industrial urban north. Middle-class African Americans migrated from urban centers to the suburbs at the end of the 1960s and the beginnings of the 1970s. Greater opportunities for interaction with people of other races, particularly whites, occurred with this migration. Now African American middle-class people were mingling with other races in their neighborhoods, schools, colleges, universities, and the workplace.

With interracial contact, more opportunities for people of different racial backgrounds to fall in love and get married were provided. Over the past 30 years, attitudes toward interracial marriages have changed dramatically. However, people who marry outside their race and their offspring continue to experience prejudice, discrimination, and stereotyping. Despite this, thousands of interracial marriages are taking place as we enter the 21st century. Although acceptance of these marriages appears to be creeping into the American psyche, life is not necessarily easy for the children of mixed parents.

Because of the increase in the number of biracial people in the United States, greater attention has been given to the issue of identity. Glazer (1997) quotes Philip Gleason:

The term "identity" has become indispensable in the discussion of ethnic affairs. Yet it was hardly used at all until the 1950s. The father of the concept, Erik H. Erikson, remarked on its novelty in . . . Childhood and Society (1950): "We begin to conceptualize matters of identity . . . in a country which attempts to make a super-identity of all the identities imported by its constituent immigrants." In an autobiographical account published 20 years later, Erikson . . . quoted this passage and added that the terms "identity" and "identity crisis" seemed to grow out of "the experience of emigration, immigration, and Americanization." (p. 99)

Even though Erikson acknowledged ethnicity in his theory, he placed that discussion in the context of a monoethnic identity and excluded a discussion of a biethnic or biracial identity. Erikson (1950, 1968) developed a theory, based on his studies and Freud's, consisting of eight stages that related to the process of one's psychological development. These stages covered the entire life span and occurred from birth to old age. He believed each of these development stages was characterized by a conflict, and each conflict contains the possibility of dual outcomes, which are referred to as *crises*. Erikson refers to positive versus negative qualities, which form part of the ego. If conflicts are worked out in a constructive way, the positive quality becomes a dominant part of the ego and enhances further development through subsequent stages. If the conflict persists, the negative quality is incorporated into the personality structure and may manifest itself in impaired self-concept, adjustment problems, and possible psychopathology.

Erikson perceived adolescence as a stage in life when an identity difficulty almost always occurs. He suggested that during adolescence individuals attempt to find out who they are in order to determine their own personal identity. According to Erikson (1968), adolescence is the bridge from childhood to adulthood. During this stage of development, people explore their different roles and make a self determination as to who they are. In other words, they define themselves through their identity. According to Zastrow & Kirst-Ashman (1993) these individuals struggle with acquiring a sense of "who they are, what they want out of life, and what kind of people they want to be." Those adolescents who do not arrive at answers are inclined to be depressed, anxious, indecisive, and unfulfilled. Erikson (1968) argues that identity confusion can show itself in a number of ways: problems with intimacy, diffusion of time perspective, diffusion of industry, and negative identity. Biracial people do not tend to resolve their identity during any one developmental period. Instead, they tend to change their identity throughout their life in response to their immediate social and familial environment as well as with the historical context of how biracial people are perceived. One might say that identity formation for biracial people is an ongoing process rather than the one that Erikson describes. So for Erikson a lack of resolution that is common to biracial people would lead to problems. This may be an indication that Erikson did not consider the issues of biracial people in his development of his life span psychological development theory.

The unique context in which biracial people grow up is described by some as a marginalized position. A marginal man, according to Kerckhoff and McCormick (1955), is "one whose socialization has not been such to prepare him to play the role assigned him in the social sphere" (p. 50). Brown (1990) states that "cultural assimilation into one or the other ethno-cultural groups presents a serious dilemma for biracial persons because it means sacrificing one or the other of their cultural frames of references" (p. 327). Growing up in a color-sensitive world, biracial people of African American and European American descent often find that they do not quite fit into the white world or the black world. Root's (1996) "Bill of Rights for Racially Mixed People" addresses this issue. She states that the bill of rights were "developed in the historical context of three interacting factors and the social forces that enable them: (1) a critical number of multiracial people of an age and in positions to give voice to concerns and injustices; (2) a biracial baby boom; and (3) a continued social movement to dismantle" (p. 6)

Although biracial people are much more accepted in society today than ever before, their search for self-identity can be an ongoing struggle filled with questions and obstacles. It may be far more difficult for biracial people to move through the developmental life cycles and develop healthy self-identities because they do not fit into one specific group. The feeling of sameness and consistency that Erikson (1950, 1968) describes may not always apply. Racial identity for biracial people is not a product of the one-drop rule or political loyalties. It is, instead, a dynamic, changing phenomenon shaped not only by the parents' racial identities and their own attitudes but also by the child's interactions with a variety of people, including peers, extended family, and community members. Through these interactions, experiences of recognition, acceptance, and belonging can facilitate a healthy, biracial, self-acceptance, and identity.

Biracial people of African American and European American descent are sometimes ostracized and stared at because they are not black enough in black neighborhoods and not white enough in white neighborhoods. They appear not to fit in either neighborhood. Because of these factors, the question that arises for interracial couples is "what about the children?" Parents, relatives, and friends of interracial couples worry that the biracial offspring will feel confused. In response to this confusion, some parents will instill in their children the belief that they are black because that is the way society will view them. Other parents will encourage an identification with the dominant group if the child is white enough to pass, and even others encourage an identity that incorporates the heritage of both parents.

The increase in black/white relationships has brought about strong interracial families in this country. These families are struggling to raise well-adjusted biracial children in a society that does not readily accept them. It appears that their struggle increases when they insist that their children be raised as proud biracial people, products of two distinct racial groups. This choice is received with fear, trepidation, and hostility from some in both racial communities and part of society in general. This hostility has been present during the discussion centered on including a biracial category in the U.S. Bureau of the Census data collection instrument. With the inclusion of that category, biracial people are no longer forced to choose one parent's ancestry over another.

One way to develop well-adjusted biracial children is to help them build positive self-esteem as a unique individual. Overmier (1990) indicates that "identifying and supporting abilities, as well as interests, independent of racial heritage" (p. 172) can accomplish this. Additionally, parents' own ability to be able to discuss and value their children's double heritage will enhance a healthy identity. McRoy and Freeman (1986) concur and indicate that "for children to view their mixed-racial background positively, the family must nurture both parts of their background by providing the child with both black and white role models" (p. 166). To further illustrate this point, Johnson and Nagoshi (1986) indicate that biracial children who are raised in a nurturing environment (family and community) experience no greater problems than monoracial children do. Positive or healthy self-image centers on the areas mentioned by

Overmier, McRoy and Freeman, and Kerwin, Ponterotto, Jackson, and Harris (1993) along with others. However, the issues faced by biracial people during the identity formation years may be crucial to their sense of self later in their lives. As Lee-St. John (2000) states, "Most of us do not think about it (race) until someone mentioned it" (p. 40). At this point, the dilemma of who they are may arise and create some doubt about their place in society. Several authors, among them Hall (2001), Lee-St. John (2000), Fukuyama (1999), Williams (1999), Bemak and Chung (1997), and Comas-Diaz (1996), collectively identified several factors that assist in a positive or healthy self-image. The factors randomly presented are as follows: (a) acceptance from others, (b) preparation from parents to deal with racism and prejudice, (c) identification with both parents, (d) acceptance of both sides of their racial heritage, (e) bridging the gap between the two distinct cultures, and (f) having a supportive family (nuclear and extended). When these things occur, the biracial persons identity will be validated, leading to a positive or healthy self-image. This may be one of the most significant events in their developmental process. Another means for developing well-adjusted biracial children is to provide them with positive role models, such as Halle Berry (entertainer), Lani Guinier (Harvard University law professor), Franco Harris (former professional football player), Stephen Small (University of California at Berkeley college professor), and Tiger Woods (professional golfer).

Education will also assist biracial children in developing a positive identity. The children should be exposed to material that reflects diversity in schools and the home. These materials need to include a wide variety of people who make up the population of America, including people who look like them. Exposure to books, posters, puzzles, and other visual material that reflect diversity and mixed heritage will enhance the child's sense of belonging.

Last, residence appears to be a major contributing factor that assists in the process of developing a healthy identity for the biracial child. Kerwin, Ponterotto, Jackson, and Harris (1993) stated that "parents discussed the choice of where to bring up their child or children as a central theme for them" (p. 225). According to Gibbs (1987), interracial families tend to seek out communities that are more tolerant of diversity. Parents do this to develop social networks with other interracial families in an effort to create a protective barrier against potential negative comments and rejection. It appears that biracial children have fewer problems of racial identity if they live in a community of interracial families than they do in a predominantly black or white community.

As the numbers of interracial families grow in America, they will continue to fight for their children's rights. As the population of biracial children continues to grow and gain confidence in their self-proclaimed identity, they will become a huge asset to America as the country struggles to free itself from the shackles of prejudice, discrimination, and racism. When these biracial children grow older, they will continue the fight for their right to self-identify. This desire for their own chosen identity currently is receiving some resistance from individuals, racial and ethnic groups, professional organizations, institutions, and the general public. In the face of this resistance, interracial couples and biracial people have organized and emerged as a political force. Parents of biracial people have developed support organizations to foster opportunities for their children to meet one another. In these organizations, they are able to interact and exchange ideas with other children who are also biracial and bicultural. Some of the organizations that deal with interracial issues are Interracial Club (Buffalo, NY); Multiracial Americans of Southern California (MASC); and Association of Multiethnic Americans. To understand the racial identity process of biracial people, an exploratory study was conducted. The results of that study are presented next.

BIRACIAL PEOPLE OF SOUTHERN CALIFORNIA

How the relationship between African Americans and European Americans manifests itself in the self-identification, behavior, and attitudes of a small sample of biracial people was examined in four areas: self-proclaimed identity, feeling of belonging, sense of value, and manner of living. According to Tucker and Mitchell-Kernan (1990), inter-racial marriage seems to be associated with having been raised in a more racially tolerant region of the country. Southern California is noted for being more racially diverse and tolerant than other areas of the country and would be expected to be a comfortable place for biracial people.

Methods

Because no list of biracial people exists, a random sample was not possible. Therefore, a purposive sample of 35 biracial people age 18 and older was used; 15 were members of MASC and 20 were not. A questionnaire was mailed to every member of MASC for collection of data. Because most members of MASC are in interracial relationships and either do not have biracial children or their biracial children are not adults yet, we ended up with a small sample. An additional snowball sample[6] of biracial people in Southern California was also obtained to supplement the sample obtained through MASC. Mailed surveys were administered to these biracial people as well. Because this sample is a nonprobability sample, these results cannot be generalized to all biracial people in Southern California. Further research is necessary to determine whether the patterns found in this study are consistent with other findings for similar samples of biracial people. Descriptive statistics were used to analyze the data.

Ethnic or racial identity of the biracial people was examined in four ways. The first was self-proclaimed identity based on the open-ended question "How do you define your racial/ethnic make-up?" The second was a summative scale formed from a series of twelve statements with response categories of "strongly disagree," "disagree," "uncertain," "agree," and "strongly agree." These questions were used to measure the extent to which biracial people exhibited a feeling of belonging to their mother's and father's racial group. Feeling of belonging was reflected in three ways: (a) their experiences with the families and people of both their mother and father, (b) emotional feelings of comfort or discomfort with respect to their mother's and father's family and people, and (c) participation in activities relating to both their mother's and father's racial group. The third way in which identity was measured was the sense of value placed on the mother's and father's racial group. Sense of value was indicated by a summative scale consisting of a series of eight questions with response categories of "strongly disagree," "disagree," "uncertain," "agree," and "strongly agree." These questions tapped at beliefs about the character of mother's and father's people. The questions used for the feeling of belonging and sense of value scales were modified from a series of questions from the Racial Identity Attitude Scale (Helms & Parham, 1990). The fourth way of measuring identity was the manner of living scale, adapted from the Cultural Identification Scale by Oetting and Beauvais (1991).[7] These questions measured an identity based on special activities or traditions, way of life that one lives or follows, and the way of life that one is successful in pertaining to the mother's group, father's group, and another's group.

Description of Sample

For purposes of this chapter, all biracial people with one African American parent were selected. Fifteen of these biracial people have African American fathers and one has an African American mother. The respondent with the African mother was dropped from this analysis so sex of the African parent would not confound the results. Schoen and Wooldredge (1989), examining marriage choices in North Carolina and Virginia, found a greater likelihood of intermarriage among more highly educated black men. The parents of our Southern California sample fit this pattern. Close to half (42.8%) of the fathers of the biracial people in the original sample of 35 respondents are African American. Only 14.3% of these African American fathers have only a high school diploma or high school equivalency, 50% have an associate degree or equivalent, 7.1% have a bachelor's degree, 14.3% have a master's degree, and 14.3% have a doctorate degree.

Education levels were found to be high for our biracial people as well as for their mothers and fathers regardless of race. Eighty percent of the 15 biracial people have a bachelor's degree or higher. The 20% of the biracial people with a less-than bachelor's degree education may be due to opportunity, because roughly 21.4% of the biracial people are age 21 or younger. Roughly one third of their mothers (33.3%) and fathers (35.7%) have a bachelor's degree or higher. Although not all parents were highly educated, all but one of the biracial people report at least a lower middle-class living or higher while they were growing up, and all but one of the biracial people report living at a lower middle-class level or better now.[8] This confirms the expectation set forth in this chapter that African Americans who enter the middle class are more likely to have contact with people of different races and, therefore, are more likely to marry a person of a different race than African Americans who are of a lower-class status. This is because middle-class people have much in common despite their racial differences.

In addition, the average age of the biracial people is 30.71 years (range = 18–44 years). One third (33.3%) of the biracial people are male and two thirds (66.7%) are female.

About half (46.7%) of these biracial people are members of MASC.

Findings and Discussion

Biracial people were separated into two groups for analysis: one group with a nonwhite, nonblack mother and a black father, and the other with a white mother and a black father.

Interestingly, lower levels of education were found for nonwhite mothers compared with white mothers. These results reflect the differential opportunities of nonwhite women compared with white women. Only 16.7% of the nonwhite mothers have a bachelor's degree, and the remaining (83.3%) have an associate's degree or less. Close to half (44.4%) of the white mothers have a bachelor's degree or higher. Although 33.3% of the African American fathers coupled with nonwhite mothers have a high school diploma, none of the African American fathers coupled with white mothers have only a high school diploma. One third (33.3%) of the African American fathers coupled with nonwhite mothers have a bachelor's degree or higher, whereas 37.5% of the African American fathers coupled with white mothers have a bachelor's degree or higher. Although this difference is small, it may indicate that African American men who are better educated have greater interaction with European Americans and, therefore, a greater likelihood of developing a relationship, marrying, and bearing children with a European American woman. A larger sample is needed before this difference can be determined to be a significant.

Also noteworthy is that biracial children with nonwhite mothers are less likely to disagree or strongly disagree with having a lot of contact with interracial families (33.3%) compared with biracial children with white mothers (44.4%). That is, biracial children with nonwhite mothers have greater contact with interracial families than do biracial children

with white mothers. This may imply that biracial children with white mothers are more assimilated in American society than biracial children with nonwhite mothers. A slightly smaller number of biracial people with nonwhite mothers (50%) report having the highest number of close friends who are white while growing up compared with biracial people with white mothers (55.6%). A larger number (50%) of biracial people with nonwhite mothers report having whites as the group most represented in the neighborhood where they spent most of their childhood compared with those with white mothers (22.2%). Likewise, a greater number (100%) of the biracial people with nonwhite mothers live in neighborhoods with the highest number of whites compared with biracial people with white mothers (33.3%). Similarly, more biracial people with nonwhite mothers report the highest number of their close friends today to be white. This may be due to a greater acceptance of nonwhite interracial couples compared with white/nonwhite interracial couples. Two minorities who cross racial lines in marriage and who are also middle class may be more accepted in a predominantly white neighborhood and accepted by white people than a black/white couple who cross racial lines. Therefore, black/white couples may feel more comfortable in a more diverse neighborhood.

Most (60%) of the biracial people agreed or strongly agreed to having a lot of contact with interracial families while growing up, whereas a small number (20%) strongly disagreed with having a lot of contact with interracial families. These results support assertions made by Gibbs (1987) and Kerwin et al. (1993) that interracial families highly consider location of residence. According to Gibbs (1987), interracial families seek more racially tolerant communities. Most (57.1%) of the biracial people lived in large cities the majority of their childhood, whereas 14.3% lived in small towns and 28.6% moved constantly.

A difference in political party is found depending on whether mother is nonwhite or white. A larger number of biracial people with nonwhite mothers are democrat (83.3%) compared with those with white mothers (66.7%). Most African American fathers coupled with nonwhite mothers are Democrat (83.3%) compared with those with white mothers (40%). Mothers follow a different pattern. Nonwhite mothers are less likely to be Democrat (0%) compared with white mothers (22.2%). Apparently, more conservative political views are associated with biracial children in black/white interracial families.

The measurement of self-proclaimed identity revealed that most biracial people prefer an identity that captures the ethnicity of both the father and the mother. Seven of the 11 responses that acknowledged the racial group of both mother and father placed an emphasis on the African American father ("black/ Asian"; black and white [sometimes just black]; "mixed: black and white"; "Afro-Asian"; "half black, half Chinese"; "mixed, black and white"; "mixed (Afro-Am/Irish Am")); and ("black and white, gray, or 'other'") whereas two of the 11 biracial people placed an emphasis on the racial group of their nonwhite mothers ("half Japanese, half African American" and "Japanese Afro-American"). One respondent selected a generic biracial identity ("biracial [multiethnic]"). These results are consistent with the pressure placed on the government to allow one to check more than one box for racial identity. Two biracial people chose an Afrocentric or color-based identity ("African American" and "black"), and one chose to deal with the dilemma of a biracial existence by eliminating race altogether in their identity ("none if I have to answer on a form, I usually put 'other,' but I don't identify myself as either or, just me!!").

Mean scores for other measures of identity were compared to determine whether a difference existed for mother and father depending on race of mother as nonwhite or white

compared with the race of father as black. The strong presence of an identity that embraces both mother's and father's racial group is apparent with an emphasis on the African American father but only when mothers are white. This is reflected in other identity measures. When black fathers' were paired with nonwhite mothers, the average for feeling of belonging to the mother's group was 39.83, whereas that for the father's group was 38.67. When African American fathers' were paired with white mothers, a different pattern emerged. The average for feeling of belonging to the mother's group was 39.00, whereas that for the father's group was 43.38. Here a distinct stronger attachment to the black father's group is apparent when compared with the attachment to the white mother's group.

When mothers are nonwhite, the average score for sense of value of mother's group was 27.83 compared with that for the father's group (28.5). When mothers are white, the scores for sense of value of mother's group were 21.38 compared with that for the father's group (26.00). So biracial people show greater attachment to black fathers over both nonwhite and white mothers; with a larger difference between white mothers and black fathers. This pattern was found to be different when ethnicity is measured by the Manner of Living scale. The manner of living of mothers and fathers were found to be similar when mothers are nonwhite (18.83) compared with black fathers (mean = 18.00). The Manner of Living of white mothers was higher (mean = 18.14) compared to the Manner of Living of black fathers (mean = 14.43). The Manner of Living scale, because it allows us to measure an attachment to a racial group that is not that of the mother or the father, reveals an interesting finding. When mothers are nonwhite, higher scores are found for the Manner of Living of another's group (mean = 13.83) and not much lower than the Manner of Living for the mother and father. However, when mothers are white, the Manner of Living score for another's group is low (mean = 6.86). This may indicate that these biracial children with minority parents are assimilating into American society as they have reached a middle-class status. Although data are not available to identify the other group for most respondents, it may be the white group that is referred to by biracial children of nonwhite mothers and black fathers.

SUMMARY AND CONCLUSIONS

This chapter discussed the way racial identity selection relates to the history of the relationship between African Americans and European Americans in the United States and how that relationship affected the social class of African Americans. Because most of the ancestors of African Americans today came to this country first as slaves, the relationship between African Americans and European Americans was established as unequal. This unequal status was institutionalized by slavery. The belief that African Americans were biologically inferior to European Americans was the justification for slavery. Therefore, slave families were not accorded the same rights and status as a European American family. That is, African American men were not accorded the status of traditional men providing for their families, and family members could easily be separated and sent in different directions. In addition, slave masters would produce biracial race offspring when they used female slaves for pleasure or breeding. The one-drop rule as a legal regulation designated that a child born to slave master and slave was still a slave because even one-drop of black blood meant that one was black and black was equated with slaves. This distinction provided numerous African American women with no fathers for their children and began the pattern of single-parent African American women.

Through the efforts of abolitionist groups and civil conflict, slavery was ended in the United States in 1865 with passage of the Thirteenth Amendment to the U.S. Constitution. Because the focus of the Civil War was on preserving the Union and freeing slaves was only instrumental in achieving that goal, the status of African Americans was not drastically changed. They were still seen as biologically inferior, but a few African Americans managed to achieve middle-class status. Even after slavery was ended, the unequal status of African Americans prevailed and manifested itself in legal statutes (e.g., Jim Crow laws). The one-drop rule, rather than a legal distinction, became a social and political one.

World Wars I and II, integration of the armed forces, the 1954 Supreme Court Decision (*Brown v. Board of Education*), and the Civil Rights Act of 1964 brought African Americans to a period in which most Americans were hopeful for integration. The African American family began experiencing changes in marriage patterns, income, and educational attainment. These changes have led to the further development of the African American middle class. The contemporary black middle class reflects not only conditions of economic prosperity but also new anti-discrimination legislation arising in response to the civil rights movement. This African American middle class differed from the old African American middle class in that it moved into mainstream white America.

The African American community's improved conditions can be seen in the increasing number of African Americans graduating from high school, attending and graduating from college, and entering graduate and professional schools. This increase in educational attainment has led to higher incomes within the African American community, and a viable African American middle class is now becoming integrated as far as employment and housing. This African American middle class is not much different from any other suburban middle-class family. The similarities have afforded them the opportunity to move about in the European American community; that is, they have begun to assimilate into American society even though they are not welcome.

With the increase in contact between African Americans and European Americans and the end of miscegenation laws, an increase in self-selected relationships between African Americans and European Americans has occurred rather than those forced through the exploitation of slaves by slave owners. This, in turn, has contributed to the biracial baby boom. In spite of this biracial baby boom, amalgamation has not occurred in great proportions, and some scholars (e.g., Milton Gordon, Peter Salins, and Nathan Glazer) have expressed concern over how African Americans have fared with respect to assimilation. Two concerns have arisen from an examination of their works. First, although African Americans are entering the middle class in greater numbers and entering into more interracial marriages, they have been blocked from attaining the full status that is supposed to be awarded Americans. Second, because African Americans have been blocked from joining American society as fully accepted members, they have formed their own cliques, clubs, and institutions, which has caused further separation. This separation has brought society to reflect more accurately a cultural pluralistic model rather than an Anglo-conformity model of assimilation. This worries those who believe that cultural pluralism divides American society and creates a question of loyalties. Because of this belief, problems arise for biracial people of African American and European American descent.

Middle-class interracial couples find their biracial children to be few in numbers, both in their communities and their schools. Sometimes these parents feel isolated and fear their children may also feel isolated. They want their biracial children to feel good about themselves. In response to this desire, many of these families work hard to get their biracial children involved with people like themselves, and

they have formed interracial organizations specifically designed for their interracial families. These organizations are critical resources for children who have limited access to other biracial people. Other families strongly encourage identification with either the minority or dominant group. Despite efforts of parents to encourage a stable identity in their children, whether that be monoracial or biracial, the offspring of interracial relationships are now facing identity issues. Questions such as "where do I fit?" "which parent do I identify with?" and "what behavior is most appropriate for me?" arise.

The results of our research relating to identity of biracial people in the categories of self-proclaimed identity, feeling of belonging, sense of value, and manner of living reveal some interesting findings. In the category of self-proclaimed identity, biracial people tended to identify with both parents but place an emphasis on their African American heritage. The results of this category clearly indicate their desire and the need for a multiracial classification within the 2000 U.S. Bureau of the Census data collection instrument. This change will provide biracial people with an opportunity to select a classification that will not deny the heritage of mother or father.

The results of the category of feeling of belonging reveal that there was little difference when both parents were nonwhite. However, when the mother was white and the father was black, there was an increased feeling of belonging to the father's group. This result may be due to the historical treatment of the offspring of the African American slave and the European American slave master. That is, history influenced by the one-drop rule and the attitudes that accompany this rule may still be operating today. Biracial children have traditionally been more accepted by the African American community than by the European American community. This differential began when European Americans denied the offspring of the unions between slave masters and slaves. Another explanation may be the sense of pride developed within the African American community during and after the civil rights movement.

The results of the identity category of sense of value replicated the findings for feeling of belonging. There was little difference when both parents were nonwhite. However, when the mother was European American and the father was African American, the biracial people appears to place a higher sense of value on the father's heritage. Clearly, choice is influenced by societal norms.

The results of the findings related to manner of living presented another pattern. The results of this category of identity indicated higher scores for the manner of living of the European American mothers rather than that of African American fathers. It should be noted that the biracial population within this study tended to be highly educated and from a middle-class or higher socioeconomic status background. Therefore, one may assume that they possess a higher level of assimilation and aspire to live in a manner similar to the dominant European American culture within this society. This may be because their social, economic, and political environments force them to interact with individuals from different racial and ethnic backgrounds, especially European Americans. In order for them to fit, feel accepted, and survive in these environments, they may find it necessary to pattern their manner of living after their European American mother. These results may be different than those for other measures of identity because of a distinction between the private and public spheres. The measures for feeling of belonging and sense of value focus on the private realm of life, whereas manner of living focuses on the public realm.

The historical analysis of the relationship between African Americans and European Americans reveals that conflict continues to exist for these two groups. The results of the empirical study indicate that biracial people of African American and European American descent identify, behave, and believe differently than those of African American and non-European American descent. This difference reflects the hierarchical arrangements that still exist between whites and people of color in the United States. The assimilation model, however, is not supported by the data in this study. Instead, an internal colonial model has more explanatory power in how biracial individuals in the 21st century identify.

An important issue that has arisen from this chapter is the question of whether a cultural pluralistic model of race relations in the United States is appropriate and gives credence to a multicultural reality or whether it reinforces the history of conflict and division that has existed between African Americans and European Americans. We believe that cultural pluralism may provide the only kind of environment that is comfortable for racial minorities in American society; however, space does not provide the opportunity to address this issue. Because cultural pluralism has recently come under attack by prominent scholars who support a model of assimilation similar to Anglo conformity, an in-depth analysis of the two competing views is warranted. Biracial people are caught up in the middle of this dilemma, and their voices need to be heard.

APPENDIX

Feeling of belonging and sense of value were scored on a five-point scale that ranged from *strongly agree* to *strongly disagree*. The statements assigned to the variable feeling of belonging to mother's group are as follows:

My mother's family has accepted me.

My mother's people have accepted me.

My mother encouraged me to identify with her ethnic/racial group.

My mother encouraged me to identify with my father's ethnic/racial group.

I believe that belonging to my mother's ethnic/racial group is a positive experience.

I feel unable to involve myself in the experiences of my mother's ethnic/racial group.

I am increasing my involvement in my mother's ethnic/racial group.

I feel an overwhelming attachment to my mother's people.

I feel very uncomfortable around my mother's people.

I find myself reading a lot of literature written by my mother's people.

My mother's people have trouble accepting me because my life experiences have been so different from their experiences.

I constantly involve myself in the political and social activities connected to my mother's ethnic/racial group (e.g., art shows, political meetings, theater).

The statements assigned to the variable sense of value placed on mother's group are as follows:

I feel that large numbers of my mother's people are untrustworthy.

I believe that my mother's people look and express themselves well.

I feel guilty and/or anxious about some of the things I believe about my mother's people.

I believe that my mother's people are intellectually superior.

I feel that my mother's people do not have much to be proud of.

In today's society, if my mother's people do not achieve, they have only themselves to blame.

The people I respect most belong to my mother's ethnic/racial group.

I believe that people should learn to think and experience life in ways that are similar to my mother's people.

The statements assigned to the variable sense of belonging to father's group are as follows:

My father's family has accepted me.

My father's people have accepted me.

My father encouraged me to identify with his ethnic/racial group.

My father encouraged me to identify with my mother's ethnic/racial group.

I believe that belonging to my father's ethnic/racial group is a positive experience.

I feel unable to involve myself in the experiences of my father's ethnic/racial group.

I am increasing my involvement in my father's ethnic/racial group.

I feel an overwhelming attachment to my father's people.

I feel very uncomfortable around my father's people.

I find myself reading a lot of literature written by my father's people.

My father's people have trouble accepting me because my life experiences have been so different from their experiences.

I constantly involve myself in the political and social activities connected to my father's ethnic/racial group (e.g., art shows, political meetings, theater).

The statements assigned to the variable sense of value placed on father's group are as follows:

I feel that large numbers of my father's people are untrustworthy.

I believe that my father's people look and express themselves well.

I feel guilty and/or anxious about some of the things I believe about my father's people.

I believe that my father's people are intellectually superior.

I feel that my father's people do not have much to be proud of.

In today's society, if my father's people do not achieve, they have only themselves to blame.

The people I respect most belong to my father's ethnic/racial group.

I believe that people should learn to think and experience life in ways that are similar to my father's people.

The Manner of Living scale was created by adding the responses to six statements with response categories of "a lot," "some," "not much," and "none," together. Responses of "a lot" were assigned a value of 3, "some" a value of 2, "not much" a value of 1, and "none" a value of zero.

The statements assigned to the variable manner of living are as follows:

1. Some families have special activities or traditions that take place every year at particular times (such as holiday parties, special meals, religious activities, trips or visits). While you were growing up, how many of these special activities or traditions did your family have that were based on . . .
2. As an adult, which special things or traditions does your family do together that are based on . . .
3. While you were growing up, did your family live by or follow . . .
4. Do you today live by or follow . . .
5. While you were growing up, was your family considered a success in . . .
6. As an adult, are you a success in . . .

Each of these statements was accompanied by three categories:

A. The way of life of your mother's ethnic/racial group.
B. The way of life of your father's ethnic/racial group
C. The way of life of another's ethnic/racial group (specify_____)

For each of the three categories, respondents were then asked to rank the manner of living with "a lot," "some," "not much," and "none."

NOTES

1.   For purposes of this chapter, African American or black and European American or white are used interchangeably.

2.   Biracial refers only to people of two racial backgrounds, and multiracial refers to people of two or more racial backgrounds.

3.   For purposes of this chapter, multiracial and mixed race are used interchangeably and refer to people of two or more racial backgrounds.

4.   "Separate, but equal" is used to refer to the situation of segregation between whites and blacks; however, equal is only a pretense.

5.   For a more detailed description of the behaviors and institutions referred to here, see Chapter 1 of Landry's (1987) *The New Black Middle Class* and Frasier's (1962) *Black Bourgeoisie*.

6.   A snowball or network sample starts with all the respondents whom the researcher is able to locate, and the sample is supplemented by referrals from the original respondents.

7.   Any modifications in these scales were made by the authors of this study and in no way should Janet Helms, Thomas A. Parham, E. R. Oetting or Fred Beauvais be held accountable for these modifications.

8.   The respondent that reported his childhood family to be "struggling just to make ends meet" was not the same respondent who reported that he and his family were "struggling just to make ends meet" today.

REFERENCES

Bemak, F., & Chung, R. C.-Y. (1997). Vietnamese Amerasians: Psychosocial adjustment and psychotherapy. *Journal of Multicultural Counseling and Development, 25*(1), 79-89.

Billingsley, A. (1992). *Climbing Jacob's ladder: The enduring legacy of African-American families*. New York: Simon & Schuster.

Blauner, R. (1972). *Racial oppression in America*. New York: Harper & Row.

Bowen, W. G., & Bok, D. (1998). *The shape of the river: Long term consequences of considering race in college and university admissions*. Princeton, NJ: Princeton University Press. (*Brown v. Board of Education*, 1954).

Brown, P. M. (1990). Biracial identity and social marginality. *Child and Adolescent Social Work Journal, 7*, 319-337.

Comas-Diaz, L. (1996). LatiNegra: Mental health issues of African Latinas. In M. P. P. Root (Ed.), *The multiracial experience: Racial borders as the new frontier* (pp. 167-190). Thousand Oaks, CA: Sage.

Cose, E. (1993). *The rage of a privileged class*. New York: HarperCollins.

Daniel, G. R. (1996). Black and white identity in the new millennium: Unsevering the ties that bind. In M. P. P. Root (Ed.), *The multiracial experience: Racial borders as the new frontier*. (pp. 211-226). Thousand Oaks, CA: Sage.

Doob, C. B. (1999). *Racism: An American cauldron* (3rd ed.). New York: Longman.

Erikson, E. H. (1950). *Childhood and society*. New York: Norton.

Erikson, E. H. (1968). *Identity: Youth and crisis*. New York: Norton.

Franklin, J. H., & Moss, A. A., Jr. (2000). *From slavery to freedom: A history of Negro Americans*. New York: Knopf.

Frasier, E. F. (1962). *The black bourgeoisie*. New York: Collier Books.

Fukuyama, M. (1999). Personal narrative: Growing up biracial. *Journal of Counseling and Development, 77*(1), 12-14.

Gibbs, J. T. (1987). Identity and marginality: Issues in the treatment of biracial adolescents. *American Journal of Orthopsychiatry, 57,* 265-278.

Glazer, N. (1997). *We are all multiculturalists now.* Cambridge, MA: Harvard University Press.

Gordon, M. M. (1964). *Assimilation in American life: The role of race, religion, and national origins.* New York: Oxford University.

Graves, E. (1998). The black wealth imperative. *Black Enterprise, 28,* 17.

Hacker, A. (1992). *Two nations: Black and white, separate, hostile, unequal.* New York: Scribner.

Hall, R. E. (2001). The Tiger Woods phenomenon: A note on biracial identity. *Social Science Journal, 38*(2), 333-337.

Helms, J. E., & Parham, T. A. (1990). Black racial identity attitude scale (Form RIAS-B). In J. E. Helms (Ed.), *Black and white racial identity: Theory, research, and practice.* New York: Greenwood Press.

Hill, R. B. (1999). *The strengths of African American families: Twenty-five years later.* New York: University Press of America.

Hirschman, C. (1983). America's melting pot reconsidered. *Annual Review of Sociology, 9,* 397-423.

Jaynes, G. D., & Williams, R. M. (1989). Blacks in the economy. In *A common destiny: Blacks and American society* (pp. 269-328). Washington, DC: National Academy Press.

Johnson, D. M., & Campbell, R. R. (1981). *Black migration in America.* Durham, NC: Duke University Press.

Johnson, R. C., & Nagoshi, C. T. (1986). The adjustment of offspring of within-group and interracial/intercultural marriages: A comparison of personality factor scores. *Journal of Marriage and the Family, 48,* 279-284.

Kallen, H. M. (1924). *Culture and democracy in the United States.* New York: Boni & Liveright.

Kelley, R., & Lewis, E. (2000). *To make our world anew: A history of African Americans.* Oxford: Oxford University Press.

Kerckhoff, A., & McCormick, T. C. (1955). Marginal status and marginal personality. *Social Forces, 34,* 50-55.

Kerwin, C., Ponterotto, J. G., Jackson, B. L., & Harris, A. (1993). Racial identity in biracial children: A qualitative investigation. *Journal of Counseling Psychology, 40,* 221-231.

Landry, B. (1987). *The new black middle class.* Berkeley: University of California Press.

Lee-St. John, T. (2000). It may be tough, but a multiracial identity is not a crisis. *Black Issues in Higher Education, 16*(25), 40.

Levine, M L. (1996). *African Americans and civil rights: From 1619 to the present.* Phoenix, AZ: Oryx Press.

Marable, M. (2000). *How capitalism underdeveloped black America.* Cambridge, MA: South End Press.

Marger, M. (1997). *Race and ethnic relations: American and global perspectives.* Belmont, CA: Wadsworth.

McCoy, M. P. (2000). *Black picket fences: Privilege and peril among the black middle class.* Chicago: University of Chicago Press.

McRoy, R. G., & Freeman, E. (1986). Racial-identity issues among mixed-race children. *Social Work Education, 1,* 164-174.

Newman, W. (1973). *American pluralism: A study of minority groups and social theory.* New York: Harper and Row.

Oetting, E. R., & Beauvais, F. (1991). Orthogonal cultural identification theory: Cultural identification of minority adolescents. *International Journal of the Addictions, 25,* 655-685.

Overmier, K. (1990). Biracial adolescents: Areas of conflict in identity formation. *Journal of Applied Social Sciences, 14,* 157-176.

Park, R. E., & Burgess, E. W. (1921). *Introduction to the science of sociology.* Chicago: University of Chicago Press.

Reynolds, A. L., & Pope, R. L. (1991). Complexities of diversity: Exploring multiple oppressions. *Journal of Counseling and Development, 70,* 174-180.

Root, M. P. P. (1996). A bill of rights for racially mixed people. In *The multiracial experience: Racial borders as the new frontier.* Thousand Oaks, CA: Sage

Salins, P. (1997). *Assimilation American style.* New York: Basic Books.

Schoen, R., & Wooldredge, J. (1989). Marriage choices in North Carolina and Virginia, 1969–71 and 1979–81. *Journal of Marriage and the Family, 50,* 19-31.

Tatum, B. D. (1987). *Assimilation blues: Black families in a white community.* New York: Greenwood Press.

Tucker, M. B., & Mitchell-Kernan, C. (1990). New trends in black American interracial marriage: The social structure context. *Journal of Marriage and the Family, 52,* 209-218.

U.S. Bureau of the Census. (1998a). *Current population reports* (Series P23-194, Population Profile of the United States: 1997). Washington, DC: Government Printing Office.

U.S. Bureau of the Census. (1998b). *Interracial married couples: 1960 to present.* Retrieved from www.census.gov/population/socdemo/ms-la/tabms-3.txt

U.S. Bureau of the Census. (1998c). *Race of child by race of householder and of spouse or partner: 1990.* Retrieved from www.census.gov/population/socdemo/race/interractab4.txt

U.S. Bureau of the Census. (1998). *Table 1. Race of Wife by Race of Husband: 1960, 1970, 1980, 1991, and 1992.* Retrieved August 8, 2002, from www.census.gov/population/socdemo/race/interractab1.txt

Williams, C. (1999). Claiming a biracial identity: Resisting social constructions of race and culture. *Journal of Counseling and Development, 77*(1), 32-36.

Zastrow, C., & Kirst-Ashman, K. K. (1993). *Understanding human behavior and the social environment.* Chicago: Nelson-Hall.

CHAPTER 9

Check All That Apply
Trends and Prospectives Among Asian-Descent Multiracials

Teresa Williams-León

California State University, Northridge

The "check all that apply" option for racial and ethnic delineation will now be available for the 2000 U.S. Census. Multiracial census respondents can now mark their multiple racial and ethnic ancestries without having to force-fit themselves into just one of the preexisting monoracially constructed categories defined by the U.S. Office of Management and Budget's (OMB) Statistical Directive 15 established in 1977. Through sociopolitical efforts of organizing and lobbying, the "critical mass" of multiracial advocates (Root, 1996b) managed to convince the OMB to make this rather significant conceptual change. The check all that apply option will undoubtedly have important political implications for racial and ethnic data collection, tabulation, and coding. Although Asian-descent multiracial individuals[1] and groups joined a coalition of lobbyists and advocates, the resulting check all that apply census option was ultimately a concerted effort on the part of many individuals and organizations.

AUTHOR'S NOTE: First and foremost, I thank Loretta Winters, Herman DeBose, and Marzie McCoy for their editorial expertise and patience. I would like to acknowledge my mentors and colleagues who have assisted in the conceptual and critical development of this chapter (before, during, and after): Don T. Nakanishi, Walter Allen, Paul Ong, Valerie Matsumoto, Dennis Arguelles, Gina Masequesmay, Edith Chen, Steven Masami Ropp, Velina Hasu Houston, H. Rika Houston, Nancy Brown, Cynthia L. Nakashima, Michael Thornton, Curtiss Takada Rooks, G. Reginald Daniel, Paul Spickard, and Maria P. P. Root. Finally, I thank Fabian León, Tracy and Nobue Williams, and Tracy Jay Williams for their inspiration and toughest of constructive critiques on this chapter's conceptualization of multiracial identity formation(s).

The mobilization of identity by Asian-descent multiracials within the last 15 years or so is a fascinating sociological example of what Michael Omi and Howard Winant (1994) call *racial formation,* or the "socio-historical process by which racial categories are created, inhabited, transformed, and destroyed" (p. 55). The galvanization of a collective identity by multiracial Asian Americans within and across shifting racial consciousnesses and contexts has resulted in the concept of "racialization" posited by Omi and Winant. Omi and Winant define racialization as "the extension of racial meaning to a previously racially unclassified relationship, social practice, or group" (Omi, 1993, p. 203). As post-civil rights Asian Pacific Islanders (APIs) underwent a pan-ethnic mobilization and racialization process, Asian-descent multiracial people—within the larger context of biracial and multiracial identity and racialized API communities—too began confronting their marginalized statuses and asserting their racial identities (Omi, 1993).

Although still in the midst of this process of "forming and transforming race," multiracial Asian Americans have contested their marginalized positionalities, organized around their multiple racial ancestries in relationship to API communities (and other multiracials as well), and transfigured their personal identities into what is now a socially recognizable and politically sustainable racial identity; they have done so in the face of social, political, and ideological opposition and increasingly within a politically intensified and ideologically variegated racial climate (Nakashima, 1996; Omi, 1993). Perhaps it is too soon to know whether the more "recently achieved" social identities of multiracial Asian Americans will persist. I speculate that the transformative process of race, as Omi and Winant have advanced, will eventually come to destroy and eliminate Asian-descent multiracial identity and space. Nevertheless, the emergence of Asian-descent multiracial identity in the public arena illustrates that the institutional recognition of identity is one that must be constantly negotiated, renegotiated, achieved, and reachieved. Out of the conflicting views and social projects[2] between, among, and within several interest groups (e.g., the state, traditional minority communities, and multiracial associates) arose the check all that apply possibility of race. At the core of this historically situated, strategic, and processual struggle for an alternative configuration of race stands the active identities of Asian-descent multiracials.

This chapter traces the sociohistorical development of Asian-descent multiracial[3] activism within the context of the "multiracial movement" (Nakashima, 1996; Spencer, 1997), locates the racialized identity mobilization of Asian-descent multiracials from within Omi and Winant's racial formation framework, and argues that Asian-descent multiracials have successfully mounted an institutional (multi-)racial identity through processes of social negotiation between and across several interest groups (e.g., the state apparatus, traditional "monoracially identified" minority communities, and representatives of the "multiracial movement"). The case of and for multiracial Asian American identity is in essence what Rebecca Chiyoko King and Kimberly McClain DaCosta (1996) frame as "racial identity in action" (see also Omi, 1993; Omi & Winant, 1994).

WILL MULTIRACIALITY BE THE NORM IN ASIAN AMERICA?

In May 1996, the *New York Times* reported that of the 1.5 million interracial marriages counted by the U.S. Census, 14% reported an African American spouse, 22% reported a Native American/Native Alaskan spouse, and 31% claimed an Asian spouse. Sociologist Larry H. Shinagawa (2000) also found that 31.2% of all API husbands and 40.4% of API wives were intermarried and that 12.3% of

API husbands were interethnically married and 12.3% were interracially married. Among the interracially married API males, 9.9% were married to European Americans. On the other hand, 16.2% of API women were interethnically married, whereas 24.2% of API women had European American spouses. Among the highest to outmarry were Japanese Americans (52%) and Filipino Americans (40.2%). APIs made up a significant share of the overall interethnic and interracial marriage statistics in the United States. This is sociologically noteworthy, considering that APIs constituted less than 3% of the total population (7.2 million) in 1990, and now they total 4.1% of the U.S. population in 2000.

The cover story for *USA Today's* September 7, 1999, issue indicates that America's future will see "diversity as the norm." The story cites a conservative projection by the U.S. Census Bureau that within the next quarter-century "among Asian Americans, the percentage able to claim some other ancestry in addition to Asian is expected to reach 36%" ("In the Future," 1999, p. 13A). The percentage of multiracial Asian Americans who claim ancestry "other than Asian" as well as rates of outmarriage has already surpassed this projection in many API communities.

A significant number of multiracial households in the United States consist of a person of Asian or partial Asian ancestry by way of adoption, marriage, or birth or a combination (Jacobs & Labov, 1995). A 1990 OMB survey found that 25% of Asian-descent children in the state of California were offspring of both Asian and European American ancestries. In that same year, the birth rate of Japanese/ European American infants outnumbered that of monoracial Japanese American infants by nearly 40% (Root, 1996a). According to the 2000 U.S. Census, about 15% of Asian-Pacific Islander Americans have reported claiming Asian and another race. That is, 1,698,126 people report themselves to be Asian-descent and Pacific Islander-descent multiracials (see Table 9.2).

No longer able to ignore this growing trend of intermarriage and multiracial identity, Asian American print media, such as *A. Magazine*, *YOLK*, *Pacific Citizen*, and *AsianWeek* have come to feature stories on interracial dating, marriage, families, and multiracial people on a regular basis. Yet despite this trajectory, the membership of interracial families and multiracial Asian Americans within APA communities overall has remained tenuous (Houston & Williams, 1997).

In many instances, multiraciality has indeed become the norm in API communities. Perhaps the critical questions involve not whether multiraciality will become the norm but rather, when it does (or, moreover, now that it has), (a) how will Asian-descent multiracials continue to navigate their entry into and forge linkages with API communities?; (b) how will API communities receive and respond to multiracial Asian Americans' negotiation efforts?; (c) as this interactive, dynamic process of negotiations (between Asian-descent multiracials and API communities) is undertaken within and across racialized and pan-ethnically organized community boundaries, how will API communities be affected and transformed in their relationships among each other and with non-API communities?; and (d) how will this guide, influence, and prescribe the racial and ethnic categorizations and options of APIs (see Espiritu, 1992; Tuan, 1999; Waters, 1990)?

1967–1990S: MULTIRACIAL IDENTITY COMES OF AGE

In 1967, when the U.S. Supreme Court struck down long-held antimiscegenation laws, the legal marital unions between individuals across racial boundaries became possible. Thus, for the most part, as an unanticipated extension of the 1960s integrationist thrust, interracial marriages have taken place in larger numbers in the post-civil rights era than in any other time in U.S. history. Nearly 20 years after the civil rights movement, ideological conservatism regained political center stage and began reconstructing U.S. social arrangements, which ironically corresponded with the increasing visibility of interracial families and multiracial individuals. During this period of the "biracial baby boom" (Root, 1992b, p. 1), hundreds of thousands of multiracial people born during and after the civil rights movement were "coming of age" during the Reagan-Bush regime and the MTV age of music videos. The decade of the 1980s witnessed a new and different consciousness surrounding mixed-race issues (Root, 1992a, 1996b; Zack, 1995).

In the 1980s, interracial couples and families began organizing community-based associations such as I(nterracial)-Pride (Berkeley, CA), Multiracial Americans of Southern California (MASC; Los Angeles, CA), Biracial Family Network (Chicago, IL), Honor Our New Ethnic Youth (Eugene, OR), and The Interracial Family Circle (Washington DC). From early on, Asian-descent multiracials played an integral role in the founding of these mainstream multiracial organizations, connecting scholarship to multiracial activism, and forming specifically Asian-descent multiracial associations. I-Pride, the first multiracial organization, founded in 1979 and incorporated in 1982, was headed by president and chief organizer George Kitahara Kich (Brown & Douglass, 1996). Kich (1982) is one of four social scientists credited for having pioneered research on Asian-descent multiracial identity in the early 1980s, along with Christine C. Iijima Hall (1980), Michael Thornton (1983), and Stephen Murphy-Shigematsu (1986).

In the backdrop of neoconservatism, multiracial community organizations in cities across the United States began to flourish. In the 1990s, certain segments of the multiracial community found allies among political conservatives such as Newt Gingrich and John Sununu. This sector of the multiracial movement's alliance with the political right gave traditional racial minority communities all the more reason to doubt the significance of multiracial identities as a legitimate contribution to the eradication of structural inequality and racial injustice.

Mainstream news media, such as *The Los Angeles Times, The New York Times, The Wall Street Journal, TIME,* and *USA Today* began frequently highlighting stories on interracial/interethnic marriages and multiraciality. In fall of 1993, a special issue of *TIME* printed a computer-simulated multiracial woman on its cover. The cover read, "Take a good look at this woman. She was created by a computer from a mix of several races. What you see is a remarkable preview of . . . The New Face of America" (1993). A few years later, golf sensation Tiger Woods's proclamation of his "Cablinasian" identity would further fuel the public discourse on multiraciality.

Jon Michael Spencer (1997) devoted his 170-page *The New Colored People: The Mixed-Race Movement in America* to discrediting the multiracial movement, lauding the rule of hypodescent (particularly its application to black identity), likening the U.S. multiracial population to coloreds in South Africa and ultimately rejecting any legislative recognition of "the new colored" (pp. 56-57). Spencer's analysis of Asian-descent multiracials is limited and perhaps simplistic. Yet it addresses an important critique of the pan-racial, pan-ethnic formation of the multiracial movement, in which racial stratification among the multitude of Asian-descent multiracial possibilities (e.g., the exclusion of Asian-African American multiracials among Asian Americans and white Americans) is purposely left unconfronted for the benefit of the "elite" (i.e., in the case of Asian-descent multiracials, the Asian-European Americans) to exploit the numbers and resources that pan-racial, pan-ethnic structures can garner (Omi, 1993, p. 204). Excerpting research findings from social scientists who have examined

Asian-descent multiracial identity and citing an *A. Magazine* article on multiracial Asian Americans, Spencer (1997; see also Hall, 1992; Nakashima, 1992; Ragaza, 1994; Williams, 1992) weaves together a convincing thesis that Asian-African American multiracials do not enjoy the same level of acceptance as do their Asian-European American multiracial counterparts. That is all the more reason, Spencer purports, for multiracial Asian-African Americans to embrace the "one-drop rule" as mixed blacks have done so for centuries. Spencer (1997) argues that

> with the racism mixed-race blacks face from the white and Asian communities in the United States (and elsewhere in the world), it makes sense that the one-drop rule would be viewed by blacks and many mixed-race blacks as a necessity. It makes sense not simply for the sake of mixed-race blacks having a 'steady home' but for the sake of the black community being able to maintain a healthy cohesiveness. After all, that cohesiveness has allowed us to fend off the racism that all of us—'race' and 'mixed race'—must endure. (p. 57)

It is not only the monoracially identified racial minority representatives who have promoted, pondered, opposed, and denounced the viability of multiracial recognition. Many prominent multiracial individuals have also questioned, "Is [being] biracial enough?" (Jones, 1995) and "Is multiracial racial status unique?" (Thornton, 1992). It is one thing to accept and make sense of the complexity and multiplicity of one's personal "mixed" identity, some would argue; however, to make the political quantum leap of having that identity socially and politically affirmed with a Census category has served to entice controversy and invite debate among fellow multiracial individuals.

In her critique of the multiracial movement, journalist and writer Lisa Jones (1995), who is of European and African American ancestries, interrogates the essentialist

articulations of multiraciality that many biracial and multiracial advocates used in denouncing essentialist applications of monoraciality. She puts forth,

> *Are we special?* The census movement and its "interracial/biracial nationalists," as I refer to them playfully, claim biraciality as a mark of "racial" singularity, one that in America (where most racial groups are multiethnic and multicultural) has little grounding. Their insistence on biraciality's unique status borders on elitism. They marvel at the perks of biraciality: That biracials have several cultures at their disposal. (Though don't we all as Americans?) They say things like "biracial people are free of bias because they embody both black and white." Can you fight essentialism with essentialism? Are we to believe that all biracials are chosen people, free of prejudice, self-interest, and Republican Christian fundamentalism?
>
> By proclaiming specialness aren't biracials still clinging to the niche of exotic other? "How could we not love them, they're so cute," boasted one white mother active in the census movement of her biracial children. Minus butter-pecan skin and Shirley Temple curls would they be less of an attractive proposition? (pp. 58-59)

Jones's point about "fighting essentialism with essentialism" directly challenges the notion of multiraciality being a new and separate identity that has been espoused by those such as playwright Velina Hasu Houston. Houston has recounted her childhood experience in the book *War Brides of World War II* (Shukert & Scibetta, 1988) and in the film *Doubles: Japan and America's Intercultural Children* (Life, 1996) when she asked her father why he was chocolate and why her mother was vanilla. Houston's father brought home a carton of neopolitan ice cream and demonstrated that when the strawberry stripe (her Native American ancestry), the chocolate stripe (her African American ancestry), and the vanilla stripe (her Japanese ancestry) were fully blended, it produced "a new brown tone," distinct from the original strawberry, chocolate, and vanilla stripes (Life, 1996; Shukert & Scibetta, 1988). Houston's neopolitan ice cream metaphor reflects a kind of primordialist view of multiraciality (i.e., a new race, neither chocolate nor vanilla), as does the single multiracial category that had been advocated by some multiracial representatives during the Census debate (Njeri, 1991).

Sociologist Michael Thornton (1992), also of Japanese and African American ancestries like Houston, on the other hand, argues that although multiracial realities must be appreciated, an official recognition is not warranted. Thornton explains,

> In comparing people of so-called multiracial status to monoracials, it is clear that the former have a different flavor to their lives. Society defines race as distinctive and homogeneous; multiracial people experience it as multidimensional. That background should and must be appreciated in and of itself. But that experience is irrelevant in a social sense. Race is a social and political tool not meant to reflect the range of experience or the diversity found within any group to any great extent. By definition, racial labels are tools used to categorize and to separate and/or exclude. There remains insufficient social justification to exclude multiracials from other groups. While there is experiential rationale for identifying a unique experience, that alone is not reason enough, and does not provide a consistent basis, to describe multiracials as one sort of people. (p. 325)

The unfolding debates around multiracial identity have illustrated the complex and dynamic nature of racial constructions as well as the contextual and strategic dictates of racial mobilization, in this case multiracial mobilization (Omi, 1993). The racialization process of multiracial Asian Americans further demonstrates how the differences and multiplicity within and among this diverse combination of peoples have often been minimized

and dissolved, as Spencer noted. Even as Asian-descent multiracials have attempted to (and continue to) organize around the sole similarity of shared "Asian-descent mixed heritage" (Asian being a pan-ethnic organization itself), the complex web of social arrangements that include U.S. racial/social stratification systems, the historical conflicts among Asian groups and intra-Asian hierarchies, and cross-racial differences and antagonisms (e.g., black-Korean, Asian-white, Asian-Latino) have had to be downplayed and neglected. Thus, among Asian-descent multiracials perhaps, like among pan-ethnically organized Asian Americans, the elite of that group (e.g., Asian-European American multiracials and among them, specifically, Japanese-descent multiracials) have come to represent and even define multiracial Asian Americans. Thus, the critique of multiraciality by those like Spencer and Jones is well warranted on the one hand.

During the shifting sociopolitical climates between the late 1960s and the early 1990s, the population of multiracial people skyrocketed, developing a multiracial critical mass during this period. The contested interests of the traditional minority communities and multiracial advocates as well as the response of the state apparatus came to a head in the early 1990s. Discourses on why, whether or not, and how individuals who identify with multiple racial and ethnic ancestries ought to be socially acknowledged and politically represented evolved. Interestingly, Asian-descent multiracials would contextually and strategically coalesce with the larger multiracial movement, among them organizations like I-Pride, MASC, and Association of Multiethnic Americans (AMEA), especially around the Census issue. Although I-Pride, MASC, and AMEA have been seen as general (i.e., black-white) multiracial organizations, they have had Asian-descent multiracial individuals as part of their leadership and membership. One of the founders and the first president of I-Pride was George Kitahara Kich. Being part of a "multiracial bloc" to convince the state to consider an alternative (multi-) racial option and to argue for legislative recognition proved to be more advantageous.

IDENTITY IN ACTION: ASIAN-DESCENT MULTIRACIALS ORGANIZE

Much of the popular discourse on multiraciality, like that of race, has been framed within the duality of black-white relations despite the rapidly changing dynamics of race and multiraciality. Because of the predominantly black-white dynamics of many multiracial organizations and perhaps the overall view that black-white multiraciality possesses an urgency that other multiracial mixes do not have or cannot understand, multiracial Asian Americans began organizing their own associations. As early as the mid-1980s, Asian-descent multiracials began grassroots efforts to establish social, cultural, and educational organizations that would address their issues. In northern California, Multiracial Asians International Network (MAIN), formed by psychologist George Kitahara Kich and ethnic studies scholar Cynthia L. Nakashima, and in southern California, The Amerasian League, led by playwright Velina Hasu Houston, community activitist H. Rika Houston, and attorney Philip Tajitsu Nash, pioneered community-based organizing for Asian-descent multiracials. These associations put together potlucks, monthly gatherings, conferences, forums, poetry readings, and panel discussions within Asian American community venues throughout the late 1980s and early 1990s. The Amerasian League even managed to print and distribute a few issues of its newsletter. One of the more memorable public interventions taken by The Amerasian League was during the 1990 Miss Saigon controversy. When a Welsh actor was cast for the part of a French-Vietnamese Eurasian, a massive Asian American response was spawned (Drake, 1990; Shirley, 1990). The Amerasian League, represented by Velina Hasu Houston (1990), contributed a mixed-race perspective to this public debate that was explosively framed as Asian American versus white.

University students also began forming groups on college campuses: University of California Berkeley's MISC, Stanford University's Half Asian People's Association (HAPA), University of California, Santa Barbara's Variations (formerly VariAsians), University of California, Santa Cruz's Students of Mixed Heritage, University of California, Irvine's "Shades," among others. Universities and colleges in the Midwest and on the East Coast also saw their share of multiracial students' organizing campus forums and groups. Asian-descent multiracial individuals played key roles in establishing many of these student-based organizations.

Many of these earlier community-based and student-initiated associations from the late 1980s and early 1990s (e.g., MAIN, The Amerasian League, HAPA, MISC) have dissolved. However, they set the foundation and started the social momentum for constructing multiracial (and especially Asian-descent multiracial) spaces; they began the early stages of galvanizing Asian-descent multi-racial identity as well as the process of transforming a personal identity of marginality and exclusion into a politically recognizable identity; they organized around their multiracial identity and status while attempting to forge alliances with other racialized communities (in particular API communities and the larger multiracial movement). Most importantly, these early organizations became the forerunners to an Asian-descent multiracial organization, Hapa Issues Forum (HIF), that has successfully created sociocultural linkages between university student activism and the API community at large and has managed to sustain itself as a viable multiracial Asian American institutional representative since 1993. Rebecca Chiyoko

King and Kimberly McClain DaCosta (1996) discuss how shared "dissemblance" of Asian-descent multiracials (although predominantly of Japanese descent during the inaugural phase of HIF in 1993–1994) became an important impetus among many interrelated factors that fueled the formation of HIF. They explain,

First, members of HIF "live" their political agenda every day. Underlying participation in the organization is a common bond of wanting to "resist" and "redo" racial categories. In this sense, there is a high level of agreement among members that they have experienced the "dissemblance" in having to "choose" one race or the other, on college entrance forms and so on. They actively identify themselves as hapa in their everyday life. Via an internal process, members have taken the existing racial frameworks and internalized them to such an extent that they realize they are standing between racial categories as they exist now but that they have the "right" to individually assert their identities as mixed people. (p. 232)

After several initial attempts at organizing Asian-descent multiraciality (by groups such as MAIN, The Amerasian League, MISC, HAPA, and Variations), HIF emerged as a self-sustaining, issues-oriented association that would come to address social, educational, and political issues for multiracial Asian Americans in relation to API communities. HIF is a case example as to how the "personal" can transfigure into the "institutional." Today the national chapter of HIF is headquartered in the San Francisco Bay area run by 20-something and 30-something Asian-descent multiracial professionals. At the dawn of the new century, HIF now claims chapters on and off college campuses throughout California with talk of chapters forming "east of California." HIF has become the institutional voice of HAPA issues, continuing to work closely with API community organizations and multiracial associations on a plethora of social, cultural,

educational, and political agendas. They supported AMEA's check all that apply position on the Census issue and claimed temporary victory in regard to the state's concession.

1990 CENSUS AS A PRECURSOR TO "CHECK ALL THAT APPLY"

Multiracial Asian Americans now make up a major portion of the multiracial (mixed race) population as a whole. For example, of the 1,037,420 children from interracial households reported by the U.S. Census Bureau, nearly half (466,580) were in families in which one parent identified as Asian and the other parent as white. Thus, when the statistical analysis of the 1990 Census data took place, it was not a great astonishment that nearly a quarter million people indicated a multiracial designator through a write-in campaign for the race and ethnicity categories. According to Maria P. P. Root (1996a), a leading scholar in the multiracial identity,

Among the top 10 categories [of those who identified as mixed] (217,656 people), four could not be retrofitted into the five-race framework (mixed, mulatto, biracial/interracial, or Creole). These people were converted to "others." The remaining six categories [were] black and white, white and black, Eurasian, Amerasian, white Japanese and white Filipino [sic]. In these categories, most people were assigned a monoracial classification based on the first race they . . . listed. In an exception to this rule, those identifying as Eurasian were classified as Asian rather than white. (pp. xvii-xviii)

Four of the 10 multiracial categories marked by multiracial individuals specifically indicated Asian ancestry as part of their racial enumeration. The Asian-descent multiracial markers listed by the respondents were Eurasian, Amerasian, white Japanese, and white P/Filipino. The specific Asian ethnicities (Japanese and P/Filipino) put forth by multiracial respondents corresponded with the data that these two groups experienced the highest rates of outmarriage among Asian Americans as a whole.

As a result of the 1990 Census and the lobbying efforts of multiracial organizations like Project RACE (Re-classify All Children Equally), AMEA, and HAPA Issues Forum, the 2000 Census will now include multiple racial check-offs as an option for individuals to delineate their multiple racial/ethnic ancestries. How the Census will tabulate and record these data has yet to be confirmed. Although official multiracial recognition continues to draw out different viewpoints from opponents and proponents, multiraciality as a "viable identity" (Lott, 1999, p. 99) choice among a significant portion of Asian Americans has now been concretized. However, the road to achieving multiracial recognition forked into two separate directions, and a rift developed between two separate multiracial camps: those who promoted a single multiracial category separate from the five pre-existing racial/ethnic designations and those who supported a multiple check-off option.

Y2K SHOWDOWN: A SINGLE MULTIRACIAL CATEGORY VERSUS MULTIPLE CHECK-OFFS

The issue of a government-sanctioned official multiracial category became perhaps the sole unifying issue for multiracial advocates during the 1990s. Recognition of multiracial people by the U.S. Census was one of the only tangible rallying mechanisms for this diversely pan-racial, pan-ethnic community of people whose only commonality was that its members identified with more than one racial and ethnic ancestry. Thus, any mention of multiracial identity or advocacy for multiracial individuals had come to be identified with this single issue. It had also become an issue that

contested possible alliances between people who identified as multiracial and representatives of traditional racial minority communities.

All pretest indicators had shown that recognizing multiracial individuals would not have any significant effect on the preexisting five OMB categories defined by the Statistical Directive 15 since 1977 (e.g., white, black, Hispanic, Asian Pacific Islander, and Native American/Alaskan Native). Although their reasons for the disapproval of a multiracial recognition varied, all traditional minority communities were united in their opposition for a multiracial category from the very beginning. Many minority representatives explained that an important personal versus sociopolitical distinction had to be made when asserting racial identity, one area of which is the acknowledgment and affirmation of one's personal identity (which seemed to be what many multiracial advocates were purporting). Another area (and one that concerned minority communities the most) is the historically and structurally disadvantaged status of racial minority groups (which minority representatives argued that multiracial individuals did not suffer). Rather, if multiracial people did experience disadvantaged status, most concurred, it was due to the minority status of a single-race group to which multiracials were bound by birth and ancestry. Furthermore, the onus would be placed on those who advocated official multiracial recognition to demonstrate why and how multiracial people were disadvantaged and deserved categorical monitoring by the OMB. The issue of disadvantaged status for multiracial people loomed large. Are multiracial people in fact disadvantaged because (a) they are mixed, (b) they possess particular racial minority statuses as part of their racial mixture, or (c) both?

At the hearings before the Subcommittee on Census, Statistics, and Postal Personnel, Henry Der (1994) of the National Coalition for an Accurate Count of Asians and Pacific

Islanders, questioned whether multiracial people in fact constituted a viable group with a shared history, a sense of peoplehood, and a collective identity. In 1994, he testified,

> because existing federal civil rights laws and programs are premised largely on exclusive membership in a racial group, it becomes difficult to ascertain the salience of biraciality or multiraciality in relationship to the specific provisions and intended benefits of these Federal laws and programs. There are for sure numerous combinations of biraciality and multiraciality. What can be stated about common experiences shared by biracial or multiracial persons?"(p. 43)

He went on to argue that

> biracial or multiracial persons have the burden to document what distinct experiences or disadvantagement, in contrast to persons of protected single race backgrounds, they have had because of their biraciality or multiraciality before the decision to establish a multiracial or biracial category would be appropriate. (p. 44)

Traditional minority communities agreed on their shared opposition to any recognition of multiracial identity, whereas multiracial representatives and advocates almost immediately found themselves at odds with one another as to how an official Census recognition for multiracial people would be carried out.

Eventually, the multiracial community split into two separate camps. Atlanta-based Project RACE pushed for a single multiracial category. Led by Susan Graham, Project RACE advocated the addition of a new category to the preexisting five racial and ethnic boxes. Graham (1995) testified before the U.S. House of Representatives, listing the "heart-rending stories" of multiracial people all over the country who were "forced to deny the race of one of their parents." Project RACE's argument largely hinged on the self-esteem of biracial children. In addition, the

multiracial category, Project RACE proposed, would help to enhance the self-esteem of biracial children who would no longer be force-fitted into inaccurate single racial categories.

West Coast-based AMEA, on the other hand, did not support a separate and exclusive multiracial/multiethnic category. Rather, headed by multiracial individuals such as Ramona Douglass and Carlos Fernandez, AMEA promoted a multiple check-off option. In his testimony to the Subcommittee on the Census, Statistics, and Postal Personnel of the U.S. House of Representatives in 1993, Fernandez (1995) said, "There is no particular legal implication that we can see arising from the adoption of a 'multiracial/multiethnic' category, though we see legal problems arising from the current requirements of the OMB Directive 15" (p. 204). AMEA developed its case for a check all that apply option from a public policy vantage point. AMEA representatives articulated the needs assessment of multiracial/multiethnic individuals, public health and public school considerations, and international concerns. Most importantly, AMEA supporters (among them HAPA Issues Forum) saw the check all that apply option as disrupting and transgressing the exclusive and binary constructions of U.S. racial categories within the existing system.

The bitter division between multiracial advocates who promoted a separate, single multiracial category and those who proposed a multiple check-off solution reflected the differences in leadership of these organizations (Project RACE and AMEA, respectively) and their political affiliations and allegiances. Susan Graham, a monoracially identified European American mother of biracial children and Project RACE spokesperson, gave the issue of biracial children's self-esteem primacy over concerns of traditional minority communities. Project RACE's position did not do much to appease the well-organized minority communities, who opposed any recognition of multiracial identity from the very beginning. AMEA organizers, on the other hand, sought to ally themselves with traditional minority groups on some level. They indicated that multiracial recognition should not result in adverse impacts on racial minority communities for the purposes of resource acquisition and allocation. In the end, the OMB sided with AMEA's proposal.

The social, political, and cultural acknowledgment of multiracial identity has often been dismissed as a quest for the apolitical, personal affirmation of more privileged, lighter-skinned, middle-class mixed-race individuals (Graham, 1995; Jones, 1995; Spencer, 1997). The position that Project RACE took on the Census issue perhaps exacerbated this perception of psychologically self-absorbed and naive multiracial adults and interracial parents of multiracial children. The issue of public recognition seemed to pale in comparison to the "survival challenges" that traditional minority communities were facing: high rates of poverty, teenage pregnancy, drug abuse and addiction, crime, racialized hate violence, police brutality, the glass ceiling in employment, university admissions, anti-immigration policies, bilingual education, lack of access to society's resources, and structural inequality (assuming that these issues do not affect the quality of life for and life chances of multiracial people). Thus, most of the opposition to multiracial identity recognition remained even after the OMB's decision to have a check all that apply option.

2000 CENSUS: THE PRELIMINARY EFFECTS OF "CHECK ALL THAT APPLY"

Asian American and Pacific Islander communities, like other racialized minority communities, had expressed their concerns over the new option to check more than one box on the 2000 Census. The greatest fear was loss of numbers as a result of "racial defection."

However, the 2000 Census data (including the stand alone and multirace categories) have not had a declining effect on single-race (i.e., whites, blacks, Asians, Pacific Islanders, Native Hawaiians, American Indians/Native Alaskans) and single-ethnicity (i.e., Latinos/Hispanics) groups. Table 9.1 presents a general breakdown of U.S. racial/ethnic figures from the 2000 Census.

The 2000 Census with the multiple check-off option gave way for the statistical ability to confirm the national presence and importance of multiple-race or multiracial populations. In the last decade, the visibility of high-profile Asian-descent and Pacific Islander-descent multiracials such as Tiger Woods, Ann Curry, Lou Diamond Phillips, Andrew Cunanan, Apolo Ohno, Paul Kariya, Sean Lennon, Jennifer Tilly, Dean Cain, Kristin Kreuk, Keanu Reeves, Sophia Choi, and Dwayne "The Rock" Johnson—all of whom possess their own unique public identity that may or may not include the acknowledgment of Asian/Pacific Islander ancestry—seemed to reify that Asian and Pacific Islander-descent multiracials are now an integral part of America's popular imagination.

Despite multiracial identity being "all the rage" in American popular culture, when one examines the overall U.S. population, the percentage of people who identify with more than one race is still statistically small. An overwhelming majority of U.S. residents reported as identifying with one race (97.6%). Only 2.4% of the total U.S. population identified with two or more races and less than 1% responded that it identified with three or more races. Table 9.2 shows Asian-descent and Pacific Islander-descent multiple-race or biracial populations.

From 1990 to 2000, the Asian American population grew from 7.2 million to 10.2 million, or 3% to 4.1% of the total U.S. population. In addition to the multiple check-off option in the 2000 Census, Native Hawaiians and Pacific Islanders were eliminated from the

Table 9.1   U.S. Population (Racial/Ethnic Breakdown, 2000)

Population	Number	%
Overall	281,421,906	100
Whites	211,460,626	75.10
Blacks	34,658,190	12.30
Latinos	35,305,818	12.50
American Indian	1,865,118	0.70
Native Alaskan	97,876	0.05
Asians	10,242,998	4.10
Native Hawaiian and other Pacific Islanders	398,835	0.10
Some other race	15,359,073	5.50
Identification w/one race	274,595,678	97.60
Identification w/two or more races	6,826,228	2.40
Identification w/three or more races	458.153	0.20

SOURCE: Data retrieved from http://factfinder.census.gov.

Table 9.2   2000 Multiple-Race Populations (Identification With Two Races)

	Number	%
Two or more identifications	6,826,228	2.4
Asian/white	868,395	0.4
Asian/black	106,782	0.0
Asian/Native Hawaiian/Other Pacific Islander	138,802	0.0
Asian/Latino	63,354	0.0
Asian/American Indian/Native Alaskan	52,429	0.0
Asian/some other race	249,108	0.1
Native Hawaiian/other Pacific Islander/Latino	33,980	0.0
Native Hawaiian/other Pacific Islander/white	112,964	0.3
Native Hawaiian/other Pacific Islander/black	29,876	0.0
Native Hawaiian/other Pacific Islander/American Indian/Native Alaskan	7,328	0.0
Native Hawaiian/other Pacific Islander Some other race	35,108	0.0
Asian and Pacific Islander-descent bimultiracials Who identify with two races	1,698,126	0.6

SOURCE: Data retrieved from http://factfinder.census.gov.

Asian Pacific Islander category and received their own separate designation. Apparently, this did not affect the overall Asian American count. When Pacific Islanders are added to the Asian American population, the overall 2000 API population increases only by about 0.1% to 4.2%. However, when *all bi-/multiracial people who identify with two or more races* are considered, Asian and Pacific Islander-descent biracials make up 25% of all biracially identified people in the United States. That is, of the 6,826,228 individuals reported to identify with two or more races, 1,698,126 are of Asian and Pacific Islander ancestry. Although those who identify as bi-/multiracial are still a small minority, these data indicate and confirm that of those who identify as bi-/multiracial, a significant portion are of Asian and Pacific Islander ancestries.

Racial and bi-/multiracial discourses in the United States are still heavily focused on black/white relations, even as Asian Americanist scholars continue to identify and challenge the limited nature of this racial focus. For example, when the number of black/white biracials counted in the 2000 Census (784,764) are examined and compared with the number of Asian/white biracials (868,395) and Native Hawaiian or Other Pacific Islander/white biracials (112,964), there are almost 200,000 individuals *more* who identify as Asian and Pacific Islander/white than there are those who identify as black/white biracials. To further illuminate how the insistent black/white focus of mixed-race identity is limited, the largest categories of part-white biracials for 2000 are (a) some other race-white, including Latinos[4] (2,206,251) (excluding Latinos, this category of "some other race-white" drops to 731,719); (b) Latino-white (1,474,532); and (c) American Indian/Native Alaskan-white (1,082,683). What these figures actually tell us is that Asian American, Pacific Islander, African American, Latino, and American Indian/Native Alaskan communities, regardless of the OMB's designation of that community as a race or ethnicity, have their own dynamic histories of conquest, colonial domination, antimiscegenation laws, segregation, blending, marriage, exogamy/endogamy, rules of hypodescent, and, therefore, their own unique relationship to bi-/multiracial identification. For example, the 2000 Census data reveal that only 784,764 black/white individuals identified with two races. However, when we consider the history of interracial blending within and across Black America, this has contributed to more than 90% of African Americans being an admixture of black, white, and Native American ancestries. For most black Americans,

because of their particular racialized history, lineage and identity are often incongruent.

What can be said of Asian Americans? Although pre-World War II Asian Americans have been viewed as having a pan-ethnic but monoracial constructionist history because of racial exclusion by mainstream American society and Asian ethnocentrism, racial/ethnic blending by way of intermarriage and interracial sexual unions between Asians and non-Asians has always existed (Espiritu, 2001; Spickard, 2001; Williams-León & Nakashima, 2001). Because of racial mores, institutional barriers, and the racial positionality of Asians in America, interracial unions and marriages between Asians and non-Asians did not take course in significant numbers until the post-World War II period.

Throughout the 1990s, racialized minorities voiced their opposition to any recognition of multiple racial identifications during the push for a check all that apply option for the 2000 Census. Asian Americans, whose various communities have high outmarriage rates, also joined in for the most part to oppose multiracial identification by the Census. Asian Americans and other racialized communities were suspicious as to how these data would be tabulated and used. After all, these data are important for resource distribution. California has witnessed the employment of multiracial people to promote Proposition 209 (which did away with affirmative action) and now the racial privacy initiative. Thus, these fears and concerns of what a multiple check-off option on the Census might mean for their communities were not unfounded. One of the main arguments was the possibility of the loss of numbers resulting from a potential racial defection. However, the data in Table 9.3 reveal that numbers can be increased or inflated if bi-/multiracially identified individuals are counted as part of the racial/ethnic group categories.

All the Asian American and Pacific Islander groups increase in numbers when the various

Table 9.3   Asian Americans and Pacific Islanders (Single- and Multiple-Race Enumeration)

Asian/Alone	*Alone or in Combination With One or More Other Categories of Same Race*	*Alone or in Any Combination*	*Pacific Islander*
Asian Indian	1,678,765	1,718,778	1,899,599
Bangladeshi	41,280	46,905	57,412
Cambodian	171,937	183,769	206,052
Chinese, except Taiwanese	2,314,537	2,445,363	2,734,841
Filipino	1,850,314	1,908,125	2,364,815
Hmong	169,428	174,712	186,310
Indonesian	39,757	44,186	63,073
Japanese	796,700	852,237	1,148,932
Korean	1,076,872	1,099,422	1,228,427
Laotian	168,707	179,103	198,203
Malaysian	10,690	15,029	18,566
Pakistani	153,533	164,628	204,309
Sri Lankan	20,145	21,364	24,587
Taiwanese	118,048	132,144	144,795
Thai	112,989	120,918	150,283
Vietnamese	1,122,528	1,169,672	1,223,736
Native Hawaiian	140,652	145,809	401,162
Samoan	91,029	96,765	133,281
Tongan	27,713	29,940	36,840
Guamanian/Chamorro	58,240	59,487	92,611
Fijian	9,796	9,965	13,581

SOURCE: Data retrieved from http://factfinder.census.gov.

combinations are enumerated as part of their racial count. In particular, Filipino, Native Hawaiian, Chamorro, Indonesian, Samoan, and Japanese populations experience substantial increases when multiple racial and ethnic ancestries are figured into the "alone" category. These sharp increases may tell us about the histories of interracial/interethnic blending among these groups as well as the much-talked-about trend of marrying outside of one's ethnicity and race among all the Asian and Pacific Islander groups documented by the Census Bureau (especially among Filipinos, Native Hawaiians, Chamorros, Indonesians, Samoans, and the Japanese). Perhaps the consideration of multiple ethnic and racial combinations in counting Asian Americans and Pacific Islanders could be of great use in understanding community needs and demographic trends without necessarily falling into the zero-sum trap that outmarriage equals loss of numbers.

CONCLUSION

The nearly 20-year effort of organizing—at times taking place in disjointed patterns and at other times in a more collective fashion—Asian-descent multiracials has successfully negotiated membership into a variety of community settings. Organizations have seized structural conditions and opportunities to mount and sustain what is becoming a socially recognizable identity. Some may question whether multiracial Asian Americans and their newly achieved political voice are transitory phases in the process of racial/ethnic absorption into the American mainstream. According to Williams, Nakashima, Kich, and Daniel (1996),

> Multiracial identity has been seen as temporary and transitional—a stage in [the] development before people either become an appendage to the subordinate racial group through social customs and hypodescent laws or become part of the superordinate group through straight-line assimilation into the core society. (p. 379)

It would be useful perhaps to understand the situational and instrumental nature of this racial (i.e., Asian-descent multiracial) dynamic (Espiritu, 1992; Omi & Winant,

1994; Williams-León & Nakashima, 2001). The emergence of Asian-descent multiracial identity in the public arena illustrates that the institutional recognition of identity is one that must be constantly and continually forged through negotiations and renegotiations. The check all that apply possibility of race begotten by the political mobilization of multiracial organizations, including Asian-descent groups and individuals, indicates that multiracial Asian Americans—distinct yet with amorphous boundaries and simultaneously interlocked with several racialized communities—have achieved a certain level of social legitimacy and institutional sustenance (Williams et al., 1996). At the center of this processual struggle for an alternative and possibly transgressive configuration of race persists the active identities of Asian-descent multiracials.

NOTES

1.   "Asian-descent multiracials" or "multiracial Asian Americans" are defined as individuals who claim multiple racial and ethnic ancestries as part of their identities in which at least one of the ancestries is Asian. "Mixed-race Asian American" and "mixed Asian" (as well as specific mixtures: multiracial Asian-European American; multiracial Asian-African American) also refer to the subjects of this article. I argue in addition that Asian-descent multiracial can and should incorporate multiethnic Asian Americans who are mixed Asian (e.g., Filipino-Japanese, Korean-Thai) and transracially adopted Asian Americans, who may be monoracially identified but are multiracial via adoption. This article, however, focuses on mixed-race Asian Americans when using the terms Asian-descent multiracials and multiracial Asian Americans. Although I interchangeably use Asian-descent multiracials and multiracial Asian Americans, the differences in the terminology suggest different racial emphases. Asian-descent multiracial gives multiraciality racial primacy (i.e., the noun). Asian descent signifies a secondary descriptive (i.e., the adjective that describes the noun) marker (e.g., "What kind of 'multiracial' is Keanu Reeves? He is an Asian-descent one."). With the usage of Asian-descent multiracial, one's Asian-descent ancestry is situated within a central (or core) multiracial identity. On the other hand, the term multiracial Asian American anchors one's multiraciality within an Asian American identity and context. (e.g., "What kind of Asian American is Tiger Woods? He is a multiracial one."). The Native Hawaiian-appropriated term "Hapa" is another name to describe multiracial people relationally to Asian-Asian Americans and Pacific Islanders. In this article, Tiger Woods is an Asian-descent multiracial, but in

another context, he could described as a multiracial African American or a Native American-descent multiracial. Therefore, I purposely use the terms Asian-descent multiracials and multiracial Asian Americans interchangeably to suggest that there are a plethora of multiracial identifications and racialized emphases. Multiracial individuals can and do accent certain aspects of their identity (as do all people) depending on context and situation. (Multiracial people "do race" but also have "race" done to them; see Williams, 1996, 1997).

2. Omi and Winant (1994) postulate that "racial formation is a process of historically situated *projects* in which human bodies and social structures are represented and organized." (pp. 55-56). They also argue that a racial project is *"simultaneously an interpretation, representation or explanation of racial dynamics, and an effort to reorganize and redistribute resources along particular racial lines* [italics added]" (pp. 56). Thus, efforts to mobilize multiracials, challenge the state to reconfigure the racial categories, and incorporate multiracials are in essence a "racial project."

3. I do not discuss an important transnational group of Asian descent-multiracials often referred to as "Amerasian." Amerasian children have been born as long as the U.S. military has been in Asia. As U.S. military, business, and missionary ventures expanded into Asia during the late 19th century and throughout the 20th century, transnational, multiracial Amerasians were born in the Philippines, Japan, Okinawa, Korea, Taiwan, Thailand, Vietnam, Cambodia, and so on. Further U.S. military presence in Asia (Central and South Asia and the Middle East) post-September 11, 2002, will likely see the continued re-emergence of multiracial/multiethnic, transnational children born from unions between American servicemen and women and Central/South Asian and Middle Eastern women and men.

4. Latinos or Hispanics are not considered a race by the Census but rather as an ethnic designation.

REFERENCES

Brown, N. G., & Douglass, R. E. (1996). Making the invisible visible: The growth of community network organizations. In M. P. P. Root (Ed.), *The multiracial experience: Racial borders as the new frontier* (pp. 323-230). Thousand Oaks, CA: Sage.

Der, H. (1994). Statement of Henry Der, National Coalition for an Accurate Count of Asians and Pacific Islanders. In *Review of federal measurements of race and Ethnicity: Hearing before the Subcommittee on Census, Statistics, and Postal Personnel* (House of Representatives, Serial No. 103-7). Washington, DC: Government Printing Office.

Drake, S. (1990, August 9). Cancellation of "Miss Saigon" plays as a tragedy. *Los Angeles Times*, pp. F6-F8.

Espiritu, Y. L. (1992). *Asian American panethnicity: Bridging institutions and identities*. Philadelphia: Temple University Press.

Espiritu, Y. L. (2001). Possibilities of a multiracial Asian America. In T. Williams-León & Cynthia Nakashima (Eds.), *The sum of our parts: Mixed heritage Asian Americans* (pp. 25-34). Philadelphia: Temple University Press.

Fernandez, C. (1995). Testimony of the Association of MultiEthnic Americans. In N. Zack (Ed.), *American mixed race: The culture of microdiversity* (p. 204). Lanham, MD: Rowman & Littlefield.

Graham, S. (1995). Grassroots advocacy. In N. Zack (Ed.), *American mixed race: The culture of microdiversity* (pp. 187-188). Lanham, MD: Rowman & Littlefield.

Hall, C. C. I. (1980). *The ethnic identity of racially mixed people: A study of black-Japanese.* Unpublished doctoral dissertation, University of California, Los Angeles.

Hall, C. C. I. (1992). Coloring outside the lines. In M. P. P. Root (Ed.), *Racially mixed people in America* (pp. 326-329). Newbury Park, CA: Sage.

Houston, V. H. (1990, August 13). The fallout over "Saigon": It's time to overcome the legacy of racism in theater. *Los Angeles Times.*

Houston, V. H., & Williams, T. K. (Eds.). (1997). No passing zone: Artistic and discursive writings by and about Asian-descent multiracials. *Amerasia Journal, 23*(1).

In the future, diversity will be the norm. (1999, September 7). *USA Today,* p. 13A.

Jacobs, J., & Labov, T. (1995, August). *Sex difference in intermarriage: Asian exceptionalism reconsidered.* Paper presented at the meeting of the American Sociological Association, Washington, DC.

Jones, L. (1995). Is biracial enough? Or, what's this about a multiracial category on the census? A conversation. In L. Jones & A. Rogers (Eds.), *Bulletproof diva: Tales of race, sex, and hair* (pp. 53-68). New York: Anchor Press.

Kich, G. K. (1982). *Eurasians: Ethnic/racial identity development of biracial Japanese/white adults.* Unpublished doctoral dissertation, Wright Institute of Professional Psychology, Berkeley, CA.

King, R. C., & DaCosta, K. M. (1996). Changing face, changing race: The remaking of race in the Japanese American and African American communities. In M. P. P. Root (Ed.), *The multiracial experience: Racial borders as the new frontier* (pp. 227-244). Thousand Oaks, CA: Sage.

Life, R. (Producer). (1996). *Doubles: Japan and America's intercultural children* [Documentary film]. United States and Japan: Sasakawa Peace Foundation, The Freeman Foundation, The Japan-United States Friendship Commission, The Japan Foundation, AIG and ANA.

Lott, J. T. (1999). Asian Americans: From racial category to multiple identities. Walnut Creek, CA: Altamira.

Murphy-Shigematsu, S. (1986). *The voices of Amerasians: Ethnicity, identity, and empowerment in interracial Japanese Americans.* Unpublished doctoral dissertation, Harvard University.

Nakashima, C. L. (1992). An invisible monster: The creation and denial of mixed-race people in America. In M. P. P. Root (Ed.), *Racially mixed people in America* (pp. 162-180). Newbury Park, CA: Sage.

Nakashima, C. L. (1996). Voices from the movement: Approaches to multiraciality. In M. P. P. Root (Ed.), *The multiracial experience: Racial borders as the new frontier* (pp. 79-100). Thousand Oaks, CA: Sage.

The new face of America [Special issue]. (1993, Fall). *Time.*

New York Times. (1997, May 16).

Njeri, I. (1991, January 13). Call for census category creates interracial debate. *Los Angeles Times,* pp. E1, E9-E-11.

Omi, M. (1993). Out of the melting pot and into the fire. In *State of Asian Pacific America: Policy issues to the year 2020.* Los Angeles: LEAP Asian Pacific American public Policy Institute and UCLA Asian American Studies Center.

Omi, M., & Winant, H. (1994). *Racial formation in the U.S.: From the 1960s to the 1990s.* New York: Routledge.

Ragaza, A. (1994). All of the above. *A. Magazine, 3*(1), 21-22, 76-77.

Root, M. P. P. (Ed.). (1992a). *Racially mixed people in America.* Newbury park, CA: Sage.

Root, M. P. P. (1992b). Within, between, and beyond race. In M. P. P. Root (Ed.), *Racially mixed people in America.* Newbury Park, CA: Sage.

Root, M. P. P. (1996a). The multiracial experience: Racial borders as a significant frontier in race relations. In M. P. P. Root (Ed.), *The multiracial experience: Racial borders as the new frontier* (p. xv). Thousand Oaks, CA: Sage.

Root, M. P. P. (Ed.). (1996b). *The multiracial experience: Racial borders as the new frontier.* Thousand Oaks, CA: Sage.

Shinagawa, L. H. (2000). Contemporary Asian American sociodemographic status. In T. Fong & L. H. Shinagawa (Eds.), *Asian Americans: Experiences and perspectives.* Upper Saddle River, NJ: Prentice Hall.

Shirley, D. (1990, August 9). The fall of "Miss Saigon" [Calendar section]. *Los Angeles Times,* p. F1.

Shukert, E. B., & Scibetta, B. S. (1988). *War brides of World War II.* New York: Penguin Books.

Spencer, J. M. (1997). *The new colored people: The mixed-race movement in America.* New York: New York University Press.

Spickard, P. (2001). Who is Asian? Who is Pacific Islander? Monoracialism, multiracial people and Asia American communities. In T. Williams-León & C. Nakashima (Eds.), *The sum of our parts: Mixed heritage Asian Americans* (pp. 12-24). Philadelphia: Temple University Press.

Thornton, M. C. (1983). *A social history of a multiethnic identity: The case of black Japanese Americans.* Unpublished doctoral dissertation, University of Michigan.

Thornton, M. C. (1992). Is multiracial status unique? The personal and social experience. In M. P. P. Root (Ed.), *Racially mixed people in America* (pp. 321-325). Newbury Park, CA: Sage.

Tuan, M. (1999). Neither real Americans nor real Asians: Multigeneration Asian ethnics navigating the terrain of authenticity. *Qualitative Sociology, 22*(2), 105-125.

Waters, M. (1990). *Ethnic options: Choosing identities in America.* Berkeley: University of California Press.

Williams, T. K. (1992). Prism lives: Identity of binational Amerasians. In M. P. P. Root (Ed.), *Racially mixed people in America* (pp. 280-303). Newbury Park, CA: Sage.

Williams, T. K. (1996). Race as process: Reassessing the "what are you?" encounters of biracial individuals. In M. P. P. Root (Ed.), *The multiracial experience: Racial borders as the new frontier.* Thousand Oaks, CA: Sage.

Williams, T. K. (1997). Raceing and being raced: The critical interrogation of passing. *Amerasia Journal, 23*(1), 61-65.

Williams, T. K., Nakashima, C. L., Kich, G. K., & Daniel, G. R. (1996). Being different together in the university classroom: Multiracial identity as transgressive education. In M. P. P. Root (Ed.), *The multiracial experience: Racial borders as the new frontier.* Thousand Oaks, CA: Sage.

Williams-León, T., & Nakashima, C. L. (2001). Reconfiguring race, rearticulating ethnicity. In T. Williams-León & C. Nakashima (Eds.), *The sum of our parts: Mixed heritage Asian Americans* (pp. 3-12). Philadelphia: Temple University Press.

Williams-León, T., & Nakashima, C. L. (2001). *The sum of our parts: Mixed heritage Asian Americans.* Philadelphia: Temple University Press.

Zack, N. (Ed.). (1995). *American mixed race: The culture of microdiversity.* Lanham, MD: Rowman & Littlefield.

CHAPTER 10

Beyond Mestizaje

The Future of Race in America[1]

GREGORY VELAZCO Y TRIANOSKY

California State University–Northridge

Since its inception, the United States has been obsessed with the idea of race. Moreover, despite many subtle transformations and variations, our dominant racial ideology has remained bipolar. We have always conceived ourselves, in the well-known words of the Kerner Commission, as two nations, "one black, one white—separate and unequal" (National Advisory Commission on Civil Disorders, 1968; O'Brien, 1996; Schwarz, 1997).

There are some who think that the increasing presence and visibility of Latino/as in our society will help to cure this "bipolar disorder." In its more romantic versions, the thought is that somehow "brown" helps to bridge the gap between "black" and "white": that our mere presence as a *mestizo* or mixed-race people can perhaps help Americans to see black and white as at best end-points on a continuum rather than as eternal and irreconcilable opposites. In this chapter I explore a less romanticized, more critical version of this thought primarily by examining the relationship between Latinos and the dominant Anglo culture in the United States.

MESTIZAJE IN LATIN AMERICA

It is true that the central racial and cultural reality of Latino life is that everyone is *mestizo*. Most of us are mixed by blood: descendants of Spanish conquerors and either African slaves or American Indian peoples or

AUTHOR'S NOTE: I thank Sally Haslanger, the members of the Race & Racism Reading Group at the University of Michigan (1995–1997), George Uba, the members of the Reading Group on the Social Construction of Race at California State University, Northridge (1998–2000), and, most of all, Harry Trianosky and Anne J. Burset Torres de Trianosky, my parents.

both. Even those who claim not to be mixed by blood are plainly mixed by culture; Latino cultures are clearly and fundamentally distinct from their Spanish ancestors. Even the newest immigrants to Latin America are mixed by language, for the Spanish that Latino/as speak always reflects, although not always honestly and without shame, the words, concepts, and accents of the three great cultural streams whose tragic and powerful coming-together was *la conquista*, the Conquest, the birth of Latino peoples.

It is important not to romanticize the racial ideologies of Latin America, however. *Mestizaje* in all its protean forms is a central reality; however, this does not mean it is an openly acknowledged reality. Many Latino/as live in a curious state of "doublethink," which Orwell described as the ability to believe something while simultaneously acknowledging the conditions that establish its falsehood. There is a well-known saying in Cuba and Puerto Rico: "*El que no tiene de Congo es de Carabalí; ¿y para el que no sabe na', tu abuela 'donde 'sta?*"[2] Although my family has been in Puerto Rico at least since the 1500s, my mother always insisted that we were "Spanish, not Puerto Rican," and she and my grandmother never went out in the sun without parasols, lest we "out" our Yoruba ancestry by a too-brown skin. Thus, in Latin America, the acknowledgment of our *mestizo* character frequently coexists with its denial, disarming its power to subvert our racialized understandings of ourselves.[3]

MESTIZAJE IN THE UNITED STATES

Will our presence in the United States help to undermine racist ideology here? It is certainly true that Latino/as are an increasingly large part of the American population. Our birth rate is the highest of any ethnic and racial group in the United States, and by some estimates one third of the American population will have some Latino/a blood by the year 2040. The 2000 Census indicates that we may already constitute the largest minority in the United States, depending on how the final results are tabulated.

As we thus move into the mainstream of American society, we become doubly mixed, doubly *mestizo*. We are mixed for the second time by culture, through our encounter with the dominant culture in this new land. We are mixed for the second time by race, as we intermingle with our new Anglo-European cousins. Thus, we become Puerto Rican-Americans, Mexican-Americans, Cuban-Americans. "*Una mano pa' 'lante, y una mano pa' 'tras*",[4] as Celia Cruz sings. This racial and cultural second mixing I call the *Nuevo Mestizaje*. Aurora Levins Morales describes it well:

> I am a child of the Americas,
> a light-skinned *mestiza* of the
> Caribbean,
> a child of many diaspora, born
> into this continent
> at a crossroads.
> I am a U.S. Puerto
> Rican Jew,
> a product of the ghettos of
> New York I have never
> known.
> An immigrant and the daughter and
> granddaughter of immigrants.
> I speak English with passion: it's the
> tongue of my
> consciousness,
> a flashing knife blade of crystal, my tool,
> my craft.
> I am Caribeña, island grown.
> Spanish is in my
> flesh,
> ripples from my tongue, lodges in
> my hips:
> the language of garlic
> and mangoes,

the singing in my poetry, the flying
gestures of my
hands.
I am of Latinoamérica, rooted in the
history of my
continent:
I speak from that body.
I am not african. Africa is in me, but I
cannot return.
I am not taína. Taíno is in me,
but there is no way
Back.
I am not european. Europe lives in me,
but I have
no home there.
I am new. History made me.
My first language
was spanglish.
I was born at the crossroads
and I am whole.

—Aurora Levins Morales (1990)

Of course, the *Nuevo Mestizaje* is only new for us Latino/as, because race mixing has always been widespread in the United States (see, e.g., Ball, 1998; Gordon-Reed, 1998; Piper, 1992). Nonetheless, the idea of *mestizaje* remains radical here. The American bipolar racial ideology continues to deny the reality of widespread race mixing between white and nonwhite; and America's continuing fascination, if not obsession, with miscegenation reveals that conceptions of white racial purity remain a significant feature of American culture.[5]

Perhaps for this reason, in the 19th century, as immigrant groups that historically were conceived as nonwhite began to mix with earlier Anglo-European settlers, racial categories flexed so that while these groups were slowly assimilated, the line between white and nonwhite remained relatively clear. Thus, the Irish, the Slavs, and the Italians (and southern Mediterraneans generally), who were typically not seen as white when they arrived, have "become white," to use Noel Ignatiev's vivid

phrase. The color line in the United States is like the national boundary between the United States and Mexico. It has moved around, but no matter where it locates itself it almost always remains clearly defined.[6]

If this is right, however, then it is difficult to believe that either the mere presence of Latino/as in increasingly visible numbers or our continued mixing into the already-white population will yield any different result. We will, over time, simply become "white."[7] Failing that, we will be assigned to the "black" category.

It follows that the *Nuevo Mestizaje* will not automatically provide a cure for America's bipolar disorder. Nonetheless, perhaps a more critical deployment of the notion of *mestizaje* can accomplish this goal.

CULTURAL IDENTITY IN A STRANGE LAND

We can begin with a fundamental and widely recognized truth: Racial categories are socially constructed.[8] This much should already have been suggested by the historical malleability of the concept of race. The construction of racial categories in America in particular is typically organized around several familiar racist assumptions:

- Putative, salient phenotypic differences are taken to signal underlying differences in "nature."
- Putative, salient differences in character and behavior (culture) are taken to signal underlying differences in "nature."
- An essential, underlying difference in "nature" is posited between blacks and whites.

Because of the emphasis that everyday racial epistemology places on phenotypic difference, it is easy to take it for granted that the first assumption is the most fundamental. In point of fact, however, it is the second assumption about culture and its relation to underlying nature that is the most powerful determinant of how racial categories are constructed in America.[9] In fact, the first assumption, central as it is to our familiar racist epistemology, can even be discarded depending on how cultural differences are understood. For example, Noel Ignatiev (1996) quotes the well-known and vicious 19th-century American canard, "An Irishman is a nigger turned inside out." On the surface, this intended slander against the Irish seems to involve discounting what to us are obvious phenotypic points of contrast between Irish immigrants and black Americans in favor of putative similarities in character and behavior. At a deeper level, however, this attempted slander puts pressure on the first assumption about racial categories, for the "inside-out" trope suggests that the alleged cultural similarities are rooted in biological isomorphisms that are obscured by mere phenotypic differences. "Inside" the trope implies, Irish immigrants are really the same as black Americans. Thus, because the perceived similarities in culture and behavior are reified—made to appear manifestations of a shared nature—the trope presses us to divest salient differences in phenotype of their familiar role as signs of divergent natures.

Now it might seem as though what happens ultimately is that race follows phenotype, because despite their putatively shared inner nature, Irish immigrants were not placed in the same racial category as black Americans. This, in turn, might suggest that it is our (culturally intransigent) perceptions of phenotypic salience that always trump in the construction of race. However, this puts the emphasis in the wrong place. The touchstone of American racial ideology is always the distinction between whites and nonwhites. The point of the canard under discussion is not that the Irish are black but that they are *not white*.[10]

In short, I am suggesting that the key supposition in the racial ideology that divided Irish immigrants from whites in the late 19th century was the notion that the character and behavior that the former supposedly shared with black Americans revealed an underlying essential "nature" also shared with black Americans. Given this notion, then, the third assumption mentioned previously settles the matter: No group that shares the essential nature of black people could possibly be white.[11] This is the deep insight suggested by the provocative title of Ignatiev's well-known book, *How the Irish Became White*. Irish immigrants became white not by changing their appearance or phenotype—still less by changing whatever underlying nature one might think they possessed—but by redefining their relationship to the dominant culture. As a group, they internalized its racial attitudes, particularly toward black people, and they found places for themselves in the dominant culture as border guards along the racial divide: in unions, on police forces, in classrooms, and in the church. Once their character and behavior had assimilated to the dominant culture in these and many other ways, however, it became possible for white society to reinterpret their phenotype, and their underlying nature, as simply another variation on the theme of whiteness. In this way, they came to be seen as phenotypically—and essentially—white. I conjecture that the same sort of story could be told about other immigrants to the United States who were initially categorized as nonwhite (e.g., Arabs, Greeks, Italians, and perhaps Slavs). They became white by a transmogrification of culture or patterns of character and behavior, and not by some objectively describable change in phenotype.[12] Perhaps, therefore, we can understand the logic of *mestizaje* or mixed-race identities by exploring the logic of the mixed-cultural identities that define the experience of Latino/as and many other immigrants to the United States.

For immigrants and other exiles, culture is mixed from the moment they arrive in this new world. The home culture is shared against the backdrop of a new, alien culture. However much "Little Italy" or "Mexicantown" is like the old country, it is almost always defined by a small space in comparison to the one staked out by the dominant culture. Moreover, that small space is almost inevitably one that, despite the best efforts of the elder generation, is pervaded by the influence of the new world that surrounds it.

The contrast between the home culture of the ghetto or the *barrio* and the dominant alien culture is particularly acute for the children of immigrants in a mass-media society. In a strange land the home culture is characteristically transmitted by personal contact. It is the parish deacon who runs the Ukrainian-language school. It is the grandmother and her sisters who know how to make the traditional Syrian dishes or tell fortunes in the trails left by the coffee grounds in one's cup. It is the corner grocer who will speak to the children only in Spanish or who corrects their too-casual, Americanized manners.

Thus, in the first instance, the tie between the children of immigrants and the home culture is hardly ever abstract or impersonal. It typically consists of concrete memories of sights, sounds and smells, words and phrases, and the faces, the voices and the touch of the people we grew up with. This is why Mario Puzo, who grew up in Brooklyn, upon visiting his parents' home town in Sicily for the first time when he was in his 30s, said that the faces, the accents, the gestures, and the actions of the people he met there seemed so very familiar to him. He was tied to them and so to the lived culture of that Sicilian town by the intensely personal experiences and emotions in the small space that was the center of his Brooklyn childhood.

This explains why, for the immigrant child, a child of parents cast ashore in a strange land, our emotional attachment to the home culture is typically some function of our emotional attachments to those who brought it to us. Our relationship to the home culture is thus shot through with the feelings, neuroses, and ambivalence that

define our relationships with those in whose lives we first intimately experienced that culture. In living with us, and so in living out their culture with us, they became its embodiment in our lives. It should not be surprising then that what we learn to love, hate, fear, and admire in the home culture are the ways of that culture as they are embodied in the people who bring it intimately to life for us.[13]

This is the lesson that Adrienne Rich's father understood, perhaps instinctively but too well. Rich is the daughter of a Jewish father and an Anglo southern mother. In her powerful essay, "Split at the Root: An Essay on Jewish Identity," Rich (1986) describes her embrace of a Jewish identity and heritage that her father had quite deliberately rejected both for himself and for his children. Her father's emotional absence is one of the dominant themes in Rich's descriptions of him. This absence is apparently the result of deliberate choice. Arnold Rich's mother came from a Sephardic family that, it appears, had already become highly assimilated in Vicksburg, Mississippi. His father, however, was an Ashkenazic immigrant from Austria-Hungary. Arnold Rich, himself a professor of pathology at Johns Hopkins University, was driven by a commitment to assimilation. Perhaps, like so many children of immigrants, he had come to see his father's home culture through the eyes of this new world, and so, having learned to be ashamed of it, did not wish to visit it on his children. Perhaps he thought more strategically, believing that taking on the traditions and manners of his father's home culture would only serve to set his daughter apart from the Gentile world in which he expected her, like him, to make her way. In any case, he does not even mention his father or his father's relatives. His Sephardic-Southern mother lives with them 6 months out of each year. However, she, Adrienne Rich says, "was a model of circumspect behavior . . . ladylike to an extreme," and "always tuned down to some WASP level [that] my father believed, surely, would protect us all" (p. 111). Rich comments, "If you did not effectively deny [your Jewish] family and community, there would always be a remote cousin claiming kinship with you who was the 'wrong kind' of Jew . . . uneducated, aggressive, loud" (p. 112).

To ensure that his daughter—and he himself—will be at home in the "tuned-down," genteel, Gentile public world, Adrienne Rich's father obscures the Jewish elements in his own upbringing and their natural expression in his day-to-day life. He cannot celebrate the High Holy Days or even acknowledge them in any fashion, however secularized. He cannot sing the songs, tell the jokes, or speak the languages he must have heard in his youth from his father or his father's relatives. He cannot reminisce about the stories he probably heard from his own father about his grandparents or other relatives. He cannot share the books or the wisdom that one imagines his father shared with him.

Emotional intimacy and attachment are characteristic and very powerful modes of the transmission of culture for the children of immigrants. For this reason, it is perhaps inevitable that to silence his Jewish heritage, Rich's father must silence himself. Perhaps it is only through the death of emotional intimacy with his daughter and his wife that he is able to suffocate the reproduction of his home culture in her life and the life of his household. Perhaps it is only through the effort to reconnect with the withheld culture that Rich can find an intimate emotional connection to the father, now deceased, in whose person it was withheld.[14]

The contrast between the modes of transmission of the home culture and of the dominant American culture for the children of immigrants is striking. The influence of the mass media is primary in the transmission of the dominant culture in the United States; and this influence is as impersonal as it is pervasive.

Eritrean children learn about Teletubbies from the television show, and Korean children learn about McDonald's from Ronald McDonald and the ubiquitous golden arches.

The culture that is transmitted by personal means is always altered, often in minute and unpredictable ways, by the personal character of its transmission. It is constantly reinterpreted by those who embody it and police it for one another and for their children. The transmission of culture by personal means is like a highly complex, multivoiced version of the children's party game of "Telephone," in which each hears in an intimate whisper the substance of what the other has learned from those who went before. The end result is always a humorous surprise, precisely because it is recognizably a transmogrification—a morph, although usually a barely coherent one—of the message with which the game began.

In contrast, the memories and impressions that enable mass culture to reproduce itself in the lives of immigrant communities are not idiosyncratic. They do not fade or get reinterpreted like personal memories. Instead, they are continually remanufactured, reproduced, and corrected in a uniform, mechanical (or electronic) way that is virtually impossible to duplicate through the everyday activities of ordinary people. This was Andy Warhol's great insight into the nature of mainstream American culture. In mass culture, although there is constant change, there is also a constant, dunning repetition of literally the same lessons. Moreover, the work of correcting misinterpretations and managing people's responses is almost automatic; consequently, our attachment to mass culture will in all probability lack the depth and emotional resonance of our attachments to a culture embodied primarily in the unique and idiosyncratic lives of those close to us.[15]

This simple tale of two cultures has several implications for the construction of culturally mixed identities.

For us, the children of immigrant parents, the struggle over who we are is almost always a personal one. To embrace the home culture is to embrace the people who embodied it for you. On the other hand, to be angry or ambivalent toward those people is inevitably to experience the home culture with anger and ambivalence as well.

For me as the child of a Nuyorican mother and Puerto Rican grandparents, for example, to embrace the culture and the heritage that my mother's family gave me is to embrace her and the experiences that her presence framed for me. The defining memories of *la cultura nuestra* (our culture) for me will always be listening to the *coquís* (tree frogs) from the screen door of my grandmother's house in Yauco, "*el pueblito de café*" (the town of coffee); encountering the sharp wit and the passionate, even melodramatic, gestures that accompanied the retelling of any event; smelling "*café y pan*" (coffee and bread) in the morning, with the underlying sweetness of heavily sugared, milky coffee; finding in a Miami schoolyard in the fall of 1963 that for the first time, I had peers who also spoke Spanish. When my mother died 16 years ago, I began to understand that if I continued to "pass," speaking only English and living (as best I could) as a member of the dominant culture—if I put aside all of these powerful and intimate memories, burying them as nothing more than fragments of the past—then I would have lost her truly and completely. My resolution to reclaim the heritage and the language of my childhood—to own the cultural identity embodied in my childhood memories, and to endow it with positive significance—is a reconfiguration of my determination to keep her alive in my life. My love for the Spanish language, my pride in being part of *La Raza*, and my devotion to its children and its future are thus reconfigurations of my love, pride, and devotion to my mother and to her Puerto Rican family.

Yet silence, ambivalence, and anger can constitute emotional attachments as powerful as love and respect. Richard Rodriguez' father is for him the living agent of *el machismo*, the traditional culture of the Mexican man who is, as the old *dicho* (saying) quoted by Rodriguez (1983, p. 128) has it, "*feo, fuerte y formál*" (rugged, strong, and reserved).[16] However, this understanding of who his father is takes a cruel twist for the young Rodriguez. When he is 7 or so, his parents accede to a request from his teachers that they speak only English at home. Suddenly deprived of the language in which intimacy has always been expressed, the child of 7 is "increasingly angry," "pushed away," "[his] throat twisted by unsounded grief":

> In an instant, they agreed to give up the language (the sounds) that had revealed and accentuated our family's closeness. The moment after the [teachers] left, the change was observed. '*Ahora*, speak to us *en inglés*,' my father and mother united to tell us. (Rodriguez, 1983, pp. 21-22)[17]

The hesitation and the silence that this reliance on an alien and poorly understood language introduced into a previously voluble and expressive household henceforth define much of his relationship to his father.[18] Yet despite the title of his extended and perceptive narrative, *Days of Obligation: An Argument With My Mexican Father*, even there we are given only glimpses of the elder Rodriguez, and we are left to infer the character of his son's relationship to him. Rodriguez is more forthcoming, however, in his expressions of contempt and hatred for the Mexico from which his father came. In one discussion of *machismo*, he says:

> In its male, in its public, in its city aspect, Mexico is an archtransvestite, a tragic buffoon. Dogs and babies cry when Mother

Mexico walks abroad in the light of day. The policeman, the Marxist mayor—Mother Mexico doesn't even bother to shave her mustachios. Swords and rifles and spurs and bags of money chink and clatter beneath her skirts. A chain of martyred priests dangles from her waist, for she is an austere, pious lady. Ay, how much—clutching her jangling bosoms; spilling cigars—how much she has suffered! (Rodriguez, 1992, p. 62)

If this is how he sees Mexico when it is figured as a man, then what is he to make of his own father's identity as a Mexican man, *el Mexicano, el macho*? On the one hand, Rodriguez himself is tied to this identity because of the power of the emotions that bind him so tightly to his father. Yet at the same time he himself is silenced in his discussion of his father, just as his father remains rugged, strong, and silent even with his own son. Even the betrayal of intimacy that occurred when the younger Rodriguez was 7—perhaps that most of all—cannot be discussed between father and son. The traditional identity by which they are both shaped in different ways, reinforced by the unnamed reality of that intimate betrayal that tore away the very language in which they could communicate intimacy, will not permit anything else between them. Perhaps it is the expressions of anger and resentment at this loss that are re-presented in his adult life as contempt and hatred for the culture that his father embodies, when that culture is imagined as a man. Perhaps it is such transmogrified anger and resentment that are expressed in Rodriguez' felt distance from the culture of his parents, his near-neurotic inability even to pronounce Spanish words correctly, let alone speak the language (Rodriguez, 1983 p. 23), and in his insistent opposition to bilingual education programs that might preserve the language of his childhood.

I suggest that for both Rodriguez and me, the depth and the character of our attachments to our home cultures—our identities as Chicano, *boricua*, Latino, *Mexicano*, Nuyorican—are a function of the emotional depth and the valence—positive or negative—that we find in our intimate relationships to those in whom this culture came alive for us: mother, father, grandmother, uncle, and aunt.

The culture so learned is characteristically idiosyncratic, and never exclusionary. This is the second implication of our tale of two cultures. The idiosyncratic nature of the newly reproduced immigrant culture is a consequence of the disruptive force of emigration. This is particularly true if the first immigrants live in small, fragmentary communities. Here the reproduction of the home culture may well take place *sans* the policing or homogenizing function exercised by larger, more well-entrenched versions of the home culture. What is typical among the few families in a small, struggling community may turn out to be quite different from what was typical back home. For instance, traditional public rituals that require churches, large groups of people, and the use of public space may be absent, and in their absence, children may grow up without a life that revolves around the religiosity that such rituals confirm. To take another example, "dating outside one's group" may be a much more viable option that it would ever have been "back home"; and the sense of identification with the romantic and marital values of one's parents may be correspondingly weakened.[19]

Furthermore, in a mass culture like this one, even in large, comparatively stable immigrant communities, the character of the home culture as it is reproduced here is suffused with the tensions and ambiguities of the ongoing negotiations between the new generation who is being taught the home culture, the older generation who is teaching it, and the dominant mass culture that now pervades all their lives.[20]

The transmission of culture from immigrants to their children is, of course, only one example of a tendency toward the chaotic and idiosyncratic that is characteristic of cultural reproduction during times of social, political, and economic upheaval. However, because change is the only constant, the character of a culture is almost constantly in flux. A culture is like a great river system. From its headwaters to the delta, there is not one major characteristic of the Amazon that does not vary as the river progresses: its rate of flow, its depth, its area, the habitats it forms, and the quantity and variety of life it sustains. Yet despite these profound transformations, it is always the Amazon.

This metaphor for cultural identity should also suggest the nonexclusionary character of the home culture as reproduced in the new world, for two such river systems will not always be discrete. In South Carolina, for example, the Ashley and the Cooper Rivers share a mouth, the Quiganonsett Bay; and yet they remain two different rivers, each with its own origin and path. In the same way, no child of immigrant parents—and particularly no child living within the larger mass culture of the United States—can possibly belong only to the home culture. Every child of the Americas is, like Levins Morales, Rich, Rodriguez, myself, and all the millions of other who grew up here in immigrant families, a child of many cultural streams at once. Almost all Puerto Rican Americans, for instance, are part of a living and continually evolving Puerto Rican culture. Thus, almost every Puerto Rican American is, culturally speaking, a Latino. At the same time, we are the latest in a long line of inheritors of the dominant, mass Anglo culture. Thus, we are Latino/as and we are also Anglos. We, the children of immigrants, are, perforce, the *Nuevos Mestizos*. We live in a newly mixed culture that is continuous with two distinct cultural traditions. We have two cultural identities; or rather one identity that is at once a recognizable morph of two very different cultural inheritances.[21]

The Nuevo Mestizaje is constantly threatened by assimilation. Here is the third implication of my prior remarks. I have stressed that the *Nuevo Mestizaje* is not simply the offspring of the coming together of two cultures. For this reason the metaphor of the two streams is too simple. To vary the metaphor, the gravitational field of the mass culture that surrounds us exerts a constant and powerful pull. Thus, to take only one example, which elements of our home cultures are most easily preserved in a mass culture depends in part on which elements are most easily commodified at this particular historical juncture. After all, it is much easier to teach children to celebrate *El Dia de los Muertos*[22] when it is front-page news in the "Style" section of the local paper every October and November. It is much easier to appreciate Frida Kahlo's self-martyrdom when it resonates so facilely, if falsely, with a self-obsessed, self-mutilating mass culture. We learn about ourselves through the eyes of others; and quick, power-ful lessons are learned when electronic eyes so tirelessly represent the saleable part of us to ourselves: We are creative, we are emotional; we are good gardeners, good dancers; our food has "zest" (that pallid English translation of "*sabor*"); we are loyal and family oriented. We are in constant danger of becoming nothing more than animated promos that sell CDs, Hallmark cards, and Pace Picante Sauce.

The danger is particularly acute, however, when what we represent in the mass market are the fears and anxieties of the dominant culture. When the electronic eyes reflect back to us images of drug dealers, gang-bangers, convicts, welfare mothers, lazy, dishonest workers, sex-crazed Romeos, and all the rest of the sorry litany of images of Latino/as that still fill the screens, we may too easily learn to become what we see, this time at great cost in human suffering.

These images are sadly familiar. They are simple variations of the dominant culture's entrenched and stereotyped portrayals of African American people. Thus, although this is not usually understood, they all invite one or another form of assimilation. After all, for us to assimilate is for us to come to define ourselves by some niche that is established for us by this New World in which we have come to labor and to live. We can assimilate by becoming white, or by becoming what the dominant culture represents as black, or by becoming Carmen Miranda and *salsa picante*. If we choose the third of these options, we find ourselves in danger of being engulfed by a mass culture that has been busily defining a place for people like us at least since the time of the Mexican-American War by making commodities out of caricatures of our culture. Perhaps the second of these options is even more obviously destructive; and the first may even seem innocuous by comparison. However, to vary the metaphor, all three describe forms of assimilation that herald the death of that branch of the home culture that was newly born here in America, and its reanimation as a zombie, a creature without a soul or will of its own.[23,24]

RACE AND CULTURE: RESISTANCE IS NOT FUTILE

The challenge of the *Nuevo Mestizaje* is the forging of a lived racial identity, the very terms of whose existence undercut the bipolar ideology of black and white. The key to meeting this challenge is to live out the conception of racial identity expressed in the rich, extended metaphor of the river. Thus, the new identity we negotiate in this new world must be, and represent itself as being, a part of several different streams, at once continuous with several distinct racialized identities. How does our discussion of the culture of immigrants help us do this?

Let us return to the story of how culture triumphed over phenotype in the case of the Irish. The lesson here for us Latino/as, as for so many immigrant groups in the last 150 years, is that we can cross the color line by crossing the culture line. If we become acculturated to being in the world as Anglos are, then for us as for Sicilians and Neapolitans, for example, our phenotype will be reinterpreted as a variant of white. Thus, the color of our skins need constitute a racial barrier for us to no greater an extent than it did for them.[25]

It follows that for us, as for other immigrant groups that were originally seen as racially distinct, our racial identity as either white or nonwhite rests on a complex series of choices and responses that we negotiate between the dominant culture and our home culture. Here the contrast with the position of black people in America is profound; for black people as such cannot become white. As elastic as the American notion of whiteness has been, it has always been anchored in one firm and invariant truth: To be white is not to be black.[26] Hence, no degree or variety of assimilation to Anglo culture can authorize the reinterpretation of black phenotypes as white.[27] Black people in the United States cannot do what the Irish, the Italians, and various other immigrant groups have done, namely transform their racial identity by altering their behavior and character. In fact, for black people the constant struggle to define their own racial identity is constituted in no small measure by the struggle not to become the stereotype, assimilating to the degrading and dehumanizing roles set aside by the dominant culture for those of African descent.

In short, our determined refusal as Latino/as to become white is the refusal to allow our home cultures to be drowned in the Ocean Sea of American mass culture.[28] This refusal constitutes a decision to set ourselves apart, to define our racial identity as distinct from that of white people in a way that the Irish and the Italians and various other immigrants to the United States chose not to do. This refusal positions us with African Americans, facing "a common struggle," to adapt DuBois' famous phrase: the struggle to resist assimilation to the stereotypes of black character and behavior, and instead to define our own racial identity.

This commonality of struggle with black people is more than just an alliance of disparate groups, however. Our mutual struggle to define ourselves against these stereotypes should remind us of the companion phrase that DuBois used: "a common history." It should remind us that our own history as Latino/as is as much the history of Africans in the new world as it is of the Spanish.[29] In the identity we define for ourselves here, therefore, we must not reproduce the characteristically Latin American misrepresentations, subordinations, and erasures of the African elements in our history and our culture.[30] Our double refusal to either become white or become the black stereotypes should thus serve to affirm our intimate relationship to African American peoples.

At the same time, this double refusal points to our potential to undermine America's racial ideology of black and white. We do this by living out a new, nonexclusionary conception of race that expresses the notion that a people can be real and legitimate descendants of several distinct, racialized cultural streams at one and the same time. This is the conception of race embodied in the metaphor of the river. Thus, I have said that we must refuse to become white, thereby losing all but a nostalgic connection to our home cultures, and alleging our cultural and racial distance from peoples of African descent. On the other hand, we must also affirm that we are indeed among the new and legitimate inheritors of Anglo culture. As we negotiate our relationships with the dominant culture, we become part of the stream that defines it. As DuBois (1989) said in *Souls of Black Folk*:

> I sit with Shakespeare and he winces not. Across the color line I move arm in arm with Balzac and Dumas. . . . I summon Aristotle and Aurelius and what soul I will, and they come all graciously with no scorn nor condescension.(p. 76)[31]

In the same way, I have said that we must refuse to become the stereotype by assimilating to the roles that Anglo culture defines for black (and Latino/a) people. However, we must at the same time acknow-ledge and embrace our status by birth, by culture, and by language as a part of the great stream of the African diaspora; and so our intimate relationship to the African dia-spora communities of the United States.

Finally, of course, we must weave these elements into an identity that is also a recognizable part of the Latino/a cultural stream. There is no one right way to live out a racial identity that is at once continuous with three distinct racialized streams. Nor is the prospect an easy one. Each of us must live out the challenge of weaving together multiple strands of identity in a world that always tries either to unravel them or to dye them all a single color. This is the site of the struggle and creative tension that Anzaldua (1987) describes so powerfully in *Borderlands/La Frontera*. Yet by living in this way, we embody a rejection of the idea of racial identities as mutually exclusive. By openly living out several racial identities at once, we can perhaps transform the character of each, so that black and white will no longer be mutually exclusive, polarized identities.

ELEMENTS OF SUCCESSFUL RESISTANCE

Perhaps this will sound less utopian if I close with some very brief remarks about the conditions required for successful resistance to assimilation in all its forms, with particular attention to the risks of commodification.

First, successful resistance to assimilation in all its forms requires recognizing the true nature of the conflict that defines our lives as *nuevos mestizos*. Our case is not the same as that of the Armenian refugees settling in early 20th-century Persia, for example, or the enslaved Yoruba brought to the Dahomey court in the early 19th century. The power of American mass culture to shape our understanding of ourselves, and thus our understanding of the cultures that we brought with us, is perhaps unequalled in human history. Bilingual education, Spanish-language newspapers, and our own foods will not suffice—although they may be necessary—to create a space in which we can nurture a genuinely new *mestizo* culture. We must also find ways to subvert mass culture or at least to shatter the flickering glamour it casts over us.

Second, given the nature of the conflict, the constant renewal of strong, positively valenced, personal and emotional attachments to our home culture is essential. After all, if it is through the depth of our positive emotional attachments that we children and grandchildren of immigrants acquired our commitments to the home culture, then it is surely through nurturing and expanding these attachments that we can strengthen and renew them. It is for this reason that to "forget where we came from" is the surest path toward assimilation in some form and thus toward being co-opted by bipolar ideology rather than resisting it.[32] Moreover, if our resistance is to have a real impact on the racist ideology that is America's own bipolar disorder, then we Latinos/as must also prize, valorize, and constantly renew strong personal and emotional attachments to African American communities. If we allow the pressure to become white to divide us from our African American kin, we will have come here only to repeat the betrayals of our own past. Race ideology in America can only be destroyed if Latino/as and others like us confront directly the question of whether to leave African American people behind in our struggles to define who we are.[33,34]

Third, successful resistance requires finding ways to sustain endlessly creative responses to the endlessly creative lust of mass culture for commodification. There is no element of any home culture, however sacred or intimate, that cannot be commodified. This means that whenever some element of our home culture calls attention to itself, for instance by being wielded as an instrument of resistance, it is immediately in danger of commodification. This is one disturbing aspect of the increasingly widespread use of traditional images of *la Virgen de Guadalupe* as *objets d'art* (e.g., alongside pastel colors and Georgia O'Keefe prints in mass-marketed southwestern home fashion). Successful resistance requires constant, vigilant reinvention of the symbols of resistance, in the present example, for instance, through the kinds of creative reworkings of the image of *la Virgencita* found in the work of many contemporary Chicana/o artists.

Finally, just as our resistance to assimilation and the racial ideology that informs it requires a new understanding of the fluidity of race, so also it requires a more subtle understanding of culture. To regard the changes in our traditions that are fomented by mass culture as a loss of authenticity is to misunderstand the nature of culture. There is no single form or morph of our culture that can claim to be more truly and essentially Latino/a than any other. Cultures are constantly altered by their interactions with each other.[35] Indeed, to all outward appearances, a culture sometimes disappears entirely, continuing only as a current beneath the surface, like the great westerly streams in the Atlantic that brought Columbus across the Ocean Sea from the coasts of Africa to the new world of the Caribbean. The prospect of our cultures being swallowed up by a mass culture that engulfs us from every side is indeed a horrifying one. However, the horror is not that the result would be something ersatz, a mere simulacrum that is somehow less truly Latino/a than what preceded it. Instead, what makes the prospect of being engulfed by mass culture so disturbing is the threat it represents to the autonomy of our culture. Cultural change has always proceeded by the endless elaboration of creative, individual responses to and interpretations of what has gone before. The evil of mass culture is that it straitjackets this creativity and dulls our individuality. This is what I meant by saying that our assimilation in any form would leave Latino/as in America only a zombie culture. It is precisely the fear that Latino/a/a culture will continue, its soul replaced by the animus of a dead racial ideology, that should mobilize our greatest and most noble efforts.

> The most beautiful word in
> the American language is
> Resist. (Tyler, 1994)

NOTES

1. A brief remark on methodology may be helpful. This chapter is certainly not written from a social-scientific perspective, as I think the reader will see very quickly. In many respects I am following in the footsteps of writers like Adrienne Rich and Richard Rodriguez, whom I quote fairly extensively. These writers address larger social and cultural issues indirectly, through autobiography and anecdote, as I have attempted to do. Naturally, my own training as a philosopher skews this attempt in what I hope are useful ways.

2. Loosely, "Those who aren't descended from the peoples of the Congo are descended from the Carabalí (a group from the Calabar Coast, in the south of Nigeria); and for he who claims he knows no such thing [about his own family], where are you hiding your grandmother?" (The shift from third person to second person is in the original Spanish.)

3. It is also important to note that historically notions of *mestizaje* have been shaped and deployed to underwrite highly repressive account of national identity, directing the marginalization or even the destruction of Latin American Indian peoples who would not or could not "mix in." This took place in Mexico, parts of Central America, and parts of South America as well. The reconstruction of the notion on which work like mine is based began with Gloria Anzaldua's appropriation of it in her well-known *Borderlands/La Frontera: The New Mestiza* (1987). It is in recognition of her pioneering work and its impact on this chapter that I adapt the phrase "The *Nuevo Mestizaje*" from her title.

4. One hand reaching forward (toward the future in the United States) and one hand reaching back (toward the past left behind in Cuba).

5. The climactic scene in the notorious *Turner Diaries* is one in which (a) all black, Asian, and Latino people are removed from the newly established white territory (their fate unspecified); (b) all white people who "collaborated" with people of color (e.g., by doing business with them or sleeping with them) are lynched; and (c) all the offspring of mixed-race sexual liaisons are lynched as well. It is Point c that reveals how strong the fear of race mixing continues to be, at least in the darker recesses of the dominant culture. Even if one accepts, for the sake of argument, that the races should be separated and that cross-race liaisons are immoral, the offspring of such a liaison obviously have done nothing immoral. Yet their punishment, described in explicit detail, is far harsher than

that of the group described in Point a, the other group who has done nothing presumed immoral. They must be eradicated, the very fact of race mixing blotted out (McDonald, 1996). What is perhaps most disturbing about this scenario is its historical continuity with Thomas Jefferson's 1778 proposed criminal code for the Commonwealth of Virginia, in which he proposes that it be illegal for free Negroes to enter the state, and that emancipated Negroes be required to leave within 1 year of their emancipation. The code also proposes that any white woman having a child by a Negro would be required to leave the state within 1 year. The historian William Cohen comments that "the individual who violated these regulations would be placed '*out of the protection of the laws*.'" [italics added] (O'Brien, 1996). Nor is the fear of miscegenation all a matter of history and fiction. During the week of March 12, 1999, CNN's Web service announced that the Alabama state legislature was considering a bill to repeal its antimiscegenation law. Some legislators were optimistic about its prospects for passage although State Representative Phil Crigler was quoted as saying that he was personally opposed to interracial marriage and that the bill was just "racial grandstanding." The bill did not pass, and a similar bill died in committee the subsequent year. Alabama finally repealed its antimiscegenation law by referendum in November 2000, by a vote of 60% to 40%. South Carolina repealed its antimiscegenation law by referendum in November 1998. Such laws were declared unconstitutional by the U.S. Supreme Court in *Loving v. Virginia*, 388 U.S. 1 (1967).

6. See Noel Ignatiev's well-known book, *How the Irish Became White* (1996), especially his analysis of how the contestation of the category of whiteness was played out on the field of labor politics in the second half of the 19th century. Even American Indians can become white, as is suggested, for example, by the definition of "white" in the Virginia miscegenation statue contested in the *Loving* case. Needless to say, there is only one group that as a group can never ever "cross over" the color line in the United States, namely, African Americans. See discussion on p. 185.

7. However, for various economic and political reasons the process of whitening may be much more prolonged and painful, at least for some groups of Latino/as, than it ever was for earlier immigrant groups.

8. The *locus classicus* for the elaboration and defense of this thesis is Michael Omi and Howard Winant (1986).

9. I return to the third assumption later.

10. There are still interesting traces of racism against the Irish to be found in American culture. For example, in the film "The Great White Hype" (Hudlin, 1996), Irish Terry Conklin's trainer is an English fellow who says of Conklin, "You are the Great White Hope—well, you're Irish, so you're almost white." He also defends himself against Conklin's accusations of racism by saying, "I'm not racist! I'm English, and I'm training you even though you're Irish!" (The trainer is played by John Rhys-Davies, who is, in fact, Welsh; and the running joke in the film is that the Conklin character, played by Peter Berg, is, in fact, not Irish. Hudlin, the director of the film, is African American.)

11. The period cartoons Ignatiev includes in his book juxtapose Irish immigrants and black Americans in contrasting dress but in parallel poses and similar facial expressions.

12. Reflection on the extraordinary fact that, for example, southern Italians are now regarded as white whereas most Puerto Ricans are not should dissuade us from the temptation to think that there is some objective scale of phenotypic similarity and that only groups that are close enough on that scale to English or northern European immigrants can deploy the strategy of cultural assimilation to

become white. Many southern Italians are darker than many African Americans and Puerto Ricans, and yet the former have become white and the latter in the first instance cannot and in the second instance have not, at least thus far. In the same way, although it is always risky to speculate about shifts in racial categories that are still in progress, I think it is fairly likely that East Indians and Japanese Americans are well on their way to becoming white, although it is difficult to imagine any scale of phenotypic similarity that would strike most Americans today as objective on which these groups were more similar to the English than, for example, most Puerto Ricans are. In this connection there is an interesting history yet to be written regarding groups like the Pashtun in Pakistan and Afghanistan, the Tutsi in Rwanda, and the descendents of the Mogul conquerors in northern India and Pakistan, all of whom have been told by European colonizers at one point or another that they were racially more closely related to white Europeans than their equally dark-skinned neighbors.

13.   It is an important and difficult task to distinguish genuine emotional attachment from mere nostalgia of the sort that attends St. Patrick's Day celebrations, and also from political commitment, both of which can be present without strong emotional attachment. I will not attempt to spell out these distinctions here. It is worth noting, however, that real emotional attachment is characteristically particular, whereas nostalgia can be entirely general.

14.   On the other hand, it is possible that the dynamic I describe had already evolved in the relationship between Arnold Rich and his father, and that the former was merely reproducing it in his relationship with Adrienne Rich. This would change the story I have interpolated, although it would not affect the point.

15.   This is not to deny the power and the importance of personal means of transmission within the dominant American culture. The point is certainly not to romanticize immigrant cultures, nor to criticize Anglo-American culture as such. However, to the extent that Anglo-American culture has been transformed—not to say hijacked—by mass forms of cultural transmission, and that personal means of transmission characterize not just immigrant cultures but perhaps many of our home cultures as well, Anglo-American culture has become profoundly corrupted and corrupting. One poignant cultural lesson of globalization is that this corruption is a powerful and infectious agent. But see footnote 32 and the attendant discussion.

16.   Compare his *Days of Obligation: An Argument With My Mexican Father* (New York: Penguin Books, 1992), p. 56.

17.   "Now, speak to us in English"(Rodriguez, 1983, pp. 21-22). The passive voice in the penultimate sentence of this quotation serves to emphasize the experience of alienation. Rodriguez' later insistence that "intimacy was not stilled by English" (p. 32) seems unconvincing.

18.   Compare his description of his father's descent into near-complete silence after the switch to the use of English at home (Rodriguez, 1983, pp. 24-25); and his remarks about the silence of his father regarding private emotional matters, even at home with the family (p. 185).

19.   Interestingly, practically the only two topics of discussion on Web sites run by and for Armenian American high school and college students are the Armenian Genocide and the appropriateness of romantic relationships with *odars* (those who are not of Armenian descent).

20.   These negotiations will proceed quite differently depending on the reasons for the first generation's having come here to begin with. For parents who came to the United States from a small town in Japan, for example, eager to leave behind a place where "the nail that sticks up must be hammered down," the newly negotiated version of the home culture may be far more heavily influenced by American individualism than the culture back home would have been.

21.   This extended metaphor should also reinforce the insight that the newly minted culture created by immigrants is no less authentically Puerto Rican, Mexican, Ashkenazic, and so on, than the home culture it reproduces. Just as there is no one part of the Amazon River system that is more truly or authentically the Amazon than any other, so cultural authenticity is not a matter of fidelity to some preestablished cultural paradigm. Instead, cultural authenticity is a matter of causal continuity coupled with sufficient and persistent similarities. As I have implied earlier in the discussion of Adrienne Rich, one might say that each stage of a culture's history must always be a recognizable morph of the previous stages. It follows that no one group can ever claim a monopoly on the ownership of a culture, whether it be middle-class Mexicans in the D.F. (Mexico City) looking contemptuously on Mexican Indians, white Cubans in Miami speaking disdainfully of the *Marielitos* (poor and working-class Cubans, mostly of color, who arrived in the United States during the Mariel boatlift, April–September 1980), or Mexicans calling their Chicana/o cousins *pochos* (a contemptuous term for Mexican Americans who do not speak Spanish well). I return to this point briefly at the conclusion of this chapter.

22.   "The Day of the Dead" is a traditional religious celebration that takes place on November 2 in certain parts of Mexico.

23.   *Merriam-Webster's Collegiate Dictionary* gives as its entry for "zombie" the following: "Etymology: Louisiana Creole or Haitian Creole *zōbi*, of Bantu origin; akin to *Kimbundu nzúmbe*, [which is apparently a Bantu phrase for] 'ghost.' 1871. 1. Usually zombi. (a) the supernatural power that according to voodoo belief may enter into and reanimate a dead body; (b) a will-less and speechless human in the West Indies capable only of automatic movement who is held to have died and been supernaturally reanimated."

24.   As the influence of mass culture becomes more and more global, the conflicts between home cultures and mass cultures will be played out for those who stay behind perhaps as much as for those who emigrate to the United States. Thus, as mass culture seeks to master and subjugate the Other through commodification, the result of this conflict may be the zombification of newborn *mestizo* cultures throughout the world.

25.   I have spoken to Italian Americans whose grandparents were put into segregated classrooms with black students in New York City when they first arrived in this country.

26.   It is important not to confuse becoming white with passing. The latter is a kind of masquerade, albeit a very serious one. It involves concealing facts about origin and perhaps phenotype as well (e.g., by hair straightening and skin lightening). Becoming white, in contrast, involves a genuine alteration in racial identity, and a consequent reinterpretation of one's phenotype—and indeed of the racial significance of one's place of origin—as legitimate forms of whiteness.

27.   The exact relationship between phenotype and racial identity is a complex matter. See my "Radical Race: Redefining Our Conception of Race" (Velazco y Trianosky, 2002).

28.   "The Ocean Sea" was the pre-Columbian European name for the mythical great ocean that surrounded the conjoined land mass of Europe, Africa, and Asia.

29.   To take only one lesser-known but dramatic example, the famous anthropologist Gonzalo Aguirre Beltrán claims that the number of Africans brought to Mexico during three centuries of colonization was, in fact, somewhat greater than the number of Spaniards who immigrated to Mexico during that same period (see Beltrán, 1948-1949).

30.   A great deal of work has been done on the African presence in Latin America. In addition to Aguirre Beltrán's work on Mexico, two helpful studies are

Claudio Esteva-Fabregat's *Mestizaje in Ibero-America* (1995) and Richard D. E. Burton's *Afro-Creole: Power, Opposition and Play in the Caribbean* (1997). There is also an excellent bibliography of scholarly work to be found on the African presence in Mexico at www.afromexico.com.

31.   I do not mean to imply that DuBois would share my epistemological assumptions here.

32.   Ironically, we can often resist the globalization of mass culture by means of the globalization of "personal technologies" (i.e., technologies that enable personal contacts that previously would have been impossible or very difficult: cars, plane flights, telephones, modern postal systems and perhaps even e-mail).

33.   I do not mention the issue of our political commitments to black communities, although these are obviously very important as well. That is a topic for another publication.

34.   This raises the question of what the relationships might be between our newly forged racial identity and that of other groups in the United States, including both American Indians as well as more recent immigrants from various parts of Asia and other places in the world. To answer this important question is beyond the scope of this chapter, but perhaps it will suffice here to note two things. First, virtually all these other groups have been and continue to be part of Latin America as well and so may well be part of the great stream of Latino/a history that grounds our identity. This is dramatically clear in the case of indigenous peoples, of course. However, one also thinks of the Koreans involved in the garment trade in Central America, for example, or the Japanese communities in Peru. Second—and were it not for the inflammatory nature of race ideology in the United States this might go without saying—we can and should live on terms of affection, intimacy, and respect with peoples of other races, even if, in fact, our history and theirs somehow happen not to intersect in any significant way.

35.   This is a point that Richard Rodriguez has made particularly eloquently in his testimony before the Penn Commission, June 12, 1997. See the transcript at the Penn Commission's Web site: http://www.upenn.edu/pnc/.

REFERENCES

Anzaldua, G. (1987). *Borderlands/La Frontera: The new mestiza*. San Francisco: Spinster/Aunt Lute Books.

Ball, E. (1998). *Slaves in the family*. New York: Farrar, Strauss, & Giroux.

Beltrán, G. A. (1948-1949) Los Negros en Mexico [Blacks in Mexico]. Retrieved August 8, 2002, from www.folklorico.com/peoples/negros.html

Burton, R. D. E. (1997). *Afro-Creole: Power, opposition and play in the Caribbean*. Ithaca, NY: Cornell University Press.

DuBois, W. E. B. (1989). Of the training of black men. In W. E. B. DuBois (Ed.), *Souls of black folk* (p. 76). New York: Bantam Books.

Esteva-Fabregat, C. (1995). *Mestizaje in Ibero-America*. Tucson: University of Arizona Press.

Gordon-Reed, A. (1998). *Thomas Jefferson and Sally Hemings: An American controversy*. Charlottesville: University Press of Virginia.

Hudlin, R. (Director). (1996). *The great white hope*. Los Angeles: Twentieth-Century Fox.

Ignatiev, N. (1996). *How the Irish became white*. London: Routledge.

McDonald, A. (1996). *Turner diaries: A novel*. Fort Lee, NJ: Barricade Books.

Morales, A. L. (1990). *Getting home alive*. Milford, CT: Firebrand Books.

National Advisory Commission on Civil Disorders. (1968). *Report of the National Advisory Commission on Civil Disorders*. New York: Bantam Books.

O'Brien, C. C. (1996). Thomas Jefferson: Radical and racist. *Atlantic Monthly, 278,* 53-74.

Omi, M., & Winant, H. (1986). *Racial formation in the United States: From the 1960s to the 1980s*. New York: Routledge.

Piper, A. M. S. (1992). Passing for white, passing for black. *Transition, 58,* 4-32.

Rich, A. (1986). Split at the root: An essay on Jewish identity. In A. Rich (Ed.), *Blood, bread, and poetry* (pp. 100-123). New York: W. W. Norton.

Rodriguez, R. (1983). *Hunger of memory: The education of Richard Rodriguez*. New York: Bantam Books.

Rodriguez, R. (1992). *Days of obligation: An argument with my Mexican father*. New York: Penguin Books.

Schwarz, B. (1997). What Jefferson helps to explain. *Atlantic Monthly, 279,* 60-72.

Tyler, M. (1994). The most beautiful word in the American language. In M. Algarín & B. Holman (Eds.), *Aloud! Voices from the Nuyorican Poets' Café*. New York: Owlet Books.

Velazco y Trianosky, G. (2002). *Radical race: Redefining our conception of race*. Unpublished manuscript, available from the author.

CHAPTER 11

Colonization, Cultural Imperialism, and the Social Construction of American Indian Mixed-Blood Identity

Karren Baird-Olson

California State University, Northridge

> *By 1830 at the latest, the notion of defining "Indianness" in terms of race had been rendered patently absurd. It has been reliably estimated that something approaching half of all Native people still residing east of the Mississippi River were at that point genetically intermixed not only with one another, but with "Negroid and Caucasoid racial stock," a demographic pattern which would spread rapidly westward over the next half-century. There is little if any indication, moreover, that most indigenous societies viewed this increasing admixture as untoward or peculiar, much less threatening, in and of itself (this is as opposed to their often bitter resistance to the cultural, political, and material encroachments of Euro-American "civilization").*
>
> — Ward Churchill (1999, p. 43)

Governmental recording of blood quantum to determine American Indian identity is the product of a racialized political and legal system. The use of fractions of blood degree as the primary means of categorizing social groups was legally recognized as early as 1705 and later supported by scientifically racist theories and the ongoing hegemonic strategy designed to create the illusion that American Indians[1] "vanish" when their White or other non-Indian blood quantum reaches a certain level, typically considered to be three fourths. Today, this technique is called statistical genocide.

The fate of the offspring of widespread First Nation miscegenation has been a matter of concern since the colonizers of the 1400s and 1500s came into the lands of the indigenous peoples of the Northeast, Southeast, and Southwest. Initially, although both First Nations and Europeans sought political marriages to protect economic and political interests, the invaders and colonizers racialized ideologies created a social issue: What would be the fate of "mixed-blood" offspring? In contrast, traditional American Indian nations did not view the fate of the children of their members and the Europeans as being problematic because First Nations determined membership by family lineage, marriage, adoption, or naturalization (obtained through long-term membership and commitment to the various communities).

Today many Indians are not fully aware, and most non-Indians have no idea of the personal and cultural implications resulting from the use of blood degree to determine ethnic group membership. Buying into dominant culture materialism and internalizing racialized thinking, an important number of First Peoples continue to play a role in their own potential vanishment. Not only is individual identity at stake, but this form of fratricide also contributes to the loss of traditional cultural values and practices, the erosion of sovereignty, and the diminishment of the remaining land. Contemporary Native America in the United States covers 4% of the land" (LaDuke, 1999, p. 2).

In this position chapter, I first address the role of language in reflecting the importance of a social issue. After refuting the myth of widespread American Indian racial purity, I then examine the confusion resulting from six historical and contemporary definitions of American Indian identity and theories of the etiology of racialized thinking leading to the exclusion of mixed bloods as well as the personal, cultural, and national consequences of denying multiethnic First Peoples. I conclude with a discussion of alternative choices needed to regain culturally relevant First People identity and to preserve national sovereignty. Traditional criteria used to determine American Indian identity, including the wisdom of considering the well-being of seven future generations, thus resurrecting the traditional meaning of membership in First People nations, could refute multiracial critic Rainer Spencer's claim "that advocates of multiracialism never challenge, destabilize or move outside the American racial paradigm, but instead always operate comfortably within its confines" (Spencer, 1999, p. 89). Although Spencer's treatment of the American Indian multiracial experience is far from adequate and even inaccurate at times, his call for deracializing human categories, as will be seen, is valid, and his discussion of the danger of conflating race and culture insightful and important.

STICKS AND STONES: WHAT'S IN A NAME?

The statement that language reflects the importance of a social concept or social issue is a truism that is graphically illustrated in the study of American Indian identity. Just as the Alaska indigenous have many words to describe snow in all of its forms, so are there many English words for the descendants of First Peoples and non-Indians. As early as the 1500s, the terms *breed*, *half breed*, and *mixed blood* appeared in historical records to describe the descendants of Indians and the newcomers to the American continent.[2] A

Box 11.1   Mixed-Blood English Labels

mixed blood	mixed ancestry
half breed	Other race
breed	blended race
Metis	bipolar Indians
part Indian	multiracial identity
Black Indian	multiethnic identity
mulatto	ethnically diverse
Creoles	racially diverse
landless Indians	multiheritage
some Indian	modern mixed blood
hidden ancestor Indian	urban Indian
cross-bloods	urban multitribalism
cross-racial	Pan Indian
biracial	supratribal
racially mixed	multicultural
mixed children	postmodern tribal blood
mixed race	Cablinasian
mixed identity	

---

review of academic and lay literature reveals 36 English language labels used to describe the descendants of the colonizers and the indigenous of the Americas. Box 11.1 lists the names arranged in approximate chronological order from the earliest to the most recent. Six of the 36 terms have reached the status of proper nouns as indicated by the initial capital letters. The list would be greatly extended if all of the numerous Spanish words for the offspring of the conquistadores were included.

All share the common theme of racialized meanings. Some are used both for American Indian mixed bloods and in a more general sense. Depending on the social contexts in which the labels are used, most have potentially negative connotations. For instance, *bipolar* implies mental illness.

For the purposes of this chapter, the label *mixed blood* is used most often, given its widespread lay usage; however, a number of the other labels will be used at times as synonyms for all of the various ethnic/national combinations of the descendants of European American "sanctified" unions with American Indians, non-"sanctified" relationships between Indians and non-Indians, and sexual assault against Indian women by non-Indian males.

As is discussed in the next section, in the 2000 U.S. Census 1,643, 345 American Indians reported descent from two or more races. At the beginning of the 21st century, at least 40% of American Indians are mixed blood.

Counting Indians

Widespread American Indian racial purity is a myth given the age-old tradition of intertribal marital unions and more than 400 years of contact with non-Indians and the consequent high numbers of exogenous relationships.

When the first wave of European settlers came to the Americas in the early 1600s, the best population estimation is that at least 18 million Indians lived in North America (Snipp, 1996). Although traditional American Indians comfortably accepted the offspring of the Europeans and their own peoples, Europeans as a rule were not as comfortable forcing American Indians of multiple ancestry to "choose up sides." By 1900 the official count for American Indians in the United States was 237,196 (Snipp, 1989). This low count was due to not only genocide and disease but also to the very real physical and social dangers of acknowledging one's Indian ancestry.

Regardless of ongoing social stigma, particularly in Indian Country,[3] by the late 1980s demographic findings supported the lay observation that the rate of racial intermarriage for American Indians was not only very high but also the highest of all American racial categories. Less than half of American Indians married other Indians, whereas Whites, Blacks, and Asians had racial endogamy rates of 95% and higher (Sandefur & McKinnell, 1986; Snipp, 1989; Thornton, Sandefur, & Snipp, 1991).

In addition, Snipp (1989) argues that urban Indians have been far more likely to intermarry with other racial ethnic groups. Although Snipp does not fully explain this marriage pattern other than to focus on migration patterns, the high rates of urban outmarriage can be attributed to American Indian retention of traditional inclusive values that recognize the relationship of all human beings, romantic ideas of certain groups of urban non-Indians about First Peoples, and a limited marriage pool of eligible American Indians in urban areas. However, since the 1970s, recognizing the cultural and political dangers of nontribal marriages, a growing number of both urban and reservation Indians talk about the need for more endogamous marriages, albeit

not yet acting in significant numbers on the realization.

When the 1990 Census was conducted, 1,878,284 people were identified as American Indian and, given the high intermarriage rates, there was no reason not to hypothesize that a considerable number of First Peoples were of mixed blood or mixed-race descent. During the last decade of the 20th century, interest as well as concern about the fate of multiethnic American Indians paralleled the growing attention to other multicultural or multiheritage groups throughout the United States. The important exception to this parallel is a growing awareness of the relationship between identity and the maintenance of American Indian sovereignty.

The various fears of academic and "racial minority activists" about including mixed-race categories in the 2000 Census are reflected in the following observation by multiracial critic Ranier Spencer in his 1999 book *Spurious Issues: Race and Multiracial Identity Politics in the United States*:

> My opposition to a federal multiracial category is explicitly based on the damage such a category would do to civil rights compliance monitoring and on the way it would validate race concept and not on some notion of the loss of Afro-American members or political power. (Spencer, 1999, pp. 191-192)

In addition to problematic caveats, given sovereignty status and other legal precedence, about the potential danger of erosion of civil rights compliance that mixed-race categories would create for American Indians, social observers underestimated population growth for American Indians. Exceeding population predictions, the 2000 U. S. Census revealed an unexpected growth for American Indians and Alaska Natives. American Indians who identified as only one race numbered 2,475,956, or 0.9%, of the total U.S. population (up from

0.7% in 1980, which did not make mixed-blood distinction and 1% higher than 1999 projections). As is noted in Table 11.1, American Indian and Alaska Native multiple-race combinations, American Indian and Alaska Native alone or in combination with another race or other races number 4, 119,301, or 1.5%, of the total 2000 U.S. population. Multiracial American Indians and Alaska natives who did not self-identify as indigenous alone for the Census number 1,643, 345, a count that is significantly lower than the estimated 20 to 30 million persons who probably have Indian ancestry (Forbes, 1998, p. 120). Undoubtedly, this multiple-race undercount was largely facilitated by widespread political activism throughout Indian Country warning people of potential resource allocation problems that could result from self-identifying in more than one race category.

American Indians who indicated both Indian and another race ancestry such as African American, Asian, Native Hawaiian and Other Pacific Islander, or some other race in the 2000 U.S. Census made up 22.3% of the two-race category. American Indian combinations with other racial groups were 46.3% of the total U.S. three-race category, 66.6% of the four-race category, and 95.6% of the five-race category. American Indians were one of the groups included in the six-race category of 823 respondents.

More specifically, descendants of White, American Indian, and Alaska Natives unions made up 15.9% of the U.S. population of two or more races. Descendants of Black or African American and American Indian and Alaska Native unions made up 2.7% of the total U.S. population of two or more races. Descendants of First Peoples and African Americans made up 20.3%, or one of five, of the total American Indian and Native Alaska multiple-race categories.

Identification as indigenous is shaped by multiple social forces. I now review six definitions of identity: biological and phenotypical; self-reflection and personal identification; geography and place; community and culture; ancestry and family descent; and legal definitions.

A Matter of Definition

Ethnic groups are actively involved in the construction and reconstruction of identities, *negotiating boundaries, asserting meanings, interpreting their own pasts, resisting the imposition of the present, and claiming the future* [italics added]. Neither actions nor circumstances alone create groups, for our actions depend on how we interpret circumstances, and circumstances ultimately are the products of human actions. Identities are created, elaborated and re-created in the interaction between the two. (Cornell & Hartman, 1998, p. 101)

Many mixed-bloods have feared asserting their Native identity . . . many were forced to "become" white or black by forgetting about being Native . . . today many of the same mixed-bloods have children and grandchildren to claim *all* of who they are . . . to claim something greater than color . . . they claim culture . . . they claim a new and stronger community. (Jolivette, 2000, p. 21)

"I am Indian because I know what it is to be Indian: the protocols, the jokes, the knowledge of shared history, the racism and struggle that are a part of who we are. Trying to identify me as a number is fucked." (Lobo, 2001, p. 81)

The concept of race is a social construction. In other words, race is defined and shaped by reigning ideologies and powerful actors within a specific social context (Cohen, 1998). Research in biology and other sciences has demonstrated that more physical variation exists within racial groups than between them. Nowhere is this more clearly seen than when a universal definition of Indian is

Table 11.1   American Indian and Alaska Native Multiple-Race Combinations[a]

Two Races		% of 2 Races
White; American Indian and Alaska Native	1,082,683	17.0
Black or African American: American Indian and Alaska Native	182,494	2.9
American Indian and Alaska Native; Asian	52,429	0.8
American Indian and Alaska Native; Native Hawaiian and Other Pacific Islander	7,328	0.1
American Indian and Alaska Native; Some Other Race	93,842	1.5
TOTAL	1,418,776	22.3

Three Races		% of 3 Races
White, Black, or African American, American Indian or Alaska Native	112, 202	27.3
White; American Indian and Alaska Native; Asian	23,766	5.8
White; American Indian and Alaska Native; Native Hawaiian and Other Pacific Islander	4,843	1.2
White; American Indian and Alaska Native; Some Other Race	29,095	7.1
Black or African American; American Indian and Alaska Native; Asian	5,798	1.4
Black or African American; American Indian and Alaska Native; Native Hawaiian and Other Pacific Islander	998	0.2
Black or African American; American Indian and Alaska Native; Some Other Race	7,023	1.7
American Indian and Alaska Native; Asian; Native Hawaiian and other Pacific Islander	3,063	0.8
American Indian and Alaska Native; Asian; Some Other Race	2,544	0.6
American Indian and Alaska Native; Native Hawaiian and Other Pacific, Islander; Some Other Race	586	0.1
TOTAL	189,923	46.3

Four Races		% of 4 Races
White; Black or African American; American Indian and Alaska Native; Asian	10,672	27.8
White; Black or African American; American Indian and Alaska Native; Native Hawaiian and Other Pacific Islander	988	2.6
White; Black or African American; American Indian and Alaska Native; Some Other Race	4,645	12.1
White; American Indian and Alaska Native; Asian; Native Hawaiian and Other Pacific Islander	6,450	16.8
White; American Indian and Alaska Native; Asian; Some Other Race	1,099	2.9
White; American Indian and Alaska Native; Native Hawaiian and Other Pacific Islander; Some Other Race	309	0.8
Black or African American; American Indian and Alaska Native; Native; Asian; Native Hawaiian and Other Pacific Islander	750	1.0
Black or African American; American Indian and Alaska Native Asian; Some Other Race	334	0.9

(Continued)

Table 11. 1 *(continued)*

Black or African American; American Indian and Alaska Native; Native Hawaiian and Other Pacific Islander; Some Other Race	111	0.3
American Indian and Alaska Native; Asian; Native Hawaiian and Other Pacific Islander; Some Other Race	207	0.5
TOTAL	25,565	66.6
Five Races		*% of 5 Races*
White; Black or African American; American Indian and Alaska Native; Asian; Native Hawaiian and Other Pacific Islander	6,611	80.0
White; Black or African American; American Indian and Alaska Native; Asian; Some Other Race	724	8.8
White; Black or African American; American Indian and Alaska Native; Native Hawaiian and Other Pacific Islander; Some Other Race	68	0.8
White; American Indian and Alaska Native; Asian; Native Hawaiian and Other Pacific Islander; Some Other Race	639	7.7
Black or African American; American Indian and Alaska Native; Asian; Native Hawaiian and Other Pacific Islander; Some Other Race	216	2.6
TOTAL	8,258	95.6
Six Races		*% of 6 Races*
White; Black or African American; American Indian and Alaska Native; Asian; Native Hawaiian and Other Pacific Islander; Some Other Race	823	100.0
Grand Total	1,643,345	40.0%

SOURCE: Adapted from Grieco and Cassidy (2001).
[a] Rounded percentages.

sought. One dimensional images of Indian often take three forms: Indian princess, who, of course, marries a White male savior; warrior, particularly the Plains Indian image; and the offensive sports mascots, blatantly presented as a tribute to the Indian warrior stereotype. In reality, there is wide variability in criteria, standards of proof of Indian ancestry, and "Indianness."

During the last three decades, "AIM identity police" as well as other "Purity Police" (Churchill, 1999, p. 53) have appeared, violating traditional cultural criteria for group membership as well as supporting the colonizer's bureaucratic "identity policy." Sadly, as anyone who has spent any thoughtful time in Indian communities knows, often the most fanatical of the Purity Police have little else going for themselves but to play "Indian" in certain places and social circles. On a more macrolevel of analysis, an honest analysis of politics in Indian Country will acknowledge that the "who is more Indian" game not only contributes to internal divisions within indigenous communities but also provides American Indian pawns used in ongoing genocidal practices for those interested in controlling the assets of First Peoples.

Biological Determinism and Phenotypical Characteristics

The view of American Indians as "primitive" and culturally "pure" derives from early anthropologists who attempted to salvage Indian cultures and ways of life through photographs and detailed ethnography that portrayed Indians in a primitive state untouched by civilization. These characteristics and images have created an ideal type of American Indian against which Indian tribes and peoples are today compared, and any deviation from this is seen as evidence of cultural assimilation and/or biological amalgamation. (Gonzales, 1998, p. 218)

"What does Indian look like?" "Funny, you don't look like one." "Are you an authentic Indian?" (Taylor, 1996)

The static, racialized phenotypical image of American Indian is refuted in Figure 11.1. In the picture taken in July 2001 on a northwestern Plains Indians reservation, identify (1) those who are federally enrolled tribal members, (2) those who are of American Indian descent, (3) those who have limited tribal enrollment status, and (4) those who are not of American Indian descent (answers follow the references at the end of this chapter.) Only 3 of the 18 family members and friends are non-Indian. Of the 15 group members of American Indian descent, 8 are enrolled and 1 has limited enrollment status. The remaining 6, two fifths of the American Indians in the picture, are not federally recognized. For instance, two of the children are Assiniboine, Blackfeet, Lakota, and Wyandot, yet they are not federally enrolled.

In addition, consider the "new" faces of five well-known public figures of multiple-race descent, including American Indian heritage: Tiger Woods, Ben Nighthorse, Lou Diamond Phillips, Johnny Cash, and Cher. Furthermore, a significant number of local and national First People leaders, bridge leaders, and spokespersons, including American Indian movement (AIM) activists, are mixed bloods. A careful social observer is challenged to identify a definite phenotypical image of "full blood" and most certainly that of "mixed blood." Thus, using phenotypical characteristics as the primary indi-cator of American Indian typically results in erroneous identification, revealing the absurdities of phenotypical characteristics as a primary means of ascertaining American Indian lineage.

In addition to being subjected to stereotypical phenotypical images of what "pure" and mixed-blood" American Indians are supposed to look like, more recently American Indians of both one-race and multiple-race descent have been challenged by racialized and sexualized claims by social observers. For example, Springwood and King (2000) continue to play the "who-had/has-it-the-worse" game by claiming that Blacks have been more hypersexualized than Indians.

Although imperialist nostalgia for the Indian centered on courage, a sexualized wildness, bellicosity, and warring aggression, a particular nostalgia also emerged surrounding black Americans. Although these white discourses of racialized longing overlapped in some ways in the white imagination—for example, both the black and Indian body were hypersexualized—blackness arguably was ever more "grotesque" and polluting than was Indianness. (p. 169)

After examining 19th- and 20th-century representations of blackness as clown, physically distorted size, dirty, and so on, the

Figure 11.1   A Photograph of an American Indian Extended Family and Friends, 2001

authors conclude that the "darker" a person is, the greater is the stigma. Although a discussion of the relationship of color to hypersexualization is needed, unfortunately, Springwood and King are not adequately familiar with historical and contemporary media representation and lay images of First Peoples. Particularly in Indian country, mixed-blood status is even lower than "full bloods" (see later discussion of Davis's rules of status). In addition, Springwood and King are apparently not aware of the extensive harm perpetrated on both mixed bloods and full bloods not only by the savage warrior and drunken Indian stereotypes but also by the seemingly benign one-dimensional Hiawatha, noble warrior, and other reductive romanticized images.

Springwood and King do acknowledge the racialized images of mascots, yet they need to do better homework regarding American Indian images on the various frontiers of westward expansion and in Indian country today before making such a broad comparative claim about the relationship of hypersexualization to the degree of color. For instance, a significant number of AIM members have been and are mixed blood, a group of men and women, especially those who are non-Christian, who are often much feared and reviled in Indian Country and certain urban centers. This distrust of AIM leaders such as Leonard Peltier and Russell Means as well as less-known mixed bloods refutes misinformed claims that mixed blood Indians are not adequately "courageous, sexually wild" (Springwood & King, 2000) to be perceived as a serious threat.

Self-Reflection and Personal Identification

Many unenrolled people who claim Indian descent do not have exploitation on their minds; they are the victims of racist policies ... *It still remains to be explained how people who value family so dearly rationalize tribal enrollment criteria that operate to exclude so many family members* [italics added]. (Meyer, 1999, p. 242)

"[H]idden ancestries" were often present in [interview respondents] who had very strong identifications with only those parts of their identities they "claimed" or recognized. Of course, the selective identification ... is not just the choice of the individual. A large part of this simplification occurs when parents decide what they will tell their children about who they are and who their ancestors are. (Waters, 1998, p. 238)

In addition to phenotypical stereotypes of American Indians, myths of identity choice abound. Ethnic switching, acknowledging one's indigenous ancestry, cannot be conflated with ethnic fraud, a conscious choice to claim Indian ancestry for economic gain. Widespread ethnic fraud is more of an urban and reservation myth than a reality: Everyone talks about it, but no one has done any actual counting of incidence rates of fake Indians taking jobs, scholarships, producing art, and so on. This task, of course, is complicated by using colonizer's definitions of who is Indian. Incidents of "Indians of convenience" is also overexaggerated; as with ethnic fraud, a few incidents are used as a basis to make the highly problematic generalization of a larger population. Although incidents of both ethnic fraud and ethnic convenience do exist, such designations are parallel to the images of the "Welfare Queen," the lazy, promiscuous sinner seeking undeserved gain. When First

Peoples support these claims of rampant fraud, their behavior manifests the internalized ideology of capitalists who argue the need to ruthlessly compete for resources.

Contemporary self-reflection leading to personal identification of one's Indian ancestry is, in most cases, not so much based on the sinister motive of committing ethnic fraud, ethnic switching, or convenience for material gain but, rather, is rooted in the opportunity to come out of hiding, a product of family secrets, and the universal human search for meaning. The legacy of family silence comes from a not-so-distant time when the comment was often made in Indian Country that "a good Indian was a dead Indian," an opinion followed by actions to ensure that there were more dead Indians than live ones and, as recently as the 1960s, the hanging in public places of signs that read "No Indians and dogs allowed."

The rates of structural and interpersonal victimization are still unacceptable. A National Institute of Justice study found that per capita rates of violence against American Indians are more than twice those of the U.S. population (Greenfeld & Smith, 1999). American Indians aged 18 to 24 experienced the highest per capita rate of violence of any racial/ethnic age group, about one violent crime for every four members of this age cohort (Greenfeld & Smith, 1999). American Indian women's rates of violent crime is nearly 50% higher than that reported by Black males (Greenfield & Smith, 1998). Unlike other ethnic or racial group victims whose offenders are usually from their own group, at least 70% of the offenders of American Indian victims are not American Indians (Greenfeld & Smith, 1999), a tragic reality that undoubtedly indicates the continuance of deep prejudice expressed in the form of violent discriminatory acts or hate crimes.

Dismal as these statistics are in terms of human suffering and social loss of the talents of all human beings of American Indian descent, since the Civil Rights Movement the social climate, both physically and psychologically, has become a bit safer for First Americans within certain social contexts. The increased social acceptance is to be found primarily in liberal middle- and upper-class urban communities but not necessarily in reservation and reservation borderline, middle- and upper-class non-Indian circles.

Increased self-identification as American Indian has more to do with cultural capital, cultural empowerment, and cultural renaissance. Newly found or newly expressed indigenous identity is more than seeking material gain, particularly in a world where one's physical safety as well as psychological well-being remains largely problematic. Ethnic identity has a symbolic component, particularly when human beings seek meaning for their individual lives as well as their collective lives. This search for meaning becomes more profound for both dominant and subordinate groups when a dominant group seeks to separate itself from a subordinate group, a distancing that becomes more pronounced if the hegemonical group has ruthlessly and consistently misused the other.

Consider the experience of the Lumbees seeking federal recognition. Their request for dominant culture's official acknowledgment was more than resource competition as some social observers have argued (see, e.g., Nagel, 1998, 2000). What small monentary compensation that this nation would receive could not offset the human costs of seeking federal recognition. The identity conflict is symbolic. If the Lumbees are federally recognized, then mixed-blood Indians, in this case, Black Indians, will have been given a new, formal affirmative status. Alternatively, consider the mid-1990s experience of a Midwest university student activist who was elected president of the American Indian student organization. Branded as a traitor by African American students and labeled as an imposter by colonized American Indian students, bearing the

phenotypical characteristics of his African ancestors and following the cultural path he had learned from his American Indian grandmother who had reared him, the young man had little if any material thing to gain. His rationale was his respect for his grandmother as well as his demonstrated support for a cultural way that he saw as healthier and more balanced than the dominant culture worldview and values.

Geography and Place:
Urban and Reservation

The rift between urban and reservation Indian people is artificial and imposed. It derives in large part from the federal policy that excluded off-reservation Indians from tribal treaty rights, as clearly acknowledged in Title 8 (Urban and Rural Non-Reservation Indians) of the American Indian Policy Review Commission. (Straus & Valentino, 2001, p. 86)

Off-reservation and urban Native Americans experience complex, sociopolitical identity problems. . . . Nearly all such problems and social conflicts are historically based, either present in actual governmental policies or in the perceptions of tribal members living in urban areas. (Fenelon, 1998, p. 273)

Some scholars (see, e.g., Nagel, 2000, p. 115) overexaggerate the tension between urban and reservation Indians. In the first place, the Eurocentric dichotomous categories of urban and reservation as rural are misleading. Not all reservations are rural; more importantly, reservations are "homelands" carrying symbolic importance of spiritual and family connections (see, e.g., Jeffredo-Warden, 1999) that are far stronger for First Peoples than are rural roots for many non-Indians who may have been born and grown up in country homes, places often viewed as merely stopping points on the way to far greater things in the cities. The circular migration between urban communities and the ties to the "rez" is constant and cannot be captured in a static snapshot such as that provided by the U.S. Census. In addition, state, country, and other Eurocentric geographical boundaries are relatively recent for all groups. For example, only slightly more than 100 years have passed since the Assiniboine were forced to restrict their homeland to two reservations in Montana and a reserve in Canada, and, more recently, the relocation program of the 1950s pressured many to relocate and create new communities in various urban sites. Thus, a growing number of Assiniboine as well as members of other nations recognize place as a connection between land and symbol, a concept essential in the maintenance of American Indian identity. When tension between reservation Indians and their urban cousins does arise, the conflict is more often about lack of respect for traditional ways and appreciation of the challenges of reservation life, attitudinal and behavioral attributes that are not unique to either reservation or urban Indians.

Parallel to the legal concept of Indian Country, place can be both land and community; however, the homelands of the reservations may carry more symbolic weight. In an urban environment, the concept of community is not always limited to a concentrated physical area but can be spread throughout a city. When community members are scattered over varying distances, within an urban setting or physical separation from the home reservation or land, community membership is determined by criteria such as those identified by scholar Susan Lobo (2001). The following four criteria, not necessarily listed in order of importance with the exception of the appearance criterion, dovetail with traditional membership criteria: birth, marriage, adoption, and naturalization.

1. *Ancestry.* Does a person have Indian relatives and ancestors, and function as a member of an Indian extended family?

2. *Appearance.* Does a person look "Indian"?

3. *Cultural knowledge*: Is the person knowledgeable of the culture of their People and of those pan-Indian values and social expectations shared within the urban Indian community?

4. *Indian community participation*: Does the person "come out" for Indian events and activities in the Indian community and contribute to the community well-being? (Lobo, 2001, p. 81)

Lobo further notes that "the weight and combination given to these elements to determine Indian identity vary situationally and, to some extent, are always under community assessment, shifting with the changing times" (p. 81). For instance, the "appearance" of a "blue-eyed Indian" or a "light skinned brother" becomes a moot criterion of ancestry when family lineage, cultural knowledge, or Indian community participation is well established.

Community and Culture

There is a . . . phenomenon [in any community] which, while nearly always implicit in social analyses that focus on discourse, has not received as much explicit attention as speech has. I refer to *silence*. Silence, too, can work as an active force in constituting and/or transforming cultural and ethnic identities; far from being a neutral and passive background, silence can . . . act to shape individual identifies and group social life in profound . . . ways. (Jackson, 1998, p. 228)

George: I'm almost non-Indian compared to most of the people that are supposed to be real Indians.

Paul: Yeah, You said that before. Why do you feel that way? What are you thinking about?

George: Being brought up White. With the Whites. Because I don't know my culture.

Paul: Do you get that, like from other Indian people then? That uh

George: That's just how I feel, and what I think.

Paul: So you feel less an Indian than other people?

George: Right. (Spicer, 1993, pp. 344-345)

How is community and culture recognized in a world that has long demanded silence of American Indians? Using a genre of humor known as "Indian humor," a form of social satire, social observer and scholar Angela Gonzales has provided still another list of "a few critical characteristics that are believed to express the essential qualities of Indianness. As a litmus test for identity, the extent to which an individual meets these criteria is used as a measure of their Indianness" (Gonzales, 2001,). Gonzalez's tongue-in-cheek six criteria for qualifying as the Essential Indian are these:

- Residence (current or previous) on an Indian reservation
- Enrolled member of federally recognized Indian tribe
- Documented Indian blood quantum—the higher the percentage, the greater one's Indianness
- Stereotypically identifiable Indian features or style of dress—long straight black hair, dark eyes, brown skin, "chiefly looks" or "doe-eyed, comely beauty," leather moccasins, ribbon shirt, beaded, silver, or turquoise jewelry
- Ability to speak a tribal language or demonstrable use of Indian colloquialism, i.e. "mother earth," the great spirit," "the two-legged, the four-legged, the winged," "a-ho," etc.
- Publicly practice what is believed to be American Indian spirituality—powwow dancing, drumming, "sweating," or burning cedar, sage, or sweetgrass (p. 175).

In addition to the three imposed criteria of blood quantum, enrollment status, and phenotypical characteristics, four of the six criteria

have cultural components. Ancestry is recognized partially by reservation residence as well as by secular and spiritual practices.

On a more serious note, Lobo (2001) has identified four community and culture criteria characterizing the American Indian community in the San Francisco Bay. These biological and phenotypical free criteria are also found in other communities with large Indian populations such as Chicago, Los Angeles, and Denver as well as in noncolonized enclaves in reservation communities.

> The American Indian community . . . is characterized . . . on a general level as a social group in which: 1. community members recognize a shared identity; 2. there are shared values, symbols, and history; 3. basic institutions have been created and sustained; and 4. there are consistent features of social organization such as those related to social control, and the definition of distinctive and specialized gender- and age-related roles. (Lobo, 2001, p. 75)

The benefits of any community, reservation tribes, or "urban tribes" such as that found in the urban San Francisco American Indian community, according to Lobo, "gives a sense of belonging, meets a need to look inward to this social entity, and fosters a feeling of responsibility to contribute to the well-being of the members via support of the community and flourishing of urban institutions" (p. 75).

Traditional criteria of membership provided a means of belonging, including roles for the offspring of the initial contacts with non-Indians. The split between modern (i.e., mixed blood) and traditional (i.e., full blood) is a devisive construct resulting from the long-time impact of cultural conflict. A specific demonstration can be found in the long history of non-Indians marrying Alaska women and being incorporated into indigenous communities. After the official arrival of Russians to the Alaska area, bringing colonization in 1741 (Sprott, 1998, p. 216), initially the offspring of the foreigners and the indigenous women were given an inclusive role in the community; later, however, the mixed-blood children were given a class designation labeled Creoles.

In other parts of Indian Country, given the violation of sovereignty rights and the consequent great numbers of non-Indians living or working on a majority of reservations, "rez" Indians may not only have a limited indigenous marriage pool but also may have greater exposure to potential non-Indian partners. In addition, given rampant discrimination in Indian country as well as the sparse American Indian populations, reservation mixed-blood Indians have little choice about their identities because they are "known" as Indian by the White community as well their indigenous communities. "Blue-eyed Indians" do not "pass" unless they move elsewhere and cut off all major ties to family and friends, an alienation that would be highly problematic. Thus, culture and community are primary influences in the construction of identity for Americans of multiple ancestry.

Colonizer criteria do not recognize the fate of American Indians whose ancestors were not given formal federal recognition nor those whose ancestors refused to have their identity validated by the White man. Nor do these criteria acknowledge the loss of the rapidly growing population of American Indians who may be "full blood" or "nearly full blood" but are not enrolled because their ancestry comes from two or more indigenous groups and their bloodline from any one of the groups is not enough to meet the one-fourth quantum requirement.

Retribalization is occurring in both urban and on- and off-reservation communities (Nagel, 1995, 1996, 2000; Straus & Valentino, 2001; Weibel-Orlando, 1991); unfortunately, in that process, adequate attention has not yet been given to recognition of all members of those communities, in particular the cross-bloods and postmodern tribal blood Indians

(Vizenor, 1990). Traditionally rooted inclusion of all First People communities is an essential component of cultural renaissance.

Ancestry and Family Descent

The White man thinks in terms of numbers. Indians think in terms of human beings. (Russell Means)[4]

"Who's your Grandma?" is a question often asked when American Indians first meet. If the first meeting is in an urban setting or on another reservation, the lineage question often follows the establishment of place of family origin and is used primarily as an additional point of reference. One's federal enrollment status is rarely asked, except by Purity Police. Family recognition of its own members is not given full respect by the Identity Police. Traditionalists would never think of dividing the essence of one's grandmother into fractions when accounting for her descendants and determining who is a "real Indian."

Table 11.2 demonstrates the dehumanizing use of blood quantum to determine American Indian identity rather than simple ancestry. The tragic consequences of using blood quantum as the primary criterion rather than unquantified family ancestry for determining individual identity and group membership is further amplified when one reflects on the social implications of the often unrecognized practice of the criminal justice system: counting anyone of "known" Indian blood regardless of blood quantum level, whereas at least a federally recognized one-fourth blood quantum is required if an American Indian seeks educational or health services agreed on in her nation's treaties with the United States.

Legal Definitions and the Colonizer's Blood Quantum

How does "enrolled" make a mixed person more Indian than "non enrolled"? (Tom Giago)[5]

Table 11.2 Chart to Establish Degree of Indian Blood

	N1*	1/16	1/8	3/16	1/4	5/16	3/8	7/16	1/2	9/16	5/8	11/16	3/4	13/16	7/8	15/16	4/4
1/16	1/32	1/16	3/32	1/8	5/32	3/16	7/32	1/4	9/32	5/16	11/32	3/8	13/32	7/16	15/32	1/2	17/32
1/8	1/16	3/32	1/8	5/32	3/16	7/32	1/4	9/32	5/16	11/32	3/8	13/32	7/16	15/32	1/2	17/32	9/16
3/16	3/32	1/8	5/32	3/16	7/32	1/4	9/32	5/16	11/32	3/8	13/32	7/16	15/32	1/2	17/32	9/16	19/32
1/4	1/8	5/32	3/16	7/32	1/4	9/32	5/16	11/32	3/8	13/32	7/16	15/32	1/2	17/32	9/16	19/32	5/8
5/16	5/32	3/16	7/32	1/4	9/32	5/16	11/32	3/8	13/32	7/16	15/32	1/2	17/32	9/16	19/32	5/8	21/32
3/8	3/16	7/32	1/4	9/32	5/16	11/32	3/8	13/32	7/16	15/32	1/2	17/32	9/16	19/32	5/8	21/32	11/16
7/16	7/32	1/4	9/32	5/16	11/32	3/8	13/32	7/16	15/32	1/2	17/32	9/16	19/32	5/8	21/32	11/16	23/32
1/2	1/4	9/32	5/16	11/32	3/8	13/32	7/16	15/32	1/2	17/32	9/16	19/32	5/8	21/32	11/16	23/32	3/4
9/16	9/32	5/16	11/32	3/8	13/32	7/16	15/32	1/2	17/32	9/16	19/32	5/8	21/32	11/16	23/32	3/4	25/32
5/8	5/16	11/32	3/8	13/32	7/16	15/32	1/2	17/32	9/16	19/32	5/8	21/32	11/16	23/32	3/4	25/32	13/16
11/16	11/32	3/8	13/32	7/16	15/32	1/2	17/32	9/16	19/32	5/8	21/32	11/16	23/32	3/4	25/32	13/16	27/32
3/4	3/8	13/32	7/16	15/32	1/2	17/32	9/16	19/32	5/8	21/32	11/16	23/32	3/4	25/32	13/16	27/32	7/8
13/16	13/32	7/16	15/32	1/2	17/32	9/16	19/32	5/8	21/32	11/16	23/32	3/4	25/32	13/16	27/32	7/8	29/32
7/8	7/16	15/32	1/2	17/32	9/16	19/32	5/8	21/32	11/16	23/32	3/4	25/32	13/16	27/32	7/8	29/32	15/16
15/16	15/32	1/2	17/32	9/16	19/32	5/8	21/32	11/16	23/32	3/4	25/32	13/16	27/32	7/8	29/32	15/16	31/32
4/4	1/2	17/32	9/16	19/32	5/8	21/32	11/16	23/32	3/4	25/32	13/16	27/32	7/8	29/32	15/16	31/32	4/4
1/32	1/64	3/64	5/64	7/64	9/64	11/64	13/64	15/64	17/64	19/64	21/64	23/64	25/64	27/64	29/64	31/64	33/64
3/32	3/64	5/64	7/64	9/64	11/64	13/64	15/64	17/64	19/64	21/64	23/64	25/64	27/64	29/64	31/64	33/64	35/64
5/32	5/64	7/64	9/64	11/64	13/64	15/64	17/64	19/64	21/64	23/64	25/64	27/64	29/64	31/64	33/64	35/64	37/64
7/32	7/64	9/64	11/64	13/64	15/64	17/64	19/64	21/64	23/64	25/64	27/64	29/64	31/64	33/64	35/64	37/64	39/64
9/32	9/64	11/64	13/64	15/64	17/64	19/64	21/64	23/64	25/64	27/64	29/64	31/64	33/64	35/64	37/64	39/64	41/64
11/32	11/64	13/64	15/64	17/64	19/64	21/64	23/64	25/64	27/64	29/64	31/64	33/64	35/64	37/64	39/64	41/64	43/64
13/32	13/64	15/64	17/64	19/64	21/64	23/64	25/64	27/64	29/64	31/64	33/64	35/64	37/64	39/64	41/64	43/64	45/64
15/32	15/64	17/64	19/64	21/64	23/64	25/64	27/64	29/64	31/64	33/64	35/64	37/64	39/64	41/64	43/64	45/64	47/64
17/32	17/64	19/64	21/64	23/64	25/64	27/64	29/64	31/64	33/64	35/64	37/64	39/64	41/64	43/64	45/64	47/64	49/64

(Continued)

Table 11.2   (Continued)

	19/64	21/64	23/64	25/64	27/64	29/64	31/64	33/64	35/64	37/64	39/64	41/64	43/64	45/64	47/64	49/64	51/64
19/32	19/64	21/64	23/64	25/64	27/64	29/64	31/64	33/64	35/64	37/64	39/64	41/64	43/64	45/64	47/64	49/64	51/64
21/32	21/64	23/64	25/64	27/64	29/64	31/64	33/64	35/64	37/64	39/64	41/64	43/64	45/64	47/64	49/64	51/64	53/64
23/32	23/64	25/64	27/64	29/64	31/64	33/64	35/64	37/64	39/64	41/64	43/64	45/64	47/64	49/64	51/64	53/64	55/64
25/32	25/64	27/64	29/64	31/64	33/64	35/64	37/64	39/64	41/64	43/64	45/64	47/64	49/64	51/64	53/64	55/64	57/64
27/32	27/64	29/64	31/64	33/64	35/64	37/64	39/64	41/64	43/64	45/64	47/64	49/64	51/64	53/64	55/64	57/64	59/64
29/32	29/64	31/64	33/64	35/64	37/64	39/64	41/64	43/64	45/64	47/64	49/64	51/64	53/64	55/64	57/64	59/64	61/64
31/32	31/64	33/64	35/64	37/64	39/64	41/64	43/64	45/64	47/64	49/64	51/64	53/64	55/64	57/64	59/64	61/64	63/64

SOURCE: Department of Interior, Bureau of Indian Affairs, Phoenix area office. *Tribal Enrollment*. (Washington: Government Printing Office, 1990).

NOTE: To determine the degree of blood of children, find degree of one parent in left column and the other parent in the top row; read across and down. For example, if a child has parents with 11/16 and 5/8 degrees of blood, then that child would be 21/32 degree Indian.

*Non-Indian.

Giago's question further illustrates the arbitrary and politicized racialization of categories (Forbes, 2001) and the resultant provocative tension within American Indian communities, particularly in terms of identity. Race and ethnicity scholar F. James Davis (2000, pp. 106-107) has identified seven status rules for racially mixed persons rooted and reinforced by informal as well as formal social control mechanisms. The first five of the rules, which are not mutually exclusive, are useful when attempting to understand the inconsistency of the social status of mixed bloods in the Americas. The first rule addressing hypodescent, commonly known as the "one-drop rule," assigns all racially mixed persons of the same racial identity and status as that of the socially subordinate group. This rule held for U.S. indigenous until the inception of the reservation system and imposition of the blood quantum criteria for federally recognized Indians and still holds for nonrecognized Indians of certain backgrounds.

The second status rule assigns all mixed-heritage persons to an in-between status, making them politically powerless, an extremely vulnerable status, especially during times of crisis. This rule applies to all mixed-blood American Indians, caught between blood quantum requirements and nonacceptance by non-Indians and, at times, by their own peoples. The third rule assigns persons of mixed ancestry a status lower than that of either parent group, as in the case of the Metis of Canada and Montana and other "landless Indians" in the United States and Canada.[6]

Davis's fourth rule, a claim that many Mestizos would refute, assigns mixed persons such as Mestizos of Mexico a status higher than that of either parent group. The fifth rule allows the status to vary widely between the parent groups, depending more on education and wealth than on race. Davis claims that the status of lowland indigenous of Latin America and most of the Caribbean illustrate

this rule, yet he does not acknowledge the lower status of known Tiano Caribbean descendants (Barrerio, 1989). As has been pointed out in this chapter, in contradiction of Davis's romanticized fourth and fifth status rules, in the great majority of cases mixed-blood status for American Indians has been less than that of both parent groups.

Mixed-race identity conflict for First Peoples can be traced to the formalization of the concept of blood quantum in 1705, when the Colony of Virginia adopted a series of laws denying civil rights to any "negro, *mulatto*, or *Indian*" [italics added] (Knepper, 1998; Pascoe, 1999). The Colony's legal definition of mulatto stated: "The child of an *Indian* [italics added], and the child, grandchild, or great grandchild of a negro shall be deemed accounted, held, and taken to be a mulatto." As a result of these racialized categories, all three groups have been treated as legally inferior persons.

Other colonies and states soon followed the Virginia model of using blood quantum as a legal means of determining who could have the privileges accorded to White persons, thereby further diminishing the status of both one-race and multiple-race members of oppressed groups in the United States. For instance, Alabama added a code that partially read:

> [A]ll negroes, mulattoes, Indians and all persons of mixed blood, to the third generation inclusive, though one ancestor of each generation may have been a white person, whether bond or free; shall be taken, and deemed incapable in law, to be witnesses . . . except for or against each other.

North Carolina's new code prohibited marriages between White persons and "an Indian, Negro, Mustee, or Mulatto . . . or any person of Mixed Blood to the Third Generation." The result for American Indians was parallel to the one-drop rules for African Americans: A part-Indian of one-eighth American ancestry (Indian) and seven-eighths European ancestry did not have sufficient European "blood" to be accorded the legal and other social privileges of whiteness.

By 1866, the state of Virginia put a new and more restrictive twist on degree of blood codes: "Every person having one-fourth or more Negro blood shall be deemed a colored person, and every person not a colored person having one-fourth or more Indian blood shall be deemed." Forbes (1998) and other scholars think that perhaps this blood quantum limit is where the Bureau of Indian Affairs (BIA) concept of one-quarter blood quantum originated.

In the 20th century, Virginia broadened the term *colored* to include all Indians with any trace of African ancestry, if living off-reservation, and with more than 1/32 African ancestry, if living on either the Pamunkey or Mattaponi reservations.

In the latter part of the 19th century, the federal government began to follow state practices of using "degree of blood" such as "full," "one half," and "one fourth" to determine tribal membership in Indian nations that had treaties or other formal agreements with the United States. This practice was an extension of the earlier system of identity racialization and a deliberate, openly acknowledged key step in anticipation of terminating Native American tribes and consequently ending treaty obligations.

Once the formal "Indian wars" had ended and Congress stopped entering into treaties with Indian nations in 1871, one of the most draconian efforts used to terminate American Indians was enacted with the passage of the General Allotment Act of 1887 (also known as the GAA or Dawes Act), designed to more quickly assimilate Indians by ignoring traditional relationships to the land, Mother Earth, and promoting individual ownership of land (a very foreign concept among most tribes). The Act required all American Indians of federally recognized nations to own parcels of land and encouraged them to become "civilized agriculturalists." Individual allotments were to be held in trust for 25 years. In less than 20 years after the passage of the Dawes Act, given the increasing political pressure of the continuing westward expansion and desire for more land, the Burke Act of 1906 was passed authorizing allotments to be taken out of trust if the allottee was deemed competent. Competency of allottees was often determined without notifying the allottees or without informing them of the consequences of taking land out of trust status. When the land was taken out of trust, a fee patent status was given to the land in question, thereby allowing full ownership of the land by the owner and making the land subject to state and taxes. Given widespread poverty, lack of complete understanding of the Eurocentric concept of land ownership, and the implications of owing taxes, much land was lost to non-Indian American and European immigrant homesteaders and real estate speculators through inability to pay taxes and the fraudulent activities of land speculators, such as serving as witnesses to the "competency" of vulnerable American Indian allottees. Between 1887 and 1934, approximately 90,000,000 acres of tribal land was loss from the sale of "surplus" lands (land left after reservations were divided up into individual allotments) and the alienation of allotments.

Targets for potential fee patent competency and consequently land loss were "the right kind of Indians." These people, almost inevitably male, were those who could be most easily manipulated and/or co-opted into supporting assimilation policies such as land-grabbing policies. Women were rarely considered "the right kind of Indians," and they were often very active in resisting colonization and assimilation policies. Occasionally, persons with greater amounts of White ancestry were said to be more competent than those with lesser amounts and were given fee patents to their lands, a status that was promoted by BIA officials and land-hungry fee patent supporters, who argued that the change of land status would result in three forms of cultural capital: the removal of wardship restrictions, the ability to sell property, and the right to vote in state and federal elections. In a significant number of Indian communities, the myth of light-skinned mixed bloods being largely responsible for the major land loss is still recited as widespread reality, although historical record demonstrates that large numbers of full bloods also were manipulated into selling their birth rights.

PERSONAL AND CULTURAL CONSEQUENCES OF DENYING ONE'S OWN

Yes, we are between two fires, the Red and the White. Our Caucasian brothers criticize us as a shiftless class, while the Indians disown us as abandoning our own race. We are maligned and traduced as no one but we of the "despised breeds" can know. (Mourning Dove, Cognea, the Half Breed, 1927)[7]

[The American Indian Holocaust] exhibit is very informative. Our Native peoples, "federally" recognized and unrecognized, full blood and mixed-blood, from North, South, and Central America, need to unite and free our minds from the colonial borders and governments imposed on our hemisphere. An exhibit-goer reaction, May 1996 (Ramirez, 2001, p. 249)

Advocates for the colonizers' blood quantum identity criteria, with far less justification, are the 21st-century ideological descendants of the pitiful "hang around the Fort" ancestors. The identity of mixed-blood human beings are defined by both the cultural constructs to which they are connected and the multiple categories from which they are excluded. Excluding mixed-blood American Indians blames the victims of the initial

American holocaust (Romero, 2001) and its more recent forms: the government and mission boarding schools, relocation, tribal termination, foster placements, and disproportionate representation in the military and prisons. The internalization of blood quantum criteria to determine identity has promoted in-group conflict, leaving First Peoples and their descendants fighting each other under the table for the pitiful scraps thrown by the lord and lady of the manor. We fight with each other for inadequate health care and educational scholarships, underpaid jobs, and pitiful fees for land claims and mineral and resource rights, and land leases. We exclude our own from the life-affirming cultural paths of traditional indigenous nations.

A growing number of scholars and social observers are recognizing the lessons of a balanced life taught by traditional leaders and spiritual mentors. Reclaiming all of our own leads to healing rather than a weakening of the traditional ways. If we do not, our people will experience more cultural loss and as a result more psychological harm.

Psychological and Personal Consequences

The majority of us [city-raised Indian people] walk around with this hole in our heart. We know we're different, that there's a piece of our life that is missing.— Michelle Duncan (Jackson, 1998, p. 189)

As has been pointed out, at least 40% of American Indians are mixed blood. Thus, two of five, and undoubtedly more, given the exclusion of multiple heritage indigenous, suffer from personal loss, grief, and anger contributing to disproportionate numbers of youth suicide, alcoholism, educational underachievement, crime victims, and criminal justice correctional representation (see, e.g., DeLeane O'Nell, 1996; Waldram, 1997). Claiming multiracial identity is not a matter of a "frivolous ground [for] self-esteem" (Spencer, 1999, p. 191) for American Indians of mixed-blood descent.

Pain resulting from the trauma of structural racism and/or interpersonal violence and consequently internalized or expressed through inappropriate means is an issue for all in Indian Country and, to a large degree, in most urban communities (see, e.g., Peters, 1998; Van Buren, 2001). One particularly poignant form of pain is related to the process of how Indianness is defined by American Indians and non-Indians (Mihesuah, 1999, p. 14). This emotional trauma is accentuated among mixed-blood American Indians, who often are not accepted by either Indians and non-Indians. American Indian youth have the highest rates of suicide of any ethnic group in the United States. If at least 40% of American Indian youth are of mixed-race background, a major portion of the identity conflicts that have contributed to youth suicide undoubtedly have to do with mixed-race issues. For example, in some homes, the non-Indian parent teaches Christian values that condemn or trivialize traditional spiritual beliefs and practices of the traditional Indian parent, creating major psychic conflicts for his or her child and thus contributing to alienation, a prime causal factor in many suicide attempts and completed suicides.

Depression and alcohol and other chemical abuse cannot adequately account for the high rates of suicide in either American Indian youth or adults. A growing body of literature such as Christine T. Lowery's (1998, 2001) study of life histories of urban American Indian males demonstrates the relationship of their alcoholism, often called in Indian country "a slow form of suicide," to identity issues. Three of the four men in her study were mixed blood.

In addition to the social crisis of disproportionate rates of suicide, American Indians and Alaska natives have the highest victimization rates of any ethnic group in the United

States. An important part of this criminal victimization is related to identity issues, including the low status of mixed bloods. Furthermore, as has been pointed out earlier, the criminal justice system casts a wide net for Indian offenders, the vast majority of whom have also been victims. Classifying anyone of known Indian descent regardless of blood quantum or enrollment status sends the inescapable message that mixed bloods are not valued enough to be accepted as Indians for other purposes but are Indian enough to be processed through the federal courts.

Sovereignty and Cultural Loss

In addition to individual alienation for mixed bloods, Indian communities lose cultural ground when they join the John Wayne group by emulating the adversarial system of the European American civil and criminal justice system rather than reviving the traditional restorative and peace-making justice systems in which healing for all involved—victim, offender, and community—is more important than inflicting more harm for all through the use of legalized revenge.

Furthermore, recognizing mixed-blood identity is essential for preservation of American Indian national sovereignty and, consequently, individual well-being. The assaults on American Indian identity continue with the continued reliance of blood quantum. In 2000 the Department of Interior proposed changes in the way the BIA calculates a Certificate of Degree of Indian or Alaska Native Blood (CDIB). As in the past, the proposed changes continue to perpetuate the racist blood quantum, ignore membership criteria of tribes, and play a role in Indians terminating themselves. The major problem with the proposed changes is the premise that "Indian blood" can only be based on Indian ancestry computed from so-called federally recognized tribes. This type of tribe must be listed in the

Federal Register as a tribe recognized by the Secretary of the Interior, thus excluding anyone whose American Indian or Eskimo Inuit ancestry derives from a terminated tribe, an administratively deleted tribe, a Canadian, Greenlandic, Mexican or other non-U.S. group, any state-recognized tribe (as along the East Coast), or perhaps from any newly organized tribe. Thus, a person who is one-eighth Wyandot from the Oklahoma Wyandot reservation, one-eighth Wyandot from the Kansas state-recognized group, and one-eighth Wyandot from Canada can only be counted as one-eighth American Indian. Also, obtaining federal recognition is a very expensive and difficult political task, as more than 200 Indian groups, including groups with little power and a large number of mixed-blood members such as the Tongua and Acjachemen in southern California, can testify (Coker, 2001).

Limiting membership limits political constituency. Restrictive membership also limits access to positive and constructive traditional cultural values, promoting balance between collectivistic and individualistic values such as learning to share and to value generosity rather than hoarding and greed; demonstrating a lived recognition of the connections between mind, body, and spirit; providing community and emotional space to appreciate the here and now; and encouraging decision making that seriously considers the well-being of seven generations to come.

ALTERNATIVE PATHS TO INDIGENOUS IDENTITY

[Will American Indians] continue to allow themselves to be defined mainly by their colonizers, in exclusively racial/familial terms (as "tribes"), or . . . will [they] (re)assume responsibility for advancing the more general and coherent political definition of themselves they once held, as *nations* defining

membership/citizenship in terms of culture, socialization, and commitment to the good of the group. (Stiffarm & Lane, 1992, p. 45)

I have always believed that the Great Creator had a great design for my people, the Cherokees. I have been taught that from my childhood up and now in my mature manhood I recognize it as a great truth. Our forces have been dissipated by the external forces, perhaps it has been just a training, but we must now get together as a race and render our contribution to mankind. We are endowed with intelligence, we are industrious, we are loyal and we are spiritual but we are overlooking the Cherokee mission on earth, for no man nor race is endowed with these qualifications without a designed purpose. . . . *Our Mixed-bloods should not be overlooked in this program of a racial awakening* [italics added]. Our pride in our ancestral heritage is our great incentive for handing something worth while to our posterity. It is this pride in ancestry that makes men strong and loyal for their principal in life. It is this same pride that makes men give up their all for their Government. (Redbird Smith, early 1900s; Chad Smith's great-grandfather)[8]

American Indian nations are political groups, nations within a nation, that potentially have the power to determine national citizenship. Indian country political divisions about the uncritical acceptance of racialized categories of identity are increasing. As in the past, some have adopted, consciously or unconsciously, the racialized paradigm and have blindly accepted the "scarce resources" justification of their colonizers. Today, given the establishment of a critical mass of biculturally educated indigenous, significant population growth, a expanding economic base, and the important cultural renaissance throughout Indian Country (see, e.g., Nagel 1998), First Peoples currently have not only an expanding resolve but also resources needed to build a national political constituency in addition to local and state Indian constituencies that are large enough to have meaningful political clout.

First Peoples need to continue to take back the power to name, specifically to reclaim, the right to determine Indian nation membership. If we do not, the oppressed have become the oppressors: By denying our relatives, we have turned on our own. As long as we do not cast aside the colonizer's rules about blood quantum, phenotypical stereotypes, and other forms of racialized thinking with all of its issues of power, status, and prestige, both mixed bloods and full bloods will remind the "colonized other," a demonstration of internalized oppression. The time is past for a paradigm shift.

The shift in consciousness is not just about reclaiming material resources but also about fully using human capital, both of which are mandatory steps if we are to stop genocide as well as ethnocide. The concurrent dialogue needs to become broader, better informed, and framed in a more systematic manner. Such an ideological and, consequently, political move does not negate or prohibit individual desires to buy into the materialist goals of the "American Dream," but the changes do provide a wedge against selling one's heritage for a "buck" (no pun intended). The short-term concerns about civil rights monitoring are valid but shortsighted; in the long term, such a materialistic approach will become dangerous, putting all of our eggs into one basket that can easily be crushed, particularly for American Indians when civil rights monitoring does not include monitoring the loss of sovereignty rights, the land, its resources, or the loss of cultures. Thus, First Peoples need to move rapidly toward relaxation of ethnic boundaries, away from restrictive colonizer criteria, and toward more indigenous inclusion, especially of all of our mixed-blood members. The acceptance of all of our relatives, regardless of degree of blood, may hasten achievement of the goal of egalitarian pluralism (horizontal as opposed to vertical pluralism) within the American landscape. Increased membership is an essential route of developing meaningful political constituency. Such gains will far outweigh any fears about perceived losses. Rather than worrying about affirmative action rights, First Peoples need to focus on obtaining economic self-sufficiency, promoting cultural viability, and using the powerful tools of treaty and constitutional rights.

Cultural competence and viability can be recreated or strengthened by the use of "citizen" training and testing roughly similar to that required of U.S. immigrants who wish to become naturalized citizens. Such policies will help to offset tragic scenarios such as that which happened to the Flathead in Montana in the 1950s when federal officials claimed that the Flathead were so acculturated or assimilated that they no longer needed federal services or protection. The result was that Flathead tribal leaders having bought into the myth that "blood quantum" is a measure of integration into the group as well as a measure of commitment to the group adopted a stricter set of blood quantum rules for membership. A team of traditional elders or leaders well versed in Indian law and sovereignty issues could have helped make the clear distinction between the benefits of short-term material culture assimilation and the benefits of long-term cultural values that do not exclude members of one's own family.

Alternative Paths and Hard Choices

Indian communities throughout the United States, federally recognized nations as well as nonrecognized nations and other groups, need to address the following three paths and make some difficult choices about individual and cultural survival. First, given the high rates of "out breeding," continuing to accept the colonizer's criteria for American Indian membership is to continue the present fast track of fratricide. A few Indian nations may survive, but their status would be like that of Monaco's, symbolic and romantic without meaningful power. Second, the exclusion of mixed bloods will continue to create more new groups such as the Metis, people with even less status and power than the original Indian nations. Certainly, the creation of such marginalized groups is both counterproductive in terms of building political constituencies and inhumane in treating one's relatives in such a manner. A third path is currently being taken by a growing number of Indian nations such as one group of the Cherokee and the Umatilla by eliminating Eurocentric blood quantum criterion and using traditional family lineage and other criteria to determine membership.

The following model for determining First People identity has been developed over the last 40 years by listening to personal and political discussions, studying and teaching Indian law and policies, analyzing the experiences of sovereignty loss and retention, and respecting and taking part in cultural renaissance throughout Indian Country.

A New Model for Determining American Indian Identity

Colonization has made many indigenous people economically paranoid; many have internalized the oppression, including self-aggrandizing, materialistic values, and have projected the colonizer's greed onto each other by excluding each other. We need to take back our lives and name our own future.

The following suggestions are intended to expand and to encourage the emerging and more thoughtful dialogue on American Indian identity and its relationship to retention of sovereignty and culture. The suggested model is culturally inclusive, recognizing the modern reality of the adoption in varying degrees of the U.S. material culture (cars, television, washing machines, *ad infinitum*), yet retains the most wholesome values of traditional cultures such as generosity and sharing that ensure that one's material gain is not at the expense of another's well-being.

If we want to stop playing a role in terminating ourselves, we must first do away with the federal blood quantum as the primary means of determining American Indian membership. Instead, First Peoples can replace this fratricidal criterion with the following four traditionally based criteria framed within the social context of contemporary life.

Family Lineage. Human beings of multitribal descent can use traditional means to recognize all of their ancestral cultures. If questions exist regarding division of material resources, there needs to be a Pan Indian decision, such as following the mother's lineage in this matter alone, to help offset intertribal squabbling over any miserable financial incentive that may make one tribal lineage appear to be more materially attractive.

Marriage. Again, as in the traditional past, if the person comes with the right motives, a good heart, demonstrated by actions rather than words alone, then the respective nation will provide formal means of incorporating the spouse as a fully accepted member, thus ensuring the well-being of the children as well as the long-term survival of the nation. A council of traditional elders and medicine people, women and men, could develop the criteria for this social inclusion if traditional ceremonies and other formal mechanisms have been lost or need to be updated. If needed, this criterion should include cultural and sovereignty literacy.

The federally enrolled American Indian members in the group picture are indicated by an E; American Indians who have limited tribal enrollment status are indicated by LE; non-enrolled American Indians are indicated by NE; and non Indians are indicated by NI.

Adoption and Naturalization. American Indians have a long history of adopting other human beings. To protect the retention of culture, literacy tests (in particular, respect for traditional spiritual values, even though the person may be a practicing member of another faith tradition) need to be developed. Also, a means of evaluating baseline knowledge in sovereignty issues and Indian legal issues must be developed for adopted and naturalized American Indian "citizens."

Literary Requirements for All Official Representatives. The imposition of the reservation system, boarding schools, and other bitter fruits of colonization has resulted in the unfortunate lack of acceptable levels of cultural and sovereignty knowledge of many tribal members (see, e.g., McBeth, 1963). Those who are not legally and consequently politically literate, especially official leaders such as tribal board members, can be sent to educational programs such as that recently started at Portland State University, Oregon, where Indian and non-Indian leaders learn about American Indian law and policies. Those who are not culturally literate can be mentored at all educational levels by traditional guides (Grantham-Campbell, 1998). Each nation can determine its evaluation techniques for cultural competency.

Mitakuye Oyasin (We are all related.
Lakota/Dakota/Nakoda)
Tsonkwadiyonrat (We are one spirit.
Wyandot)

NOTES

1. In this chapter, the names American Indians, American Indians and Alaska Natives, Native Americans, First Peoples, Indigenous, and so on are used interchangeably.

2. Today more than 700 native nations on the North American continent have survived. Five hundred and fifty eight Indian nations are federally recognized by the United States.

3. Indian Country is a legal concept rather than a physical space located only in the West. Vine Deloria, Jr., and Clifford M. Lytle point out that today the concept "has been elevated by federal law above other ideas because it transcends mere geographical limitations and represents that sphere of influence in which Indian traditions and federal laws passed specifically to deal with the political relationship of the United States to American Indians have primacy" (1985, p. 58).

4. Extemporaneous talk at the Trail of Broken Treaties occupation of the Bureau of Indian Affairs building, Washington, D.C., November 1972.

5. From an editorial in the newspaper *Indian Country*.

6. Metis (pronounced May-tees, Metiss, or Mechef) of northern United States and Canada are estimated to number nearly 1,000,000 (Anonymous, 2001, p. 16).

7. From the author's personal files.

8. Quotation from Chad Smith's Web site at www.chadsmith.com.

REFERENCES

Anonymous. (2001). Looking back: The Metis conference [1981]. *Meeting Ground: D'Arcy McNickle Center for American Indian History, 44,* 16-17.

Barrerio, J. (1989). Indians in Cuba. *Cultural Survival Quarterly, 13*(3), 59-60.

Churchill, W. (1999). The crucible of American Indian identity: Native tradition versus colonial imposition in postconquest North America. In D. Champagne (Ed.), *Contemporary Native American cultural issues* (pp. 39-67). Walnut Creek, CA: AltaMira Press.

Cohen, D. S. (1998) Reflections on American identity. In J. Ferrante & P. Brown, Jr. (Eds.), *The social construction of race and ethnicity in the United States* (pp. 239-248). New York: Longman.

Coker, M. (2001, November 28). This is where we pray: As earthmovers move in, local Indians move to save their sacred land. *OC Weekly.* Retrieved from www.ocweekly.com

Cornell, S., & Hartman, D. (1998). *Ethnicity and race: Making identities in a changing world.* Thousand Oaks, CA: Pine Forge Press.

Davis, F. J. (2000). Black identity in the United States. In P. Kivisto & G. Rundblad (Eds.), *Multiculturalism in the United States: Current issues, contemporary voices* (pp. 101-111). Thousand Oaks, CA: Pine Forge Press.

DeLeane O'Nell, T. (1996). *Disciplined hearts: History, identity, and depression in an American Indian community.* Berkley, California: University of California Press.

Deloria, V., Jr., & Lytle, C. M. (1985). *American Indian, American justice.* Austin: University of Texas Press.

Fenelon, J. V. (1998). Discrimination and indigenous identity in Chicago's native community. *American Indian Culture and Research Journal, 22*(4), 273-303.

Forbes, J. D. (1998). Indian and black as radically different types of categories. In J. Ferrante & P. Brown, Jr. (Eds.), *The social construction of race and ethnicity in the United States* (pp. 120-122). New York: Longman.

Forbes, J. D. (2001). Blood quantum: A relic of racism and termination. *Indian Times, 10*, 9, 11.

Gonzales, A. A. (1998). The (re)articulation of American Indian identity: Maintaining boundaries and regulating access to ethnically tied resources. *American Indian Culture and Research Journal, 22*(4), 199-225.

Gonzales, A. A. (2001). Urban (trans) formations: Changes in the meaning and use of American Indian identity. In S. Lobo & K. Peters (Eds.), *American Indians and the urban experience* (pp. 169-185). Walnut Creek, CA: AltaMira Press.

Grantham-Campbell, M. (1998). It's okay to be native: Alaska native cultural strategies in urban and school settings. *American Indian Culture and Research Journal, 22*(4), 385-405.

Greenfeld, L. A., & Smith, S. K. (l999, February). *American Indians and crime* [NCJ 173386]. Washington, DC: U. S. Department of Justice, Office of Justice Programs, Bureau of Justice Statistics.

Grieco, E. M., & Cassidy, R. C. (2001, March). *Overview of race and Hispanic origin: Census 2000 brief.* Washington, DC: U.S. Department of Commerce, Economics and Statistics Administration, U.S. Census Bureau.

Jackson, D. D. (1998). This hole in our heart: Urban Indian identity and the power of silence. *American Indian Culture and Research Journal, 22*(4), 227-254.

Jeffredo-Warden, L. V. (1999). Perceiving, experiencing, and expressing the sacred: An indigenous southern California view. In V. J. Matsumoto & B. Allmendinger (Eds.), *Over the edge: Remapping the American west* (pp. 329-338). Berkeley: University of California Press.

Jolivette, A. (2000, spring). Is red really red? A critique of American Indian renewal. *American Indian Studies Review Journal, 20*, 19-21.

Knepper, P. (1998). Historical origins of the prohibition of multiracial legal identity in the States and the nation. In J. Ferrante & P. Brown, Jr. (Eds.), The *Social Construction of Race and Ethnicity in the United States* (pp. 123-130). New York: Longman.

LaDuke, W. (1999). *All our relations: Native struggles for land and life.* Cambridge, MA: South End Press.

Lobo, S. (2001). Is urban a person or a place? Characteristics of urban Indian country. In S. Lobo & K. Peters (Eds.), *American Indians and the urban experience* (pp. 73-84). Walnut Creek, CA: AltaMira Press.

Lowery, C. T. (1998). From the outside looking in: Rejection and belongingness for four urban Indian men in Milwaukee, Wisconsin, 1944-1995. *American Indian Culture and Research Journal, 22*(4), 361-383.

Lowery, C. T. (2001). Rejection and belonging in addiction and recovery. In S. Lobo & K. Peters (Eds.), *American Indians and the urban experience* (pp. 277-290). Walnut Creek, CA: AltaMira Press.

McBeth, S. J. (1983). *Ethnic identity and the boarding school experience of west-central Oklahoma American Indians.* New York: University Press of America.

Meyer, M. L. (1999). American Indian blood quantum requirements: Blood is thicker than family. In V. J. Matsumoto & B. Allmendinger (Eds.), *Over the edge: Remapping the American west* (pp. 231-249). Berkeley: University of California Press.

Mihesuah, D. A. (1999). American Indian identities: Issues of individual choice and development. In D. Champagne (Ed.), *Contemporary Native American cultural issues* (pp. 13-38).Walnut Creek, CA: AltaMira Press.

Nagel, J. (1995, December). American Indian ethnic renewal: Politics and the resurgence of identity. *American Sociological Review, 60*, 947-965.

Nagel, J. (1996). *American Indian ethnic renewal: Red power and the resurgence of identity and culture.* New York: Oxford University Press.

Nagel, J. (1998). Resource competition theories. In J. Ferrante & P. Brown, Jr. (Eds.), *The social construction of race and ethnicity in the United States* (pp. 249-267). New York: Longman.

Nagel, J. (2000). The politics of ethnic authenticity: Building Native American identities and communities. In P. Kivisto & G. Rundblad (Eds.), *Multiculturalism in the United States: Current issues, contemporary issues* (pp. 113-124). Thousand Oaks, CA: Pine Forge Press.

Pascoe, P. (1999). Race, gender, and the privileges of property: On the significance of miscegenation law in the U.S. west. In V. J. Matsumoto & B. Allmendinger (Eds.), *Over the edge: Remapping the American west* (pp. 215-230). Berkeley: University of California Press.

Peters, K. M. (1998). Continuing identity: Laguna Pueblo railroaders in Richmond, California. *American Indian Culture and Research Journal, 22*(4),187-198.

Ramirez, R. (2001). Healing through grief: Urban Indians reimagining culture and community. In S. Lobo & K. Peters (Eds.), *American Indians and the urban experience* (pp. 249-264). Walnut Creek, CA: AltaMira Press.

Romero, J. (Writer and Producer). (2001). *American holocaust: When It's over, I'll be an Indian* [Video documentary]. Los Angeles: Spirit World Productions.

Sandefur, G. D., & McKinnell, T. (1986). American Indian intermarriage. *Social Science Research, 15,* 347-371.

Snipp, C. M. (1989). *American Indians: The first of this land.* New York: Russell Sage Foundation.

Snipp, C. M. (1996, November). A demographic comeback for American Indians. *Population Today, 24,* 4-5.

Spencer, R. (1999). *Spurious issues: Race and multiracial identity politics in the United States.* Boulder, CO: Westview Press.

Spicer, P. (1993). Drinking, foster care, and the intergenerational continuity of parenting in an urban Indian community. *American Indian Culture and Research Journal, 27*(4), 335-360.

Springwood, C. F., & King, C. R. (2000). Race, power, and representation in contemporary American sport. In P. Kivisto & G. Rundblad (Eds.), *Multiculturalism in the United States: Current issues, contemporary voices* (pp. 161-174). Thousand Oaks, CA: Pine Forge Press.

Sprott, J. E. (1998). The mingling of Alaska Natives with foreigners: A brief historical overview. In J. Ferrante & P. Brown, Jr. (Eds.), *The social construction of race and ethnicity in the United States* (pp. 216-222). New York: Longman.

Stiffarm, L. A., & Lane, P., Jr. (1992). The demography of native North America: A question of American Indian survival. In M. A. Jaimes (Ed.), *The state of native America: Genocide, colonization, and resistance.* Boston: South End Press.

Straus, T., & Valentino, D. (2001). Retribalization in urban Indian communities. In S. Lobo & K. Peters (Eds.), *American Indians and the urban experience* (pp. 85-94). Walnut Creek, CA: AltaMira Press.

Taylor, D. H. (1996). *Funny, you don't look like one.* Penticton, British Columbia: Theytus Books.

Thorton, R., Sandefur, G. D., & Snipp, C. M. (1991). American Indian fertility patterns: 1910 and 1940 to 1980. *American Indian Quarterly, 15,* 359-367.

Van Buren, R. (2001). *Voices of American Indian women: Constructing identity.* Paper presented at the annual meeting of the Pacific Sociological Association, San Francisco.

Vizenor, G. (1990). *Crossbloods: Bone courts, bingo and other reports.* Minneapolis: University of Minnesota Press.

Waldram, J. B. (1997). The way of the pipe: Aboriginal spirituality and symbolic healing. In *Canadian prisons*. Peterborough, Ontario: Broadview.

Waters, M. C. (1998). Choosing an ancestry. In J. Ferrante & P. Brown, Jr. (Eds.), *The social construction of race and ethnicity in the United States* (pp. 235-238). New York: Longman.

Weibel-Orlando, J. (1991). And the drumbeat goes on . . . urban Indian institutional survival into the new millennium. In S. Lobo & K. Peters (Eds.), *American Indians and the urban experience* (pp. 95-113). Walnut Creek, CA: AltaMira Press.

CHAPTER 12

"Race," "Ethnicity," and "Culture" in Hawai'i
The Myth of the "Model Minority" State

LAURA DESFOR EDLES

California State University, Northridge

In the last several years, there has been a surge of interest in "multiracial" peoples and identity. The phenomenal young golfer, Tiger Woods, whose Thai, African American, Native American, and Irish roots are well known, has undoubtedly (if not unwittingly) been the single most influential person in raising "multiracial" consciousness in the United States, the single most prominent (if not inadvertent) spokesperson for "multiracialism." Of course, the option to identify oneself as more than one race in the 2000 U.S. Census has been the single most important "official" institutional act in the recent affirmation and legitimization of "multiracialism."[1]

However, as students of "race" and "ethnicity" well know, the phenomenon we call "multiracialism" has been a part of American history from the start. Since the forced migration of Africans in the 16th century, many, if not most, American-born "blacks" have been of "mixed blood," with both American Indian and European ancestry.[2] Similarly, some 85% of "Mexicans" have "mixed" indigenous and Spanish roots, which is why, at least since the 1980 census, social scientists and demographers have tended to construe "Hispanic/Latino" and so on as an "ethnic" rather than "racial" identity.[3]

Yet in my view, one of the most important and misunderstood cases of "multiracialism"

AUTHOR'S NOTE: This chapter is based on a paper presented at the Pacific Sociological meetings in San Francisco, California, in April 2001. I thank Tina Wilson, C. Reginald Daniel, Loretta Winters, Herman DeBose, Jon Okamura, Eldon Wegner, Herb Barringer, Jit Singh, Noel Kent, Orlando Garcia-Santiago, Chuck Petranek, Miriam Stark, and Bill Teter for their helpful comments and suggestions and help in collecting data. Finally, *mahalo* to the students at the University of Hawai'i, Manoa, who took the time to share their thoughts with me and respond to my survey.

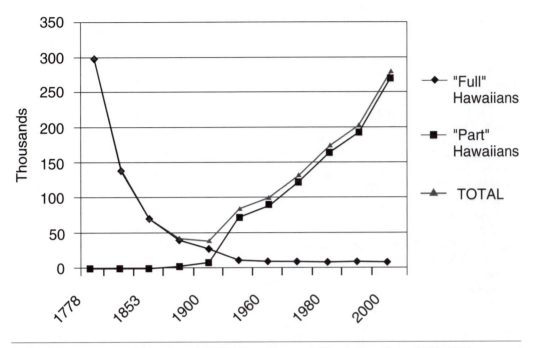

Figure 12.1   Estimated Number of "Full" Hawaiians and "Part" Hawaiians, 1778–2000

and "multiculturalism" in the United States is that of the state of "Hawai'i." Hawai'i has been multiracial at least since colonization in the 1700s. With the introduction of European communicable diseases, many "pure" Hawaiians died; there were some 300,000 native Hawaiians on the arrival of Captain Cook but only 58,000 a century later (Barringer & Liu, 1994). However, because of intermarriage, the number of "part Hawaiians" rose from about 7,000 in 1900 to more than 280,000 today (Figure 12.1).[4]

In addition, because of the institutionalization of a plantation economy and the importation of workers from China, Japan, Korea, and the Philippines as well as the colonization by Europeans and European Americans, there has been a historic trend toward an increased frequency of intergroup marriage in Hawai'i and, consequently, "multiracial" progeny (Johnson &

Ogasawara, 1988). Indeed, as shown in Table 12.1, 21.4% of the population in Hawai'i identified themselves by two or more races in the 2000 Census compared with only 2.4% of the national population.

It is primarily for this reason—high rates of intergroup contact and marriage—that many people view Hawai'i as a "racial" or "multiracial" paradise. For tourists as well as mainstream academics alike, Hawai'i is a "laboratory of race relations" where peoples of sharply differing traditions are able to live together in harmony with one another, where diverse "races" have fused through intermarriage (Okamura, 1980, p. 122). For instance, Davis (1991) maintains that "the history of the [Hawaiian] islands has generally not been racist. . . . There has been no systematic racial segregation and discrimination, either de jure or de facto, and people generally are scornful of anyone who

Table 12.1   Race and Ethnicity in Hawai'i—2000 Census

	Number	Percentage
One race	952,194	78.6
White	294,102	24.3
Black or African American	22,003	1.8
American Indian or Alaska Native	3,535	0.3
Asian	503,868	41.6
• Asian Indian	1,441	0.1
• Chinese	56,600	4.7
• Filipino	170,635	14.1
• Japanese	201,764	16.7
• Korean	23,537	1.9
• Vietnamese	7,867	0.6
• Other Asian	42,024	3.5
Native Hawaiian and Other Pacific Islander	113,539	9.4
• Native Hawaiian	80,137	6.6
• Guamanian or Chamorro	1,663	0.1
• Samoan	16,166	1.3
• Other Pacific Islander	15,573	1.3
Some other race	15,147	1.3
Two or more races	259,343	21.4
Race alone or with other races		
White	476,162	39.3
Black or African American	33,343	2.8
American Indian or Alaska Native	24,882	2.1
Asian	703,232	58.0
Native Hawaiian and other Pacific Islander	282,667	23.3
Some other race	47,603	3.9
Hispanic or Latino and race		
Hispanic or Latino (any race)	87,699	7.2
• Mexican	19,820	1.6
• Puerto Rican	30,005	2.5
• Cuban	711	0.1
• Other Hispanic or Latino	37,163	3.1
Not Hispanic or Latino	1,123,838	92.8
• White alone	277,091	22.9

exhibits racial prejudice" (p. 111). Indeed, even in her ground-breaking book, *The Multiracial Experience,* Maria Root (1994) laments that even in Hawai'i people living there have "been exposed to considerable negativity" regarding racial mixing (p. xxiii), which implicitly affirms the myth of Hawai'i as a multiracial panacea.

In short, Hawaii has become our "model minority" state, the state that epitomizes what a multiracial, multiethnic, multicultural melting pot should look like. "Harmonious Hawaii" is a model minority state that symbolically opposes not-model-minority states, such as California, where people do not "just get along." In contrast to "harmonious Hawai'i," not-model-minority states (e.g., California) are plagued by interracial violence (e.g., the Rodney King verdict and its aftermath); in addition, in not-model-minority states, people wave the "race card" at the drop of a hat, blaming "race" for their social and personal ills. In sum, whether applied to an individual or an entire state, the model minority myth is itself an expression of an extraordinarily loaded, binary racial code. The sacralization of certain minorities inherently involves the profanation of others (Edles, 2002).[5]

Of course, just as there are significant historical, theoretical, and empirical problems with the original model minority myth, there are significant historical, theoretical, and empirical problems with the myth of Hawai'i as the model minority state. The two most important (albeit interrelated) problems are (a) that the myth of Hawai'i as a model minority state is grossly, historically inaccurate; and (b) that the myth of Hawai'i as a model minority state grossly misconstrues the complex workings of racialization.

Specifically, the first problem with the myth of Hawai'i as the model minority state is that it grossly ignores the colonial history of Hawai'i. The fact is that contemporary Hawaiian culture is rooted not in the happy, melding of diverse cultures but in the violent imposition of American institutions on Hawaiians and the immigrant plantation groups through armed revolution and the penal sanctions of the contract labor system (Okamura, 1980, p. 123). To say that Hawaiian culture reflects a multiracial paradise ignores that Native Hawaiians have been nearly decimated by colonization and that, consequently, Native Hawaiians have the highest poverty rates, infant death rates, suicide rates, and incarceration rates in the state of Hawai'i today (see Barringer & Liu, 1994; Castberg, 1998), although akin to their native counterparts on the "mainland,"[6] Native Hawaiians continue to struggle for autonomy and self-determination. Moreover, to imagine Hawai'i as a multiracial paradise ignores that historically social relations among the various plantation groups—Japanese, Chinese, Koreans,

Filipinos, Portuguese—and the wider Hawai'i society have not been particularly amicable. The fascinating thing about Hawai'i is that historically it has combined high rates of intermarriage and a genuine "aloha" spirit, with a tremendous cognizance of "race" and "ethnicity" that is the polar opposite of what on the "mainland" we call "color-blindness" or "cultural pluralism." In short, what Hawai'i exhibits to a much greater degree than most places in the United States is a very complex racial/ethnic code, a very nuanced system of racial/ethnic stratification (see Grant & Ogawa, 1993).

The second problem with the myth of Hawai'i as our model minority state mirrors the problem with the original model minority myth: Both overindividualize "race"; that is, they work strictly at the level of the individual. Hawai'i is imagined as a multiracial paradise because it is imagined that the people in Hawai'i are not "racist." Thus, whether in its individual or state version, the model minority myth infers that "race" is an individual problem and that the solution to racism is individual as well. Nowhere is this overindividualization of how "race" works more evident than in the romantic conceptualization of Hawai'i as the state in which the problem of racism has been solved through *intermarriage.* Although there are certainly many wonderful things about intermarriage, to say that intermarriage is the solution to the problem of racism is not a whole lot more logical than saying that heterosexual marriage is the route out of sexism. The notion that one cannot possibly be racist if he is married to a person of another "race" (at least against that race) is almost as absurd as saying that one cannot possibly be sexist because he is married to someone of the opposite gender. (Can you imagine a man saying, "I can't be sexist; some of my best friends—indeed, even my wife and my mother—are women!") Surely the fact that historically in Hawai'i (as well as the "mainland") the intermarriage rates for Asian women and white men are far higher than that of white women and Asian men indicates that something else is going on here rather than strictly racial accommodation. (Almost three quarters of intermarriages for Asian Americans are comprised of white male/Asian American female pairings; Root, 2001, p. 187). Even if one blames those rates on demographic variables (i.e., the "over-supply" of Asian women), which is dubious, surely the advertisements directed at white military men make it quite clear. These ads bluntly state things such as "Tired of those white feminist bitches? Get a subservient wife from Vietnam!" Surely these ads indicate that whether "racism" or "sexism" is defeated or not depends on what is going on, or what happens, within an "interracial" relationship/marriage.

Put in another way, the motivation behind and impact of interracial marriage in a particular environment is an *empirical* question that warrants further exploration. This is, indeed, one of the central questions undergirding my research. In this chapter I explore, first, the history of "race" and "ethnicity" in Hawai'i. As indicated previously, I am particularly interested in the case of Hawai'i because it has historically combined high rates of intermarriage (so often posed as the solution to racism) with a tremendous cognizance of "race" (which is the polar opposite of that other solution to racism so often touted on the "mainland": color-blindness) and ethnicity. Second, I attempt to resolve some theoretical dilemmas uncovered by this historical examination of "race" and "ethnicity" in Hawai'i. Specifically, I argue that social scientists have tended to either misconstrue or ignore the role of culture in the complex process of racialization and identity formation; but the case of Hawai'i helps illuminate the complex relationship among "race," "ethnicity," and "culture."

THEORETICAL AND METHODOLOGICAL BACKGROUND: A DISCURSIVE APPROACH TO "CULTURE," "RACE," AND "ETHNICITY"

Colloquially, "race" is used to refer to obvious physical differences between groups. However, as most social scientists know, scientifically the concept of "race" is untenable. No matter what system of classification is used—anatomical (e.g., skin color, hair texture, body and/or facial shape) or physiological (e.g., metabolic rate, genetic diseases, hormonal activity, or blood characteristics), differences among individuals of the same group (or racial type) are greater than those found between groups. The one thing on which biologists, geneticists, and physical anthropologists agree is that "pure" races do not exist today (and they may have never existed; Edles, 2001; Marger, 1997, p. 20).

For this reason, since the 1920s many social scientists have abandoned the concept of "race" altogether, replacing it with the study of ethnicity, which is explicitly construed as a social (rather than a biological) category. According to Weber's (1922/1968) classic definition, an ethnic group is one whose members "entertain a subjective belief in their common descent because of similarities of physical type or of customs or both, or because of memories of colonization and migration" (p. 389). Meanwhile, other analysts, such as Alba (1992), slide "race" in as a special *kind* of ethnic group: "A racial group is . . . an ethnic group whose members are believed, by others if not also by themselves to be physiologically distinctive."

However, the problem with throwing the "race" concept out altogether or subsuming it under "ethnicity" is that "race" and "ethnicity" are both fundamental categories of perception and experience in modern (and postmodern) society. Next to gender, "race"

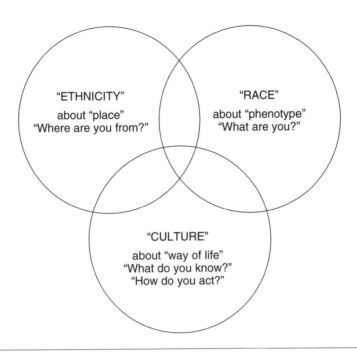

Figure 12.2   "Ethnicity," "Race," and "Culture"

and "ethnicity" are fundamental ways we order our experience and organize meaning. Put in another way, what makes "race" recognizable across space and time is "the deeply held—though biologically untenable—schema of 'separation of human populations by some notion of stock or collective heredity of traits'" (Anthias & Yuval-Davis, 1992, p. 2, cited in Jung, 1999, p. 363). Race "provides people with a deep sense of belonging to an imagined and limited community" (Jung, 1999, p. 363); just because "race" is biologically untenable, we must not ignore this deep sense of belonging and the social consequences that such belonging and categorization creates.

Nevertheless, the question remains, how can we use the concept of "race" without reaffirming the erroneous perception that these differences are phenotypical, biological, or somehow "hard-wired"? As Loveman (1999) quite rightly points out, ironically, many social scientists and demographers

briefly acknowledge that "race" does not really exist, but they then proceed to use the "race" concept and racial categories as they were real. I use the term *racism* to refer to a specific kind of racialized system of meaning, a system of meaning in which (implicitly or explicitly) physical "racial" differences between groups are assumed to reflect internal (moral, personality, intellectual) differences between groups and that these differences are organized both biologically and hierarchically (i.e., on the basis of genetic inheritance, some groups are innately superior to others).

My definition of "race" is similar to that of Eduardo Bonilla-Silva (1999, p. 903), who conceptualizes "race" as a social category that evokes the language of phenotype (i.e., "What are you?"), whereas "ethnicity" is a social category that primarily refers to and evokes the language of place (i.e. "Where are you from?"; Figure 12.2).

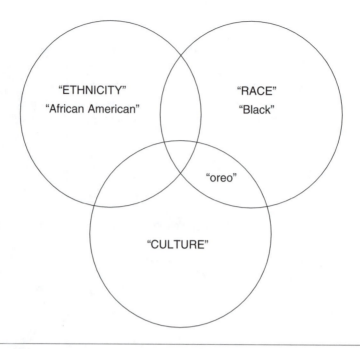

Figure 12.3   Ethnic, Racial and Cultural Dimensions of "African American"/"Black"

In our common vernacular, "ethnically" similar people may be "racially" (i.e., perceived as "phenotypically") different (e.g., "Cubans" can be dark-skinned ["black"] or light-skinned ["white"]; whereas "racially" similar people [perceived as "black"] might have completely different "ethnic" backgrounds [Haitian, Cuban, Senegalese]). For me, shifts in discourse over time and among social groups (e.g., away from "racial" terms ["colored" to "Negro" to "black," "white"] and toward "ethnic" terms ["African American," "European American"]) reflect changes in how people think about and perceive social identity and categorization. Thus, as shown in Figure 12.3, although the terms "black" and "African American" are often used interchangeably, "black" is, in fact, primarily a "racial" term that emphasizes the perception of "phenotypical" differences, whereas "African American" is primarily an "ethnic" term that emphasizes a

common African heritage. For instance, the term "black" is commonly used (or, I argue, should be used) when discussing the phenomenon of "racial profiling," or what in African American communities is sometimes called DWB ("driving while black"; i.e., the allegation that police officers stop people who appear "black," in other words, because of their *appearance,* whether they are a tourist on a 10-day tour from Jamaica or a 10th-generation "African American"). By contrast, the term "African American" refers to people of African ancestry who grow up in the United States. The term "African American" implies that African Americans are not the same as "Africans" nor are they the same as "Brazilians," who also share an African heritage.

However, as shown in Figure 12.2, in contrast to Bonilla-Silva, in my work I also use a third category—"culture"—alongside "race" and "ethnicity." "Culture" is primarily

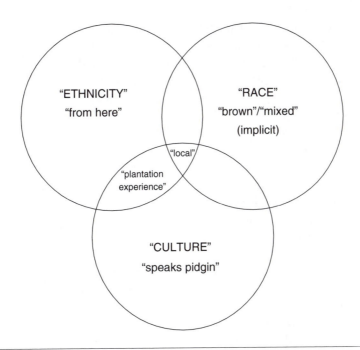

Figure 12.4   "Ethnic," Racial," and "Cultural" Dimensions of "Local"

about "ways of life," most important language. Culture evokes questions such as "What do you know?" and "How do you act?"(although these questions tend to be implicit rather than explicit). Both on the "mainland" and in Hawai'i, culture is often at the heart of xenophobia (fear of foreigners) as well as anti-immigrantism (although, to be sure, xenophobia and racism often go hand in hand).[7]

Interestingly, as shown in Figure 12.3, neither "black" nor "African American" explicitly contains a cultural component. One is not generally deemed black or African American because of the way one acts or because of one's way of life. (For this, one generally uses the term "black" or "African American" *culture*). However, slang, derogatory ethnic/racial terms often implicitly contain cultural referents. For example, as shown in Figure 12.3, previously popular terms such as "Uncle Tom,"

and "oreo" (the symbolic equivalent—and root—of a "local" term in Hawai'i: "coconut") means that though one looks "black" (appears "black" "on the outside"), one acts "white," (is "white" "on the inside"); i.e., one does not act within the norms and behavioral codes, particularly the language, of "black culture."[8]

As we will shortly see, by contrast, in Hawai'i, "racial" and "ethnic" discourse is explicitly laced with significant cultural referents. This is particularly obvious in the case of "local" identity, a category of experience and meaning that first emerged with a strong racial sense but now has primarily cultural connotations (Figure 12.4).

This empirical finding is discussed in greater detail later. In my open-ended survey of 128 students at the University of Hawai'i, Manoa, more than 90% (116/128) of the students surveyed used cultural variables to define being "local" (e.g., way of life, food, music, attitude), whereas less than 9% (11/128) said that being "local" meant being a particular "race" and 13% (17/128) defined "local" by referring to a specific "ethnic" heritage.

Nonetheless, this does not mean that there is an absence of racialization and racism in Hawai'i. Rather, Hawai'i exhibits an extraordinarily complex system of racial/ethnic codes, in which "race" and "ethnicity" are often implicit rather than explicit. These intricate, often implicit, systems of meaning about "race" and "ethnicity" are rooted in the extraordinary "multiracial," "multiethnic," and "multicultural" history of Hawai'i. Thus, we begin with a brief history of "race," "ethnicity," and "culture" in Hawai'i; we then turn to our sociological analysis of multiculturalism, multiracialism, and "local" identity.

THE MULTIRACIAL, MULTIETHNIC, AND MULTICULTURAL HISTORY OF HAWAII

The first inhabitants of Hawai'i were Polynesians who came to Hawai'i from the Marquesas Islands and Tahiti around 450 A.D. A second wave of Polynesians came to Hawai'i between the 11th and 14th centuries, bringing with them a more "developed" culture as well as new food plants, language, customs, and a more stratified social system.[9] There were at least 300,000 and possibly as many as 800,000 Hawaiians in the mid-1700s (Haas, 1998a, p. 23). The islands, divided into four separate kingdoms (Hawai'i, Maui, Oahu, and Kauai), were engaged in intense rivalry and warfare from 1650 until 1795, when, with the aid of newly acquired Western firearms and ships, King Kamehameha I consolidated the islands (except Kauai) under his rule (Merry, 2000, p. 52).[10]

From the 13th to the early 19th centuries, there were few visitors to the remote Hawaiian islands, and thus visitors, mostly shipwrecked seamen, were warmly welcomed with a spirit of *aloha,* a welcome that combined joy and respect. Reports indicate that Japanese ships arrived in Hawai'i as early as the 13th century; the first Europeans to arrive were said to be two Spanish explorers who survived a shipwreck in 1521 and then made their way to Hawai'i and intermarried with the native population (Haas, 1998a, p. 23). A Chinese man was reported to be living in Hawai'i as early as 1794 (Glick, 1980, p. 1), and there were "firsthand" reports of Japanese and Chinese arriving in Hawai'i beginning in the early 1800s and marrying Hawaiian women.

This is not to say that the relations between Hawaiians and Europeans were always amicable. Rather, they were often violent, as was the case with the English Captain James Cook, who inadvertently arrived in Hawai'i in 1778. Scholars concur that Cook and his crew were welcomed initially and that King Kamehameha I was eager to trade for Western goods; nevertheless, conflict between Cook and his crew and native Hawaiians soon broke out, and Cook was killed in 1779 after he tried to take a chief hostage in order to retrieve a small ship hijacked by several Native Hawaiian warriors (Haas, 1998a).[11] Cook's death brought about extensive retaliatory killings by the British; in 1790, some 100 Hawaiians were massacred in retaliation for the killing of a single European guarding a boat stolen for its coveted nails (Merry, 2000, p. 44).

Even before the arrival of Captain Cook, non-Hawaiian visitors and inhabitants of the islands were called "*haole,*" which is commonly translated as "foreigner."[12] However, because most of the foreigners were "white" Europeans, *haole* took on racial, and later, class connotations (Figure 12.5).

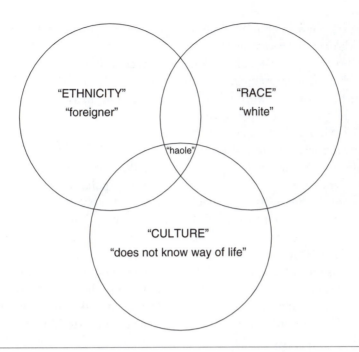

Figure 12.5 "Ethnic," "Racial," and "Cultural" Dimensions of "Haole"

By 1790, there were about 10 *haole* men living in Hawai'i; they congregated around King Kamehameha and married high-status Hawaiian women (Whittaker, 1986, pp. 25-27). The *hapa haole* ("half/half") children of these mixed marriages were accorded high status (Haas, 1992, p. 50), closely identifying with their mother's Hawaiian family and relatives.[13] Missionaries, primarily from New England, began arriving in Hawai'i in 1820. The missionaries sought to extinguish the polytheistic native Hawaiian religion, including the *kapu* system once and for all, to clothe the native Hawaiians in Western dress, and to teach them the basic tenets of "civilization." Interestingly, the American Board of Commissioners for Foreign Missions (ABCFM) mandated that missionaries to Hawai'i must be married before departure; previous experience in Tahiti had established that in the midst of a Polynesian community, celibate men were at risk (Turnbull & Ferguson, 1997, p. 100).

The missionaries preached that the decimation of the Native population—from more than 300,000 in 1778 to 71,000 in 1853 (see Figure 12.1)—was evidence of spiritual and moral malaise. Missionary physicians recognized that native Hawaiians were suffering from Western diseases, but they took "social Darwinism" for granted and maintained that indigenous peoples were dying because they were biologically, or racially, inferior. Of course, the dominant Western view of the 19th century was that racial inequality (i.e., white supremacy) was a function of the "laws of nature" ("manifest destiny") ordained by God. Thus, for instance, in his 1854 *Essay on the Inequality of the Races*, Count Joseph Arthur de Gobineau referred to Hawaiians as a mixture of black and yellow peoples, who were dying off as a result of miscegenation and thus needed the wisdom of the whites to advance themselves (Haas, 1992, p. 51).

Distraught by the catastrophic annihilation of their people by disease, many *ali'i*

(Hawaiian royalty)— most important Queen Ka'ahumanu, who became regent in 1825— converted to Christianity. To Ka'ahumanu, it seemed that the missionaries spoke for a new and powerful god, Jehovah, and that Christianity might provide the new source of *mana* she needed (Merry, 2000, pp. 40-41).[14] In addition, the *ali'i* were fascinated by the strategic usefulness and transcendent power of *palapala* (the written word) that the missionaries brought; all the chiefs wanted to be able to read and write, and they quickly started writing letters to each other and teaching their children (Merry, 2000, p. 64).

The *ali'i* may also have been attracted to Christianity as a way to control the increasing number of unruly sailors and resident foreigners in the booming port towns (Merry, 2000, p. 67). Between 1824 and 1852, some 5,016 vessels sailed into the harbor at Honolulu, and from these ships, some 100 to 200 seamen deserted (or were "discharged" to Honolulu to idle in grog shops and brothels or sign on to another crew later) per year (Whittaker, 1986, pp. 26-27). By 1828, some 400 foreigners (mostly American and European men) were estimated to be living in Honolulu; and King Kamehameha I began to take action against the drifters and adventurers "of low character" who formed alliances with Hawaiian women, married them, and then abandoned them (Whittaker, 1986, pp. 27-28). In 1840 some members of the Hawaiian legislative council argued that unnaturalized foreigners should not be allowed to marry Hawaiians at all because after a year or so (and sometimes within a month), the husband often returned to his own country, deserting his wife; and the women were left in destitution (Greer, 1970, p. 78). Foreigners, both visiting and resident, were outraged by the naturalization requirement, and thus an alternative oath was set out, a bond of not more than $1,000 to the minister of the interior, pledging faithful performance of marital and parental duties (Greer, 1970, p. 78). By 1848 there were between 1,300 to 1,500 foreigners living in Hawai'i, in comparison to the some 100,000 Native Hawaiians.

The Plantation Economy

In the second half of the 19th century, the economic, political, social, demographic, cultural, and racial/ethnic landscape of Hawai'i drastically and irrevocably changed. *Haole* entrepreneurs convinced the Hawaiian monarchy to privatize the land (before that land was not for sale; it was held in common on behalf of the people by the monarchs). An 1841 law had allowed the *ali'i* to lease land to foreigners for up to 55 years, but still the *haole* were not satisfied. Thus, in 1848, the monarchs divided the Hawaiian land up in what is called *The Great Mahele*. Now Native Hawaiians could own "private property," but they had to file a claim for their own *kuleana* (land where they lived and to which they put productive use) and pay hefty fees to survey the land and register their titles. If they failed to do so, others could file claims of adverse possession. Meanwhile, *haole* entrepreneurs (many children of missionaries) entreated the Native Hawaiians to sell at profits that seemed staggering. Thus, many native Hawaiians soon became tenants on land owned by others. Indeed, by 1886 foreigners owned two thirds of Hawaiian land.

Sugar was a particularly lucrative crop, and *haole* entrepreneurs set up plantations to harvest sugarcane (and later pineapple). Power was soon consolidated in the five largest sugar companies, later known as "The Big Five"— Castle & Cooke, Ltd; Theo H. Davies, Ltd.; H. Hackfeld & Co (later American Factors); C. Brewer & Co; and Alexander and Baldwin, Ltd—who treated government as an extension of the plantation system. The Hawaiian monarch Queen Lili'uokalani attempted to break up the control of the "Big Five," but her efforts backfired. In an illegal *coup d'etat* in 1893, the Big Five ordered 162 troops to disembark from the USS *Boston* and seize the government building and place the queen under house arrest in the palace, demanding that she relinquish her sovereignty. The leaders of the conspiracy declared the dissolution of the monarchy and proclaimed a provisional government under martial law, pending annexation by the United States.[15] In 1896, the U.S. Congress voted to annex Guam, Hawai'i, the Philippines, and Puerto Rico. The annexations were made by a joint congressional resolution, not a treaty; there was no referendum in Hawai'i or in the other newly acquired "possessions."

As indicated previously, the native Hawaiian population was rapidly declining as a result of disease (see Figure 12.1), and many Native Hawaiians refused to work on the *haole* plantations. Thus, *haole* landlords began to import "aliens" from China and later Japan to work on the plantations. A few Europeans (mostly from Portugal) came as contract laborers, but because of their "white" skin and European origins they became plantation "managers." According to the Masters and Servants Act of 1850—a revealing title if there ever was one—the costs of transporting Chinese or other workers to Hawai'i were to be paid by means of lengthy work contracts, which could be broken only under penalty of a jail sentence, thereby creating a condition of legal peonage. Thus began the system of institutionalized racial discrimination, in which plantation managers paid different wage rates to workers of different nationalities and genders for the same work.

In other words, by the end of the 19th century, Hawai'i was not a "multiracial melting pot" but a multiethnic caste society in which *haoles* and a few upper-status Native Hawaiians and *hapas* lived the good life, Portuguese became plantation supervisors,

Chinese and Japanese became plantation laborers, and lower-status Native Hawaiians tried to eke out an existence through traditional subsistence agriculture or as unskilled workers in the towns (Merry, 1998). For example, on one sugar plantation in Honoka'a, north of Hilo, Portuguese laborers were paid $15 to $16 a month in 1885, whereas newly arrived Japanese were paid $9 for the same work (Merry, 2000, p. 143). Most revealing of the mind-set of this era are labor documents that list workers in categories that merge plantation tasks with race and gender. For instance, see the manager's report from the Olaa Sugar Company in 1901 and 1902 (the first few years of its operation) shown in Table 12.2.

As Sally Engel Merry (2000) points out,

This curious list of employees, similar to that provided in other plantation manager's reports, blends occupation, nationality, and gender as if they all refer to the same thing. . . . work is so deeply understood in categories of race and gender that these identities stand in for occupational identities, just as the first three categories of occupation similarly encode a racial and gender destination of haole (white) male, although this identity is implicit. (p. 142)

Unhappy with this discrimination, workers went on strike from time to time. After the turn of the century, *haole* plantation owners sought to circumvent strikes by importing workers from new lands, such as Korea and, especially after the turn of the century, the Philippines, most of whom were illiterate. Between 1915 and 1933, Filipino males were typically paid $18 to $20 a month, whereas Filipino women were paid $12 to $14 (Merry, 2000, p. 143). Although conditions improved for other ethnic groups on the plantations, Filipinos became virtual serfs (Abbott, 1967, cited in Haas, 1998a, p. 37). Plantation owners evicted social workers who tried to teach English to Filipinos. Trade

Table 12.2   Manager's Report From the
Olaa Sugar Company, 1901 and
1902

	1901	1902
Management and office	11	13
Lunas[a]	34	14
Mechanics	42	18
Chinese cane cultivation contractors	21	46
Japanese cane cultivation contractors	399	577
Japanese day laborers	805	424
Japanese day women	38	6
Chinese	206	2
Portuguese	100	91
Hawaiians	20	9
Porto Ricans[b]	220	85
Porto Rican women	17	2
Other nationalities	19	7
Sundry clearing contracts	550	—

SOURCE: Merry (2000, p. 142).
[a]Lunas = "foremen."
[b]Porto Ricans = Puerto Ricans.

union organization was hampered by the fact that plantation owners could deport any alien who refused to accept labor conditions.

In 1924, after 8 months of strikes, Filipino workers protested eviction from their homes by taking two strike breakers as hostages. Sheriff's deputies arrived to quell the disturbance and shot 16 strikers dead. Four law enforcement officers also died in what has become known as the Hanapepe Massacre, and some 60 Filipinos subsequently served jail sentences of 4 years. In the ensuing investigation, Filipinos were deemed "subjects" without constitutional protections under American law (Wright, 1972, p. 59, cited in Haas, 1998a, p. 39), and Pablo Manlapit, an attorney who led the strike, was deported to the Philippines.

Picture-Brides

By 1890, most of the population in Hawai'i was not native Hawaiian: The Census reported a total population of about 90,000, with 41,000 Hawaiians, 15,000 Chinese, 12,000 Japanese, 9,000 Portuguese, 2,000 Americans, 1,300 British, and 1,000 Germans (Fu & Heaton, 1997, p. 14). Most of the "alien" laborers, who came in waves from China, Japan, Korea, and the Philippines, were male. Consequently, there was a shortage of "marriageable" women. However, between 1885 and 1924, some 70,000 women migrated from Japan to Hawai'i and the United States. Many of these women were picture brides, others prostitutes; some fell partly within these categories. Interestingly, some Japanese women became picture brides with the intention of *migration* (not marriage), and many others were lied to about their prospective husbands (e.g., about their age, health, economic status), and ended up deserting their husbands within a year of migration. Indeed, Mengel (1997, p. 24) found that of 110 divorce records between Japanese workers from 1885 to 1908, 84 were petitioned by the wives and only 24 were filed by the husbands. Mengel (1997, p. 23) suspects that many subsequent marriages were interracial and, therefore, that the rate of interracial unions of Japanese immigrants and others is much higher than previously assumed (although there is a lack of data on this). Nevertheless, the high number of Japanese women in Hawai'i meant that fewer Japanese intermarried. In 1930, the male-female ratio was only 1.6:1, far lower than that of other immigrant groups (Spickard, 1989, p. 75).

MULTICULTURALISM, MULTIRACIALISM, AND "LOCAL" IDENTITY

Generally, the term "Hawaiian" refers to the people who inhabited the islands before the coming of Europeans and Americans in the 18th and 19th centuries. Hawaiian activists and scholars such as Trask (1996, p. 906) use the term "*Native* Hawaiian" to emphasize that Hawaiians are "not immigrants." In either case, the point is that the terms "Hawaiian" and "Native Hawaiian" refer only to a small fraction of Hawai'i's population (see Table 12.1). The vast majority of those who live in Hawai'i today are not "Hawaiian" or "Native Hawaiian."

Thus, in the last century, the term "local" has emerged to refer to people who are born and raised in Hawai'i who are of Hawai'i but not necessarily descendants of the original aboriginal peoples. However, given the extraordinarily raced, colonial history of Hawai'i, it should come as no surprise that the term "local" is not only about "place of origin" but that it also has significant "race" and "class" connotations. Historically, the term "local" has meant "working class people of color in Hawai'i," particularly those with "plantation" backgrounds as opposed to *haole* elites (see Figure 12.4). This meaning of "local" was crystallized and affirmed in the 1930s in the Massie case. As John Rosa (2000, p. 100) points out, the Massie case did not cause "local" identity to emerge, but it became a means to express "local" identity.

The Massie Case

The military population in Hawai'i is and was largely segregated from the mainstream on military bases. However, one evening in 1931, Thalia Massie, the white, 20-year-old wife of naval Lieutenant Thomas Massie, walked home from a nightclub in Waikiki. Arriving home with her face bruised and her lips swollen, she claimed that she had been raped. Five young men who happened to be having an altercation with a couple in another car at about the same were arrested. Two (Joseph Kahahawai and Ben Ahakuelo) were Native Hawaiian; two (Horace Ida and David Takai) were Japanese American, and one (Henry Chang) was half Native Hawaiian and half Chinese. Massie identified the five men as

her rapists, and the five "local" men were put on trial. However, a jury found the evidence slim and refused to bring in a verdict. Defense attorneys argued that the youths would not have had enough time to commit the crime after leaving a dance at the Aloha Amusement Park and before being in a near traffic accident in downtown (Rosa, 2000, pp. 95-96).

Incensed that "justice" had not prevailed, the Massies resorted to vigilantism. A group of Navy men abducted one of the defendants, Horace Ida, from a speakeasy in downtown Honolulu, beat him, and nearly threw him over the Pali (a famous cliff on O'ahu) when he refused to admit to the rape of Thalia Massie. A month later, another defendant, Joseph Kahahawai, fared much worse. Thomas Massie, Grace Fortescue (Thalia Massie's mother), and two subordinate naval officers tried to force a confession of Joseph Kahahawai (who was called the "darkest" of the youths) and ended up killing him with a single gunshot to the heart. The Massie-Fortescue group hired the famous "mainland" attorney, Clarence Darrow, to defend them, but they were found guilty of manslaughter by a jury of "local" men and sentenced to up to 10 years in prison. However, minutes after the group was sentenced, they were escorted across the street to the territorial governor's office in 'Iolani Palace. There Governor Lawrence Judd commuted the sentence to just 1 day of detention. The Massie-Fortescue group spent half a day signing papers and posing for press photos on the balcony of Iolani Palace and were then freed. Within a week, Thalia Massie and all the members of the Massie-Fortescue group left the islands, never to return (Rosa, 2000, p. 96).

Hawai'i residents were outraged. For "local" Asians and Native Hawaiians, this was an example of "*haole* justice." The Japanese American newspaper, the *Hawai'i Hochi*, lambasted the Territory's *haole* leadership as "traitors to Hawai'i in the eyes of the common people" (Rosa, 2000, p. 96). Of course, the main point here is that the Massie case crystallized and reaffirmed the structural as well as symbolic opposition between "locals" ("brown" working class) and "*haoles*" (white elites). The five "local" boys arrested for the rape of Thalia Massie grew up in Kalihi-Palama (a working class district of Honolulu) and had attended Kauluwela Elementary School. They were members of a new generation that in contrast to their parents on rural plantations (with ethnically segregated housing), inhabited city spaces with a denser and more diverse population. The Kauluwela boys spoke "Pidgin," an urban variant of Hawai'i Creole English (HCE) that had emerged from the plantation experience and later developed in public elementary schools. They also shared a common Americanized youth culture (e.g., sports teams, school activities, dances, movies; Rosa, 2000, p. 98). This meaning of "local" is illustrated in Figure 12.4.

Jon Okamura's (1980) classic explanation for the emergence of "local" identity in Hawai'i parallels E. P. Thompson's conception of class in *The Making of the English Working Class* (1963), except that "local identity" is more nuanced because it has racial, ethnic, and gender as well as class dimensions (Rosa, 2000, p. 99). Okamura (1980) first pointed out that the interethnic accommodations (for which Hawai'i is so often praised) arose out of "a social system primarily distinguished by the wide cleavage between the Haole planter and merchant oligarchy on the one hand, and the subordinate Native Hawaiian and immigrant plantation groups on the other." Rosa maintains, however, that it is not only the "shared" stratification experience but the shared "talk story" and cultural production of that experience that reaffirms "local" identity. Thus, for instance, each retelling of the Massie case reaffirms the symbolic opposition between (good) "local" boys (brown working class men of Hawai'i) and the (bad) *haole* elite. One of the most blatant, exaggerated displays

of this symbolization was in the 4-hour CBS television miniseries, *Blood and Orchids*, produced in the 1980s. Although the real Massie-Fortescue group was caught red-handed while trying to dispose of the body of Joseph Kahahawai; in the fictionalized *Blood and Orchids* account, the Native Hawaiian is shot dead in a courtroom full of witnesses, and then the rape victim vindicates the youth by screaming, "No, they didn't do it! They were innocent!" (Rosa, 2000, p. 107).

The "Deracialization" of "Local" Identity

Yet given that the term "local" distinguishes people who are born and raised in Hawai'i from nonresidents and newly arrived *haole*, it should come as no surprise that "local" has even been appropriated by working-class whites (especially surfers) to distinguish themselves from nonresidents and newly arrived *haole* (especially military *haole*). As shown in Figure 12.6.

The term "local *haole*" tends to mean that even though one is "white," he is nevertheless aware of, understands, and "appreciates" Hawai'i, especially "knowing" "local" food and customs and appreciating the ocean and the land. Put in another way, the symbolic opposite of "local *haole*" is "mainland *haole*" (or even "fuckin' *haole*," one of the most commonly heard racial epithets in Hawai'i today); it refers to a particular *kind* of *haole*: arrogant, assertive, and usually upper-middle class, especially tourists and recently arrived military men and women (which accords with the symbol of the "Ugly American"). As one self-identified "local *haole*" (a white boy from Palolo) states, "It's ["local *haole*"] an immersion into a culture that becomes your own. You rise above being a *haole* and become a "local *haole*" (Rohrer, 1997, p. 151).[16]

Interestingly, this cultural distinction between those who "know how to act" and

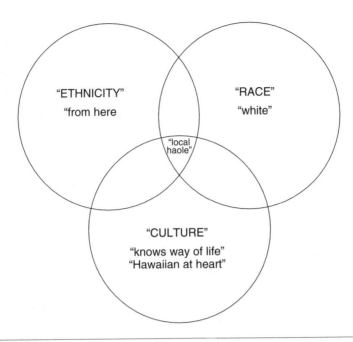

Figure 12.6 "Ethnic," "Racial," and "Cultural" Dimensions of "Local *Haole*"

those who do not, is typical of "old" immigrant groups. Symbolically, it is analogous to epithets like "wetback" and "FOB" ("Fresh of the Boat"). The differentiation of "new" and "old" immigrants emerges because as "old" immigrants learn "new" ways of life, they are embarrassed by, and do not want to be confused and associated with, those of similar ethnic/racial background who do not act "appropriately." As one "mainland *haole*" interviewed by Whittaker (1986) states:

> You see another new arrival come, and you find him being very obnoxious in his approach and attitude, and you realize that he's not doing anything you didn't do when you first got here. You see the eyes of [local] people around him, and you feel they're feeling even stronger what you're beginning to feel. It takes a while, more than a year of sitting around, to be able to see the difference. (pp. 153-154)

In the summer of 2001, I conducted an informal mini-survey of 128 students at the University of Hawai'i, Manoa.[17] In addition to a few standard demographic questions, I asked one open-ended question: "What does being "local" mean to you?" I found that more than 90% of the students surveyed at least mentioned some kind of "cultural" criteria in their definition of "local."[18] For instance, "being 'local'" meant "a state of mind more than anything. It's being familiar with the language, culture, customs, arts, etc. of the place you are in" or "being local to Hawai'i is a feeling, something deep down inside that ties you to this land and its people, truly understanding the way of life here, clothes, language, eating habits."[19]

Moreover, several students (12/128, or 9%) explicitly rejected "racial" or "ethnic" definitions of "local," while affirming a "cultural" one (e.g., "No matter what ethnicity/race you are, if you have the aloha spirit deep inside you then I feel you are local") or

"Local" means having a value system where family, friends, respect, and aloha

[are] your top priorities. It means living life at a slower pace, taking the time to enjoy the simple things in life. We live in a beautiful place so why not take the time to enjoy it. "Local" doesn't mean that you're a specific ethnic group. . . . it is the quality of your heart and the positive intentions that you have for yourself and others.

Local means that you have been accustomed to the culture, the native language, dress code, food, etc. . . . It means that you can fit in with the natives, but don't have to look exactly like them. It's where you are comfortable with everyone and the place. . . . you will also enjoy living there. It doesn't matter how long you have lived there or if you're not the race. It's when you can say you are a part of their own community.[20]

Ironically, however, these pointedly inclusive "cultural" definitions of "local" are themselves a response to the implicit assumption that "local" *does* mean a specific "racial" and/or "ethnic" group. (This is most readily apparent in the last example, in the phrases "the race" and "their own community"). As one respondent states, "It is easier to consider a Hawaiian person local than [an] Asian person. Contrarywise [sic], it is easier to consider an Asian local than a white person. I believe it is hardest to consider white people local." And another respondent maintains:

Local to me means being born here. But it depends because you could be born elsewhere and brought to Hawai'i at a very early age and still consider yourself local. . . . "Local" also means living in Hawai'i and absorbing the culture of Hawai'i. For example, wearing rubber slippers, eating the plate lunches. . . . But on the other hand, "local" also involves race. Even if you were born here but [were] caucasian, it would be harder to believe that you were local. But if an Asian from the mainland came, everyone would make the mistake of thinking that they were "local."

In the same vein, another respondent states:

You can tell when people are "local" because they speak pidgin English, wear "rubber slippers," etc. Even though haoles live here, many people don't consider them to be local because of their ethnicity. They may have been [born] here and follow the local customs, but people still consider them to be outsiders."

In addition, the implicit link among "culture," "race"/"ethnicity," and "local" identity in Hawai'i is apparent in that the "values" at the heart of being "local" (e.g., "quiet," "reserved," prioritizing "family," the *aloha* spirit) are commonly perceived as "Hawaiian" and/or "Asian" values and/or historically linked to the "plantation experience." "Local knowledge" holds that the *aloha* spirit and interracial/interethnic tolerance were borne of the culture of the Native Hawaiians as well as the interracial, intercultural, interethnic life on the plantation. For instance, one respondent maintains:

I think local is . . . a culmination of the various cultures that have come to live in Hawai'i along with a shared history. As for the aspects of this local culture, it remains subjective, but shared thoughts of family as important and to be respected. There is a shared food, music, and pop culture. The shared history is immigration, sugar, etc.

Indeed, almost one quarter of the respondents (24%) explicitly mentioned some type of "multiculturalism," or knowledge, tolerance, and acceptance of the diverse cultures that make up Hawai'i, as part of their definition of being "local." For instance, "being local means to me that I am a part of a unique blend of cultures and nationalities that try to live together in a harmonious manner" and "although everywhere we go is filled with stereotypes and discrimination, Hawai'i still exists as a 'melting pot'. Welcoming other people to the islands with open arms, you can be perceived as local." In sum, for the vast majority of respondents, being "local" is, above all, about having a special interethnic, multiracial awareness as well as the *aloha* spirit, and *haoles* who live in Hawai'i can learn to practice this too.

The Rejection of "Local" Identity

Significantly, however, this positive, inclusive, cultural definition of "local"—and indeed the very concept of "local"—is not universally accepted and used throughout Hawai'i. For many people in Hawai'i, whether they live in Hawai'i and practice *aloha* or not, *haoles* are still *haoles*, just *haoles*, period. For these folks, the term "local *haole*" itself is a *haole* term that for the nonwhite majority in Hawai'i is just another example of white appropriation of Hawaiian culture. As Rohrer (1997) points out, "It seems so hard for white people to appreciate another culture without appropriating it. Perhaps it is because we have a hard time really knowing who we are" (p. 158).

Most important, this white response to *haoleness*—to reject any association with white history and power—is typical of *haoleness* (on the "mainland" as well as in Hawai'i). White people want desperately to not be blamed for the past or what white folks may be currently doing (Rohrer, 1997, p. 150); they want to be seen as "individuals."[21] The problem is, of course, that we are not all "simply who we are" ("individuals")—"flat, cardboard cut-outs with no history, no context, no relationships to power, no nothing." White people try desperately to "wiggle free" from their historical, structural, and symbolic location, but this in itself is also a reflection of white privilege (Rohrer, 1997, p. 150).

It is precisely for this reason that Native Hawaiian activists such as Huanani Kay Trask reject the term "local" altogether. For Trask, the term "local" has an insidious side; "local" identity is an inherently political identity used by those who wish to gloss over and

minimize the historical differences between natives and nonnatives. In Hawaiian tradition, Trask (2000) roots Hawaiian identity firmly in the land: "The lesson of our origins is that we are genealogically related to Hawai'i, our islands, as family. We are obligated to care for our mother, from whom all bounty flows." "'Locals' have no indigenous land base, traditional language, culture, and history that is Native to Hawai'i" (pp. 1-2). In short, for Trask (2000) there are only two kinds of people in Hawai'i: Hawaiians and settlers. Trask states, "Hawaiians are Native to Hawai'i. Everyone else is a settler."[22]

Indeed, although until 1997 the U.S. Census and other federal agency directives legally designated Asian Americans and Native Hawaiians as part of the same race (Asian and Pacific Islander), in 1997 Native Hawaiians achieved recognition as a separate category: Native Hawaiian and Pacific Islander.

Similarly, many Native Hawaiians reject the widespread appropriation of the term *kama'aina*, which means literally "children of the land," by those who live in Hawai'i. Like many things Hawaiian, the term *kama'aina* has been commercialized. There are *kama'aina* airline deals and hotel rates, and so on, and *kama'aina* is commonly used today to refer simply to those who live in Hawai'i, whether they are "local" or *haole*, on temporary military duty, or 10th generation (Rohrer, 1997). However, most Native Hawaiians believe that *haoles* should never claim this status, and in the last few years Trask has rejected this status for "settlers of color" as well.

CONCLUSION

The number of "pure" Hawaiians has so sharply declined that demographers expect the eventual elimination of this entire category. In "mainland" terms, most "Native Hawaiians" (and certainly the most prominent activists) are actually of "mixed blood." Prominent activists such as Trask are commonly criticized for ignoring their "mixed" heritage (and for being "antiwhite"). However, Native Hawaiians such as Trask do not use the concept of "mixed blood"; they distinguish only between those who have *genealogical* roots to the *land* (Native Hawaiians) and those who *don't* (settlers)—period. Of course, "locals" (including first, second, third, or fourth generation "local *haoles*" using self-designations) contend that they are also connected to the land. They emphasize that they were born in Hawai'i, and/or they perceive and portray themselves and others as acting contiguously with the sacred elements of Hawaiian culture, sometimes even learning Hawaiian and adopting traditional Hawaiian notions of the sacred.[23]

Put in another way, "locals" both *haole* and not (using self-designations), commonly emphasize their familiarity with and integration in local culture. In addition, "local *haoles*" often insert their *haole* status into the Hawaiian ethnic and racial mosaic, to put a multicultural gloss on *haole*, just as "locals"

who are of "mixed" or "Asian" background, commonly emphasize their ethnic roots (especially if they are "mixed"). As we have seen, this awareness and appreciation of multiculturalism is itself understood as part of "being local" in Hawai'i. Being "local" is being fluent in (having cognizance and facility with) "ethnic" and "racial" symbolization, especially ethnic foods, customs, and lore. This fluency with racial and ethnic symbolization is both integral in the sacred spirit of *aloha* and its flipside: stereotypes and prejudice. Although the former (i.e., the spirit of *aloha*, that famous tolerance for racial and ethnic diversity, including intermarriage) has perhaps received most scholarly and popular attention, the latter (fluency in stereotypes and prejudice) must not be ignored. As one respondent states, "I think 'local' is another way of categorizing people like race is used." Similarly, another maintains that "it [local] is a term that is overemphasized in today's global scheme. The term is a prejudice in a way, since you exclude a group of people because of something they could not help."[24]

NOTES

1. As will be discussed, I use quotation marks to reflect that I am talking about the *social perception and experience* of "race" (not a biological concept of "race"). Were it not so cumbersome, I would use the phrase "the social perception and experience of race" (rather than the term "race"); quotation marks are shorthand for this meaning. Hunt (1997) uses a similar device; rather than say "black" or "white" respondents, he says "white-raced" and "black-raced" informants and so on. Of course, that "race" does not "really" exist problematizes the concept of "multiracialism." For more on this topic, see Spencer (1999). For an insightful discussion of "racial" versus "ethnic" identity, see Waters (1999).

2. Of course, "Native Americans" also have "mixed" roots. In colonial times, some American Indians had relationships with "whites" and became part of the "white" population. Meanwhile, some Indian tribes welcomed "maroons" (runaway slaves) and "black" freed persons, and some "Indians" were absorbed within the "black" population (Davis, 1991, p. 136).

3. As Gloria Anzaldúa and Cherríe Moraga (1981) emphasized more than two decades ago, American Latinos/as have an ambiguous, labyrinthine identity; the *"mestizo* worldview"—*mestizo* stemming from the Latin term "to mix"—is ambivalent. Similarly, the Mexican-born writer, Ilan Stavans (1995) quips, "Divided we stand, without a sense of guilt. Gringolandia, after all, is our ambivalent, schizophrenic *hogar*" (pp. 17-18).

4. As Barringer and Liu (1994) point out, "pure" and "full" ancestry are self-designations that may not be "genetically" accurate (p. 2). Although 9.4% of Hawaii's population checked only "Native Hawaiian" in the 2000 Census, most demographers maintain either that virtually all Native Hawaiians today are of mixed ancestry or that the number of "pure" Hawaiians is only about 8,000. See Nordyke (1989), Ikeda (1987), and Barringer and Liu (1994, pp. 2-4).

5. This symbolization is readily apparent in mainstream media accounts of Hawai'i's high percentage of mixed-race people. As reported in the *Honolulu Advertiser* (Bricking, 2001), "Hawai'i has the highest percentage of mixed-race people in the nation, followed by the increasingly diverse state of California. The difference in Hawai'i . . . is that there really is a sense of 'aloha.'"

6. Although the term "mainland" is still widely used in Hawai'i to refer to the continental United States, many Hawaiian activists and scholars prefer the term "continent" because "mainland" implies a position of privilege (or at least "continent centeredness") and hence domination. As one writer stated, "For me, Hawai'i is the 'main land'!" However, in this article, I use "mainland" (rather than "continent") because, outside of Hawai'i, readers sometimes misinterpret "the continent" as meaning Europe.

7. Perhaps because he ignores "cultural" variables, Bonilla-Silva (2000) confuses racism with xenophobia in his discussion of "the racial ideology of the Western nations of the World System":

> Politicians of all hues routinely make inflammatory racial comments. In Germany Chancellor Helmut Schmidt said after his 1980 re-election that although the integration of immigrants was very important "it's not easy for Germans who live in an apartment house and don't like the smell of garlic to have to put with it [sic] and even have a lamb slaughtered in the hallway.". . . Analogously, Margaret Thatcher said in 1979 that "some people have felt swamped by immigrants. . . . once a minority in a neighborhood gets very large, people do feel swamped. . . . Jacques Chirac, France's current president, made a public remark about the "smell" of immigrants. (p. 188)

In short, these are xenophobic (or anti-immigrant) comments, not *racial* comments, though, to be sure, xenophobia and racism often go hand in hand.

8. Similarly, in Hawai'i, the adjective "haolified" is used to mean that one is "white" on the "inside," and parallel to "oreo" are the terms "coconut" ("brown on the outside, white on the inside") and "banana" ("yellow on the outside, white on the inside").

9. Hawaiians share significant similarities with Tahitians and other central Polynesians; most important, the Hawaiian language bears a close resemblance to Tahitian, Samoan, Tongan and New Zealand Maori languages, indicating a common cultural root among people of these islands, and Hawaiians also share similar physical features, traditions, and artifacts (such as fishhooks, adzes, and ornaments) with Tahitians and other central Polynesians (Elbert, 1953, as cited by Fu and Heaton, 1997, pp. 9-10).

10. "Mainland" and *"haole"* historians and political scientists often refer to "pre-contact" Hawaiian society as "feudal," meaning that a class of *ali'i* ("nobility") imposed hierarchical control over the *maka'ainana* ("commoners"),

who cultivated food and developed fishing grounds sufficient to feed the population. But analysts such as Trask (1999, pp. 4-5) firmly reject this "feudal" image. While she acknowledges that the *maka 'ainana* ("people of the land") were "subordinate" to their *ali 'i* "caretakers," Trask maintains that because the *maka 'ainana* were free to move with their *'ohana* (extended families) to live under an *ali'i* of their choosing, while the *ali'i* increased their status and material prosperity by having more people living within their *moku*, or "domain", "the result was an incentive for the society's leaders to provide for all their constituents' well-being and contentment" (p. 5) Indeed, states Trask (p. 4) "the economy of pre-*haole* [not "pre-contact"] Hawai'i depended primarily on a balanced use of the products of the land and sea . . . there was no basis for economic exploitation in pre-*haole* Hawai'i."

11.   There is heated debate as to whether or not the Hawaiians conceived of Cook as one of their own "gods," Lono, or whether that is Western mythology (see Obeyesekere, 1992; Sahlins, 1995). In addition, scholars debate as to whether Cook was killed for "political" (e.g., questions about power and control) or "religious" (for its cosmic value) reasons. Nevertheless, anthropologists agree that the distribution of his bones indicates that Cook was treated as a sacrificial victim and adversary of the king (Sahlins, 1995, p. 85).

12.   *Haole* is also sometimes translated as "stranger" or "outsider." Some analysts (e.g., Geschwender, Carroll-Seguin, & Brill, 1988, p. 516) maintain that *haole* combines two Hawaiian words—*ha* (breath) and *ole* (without)—and originally referred to those who could not speak Hawaiian. However, other scholars (e.g., Pila Wilson) insist that *haole* has neither macron nor glottal stop and thus did not mean "without breath"; it meant simply "foreigner." Significantly, in contrast to most scholars, Huanani-Kay Trask (1999, p. 19) incorporates "race" into her definition of *haole*; she defines *haole* as "white foreigner."

13.   Adams (1937) hypothesized that the earliest "part-Hawaiians" were adopted and accepted as "Hawaiians," which accounts for the lack of "part-Hawaiians" in eighteenth and early nineteenth century data. The 1853 census record showed only 983 "part-Hawaiians (the actual term used was "part-Native"); but by 1900 there were 7,857 Part-Hawaiians" on record (Fu and Heaton, 1997, p. 23). Interestingly, the categorization of "part-Hawaiians" has changed several times in the 20th century. The 1910 and 1930 censuses as well as Thrum's *Hawaiian Almanac and Annual* (1920) distinguished "Asiatic-Hawaiians" from "Caucasian-Hawaiians"; the 1940, 1950, and 1960 censuses used only the category "part-Hawaiian"; and the 1970, 1980, and 1990 censuses no longer distinguished between Hawaiians and part-Hawaiians, largely due to the fact that "full-blooded" Hawaiians were so few and their accurate count was so difficult. The state of Hawai'i, on the other hand, continues to try to distinguish "part-Hawaiians" and "Native Hawaiians," which is why there is significant discrepancy in Hawai'i state and U.S. Census Bureau data (see Fu & Heaton, 1997, pp. 23-24; Barringer & Liu, 1994, pp. INT-4-6).

14.   As Sally Engel Merry (2000, p. 63) points out, conversion to Christianity was consistent with traditional Hawaiian politico-religious practices, in that it was a common practice for chiefs or kings to take a new god for his or her personal god and to build temples and make offerings to that god in the hope of support for his endeavors.

15.   A prominent *hapa*, Robert Wilcox, organized a plot to restore Lili'uokalani to her throne through a counterrevolution, but the plot was uncovered and crushed.

16.   See Rohrer (1997) for an excellent autobiographical and analytical essay on managing *haole* identity.

17.   I collected questionnaires from 142 students enrolled in sociology and ethnic studies courses at the University of Hawai'i, Manoa, in the first and second summer sessions of 2001 as to what it means to them to be "local." However, I eliminated from the data set surveys of 11 students who were new to Hawai'i (i.e., in Hawai'i only for the summer session or less than a year) and 3 who did not answer the question, "How long have you lived in Hawai'i?," leaving a final sample size of 128. Although I will be analyzing these data in more depth in the future, my preliminary findings are consistent with those of other informal studies (e.g., Teter, 1998).

18.   I coded the responses by looking for a variety of cultural variables, including (a) food (e.g., eats "plate lunches"), (b) clothing (e.g., "wears slippers"), (c) language ("speaks pidgin"), (d) way of life ("goes to potlucks"), (e) attitude (e.g., has the "aloha spirit"), (f) knowledge (e.g., "knows where everything is"), and (g) specific values (e.g., "appreciation of the land"). More than 90% of the students surveyed mentioned at least one of these cultural variables in their definition of "local."

19.   Similarly, "being local is more than just being born and raised in Hawai'i, more than just knowing all the cool 'local' spots, or knowing how to speak pidgin; it is claiming a responsibility to/for this place—to the land and all of its peoples."

20.   Another student who identified her "race" as "local" and her "ethnicity" as "Hawaiian, Chinese, German, Irish, English," maintains:

> I believe that being local means integrating well into the society and culture that [you're] living in. Being "local" can also mean being of the ethnic background where you are, i.e. being Hawaiian in Hawai'i. My mom is full [caucasian] and from Michigan originally but has been living in Hawai'i for over 25 years so she is considered as a "local."

21.   See the Huanani-Kay Trask/Joey Carter (1990) debacle, as cited by Rohrer (1997).

22.   Elsewhere Trask states: "Beyond our cultural difference, the legal history of Hawaiians places us in a separate category from that of immigrants to Hawai'i. Hawaiians are the only people who have legal and historical rights to lands in Hawai'i based on aboriginal occupation" (cited in Yamamoto, 1999, p. 293).

23.   For instance, one "Caucasian" woman who has lived in Hawai'i 13 years, states:

> For people like me who would like to live here for the rest of my life we wish we could fit in. Ever since I came here, I have been trying to learn how to speak "pidgin." In trying to fit in, and also because I like the Hawaiian language, the Hawaiian culture, I have studied Hawaiian language formally for four semesters. . . . taken Hawaiian literature. . . . Hawaiian studies, Hula Kahiko. . . . Also, I have got [sic] myself a Hawaiian boyfriend, replete with Hawaiian parents, three Hawaiian "brothers-in-law" and sister-in-law. My "father-in-law" has homestead land on Molokai, where he was born and raised. They practice many Hawaiian traditions such as cooking pua'a in the imu, and making raw squid with kukui, which is my favorite dish.

24.   In a parallel way, Darrell Lum (1998, p. 11) points out that on one hand, the typical "local" question, "What school you went?," has "its roots in the native Hawaiian way of identifying oneself by geography and genealogy"; "what school you went?" is "fundamentally an effort to discover how we are connected." (This is most evident in that it is typically followed by, "Do you know my cousin . . . " and so on). However, at the same time, "What school you

went?" is also symbolically loaded, because schools in Hawai'i are notoriously divided on class and ethnic lines, most obviously in the public/private school distinction. Thus, "what school you went?" serves to place one in terms of preexisting categories (e.g., rich white/Japanese [Punahou] or working class Native Hawaiian [Kamehameha]). (Punahou is one of the most prestigious private schools in Hawai'i. It was started by missionary families in the mid-1800s to educate their own children separately. The student population is disproportionately white and Japanese. Kamehameha was established in 1887 through the will of Princess Bernice Pauahi Bishop. Although presumably any child can apply for admission to Kamehameha, children of Native Hawaiian ancestry are given priority; and the student population is almost exclusively Native Hawaiian. Kamehameha enrolls one fourth of all Native Hawaiian children; most of the rest attend public schools (Haas, 1998b, p. 208; Rohrer, 1997, p. 160).

REFERENCES

Abbott, W. (1967). *The American labor heritage.* Honolulu: Industrial Relations Center, University of Hawaii.

Adams, R. (1937). *Interracial marriage in Hawai'i.* New York: Macmillan.

Alba, R. (1992). Ethnicity. In E. F. Borgatta & M. L. Borgatta (Eds.), *Encyclopedia of sociology* (Vol. 2, pp. 575-584). New York: Macmillan.

Anthias, F., & Yuval-Davis, N. (1992). Racialized boundaries: Race, nation, gender, color, and class and the anti-racist struggle. New York: Routledge.

Anzaldúa, G., & Moraga, C. (1981). *This bridge called my back: Writings by radical women of color.* Watertown, MA: Persephone Press.

Barringer, H., & Liu, N. (1994). *The demographic, social, and economic status of native Hawaiians, 1990.* Honolulu: Alu Like.

Bonilla-Silva, E. (1999). The essential social fact of race. *American Sociological Review, 64,* 899-906.

Bonilla-Silva, E. (2000). This is a white country. *Sociological Inquiry, 70,* 188-215.

Bricking, T. (2001). Hawai'i's mixed plate of races complicates census. *Honolulu Advertiser.* Retrieved from www.the.honoluluadvertisercom/article/2001/May/18

Castberg, A. D. (1998). Crime and justice. In M. Haas (Ed.), *Multicultural Hawai'i* (pp. 253-266). New York: Garland.

Davis, F. J. (1991). *Who is black?* University Park: Pennsylvania State University Press.

Edles, L. D. (2001). *Cultural sociology in practice.* Malden, MA: Blackwell.

Elbert, S. (1953). Internal relationships of Polynesian languages and dialects. *Southwestern Journal of Anthropology, 9,* 147-173.

Fu, X., & Heaton, T. (1997). *Interracial marriage in Hawai'i, 1983–1994.* Lewiston, NY: Edwin Mellen Press.

Geschwender, J. A., Carroll-Seguin, R., & Brill, H. (1988). The Portuguese and haoles in Hawai'i: Implications for the origin of ethnicity. *American Sociological Review, 53,* 515-527.

Glick, C. (1980). *Sojourners and settlers: Chinese migrants in Hawai'i.* Honolulu: University of Hawai'i Press.

Grant, G., & Ogawa, D. (1993). Living proof: Is Hawaii the answer. *Annals of the American Academic of Political and Social Science, 530,* 137-154.

Greer, R. (1970). Honolulu in 1847. *Hawaiian Journal of History, 4,* 59-95.

Haas, M. (1992). *Institutional racism: The case of Hawai'i.* Westport, CT: Praeger.

Haas, M. (1998a). A brief history. In M. Haas (Ed.), *Multicultural Hawai'i: The fabric of a multiethnic society* (pp. 23-52). New York: Garland.

Haas, M. (1998b). Elementary and secondary education. In M. Haas (Ed.), *Multicultural Hawai'i: The fabric of a multiethnic society* (pp. 205-228). New York: Garland.

Hunt, D. (1997). *Screening the Los Angeles riots*. Cambridge, UK: Cambridge University Press.

Ikeda, K. (1987). *Demographic profile of native Hawaiians: 1980–1986*. Honolulu: University of Hawai'i, Department of Sociology.

Johnson, R. C., & Ogasawara, G. (1988). Within- and across-group dating in Hawai'i. *Social Biology, 3*, 103-109.

Jung, M.-K. (1999). No whites, no Asians: Race, Marxism, and Hawaii's preemergent working class. *Social Science History, 23*(3), 357-393.

Kuykendall, R, & Day, A. G. (1953). *The Hawaiian kingdom* (Vol. 1, pp. 1778-1854). Honolulu: University of Hawai'i Press.

Loveman, M. (1999). Is "race" essential? *American Sociological Review, 64*, 891-898.

Lum, D. (1998). Local genealogy: What school you went? In E. Chock, J. R. Harstad, D. H. Y. Lum, & B. Teter (Eds.), *Growing up local: An anthology of poetry and prose from Hawai'i*. Honolulu, HI: Bamboo Ridge Press.

Marger, M. (1997). *Race and ethnic relations: Global perspectives* (4th ed.). Belmont, CA: Wadsworth.

Mengel, L. (1997). Issei women and divorce in Hawai'i, 1885–1908. *Social Process in Hawai'i, 38*, 18-39.

Merry, S. E. (1998). *Christian conversion and racial labor capacities: Constructing racialized identities in Hawai'i*. Paper presented at the New World Orders? conference, University of California, Irvine.

Merry, S. E. (2000). *Colonizing Hawai'i*. Princeton, NJ: Princeton University Press.

Nordyke, E. (1989). *The peopling of Hawai'i* (2nd ed.). Honolulu: University of Hawai'i Press.

Obeyesekere, G. (1992). *The apotheosis of Captain Cook: European mythmaking in the Pacific*. Princeton, NJ: Princeton University Press.

Okamura, J. (1980). Aloha kanaka me ke aloha 'aina: Local culture and society in Hawai'i. *Amerasia, 7*, 119-137.

Rohrer, J. (1997). Haole girl: Identity and white privilege in Hawai'i. *Social Process in Hawai'i, 38*, 140-161.

Root, M. (1994). The multiracial experience: Racial borders as a significant frontier in race relations. In M. Root (Ed.), *The multiracial experience: Racial borders as the new frontier* (pp. 140-161). Thousand Oaks, CA: Sage.

Root, M. (2001). *Love's revolution: Interracial marriage*. Philadelphia: Temple University Press.

Rosa, J. (2000). Local story: The Massie case narrative and the cultural production of local identity in Hawai'i. *Amerasia Journal, 26*, 93-115.

Sahlins, M. (1995). *How "natives" think—about Captain Cook for example*. Chicago: University of Chicago.

Spencer, R. (1999). *Spurious issues: Race and multiracial identity politics in the United States*. Boulder, Co: Westview.

Spickard, P. (1989). *Mixed blood*. Madison: University of Wisconsin.

Stavans, I. (1995). *The Hispanic condition*. New York: HarperCollins.

Teter, B. (1998). Listening with an outsider's ear. In E. Chock et al. (Eds.), *Growing up local: An anthology of poetry and prose from Hawai'i* (pp. 348-349). Honolulu: Bamboo Ridge Press.

Thompson, E. P. (1963). *The making of the English working class*. New York: Random House.

Thrum, T. G. (1920). *Hawaiian almanac and annual.* Honolulu: Thomas Thrum.

Trask, H.-K. (1996). Feminism and indigenous Hawaiian nationalism. *Signs, 21,* 906-916.

Trask, H.-K. (1999). *From a native daughter* (2nd ed.). Honolulu: University of Hawai'i Press.

Trask, H.-K. (2000). Settlers of color and "immigrant" hegemony: "Locals" in Hawai'i. *Amerasia Journal, 26,* 1-24.

Turnbull, P., & Ferguson, K. E. (1997). Military presence/missionary past: The historical construction of masculine order and feminine Hawai'i. *Social Process in Hawai'i, 38,* 94-107.

Waters, M. (1999). *Black identities: West Indian immigrant dreams and American realities.* Cambridge, MA: Harvard University Press.

Weber, M. (1968). *Economy and society,* volume 1. Berkeley: University of California Press. (Original work published 1922)

Whittaker, E. (1986). *The mainland haole: The white experience in Hawai'i.* New York: Columbia University Press.

Wright, T. (1972). *The disenchanted isles: The story of the second revolution in Hawai'i.* New York: Dial.

Yamamoto, E. (1999). *Interracial justice.* New York: New York University Press.

CHAPTER 13

Multiracial Identity in Global Perspective[1]

The United States, Brazil, and South Africa

G. REGINALD DANIEL

University of California, Santa Barbara

WHITE OVER BLACK: THE COMPARATIVE-HISTORICAL DIMENSION

The Dichotomous Racial Hierarchy

The issues surrounding multiracial identity in the United States, Brazil, and South Africa are not limited to the experience of individuals of predominantly African and European descent. Moreover, during the past decade, the black/white paradigm for understanding racial formation has been challenged as inadequate. Nevertheless, there are several reasons for focusing on the significance of multiracial identity as it relates to the social construction of blackness.[2] First, the history of African slavery and the unique legacy of attitudes and policies that crystallized around individuals of African descent in Brazil, South Africa, and the United States make a comparative-historical analysis useful. Second, although the law in

the United States and South Africa has been preoccupied with race in general, the specificity of the place of blackness in United States jurisprudence, combined with the eradication of formal expressions of racism in the United States and South Africa and the dismantling of the myth of racial democracy in Brazil, makes a contemporary comparative analysis of multiracial identity particularly meaningful. Furthermore, the black/white paradigm, as well as the historic treatment of individuals of African descent in all three countries, has been the touchstone for the treatment of all racialized "others." Despite limitations in application to those racial others, the black/white paradigm has provided a context in which their experiences have been grounded and the construct in which they continue to be framed.

The U.S. racial order, like those in Brazil and South Africa, was an outgrowth of Europe's rise to global dominion in the

16th century. Consequently, blackness and whiteness have represented the negative and positive designations, respectively, in a dichotomous hierarchy grounded in African and European racial and cultural differences. Brazil's long history of extensive racial (geno-phenotypical, ancestral) and cultural (beliefs, ideals, meanings, values, customs, artifacts) blending, however, led to fluid racial/cultural markers and a racial order that acknowledged multiracial individuals (*pardos*). Accordingly, these dynamics led to a more attenuated dichotomization of blackness and whiteness. In addition, there has been an absence of legalized barriers to equality in both the public and private spheres. Some have argued, therefore, that class and cultural, rather than racial, signifiers have come to determine one's identity and status in the social hierarchy (Daniel, 2000; Davis, 1991; Degler, 1971).

As with Brazil, South Africa has acknowledged multiracial individuals (coloureds), who historically have been circumscribed to a structurally intermediate status separate from and significantly subordinate to the dominant whites but also separate from and somewhat superior to other nonwhites, particularly blacks. Although the social positioning of those individuals designated as multiracial in both South Africa and Brazil has been intermediate in the ternary racial order, overall their location has been much closer to subordinate blacks than dominant whites. Therefore, in keeping with the dichotomous racial hierarchy originating in Eurocentric dynamics, the primary racial divide in terms of the distribution of wealth, power, privilege, and prestige is between whites and nonwhites and only secondarily between the black and multiracial populations (Fredrickson, 1981; Goldin, 1987).

The "One-Drop Rule" of Hypodescent

The United States, characterized by an extreme dichotomization and hierarchical valuation of blackness and whiteness, has historically maintained a binary racial order that recognizes no intermediate (or multiracial) identity and status. Yet unlike Brazil, whites in the United States and South Africa variously implemented the rule of hypodescent, which relies on ancestry as a primary criterion in determining racial categorization. It determines racial group membership of the offspring of interracial unions between whites and nonwhites based exclusively on the nonwhite background to draw social distinctions between the dominant whites and the subordinate groups of color. The rule of hypodescent was implemented primarily in the area of interracial sexual relations and, more specifically, interracial marriages to preserve white racial and cultural "purity."

This device has also helped maintain white racial privilege by supporting other legal and informal barriers to equality in most aspects of social life. These barriers have existed in public facilities and various areas of the public sphere (e.g., political, economic, educational) as well as the private sphere (e.g., residential, associational, interpersonal), particularly the area of miscegenation. These restrictions reached extreme proportions with Jim Crow laws in the United States at the end of the 19th century and apartheid in South Africa in the mid-20th century (Davis, 1991).

The rule of hypodescent has been such an accepted part of the U.S. fabric that its oppressive origins have often been obscured. The rule has been applied in differing degrees to the first-generation offspring of European Americans and Americans of color (e.g., Native American, Asian American, Latina/o American). Successive generations of individuals whose lineage has included a background of color, along with European ancestry, however, have been more flexible. These individuals have not invariably been designated exclusively or even partially as members of that group of color if the background is less than one fourth of their lineage. Furthermore, self-identification with that background has been more a matter of choice (Davis, 1991).

This flexibility has not been extended to individuals of African American and European American descent. The first-generation offspring of African Americans and European Americans, as well as later generations of individuals whose lineage has included African American, along with European American ancestry, have experienced the most restrictive rule of hypodescent (the one-drop rule). This mechanism designates as black everyone with any African American ancestry ("one drop of blood"). The one-drop rule of hypodescent thus precludes any notion of self-identification and ensures that all future offspring of African American ancestry will be socially designated as black (Daniel, 2001).

The rule emerged in the late 17th century, but over the course of the 18th century it gained currency as the customary social, informal, and "commonsense" definition of blackness and became definitive by the 1920s (Daniel, 2001; Davis, 1991). Rules of hypodescent specifying other amounts of African American ancestry defining legal blackness had existed since the colonial period. Yet the one-drop rule did not become a normative part of the legal apparatus in the United States until the early 20th century (circa 1915).

EITHER BLACK OR WHITE: THE U.S. RACIAL ORDER

The Colonial Foundation

Gilberto Freyre's monumental study of Brazilian race relations is largely responsible for notions about the exceptional openness to miscegenation with people of African descent on the part of the Portuguese colonizers of Brazil and the altruistic motives underlying their differentiation of multiracial individuals from blacks and Native

Americans. Such arguments, however, had more to do with racial romanticism than reality. Irrespective of the national and cultural origins of the colonizing Europeans, miscegenation and the social differentiation of multiracial individuals from other nonwhites were motivated primarily by self-interest and were closely related to respectively the ratio of European men to women and the ratio of whites to nonwhites (Bender, 1978; Daniel, 2000; Degler, 1971).

In Brazil and other areas of Latin America, including English-speaking areas such as Jamaica as well as "Latin North America" such as the lower Mississippi Valley, the Gulf Coast, and South Carolina, the colonizing Europeans were a minority and mostly single males. Africans and Native Americans were a majority of the population. Rape, fleeting extramarital relations, as well as extended concubinage and common-law unions between white men and women of color were approved, if not encouraged, by the prevailing unwritten mores. There were, however, legal barriers to interracial marriages during most of the colonial period and formidable social prejudice against these relationships that continued long afterward. Moreover, wherever whites were greatly outnumbered, multiracial individuals not only occupied an intermediate position in the racial hierarchy but also collaborated with whites in preserving the racial status quo (Bender, 1978; Daniel, 2000; Nash, 1982).

In contrast to Latin America, the balance between European males and females in colonial Anglo-North America (the northeastern and upper southeastern United States) made possible the reestablishment of European patterns of domestic life and precluded permissive attitudes toward miscegenation. Accordingly, the standard social unit remained the white family formed by legal marriage. This was particularly true of New England. In that region, not only did Europeans emigrate with families but the early parity between the sexes

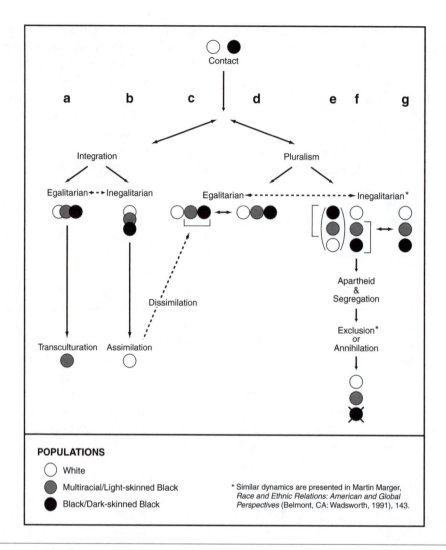

Figure 13.1　Pluralist and Integrationist Dynamics

also meant that single males found a sufficient number of females.

If demographics in Anglo-North America made racial and cultural blending less common than in Latin America, they did not prevent it altogether (Bender, 1978; Daniel, 2000; Nash, 1982; Spickard, 1989). Although whites dominated the 13 colonies, there were also African American centers of reference that were smaller but of equal demographic significance and, at times, necessitated the accommodation of differences

in beliefs, ideals, values, customs, and artifacts in the manner of egalitarian pluralism. This type of pluralism is captured in the "d" circle in Figure 13.1.

The pluralistic relationship is indicated by the fact that the circles are separated, as opposed to being linked, because they are in the integrationist half of the chart. The relationship is horizontal (egalitarian) and results in the equal valuation of the gray, black, and white circles.

These same factors also allowed a significant blending in perceptions of time, aesthetics, and approaches to ecstatic religious experience in the manner of egalitarian cultural integration. Even the distinctive linguistic features of the southern dialect are a Creolization of West African and Old English speech patterns (Daniel, 2001; Nash, 1982; Sobel, 1987). This dynamic is captured in Figure 13.1.a. The integrative relationship is indicated by the fact that the circles are linked. The relationship is horizontal (egalitarian) and, therefore, not premised on the dominance of any one circle. Also, the outcome of this dynamic is a blend of the white, gray, and black circles. Although this composite is similar to the intermediate gray circle it is not in fact the result of its dominance.

The integration of beliefs, ideals, values, customs, and artifacts through intermarriage or social intercourse, however, certainly did not extend to equitable treatment in the educational, political, and economic arenas, which tended to follow the pattern of inegalitarian pluralism typified by apartheid. This dynamic is captured in Figure 13.1.f. The pluralistic relationship is indicated by the fact that the circles are separated, as opposed to being linked, as they are in the integrationist half of the chart. In addition, the relationship between the circles is not only vertical (inegalitarian) and thus hierarchical, but more important, the gray and black circles are bracketed into one category. This results in the exclusion of both the gray and black circles, despite the somewhat higher positioning of the gray circle in relation to the white. Nevertheless, by the end of the colonial period, blacks and whites had forged a new southern culture that was a transcultural blend of both (Daniel, 2000).

Also, during the early 17th century, the number of blacks in Anglo-North America was comparatively small, and the distinction between white indenture and black slave was less precise than that between bonded and free. Consequently, a number of African-descent Americans were able to enjoy a measure of freedom in the public sphere and in some cases become independent landowners and employers of servants and owners of slaves. In the private sphere, phenotypical differences were accommodated, and no laws prohibited the commingling of ancestral lines, despite strong social prejudice against miscegenation. This is indicated by the small, but not insignificant, number of blacks and whites of both sexes who intermarried or formed common-law unions of some duration and had legitimate offspring, alongside more widespread clandestine and fleeting liaisons that involved births outside of wedlock. Most of the latter, however, were between white masters and indentured (or slave) women of African descent and involved concubinage and rape (Bender, 1978; Daniel, 2000; Nash, 1982; Spickard, 1989).

Given the initial shortage of women, both African and European American, as well as the harsh realities of frontier life in 17th-century Anglo-North America, marriages and other sexual relationships were frequently formed out of simple opportunity, which contributed to widespread miscegenation. This was particularly true of relationships between European American servant women and African American men, both slave and free, who were the largest source of multiracial offspring in the early colonial period. In addition, free white men also married African slaves, who were often the only women they knew.

Irrespective of the ratio of blacks to whites, both African Americans and European Americans exhibited a remarkable capacity over the course of the 18th century to achieve a balance between the sexes in their respective communities except in areas on the newly opening frontier. The tendency of both African American and European American women to survive at a higher rate than men, despite their initially smaller numbers, was counterbalanced by the continuous flow of European males into the free population as well as the movement of African and

European males into the population of bond laborers. This was due to the larger ratio of men to women imported as indentures and slaves (Bender, 1978; Daniel, 2001; Davis, 1991; Nash, 1982; Spickard, 1989).

Over the course of the 17th century, African slaves replaced European indentures as bonded labor to the degree that slavery became an entrenched fact of colonial life. As the African-descent population expanded to meet labor needs, barriers were erected between African Americans and European Americans, particularly indentured white servants. Codes were promulgated to solidify the distinction between slave and free, which ultimately came to mean the distinction between black and white. Simultaneously, several of the southern colonies and some northern colonies began enforcing laws that criminalized sexual relations and intermarriage between whites and blacks (Bender, 1978; Daniel, 2000; Nash, 1982; Spickard, 1989). Intermarriage carried painful social consequences even in those locales where it was allowed. It is highly significant, however, that the first antimiscegenation legislation passed by Virginia and Maryland in the 1660s and 1680s was largely concerned with regulating interracial sexual relations and marriages between European women—particularly indentures—and slave men of African descent (Daniel, 2001; Davis, 1991; Spickard, 1989).

The earliest laws did not actually forbid interracial unions but sought to discourage miscegenation by imposing stiff fines or severe penalties ranging from banishment to whippings or locking white indentured women into additional terms of servitude. They also stipulated that children born of these relationships would be held in bondage for extended periods of time. With the passage of these and similar statutes, white slave owners actually had an economic incentive to coerce black slave men and white indentured women into marriage to increase the

number of bound servants, despite the social antipathy toward such unions. So widespread was this abuse that in 1681 an act was passed in Maryland that imposed stiff fines on masters and ministers performing such marriages (Davis, 1991; Tenzer, 1990). Later statutes stipulated that free white men who married interracially or became sexually involved with African American women, slave or free, were to incur the same fines and penalties imposed on free white women. By the middle of the 18th century, laws did not merely discourage interracial sexual relations and marriage but outlawed them altogether (Davis, 1991; Tenzer, 1990).

This was particularly the case with black male/white female unions, whether marriages or sexual relations outside wedlock. To some extent, these relationships were less common and carried a greater social stigma because of the initial shortage of available white women. Even after the number of white women in all colonies—particularly in the upper South—approached that of white men, however, black male/white female unions were frowned on in practice, even when they were not forbidden by law. These relationships threatened the sanctity of white womanhood and the integrity of the white family, both of which were pivotal to preserving the racial purity of the European American community and to perpetuating the transmission of white wealth, power, privilege, and prestige down through the generations. Even in those colonies—and eventually those states—where interracial unions between blacks and whites were allowed, these relationships, whether informal unions or legal marriages, carried painful social consequences (Daniel, 2001; Davis, 1991; Spickard 1989; Tenzer, 1990).

Such restrictions alone did not markedly decrease the rate of miscegenation, however. The key change was a shift in public attitudes. Rape and extended concubinage involving white slave masters (or overseers) and women of African descent, whether slave or free, continued to be tolerated (and would become the source of most subsequent miscegenation). These relationships had no legal standing, posed little threat to the slave system, and would become the source of most subsequent miscegenation. Marriage, on the other hand, reflected an assumption that the two parties were social equals (Berlin, 1974; Daniel, 2001; Davis, 1991; Nash, 1982; Spickard, 1989).

From Servitude to Fettered Freedom

The Anglo-North American patriarchy thus established an economic and political system, as well as a cultural ideology, grounded in racial, gender, and class oppression. White male slave owners had the power to control not only the productive labor of African American men but also the productive and reproductive labor of African American and European American women (Daniel, 2001; Davis, 1991; Nash, 1982). If legislation and public pronouncements were relatively unsuccessful at controlling miscegenation, there was little cause for real concern so long as it was restricted largely to white male exploitation of African American women, especially when these men disowned their mulatto offspring, which they usually did. What was feared was not the racial blending itself as much as the implicit challenge mulattoes presented to white domination and the subordination of blacks. As slavery became entrenched, the primary need was for plantation labor. Consequently, the practice of disowning mulatto offspring had the dual advantage of divesting the mulatto offspring of white slave masters of the privileges associated with paternity and increasing the number of individuals held in bondage (Daniel, 1996; Davis, 1991; Nash, 1982).

The overwhelming numbers of whites in Anglo-North America diminished any need for collaborating with multiracial individuals to protect their dominant status and precluded the social differentiation of multiracial individuals from whites and blacks. Indeed, European Americans enjoyed the luxury of a numerical superiority that is probably unparalleled in the annals of European colonization. There is little evidence that mulattoes were accorded higher status than blacks, preferred as house servants or concubines, or given preferential liberation over blacks. A disproportionate number of free coloreds were multiracial and performed an important role in the artisanal and skilled trades. Yet whites were always in abundant supply (Bender, 1978; Daniel, 2001; Davis, 1991).

Up to the time of the American Revolution, the legal status of free mulattoes (and free people of color generally) was ambiguous at best. Whites chipped away at their rights as early as the 1660s. In the early 18th century, when slaves began pouring into the colonies, mulattoes' status rapidly deteriorated. Some southern legislatures made private emancipations by slave owners more difficult, discriminated against free mulatto women through taxes, and denied equal rights to free mulattoes in a wide range of categories, including the right to vote and carry a firearm. As the numbers of free coloreds increased in the late 18th century, Anglo-North Americans became more concerned with racial demarcations. Some states barred free people of color from holding office, serving in the militia, and testifying against whites, placed restrictions on interstate travel and migration, and required them to carry passes giving proof of their free status or risk being fined, expelled from the state, or, even worse, being kidnapped or reenslaved (Berlin, 1974; Daniel, 2001; Davis, 1991; Spickard, 1989).

The Darkening of the Light

The ancestral quantum defining legal blackness varied from legislature to legislature. In most of Anglo-North America, any individual with one-sixteenth to one-eighth African ancestry would be subject to the laws regulating free people of color. Informally, however, any African ancestry—the one-drop rule—was used to classify a person as black lest large numbers of mulattoes slip into the ranks of whites. Even those few individuals who have "passed" into the white population necessarily have been predominantly of European descent and carried very few, if any, genes inherited from West African forebears into the European American community. Consequently, only about 1% of the genes of European Americans are derived from West African ancestors, although the total of European Americans with West African antecedents numbers in the millions (Davis, 1991).

The legacy of these policies would manifest itself throughout westward expansion and throughout the 19th century and into the 20th century, except for a brief retrenchment during Reconstruction (1865–1879). States enacted legislation not merely to prohibit interracial sexual relations and marriages by imposing heavy fines and penalties but also by making interracial marriages legally null and void. By 1915 the one drop-rule had become the official definition of blackness in Anglo-North America as well as in areas of "Latin" North America (the lower South), annexed by Anglo-North America (from Spain and France) during the first half of the 19th century (Daniel, 2001; Davis, 1991).

The region displayed a ternary racial order originating in demographics similar to those that prevailed in Brazil. There were fewer free coloreds in the lower South than in Brazil, and their social elevation was not so overt. Despite the deplorable conditions in the North and the South, free coloreds in Charleston, Savannah, and the gulf ports of Natchez, Mobile, Pensacola, and New Orleans enjoyed the most secure position of free people of color anywhere in North America. With

Anglo-Americanization, however, multiracial individuals in the lower South lost their intermediate status as the ternary racial order polarized into black and white (Berlin, 1974; Daniel, 2001; Davis, 1991).

The Multiracial Consciousness Movement

The one-drop rule, by codifying the dichotomization and hierarchical valorization of blackness and whiteness, underpinned a generalized system of inegalitarian pluralism. All contact between individuals of African descent and whites was restricted in most aspects of social life. At the end of the 19th century, draconian measures were taken to ensure these restrictions with the institutionalization of Jim Crow segregation. Yet the one-drop rule had some unintended consequences. Its purpose was to draw boundaries solidifying subordinated racial identity, but it also made possible the mass mobilization that led to the end of Jim Crow segregation. The dismantling of Jim Crow segregation, particularly the removal of the last legal prohibitions against intermarriage in 1967 (*Loving v. Virginia*) and the implementation of civil rights legislation during the 1950s and 1960s, in turn dissolved the formal mechanism barring individuals of African descent from having contact with whites as equals. Not only has there been a significant increase in the number of interracial intermarriages, but many of these couples also have sought to bring both black and white backgrounds to the identity of their offspring and thus challenge traditional racial categories and boundaries originating in the rule of hypodescent (Daniel, 2001).

By the 1990s, a coalition of more than 40 grass-roots organizations representing the interests of this growing population of interracial couples and their offspring became the basis of a multiracial consciousness movement that lobbied for and successfully brought about changes in official racial classification (such as in the decennial census) that would make possible a "multiracial identification." (Traditionally, individuals have been required to identify with only one racial background on official forms.) This network encompasses individuals from various racial backgrounds. Because of the challenges presented by the one-drop rule, this consciousness has attracted a significant number of black and white couples and their "first-generation" children as well as a smaller number of "multigenerational" individuals. The latter have backgrounds that have been blended for several generations and have been socially designated as members of the various traditional U.S. racial groups (e.g., European American, African American, Native American, Latina/o American). However, these individuals have resisted identifying solely with those socially assigned communities (Daniel, 1992, 2001).

Individuals and organizations representing communities of color (e.g., African American, Latina/o, Native American, Asian American, Pacific Islander) expressed concerns about the addition of a multiracial identifier on the census. Various African American leaders and organizations expressed the most vocal opposition. They argued that most if not all African Americans have some European and, in many cases, Native American ancestry (although most identify solely with the African American community). They feared that many individuals would designate themselves as "multiracial" rather than black to escape the continuing social stigma associated with African Americans. Moreover, critics maintained that multiracial identity in the United States would rearticulate the racial orders that have historically typified Brazil and South Africa. Correspondingly, they argued that multiracial individuals, particularly those who more closely approximate European Americans in terms of physical appearance, would be co-opted into the mainstream of society as

provisional whites (as has been the case in Brazil), whereas the black masses would remain on the periphery. Others asserted that multiracial individuals would be granted a structurally intermediate status in a manner similar to South Africa (Daniel, 1992, 2001).

In addition, critics argued that the rule of hypodescent, if originally oppressive, has also been a means of mobilizing communities of color in the struggle against white racial privilege. More important, this mechanism has prevented a reduction in the number of individuals who would be counted as members of the traditional communities of color. These numbers are needed to enforce and support civil rights legislation and claims tracking patterns of discrimination and were important for achieving social and economic equity through such programs as affirmative action. By virtue of this opposition, the Office of Management and Budget (OMB), the branch of the government responsible for implementing changes in federal statistical surveys, rejected proposals to make multiracial a legitimate official means of self-identification on the 1990 census. However, in 1993 the OMB began a comprehensive review process to discuss possible changes in this direction on the 2000 U.S. Census. After extensive cognitive research and field testing, on October 30, 1997 the OMB approved changes that would allow multiracial individuals to identify themselves as such on official forms (Daniel, 2001).

The OMB proposed a format that reads: "What is this person's race? Mark [X] one or more races to indicate what this person considers herself/himself to be." This format was chosen partially in response to the support it received from the various federal agencies that require data on race and ethnicity. More important, the data could be counted in each of the existing official single-racial categories with which multiracial individuals identified, including the historically "underrepresented" racial components in their background for the purposes of enforcing civil rights legislation and in meeting affirmative action guidelines.

Although some questions remained as to how the multiple response data actually would be tabulated to achieve these goals, this format also received support from civil rights organizations such as the National Association for the Advancement of Colored People (NAACP), Urban League, Congressional Black Caucus, and Mexican American Legal Defense and Education Fund (MALDEF). The federal agencies continue to review various approaches for tabulating data on individuals who mark more than one race. Whatever the outcome for tabulating multiple racial responses, the United States is moving toward a ternary racial order that would recognize multiracial individuals (Daniel, 2001).

BLACK INTO WHITE: REARTICULATING THE BRAZILIAN RACIAL ORDER

The Colonial Foundation

African American concerns surrounding multiracial identity are not limited to the impact it may have on the collection of data needed to support of civil rights legislation and tracking patterns of racial discrimination. There are also fears that this identity will perpetuate a divisive and pernicious "colorism." This phenomenon has historically granted the preferential treatment of individuals who more closely approximate whites in terms of consciousness, behavior, and phenotype within the African American community and to some extent in the larger society.

Therefore, opponents contend that multiracial identity will exacerbate this trend and replace the U.S. binary racial order with the ternary and a more fluid, yet equally hierarchical, racial order typical of Brazil, which differentiates its population into whites (*brancos*), multiracial individuals (*pardos*), and

blacks (*pretos*).[3] Black and white are relative on a continuum of intermediate grays but represent the negative and positive extremes, respectively, in a dichotomous racial hierarchy, in which physical appearance, in conjunction with socioeconomic and cultural factors rather than ancestry, has come to determine one's race and status in the social order (Daniel, 1992, 2000; Skidmore, 1993).

In Brazil, where whites were greatly outnumbered by blacks from early in the colonial era to well into the 19th century, multiracial individuals occupied an intermediate position in the social structure. Mulatto slave offspring were often assigned tasks that symbolized greater personal worth and required greater skill (e.g., domestics and artisans). The scarcity of white women mitigated opposition from the legal wife and enhanced the likelihood that these offspring would be the recipients of socially tolerated demonstrations of affection as well as economic and educational protection. Furthermore, mulattoes were given preferential liberation over blacks, who overwhelmingly were slaves. This made it possible for multiracial individuals in the early colonial period to enter the free classes where they filled interstitial roles in the economy— particularly in the artisinal and skilled trades—because of a shortage of European labor and for which the use of slave labor was considered impractical (Bender, 1978; Daniel, 2000; Degler, 1971; Klein, 1972; Russell-Wood, 1972).

Free colored urban artisans, long before abolition, advanced from these interstitial positions into the arts, letters, and liberal professions (including medicine, engineering, law, and the civil service), although they were barred from holding public office, entering high-status occupations in the clergy and governmental bureaucracy, experienced limitations on educational attainment, and were denied equal rights in a variety of categories. In addition, free coloreds did not achieve vertical mobility through direct competition in the open market; rather, they achieved it through the support of patrons in the white elite who always controlled their advancement. It should come as no surprise, therefore, that these mulattoes feared that the end of slavery would threaten their position in the labor market. Thus, they were reluctant to oppose slavery, tended to eschew all forms of alliance with slaves, and proved to be valuable allies in preserving the racial order (da Costa, 1985; Daniel, 2000; Degler, 1971; Klein, 1972; Russell-Wood, 1972).

So reliable were mulattoes that the distant Portuguese monarchs viewed free colored militia as a balance wheel against independence-minded whites. Both the Portuguese crown and Brazilian slaveholders, as early as the 17th century, relied on the free coloreds to help expel Dutch invaders and thus secure Brazil's territorial borders against foreign interlopers. The planter class also used their services in local militia as a means of protecting their property and in the suppression of slave uprisings as well as the capturing and returning of fugitive slaves. European Brazilians, by granting mulattoes a social location superior to that of blacks and Native Americans but significantly inferior to that of whites, won their loyalty in efforts to exclude blacks and Native Americans from power without simultaneously undermining white domination and control. The process of abolition signed and sealed this racial contract and made it possible for whites to continue to rely on mulatto support long after slavery. As long as blacks were retained in the least remunerative sectors of the secondary labor force—agricultural, industrial, and service laborers—mulattoes settled for token integration into the skilled trades, the petty bourgeoisie, intelligentsia, and primary labor force composed of white-collar workers (Burdick, 1992; Cohen & Greene, 1972; Daniel, 2000; Degler, 1971; Klein, 1972; Russell-Wood, 1972).

The Brazilian racial order has thus ensured that African Brazilians, collectively speaking, are denied the privileges of whites, but mulattoes are at the same time rewarded in proportion to their cultural and phenotypical approximation to the European ideal. The inegalitarian nature of this type of integration is captured in Figure 13.1.b. Both the gray and black circles are in a subdominant position. However, the positioning of the gray circle is not only intermediate, and thus comparatively less subdominant than the black circle, but it is also linked with the dominant white circle because of its closer somatic approximation to the latter. By virtue of this dynamic, select multiracial individuals have been allowed token vertical socioeconomic mobility into the bourgeoisie through an informal window of opportunity that historian Carl Degler (1971) calls the "mulatto escape hatch." Degler does not imply that the masses of mulattoes in Brazil gain access carte blanche to these prestigious ranks of whites by virtue of the fact that they are mulatto as opposed to black. Rather, he argues that the escape hatch is an informal social mechanism by which a few "visibly" multiracial individuals, for reasons of talent, culture, or education, have been allowed vertical socioeconomic mobility into the middle class and with it the rank of situational whiteness.

In its broadest sense, however, the escape hatch is a device that has made it possible for other millions of individuals whose ancestry has included African forebears but who are phenotypically white or near white to become officially white. This aspect of the escape hatch indicates that the social construction of whiteness, as well as the extension of white racial privilege in Brazil, is more inclusive compared with the United States, where the one-drop rule can transform into black an individual who appears otherwise white.

The Myth of Racial Democracy

Brazil's history of pervasive miscegenation and its absence of legalized barriers to equality should not obscure the fact that "white" is synonymous with being superior and "black" with being inferior. The ruling elite is overwhelmingly of European descent and European in manners. It also has implemented covert and overt forms of discrimination that have kept the African Brazilian masses in a de facto subordinate status both before and after the abolition of slavery. Furthermore, if miscegenation made the line between black and white imprecise at best, and became a central tenet in the 20th-century evolution of Brazil's concept of racial democracy, racial and cultural blending was not posited on egalitarian integration. In other words, there was not a random blend of European, African, and by extension, Native American traits seeking its own "natural" equilibrium. In this scenario, equal value would be attached to each of these racial and cultural constituents through a reciprocal transracial/transcultural process (Figure 13.1.a), which Gilberto Freyre referred to as "metaracial brunettism" (do Nascimento, 1979). Rather, it was a process of inegalitarian integration (or assimilation in disguise; Figure 13.1.b), an unnatural contest between unequal participants artificially manipulated to purify the Brazilian pedigree and culture of its vast accumulation of "inferior" African (and Native American) traits with the goal of perpetuating only one: the European (Daniel, 2000; Degler, 1971; do Nascimento, 1979; Klein, 1972; Russell-Wood, 1972; Skidmore, 1974).

Some of these attitudes reflect the indigenous toxins of Brazil's own racial ecology. Nevertheless, this "whitening" ideology was also part of Brazil's compromised response to 19th-century European and European American theories of the evils of miscegenation (Skidmore, 1974). To understand the seriousness of this matter, consider that by the latter half of the 19th century the majority of Brazilians, despite official claims to the contrary, were de facto *mulato claro* (clear [light]-skinned mulatto) or *claramente mulato* (clearly mulatto) in terms of ancestry or phenotype (Coutinho, 1989). Not even the most phenotypically and culturally European individuals of the elite could be certain that their genealogy was free of African ancestry and, therefore, insulated from the stigma of slavery and the "evils" of miscegenation. If miscegenation was the disease, whitening through miscegenation became the cure.

Thus, the Brazilian state encouraged European immigration, particularly from Germany, and passed legislation restricting the immigration of blacks. This was matched by the tendency of many individuals to seek a spouse more apparently European in culture and physical appearance than themselves plus the desire to assimilate anything from ideas to cultural artifacts that tasted of Europe and, by extension, the United States. At the same time, the majority of blacks and mulattoes were excluded de facto from having contact with whites as equals. This informal inegalitarian pluralism (Figure 13.1.f) was envisioned as the final solution that eventually would eliminate African Brazilians through the "laissez-faire genocide" of sharply lower levels of education and higher rates of poverty, malnutrition, disease, and infant mortality (Daniel, 2000; Degler, 1971; Haberly, 1972; Klein, 1972; Russell-Wood, 1972; Skidmore, 1974).

Despite the absence of legalized barriers to equality in Brazil compared with the United States, Brazil's image as a racial democracy began to erode under the weight of data compiled in the 1950s by both Brazilian and foreign social scientists. These scholars, most of whom were part of a United Nations Educational, Scientific, and Cultural Organization (UNESCO)-sponsored project, used the latest research techniques to reveal a complex web of correlations among physical appearance, culture, and class in determining social stratification. Comprehensive data were lacking, important regional variations existed, and opinions varied on how phenotype might affect future social mobility. There was a general consensus, however, that Brazilians who were phenotypically more African were disproportionately found at the bottom of society in terms of education and occupation. Journalists soon found anecdotal evidence that confirmed the existence of a subtle, yet unmistakable, pattern of racial discrimination in social relations (Skidmore, 1992–1993).

Racial discrimination in Brazil was more complex than in the United States and had never been codified since the colonial era. Furthermore, Brazilians could still tout the fact that they had avoided the violent urban uprisings and distorted white supremacist ideology of the United States. Nevertheless, the growing body of evidence not only made the Brazilian elite cautious about discussing their society's race relations but also, paradoxically, made the myth of racial democracy an even more crucial official ideology. It was staunchly defended by Brazil's ruling elite and reinforced by the series of military dictatorships that dominated the Brazilian political scene between 1964 and 1985 (Skidmore, 1992–1993).

During this period, further research and discussion on the problem of racial inequality were severely censored by claims that no such problem existed. In 1969, this resulted in the "involuntary" retirement of university faculty branded as subversives for doing research on Brazilian race relations. The political machinery of the state also decreed that any efforts to mobilize along racial lines were "racist," "subversive," a threat to national security, and punishable by imprisonment. Individuals who were inclined to organize to address a problem that the state declared did not in fact exist, therefore, were themselves viewed as creating a

problem and accused of having been infected with a contagion imported from the United States. Many individuals were imprisoned; others became voluntary exiles or were forcibly deported (Skidmore, 1992–1993).

The intense censorship of public discussion on racial issues was paralleled by the fact that no racial data were collected on the 1970 census. The principal reason given for the decision was that previous data had been notoriously unreliable, because definitions of racial categories lacked uniformity. In actuality, government officials sought to promote the notion that racial criteria were insignificant in determining the distribution of societal wealth, power, privilege, and prestige and were thus meaningless statistical categories. Part of their strategy for achieving this was to deprive researchers (and, therefore, the public and politicians) of nationwide figures that would make it possible to document the deplorable conditions endured by African Brazilians in terms of education, jobs, income, and health (Skidmore, 1992–1993).

The Black Consciousness Movement

The veil of silence cast over the discussion of racial inequality in Brazil was raised in the 1970s during the gradual liberalization of the sociopolitical ecology: the *abertura democrática*, or democratic opening. Beginning in 1978, in several major cities (primarily in the industrialized Southeast), African Brazilian activists took advantage of the celebration of the abolition of slavery in May 1978 to organize protests against police brutality, mistreatment at the hands of public agencies, and an overt act of discrimination in which three African Brazilian youth were barred from a yacht club. None of these events was unusual in and of themselves (Andrews, 1991; Mitchell, 1985). Nevertheless, growing covert racial tension, the lifting of authoritarian rule in Brazil, and the civil rights movement in the

United States combined to set the stage for the formation of the Unified Black Movement: the MNU (*O Movimento Negro Unificado*). (Unified Black Movement is the official name of the organization and should probably be in upper case.)

The MNU's vision of Brazil diverged from the official assimilationist ideology. Activists proposed a mosaic of mutually respectful and differentiated, or dissimilated if not mutually exclusive, African Brazilian and European Brazilian racial/cultural centers of reference in the manner of egalitarian pluralism (Figure 13.1.c). The premises and goals of the black consciousness movement are best captured in Figure 13.1.c. The black and gray circles are bracketed by virtue of their shared dissimilarities to the white. The goal is to establish a horizontal (as opposed to hierarchical) and thus egalitarian relationship that valorizes the two previously subdominant and excluded circles. Both whites and blacks would have equal access to all aspects of the public sphere, with the option of integrating in the private sphere in the manner of egalitarian integration. In this case, the selective pattern would be voluntary rather than mandated by whites, such that if and when African Brazilians choose to integrate they do so as equals (Daniel, 2000).

Nevertheless, the MNU met with hostility from some sectors of the political and cultural establishment. Their goal of achieving a more equitable society by mobilizing an African Brazilian plurality was labeled "un-Brazilian" and a mindless imitation of the United States civil rights movement. Others described the MNU's tactics as racist in the manner of a reverse type of apartheid. The contrast between these two types of pluralism is captured in Figure 13.1.e and 13.1.f. The pluralistic relationship is indicated by the fact that the circles are separated, as opposed to linked, because they are in the integrationist half of the chart. The relationship in Figure 13.1.e is not only vertical (inegalitarian) and thus

hierarchical, but also the positions of the previously subdominant black and dominant white circles in Figure 13.1.f are reversed.

African Brazilian activists received warmer, if somewhat tentative, support from intellectuals, students, progressive sections of the church, and workers committed to political and social change. Many of these individuals, however, have socialist leanings and view African Brazilians as part of a larger transracial proletariat. They consider racism to be an epiphenomenon of class inequality and argue that one automatically addresses the former by addressing the latter. They agreed that the racial prejudice and discrimination directed against African Brazilians has led to gross inequalities in educational, socioeconomic, and political attainment. However, these activists have focused their attention primarily on the poor, the unemployed, and nonliterate. They believe that singling out African Brazilians for special treatment would deviate from the main course of social reform (Skidmore, 1992–1993).

The MNU enjoyed a significant amount of publicity in the late 1970s and early 1980s but has received greater attention from academics abroad than in Brazil. Since its inception, the MNU has tended to be dominated by individuals from the urban bourgeoisie and has been plagued by class divisions. These factors have prevented the MNU from garnering broad support from other urban and, in particular, rural sectors of the African Brazilian community, which remain largely unaware of its existence. Notwithstanding the MNU's lack of success in gaining broad support for a race-specific political agenda or organizing a large race-based electorate in governmental politics, it is, nonetheless, part of a larger black consciousness movement encompassing various social, cultural, and political organizations and activities. This can be seen in the revitalization of African-derived religious and musical expression and an upsurge in African

Brazilian literature, much of which has been published in modest editions at authors' expense. Militant African Brazilian action groups have gained the support of the leading national labor confederation and from domestic employees. Prominent African Brazilians (particularly artists and entertainers) have become willing to speak out publicly about their experiences with racial discrimination (Hanchard, 1994; Skidmore, 1992–1993).

The MNU's efforts also have been aided by a new generation of social scientists. These researchers, most of whom are white, not only helped get the race (or color) question reinstated on the 1980 census but also were funded with a grant from the Ford Foundation to provide analyses of the 1940, 1950, and 1980 censuses and the National Household Surveys of the 1970s and 1980s. As a result, they verified glaring disparities in the areas of health, income, and education between whites, who make up approximately 54% of the population, and African Brazilians, who make up approximately 46% (Skidmore, 1992–1993). For example, analyses of 1980 census data indicate that on the whole school attendance has increased for all Brazilians. Yet black and multiracial children of all ages display a lower probability of attending school. They also tend to enter school later and leave school earlier. In terms of employment, black and multiracial individuals are concentrated in jobs that require less skill and are less remunerative. Moreover, wage differentials persist among the black, multiracial, and white populations even when controlling for education and job experience (Nobles, 2000).

It is true that mulattoes have been able to enter the primary occupational tier as schoolteachers, journalists, artists, clerks, or low-level officials in municipal government and tax offices and get promoted more easily. They also earn 42% more than their black counterparts. It is equally true that rates of intermarriage and residential integration among

mulattoes and whites are comparatively higher than between whites and blacks, and that the multiracial population does occupy an intermediate position in the Brazilian racial hierarchy. Moreover, the presence of African ancestry in one's genealogy or some phenotypically African traits does not preclude a self-identification or social designation as white. Consequently, the credentials distinguishing someone who is white from someone who is multiracial are ambiguous.

Nevertheless, whites earn another 98% more than mulattoes, and the intermediate positioning of the majority of those 40% of Brazilians who are considered multiracial is much closer to blacks than whites. For the most part, they are excluded from professions in medicine, law, academia, upper-level government, and the officer and diplomatic corps. Even entry-level jobs in the primary labor force that require a "good appearance," such as receptionists, secretaries, and bank tellers, or even minimal authority, such as entry-level federal employees, are effectively closed to the majority of mulattoes. The multiracial population, along with the 6% of African Brazilians who are designated as black, remain disproportionately concentrated at the bottom of society in the secondary labor force composed of agricultural and industrial workers, service employees, janitors, porters, laundresses, day laborers, and domestic servants or in the ranks of the underemployed and unemployed. Moreover, black and multiracial individuals in the proletariat, as both children and adults, are routinely subjected to police harassment, often resulting in murder (Burdick, 1992; Dzidzienyo, 1987; Lovell-Webster; 1987; Margolis, 1992; Nobles, 2000; Reichmann, 1995; Telles, 1992, 1993).

Whites and African Brazilians do experience similar disadvantages at the undermost levels of society, which gives credence to the notion that social inequality is based primarily on class. Data indicate, however, that whites supersede these disadvantages in higher rates of tangible returns in terms of wealth, power, privilege, and prestige once they have made educational gains. Whites are not only seven times more likely than African Brazilians to be college graduates, but African Brazilian professionals such as physicians, teachers, and engineers also earn 20% to 25% less than their white counterparts (Goering, 1994; Hasenbalg, 1985; Lovell-Webster & Dwyer, 1988; Margolis, 1992; Reichmann, 1995; Silva, 1985; Simmons, 1988).

Furthermore, if the achievements of individual African Brazilians can be pointed to as examples of meritocracy in action, they also divert attention from the fact that blacks and mulattoes not only find it more difficult to break out of the proletariat but also suffer increasing disadvantages as their vertical class mobility increases. Whites are more successful at intergenerational transferal of their achieved status given the same starting point. African Brazilians are handicapped by the cumulative disadvantages of previous, as well as persistent, racial discrimination. These factors hamper and erode, if not preclude, their ability to pass on wealth, power, privilege, and prestige from generation to generation. This is due precisely to the superordinate and subordinate ascribed racial status respectively assigned to whites and African Brazilians (Hasenbalg, 1985; Silva, 1985; Winant, 1994). These and other findings underscore the significance of race, quite apart from culture or class, and its role in determining social inequality. More important, they point to the fact that in terms of overall socioeconomic stratification, the racial divide is primarily located between whites and all "others"—as is the case in the United States—and only secondarily between the black and multiracial populations.

Previously, discussion on Brazilian race relations relied heavily on "qualitative" data and was primarily framed in the context of historical and anthropological discourse. Historians focused on laws, traveler's accounts, memoirs, parliamentary debates, and newspaper articles in which anecdotal accounts remained the standard source of information. They generally neglected researching police and court records, health archives, personnel files, and other sources from which they might have constructed time series. When such sources were consulted, it was generally to study slavery. Historians did not hesitate to draw conclusions about the historical nature of the Brazilian racial order. Yet they seldom studied contemporary race relations. Anthropologists generally studied African-derived religious and linguistic systems and creative expression in the arts. When they did examine race relations, their focus was primarily on the ambiguity and situational nature of racial markers (Skidmore, 1992–1993). They provided little analysis of the role of race in determining larger structural issues (e.g., education, income, and occupation).

The new generation of sociologists, following in the footsteps of their predecessors in the 1960s, however, has provided activists with the necessary quantitative data to wage their struggle for social change at the level of unions, courts, employers, and the media. Nevertheless, there is no in-depth overview of the post-1976 statistics. Much more data on, for example, health, housing, education, and family structure are needed, yet census forms are designed to collect only the most basic information. Furthermore, it has been difficult for researchers to gain access to data already gathered: Most of the important information has never been published. The data are available only on tapes, and researchers were denied access to these sources for years. When the tapes were released, they were made available only at great expense to users. A group of researchers, in response to these obstructionist procedures, has pressured the Census Bureau to release future data on a timely and accessible basis (Skidmore, 1992–1993).

The 1988 Constitution, for the first time in Brazilian history, outlawed racism. It declared that "the practice of racism constitutes a crime that is unbailable and without stature of limitation and is subject to imprisonment according to the law." Yet the Preliminary Study Commission on the New Constitution, which was organized in 1985, omitted the names of the three African Brazilians who had been recommended by the recently deceased President Tancredo Neves. Only after vigorous protest by African Brazilian organizations was the name of one African Brazilian added (Daniel, 2000). Furthermore, the antiracist article in the Constitution of 1988, like the Afonso Arinos Law of 1951, which outlawed racial discrimination in public accommodations, is more rhetoric than commitment. Even with the passage of the necessary enabling law (the *Lei Caó*), Brazilian civil rights lawyers have found it difficult in practice to establish a legal basis for their criminal complaints. There were no African Brazilians on the Ministry of Justice's 1984 committee to publish five books on the centennial of the abolition of slavery. Although African Brazilians mounted massive public demonstrations against racism during the centennial in the spring of 1988, a barrage of academic papers and civic ceremonies extolling Brazil's genius in having allegedly liquidated slavery without such upheavals as the U.S. Civil War largely overshadowed their protests (Reichmann, 1995; Skidmore, 1992–1993).

Although Geledés, a São Paulo-based non-governmental organization focusing on the problems of African Brazilian women, pressed at least 62 cases of racial discrimination before the courts, by 1992 only four cases had been brought to trial. Governor Franco Montoro in São Paulo (and his successor, Orestes Quércia) and Leonel Brizola during his first term as mayor of Rio de Janeiro initiated policies to move against racial discrimination. They placed African Brazilians in prominent positions and,

respectively, created the Council for the Participation and Development of the African Brazilian Community and prohibited employers from requiring domestics to use separate stairwells and elevators. However, these initiatives were largely undermined by their successors, sometimes blatantly. There has been some discussion of compensatory measures in the manner of affirmative action to ensure equal representation of African Brazilians in the public sphere in proportion to their numbers in the population. Such tactics, nevertheless, are viewed with suspicion or as a form of reverse discrimination that would aggravate rather than resolve the problem of racial inequality (Daniel, 2000; Reichmann, 1995).

Black Identity and the Decennial Census

African Brazilian activists, however, regard their battle as only in its preliminary stages. Since 1978, they have sought to awaken more individuals to the fact that Brazil's racial democracy ideology is a myth. They argue that contrary to its egalitarian rhetoric, the racial democracy ideology has translated into inegalitarian integration (i.e., assimilation) for a privileged few multiracial individuals (and some rare blacks), who are thus co-opted into an alliance as "insiders."[4] This, in turn, has obscured the pervasive inegalitarian pluralism originating in de facto, if not de jure, apartheid, which perpetuates gross inequities between whites and the African Brazilian masses in the areas of education, jobs, income, and health.

The Brazilian Institute of Geography and Statistics (IBGE), and more specifically the Department of Social Studies and Indicators within the IBGE (the agency responsible for collecting census and other demographic data) fully documented these disparities between whites (*brancos*) and the African Brazilian masses (*negros*) when it changed its policy in 1980 and began analyzing and publishing racial data in binary form (Nobles, 2000). The impetus for this seemingly routine decision by a group of government researchers and technocrats appears to have originated to some extent in the IBGE's own analysis of the 1976 and 1980 data. This procedural change was no doubt a response in part to demands made by African Brazilian activists and similar recommendations made by the new generation of social scientists. Consequently, this change had broad implications. Although IBGE had not abandoned the traditional three-category concept of color (or four if one includes the category of "yellows," *amarelos*, used to designate individuals of Asian ancestry), it had moved toward a conceptualization of Brazilian race relations in which both the *preto* and *pardo* populations are considered a single racial group (Andrews, 1991; Nobles, 2000).

Black consciousness movement activists have placed a great deal of emphasis on this survey data documenting the inequalities between whites and the African Brazilian masses, which confirms their argument that the socioeconomic status of *pretos* and *pardos* is similar. In addition, the movement's specific concern with statistical data on the census is directly related to the strategy of identifying its constituency as a numerical majority. Individuals who identify themselves as *preto* on the census in Brazil have never been more than 10% of the population. Yet if this 10% is combined with the roughly 42% who identify as *pardo*, the total would exceed 50%. Movement activists have strong sentiments concerning this fact, and in a significant amount of movement discourse and writing they have employed an expanded definition of blackness based on African ancestry rather than on color. This supports their claim that the percentage of African Brazilians (or African-descent Brazilians) ranges from 50% to as much as 80% (Nobles, 2000).

Beginning in 1990, African Brazilian organizations, along with nine governmental agencies (including development groups and research centers), gained the support of *Instituto Brasileiro de Análisis Sociais e Económicas* (IBASE) in mounting a joint publicity campaign with funds from the Ford Foundation and *Terra Nuova* (an Italian agency for cooperation), directing all Brazilians to be more "conscientious" in filling out the racial question on the 1990 census. The spirit of the campaign was captured best in its poster and brochure slogan *"Não Deixe sua Côr Passar em Branco. Responda com Bom C/Senso"* ("Don't let your color be passed off as white. Respond with good [census] sense"). This slogan used a play on words between census (*censo*) and sense (*senso*) to address the tendency of individuals to identify themselves on previous surveys with a lighter color (racial) category than their "actual" phenotype might warrant. Over time, this process of racial alchemy has led to a "distortion" of racial demographics. Consequently, blacks numerically have lost much and gained nothing; multiracial individuals have gained more than they have lost, and whites have made substantial gains (Nobles, 2000).

The goal of the census campaign was to expose the reality behind the myth of racial democracy. More specifically, it was aimed at getting African Brazilians to identify with the concept *negro* rather than the color codings *preto* and *pardo* to affirm a politicized racial identity. Furthermore, *pardo* includes all possible types of blended backgrounds and, therefore, was considered so general as to be meaningless. It also stirred controversy because it was considered to be a remnant of the racial divisiveness of the past. The census was canceled that year because of problems between the Ministry of the Economy and the Census Bureau. Although the census was finally taken in 1991, strikes by census staff short-circuited dialogue among campaign organizers, the Bureau administrators, and enumerators that potentially would have resulted in changing the wording on the census questionnaire from *branco* (whites), *pardo* (multiracial), and *preto* (black) to reflect the *branco* (whites) and *negro* (African Brazilian) distinctions (Nobles, 2000).

Color data for the 1991 census (released in 1995) are consistent with previous censuses, which indicate a progressive decline in the percentage of individuals identifying as black (*preto*) and white (*branco*). Yet the percentage of Brazilians identifying as white still remained more than half of the population (52%), whereas those who identified as black (*preto*) decreased slightly from 5.9% in 1980 to 5%. The percentage of individuals identifying as multiracial (*pardo*) increased from 38.8% in 1980 to 42% in 1991. This is also in keeping with previous trends and is unlikely attributable to the census campaign (Nobles, 2000).

Indeed, the data suggest that the campaign had little or no impact on racial preferences. The campaign effort was constrained by a limited staff and inadequate financial resources. Despite its national aspirations, the campaign activities were largely centered in the city of Rio de Janeiro. It thus remains unknown how the masses of Brazilians would have responded to the campaign's goals had they been aware of it (Nobles, 2000). What is clear, however, is that the actual number of individuals who comprise the black consciousness movement is extremely small (perhaps as many as 25,000 active members) compared with its claimed African Brazilian constituency of approximately 73 million people, which is half of Brazil's population (Burdick, 1992).

Yet the 1991 census data weakened neither the legitimacy of the black consciousness movement nor activists' resolve in continuing their campaign goals in terms of the 2000 census. Indeed, the current open discussion about census methods within the IBGE and in the media is directly, if not completely, attributable to the campaign. More important, the 2000 census figures do show an increase in the numbers of Brazilians that decided to assume their blackness. Preliminary tabulations indicate that 6.2% of the respondents identified as *preto*, which is a slight increase over the 5% on the 1991 census. At the same time, there was a decrease in the number of individuals who identified as *pardo* (42.6% in 1991 to 39.1% in 2000). In the state of Bahia, which contains the largest number of *pretos* and *pardos* (75.7%), the increase in the proportion of *pretos* was even more significant. The proportion of *pretos* increased from 10.2% in 1991 to 13.1% in 2000; the proportion of *pardos* fell from 69.3% in 1991 to 62.5% in 2000. The *pardo* population is largest in the North (63.5%) and Northeast (59.8%) whereas the Central West region indicates a relative balance between whites and African Brazilians, including both *pretos* and *pardos* (IBGE, Censo Demográfico, 2000).

That said, the census indicates that the majority of Brazilians (53.7%) still identify as *branco*, whereas 39.1% identify as *pardo*, 6.2% as *preto*, 0.5% as *amarelo*, and 0.4% as Indígena (Native American). As expected, the majority of those who consider themselves white live in the in the South (84.2%) and Southeast (62.4%) regions where there was a significant influx of European immigrants mainly from Italy and Germany. In the Southeast, 62.4% of the respondents identified as *branco*, 30% as *pardo*, and 6.6% as *preto* (IBGE, Censo Demográfico, 2000).

If the small increase in the numbers of *pretos* on the 2000 census can be attributed to the census campaign these figures indicate nonetheless that the black consciousness movement has a difficult task of consolidating its actual and potential constituents into a politically conscious collective subjectivity. Activist claims of representing an African Brazilian majority (or a large plurality) based on census data and actually mobilizing individuals into a collective subjectivity as *negros* are entirely separate, if related, tasks (Nobles, 2000). To do this, the black consciousness movement will need to convince vast numbers of individuals who self-identify as *pardo* (or even as *brancos*) to view themselves as part of a larger African Brazilian (*negro*) constituency or even as partners in a common cause with blacks.

Activists believe that the absence in Brazil of the original negative factor of legal discrimination typified by the United States—which was buttressed by the one-drop rule—along with pervasive miscegenation, and the greater fluidity and ambiguity of racial identities and markers, have made racial cohesion more difficult in Brazil. This has resulted in a less unified voice against the brutalities of racial discrimination and undermined the social progress of African Brazilians collectively. A major portion of the black consciousness movement's energy has thus been devoted to forging an African Brazilian plurality and political consciousness in the absence of that original negative factor by convincing more individuals to assume their blackness. Correspondingly, many activists believe that the United States one-drop rule of hypodescent should be adopted in Brazil as a form of "strategic racial essentialism" that would make possible the mass mobilization of African Brazilians in the struggle for racial equality just as it has mobilized African Americans (Spivak, 1996).[5]

Activists have sought to achieve this by constructing clear boundaries of racial identities, as well as undermine the superior valuation attached to whiteness (or more specifically, expand the boundaries of blackness and contract those of whiteness). In addition, activists argue that Brazilian society is not an integrated, or in fact, a whiter one but, rather, is comprised of distinct pluralities of racial/ethnic groups that can nonetheless rightfully lay claim to Brazilian citizenship and identity. Accordingly, they have sought to shift focus away from distinctions made between the black and multiracial populations

(and based on the color designations of *pardo* and *preto*) and rearticulate a new African Brazilian identity. The goal has been to sensitize individuals to the idea of ethno-racial origins (that is African ancestry) and assign positive value to that identity by means of the term *negro*. This designator would replace not only the existing color term *preto* but the term *pardo* as well (Nobles, 2000; Robinson, 1994, Skidmore, 1992–1993).

Yet the black consciousness movement's definition of *negro*, or African Brazilian, as anyone of African descent poses some serious logistical problems particularly considering the racially blended backgrounds as well as phenotypes of a significant number of whites. This is not to suggest that it is either possible or even desirable to dismiss the movement's concerns with identity politics. Given the programmatic effort to prevent the formation of a radical African Brazilian subjectivity, or plurality, the strengths of the black consciousness movement's perspective are undeniable: the fostering of pride, group solidarity and self-respect in the manner of egalitarian pluralism and a critique of the ideology of token inclusion in the manner of inegalitarian (or assimilationist) integration as well as pervasive exclusion in the manner of inegalitarian pluralism (or apartheid). Also, there can be no denying that a racialized African American identity premised on the one-drop rule has been a potent force in forging cultural and political mobilization in the United States. But the effectiveness of this device as an organizing principle when applied to the Brazilian terrain is inherently fraught with irreconcilable contradictions.

Although self-definition as *negro* ultimately seems to be the criterion utilized to resolve this dilemma, some tension has arisen over who is "authentically" African Brazilian (Burdick, 1992, 1998). In practice, this has resulted in a strong ideological rejection of terminology referring to racially intermediate phenotypes. Activists argue that such distinctions have long been part of the white ruling elite's strategy of "divide-and-rule," which has prevented African Brazilians from becoming a united political force. In fact, some observers have noted that in seminars and conferences where black consciousness movement participants are present individuals have been chastised and corrected when they inadvertently use one of the intermediate terms (e.g., *mestiço, mulato*).

Yet this rejection of such intermediate racial terminology may also alienate many individuals who unequivocally acknowledge they are the descendents of slaves, and genuinely wish to valorize their African ancestry, but who honestly cannot translate these sentiments into adopting the designator *negro* as an appropriate means of self-identification (Burdick, 1992, 1998). Some researchers suggest that this disconnection from the term *negro* may be attributable to the fact that these individuals are aware that their social experiences have been qualitatively different from those of individuals at the darker end of the color spectrum. In addition, there is still some question as to whether or not and to what extent the black consciousness movement can embrace individuals who generally would be considered "phenotypically white" in Brazilian terms but who assume an African Brazilian identify based on the movement's definition of *negro* as anyone of African ancestry. What is clear, however, is that activists may need to rethink the prerequisites for involvement in the black consciousness movement. This could conceivably expand movement discourse to embrace the experiences of a wider group of individuals who might become actively engaged in the antiracist struggle (Burdick, 1992, 1998; Neves, 2002).

Yet activists in the black consciousness movement in Brazil, much as those in the multiracial consciousness movement in the United States, have been most immediately concerned with encountering and reforming the racial state through the collection of census racial data. This is a logical strategy given the state's role not only in the collection of racial data but, more important, in the maintenance of racial categories and thus the formation of identities. By questioning the legitimacy of and demanding changes in extant racial categories, activists forced recognition and discussion of the role of the census in buttressing certain ideas about race and displacing others (Omi & Winant, 1994).

The black consciousness movement was unsuccessful in persuading the Census Bureau to use *negro* as an official designator in collecting data on either the 1990 or 2000 census. The term has a political connotation that officials of the racial state do not wish to encourage. Nonetheless, on the 2000 census, the IBGE did consider retaining the term *pardo*, with a suboption that would allow Brazilians to acknowledge African ancestry. *Branco, preto, amarelo*, and *Indígena* (Native American) would be retained. (Traditionally, the indigenous population was listed under the category *pardo*. However, it appeared as a separate racial category beginning with the 1990 census.) More important, Brazil's President Henrique Cardoso requested that the IBGE continue its policy of grouping *pretos* and *pardos* together as nonwhites, although this grouping would not appear in actual tabulations. In other words, the IBGE would continue to count by four separate categories, but for the purposes of public presentation and certain statistical work in the presentation of data and some of the cross-tabulations the relevant categories would be whites and nonwhites, if not *negro* and *branco* (Nobles, 2000).

Official Brazilian racial discourse has thus begun to place greater emphasis on the white/nonwhite, if not *branco/negro* designations, in a manner similar to the black/white dichotomy that has characterized the U.S. racial order. Yet the black consciousness movement's calculated African Brazilian (negro) majority, which it claims as its constituency, is not considered by officials as an actual majority but rather an abstraction that exists only on paper. Indeed, the full social, economic, and political import of regarding Brazil as a nation with an African Brazilian majority has not yet registered in the public consciousness.

Some entities have established certain modest percentages (or quotas) of positions that must be reserved for African Brazilians (e.g. The Ministry of Agrarian Development (MDA), the Ministry of Social Security, the Labor Ministry, the Superior Federal Tribunal, the Ministry of the Chamber of Deputies, etc.). In addition, in May 2002, with details to follow in July, President Cardoso announced outlines of affirmative action programs mandating that 20% of all federal government jobs would be reserved for African Brazilians (Alvin, 2002; Hall, 2002; Jones, 2001). Yet the discussions of affirmative action have not been accompanied by the necessary legislation and implementation of public policy to achieve redistribution of political, economic, and social benefits to this new African Brazilian majority (Nobles, 2000).

Nonetheless, the black consciousness movement has been very successful in undermining the image of Brazil as a racial democracy. In fact, this was one of the main motivations behind the census campaign. Political discourse increasingly includes references to the nation's "racial diversity" (egalitarian pluralism) compared with the traditional reference to its "racial unity" (egalitarian integration), both of which are inextricably intertwined with census categories. Currently, it seems unlikely that large numbers of individuals actually will join African Brazilian political organizations. Yet many more appear willing to embrace the idea of a distinct African

Brazilian culture and experience. Several popular magazines targeting African Brazilians have been launched: *Black People* (its title is in English, and the text is in Portuguese) in 1993 and *Raça: A Revista dos Negros Brasileiros* (Race: The Magazine of African Brazilians) in late October 1996 (Burdick, 1998; Nobles, 2000).

In addition, the public and political debate has increasingly included discussions about the importance of race, quite apart from questions of class, in determining social stratification. For example, in June 1995, the prominent newspaper *Folha de São Paulo* published a special Sunday supplement titled "Racismo Cordial: A Mais Completa Analise Sobre Preconceito de Côr no Brasil" ("Cordial Racism: The Most Comprehensive Analysis of Color Prejudice in Brazil"), which was later published as a book. The study was based on a *Datafolha* survey that polled 5,000 individuals on a various questions, including the color terms individuals use in self-identification as well as their views on the prevalence of racism in Brazil. The data indicated that 89% of the respondents agreed that racism against African Brazilian exists. Based on these data, the book's introduction stated unequivocally that racism against African Brazilians was widespread in Brazil. Despite the respondents' certainty about the prevalence of racism in Brazil, only 10% stated that they themselves behaved in discriminatory ways. What is even more interesting and perplexing is that 64% of *pretos* and 84% of *pardos* stated that they personally had never felt discriminated against (Nobles, 2000).

The data on self-identification in terms of color indicated that 39% of the respondents self-identified as *branco*, 6% as *pardo*, and 8% as *preto*. Interestingly, 43% self-identified as *moreno* (or brunette), which is a term that describes a wide variety of "brunette" phenotypes, including those individuals who are designated as *preto*, *pardo*, or *branco* (if the latter have dark hair and eyes). Researchers at *Datafolha* thus recommended that *pardo* be replaced with *moreno* on census schedules. The use of *moreno* also received qualified support from demographers, who suggested that IBGE conduct further research on the subject (Nobles, 2000). However, IBGE officials have expressed no intention of adopting the term *moreno*, although they admit that *pardo* is, in significant ways, unacceptable.

Some might view the increasing support of the term *moreno*, at least in terms of the census, as an indication of the triumph of Gilberto Freyre's notion of *morenidade* (or "metaracial brunettism"). In polite conversation, however, the term *moreno* is often used as a euphemism purposely to avoid more specifically racialized terminology. If *moreno* is adopted as an official census category, the number of individuals identifying as black and white will probably decrease. This would move Brazil in the direction of a nonwhite majority but not necessarily an African Brazilian majority. Accordingly, *moreno* could easily become co-opted as yet another means of erasing racial distinctions and furthering the national project of unifying all individuals under an identity as Brazilians to deflect attention away from persistent and pervasive racial inequities. Understandably, the terms *moreno* and *morenidade* have met with a lukewarm reception among African Brazilian activists (Nobles, 2000; Telles, 1995).

BLACK INTO BROWN: REARTICULATING THE SOUTH AFRICAN RACIAL ORDER

The Colonial Foundation

Other critics suggest that multiracial identity in the United States will reproduce the South African model of multiracial identification originating in colonial patterns of race

relations that culminated in apartheid. Unlike the ternary racial order typified by Brazil, multiracial individuals in South African (coloureds) were not primarily the progeny of the blending of the two main racial groups—the dominant European (white) and subordinate Bantu-speaking African (black) populations—originating in the early colonial period. Coloureds are, for the most part, descendants of Europeans (particularly the Dutch), indigenous African Khoikhoi, and slaves imported from Asia, East Africa, and Indonesia (this importation preceded the main black/white encounter; Fredrickson, 1981; Keegan, 1996).

The original colonists were mostly single men from the social margins of a variety of European nations. This pattern of settlement continued until the arrival of British families in 1820. Considering that few European women could be enticed to immigrate to the Cape, there was a notable absence of legal prohibitions against miscegenation. Consequently, European males formed sexual liaisons and marriages with nonwhite women as they did in Brazil. The initial multiracial population was the product of unions between whites and slaves or ex-slaves of Asian or East African origin who were not accepted into the European group. This population also included the offspring of miscegenation between whites and Khoikhoi, or slaves and Khoikhoi. Eventually the unblended slaves who were freed in 1838 and a large proportion of the remaining Khoikhoi intermarried with the original coloured population. Although this increased the nonwhite ancestry among coloureds, the European contribution to this multiracial population did not cease with the abolition of slavery. White men continued to marry and take coloured women as mistresses and common-law wives, and most of their children were now incorporated into the mother's racial group (Elphick & Shell, 1988; Fredrickson, 1981; Keegan, 1996).

The legacy of this early miscegenation was the formation of a distinct population that became known in the 19th century as the Cape coloureds. The emergence of this social category in the 17th and 18th centuries can be attributed in part to the extension of the eastern Cape frontier and the conquest of Bantu-speaking Africans (blacks) during the 19th century. Both the Dutch-descended Afrikaners (or Boers) and the British-descended English-speaking populations realized that the most relevant social division was between whites and indigenous blacks. The other nonwhites or part-whites that Europeans had earlier enslaved, conquered, and taken as sexual partners had to be located within the new social order resulting from the economic incorporation of Bantu-speaking Africans into an expanding settler society (Fredrickson, 1981; Keegan, 1996; Marks, 1998).

One alternative for dealing with the coloured population would have been for whites to follow the ternary racial order typified by Brazil. In fact, the early colonial period in South Africa provided some precedent for this. Accordingly, the most phenotypically and culturally European Cape coloureds would have been assimilated into dominant group as a means of strengthening the "white" population's position in relation to "blacks" or the Bantu-speaking majority. Another option would have been to follow the U.S. binary racial order and relegate all coloureds to an undifferentiated nonwhite or black category. The trajectory that followed in the Cape Colony was somewhat of a compromise between these two alternatives.

Accordingly, multiracial individuals were allowed to find their own social location in a social order that was racially prejudiced and discriminatory but not legally segregated. Coloureds functioned as a socially disadvantaged "lower" class within the Western Cape, where most of them were concentrated, and remained the largest nonwhite segment.

Within the broader South African racial order, they eventually formed a group intermediate to whites and blacks. Yet whites did not consider the de facto intermediate positioning of coloureds in relation to the black/white dichotomy to be static, permanent, or desirable. In addition, there was a perennial debate among white supremacists as to whether coloureds belonged on the white or black side of the main racial divide (Fredrickson, 1981; Keegan, 1996; Marks, 1998).

During the 19th century, whites in the Cape Colony increasingly differentiated coloureds more sharply from themselves, as evidenced by the rise of segregation in the Dutch Reformed Church in the 1850s. By 1853, a complex, if largely informal, racial hierarchy was established in the Cape. This had not been articulated in the exclusion of all Bantu-speaking people from the franchise. Furthermore, racial ideologies had not crystallized around the distinction between Bantu-speaking and other nonwhites. Class allegiances and, to a lesser extent, religious affiliation continued to function as the principal markers for political and ideological mobilization. The critical distinction was between "heathen" and uneducated "blanket Kaffirs" and the minority of "civilized" missionary-educated blacks. "Blanket Kaffirs" were mainly confined to the eastern frontier. Those blacks who resided in the Western Cape were small in number (674), and many were educated and eligible to vote. This facilitated their inclusion into the category of the 14,000 people in the Western Cape who were defined as "coloured" (Elphick & Shell, 1988; Fredrickson, 1981; Goldin, 1987).

In addition, social discrimination against "obvious" coloureds in the Cape did not result in the rigid legal racial divide that existed between whites and mulattoes in the United States. Rather, these distinctions were maintained more by social convention well into the 20th century. There were no legal prohibitions against racial inter-marriage, and the lack of these and other overtly discriminatory measures made it unnecessary to provide legal definitions for *white* and *coloured*. Given the racially blended ancestry of many families that had earlier been accepted as whites, the situation clearly facilitated a substantial amount of "passing." There was tacit awareness and a noticeable absence of public condemnation of the fact that this phenomenon was occurring. That said, the coloureds most likely to achieve white status in the late 19th century were those who not only approximated a rather liberal notion of European physical appearance but also had some degree of wealth or education. Some of these individuals became prominent in the Afrikaner middle class (Fredrickson, 1981; Goldin, 1987; Keegan, 1996; Western, 1996).

During World War I, the large-scale urban migration of rural coloureds and poor Afrikaners, both of whom were being driven off the land, encouraged social intercourse and miscegenation at the less privileged socioeconomic level. These circumstances no doubt made possible the passing of many coloureds into an emerging Afrikaner working class. The substantially lower increase in the number of coloureds compared with whites or Africans on the census from 1911 to 1921 may be attributable in part to that process (Fredrickson, 1981; Goldin, 1987). A significant number of individuals who would otherwise have constituted the leadership of the coloured community were siphoned off by the phenomenon of passing. This situation is similar to the ternary Brazilian racial order but contrasts sharply with that in the United States. The mulatto elite in the United States was consigned to the subordinate status of blacks, identified themselves as such, and provided much of the leadership in the African American community.

Toward Racial Apartheid

Coloured identity has changed over time and has been the site of ideological and political conflict in South Africa for most of the 20th century. The term *coloured*, until the turn of the 20th century, generally referred to all non-Europeans. By 1904, this broader definition had been replaced with a more restrictive one. In contrast to the census of 1890, the Cape census of 1904 distinguished between three distinct racial groups: whites, Bantu, and coloured. The last category included all intermediate phenotypes between the first two.

Although the reconstitution of the term *coloured* and the identification of coloureds as a multiracial plurality distinct from other non-Europeans have been intertwined with the objectives of the dominant whites, they have also reflected a reorientation of allegiances and ideas among coloureds themselves (Adhikari, 1994; Goldin, 1987; Marks, 1998). Moreover, these phenomena were tied to the dramatic transformations of productive relations caused by a series of economic depressions beginning in the 1860s. The unskilled ranks in the mass of coloureds, particularly manual laborers in the docks, quarries, and municipal services, who were vulnerable to wage undercutting by cheaper African laborers, experienced massive unemployment. The small coloured petty bourgeoisie, composed of the skilled workers, artisans, clerks, merchants, and professionals, were not significantly affected by these changed economic circumstances and continued to prosper. Nevertheless, they saw the economic setbacks as an indication of even worse things to come. Through such organizations as the African Peoples Organization (APO), they formed a vanguard in the effort to mobilize a multiracial identity as a means of preventing further erosion of their few existing privileges. Their preference would have been assimilation into the white community. Denied this possibility, they sought increased social rewards superior to blacks but inferior to those of whites (Ahdikari, 1994; Goldin, 1987; Lewis, 1987; van der Ross, 1986).

The binary racial order, which emerged during the days of the Dutch East India Company and was premised on a more or less permeable white/nonwhite divide, was being replaced with a more restrictive ternary racial order that distinguished coloureds from whites and blacks (as well as from Asians). The official maintenance of a fictive white "racial purity" through enforcing the rule of hypodescent was not, however, a main feature of white supremacy in South Africa to the extent that it was in the United States. Despite the growth of segregationist policies that culminated with the institutionalization of apartheid in 1948, the Afrikaner-led National Party (NP), which finally banned coloured/white intermarriage and introduced a system of racial registration designed to end most racial passing, avoided using an unambiguous ancestry rule to determine who was coloured (Fredrickson, 1981; Goldin, 1987).

The dilemma faced by the NP had been confronted earlier by a government commission set up to consider the desirability of imitating U.S. antimiscegenation laws. In its 1939 report, the commission concluded that determining the extent of intermarriage in South Africa was very difficult and depended on one's definition of a white person. Consequently, before the implementation of apartheid, individuals who appeared to be white were not required to produce their genealogy to verify their racial credentials. Furthermore, light-skinned coloured children were routinely admitted to white schools, even though darker siblings may have been denied admission. An individual suspected of a multiracial lineage—but not obviously so—was neither rejected socially by whites nor precluded from marrying into the white community if they had some degree of wealth and education.

One could argue that this was a variation on the Brazilian "mulatto escape hatch." Unlike Brazil, however, it was not until the beginning of the 20th century that this form of vertical social mobility by multiracial individuals in South Africa involved recognition of a clearly differentiated intermediate positioning of coloureds in a ternary racial order. The possibility of more or less socially sanctioned passing declined significantly with the encroachment of apartheid. Nevertheless, in preapartheid South Africa, and to some extent during the apartheid era, individuals who could conceivably pass as whites were designated as such if they could present "evidence" supporting that fact. Generally, this was based on general knowledge of their reputation in the community if and when there was any doubt (Fredrickson, 1981; Goldin, 1987; Unterhalter, 1975).

Because there were always many whites who knew or strongly suspected they had nonwhite progenitors, it would have been unwise to inquire too closely into the antecedents of others who might have passed for white more recently. This situation contrasts sharply with that in the United States, where passing has generally been so clandestine that most of the descendants have known nothing about their African American ancestry. Furthermore, South African whites have had an incentive to augment their own numbers that European Americans generally lacked. Once they had conquered the populous African societies and incorporated many of their members into the white economy as laborers, South African whites' fear of being overwhelmed by a rebellious black majority became central to their anxieties about their survival as the dominant group. Considering that coloureds have generally numbered just over half the size of the white population (and approximately 10% to 12% of the total South African population), the former inevitably figured into the latter's calculations concerning the future balance of forces necessary to maintain domination by the white minority against the black majority (Fredrickson, 1981; Goldin, 1987).

Thus, even as they implemented apartheid with religious zeal, Afrikaners equivocated when it came to attitudes toward their coloured brethren. Boers and coloureds not only have the same ancestors but also share Afrikaans as their mother tongue. The very existence of coloureds threatened the fragile construct of the Boers as "chosen people" by virtue of the fact that one could also argue that coloureds as partial offspring of the master race were similarly endowed. Indeed, there have been serious proposals in the 20th century, even within Afrikanerdom, to grant coloureds European status or something close to it in the form of "brown Afrikaners." This may have been indicative of a tacit agreement that assimilating the lighter coloureds into the white group had certain demographic and strategic advantages. Yet the architects of South African apartheid compromised by granting coloureds the status of the "privileged oppressed" (Fredrickson, 1981; Goldin, 1987; Marks, 1998).

The Western Cape region, where the coloured population has been the largest, was the most significant locus for the evolution of coloured identity. Consequently, the NP implemented a policy whereby the region became a "labor preference area" for coloured workers to the virtual exclusion of Africans. The restriction of black employment and residence in the area was linked with attempts to make the region a coloured "homeland" similar to those that existed for the various black (i.e., African) tribal communities. It also furthered South African whites' goal of reconstituting coloured political identity through a legacy of divide and rule. Correspondingly, coloured schools were a little less deprived than black schools and coloured townships were a little less squalid. These tactics achieved

the desired end: Many coloureds viewed blacks as inferior or at least as a threat to their jobs. As long as coloureds got a few more crumbs of bread, many concluded that they might as well enjoy the meal, even if the baker kept most of the loaf. Blacks reciprocated by branding coloureds as sellouts, coined with the phrase, "black Boers" (Goldin, 1987).

The Brazilian Option

In the 1980s, the South African state under Afrikaner rule appeared to be moving toward what some referred to as the "Brazilian option" (Sparks, 1990). This was a last, desperate attempt to maintain white control, if not white domination and supremacy, in the process of dismantling apartheid. Rather than ruling principally through domination (although it is hardly absent), this trend, which Italian political theorist and activist Antonio Gramsci encapsulates with the term *hegemony*, would allow the dominant whites selectively to include their subjects and incorporate the opposition (Omi & Winant, 1994). The South African racial state thus developed alternative mechanisms by which it intended to hold off the challenge to its authority. Accordingly, coloureds, Asians, and a few educated blacks were to be co-opted into a new alliance as insiders given more, if controlled and inegalitarian, integration (i.e., assimilation) in the new racial order; the black masses (the outsiders) were to be pushed further on the periphery (Sparks, 1990).

As part of the strategy for achieving this goal, the NP leadership scrapped the coloured labor preference policy in 1984 and revised the statutes governing interracial sex and marriage—the Immorality and Mixed Marriages Acts—in 1985. The protracted struggles against the destruction of squatter communities and the determination of blacks to resist resettlement in the barren wastelands of the eastern Cape forced the state to accept the permanence of blacks in the Western Cape. Both policies were cornerstones of the NP's attempt in the 1950s to construct a distinct coloured racial plurality. Now, three decades later, the party was compelled to drop its commitment to these attempts to entrench racial divisions (Goldin, 1987).

Although the end of the policy was a political defeat for the NP, it did not result in any positive change for blacks in the region; legislative measurers that controlled all aspects of black employment and residence simply meant that from 1980 on the policy ceased to have more than a political significance. The eradication of laws prohibiting interracial sex and marriage represented another major concession on the part of the beleaguered NP leadership. However, these so-called reforms were undermined by the lack of simultaneous passage of related legislation removing the prohibitions against the coresidence of different racial groups in any residential area as well as the racial state's continued commitment to similar inegalitarian pluralist policies in virtually every other aspect of everyday existence (Goldin, 1987; Sparks, 1990).

Organizations in the Western Cape were at the forefront presenting a direct challenge to the NP's attempt to incorporate coloureds in the region by means of the coloured labor preference policy and other measures. Some of this resistance can be attributed to the fact that in South Africa, as in Brazil, the black consciousness movement that had been growing since the 1970s sought to narrow the political divide between the black and multiracial populations. Accordingly, activists redefined *black* as an all-encompassing term synonymous with nonwhite, which would unify all individuals of color, including Asians, in the struggle against their shared disenfranchisement. The United Democratic Front (UDF) sought similar goals, although it was largely committed to a platform of "nonracialism," which sought to affirm a universal humanism that

transcended racial designations (Goldin, 1987; Lewis, 1987; Sparks, 1990).

State repression, intensifying in the 1980s, dashed the fragile sense of privilege that coloureds enjoyed. Coloured communities such as Cape Town's fabled District Six, a vibrant community with jazz, street gangs, and radical politics, was razed to the ground (Western, 1996). Suddenly, coloured youth were being shot just as wantonly as blacks. The younger generation of coloureds took the lead in the development of student and community organizations committed to overcoming racial divisions between blacks and coloureds. They fought, were arrested, and died in the name of the antiracist struggle. Progressive trade unions strengthened this challenge, which forced the NP to abandon those strategies to develop a distinct but compliant coloured identity (Goldin, 1987).

Nevertheless, the NP's desire to promote a pluralistic coloured identity remained at the core of its strategy in the 1980s. It devised other methods of coping with the disaffection of coloureds and the growing challenge to its authority. This was to be achieved through the creation of a new constitution that would permit token participation (i.e., inegalitarian political integration) of Indians and coloureds in national government. At the cost of alienating many of its traditional supporters, the Afrikaner gatekeepers of the racial state were being forced to acknowledge that nonwhites would somehow have to be brought into the governing process, although NP strategists were not certain how to achieve this goal. They finally settled on a formula in which separate coloured and Indian elected representatives would be responsible for the administration of coloured and Indian affairs through what was termed the *Tricameral parliament*. The black (or African) majority, which made up three fourths of the population, would only get locally elected municipal councils. This was a veiled attempt to neutralize the influence of the militant civic and grassroots organizations that were proliferating in townships (Atwell, 1986; Goldin, 1987; Omond, 1985; Sparks, 1990).

White South Africans now had to accept that a House of Representatives for coloureds and a House of Delegates for Indians would supplement their all-white parliament. For the first time since the 1950s, some nonwhites could vote in national elections for a Tricameral parliament to be held in August 1984. Right-wing whites, who were offended by sharing power with any nonwhites, broke away from the NP. Yet the Indian and coloured parliaments were purposely formulated to severely restrict their power. Whites maintained complete authority and had the final say in decisions on national and foreign policy. Coloured political influence was circumscribed to issues affecting the infrastructure of the coloured community (e.g., education, housing, health care). Any contentious legislation relating to national and international affairs would be decided by the President's Council, which was dominated by whites.

Under the guise of reform, through the political integration of Coloureds and Asians, the Tricameral parliament thus actually strengthened the continuing inegalitarian, if somewhat attenuated, pluralism of apartheid. With separate voters' rolls for Indians and coloureds and no vote for blacks, it was merely a new version of the proverbial apartheid strategy of divide and rule. This dashed the hopes of black moderates, who sought to dismantle apartheid through the political process. Yet a few coloureds viewed the opportunity to work within the system, however limited, as a significant improvement over the previous exclusionary policies. This earned them the reputation as "sellouts" and "traitors" because overall there was widespread coloured resistance to this form of co-optation (Atwell, 1986; Goldin, 1987; Omond, 1985).

Brown Afrikaners and the "Black Peril"

The NP's "reform" failed to achieve its objectives. Resistance against the discriminatory measures grew to such an extent that it was forced to fashion new methods of coping with the growing challenge to its authority. In the run-up to the1994 democratic elections, the NP astutely identified the coloured vote as the key to its survival. This was particularly important in light of the growing prominence of the black-led ANC (African National Congress), which had been outlawed during the apartheid regime. (Fifty-five percent of Western Cape voters were classified as coloured in 1994 compared with 19% of black voters and 25% of white voters.)

The NP gained coloured support by implementing public works projects employing coloured construction crews in the erection of miles of concrete fencing around black squatter camps, much to the outrage of the squatters, while reviving the time-tested image of the *swart gevaar* (the "black peril"). Accordingly, the NP preached hysterically that droves of coloureds would lose their jobs as a result of affirmative action policies, which would be implemented for the benefit of blacks under an ANC-dominated government. The coloured elite, which had comparatively less to lose, saw through the racist appeals and generally was supportive of the ANC. Nevertheless, these scare tactics duped large numbers of the mass of proletarian coloured voters, who compete with blacks for housing, employment, and the like, into supporting the NP's platform (Goodman, 1999; Marks, 1998; Mattes, Giliomee, & James, 1996; Western, 1996).

Coloured voters cast 53% of the Cape vote for the NP compared with 33% for the ANC; the NP won 23 of the 42 seats in the provincial legislation. This outcome was reinforced in 1995 when the NP resoundingly defeated the ANC in the election for municipal councils. The national democratic elections that were held in May 1999 showed no significant shift in this voting pattern among coloureds. The emergence of coloured nationalism, particularly among the less educated and less economically prosperous masses in the Western Cape, and the deepening schism between coloureds and blacks can be accredited in part to the NP's strategy.

This can also be attributed to coloured concerns about the Mandela and successive ANC administration's affirmative action policies. In seeking to address some of the housing and employment needs of the black masses, the ANC eroded many of the few privileges that coloureds had under apartheid. Thus, the coloured masses have maintained an ambivalent attitude toward the ANC. Yet more recently, coloureds have questioned whether the NP (or its reformulations, the New National Party and the Democratic Party) best serves their interests. Many have shifted their support to the newly formed Democratic Alliance: essentially a merger of National and Democratic Party platforms without the extremism typified by the NP and sympathetic to coloured concerns, particularly about affirmative action (Goodman, 1999; Mattes, Giliomee, & James, 1996; Western, 1996).

The democratic elections have given South African blacks unprecedented power. The dissolution of formal apartheid has given whites and all nonwhites the opportunity to have contact with each other as equals as never before. Yet most South Africans still live in separate and unequal, and sometimes downright hostile, worlds. Indeed, disparities in housing, employment, education, and health remain the most inegalitarian pluralist aspects of South African life. Yet class divisions within the black and coloured communities have become more pronounced as those few affluent nonwhites begin to take advantage of the comparatively more fluid postapartheid racial

dynamics. Indeed, the divide between the haves and have-nots in the black community is coming to mirror the division that until recently had been the defining feature of black/white relations (Appelt, 2000; Goodman, 1999; James & Lever, 2001; Ramphele, 2001; Sparks, 1990; Steyn, 2001).

In addition, there are indications that sectors of the middle and upper classes in the black, white, Asian, and coloured communities may be developing a class consciousness based on similar sociocultural values and socioeconomic interests, if not an actual shared racial/cultural identification. The fact remains that although the status accorded race has changed, the relationship between race and opportunity has not been significantly modified. For white South Africans race still locates wealth, power, privilege, and prestige; for nonwhites race continues to identify disadvantages and constraints in the manner of inegalitarian pluralism. The legacy of racial apartheid endures, however informal and subtle this phenomenon might be compared with that in the past (Appelt, 2000; Goodman, 1999; James & Lever, 2001; Ramphele, 2001; Sparks, 1990; Steyn, 2001).

THE UNITED STATES: TOWARD THE BRAZILIAN AND SOUTH AFRICAN RACIAL ORDERS?

The Uncommon Denominator

Multiracial identity in Brazil and South Africa originated in colonial systems of exclusion that sought to control the potential threat to white dominance. Consequently, all nonwhites have been the targets of de facto discriminatory practices in Brazil and officially sanctioned practices in South Africa. Still, multiracial individuals in Brazil and South Africa have avoided the full brunt of racial stigma and racist policies—compared with other nonwhites—although, historically, multiracial individuals in South Africa have not typically been extended a white racial identity and white racial privilege to the same extent as in Brazil. Yet any suggestion that the new multiracial identity in the United States is necessarily a rearticulation of the Brazilian and South African models of multiracial identification ignores the significant historical-sociological differences that gave rise to those identities as well as contemporary patterns of U.S. racial relations.

It is difficult, therefore, simply to equate the new multiracial identity in the United States with those in South Africa or Brazil despite similar legacies of white domination and supremacy. The new multiracial identity in the United States seeks to expand definitions of blackness, as well as whiteness, to include more multidimensional configurations. It is indicative of an egalitarian dynamic that resists both the dichotomization and hierarchical valuation of blackness and whiteness inherited from the United States' own colonial past. Consequently, as a racial project, it does not actually rearticulate Brazilian or South African models of multiracial identification. Rather, it rearticulates a multiracial identity typified by Brazil and South Africa, without the hierarchical valuation attached to African and European racial/cultural differences (Daniel, 1992, 2001).

Brazil, South Africa, and the United States have much work ahead in liberating themselves from their colonial past to achieve full participatory racial democracies. The new multiracial identity may, therefore, be viewed as a significant step in the direction of liberating the United States from the shackles of at least one vestige of its own colonial past: the one-drop rule of hypodescent. As long as public policy deems it necessary to collect data on race/ethnicity, particularly as a means of tracking our progress in achieving equity in the area of race relations, any change

allowing for the inclusion of a multiracial identifier would alleviate the psychological oppression perpetuated by current methods of data collection. This would also change many societal attitudes reinforced by these methods, which force multiracial-identified individuals to make an inauthentic choice. It would also provide a more accurate picture of contemporary demographics.

More important, the inclusion of a multiracial identifier, regardless of the format, not only would be a logical step in the progression of civil as well as human rights but also would help deconstruct the very means by which racist ideology and racial privilege are enforced in the United States, specifically the notion of racial "purity" as well as mutually exclusive racial categories. This would call into question essentialist assumptions about racial categories and identities as well as the legitimacy of racial hierarchy. In addition, it may encourage more individuals to question the "taken-for-grantedness" of their own racial identities and ultimately open up a long-overdue national dialogue about the shared lineages that have been obscured, if not erased, in U.S. consciousness by centuries of racism.

The Common Denominator

If, however, it is true that individuals should have the right to identify with the fullness of their racial background, resistance to a multiracial identity also alerts us that any discussion on this topic must necessarily take its wide-ranging and long-term consequences into consideration. Despite its egalitarian premises, a multiracial identity is not inherently immune to the lingering effects of previous, as well as persistent, though largely insidious, toxins in the racial ecology. Accordingly, the desire to embrace a European ancestral/cultural background as a means of affirming a more egalitarian identity could be subverted. Multiracial individuals would thus be granted the status as new "insiders" who are rewarded with a greater opportunity to achieve wealth, power, privilege, and prestige. The "outsiders," the black masses, would be pushed further on the periphery of society. This would undermine the very gains in civil rights that now make the recognition of multiracial identity a possibility by disguising the fact that the status accorded to race essentially remains unchanged, although the relationship between race and opportunity would be modified, by furthering the illusion of power sharing without European Americans actually giving up structural control (Daniel, 2001).

Indeed, increased integration, made possible by the dissolution of legalized inegalitarian pluralism, has allowed only a select few African-descent Americans to gain access to wealth, power, privilege, and prestige. Many of those gains also are circumscribed and easily eroded. Furthermore, the privileged few tend to be disproportionately of more "visible" European ancestry and share similar sociocultural values, if not actual racial/cultural identification, with affluent whites by virtue of their socioeconomic status. The black masses, along with darker-skinned individuals in various other communities of color, remain disproportionately in blue-collar jobs and in the ranks of the underemployed and unemployed because of the continuing informal inegalitarian pluralism (Boston, 1988; Feagin & Sikes, 1994; Hacker, 1992; Hughes & Hertel, 1990; Keith & Herring, 1991; Landry, 1987).

Contemporary black/white relations have thus shifted away from the domination-based racial apartheid of the past. Although this transition has been uneven, pervasive formal exclusion and coercion in the manner of inegalitarian pluralism have been replaced with more informal dynamics. Moreover, these have been juxtaposed and sit in an uneasy relationship with another less pervasive trend toward white hegemony based on inegalitarian integration (or assimilation). Neither of these trends taken separately or together precludes the formation of cultures of racial resistance that seek to counter racial hierarchy by mounting racial projects in the manner of egalitarian pluralism and egalitarian integration. That said, neither do they indicate that the hierarchical relationship between blackness and whiteness that maintains white privilege has been dismantled, or that coercion and exclusion in the manner of inegalitarian pluralism are a thing of the past, or that the United States has actually achieved a racial democracy in which European Americans and African Americans interact in the manner of egalitarian integration. This trend indicates rather that the dichotomization of blackness and whiteness has been attenuated. Accordingly, the one-drop rule has ceased to be the primary factor determining the social location of African-descent Americans because of the increased currency of phenotype—particularly skin color—as a form of racial capital in combination with the increasing significance of culture and class (Daniel, 2001).

The balance between colorism in intraracial relations among African Americans and the one-drop rule in interracial relations between blacks and whites is, therefore, shifting in the direction of a more general "interracial colorism." This phenomenon originates in an inegalitarian dynamic and is reflective of the resurgence of the assimilationist paradigm that since the 1980s has redefined conservative political, social, and cultural agendas and consequently has undermined the integrity of the African American community. The new multiracial identity is not synonymous with this pathology of interracial colorism but rather is indicative of an egalitarian dynamic that seeks to resist both the dichotomization and hierarchical valuation of African American and European American cultural and racial differences (Daniel, 1992; Daniel, 2001).

Nevertheless, opponents in the African American community contend that increased interracial marriage, in conjunction with multiracial identity, will merely exacerbate the trend toward interracial colorism. Taken to its logical conclusion, this dynamic would integrate into the mainstream of society (see Figure 13.1.b) as "whites" those multiracial individuals who approximate European Americans in terms of physical appearance, whereas the black masses would be pushed further onto the periphery (see Figure 13.1.f). This would not result in a more inclusive transracial/transcultural integration wherein blacks and whites would become similar to each other (see Figure 13.1.a). It would, rather, lead to inegalitarian integration (i.e., assimilation; see Figure 13.1.b), which would ultimately increase commonalities between blacks and whites by eliminating African American racial and cultural distinctiveness.

In general, African Americans have not sought complete de facto integration in the primary structural (or private) sphere, especially as this relates to intermarriage, despite having challenged, over the last half-century, both the legal and informal inegalitarian pluralism barring them from integrating with whites as equals in the secondary (or public) and private spheres, including the area of intermarriage. Indeed, even within the African American bourgeoisie, which has the highest rate of racial intermarriage among blacks, the majority of this sector of African Americans, like the majority of African Americans, still marries within the black community (Daniel, 2001).

What is envisioned instead is a mosaic of mutually respectful and differentiated—dissimilated (see Figure 13.1.c), if not mutually exclusive—African American and European American racial/cultural pluralities (i.e., egalitarian pluralism). Both whites and blacks would have equal access to all aspects of the public sphere, with the option of integrating in

the private sphere (i.e., egalitarian integration; see Figure 13.1.a). In this case, the selective pattern would be voluntary rather than mandated by whites, such that if and when blacks choose to integrate they do so as equals.

Therefore, we should be alert to any half-hearted attack on white racial privilege that merely attenuates the dichotomization of blackness and whiteness while leaving intact the hierarchical relationship between these categories of experience. Indeed, in contrast to previous efforts to limit the parameters of whiteness through the one-drop rule, the U.S. racial order is now dismantling this device and may be expanding the criteria for racial whiteness through racial assimilation of select African-descent Americans who approximate the dominant psychosomatic norm image. This would not only bolster the numbers of individuals with insider status but also maintain the United States as an ostensibly white nation. Indeed, this would be of strategic value considering that the currently defined whites or European American population in the United States will lose its numerical majority status in this century (Daniel, 2001).

It is still not generally accepted in the United States for individuals to identify as whites while acknowledging African American ancestry, as has historically been the case with Native American and various other ancestries of color. Nevertheless, indications of a new trend may have been reflected in the public response to recent DNA evidence confirming the long-disputed contention that Thomas Jefferson had a mistress, Sally Hemings, who was of partial African descent and with whom he fathered several children. The DNA evidence indicates that Jefferson most likely fathered at least one of Sally Hemings's sons. In addition, this individual or some of his descendents apparently passed as European American. The contemporary descendents of this individual have been socialized as whites and had no knowledge of their African American ancestry. More important, the story was widely publicized in the national print media and was the focus of several segments of *The Oprah Winfrey Show*. Still, there was no public suggestion that these ostensibly European American individuals were now black, either legally or informally (Daniel, 2001).

It is possible that these individuals—and the many others who will likely emerge if more European Americans explore their genealogy—may reconsider the appropriateness of their racial socialization as well as a racial designation as whites. The important point is that they did not conceal their African American ancestry but, in fact, allowed it to become public knowledge in the national media. At no point were questions raised publicly as to whether the findings about their African American ancestry now discredited them as bona fide whites. In the past, the potentially negative ramifications would have prevented most individuals from having made such a disclosure.

It is unclear whether a similar dynamic would be extended to individuals—and to what extent—who have been socialized as African American (or even as multiracial) but select a white racial identity, while being aware of (or acknowledging) African American ancestry or displaying some African American phenotypical traits. Indications of a shift in this direction may have been suggested by audience response on a segment of *The Maury Povich Show* involving two women who were African American identified. Both guests had been socialized in the black community—as had several generations of their antecedents at least since 1840—but were phenotypically indistinguishable from European Americans. Many whites and some blacks in the audience chastised the women for not embracing both their African American and European American backgrounds, particularly considering their phenotypical whiteness. Some individuals, including some African Americans, argued that they were ostensibly white, despite their socialization and self-identification as African Americans (Povich, 1993).

Therefore, if the one-drop rule has been an unquestioned and almost sacred social concept, or "doxa," (Bordieu, 1977) with the force of nature in the U.S. racial order, the trend toward a more generalized "inter-racial colorism" indicates that European Americans may have become more willing to bend this rule. African Americans paradoxically, yet understandably, generally hold onto the one-drop rule ever more tenaciously. As noted, the rule, by solidifying subordinated racial identity and excluding African Americans from interacting with European Americans as equals, has had the consequence of legitimating and forging group identity. It is, therefore, viewed as a necessary, if originally oppressive, means not only of maintaining a distinct, but equal, African American racial and cultural plurality but also of mobilizing blacks in the continuing struggle against white privilege.

The Law of the Included Middle

The new multiracial identity is not, however, synonymous with the desire to embrace a white racial identity and, more specifically, to gain the privileges associated with whiteness. Rather, this identity is displayed by individuals who attach equal value to their European American background and identify with European Americans without diminishing the value attached to their African American background and affinity with the experience of African Americans. Accordingly, it recognizes the commonalities among blacks and whites in the manner of egalitarian integration and, at the same time, appreciates the differences in the manner of egalitarian pluralism.

It remains to be seen how many individuals imbued with this new identity will actually live out its full implications and successfully navigate the uncharted waters of the new multiracial consciousness by helping to transform the United States into a more racially democratic order. Yet individuals are active agents in constructing, maintaining, reconstructing, and deconstructing their own identities. Moreover, identities are capable of reconstructing circumstances via the actions they set in motion (Cornell & Hartmann, 1998). Racial identities are much more than an individual characteristic or some vaguely defined set of role expectations. Rather, they are ongoing phenomena that are accomplished in interaction with others and must be situated in social situations and structure.

The accomplishment of race normalizes and naturalizes the social dynamics based on race; that is, it legitimizes ways of organizing social life. This in turn reaffirms institutional practice, the racial order, and the respective power relations associated with them. The accountability of individuals to race categories is key to understanding the maintenance of these dynamics. It is a mechanism whereby situated social action contributes to the reproduction of racialized social structure and systems of domination by extension, whose entrenched ideas, practices, explicit decisions, and procedures construct dichotomous racial hierarchies that exclude, control, and constrain human agency (West & Fenstermaker, 1995).

Considering that the U.S. binary racial order, along with it racial categories, boundaries, and racial hierarchies, is continually constructed in everyday life, it also follows that under certain conditions, individuals acting as singular agents or as collective subjectivities resist pressures to conform to these social forces. The assertion of the new multiracial identity represents just such a form of resistance to the U.S. racial order, particularly commonsense notions of a black identity based on the one-drop rule, that precludes the simultaneous affirmation of a white or any other racial identity. Although this should not be viewed as a solution in and of itself to racial inequality, the new multiracial identity's radical potential as a racial project should not be underestimated any more than its reactionary potential should be overestimated.

Furthermore, discussion should not center on multiracial identity, which is not inherently problematic. The critical challenge is to dismantle the dichotomous hierarchy that underpins the U.S. binary racial order through the formation of an alternative societal consciousness. Accordingly, differentiation in the manner of egalitarian pluralism (see Figure 13.1.d) would become a prelude and counterpart to a new higher dedifferentiation in the manner of egalitarian integration (see Figure 13.1a). This integrative pluralism (or pluralistic integration) would seek to achieve the equality of similarity without perpetuating assimilation, unity without perpetuating uniformity, and build new kinds of community that are not achieved through conformity. The new multiracial identity is thus perhaps best characterized as a new archetype in the United States' s collective racial consciousness based on the "law of the included middle." As multiracial-identified individuals climb over the walls, cross the borders, and erase and redraw the boundaries that separate them, everyone will be reminded that they actually live most of their lives in the liminal gray space between the extremes of black and whites, whether or not they are conscious of that fact.

NOTES

1. Sections of my analysis of multiracial identity in Brazil and the United States draw heavily on my research (Daniel, 2000, 2001).

2. Unless otherwise indicated, the words "mulatto," "multiracial," and "biracial" are used interchangeably to refer to individuals of predominantly black and white backgrounds, although other backgrounds may be included in their lineage. "Black" generally refers to individuals who are considered to be completely (or at least predominantly) African, African American, and African Brazilian in background. However, the term is sometimes used as a synonym for "African American," "African Brazilian," "African-descent American," and "African-descent Brazilian," which encompass both "black" and "multiracial" individuals. In South Africa the term "*black*" has frequently been used to refer to all nonwhites (Africans, coloureds, and Asians). For continuity, I generally use the term *black* in a more restrictive sense as a synonym for "Africans" rather than as the more inclusive definition that includes coloureds and Asians (specifically Asian Indians) as well. However, the term *nonwhite* includes Africans, coloureds, and Asians.

3. *Preto, branco*, and *mulato* are used in everyday parlance to refer, respectively, to black, whites, and multiracial individuals. Pardo, which literally means brown, is an official term used to refer to multiracial individuals, particularly mulattoes. ("Mulatto" in Portuguese has only one "t.")

4. The escape hatch allows vertical mobility primarily in terms of phenotypical approximation to the dominant European norm image. However, external characteristics of a cultural and economic nature (e.g., speech, mannerisms, attire, occupation, income) and psychological factors, such as beliefs, ideals, values, and attitudes, are also taken into consideration. Consequently, a few exceptional blacks have gained vertical mobility in accordance with their socioeconomic and sociocultural, if not phenotypical, approximation to the dominant whites.

5. The one-drop rule, by codifying the dichotomization and hierarchical valorization of whiteness over blackness, has historically constructed European Americans and African Americans as essentialized, that is, "natural," static, and primordial superior and inferior groups respectively. Yet this device has had the unintended consequence of forging African Americans into a collective subjectivity and been strategically deployed by African Americans as a rallying point, for generations, with which to organize in protest against the very oppressive forces that created the one-drop rule if not the rule itself.

REFERENCES

Adhikari, M. (1994). Coloured identity and the politics of coloured education: The origin of the Teacher's League of South Africa. *The International Journal of African Historical Studies, 27*(1), 101-126.

Alvin, M. (2002, March). Mixed race, mixed up feelings. *Brazzil*. Retrieved from www.brazzil.com/cvrmar02.htm

Andrews, G. R. (1991). *Blacks and whites in São Paulo, Brazil, 1888–1988*. Madison: University of Wisconsin Press.

Appelt, P. (2000, August 7). Still stooges under this alliance's sun [Insight]. *Sunday Times*. Retrieved from www.suntimes.co.za/2000/08/27/insight/in12.htm

Atwell, M. (1986). *South Africa: Background to the crisis.* London: Sidgwick & Jackson.

Bender, G. (1978). *Angola under the Portuguese.* Berkeley: University of California Press.

Berlin, I. (1974). *Slaves without masters: The free Negro in the ante-bellum South.* New York: Random House.

Bordieu, P. (1977). *Outline of a theory practice* (R. Nice, Trans.). New York: Cambridge University Press.

Boston, T. D. (1988). *Race, class, and conservatism.* Boston: Unwin Hyman.

Burdick, J. (1992). Brazil's black consciousness movement. *North American Congress on Latin America Report on the Americas, 25*(4), 23-27.

Burdick, J. (1998). *Blessed Anastácia: Women, race, and popular Christianity in Brazil.* New York: Routledge.

Cohen, D. W., & Greene, J. P. (1972). Introduction. In D. W. Cohen & J. P. Greene (Eds.), *Neither slave nor free: The freemen of African descent in the slave societies of the New World* (pp. 1-23). Baltimore, MD: Johns Hopkins University Press.

Cornell, S., & Hartmann, D. (1998). *Ethnicity and race: Making identities in a changing world.* Thousand Oaks, CA: Pine Forge Press.

Coutinho, A. (1989). El fenómeno de Machado de Assis. *Brasil Kultura, XIV*(63), 8-12.

Da Costa, E. V. (1985). *The Brazilian empire: Myths and histories.* Chicago: University of Chicago Press.

Daniel, G. R. (1992). Beyond black and white: The new multiracial consciousness. In M. P. P. Root (Ed.), *Racially mixed people in America* (pp. 333-341). Thousand Oaks, CA: Sage.

Daniel, G. R. (1996). Black and white identity in the new millennium: Unsevering the ties that bind. In M. P. P. Root (Ed.), *The multiracial experience: Racial borders as the new frontier* (pp. 121-139). Thousand Oaks, CA.: Sage.

Daniel, G. R. (2000). Multiracial identity in Brazil and the United States. In P. Spickard & J. Burroughs (Eds.), *We are a people: Narrative and multiplicity in the construction of ethnic identity* (pp. 53-178). Philadelphia: Temple University Press.

Daniel, G. R. (2001). *More than black? Multiracial identity and the new racial order.* Philadelphia: Temple University Press.

Davis, F. J. (1991). *Who is black? One nation's definition.* University Park: Pennsylvania State University Press.

Degler, C. N. (1971). *Neither black nor white: Slavery and race relations in Brazil and the United States.* New York: Macmillan.

do Nascimento, A. (1979). *Mixture or massacre?: Essays on the genocide of a black People* (E. L. Nascimento, Trans.). Buffalo: State University of New York at Buffalo, Puerto Rican Studies and Research Center.

Dzidzienyo, A. (1987). Brazil. In J. A. Sigler (Ed.), *International handbook on race and race relations* (pp. 23-42). New York: Greenwood Press.

Elphick, R., & Shell, R. (1988). Intergroup relations: Khoikhoi, settlers, slaves and free blacks. In R. Elphick & H. Giliomee (Ed.), *The shaping of South African society, 1652–1840* (pp. 184-239). Middleton, CT: Wesleyan University Press.

Feagin, J., & Sikes, M. P. (1994). *Living with racism: The black middle-class experience.* Boston: Beacon Press.

Fredrickson, G. M. (1981). *White supremacy: A comparative study in American and South African history.* New York: Oxford University Press.

Goering, L. (1994, December 20). Beneath utopian facade, Brazilians uncover racism. *Chicago Tribune,* pp. 1, 11.

Goldin, I. (1987). *Making race: The politics and economics of coloured identity in South Africa.* New York: Longman.

Goodman, D. (1999). *Fault lines: Journeys into the new South Africa.* Berkeley: University of California Press.

Haberly, D. T. (1972). Abolitionism in Brazil: Anti-slavery and anti-slave. *Luso-Brazilian Review, 9*(2), 30-46.

Hacker, A. (1992). *Two nations: Black and white, separate, hostile, unequal.* New York: Scribner.

Hall, K. G. (2002, June 21). Brazil program will set aside jobs for blacks, government plans to address inequities. *Detroit Free Press.* Retrieved from www.freep.com/news/nw/ebrazil21_20020621.htm

Hanchard, M. G. (1994). *Orpheus and power: The movimento negro of Rio de Janeiro and São Paulo, Brazil, 1945–1988.* Princeton, NJ: Princeton University Press.

Hasenbalg, C. A. (1985). Race and socioeconomic inequalities in Brazil. In P.-M. Fontaine (Ed.), *Race, class, and power in Brazil* (pp. 25-41). Los Angeles: University of California, Los Angeles, Center for African American Studies.

Hughes, M., & Hertel, B. R. (1990). The significance of color remains: A study of life chances, mate selection, and ethnic consciousness among black Americans. *Social Forces, 68*(4), 1105-1120.

Instituto Brasileiro de Geografia e Estadísticas. (2002). *Demographic Census 2000. Advanced Tabulation Preliminary Results of the Sample.* Rio de Janiero, Brazil: Author.

James, W., & Lever, J. (2001). The second republic: Race, inequality, and democracy in South Africa. In C. V. Hamilton, L. Huntley, N. Alexander, A. S. A. Guimarães, & W. James (Eds.), *Beyond racism: Race and inequality in Brazil, South Africa, and the United States* (pp. 29-62). Boulder, CO: Lynne Rienner.

Jones, P. M. (2001, December 27). Brazil debates affirmative action. *Chicago Tribune*, Section 1, p. 9.

Keegan, T. (1996). *Colonial South Africa and the origins of the racial order.* Charlottesville, VA: University of Virginia Press.

Keith, V. M., & Herring, C. (1991). Skin tone and stratification in the black community. *American Journal of Sociology, 97*(3), 760-778.

Klein, H. S. (1972). Nineteenth-century Brazil. In D. Cohen & J. P. Greene (Ed.), *Neither slave nor free: The freemen of African descent in the slave societies of the New World* (pp. 309-334). Baltimore, MD: Johns Hopkins University Press.

Landry, B. (1987). *The new black middle class.* Berkeley: University of California Press.

Lewis, G. (1987). *Between the wire and the wall: A history of South African 'coloured' politics.* New York: St. Martin's Press.

Lovell-Webster, P. (1987). The myth of racial equality: A study of race and mortality in northeast Brazil. *Latinamericanist, 22*, 1-6.

Lovell-Webster, P., & Dwyer, J. (1988). The cost of being nonwhite in Brazil. *Sociology and Social Research, 72*(2), 136-138.

Marger, M. (1991). *Race and ethnic relations: American and global perspectives.* Belmont, CA: Wadsworth.

Margolis, M. (1992). The invisible issue: Race in Brazil. *Ford Foundation Report, 23*(2), 3-7.

Marks, A. (1998). *Making race and nation: A comparison of the United States, South Africa, and Brazil.* Cambridge, UK: Cambridge University Press.

Mattes, R., Giliomee, H., & James, W. (1996). The election in the Western Cape. In R. W. Johnson & L. Schlemmer (Eds.), *Launching democracy in South*

Africa: The first open election, April 1994 (pp. 108-167). New Haven, CT: Yale University Press.

Mitchell, M. (1985). Blacks and the abertura democrática. In P.-M. Fontaine (Ed.), *Race, class and power in Brazil* (pp. 120-134). Los Angeles: University of California, Los Angeles, Center for African American Studies.

Nash, G. B. (1982). *Red, white and black: The peoples of early America* (2nd ed.). Englewood Cliffs, NJ: Prentice Hall.

Neves, Francisco. (2002, May). Two Brazils. *Brazzil*. Retrieved August 9, 2002, from www.brazzil.com/cvrmay02.htm

Nobles, M. (2000). *Shades of citizenship: Race and the census in modern politics*. Stanford, CA: Stanford University Press.

Omi, M., & Winant, H. (1994). *Racial formation in the United States: From the 1960s to the 1990s*. New York: Routledge.

Omond, R. (1985). *The apartheid handbook*. Middlesex, UK: Penguin Books.

Povich, M. (Producer). (1993, July 27). Black women who look white. *The Maury Povich Show*. New York: KCAL.

Ramphele, M. (2001). Combating racism in South Africa: Redress/remedies. In C. V. Hamilton, L. Huntley, N. Alexander, A. S. A. Guimarães, & W. James (Eds.), *Beyond racism: Race and inequality in Brazil, South Africa, and the United States* (pp. 63-84). Boulder, CO: Lynne Rienner.

Reichmann, R. (1995). Brazil's denial of race. *North American Congress on Latin America Report on the Americas, 28*(6), 35-42.

Robinson, L. S. (1994, October). The two faces of Brazil: A black movement gives voice to an invisible majority. *Emerge, 6*, 38-42.

Russell-Wood, A. J. R. (1972). Colonial Brazil. In D. Cohen & J. P. Greene (Eds.), *Neither slave nor free: The freemen of African descent in the slave societies of the New World* (pp. 84-133). Baltimore, MD: Johns Hopkins University Press.

Silva, N. do V. (1985). Updating the cost of not being white in Brazil. In P. Fontaine (Ed.), *Race, class, and power in Brazil* (pp. 25-41). Los Angeles: University of California, Los Angeles, Center for African-American Studies.

Simmons, M. (1988, May 14). Brazil's blacks feel prejudice 100 years after slavery's end. *New York Times*, pp. 1, 6.

Skidmore, T. A. (1974). *Black into white: Race and nationality in Brazilian thought*. New York: Oxford University Press.

Skidmore, T. A. (1992–1993). Race relations in Brazil. *Camões Center Quarterly, 4*(3, 4), 49-57.

Skidmore, T. A. (1993). Bi-racial U.S.A. vs. multi-racial Brazil: Is the contrast still valid? *Journal of Latin American Studies, 25*, 383-386.

Sobel, M. (1987). *The world they made together: Black and white values in eighteenth-century Virginia*. Princeton, NJ: Princeton University Press.

Sparks, A. (1990). *The mind of South Africa*. New York: Alfred Knopf.

Spickard, P. (1989). *Mixed blood: Intermarriage and ethnic identity in twentieth-century America*. Madison: University of Wisconsin Press.

Spivak, G. C. (1996). *The Spivak reader: Selected works of Gayatri Chakravorty* (D. Landry & G. MacLean, Eds.). New York: Routledge.

Steyn, M. (2001). Whiteness in the rainbow: Experiencing the loss of privilege in the New South Africa. In C. V. Hamilton, L. Huntley, N. Alexander, A. S. A. Guimarães, & W. James (Eds.), *Beyond racism: Race and inequality in Brazil, South Africa, and the United States* (pp. 85-104). Boulder, CO: Lynne Rienner.

Telles, E. E. (1992). Residential segregation by skin color in Brazil. *American Sociological Review, 57*, 2, 186-197.

Telles, E. E. (1993). Racial distance and region in Brazil: Intermarriage in Brazilian urban areas. *Latin American Research Review, 28,* 141-162.

Telles, E. E. (1995). Who are the Morenas? *Social Forces, 73*(4), 1610-1611.

Tenzer, L. R. (1990). *A completely new look at interracial sexuality: Public opinions and select commentaries.* Manahawkin, NJ: Scholar's Publishing House.

Unterhalter, B. (1975). Changing attitudes to 'passing for white' in an urban coloured community. *Social Dynamics, 1*(1), 53-62.

van der Ross, R. E. (1986). *The rise and decline of apartheid: A study of political movements among the coloured people in South Africa, 1880–1985.* Cape Town, South Africa: Tafelberg.

West, C., & Fenstermaker, S. (1995). Doing difference. *Gender and Society, 9*(1), 8-73.

Western, J. (1996). *Outcast Cape Town.* Los Angeles: University of California Press.

Winant, H. (1994). *Racial conditions: Politics, theory, comparisons.* Minneapolis: University of Minnesota Press.

PART IV

RACE, GENDER, AND HIERARCHY

CHAPTER 14

Does Multiraciality Lighten?

Me-Too Ethnicity and the Whiteness Trap

PAUL SPICKARD

University of California, Santa Barbara

MULTIRACIALITY STUDIES AND WHITENESS STUDIES

The two most striking themes—some would say movements—in recent ethnic studies literature are expressions of multiraciality and studies of Whiteness.[1] There are similarities and perhaps connections between the two themes. Both depend on an understanding that race is a constructed entity rather than a biological essence. Both Whiteness studies and mutiracialism have been put forth by their advocates as expressions of antiracism. In addition, both have been accused by their detractors of selling out the interests of people of color. It is true that there are potential dangers for monoracial communities of color in both the Whiteness studies movement and the multiracial movement. It is also true that the multiracial movement has been more concerned with the psychological needs of individuals than with the needs of monoracial communities. However, as we will see,

the dangers are greater in Whiteness studies than in the multiracial idea. Critics' fears to the contrary, the acknowledgment of multiraciality, even the assertion of a multiracial identity, is not necessarily an indicator that one is abandoning one's community of color and seeking Whiteness.

The concept of multiraciality needs no introduction to readers who have made it to the 14th chapter of this book. It is true, for good or for ill, that the last decade and a half of the 20th century saw the rise of a new consciousness of racial multiplicity, both on the part of people who were claiming multiracial identities and in the minds of monoracial observers. In recent years the shelf of books on multiraciality has been growing rapidly (see, e.g., Azoulay, 1997; Ball, 1999; Camper, 1994; Daniel, 2002; Davis, 1991; Eaton, 1997; Forbes, 1993; Funderburg, 1994; Gaskins, 1999; Haizlip, 1994; Hall, 1997; Hara & Keller, 1999; Hügel-Marshall, 2001; Katz, 1997; Khanga, 1992; Kim, 2000;

Korgen, 1999; Lazarre, 1996; Leslie, 1995; McBride, 1996; McKelvey, 1999; Minerbrook, 1996; Nunez, 1995; Obama, 1995; O'Hearn, 1998; Parker & Song, 2001; Penn, 1997; Root, 1992; Root, 1996b; Scales-Trent, 1995; Senna, 1998a; Sollors, 1997; Spencer, 1997; Spencer, 1999; Spickard & Burroughs, 2000; Talalay, 1995; Tizard & Phoenix, 1993; West, 1995; Williams, 1995; Williams-León & Nakashima, 2001; Zack, 1993, 1995; and, of course, the present volume). Ethnic studies departments have begun to recognize this trend. Courses on multiraciality are taught at several universities across the country.[2] Courses and textbooks on race and ethnicity routinely now include units on multiraciality (e.g., Cornell & Hartmann, 1997; Thompson & Tyagi, 1996). In 1999 San Francisco State University's College of Ethnic Studies advertised for and hired a professor whose task was specifically to teach multiracial issues.

Alongside the heightened attention to multiraciality, the 1990s witnessed a boom in Whiteness studies. Scholars began to examine the experiences of European Americans as a racial group. The impetus came from left-wing White scholars who wanted to examine the bases and processes of White privilege so that they might undermine it. The list of books in this field is just as long as that in multiraciality studies (e.g., Allen, 1994, 1997; Almaguer, 1994; Babb, 1998; Berger, 1999; Brodkin, 1998; Bronwen, 2001; Clark & O'Donnell, 1999; Conley, 2000; Crooks, 2000; Cuomo & Hill, 1999; Curry, 2000; Delgado & Stefancic, 1997; Deloria, 1998; Dyer, 1997; Ferber, 1998; Fine, Weis, Powell, & Wong, 1997; Foley, 1997; Frankenberg, 1993, 1997; Gabriel, 1998; Goad, 1998; Hale, 1998; Haney López, 1996; Hartigan, 1999; Hill, 1997; Ignatiev, 1995; Ignatiev & Garvey, 1996; Jacobson, 1998; Kincheloe, Steinberg, Rodriguez, Nelson, & Chennault, 1998; Lazarre, 1996; Lee, 1999; Lipsitz,

1998; Nakayama & Martin, 1999; Nelson, 1998; Reddy, 1994; Rodriguez & Villaverde, 2000; Roediger, 1991, 1994, 1998; Saxton, 1990; Thandeka, 1999; "The White Issue," 1996; Wray & Newitz, 1997). The American Historical Association and the American Studies Association have held sessions on the history and culture of Whiteness. Can the establishment of faculty positions in Whiteness studies be far behind?[3]

Racial Constructions

The notion of multiraciality and the advocacy of Whiteness studies each depends on a constructivist concept of ethnicity. In a book on multiracial identity, I have argued (Spickard, 1992) that

> The process of racial labeling starts with geography, culture, and family ties and runs through economics and politics to biology, and not the other way around. That is, a group is defined by an observer according to its location, its cultural practices, or its social connectedness (and their subsequent economic, social, and political implications). Then, on looking at physical markers or genetic makeup, the observer may find that this group shares certain items with greater frequency than do other populations that are also socially defined. . . . All of this is not to argue that there is no biological aspect to race, only that biology is not fundamental. The origins of race are sociocultural and political, and the main ways race is used are sociocultural and political. (p. 16)

In *The Sweeter the Juice* (1994), one of several books on a similar theme, Shirlee Taylor Haizlip shows half of her racially mixed family creating themselves as Black people and the other half creating themselves as White. In "A Bill of Rights for Racially Mixed People," Maria Root (1996a) argues passionately that people of mixed ancestry ought not be bound by someone else's notions of racial categories or appropriate racial behavior. She argues that as a multiracial person:

I have the right . . .
> not to keep the races separate within me
> not to be responsible for people's discomfort with my physical ambiguity
> not to justify my ethnic legitimacy

I have the right
> to identify myself differently than strangers expect me to identify
> to identify myself differently than how my parents identify me
> to identify myself differently than my brothers and sisters
> to identify myself differently in different situations. (p. 7)

This is a powerful statement about race as individual choice, as something plastic that may—and perhaps must—be molded by individuals on a daily basis.

In an equally constructivist vein, Matthew Jacobson (1998) writes of Whiteness as "alchemy." He portrays the White group in American history as a coalition with ever-changing boundaries around it and constantly morphing glue holding it together. Karen Brodkin (1998) writes (although I believe her argument is overstated) about "how Jews became White folks." David Roediger (1991), in a much more careful exposition with less sweeping claims, shows how White working people in the 19th century gathered in class solidarity, in part on the basis of an increasing sense of racial solidarity. The most boldly constructivist of all the Whiteness studies writers is Noel Ignatiev (1995). He argues that Whiteness itself is not a matter of skin color, ancestry, or anything else that might be attributed to historical or biological background. Rather, he says, Whiteness is defined by the very act of oppressing Black people.[4]

Undermining Racism

The main expressions in each literature, Whiteness and multiraciality studies, assert that they are antiracist in intent and impact. Multiracialists contend their work undermines the very categories of racism. Aubyn Fulton (1997) says, "I think the existence of [interracial individuals] is corrosive to and undermining of the current racial status quo (in this context I think that 'corrosive' and 'undermining' are *good* things, since I think that the current racial status quo is a bad thing and should be corroded and undermined)." Ronald Glass and Kendra Wallace (1996) insist that

> Race cannot be ignored as a conceptual framework because of its theoretical inadequacy for capturing the phenomenon of race, nor because of its simplistic use of reified notions for historically dynamic meanings and practices. Nor can the politics of race be transcended by a mental act of some sort (like a change in belief, or an act of will) nor wished away in a fantasy of color-blindness. . . . But an even stronger challenge to race can come from people at the margins to all racial centers; that is, from people expressive of multiracial existence and evident human variation, who resist efforts to be subdued and brought within racial orders. (p. 344)

Reginald Daniel (1992) submits that people who maintain multiracial identities are "subverting the racial divide." I have written that multiracial people, by their very choice to assert a multiracial identity, are "undermining the very basis of racism, its categories" (Spickard, Fong, & Ewalt, 1995).

In similar fashion, students of Whiteness say they are interrogating and thereby undermining the processes of White privilege. Some of them call their collective project "critical White studies" (Delgado & Stefancic, 1997). Noel Ignatiev and John Garvey (1996) call themselves "race traitors." In addition, some scholars of Whiteness do, in fact, examine their subject in such a way as to critique White privilege. David Roediger (1991), echoing W. E. B. Du Bois, writes of "the wages of Whiteness":

> The pleasures of Whiteness could function as a "wage" for White workers. That is, status and privileges conferred by race could be used to make up for alienating and exploitative class relationships, North and South. White workers could, and did, divine and accept their class positions by fashioning identities as "not slaves" and as "not Blacks." (p. 13)

George Lipsitz (1998) writes of "the possessive investment in Whiteness":

> The problem with white people is not our whiteness, but our possessive investment in it. Created by politics, culture, and consciousness, our possessive investment in whiteness can be altered by those same processes, but only if we face the hard facts openly. . . . How can we account for the ways in which white people refuse to acknowledge their possessive investment in whiteness even as they work to increase its value every day? We can't blame the color of our skin. It must be the content of our character. (p. 233)

Critiques of Multiraciality and Whiteness Studies

Despite such aspirations to undermine racial privilege on the part of scholars and advocates of multiraciality and Whiteness studies, some critics have nonetheless derided each of these modes of study as tending to reinforce racial hierarchy and White privilege. Monoracialist critics say that advocacy of a multiracial interpretation encourages individuals to flee identification with communities of color and seek a middle social position, lightened by recognition of their ancestral multiplicity. Jon Michael Spencer (1997) accuses

advocates of a multiracial identity of trying to create in America a three-tiered racial hierarchy like the one he perceives to exist in South Africa: White on top, multiracial in the middle, and Black on the bottom.[5] In a more sophisticated analysis, Rainier Spencer agrees and argues that asserting multiraciality constitutes a racist embrace of the one-drop rule. Because nearly every person in America who has some African ancestry also has other ancestries, the only logical thing to do would be to call all African Americans multiracial people. To do so, he argues, would be to ignore the real social disabilities suffered by African Americans. He argues that good census data are needed to measure racial progress or the lack thereof, and that existing monoracial categories are the necessary categories of analysis. "The challenge for America," Spencer (1999) says, "lies in determining how to move away from the fallacy of race while remaining aggressive in the battle against racism" (p. 167).

Both of these critics—indeed, most of the criticism of the multiracial movement—has focused on the 1990s movement to change the racial categories employed by the U.S. Census. That is curious, for I read the census debate as a significant but ultimately minor issue in a much broader multiracial social movement (Spickard, 1999). Nonetheless, their opposition to both commonly espoused options, a multiracial category and multiple box checking, is echoed by some members of the public who identify themselves monoracially despite possessing multiple ancestries. Declaring his intention to eschew the chance to check more than one box on the 2000 Census and determined to check the "Black" box only, Michael Gelobter asks, "Should Frederick Douglass have checked white and black? Should W. E. B. Du Bois have checked white and black?" (Schemo, 2000, p. A1). For African American leaders such as Du Bois and Douglass to have acknowledged their patent multiracial ancestry, argues Gelobter, would have been for them to have abandoned common cause with other African Americans. This is the core of the monoracial argument against the expression of a multiracial identity: claiming a multiracial identity means abandoning Black America.

Critics of Whiteness studies are equally caustic. The critics complain that whatever their antiracist intentions may be, the authors of Whiteness studies place White people at the center of attention, thus distracting from the real needs of peoples of color. Noel Ignatiev wrote a book with the title *How the Irish Became White* (1995) and Karen Brodkin followed with *How Jews Became White Folks and What That Says About Race in America* (1998). Soon scholars and lay people alike could be heard to remark, "You know, once [X White group] were not White, but then they became White." This amounted to a kind of me-too ethnicity. White people were saying, "Look at us. We have race, too. We are the ones who merit attention." Significant energy in ethnic studies began to shift away from examining the lives and experiences of people of color. Instead, that attention began to go to White people, who, I contend, already were the subject of nearly the entire curriculum. Many studies of Whiteness, in this interpretation, amount to little more than me-too ethnic absorption on the part of White people.

It is that quality of self-absorption in each movement and a related individualism that are troubling. The central claim of the multiracial movement is that America must recognize the multiplicity in their identities as multiracial individuals. They tend to be opposed by the group claims of monoracially defined communities of color. Marie Hara and Nora Okja Keller (1999) have edited a stunning collection of poetry and prose by multiracial women. However, in 63 sensitive evocations of the various authors' life experiences, almost no attention is paid to group needs. It is all about their own individual identity and relationship issues. Many multiracial activists are in practical fact committed to the needs of the communities of color to which they have connections, but their multiracial claim is essentially an individualistic concern. Similarly, Whiteness studies have resulted in a significant turning away from the issues of communities of color and redirecting of that scholarly energy toward White people as a group. In addition to individualism and self-concern, both intellectual movements have a trendy quality. As Danzy Senna (1998b) writes, "Hybridity is in"; the same can be said of Whiteness.

Connecting Multiraciality and Whiteness Studies

Whatever the merits of multiraciality and of Whiteness studies, the critics have pointed to at least potentially problematic tendencies in these two intellectual movements. It now remains to be ascertained whether there is a connection between these two fields of concern. From a certain skeptical angle, one may view the assertion of a multiracial identity as a kind of Whiteness experience: centering Whiteness, decentering monoracial oppression, and de-emphasizing the needs of communities of color. This we may call the Whiteness trap.

A University of California, Berkeley, student, himself multiracial, complains about his classmates in Hapa Issues Forum, one of the multiracial groups on campus: "They're all Japanese-White kids from the suburbs who think that because they are part White their shit don't stink." Lisa Jones (1994) writes,

> By marketing themselves as anything but black, do light-complexioned entertainers such as [Mariah] Carey become, in the eyes of most Americans, de facto whites? And do Carey and other people of color who feel more at ease representing themselves by

their combination ethnic heritages, and not by race ... teach the world how to be "raceless"? Or are they positioning themselves as a separate class along the lines of South African "coloreds"? (p. 201)

There may be some evidence that the assertion of a multiracial identity is related to middle-class status and experience in White contexts. Kerry Ann Rockquemore surveyed 250 college students, each of whom had one White parent and one Black parent. She found that those raised in middle-class White neighborhoods tended to identify themselves as biracial, whereas those raised in Black communities tended to identity themselves as monoracially Black (Rockquemore, 1998).

Jon Michael Spencer (1997) suggests that White parents with Black partners who have advocated a multiracial Census category have done so partly out of a wish for their children to avoid the disabilities of being Black in American society: "[It] is not all about the self-esteem of their mixed-race children. Some of this behavior has to do with the self-esteem of these interracially married White parents who have difficulty accepting their mixed-race children choosing black as an identity" (p. 87). The most insistent advocate of a multiracial census option, Susan Graham of Project RACE, lends some support to such a suggestion when she says "Nobody can tell me my children are more black than white" (Schemo, 2000, p. A1).

Conservative activist Charles Byrd, who is also a multiracialist, says, "What we need to do as a country is get rid of these stupid [racial] boxes altogether" (Schemo, 2000, p. A9). Royce Van Tassell (2000) echoes this opinion, setting forth multiraciality as a station on the way to getting rid of talking about race entirely. Van Tassel, affiliated with a right-wing action group that sponsors the Race Has No Place Project, wants to drum any consideration of race—of the causes, patterns,

and consequences of racial discrimination—out of American public life. As evidence to support his claim that Americans do not want to think about race, talk about race, or collect data about the status of America's various racial communities, he cites a survey his group sponsored that claims that a large majority of Americans would describe a person of a Black parent and a White parent as multiracial. He skips several logical steps to the conclusion that "Americans want to reclaim their racial privacy, and they are tired of the government's intrusive race questions" (p. 5).

There are considerable grounds, then, to make the argument that multiraciality lightens. At the very least, the multiracial idea can give support to the position that the most important thing is an individual's self-identity. As in the cases of Van Tassel and Byrd, the concept of multiraciality may be used by people with malign motives to attack communities of color.

Does Multiraciality Lighten? Evidence From History

One may grant that there may be some measure of evidence for Rainier Spencer's fears. Some people who are not persons of good will—who do not support the interests of communities of color in the United States and who do not want White Americans to have to take race seriously—may welcome the multiracial movement. They may try to turn it to their ends, as a way station on the path to ignoring race (and, therefore, their own guilt) entirely. Yet does that mean that the critics' contention is true? Does multiraciality necessarily lighten? Contrary to the contentions of Spencer, Gelobter, and others, there is not much historical evidence that it does.

Consider the cases of several prominent Americans who acknowledged multiracial ancestry. Frederick Douglass was the most widely known African American of the 19th century. He was the son of a slave woman and a White man, although his features were such that he could not easily have passed for White. There was no fiercer advocate of the rights of African Americans, yet throughout his life Douglass acknowledged his White ancestry along with the Black. He insisted on traveling in an interracial social world and in his latter years married a White woman. Douglass acknowledged his multiraciality, even as he embraced Black America fully. Gregory Stephens (1999) writes of Douglass:

> In 1886, he told an audience: "[A man painting me insisted I show] my full face, for that is Ethiopian. Take my side face, said I, for that is Caucasian. But should you try my quarter face you would find it Indian. I don't know that any race can claim me, but being identified with slaves as I am, I think I know the meaning of the inquiry.' Douglass' public persona was that of a defender of the rights of Afro-Americans. But his private identity was multiethnic (p. 104).

Alice Dunbar-Nelson was a turn-of-the-century African American writer and wife of poet Paul Laurence Dunbar. She was Black in her writing and in her political commitments. However, her social world was racially mixed, and she passed for White frequently in her private life, for instance to shop in segregated White stores or to attend the theater. Reading out from Dunbar-Nelson's life to those of several of her contemporaries and successors in African American letters, Hanna Wallinger (in press) concludes that "although racial thinking determined the public utterances and creative writing of many prominent African Americans— . . . Charles Chesnutt, Wallace Thurman, Langston Hughes, Hallie E. Queen, and Josephine and Senator Blanche Bruce—it did not determine their personal lives to an exclusive degree."

Edith Maude Eaton was another of that same generation that spanned the turn of the 20th century. She has widely been honored as the foremother of Asian American fiction. The child of English and Chinese parents, she lived in North America, took the pen name Sui Sin Far, and wrote in humane and sympathetic tones about the plight of Chinese Americans. Nonetheless, although she has been honored for her public persona as a Chinese American, she lived her personal life as a White woman (Spickard & Mengel, 1997; White-Parks, 1995).

Perhaps there is no more revered figure in African American history than W. E. B. Du Bois—historian, sociologist, journalist, cofounder of the National Association for the Advancement of Colored Persons (NAACP), pan-Africanist. Indeed, a Pulitzer Prize-winning author subtitled Du Bois's story "Biography of a Race" (Lewis, 1993). Du Bois was fervently committed to his identity as an African American, to the African American people, and later to the entire African diaspora. Yet in *Dusk of Dawn*, one of several autobiographies, Du Bois discusses at great length the various strands of his European ancestry, some of it quite recent, and the degrees of his affinity with those strands. Du Bois was light of skin and European of feature, and he could easily have passed for White had he chosen to do so. He consistently recognized his multiraciality. However, that did not mitigate his embrace of Blackness or his effectiveness in serving the cause of African Americans (Du Bois, 1984).

Similar stories could be told of other important figures of African American history: Mary Church Terrell, first president of the National Association of Colored Women; Mordecai Johnson, first African American president of Howard University; Walter White, novelist and longtime executive secretary of the NAACP; Jean Toomer, herald of the Harlem Renaissance; Adam Clayton Powell, Jr., flamboyant Congress member from Harlem in the 1950s and 1960s. All these were multi-racial people who acknowledged, even embraced, their multiraciality and who nonetheless were leaders in one way or another of communities of color. Even Wallace D. Fard, the mysterious figure behind the founding of the Nation of Islam, and Malcolm X, the Black Muslims' fiery leader, were multiracial men who acknowledged their multiraciality, although they were less sanguine about it than Douglass or Du Bois.

Earlier in this chapter, I reported that Michael Gelobter asked, "Should Frederick Douglass have checked white and black? Should W. E. B. Du Bois have checked white and black?" (Schemo, 2000, p. A9). I think it is possible, given the shape of those men's careers and the contents of their public utterances, that they might well have chosen to check both "Black" and "White" boxes if they had lived to the time of the 2000 Census. Both they, and all the other individuals to whom I have just referred, identified themselves emphatically with communities of color (Black and Chinese in these cases). Yet they all also acknowledged their multiplicity and did not try to mask it. Some, like Dunbar-Nelson

and Sui Sin Far, lived part of the time on the White side of the line. Some, like Du Bois, gloried in their multiraciality even as they chose monoracial lives. Some, like Malcolm X, hated their White ancestry. However, all recognized their multiplicity even as they chose to serve communities of color. There is just not adequate historical evidence to conclude that acknowledgment or embrace of a multiracial identity necessarily lightens. The important issue for monoracial communities of color is not whether multiracial people claim their multiraciality, but whether, having done so, they continue to serve the needs of those communities of color.

The criticism of the multiracial movement—that it is a form of seeking after Whiteness—has theoretical validity: It points to a real danger. There are those who advocate a multiracial identity who also would like to do away with consideration of race in American society, who in effect would abandon the needs of communities of color. However, examining the actual lives of several multiracial people in historical context suggests that recognition, even embrace, of a multiracial identity does not mean that multiracial people fall into the Whiteness trap.

NOTES

1. In this chapter, I capitalize such words as "White," "Black," and "Whiteness" because they are used as proper nouns and adjectives, in the same way that African American, Caucasian, and European American are proper nouns and adjectives. I have met only a handful of people who could accurately be described to be the color black, and I have never met a White person without a tinge of pink, beige, or gray. I do not capitalize "multiracial" because, in my judgment, it is not yet an accepted racial designation in American society at large, as much as some people whom I respect would like it to be. I use it here, then, as a descriptive adjective. Some of the authors whose words I quote use a different capitalization scheme. I have left their words as they wrote them.

2. In recent years, they have included the University of California campuses at Berkeley, Los Angeles, and Santa Barbara; California State University campuses at Northridge, San Francisco, and San Jose; Brigham Young University—Hawai'i; the University of Hawai'i; —the University of North Texas; and Brown University.

3. Some would argue that the majority of faculty positions in the humanities and social sciences are, in fact, already dedicated to Whiteness studies. See Spickard (in press).

4.   For a more careful exposition of racial construction on the part of African Americans in the same period, see Gomez (1998). For theoretical formulations of racial construction, see Cornell and Hartmann (1997) and Spickard and Burroughs (2000). For a fuller examination of the strengths and dangers of the Whiteness studies movement, see Spickard (in press).

5.   Spencer sees only two races in America: Black and White. He offers essentially no evidence for his South African analogy.

REFERENCES

Allen, Theodore. (1994). *The invention of the white race: Racial oppression and social control.* London: Verso.

Allen, Theodore. (1997). *The invention of the white race: The origin of racial oppression in Anglo-America.* London: Verso.

Almaguer, Tomás. (1994). *Racial fault lines: The historical origins of white supremacy in California.* Berkeley: University of California Press.

Azoulay, Katya Gibel. (1997). *Black, Jewish, and interracial.* Durham, NC: Duke University Press.

Babb, Valerie. (1998). *Whiteness visible: The meaning of whiteness in American literature and culture.* New York: New York University Press.

Ball, Edward. (1999). *Slaves in the family.* New York: Random House.

Berger, Maurice. (1999). *White lies: Race and the myths of whiteness.* New York: Farrar, Straus & Giroux.

Brodkin, Karen. (1998). *How Jews became white folks and what that says about race in America.* New Brunswick, NJ: Rutgers University Press.

Bronwen, Walter. (2001). *Outsiders inside: Whiteness, place and Irish women.* New York: Routledge.

Camper, Carol. (Ed.). (1994). *Miscegenation blues: Voices of mixed race women.* Toronto: Sister Vision.

Clark, Christine, & O'Donnell, James. (Eds.). (1999). *Becoming and unbecoming white: Owning and disowning a racial identity.* Westport, CT: Bergin & Garvey.

Conley, Dalton. (2000). *Honky.* Berkeley: University of California Press.

Cornell, Stephen, & Hartmann, Douglas. (1997). *Ethnicity and race.* Thousand Oaks, CA: Pine Forge.

Crooks, Kalpana Seshari. (2000). *Desiring whiteness: A Lacanian analysis of race.* New York: Routledge.

Cuomo, Chris J., & Hall, Kim Q. (Eds.). (1999). *Whiteness: Feminist philosophical reflections.* Lanham, MD: Rowman and Littlefield.

Curry, Renee R. (2000). *White women writing white.* New York: Greenwood.

Daniel, G. Reginald. (1992). Passers and pluralists: Subverting the racial divide. In Maria P. P. Root (Ed.), *Racially mixed people in America* (pp. 91-107). Newbury Park, CA: Sage.

Daniel, G. Reginald. (2002). *More than black? Multiracial identity and the new racial order.* Philadelphia: Temple University Press.

Davis, F. James. (1991). *Who is black? One nation's definition.* University Park: Pennsylvania State University Press.

Delgado, Richard, & Stefancic, Jean. (Eds.). (1997). *Critical white studies.* Philadelphia: Temple University Press.

Deloria, Philip. (1998). *Playing Indian.* New Haven, CT: Yale University Press.

Du Bois, W. E. B. (1984). *Dusk of dawn: An essay toward an autobiography of a race concept.* New Brunswick, NJ: Transaction.

Dyer, Richard. (1997). *White.* London: Routledge.

Eaton, Winnifred. (1997). *Me: A book of remembrance*. Jackson: University Press of Mississippi.

Ferber, Abby L. (1998). *White man falling: Race, gender, and white supremacy*. Lanham, MD: Rowman and Littlefield.

Fine, Michelle, Weis, Lois, Powell, Linda C., & Wong, L. Mun. (Eds.). (1997). *Off white: Readings on race, power, and society*. New York: Routledge.

Foley, Neil. (1997). *The white scourge: Mexicans, blacks, and poor whites in Texas cotton culture*. Berkeley: University of California Press.

Forbes, Jack D. (1993). *Africans and Native Americans: The language of race and the evolution of red-black peoples*. Urbana: University of Illinois Press.

Frankenberg, Ruth. (1993). *White women, race matters: The social construction of whiteness*. Minneapolis: University of Minnesota Press.

Frankenberg, Ruth. (Ed.). (1997). *Displacing whiteness: Essays in social and cultural criticism*. Durham, NC: Duke University Press.

Fulton, Aubyn. (1997, May 30). Message posted to interracial individuals discussion list. Retrieved from www.ii-list@hcs.harvard.edu

Funderburg, Lise. (1994). *Black, white, other: Biracial Americans talk about race and identity*. New York: Morrow.

Gabriel, John. (1998). *Whitewash: Racialized politics and the media*. New York: Routledge.

Gaskins, Pearl Fuyo. (1999). *What are you? Voices of mixed-race young people*. New York: Holt.

Glass, Ronald David, & Wallace, Kendra R. (1996). Challenging race and racism: A framework for educators. In Maria P. P. Root (Ed.), *The multiracial experience* (pp. 341-358). Thousand Oaks, CA: Sage.

Goad, Jim. (1998). *The redneck manifesto: How hillbillies, hicks, and white trash became America's scapegoats*. New York: Touchstone.

Gomez, Michael A. (1998). *Exchanging our country marks: The transformation of African identities and the colonial and antebellum south*. Chapel Hill: University of North Carolina Press.

Haizlip, Shirlee Taylor. (1994). *The sweeter the juice: A family memoir in black and white*. New York: Simon & Schuster.

Hale, Grace Elizabeth. (1998). *Making whiteness: The culture of segregation in the south, 1890–1940*. New York: Vintage.

Hall, Wade. (1997). *Passing for black: The life and careers of Mae Street Kidd*. Lexington: University Press of Kentucky.

Haney López, Ian F. (1996). *White by law: The legal construction of race*. New York: New York University Press.

Hara, Marie, & Keller, Nora Okja. (Eds.). (1999). *Intersecting circles: The voices of Hapa women in poetry and prose*. Honolulu: Bamboo Ridge.

Hartigan, John. (1999). *Racial situations: Class predicaments of whiteness in Detroit*. Princeton, NJ: Princeton University Press.

Hill, Mike. (Ed.). (1997). *Whiteness: A critical reader*. New York: New York University Press.

Hügel-Marshall, Ika. (2001). *Invisible woman: Growing up black in Germany*. New York: Continuum.

Ignatiev, Noel. (1995). *How the Irish became white*. New York: Routledge.

Ignatiev, Noel, & Garvey, John. (Eds.). (1996). *Race traitor*. New York: Routledge.

Jacobson, Matthew Frye. (1998). *Whiteness of a different color: European immigrants and the alchemy of race*. Cambridge, MA: Harvard University Press.

Jones, Lisa. (1994). *Bulletproof diva: Tales of race, sex, and hair*. New York: Doubleday.

Katz, William Loren. (1997). *Black Indians*. New York: Simon & Schuster.

Khanga, Yelena. (1992). *Soul to soul: The story of a black Russian American family, 1865–1992*. New York: Norton.

Kim, Elizabeth. (2000). *Ten thousand sorrows*. New York: Doubleday.

Kincheloe, Joe, Steinberg, Shirley R., Rodriguez, Nelson M., & Chennault, Ronald E. (Eds.). (1998). *White reign: Deploying whiteness in America*. New York: St. Martin's.

Korgen, Kathleen Odell. (1999). *From black to biracial: Transforming racial identity among Americans*. Westport, CT: Praeger.

Lazarre, Jane. (1996). *Beyond the whiteness of whiteness: Memoir of a white mother of black sons*. Durham, NC: Duke University Press.

Lee, Robert G. (1999). *Orientals: Asian Americans in popular culture*. Philadelphia: Temple University Press.

Leslie, Kent Anderson. (1995). *Woman of color, daughter of privilege: Amanda America Dickson, 1849–1893*. Athens: University of Georgia Press.

Lewis, David Levering. (1993). *W. E. B. Du Bois: Biography of a race*. New York: Holt.

Lipsitz, George. (1998). *The possessive investment in whiteness: How white people profit from identity politics*. Philadelphia: Temple University Press.

McBride, James. (1996). *The color of water: A black man's tribute to his white mother*. New York: Riverhead.

McKelvey, Robert S. (1999). *The dust of life: America's children abandoned in Vietnam*. Seattle: University of Washington Press.

Minerbrook, Scott. (1996). *Divided to the vein: A journey into race and family*. New York: Harcourt Brace.

Nakayama, Thomas K., & Martin, Judith N. (Eds.). (1999). *Whiteness: The communication of social identity*. Thousand Oaks, CA: Sage.

Nelson, Dona D. (Ed.). (1998). *Capitalist citizenship and the imagined fraternity of white men*. Durham, NC: Duke University Press.

Nunez, Sigrid. (1995). *A feather on the breath of God*. New York: HarperCollins.

Obama, Barack. (1995). *Dreams from my father: A story of race and inheritance*. New York: Times Books.

O'Hearn, Claudine Chiawei. (Ed.). (1998). *Half + half: Writers on growing up biracial + bicultural*. New York: Pantheon.

Parker, David, & Song, Miri. (Eds.). (2001). *Rethinking "mixed race."* London: Pluto.

Penn, William S. (Ed.). (1997). *As we are now: Mixblood essays on race and identity*. Berkeley: University of California Press.

Reddy, Maureen. (1994). *Crossing the color line: Race, parenting, and culture*. New Brunswick, NJ: Rutgers University Press.

Rockquemore, Kerry Ann. (1998). Between black and white: Exploring the biracial experience. *Race and Society, 1*(2), 197-212.

Rodriguez, Nelson M., & Villaverde, Leila E. (Eds.). (2000). *Dismantling white privilege: Pedagogy, politics, and whiteness*. New York: Peter Lang.

Roediger, David. (1991). *The wages of whiteness: Race and the making of the American working class*. London: Verso.

Roediger, David. (1994). *Towards the abolition of whiteness*. London: Verso.

Roediger, David. (1998). *Black on white: Black writers on what it means to be white*. New York: Schocken.

Root, Maria P. P. (Ed.). (1992). *Racially mixed people in America*. Newbury Park, CA: Sage.

Root, Maria P. P. (1996a). A bill of rights for racially mixed people. In Maria P. P. Root (Ed.), *The multiracial experience* (pp. 3-14). Thousand Oaks, CA: Sage.

Root, Maria P. P. (Ed.). (1996b). *The multiracial experience*. Thousand Oaks, CA: Sage.

Saxton, Alexander. (1990). *The rise and fall of the white republic: Class politics and mass culture in nineteenth-century America*. London: Verso.

Scales-Trent, Judy. (1995). *Notes of a white black woman*. University Park: Pennsylvania State University Press.

Schemo, Diana Jean. (2000, February 12). Despite options on census, many to check "black" only. *New York Times,* pp. A1, A9.

Senna, Danzy. (1998a). *Caucasia.* New York: Riverhead.

Senna, Danzy. (1998b). The mulatto millennium. In C. C. O'Hearn (Ed.), *Half + half* (pp. 12-27). New York: Pantheon.

Sollors, Werner. (1997). *Neither black nor white yet both: Thematic explorations of interracial literature.* New York: Oxford University Press.

Spencer, Jon Michael. (1997). *The new colored people: The mixed-race movement in America.* New York: New York University Press.

Spencer, Rainier. (1999). *Spurious issues: Race and multiracial identity politics in the United States.* Boulder, CO: Westview.

Spickard, Paul. (1992). The illogic of American racial categories. In Maria P. P. Root (Ed.), *Racially mixed people in America* (pp. 12-23). Newbury Park, CA: Sage.

Spickard, Paul. (1999). Review of Werner Sollors, *Neither black nor white yet both,* and Jon Michael Spencer, *The new colored people: The mixed-race movement in America. Journal of American Ethnic History, 18*(2), 153-156.

Spickard, Paul. (in press). What's critical about white studies. In P. Spickard & G. Reginald Daniel (Eds.), *Uncompleted independence: Racial ideas in the United States.* Notre Dame, IN: University of Notre Dame Press.

Spickard, Paul, & Burroughs, W. Jeffrey. (Eds.). (2000). *We are a people: Narrative and multiplicity in constructing ethnic identity.* Philadelphia: Temple University Press.

Spickard, Paul, Fong, Rowena, & Ewalt, Pat. (Eds.). (1995). Undermining the very basis of racism, its categories. *Social Work, 40*(6), 725-728.

Spickard, Paul, & Mengel, Laurie. (1997, November). Deconstructing race: The multiethnicity of Sui Sin Far. *Books and Culture,* pp. 4-5.

Stephens, Gregory. (1999). *On racial frontiers: The new culture of Frederick Douglass, Ralph Ellison, and Bob Marley.* Cambridge, UK: Cambridge University Press.

Talalay, Kathryn. (1995). *Composition in black and white: The life of Philippa Schuyler.* New York: Oxford University Press.

Thandeka. (1999). *Learning to be white: Money, race, & God in America.* New York: Continuum.

Thompson, Becky, & Tyagi, Sangeeta. (Eds.). (1996). *Names we call home: Autobiography on racial identity.* New York: Routledge.

Tizard, Barbara, & Phoenix, Ann. (1993). *Black, white, or mixed race? Race and racism in the lives of young people of mixed parentage.* London: Routledge.

Van Tassell, M. Royce. (2000). Americans are tired of racial boxes: Vast majority want government to "leave my race alone!" *The Egalitarian, 3*(2), 1, 5.

Wallinger, Hanna. (in press). Not color but character: Alice Dunbar-Nelson's uncompleted argument. In P. Spickard & G. Reginald Daniel (Eds.), *Uncompleted independence: Racial thinking in the United States.* Notre Dame, IN: University of Notre Dame Press.

West, Dorothy. (1995). *The wedding.* New York: Doubleday.

The white issue. (1996). *Transition* [Special issue], *73.*

White-Parks, Annette. (1995). *Sui Sin Far/Edith Maude Eaton.* Urbana: University of Illinois Press.

Williams, Gregory Howard. (1995). *Life on the color line: The true story of a white boy who discovered he was black.* New York: Penguin.

Williams-León, Teresa, & Nakashima, Cynthia. (Eds.). (2001). *The sum of our parts: Mixed-heritage Asian Americans.* Philadelphia: Temple University Press.

Wray, Matt, & Newitz, Annalee. (Eds.). (1997). *White trash: Race and class in America.* New York: Routledge.

Zack, Naomi. (1993). *Race and mixed race.* Philadelphia: Temple University Press.

Zack, Naomi. (Ed.). (1995). *American mixed race.* Lanham, MD: Rowman & Littlefield.

CHAPTER 15

The Hazards of Visibility

"Biracial" Women, Media Images, and Narratives of Identity

CAROLINE A. STREETER

The republic of the United States is a society consumed by ideas of racial purity and racial denial. Therefore, the United States is also replete with fascination with racial mixing and racial difference.

— Donna Haraway (1997)

In this chapter, I examine the topic of biracial women through two lenses: media images from the United States and a small sample of creative writing and documentary videos produced by college-age women from two University of California campuses. We encounter an immediate dilemma with regard to terminology because, in media imagery, it is rarely possible to discern whether a woman depicted is "biracial," that is, has two parents of different "races."[1] For that reason, I often use the more general designation "mixed-race," especially in the first part of the chapter, which focuses on print media.[2] A second dilemma involves why one needs to know, and how one goes about determining, whether a woman depicted in a media image is of mixed race. To bring a quality of hypervigilance to the visual markers of race entails participation in the discourse that makes physical features synonymous with racial classification. Even if the goal is to ascertain "mixedness," one becomes engaged in an attempt to fix what "mixed" looks like.

The discourse of race in U.S. media is heavily weighted toward an understanding of race relations that is limited to African Americans and European Americans. In a cultural climate in which the legibility of race is restricted to "black" and "white," mixed-race people tend to be imagined as black/white or "mulatto."

Yet recent manifestations of racial/ethnic conflict such as the riots/rebellions that took place in Los Angeles 10 years ago clearly indicate how inadequate that model is (Gooding-Williams, 1993). Although in the world of popular culture the black/white racial dichotomy continues to be exploited, in recent decades many have jumped onto the lucrative multicultural bandwagon. This phenomenon has revolutionized media images, especially in advertising. Led by the Italian clothing company Benetton, advertisements increasingly depict a wide range of ethnicities as well as many types of multiracial people. The visual pleasure provided by diverse ethnic types, however, has disturbing antecedents in 19th century racial science and the ethnographic photography that accompanied European colonial expansion. The assumption that "race" and "mixed race" can be determined through the visual evidence of physical features has been used repeatedly to buttress the logic of racial hierarchies. As the black British photographer and writer David A. Bailey (1989) has commented:

> If we look at early anthropological photography we can see the process of categorisation and construction of racial difference in which cultures were either photogra-phed voyeuristically within their homelands (emphasizing physical features) or photographed and measured in studies. This is reproduced in the Benetton campaign by the categorisation of differences and the emphasis on physical features such as eyes, hair and skin color. This emphasis on physical features is also similar to the early medical and police photographs of mental, physical and social deviants. Likewise the framing and cropping of the United Contrasts [sic] of Benetton advertisements is very similar to these earlier photographs. (p. 65)

In addition to the troubling history invoked by attempts to translate physical features into racial "types," the title of this chapter, "the hazards of visibility" refers to an ongoing debate about how media images affect individuals and groups in society. Although Census 2000 made it clear that the United States has undergone dramatic demographic change, the implicit understanding of an American as a white person of Western European descent is not only deeply embedded in our national narratives but also is everywhere visible in media representations. In other words, images of white people dominate the visual culture that saturates our everyday environment. The idea that media images and the visual and textual narratives they contain affect us, although seemingly a commonsense notion, is controversial. I suggest that although women and people of color naturally enough wish to see themselves in the images with which all of us are relentlessly bombarded, we must be vigilant about the terms of our inclusion. Like ethnic advocacy groups such as the National Association for the Advancement of Colored People (NAACP), organizations such as the Association for MultiEthnic Americans (AMEA) and Multiracial Americans of Southern California (MASC), as well as magazines aimed at multiracial individuals and families like *Interrace* and *Mavin* consistently applaud the increase in representations of mixed-race people in media images as a positive development. I argue here that visibility is a complex phenomenon that should not be uncritically celebrated. As the word "hazard" indicates, a possible danger to be carefully negotiated, the stream of media images from which I analyze selected examples can be considered a kind of traffic. U.S. society is characterized by a formidable traffic in media images, in which we all may be said to participate but in which the profits and benefits are very unevenly distributed.

Many of the women in the media images that I analyze can be called "virtual girls" because their personal history is unknown to the viewer. They exist solely on the level of the image. By contrast, in the second part of the chapter, I discuss "real girls," exploring media representations of the celebrity Mariah Carey as well as writing and documentary video by college-age women. The use of the term *biracial* is more appropriate when we have evidence of how people identify, especially when, as in the writing and video, women draw substantially on autobiographical material. My analysis of texts that draw on autobiography—the narratives of identity to which the chapter's title refers—demonstrates how young women deploy the tools of feminist theory and antiracist activism to engage what it means to inhabit a biracial female body.

THE METAPHOR DANCE: WHEN DOES MULTICULTURAL MEAN MULTIRACIAL?

Print images that feature mixed-race people are a prominent example of the multicultural representations that have become ubiquitous in contemporary media. The ideology of multiculturalism that is referenced by such images emphasizes the pleasurable aspects of ethnic diversity without engaging the challenge of cultural differences and the existence of racial hierarchies and racial inequality. Multicultural images that use multiracial people envision a future that is free of such power struggles. In a recent example that I discuss more thoroughly later, in 1993 *Time* magazine imagined the future U.S. population as represented by a multiracial woman created through a computer program, featured on the issue's cover.[3] *Time* used the metaphor of the multicultural society to update that of the melting pot. Traditionally, the melting pot required ethnic groups to assimilate to a generic American

model.[4] The concept of a multicultural "stew" might appear more inclusive than the melting pot, in that it would allow for the survival of ethnic particularity, influencing the definition of "American" rather than requiring the burden of change to be fully borne by ethnic "others." However, multiculturalism in the hands of corporate interests has frequently merely facilitated the commodification of ethnic difference.

In media imagery the idealized future— free of troubling difference and conflict—has often been represented by a mixed-race child, in a move that demonstrates how multicultural ideology becomes represented by images of multiracial people. This phenomenon of conflation is especially evident when images of mixed-race children are deployed to represent visions of racial harmony deemed unthreatening because they are so "cute." In one example, a Baby Gap ad published in *O (The Oprah Magazine)* in May 2000 depicting an Afro-Asian baby girl reinforces the tenacious myth that mixed-race children are "naturally" the most beautiful (Figure 15.1).

The media's fixation on beautiful children of mixed descent provides an example of why the increase in the number of visibly racially mixed bodies depicted "positively" does not necessarily constitute a progressive move in representation. Adorable images do little to challenge the basis for social inclusion.

Just as advertising photography deploys strongly contrasting skin colors to signify racial difference, it often uses "rainbow imagery" (intermediate skin tones) to portray people of mixed descent.[5] In fact, *rainbow baby* is a term used to describe racially mixed children, particularly those of black and white heritage. The ubiquity of phrases such as "rainbow babies" and "coffee-colored children" is indicative of the tendency to infantilize the subject of mixed descent.

babyGap is spring

baby
GAP

Figure 15.1   Baby GAP, O (The Oprah Magazine), May–June 2000

An overriding concern for children, whether articulated to caution against interracial relationships or to advocate for an institutionalized multiracial classification (Graham, 1996), dovetails with trends in advertising and television, which are currently obsessed with young models and actors, and the more adolescent looking, the better (Hirschberg, 1999).

As well, in this climate, "everybody's going for the multi-ethnic girl" (Namkung, 2000).

As I have mentioned, *Time* magazine gave prominent visibility to a multiethnic girl in a special issue published in fall 1993, although this particular cover photo was computer generated (Figure 15.2).

Time's cover consisted of a "morph" based on the projected future racial and ethnic composition of the U.S. population. According to *Time*, "the image of (their) new Eve" is "15% Anglo Saxon, 17.5% Middle Eastern, 17.5% African, 7.5% Asian, 35% Southern European and 7.5% Hispanic" ("The New Face," 1993). Apparently, as Eve's face emerged on the computer screen, *Time's* staff members became heartbroken that "she doesn't exist" ("The New Face," 1993). However, the writer Danzy Senna (1998) contends

> Of course, anyone could see that women just like the computer face they had created did exist in Puerto Rico, Latin America, and Spanish Harlem. . . . As I read the article, it reminded me of an old saying they used to have down South during Jim Crow: 'If a black man wants to sit in the front of the bus, he just puts on a turban.' Maybe the same rule applied here: call yourself mixed and you just might find the world smiles a little brighter on you. (p. 14)

Senna's comments echo the suspicions of black Americans who question the purpose of a multiracial category, a critique influenced by historical attempts on the part of individuals and groups to "pass" and become reclassified as anything but black (or Negro or colored).[6] Likewise, Senna alludes to the instability of visual markers of race as well as to the importance of historical, geographic, and cultural factors in determining racialization.[7] Her critique of the ways that mixed-race people can escape the social prejudice that is aimed at people of color brings to mind what I call the "safe hybridity," represented by individuals who inhabit an intermediate racial

category. In fact, my juxtaposition of the terms *safe* and *hybridity* is intentionally paradoxical. Hybridity as conceptualized by postcolonial theorists such as Trinh T. Minh-ha and Homi Bhabha cannot be safe. Bhabha has remarked, "A strategy of hybridization does not celebrate cultural diversity, it celebrates . . . cultural difference" (Trinh, 1999, p. 28). However, the hybridization that is practiced by the *Time* magazine cover is emptied of political content through its celebration as mere curiosity—a high-tech feat. *Time* reduces hybridity to horticulture; the meaning of the woman's face is limited to her (sexually attractive) blended features.

The words on *Time's* cover make it clear that Eve is not racially "pure": "Take a good look at this woman. She was created by a computer from a mix of several races." When we consider the iconic status of blue-eyed, blonde-haired, and white-skinned femininity, not just in the United States but throughout western European and Latin American countries, *Time's* rendering of the representative American woman of the future as an olive-skinned brunette with hazel eyes could be considered progressive.[8] Nevertheless, some have contended that the image looks like a white woman.[9] Like Danzy Senna, others disagreed with the *Time* staff's lament that their Eve does not exist, finding her ethnicity conceivable, albeit ambiguous. My mixed-race friends and I concurred that Eve's hair was quite intriguing. While it is not wavy, its texture hints at a fuzziness that will be familiar to the parents of rainbow babies. Yet the magazine's cover elides the topic of miscegenation, allowing the apparently more palatable *multicultural* to stand in for *multiracial*. The magazine text invokes the narrative of immigration to account for the multiracial and multiethnic composition of their cover girl: "What you see is a remarkable preview of . . . The New Face of America. How Immigrants Are Shaping the World's First Multicultural Society."

Figure 15.2   *Time* Magazine, Fall 1993

Time's article explaining how the morphing program worked was accompanied by a grid of photographs illustrating examples of the program's generation of the "progeny" of 14 men and women of various racial and ethnic backgrounds. The grid, appearing under the title "Rebirth of a Nation—Computer Style," makes a cultural reference that should give us pause. D. W. Griffith's silent film of 1915 *The Birth of a Nation* repudiated the outcome of the United States' Civil War, especially the Reconstruction Era, during which newly enfranchised black Americans voted and held office in the southern states. The film's vicious racial stereotypes, including rapacious black men who preyed on white virgins as well as corrupt and over-sexed mulattoes, had an enduring influence on American cinema. As Lauren Berlant has commented, *Time's* reference to the film is simultaneously innocuous and deeply troubling.[10] For my purposes here, *Time's* "Freudian slip" is especially meaningful because it betrays the extent to which ambivalence about miscegenation, which, in *The Birth of a Nation*, was the most depraved result of black emancipation, persists in contemporary discourse about race.

Judging by the images of mixed-race progeny in *Time's* "Rebirth of a Nation" grid, gender categories presented unexpected complications for a computer program written to mimic biological reproduction. Many of the photos struggle for gender determinacy, and it is frequently difficult to tell whether the morph is male or female without looking at the "parents," in which case the hairstyle seems most determinative of "gender." It is intriguing that the computer program would create ambiguously gendered offspring from images of men and women, undermining the myth of heterosexual normativity, at least in cyberspace! Because the parameters by which

the program functioned are so different from those that drive genetic reproduction, it seems curious that *Time's* staff felt compelled to mimic heterosexual reproduction. Why not morph women with women and men with men? Would "gay" and "lesbian" parents render offspring with a more easily identifiable gender? In fact, *Time's* unambiguously female Eve was created by morphing the features of all seven of the women used to produce their "Rebirth of a Nation" chart.

In addition to virtual miscegenation, *Time* highlights what is actually called "crossbreeding" in their text: real live adults in interracial relationships and the children born from these unions. The subjects are presented in a format similar to the virtual morphs on *Time's* cover image and in their "Rebirth of a Nation" grid, photographed with seemingly nude torsos and looking directly into the camera lens, fully available to the viewer.[11] Looking at these images, one experiences the unsettling yet irresistible urge to compare the real-life "mixed breeds" with their morphed counterparts and to note which physical features the children have inherited from their parents. The compulsion to focus on the physical characteristics, especially the face of a person, is precisely the impulse that advertising that features mixed-race women plays on.

REBIRTH OF A NATION

Advertising makes explicit the routes by which persons might individually and collectively give a name to their desire (Berlant, 1997, p. 11).

An ad from the clothing designer Calvin Klein's campaign for the fragrance cKone highlights the ways that ethnic mystery becomes a sign of miscegenation in an image that emphasizes the vulnerable and available sexuality of a mixed-race woman. In this way, the cKone ad metaphorically fulfills the expectations raised by advertising that eroticizes interracial couples.[12] In the full-page photograph, three quarters of the space is devoted to a close-up image of the face and throat of a young woman with an Afro-Asian appearance, flanked by a partial image of a fragrance bottle (Figure 15.3).

Lighting in the photograph emphasizes the model's skin, especially its golden, luminous quality. Her skin is a shade that could be described as maple or honey, a color that is clearly located in the continuum between black and white.

An image of an Afro-Asian woman evokes a different kind of biracial subject, one whose existence was not the object of antimiscegenation law in the United States. As Phillip Brian Harper has observed, "The centrality of the white subject's interest in the phenomenon of miscegenation is indicated by the dictionary definition of the term, which characterizes it as denoting especially 'marriage between white and non-white persons'"[13] (p. 31). Instead, the model's "hapa" features conjure histories of American imperialism and military occupations in Asia as well as relationships between Asian women and black American soldiers.[14] The photograph is composed to expose the model to the viewer; the hollow in her throat and her graceful, yet fragile neck signal vulnerability.[15] If there was any doubt as to her sexual availability, the woman's alleged contact information appears in the lower third of the image. The phrase "e-mail: kristy@cKone.com" updates the proverbial scrawl in the bathroom stall for the Internet age (i.e., "For a good time call . . . ").[16] That "Kristy" strongly resembles a grown-up version of the little girl in the Baby Gap ad should come as no surprise. Although rainbow babies are celebrated as signs of racial harmony, the taboo of interracial sexuality lurking in their genetic make-up becomes full-blown in erotic images of mixed-race women.

At the same time, some advertisements represent alternative possibilities for the Baby Gap girl child's future. In the winter of 1998–1999, an ad campaign by Levi's capitalized on discourses of multiculturalism by making racial ambiguity representative of a different type of fantasy. Rather than offering the consumer the illusion of unfettered sexual access to a mixed-race woman, this campaign positioned her as the embodiment of post-civil rights era idealism, making consumption of her image a surrogate for antiracist activism. The campaign featured teenagers from a variety of ethnic backgrounds holding placards inscribed with phrases. One image depicted a young black man with dreadlocks holding a sign proclaiming, "Conformity Breeds Mediocrity." Another showed a Latino with a placard that declared, "Latinos Presente." In a third ad, two teenagers, one male and one female, both of indeterminate ancestry, held a sign saying "We Are One." The image that immediately drew my attention was of a young woman holding a sign inscribed with the words, "I can't be Prejudice [sic], I'm Mulatto [sic]" (Figure 15.4). The motto of the campaign—the phrase "What's True"—was visible on the lower right side of each advertisement.

The first time I saw these Levi's ads (in San Francisco in December 1998), only the "mulatto" images had been mounted. Multiple larger-than-life sized posters of the teenage girl were plastered over wooden partitions that were being used to delineate the construction site around a building in the Mission District (a working class Latino neighborhood undergoing intense gentrification). The young woman's hair made me nostalgic for my own teen years, when I wore an Afro "as big as a rain cloud."[17] Only later did I realize that the ad was one of a series. By the time I attempted to track them down to make photographs approximately 2 months later, they had all but disappeared. Although I eventually found all four images in an alley in

Figure 15.3 Calvin Klein, *Vibe* Magazine, August 1999

downtown San Francisco, they had been tagged with the word *uno*, which obscured the phrases on the signs held by each model.[18]

My own initial surprise at seeing the word *mulatto* used in an ad is typical of the lack of consensus about terms that mark identity. I joke with my friends that mulatto, unlike words such as *black, nigger, queer, faggot,* or even *girl,* has not been rehabilitated. By the same token, I have encountered young

Figure 15.4   Levi-Strauss Billboard Photographed in downtown San Francisco by Caroline A.
Streeter, February 1999

people of mixed black/white descent who
embrace mulatto, feeling that it describes
their heritage in a succinct and accurate way.
I e-mailed the office of consumer services at
Levi's to ask how they made decisions
regarding the language used in the billboards.
They responded:

In the "What's True" campaign we gave a
forum to all different types of people. The
campaign represents diversity in thoughts,
ideas and style, which is what the Levi's®
brand is all about. We didn't use models or
actors and the spots are unscripted, unedited,
and spontaneous. They were created with

teens off the street—not in a studio—speaking candidly about what "true" means to them.

The assertion that an advertising campaign is "unscripted, unedited and spontaneous" is misleading to say the least. In fact, Levi's response to my query could be interpreted to mean that the models are not even wearing the company's clothing. Moreover, the girl in the mulatto ad looks very groomed; she wears makeup and has manicured nails, and her hair appears styled to embody a particular aesthetic that is associated with rainbow babies, brushed out to emphasize its volume and texture.

What of Levi's claim that the ads feature teenagers "off the street . . . speaking candidly?" Although the mixed-race girl in the Levi's image may indeed describe herself as mulatto, I doubt that Levi's had no influence in the conception of the phrase that she allegedly "created" herself. By composing the ad in this way, Levi's states that "the truth" is that racially mixed people "can't be prejudice," a statement that makes the mixed-race subject the embodiment of liberation from racial discrimination. The idea that the mixed-race child represents the elimination of prejudice is part of a utopian dream adopted by many political activists during the civil rights movement. When young people from all over the United States went south to work in voter registration drives (especially during the summer of 1964), blacks and whites worked and socialized together, and became lovers (Evans, 1979). This was the nightmare that the segregationists had warned about. Such activity also contributed to the seductive mythology that if people could transcend racial barriers in their private lives, the elimination of society's racism would follow. In this sense, Levi's "What's True" image of a mixed-race teenage girl is the alternative grown-up depiction of the Afro-Asian child in the Baby Gap ad. Rather than exploiting the lure of sexual availability, the image promises liberation from social injustice.

Yet the Levi's notion of mulattoes relies on celebratory and ahistorical rhetoric that elides the vexed strategies that racially mixed subjects have deployed to negotiate hierarchies of race and color.[19] This kind of multicultural imagery makes racially mixed people symbolic embodiments of antidiscrimination while using their images to mask persistent race-based inequalities.[20] The Levi's discourse also, oddly enough, solidly reinforces the authority of the "one-drop rule." This occurs through the spelling "error" in the sentence "I can't be prejudice, I'm mulatto." The phrase evokes Ebonics, or Black English, thus inscribing blackness as effectively as the girl's Afro.[21]

The muddled messages in the advertisement also point to the contradictory expectations that Americans harbor for miscegenation. Although the outcome, mixed-race people, are expected to free the society of prejudice, they are as subject to being defined in racialized terms as anyone. Because we are confused about what racism is—Is it the articulation of taboo words? The dissemination of negative images?—it is difficult to gauge when racial language or imagery is problematic.

RAINBOW BABY

In the transition to thinking about "real girls," I begin with an analysis of the media's discourse about the well-known celebrity Mariah Carey. Carey is a unique example because her image transformed quite literally from white to black before our very eyes, a process exhaustively documented in the mainstream and African-American media over the past decade.[22] When her first album was released (1990), Carey's record company marketed her as a pop singer with no clearly defined ethnic identity. Like the biracial actress Jennifer Beals, Carey's ambiguous features enabled her to remain racially unclassified, (synonymous with being white in

America). As Carey's fame grew, journalists delving into her background soon "discovered" that she is biracial, with a European-American mother and a father of African-American and Venezuelan heritage.[23] Much was made of Carey's "passing," particularly by black journalists, and articles about her began to routinely comment on her mixed heritage as well as her attempts to articulate a biracial subjectivity.[24] Once she had been "outed"[25] Carey's music videos began to shift from rainbow imagery (with children of diverse races[26]) to representations that prominently featured black men. She also began collaborating with male and female rap and hip-hop artists on her albums. Carey's divorce from the white record executive Tommy Mottola (almost two decades her senior) after a 5-year marriage seems to have accelerated her emergence as a black female celebrity. Since her divorce in 1998, she has made appearances at venues such as the NAACP Image Awards, pursued high-profile collaborations with African American artists, and been linked romantically to a number of black male celebrities.[27] In addition, her image on magazine covers and in music videos became significantly more sexual. Magazines in particular repeatedly alluded to her single status and sexual desirability.[28] Like the cKone ads using mixed-race models, references to Carey's biracial heritage functioned to increase her sexual allure.[29]

Mariah Carey's racialized sexuality is the potent and unstable flash point that renders her image perpetually troubling. The conflation of Carey's racial heritage and her sexuality became pop cultural fodder in arenas such as the performer Sandra Bernhard's one-woman show, *I'm Still Here . . . Damn It!* (which I saw live in San Francisco in 1999).[30] Bernhard's comments on Carey demonstrate how race can be sexualized and sexuality raced. In a voice dripping with sarcasm, Bernhard related, "Mariah's been getting a little niggerish on us . . . she been seeing those rap stars and saying oh yeah baby do it, do it . . . give me some of that big black dick!" In Bernhard's discourse, Carey assumes a position analogous to how white women are often depicted in advertising that features black male/white female interracial couples: eroticized as the light-skinned vessel for a "big black dick."[31] Bernhard's humor simultaneously frames Carey as a white-looking woman and a mulatta subject, exploiting her racial ambiguity to fuel stereotypical images of white women and black men in interracial relationships as well as insatiable mulatta sexuality. Carey herself offered astute commentary on Bernhard's monologue:

> Sandra Bernhard used words that every African American I know—and definitely I, personally, find inappropriate. If my skin were two shades darker, she wouldn't have done it. . . . (C)alling me a "phony white bitch" and saying I was "acting niggerish" is acceptable because she figures, "Who's gonna stick up for her?" I think she perceives me as white, which is a common perception. And yeah, I'm a freaking mutt, I'm a triracial freak, but she implied I was a white person trying to be black. And it's offensive to me, because I've been a victim of racism on both sides. (Herman, 1999, p. 128)

Carey's statement about skin color is especially insightful, pointing to the ways in which her "white-looking" features are read as defusing Bernhard's racial slurs. Her comments imply an awareness that her body is "marked by a border condition, a position at the rim . . . neither fully inside nor fully outside" (Burgin, 1996, p. 257). Although the exploitation of Carey's image as a mixed-race woman gives us valuable information about trends in popular culture, her unique status as a pop star make it difficult to consider her "representative" of mixed-race women in everyday life. In the next section, I turn to "real girls" with less rarefied personal circumstances, from two

University of California campuses, who have explored biracial identity in autobiographical writing and documentary video.

MIXED-RACE WOMEN'S INDEPENDENT WRITING AND VIDEO

In the 1990s, the topic of multiracial identity entered the public sphere through the publication of academic texts as well as general interest literature, especially autobiography and family histories.[32] Multiracial concerns began to be addressed in national discourses of American identity, most notably in debates that preceded the dramatic shift that enabled people for the first time in the year 2000 to check more than one racial category on U.S. Census forms. As well, social organizations for multiracial individuals have proliferated on college campuses throughout the nation. Students have produced literary anthologies, films, and videos that document multiracial identity from a variety of ethnic perspectives.[33]

Young mixed-race women offer creative explorations of multiracial female identity that reach far beyond the limited parameters delineated by the media's fantasies of post-civil rights era rainbow babies. *Voices* (by the group Students of Mixed Heritage, University of California, Berkeley, 1992) and *Out of Many. One.* (Students of Mixed Heritage, University of California, Santa Cruz, 1995) are collections of autobiographical narrative, poetry, and creative writing. In both works, women make up the majority of contributors. To some observers, the proliferation of social groups for people of mixed heritage on college campuses is an indication that identifying as mixed occurs in contexts of relative privilege and material comfort, encouraging some to label the "mixed-race movement" a "middle-class phenomenon."[34] It may be that class privilege affords the opportunity to explore mixed racial

heritage. However, as expressed by the writers in *Voices* and *Out of Many. One.*, the desire for the freedom to express multiracial identity does not necessarily translate into a wish to stake out "new" racial territory. Compared with much of the academic writing by scholars of multiraciality, writing and video work by racially mixed women are far less invested in "the right to choose identity."[35] In the collectively written introduction to *Voices*, the editors of No Press Collective (1992) declare:

> We do not advocate the creation of a new racial category for people of mixed descent. If mixed people realize that "race" is a fiction, and that the constructions of racial boundaries are an illusion. . . . then the possibility of creating yet another race-based category, however fluid, is self-defeating. (p. xxvi)

It is interesting to note that although identifying as mixed is important, the creation of a census category is not a strategic move that interests the writers. A political commitment to people of color, opposition to racism, and concern about cultural erasure are all strong elements of writing and video by racially mixed people. For many of them, identification with their nonwhite heritage grounds their identities. Because they are not invested in a specific label that would identify them as a group, these racially mixed people do not act as gatekeepers to the category "mixed race."

The political perspectives in both anthologies reflect an integration of the critiques of racism, class discrimination, gender oppression, and homophobia that have been elaborated by feminists of color (see especially Anzaldúa & Moraga, 1981; Smith, 1983). Like the anthologies by women of color that seem to be the models for both *Voices* and *Out of Many. One.*, the editorial groups for the mixed-race publications emphasized the extent to which the groups functioned as community for the individual writers. The shifting, contingent, and constructed nature of these individuals' mixed-race identities, then, is mirrored in the contingent and constructed nature of their mixed-race communities. The work in anthologies by people of mixed descent reflects a critique of fragmentation that is accompanied by a simultaneous recognition of how fragmentation overdetermines social experience. The editors of *Out of Many. One.* write, "The very words 'Mixed Heritage' call to mind parts of a whole, but 'Fractions are for math, not for people.' . . . Our title (is) expressive of the struggle we have undertaken to claim our identities in their entirety" (Students of Mixed Heritage Collective, 1995, p. iv). This assertion takes a cue from feminist of color theory. Like women of color, racially mixed people want to be able to bring their whole selves to their art and their activism.

Writing by mixed-race women, as compared with writing in women of color anthologies, expresses a uniquely rigorous questioning of racial categories. In an excerpt from her poem "Collage," Tamu C. Green writes,

> A little brown girl stopped me
> at the rec. today.
> "What is you?" she asked.
> Her big sister, hovering a foot taller,
> looked interested, too.
> Wasn't it obvious?
> "White on the outside & Black on the
> inside,"
> I shrugged & said without thinking.
> But now I've got that look on my face.
> Now I'm thinking.
> Hard.
> After all, Dad said you can't be
> half Christian & half Jewish.
> Does that mean you can't be
> half Black & half White too?

> (Students of Mixed Heritage
> Collective, 1995, p. 55)

One radical potential that grows from the mixed-race movement is the possibility that

racial ambiguity will take root within "monoracial" white communities rather than being perpetually projected onto communities of color. People of mixed-race prompt the interrogation of the boundaries that define whiteness because they may be "people of color" in a white skin. Although theory has begun addressing whiteness as a political construct, it has had less to say about whiteness as lived experience, especially one that "people of color" may know. In an excerpt from her poem "Untitled II," the Chicana/white Jill Flores writes,

> Pasty blue face
> fools them into thinking
> I'm frozen harmless
> as blood swims and darts
> below my skin,
> waiting.
> Underneath,
> I am glowing
> stored energy.
> To peel away
> my disguise would
> blind them dead.

> (No Press Collective, 1992, p. 139)

Thinking about identity for biracial women of Chicana descent gives us an opportunity to investigate a different resonance for the term mulatta. In this context, the term no longer functions as the hinge that simultaneously links and separates the racial categories black and white but, rather, refers to a mestiza identity that can be traced to the indigenous, European, and African heritage of Mexico, the Caribbean, and other Latin American countries. Since the "Latin Explosion," which occurred primarily in popular music of the 1990s, we have witnessed a fascinating case of the U.S. mainstream media heralding members of a diasporic culture that is multiracial, multiethnic, and multinational and that has a long history of mulatta celebrities. Tellingly, any traces of African or Indigenous heritage among Latina celebrities tend to be erased. As I have mentioned, this erasure has its counterpart in Mexican culture, which also privileges images of feminine beauty that are blonde and anglicized. Likewise in the American popular media, images of women of color entertainers often move inexorably away from ethnic models of beauty as they become more famous. This has been a disturbing aspect of the career of the Puerto-Rican American Jennifer Lopez, arguably the most prominent female of the Latin Explosion. In just 2 years, Lopez morphed from a dark-haired ethnic beauty wearing deep-toned cosmetics, her photo appearing under the heading "Butter Pecan Rican" (in the pages of *Vibe* magazine, June 1997) to a blonde-streaked "Diva Loca" (on the cover of *Vibe*, August 1999), sporting make-up in pastel shades.

In contrast to the way that light skin and European features are valued in some Latina celebrities, Chicana-identified women of mixed descent in California report the resistance they experience to being included in the ethnic community because they are light skinned. The equation of color with racial authenticity is a strong theme expressed in Manijeh Fata's video *Soy Chicana Y Mas!/Soy Chicano Y Mas!* (1997), a work that focused on biracial students living in the Chicano ethnic theme house on University of California, Berkeley's campus (Fata, 1997). All of the light-skinned biracial Chicanas in Fata's work related the way in which their color impacts whether they will be accepted in the Chicano community at University of California, Berkeley. Although last name and knowledge of Spanish were other "ethnic badges" that influenced the acceptance of mixed-race Chicanas, several stated that skin color was the first characteristic used to judge acceptance and that other students often assumed that they were white and "passing"

in the Chicano community because of their appearance. Interestingly, the Chicanas in Fata's video declare their biracial heritage. They seek to be accepted as Chicana and Irish, Chicana and Greek, or Chicana and Persian within their Chicano community. Unlike monoracially identified people of color who either do not know about or do not acknowledge multiracial background, many mixed-race people seek to be included in their multiplicity. They refuse to repress their background in order to fit in. This identification can be a source of consternation to others. Brooke, one of the biracial women in *Soy Chicana/o Y Mas!* related an anecdote about a man who questioned her about her ethnic background and her hairstyle. The man said to her, "You're mixed right?" to which Brooke confirmed, "Yeah." He continued, "But you're not black?" and she replied, "I'm Mexican and Irish." The man said, "But you've got braids!" To which Brooke laughed, "You don't gotta be black to have braids!" In this story, we see that contemporary people of mixed-race are testing different types of racial boundaries, and they are not limited to the races/ethnicities in their "biological" heritage.

The phenomenon of not being recognized as part of an ethnic group or of being identified as part of an ethnic group with whom one does not share a heritage is a common experience for many racially mixed people. In fact, the increased social awareness of mixed race has given rise to occasions when a mixed person is identified as the "wrong" mix. For example, Jennifer Jackson (1997), a woman of black/white biracial heritage, relates in an untitled independent video her experience of frequently being mistaken for hapa, the colloquial name that has been adopted by many biracial people of Asian, especially Japanese American, descent.

This limited sample of autobiographical writing and documentary video by mixed-race women is expressive of a variety of tensions with regard to how they will locate themselves vis-à-vis the category "women of color." They identify as women of color, albeit with differences. It may be that remaining racially unidentified, or unclassified, was not politically expedient in the 1990s and may well not be in the new millennium. The refusal to identify at all racially, or the impulse to identify as racially hybrid, may be too easily co-opted in a society that fetishizes racial difference even as it manufactures a rhetoric of racial equality in a multicultural, postaffirmative action moment.

CONCLUSION

This chapter has explored the dilemma of visibility for mixed-race women by proposing that the increased representation of people of mixed descent in media images should be viewed with caution rather than celebrated uncritically. I have argued that attempts to fix the terms that describe racial mixture and to identify mixed-race women visually betray failures of language and questionable participation in troubling discourses of race. In my analysis of the "virtual girls" on the cover of *Time* magazine and in selected advertisements by The Gap, Calvin Klein, and Levi's, I investigated the media's romance with the notion of the rainbow baby and the imagined racial harmony that will characterize a multicultural society. Yet when we look closely, it is clear that a deep ambivalence about miscegenation undergirds these images, whether they are designed to seduce the viewer with a mixed-race woman's sexual availability or to convince us that buying jeans somehow constitutes antiracist activity.

The example of Mariah Carey's celebrity career is a unique phenomenon because her image became transformed when her mixed heritage was revealed. Although Carey's African American parentage became emphasized as a result of the power of the one-drop rule, we also observed the ways in which Carey's mixed status and physical appearance make her vulnerable to particular sexualized racial stereotypes.

Although I have in this chapter emphasized an interrogation of the desire to fix terms that describe racial identity and advocated a rigorous examination of media images of mixed-race women, I also acknowledge the valid impulse on the part of individuals and groups both to seek their own images in popular cultural representations and to use the language they feel best accounts for their identities. As an example of those attempts to negotiate representation in language and in visual images, the chapter investigates autobiographical poetry and documentary video by mixed-race women. These independent efforts demonstrate that mixed-race women model their creative efforts on writing by feminists of color, who express a strong critique of inequality and discrimination of all kinds and who emphasize the importance of community. Although mixed-race women question the logic of racial categories, many nevertheless tend to align themselves with people of color, while remaining mindful of how mixed heritage makes their own personal experience unique.

In a world that is overwhelmed with media images, it is tempting to simply be entertained by them, to equate their ephemeral nature with relative harmlessness. As Lauren Berlant has noted, "These materials frequently use the silliest, most banal and erratic logic imaginable to describe important things, like what constitutes intimate relations, political personhood, and national life" (Berlant, 1997, p. 12). However, as she also suggests, "developing . . . a mode of criticism and conceptualization that reads the waste materials of everyday communication in the national public sphere as pivotal documents in the construction, experience and rhetoric of quotidian citizenship in the U.S." constitutes a kind of "counterpolitics of the silly object" (p. 12). This chapter advocates studying media images of mixed-race women and the discourses that they generate with both humor and skepticism. Because of the ubiquity of these images, it is also important to seek out alternatives. Unfortunately, other options are not always easy to locate. The anthologies and videos that I discuss were distributed in very limited contexts and are not widely available. Still, the relative accessibility of writing, and to an increasing extent video technology, means that alternative narratives and images are, quite literally, being produced all the time. Although these alternatives may be as fleeting as media images, it is heartening to know that mixed-race women contribute to the stream of narrative and visual representations that reflects and shapes our popular culture.

NOTES

1. We can be certain of racial heritage only when autobiographical information accompanies a photograph, or the person's parentage is known because of celebrity status (e.g., Mariah Carey). My use of quotation marks around terms that denote racial heritage points to the problematic status of the concept of "race." Although I do not use quotation marks throughout the chapter whenever racial terms are used, the problematic status of "race" as an idea is consistently implied.

2. My use of "mixed race" includes those who are "immediately mixed," with parents of different races, as well as those who are mixed because ancestors in earlier generations of their families were of different races. This use of the term, in that it relies on "biology" or heredity, does not take into account all of the reasons why people might identify as mixed race, including ethnic and cultural identifications.

3. Several theorists have made astute analyses of this image, including Berlant (1997), Burgin (1996), Haraway (1997), and Smith (1999).

4. Such a model prompts some to wonder, "melting pot or incinerator?"— a repeated refrain in British filmmaker Ngozi Onwurah's *Coffee-Coloured Children* (1988). Onwurah's short film, which incorporates autobiographical elements, investigates the racism experienced by children of mixed descent in 1970s London.

5. Rainbow imagery can also signify racial diversity and multiculturalism in ads that use models from a variety of ethnic backgrounds with a range of skin colors.

6. Historical attempts by individuals and groups to negotiate the system of racial classification to avoid discrimination have, in many cases, involved the disavowal of black heritage. An example is the case of triracial isolate groups. See Daniel (1992).

7. Senna's comments about the ways that a culturally specific item of clothing can determine racialization is consistent with those of theorists Floya Anthias and Nira Yuval-Davis (1992), who argue against the monolithic definition of racism as skin color prejudice.

8. For example, in Mexican soap operas—"télénovélas"—the leading actresses are invariably blonde haired and blue eyed. The video artist Ximena Cuevas has created a funny and scathing comment on Mexican femininity and the cultural obsession with becoming blonde in her video, "Natural Instincts" (part of the 1998 30-minute compilation *Dormimundo Vol. 1 Incomodidad*).

9.   See, for example, Victor Burgin (1996): "Although only fifteen percent Anglo-Saxon, the woman nevertheless has the appearance of a White woman recently returned from a holiday on the Mediterranean" (p. 259). As I have written elsewhere, the reception of actresses of different racial backgrounds who portray black, white, and mixed-race heroines in film and television indicate that there is some type of "common sense" about what blackness, whiteness and "mixed-ness" look like, especially among African Americans. At the same time, it is increasingly clear that there is little stable consensus about the racial meaning of physical features (see Streeter, 2000).

10.   Can it be an accident that the new face of America is captioned with a citation of D. W. Griffith's racist nationality? (An answer: Sure, racist citation can be unconscious or unintentional; that is what makes the simple pun and other cruel and popular forms of dominant cultural privilege so hard to contest) (Lauren Berlant, 1997).

11.   "The bodies are still and naked. . . . available for erotic fantasy and consumption" (Berlant, 1997, p. 202).

12.   See my analysis of interracial imagery in advertising, "The Post 1960s 'Biracial Baby' in Contemporary Media" (Streeter, 2000).

13.   Harper (1999) cites *The American Heritage Dictionary of the English Language*.

14.   The term *hapa* originated in Hawaii to describe people of mixed ancestry (*hapa haole* or "half white"). The word has since been appropriated by people of mixed Asian descent (especially Japanese American and European American) in the United States. See King and DaCosta (1996). The woman's appearance also recalls the diverse and little-known Afro-Asian history of the United States. There are, for example, communities in the southern United States that descend from Asian male immigrants who intermarried with native African American women (Loewen, 1971). There are also communities made up of the families of African American GIs and their Asian wives (see Houston, 1991).

15.   The cKone ad simultaneously brings to mind racially mixed women in Asia as well as America's "native" "rainbow babies." Because the American military presence in many Asian countries dates from the turn of the century and continues to this day, some communities have successive generations of mixed-race Asian people in their populations. See Spickard (1989).

16.   Although I established e-mail contact with Kristy, she did not answer any of my questions about her racial heritage or ethnic identity.

17.   I take this description from a remark made in Sandler's video, *A Question of Color* (1992). For an excellent essay analyzing, among other things, contemporary popular culture's engagement with a range of symbolic meanings that are associated with the Afro hairstyle, see Davis (1994).

18.   Although I do not pursue a detailed analysis of the graffiti here, it is certainly significant that the billboard images were tagged with the Spanish word meaning "one" to obscure the placards held by the models rather than the corporate logo or the teenagers' faces. In fact, the posters had been plastered over a wall that already bore white spray-painted graffiti (like the "uno" tag), possibly indicating that the taggers returned to re-mark their turf. I can only point here to the potential for analyses of such negotiations of urban space between corporate institutions and local interests.

19.   To anyone acquainted with African-American literature, the phrase, "I Can't Be Prejudice, I'm Mulatto" will sound simplistic. Novels of the 19th and early 20th centuries in particular depict the mulatto's struggle with identity and social position as exacerbated by the way that the racial hierarchy encourages people of mixed descent to disavow blackness. Examples include William Wells Brown's *Clotel, or The President's Daughter* (1853/1969) and Frances Ellen

Watkins Harper's *Iola Leroy* (1895/1987). Early 20th-century and Harlem Renaissance novels that deal with the theme of the temptation of racial passing experienced on the part of the light-skinned African American and the spiritual impoverishment of the individual who succumbs to that temptation include James Weldon Johnson's *Autobiography of an Ex-Coloured Man* (1912/1960) and Nella Larsen's *Passing* (1929/1986.)

20. The political climate of the 1990s is characterized by significant backlash against policies of the 1960s and 1970s designed to redress institutionalized racial discrimination. Ironically, although California is in the vanguard of the ethnic diversity and demographic change that is predicted for the rest of the country, it leads the nation in the elimination of affirmative action policies and the attempt to implement measures that would limit immigrants' access to state services. See Lydia Chávez (1998).

21. In the context of the ad, the word "prejudice" is being used in an unusual way, as a noun that refers to a person. In standard English the phrase would use the adjective form of the word, as in, "I can't be prejudiced, I'm mulatto."

22. I first began to think about Mariah Carey as a morphing mulatta after hearing a paper by my colleague Dr. Laura Harris, whose description of Carey's transformation I paraphrase above. In her paper, Harris (1997) linked Carey to characterizations of the mulatta in Harlem Renaissance literature.

23. Despite Carey's Venezuelan heritage, she has not until recent years been considered Latina by the mainstream or ethnic press. Carey's career has not been represented in the media as constituting part of the "Latin Explosion" that in the late 1990s, jump-started the careers of singers Ricky Martin and Marc Anthony and actress/singer Jennifer Lopez. Such tacit reliance on the one-drop rule is an example of the paradox of mixed heritage for African Americans, as it is simultaneously acknowledged and repressed. The public perception of Carey's identity also indicates the importance of individual experience (Carey recognizes her Venezuelan heritage but does not express a Latina cultural identity) and the extent to which ethnic media respect each other's turf.

24. "In person, Carey came across, quite clearly, as a rainbow baby of African descent, skin toasted almond and hair light brown" (Jones, 1994).

25. *Outing* is a term that originated in the gay and lesbian movement. It refers to a closeted person's homosexuality being made public knowledge.

26. An example is the video for the song *Emotion* (1991).

27. Carey appeared at the NAACP Image Awards (which recognize achievement in the arts and entertainment) in 1999 to perform with the African American pop sensation Whitney Houston. Their duet, "When You Believe," was the theme song from Disney's movie *Aladdin*.

28. Carey was photographed in profile and topless with her blonde hair concealing her breasts on the February 1998 cover of *Rolling Stone*. *Vibe* magazine depicted her in a silver lamé bikini (November 1998). On the cover of a number of publications aimed at women, Carey kept her clothes on, although the magazine cover discourses did not change. She posed for the April 1999 issue of *Jane*, which was devoted to celebrities and sex. *Mirabella* recycled *Rolling Stone's* headline ("Sex and the Single Diva—How Mariah Carries On") in May 1999. Only *Glamour* has offered a more subtle cover: "Mariah's New . . . Music, Movie, Man," November 1999).

29. Carey (or at least her record company) seems willing to exploit her multiracial heritage and her sexual attractiveness to sell albums. The cover of a recent release, *Rainbow* (1999), features Carey's nubile body scantily clad in white briefs and tank top emblazoned with—what else?—a rainbow.

30. Bernhard, a Jewish-American woman, is known for performances that involve racial mimicry and masquerade. I have paraphrased quotes from her monologue based on notes taken when I saw the show.

31.   As mentioned earlier, I discuss just such depictions of interracial couples in advertising in "The Post 1960s 'Biracial Baby' in Contemporary Media" (Streeter, 2000).

32.   Examples of autobiographical literature include: Shirlee Taylor Haizlip's *The Sweeter the Juice: A Family Memoir in Black and White* (1994), Marcia Hunt's *Repossessing Ernestine: A Granddaughter Uncovers the Secret History of Her American Family* (1996), James McBride's *The Color of Water: A Black Man's Tribute to his White Mother* (1996), Scott Minerbrook's *Divided to the Vein: A Journey into Race and Family* (1996), Barack Obama's *Dreams from my Father: A Story of Race and Inheritance* (1995), Adrian Piper's "Passing for White, Passing for Black" (1996), Judy Scales-Trent's *Notes of a White Black Woman: Race, Color, Community* (1995), Gregory Howard Williams's *Life on the Color Line: The True Story of a White Boy Who Discovered He Was Black* (1995), and Rebecca Walker's *Black, White, and Jewish: Autobiography of a Shifting Self* (2001). Even as I completed the final draft of this chapter, a new text by Neil Henry appeared entitled *Pearl's Secret: A Black Man's Search for His White Family* (2001).

33.   Organizations include Kaleidoscope (University of California, Berkeley), Students of Mixed Descent (University of California, Santa Cruz), Hapa Issues Forum (University of California, Berkeley), Prism (Harvard University) and Mixed Initiative (Mills College, CA). See Namkung (2000). Publications include *Voices of Identity, Rage and Deliverance* (No Collective Press, 1992) and *Out of Many. One.* (Students of Mixed Heritage Collective, 1995). Films and videos include *Just Black? Multiracial Identity* (Twine, Warren, & Ferrandiz, 1991), *Soy Chicana Y Mas! Soy Chicano Y Mas!* (Fata, 1997), and *Children of Mixed-race: Who You Wanna Be* (Lightholder, 1997).

34.   The "mixed-race movement" refers to a variety of different activities, including changes to the U.S. Census and the myriad social clubs and creative groups that have sprung up around the country, although they tend to be concentrated on the West Coast, in urban centers, and on college campuses. In addition, the term *movement* can include the growth of curricula in academic settings that address the topic of people of mixed racial descent as well as the research that is being done in this area. The class dynamics that characterize the mixed-race movement, as well as the fact that the activities of the movement have been primarily based on gaining recognition for mixed-race identity, influences the critique that this movement has limited political potential.

35.   The idea that mixed-race people should exercise the right to choose an identity is a strongly American notion, linked to powerful ideologies of liberal humanism and the primacy of the individual. Maria P. P. Root's "Bill of Rights for Racially Mixed People" draws precisely upon these ideological references.

REFERENCES

Anthias, F., & Yuval-Davis, N. (with Cain, H.). (1992). *Racialized boundaries: Race, nation gender, colour and class and the anti-racist struggle.* London: Routledge.

Anzaldúa, G., & Moraga, C. (1981). *This bridge called my back: Writings by radical women of color.* Watertown, MA: Persephone Press.

Bailey, D. A. (1989). Product branding in the world. In P. Wombell (Ed.), *The globe: Representing the world* (p. 65). York, UK: Impressions Gallery.

Berlant, L. (1997). *The queen of American goes to Washington City: Essays on sex and citizenship.* Durham, NC: Duke University Press.

Brown, W. W. (1969). *Clotel, or the president's daughter*. New York: Arno Press. (Original work published 1853)

Burgin, V. (1996). *In/different spaces: Place and memory in visual culture*. Berkeley: University of California Press.

Chávez, L. (1998). *The color bind: California's battle to end affirmative action*. Berkeley: University of California Press.

Cuevas, X. (Director). (1998). *"Natural instincts" Dormimundo Vol. 1 Incomodidad* [Video]. Mexico City, Mexico: Producer not known.

Daniel, G. R. (1992). Passers and pluralists: Subverting the racial divide. In M. P. P. Root (Ed.), *Racially mixed people in America*. Newbury Park, CA: Sage.

Davis, A. (1994). Afro images: Politics, fashion and nostalgia. In D. Willis (Ed.), *Picturing us: African American identity in photography*. New York: New Press.

Evans, S. (1979). *Personal politics: The roots of women's liberation in the civil rights movement and the new left*. New York: Alfred A. Knopf.

Fata, M. A. (Director). (1997). *Soy Chicana Y Mas! Soy Chicano Y Mas!* [Video]. Berkeley, CA: Author.

Gooding-Williams, R. (1993). *Reading Rodney King, reading urban uprising*. New York: Routledge.

Graham, S. R. (1996). The real world. In M. P. P. Root (Ed.), *The multiracial experience: Racial borders as the new frontier*. Thousand Oaks, CA: Sage.

Haizlip, S. T. (1994). *The sweeter the juice: A family memoir in black and white*. New York: Simon & Schuster.

Haraway, D. (1997). *Modest witness @ second millenium. Femaleman meets oncomouse: Feminism and technoscience*. New York: Routledge.

Harper, F. E. W. (1987). *Iola Leroy*. Boston: Beacon Press. (Original work published 1895)

Harper, P. B. (1999). *Private affairs: Critical ventures in the culture of social relations*. New York: New York University Press.

Harris, L. (1997, November 21). *Villainous monstrous mulattas: Color, class and corrupt agency*. Paper presented at "Narratives of Resistance," Universidad de Castilla-La Mancha, Spain.

Henry, N. (2001). *Pearl's secret: A black man's search for his white family*. Berkeley: University of California Press.

Herman, J. P. (1999, May). There's something about Mariah. *Mirabella*, pp. 93-98.

Hirschberg, L. (1999, September 5). Desperate to seem 16: Hollywood's obsession with youth. *New York Times Magazine*, p. 42.

Houston, V. H. (1991). The past meets the future: A cultural essay. *Amerasia Journal, 17*(1), 53-56.

Hunt, M. (1996). *Repossessing Ernestine: A granddaughter uncovers the secret history of her American family*. New York: HarperCollins.

Jackson, J. (Director). (1997). Untitled. [Video]. Berkeley, CA: Author.

Johnson, J. W. (1960). *The autobiography of an ex-coloured man*. New York: Hill & Wang. (Original work published 1912)

Jones, L. (1994). *Bulletproof diva: Tales of race, sex and hair*. New York: Doubleday.

King, R. C., & DaCosta, K. M. (1996). Changing face, changing race: The remaking of race in the Japanese American and African American communities. In M. P. P. Root (Ed.), *The multiracial experience: Racial borders as the new frontier*. Thousand Oaks, CA: Sage.

Larsen, N. (1986). *Quicksand and passing* (D. E. McDowell, Ed.). New Brunswick, NJ: Rutgers University Press. (Original work published 1928)

Lightholder, S. (Director). (1997). *Children of mixed race: Who you wanna be* [Ethnic Studies 150 Video]. Berkeley, CA: Author.

Loewen, J. W. (1971). *The Mississippi Chinese: Between black and white.* Cambridge, MA: Harvard University Press.

McBride, J. (1996). *The color of water: A black man's tribute to his white mother.* New York: Riverhead Books.

Minerbrook, S. (1996). *Divided to the vein: A journey into race and family.* New York: Harcourt Brace.

Namkung, V. (2000). Exposure. *Mavin: The Mixed-Race Experience, 4,* 38-42.

New face of America. (1993, Fall). *Time* Magazine [Special issue].

No Press Collective. (1992). *Voices of identity, rage and deliverance* (UC Berkeley Students of Mixed Heritage). Berkeley, CA: Author.

Obama, B. (1995). *Dreams from my father: A story of race and inheritance.* New York: Random House.

Onwurah, N. (Director). (1988*). Coffee-coloured children.* New York: Woman Make Movies.

Piper, A. (1996). Passing for white, passing for black. In A. Piper (Ed.), *Out of order, out of sight: Volume I: Selected writings in meta-art 1968–1992.* Cambridge: MIT Press.

Root, M. P. P. (1996). A bill of rights for racially mixed people. In M. P. P. Root (Ed.), *The multiracial experience: Racial borders as the new frontier.* Thousand Oaks, CA: Sage.

Sandler, K. (Director/Producer). (1992). *A question of color* [Video]. San Francisco: California Newsreel.

Scales-Trent, J. (1995). *Notes of a white black woman: Race, color, community.* University Park: Pennsylvania State University Press.

Senna, D. (1998). The mulatto millennium. In C. C. O'Hearn (Ed.), *Half and half: Writers on growing up biracial and bicultural.* New York: Pantheon Books.

Smith, B. (Ed.). (1983). *Home girls: A black feminist anthology.* New York: Kitchen Table: Women of Color Press.

Smith, S. M. (1999). *American archives: Gender, race, and class in visual culture.* Princeton, NJ: Princeton University Press.

Spickard, P. R. (1989). *Mixed blood: Intermarriage and ethnic identity in twentieth century America.* Madison: University of Wisconsin Press.

Streeter, C. A. (2000). *Ambiguous bodies, ambivalent desires: The morphing mulatta body in U.S. culture, 1965–1999.* Doctoral dissertation, University of California, Berkeley.

Students of Mixed Heritage Collective. (1995). *Out of many. One.* University of California, Santa Cruz: Author.

Trinh, T. M.-Ha. (1999). *Cinema interval.* New York: Routledge.

Twine, F. W., Warren, J. W., & Ferrandiz, F. (Directors). (1991). *Just black? Multiracial identity.* New York: Filmmakers Library.

Walker, R. (2001). *Black, White, and Jewish: Autobiography of a shifting self.* New York: Riverhead Books.

Williams, G. H. (1995). *Life on the color line: The true story of a white boy who discovered he was black.* New York: Dutton.

CHAPTER 16

Masculine Multiracial Comedians

DARBY LI PO PRICE

University of California

This chapter examines constructions of masculinity, race, and multiraciality among male comedians who identify as more than one race. American comedy has historically been a popular site for expressing both masculinity and race. Masculine multiracial identities are both shaped by and mediate power relations involving meanings of masculinity, race, and mixed race. Multiracial comedians provide an alternative to dominant portrayals of mixed-race identity as a tragic situation. After providing an overview of dominant theories of masculinity, mixed race, and ethnic comedy, I examine how expressions of masculinity and mixedness among comedians exemplify, challenge, and provide alternatives to such models.

DOMINANT MODELS OF MASCULINITY AND MIXED RACE

The dominant hegemonic model of masculinity is that of the powerful man: nonfeminine, powerful, successful, independent, calm, and nonemotional. (Kimmel, 1994, p. 125). Theories of masculinity addressing race recognize white heterosexual masculinity as the standard by which other men are measured and usually fall short. In *Theorizing Masculinities,* Michael Kimmel (1994) frames the dominant model of masculinity within the context of power relations: "The hegemonic definition of manhood is a man *in* power, a man *with* power, and a man *of* power. We equate manhood with being strong, successful, capable, reliable, in control. The very definitions of manhood we have developed in our culture maintain the power that some men have over other men and that men have over women" (p. 135). Robert Connel (1995) in *Masculinities* characterizes four forms of masculinity in terms of power relations: hegemonic, complicit, subordinated, and marginalized.

In American history various groups have been configured as the less than "real men" by which white American masculinity has been contrasted. During frontier times, European Americans portrayed Native Americans as naive children of nature destined to perish under the advancement of white civilization.

At the turn of the 19th century, white Americans cast European men as effete sissies. By the mid-19th century, African American men were seen as both childish and hypersexual and, therefore, dependent on their master's rule. By the end of the 19th century, new European immigrants, especially Irish and Italians, were portrayed as effeminate. By the mid-20th century, Asian and gay men were cast as effete.

The status of multiracial masculinities varies according to specific racial combinations and sociohistorical contexts. Springing from the context of U.S. hierarchical race relations based on slavery and other systems of racially based inequality, mixed-race identities have historically been viewed as marginal because of their ambiguous status outside of recognized groups. In the first half of the 20th century, the term *marginal man* was applied to people of multiple ancestries by prominent sociologists such as Robert Park (1928) and Everett Stonequist (1937) (cited in Spickard, 1989).

Susan Purdie writes in *Comedy: The Mastery of Discourse* (1992) that dominant groups have historically marginalized subordinate groups by denying that they have a sense of humor. In American popular culture, mixed-race, Native American, Asian, and female identities have historically been portrayed as humorless or lacking a full sense of humor. Peoples identified with multiple racial or ethnic groups have been viewed primarily as targets rather than creators of humor. Christi Davies (1990) writes in *Ethnic Humor Around the World: A Comparative Approach* that peoples who are of multiple ethnicities are viewed as outside of existing categories and, therefore, the most likely to become the butts of humor (p. 314).

The status of multiracial masculinity among comedians has varied according to time, place, racial relations, and admixtures. White/black identity has historically been the most stigmatized.

Denial of Mulatto Masculinity

The racial line between white and black arose from the institution of slavery based on race. Symbolizing racial transgression, the male mulatto figure was cast as a threat to white purity and womanhood in popular culture. Whereas the female tragic mulatta became an object of white male sexual desire and a staple figure in blackface minstrel shows, the male mulatto figure was feared to the degree it was absent from minstrelsy.[1] Until the second half of the 20th century, light-skinned mulattoes had to darken their faces to perform comedy, which was not required of darker comedians who did not appear to be mixed.

The "first great African American comedian," Bert Williams (1870–1920), was born in Jamaica and, as a light-skinned person of more European than African ancestry, did not think of himself as black until moving to the United States. Williams resented having to wear blackface to perform comedy, especially since his darker partner George Walker did not have to when they performed in the early 1890s as "The Two Real Coons" and became one of America's most renowned comedy teams. Although Williams was immensely popular from the 1890s until the 1920s, when he died, he hated being limited to the emasculated persona of the blackface minstrel characterized by black make-up, an exaggerated tuxedo, white gloves, and inept stage language and coon songs of the "shuffling nigger" that he had to learn and use (Rogin, 1996, p. 43). Williams was able to neither perform as himself nor express his own opinions on stage. Bert Williams could be considered a tragic figure.

Rules of hypodescent encouraged multiracial African American comedians to identify solely as black throughout the 20th century. Richard Pryor, born of a black father and a Creole mother, initially thought of himself as orange rather than black. However, a white teacher told him firmly he was a "Negro."

Pryor responded, "But I'm orange, do I have to be a Negro?" (Haskins, 1984, p. 10). Pryor asserted his mixed ancestry in early stand-up comedy routines (Pryor, 1995, p. 74), but in accordance with dominant racial expectations he became known and identified himself primarily as black. Pryor represented a vulgar, aggressive, and hypersexual underclass style of black masculinity, embodying what Don Bogle (1996) refers to in *Toms, Coons, Mulattoes, Mammies, & Bucks* as the "foul-mouthed, iconoclastic wild man, the Crazy Nigger" (p. 259).

Although dominant racial politics historically discouraged mulatto comedy figures, partial American Indian heritage has been more widely accepted.

Acceptance of Indian Mixed Blood

Native American mixed bloods were portrayed in early 19th-century literature as genetically inferior and unable to live up to the rigors of the frontier. However, by the late 19th century, when the last of the Native American tribes were finally conquered and relegated to reservations, whites accepted partial Indian ancestry as a nostalgic symbol of the vanishing frontier, particularly if it was several generations removed.[2]

Although the decline in spatial presence of Native Americans reduced white fear of Indians, an increasing African American population increased white fear of blacks mixing with whites because, under the rules of hypodescent, the offspring of such miscegenation increased the black population rather than the white population. According to Scheik (1979), the "black problem" divided the country more greatly than the "Indian problem": "Unlike the declining red side of the half-blood, the black component of the mulatto reminded whites of what they regarded as the menace of black dominance" (p. 85). Such fears were further increased with

the dissolution of slavery as a means of control. Whereas whites saw mulatto identity as no laughing matter, they took expressions of partial Indian ancestry more lightly.

Will Rogers, the best-loved American humorist of the early 20th century, expressed an acceptable level of Indian-ness: "My father was one eighth Cherokee and my mother one fourth Cherokee, which I figure makes me about one eighth cigar-store Injun" (O'Brien, 1935, p. 24). As a light-skinned blue-eyed white-Indian with a cowboy persona (a symbol of American masculinity), Rogers's fit into the dominant image of masculinity and attained the status of an American hero. Rogers became known for his prowess as a champion horse racer, rodeo rider, and lassoer. He christened himself the "Cherokee Kid" when he started his stage career in the Wild West Show as a witty commonsense cowboy who told jokes and wisecrack social commentary between rope tricks.

Rogers asserted his Indian ancestry as a badge of masculinity distinguishing him from effeminized European identity. Rogers boasted to a Daughters of the Revolution audience: "My ancestors didn't come over on the Mayflower—they met 'em at the boat."

Exemplifying masculine individualism, Rogers joked that if audiences quit liking his act "I will bundle up my wife and three little Cherokees and burn the breeze for the tall grass of Oklahoma, get me one of those long-distance shooting guns . . . If ever I see a man coming down the road with a newspaper I will cut the gun loose and just keep on living in ignorance" (Day, 1921, p. 55). Rogers's powerful, independent, and in-control masculine multiraciality counters the "marginal man" thesis.

Affirmational Chicano Comedy

After the U.S. takeover of the northern half of Mexico in 1848, Mexican American Chicano identity emerged as between but yet neither American nor Mexican. American popular culture cast Chicanos as Mexican outcasts, and Mexican popular culture depicted Chicanos as cultural embarrassments (Hernandez, 1991, 27). Chicano comedy has played a significant role in transforming Chicano identity into a symbol of pride and, because of their ambiguous ethnic status, often addresses mixedness. Their comedy figures imbue the spirit of "rasquachismo," or multicultural resourcefulness, which affirms pride in things denigrated by the two dominant cultures.

The peladito, or comic hobo character, became the star male character of late 19th and early 20th-century Mexican American comedy troupes. A trickster-like figure, the peladito, best exemplified by Cantinflas, was poor and uneducated, had vulgar low-class habits and language, and was witty in maneuvering among Chicano, American, and Mexican cultures. Upper-class Mexicans and Mexican Americans were offended by the peladito's critical mockery of the upper classes, and the peladito was censured in Mexico during the 1920s.

The masculine pachuco figure emerged as a stylish, urban working-class deviant characterized by oversized suits, Chicano pride, defiantly exaggerated posture, and Spanglish (mixed Spanish and English) slang. Guillermo Hernandez (1991), in *Chicano Satire: A Study in Literary Culture*, describes pachuco style in the "padded, finger-length coat with wide lapels; the narrow-brimmed lid or hat; the draped pants with near pleats, ballooning to the knee then narrowing tightly at the ankle; the looping chain; doubled soled shoes" as blending aspects of "outsider" images from American popular culture's "outsiders" such as the southern dandy, the western gambler, the urban gangster, with a Chicano cultural orientation (p. 560).

Chicano comedians often joke about internal conflicts as a means of addressing inequalities between Mexican and Anglo Americans. For example, in Latins Anonymous's show "Latins Anonymous," Rick contrasts the treatment of Anglo Americans and Mexican Americans in the United States: "My American side would like to hang out with his friends, and that's called a fraternity. But when my Mexican side hangs out with his friends, it's called a street gang! I hate contradictions" (Leschin et al., 1996, p. 92). Rick compares how both masculine sides view the Rosarita Refried Bean commercial:

> My Mexican side just wants to take that Rosarita woman and put her on a kitchen table and, wango, wango, wango! and have twelve children with her. But my American side would like to get to know her better, talk to her, establish some honesty, communication, and then wango, wango, wango! and have 2.5 kids with her. (Leschin et al., 1996, pp. 91-92)

In contrast to the stereotype of Latino men as overly masculine, Asian male identity has been emasculated.

Reconfigured Hapas

Asian men have historically been stereotyped as asexual, effeminate, and nerdy. Until the 1990s the dominant image of multiracial Asians was the tragic Amerasian bastard offspring of American soldiers and Asian prostitutes (Hasu-Houston, 1997). However, better relations between the United States and Asian countries have resulted in a more favorable image for both interracial sexual relations (particularly between white men and Asian women) and their children. Hapa men were reconfigured as sexually attractive, masculine, and sophisticated in popular culture in the 1990s.

Anond Trulani, of East Indian and English descent, plays on the dominant conception that Asian men are not sexy. "My name is Anond Trulani, but people get my name wrong—Andy, Ahab, Amos. What does my name mean? It means Bristol orgasm. I'm Indian and English." "It's cool to be Indian, it's like a fashion statement, unless you're Indian." He then sings, "We're cool, we're hip, we're down, we're brown" and dances in an exaggeratedly sexually provocative way, to which women in the audience applaud. He then jokes, "I've got a confession, I'm not the lady's man. But I've had sexual experiences—I just happened to be by myself that's all. I'm going to have an arranged marriage. I haven't met her yet, unfortunately, because she's still a fetus" (live performance, The Comedy Store, Los Angeles, Dec. 13, 2000).

Hapa comedian Kip Fulbeck (2001) reflects on how many full Asian men don't like hapa men because hapas remind them of the high percentage of Asian women that prefer white guys over Asian guys as well as the high number of Asian women who are attracted to hapa men. "The other reason some full-yellow brothers hate hapas is this whole exotica crap. The whole best-of-both worlds hybrid-vigor myth of physical beauty and prowess and intelligence and mystery. Kind of like how everyone talks about mutts being better and smarter and healthier dogs than purebreds. If you want to dispel that myth once and for all, I can bring out some butt-ass ugly hapas right now, okay? They're out there, believe me." Fulbeck says some Asian men resent hapa men because "they see women swoon over Bruce or Brandon or Keanu or Russell or Tiger. They feel they get left out in the cold while Asian women jump on the hapa bandwagon" (p. 190).

In "Talking Shop," Fulbeck jokes about how when it comes to the issue of Asian women dating out that both Asian women and men thought he must be on their side: "The men think 'well, you're an Asian man, you know what it's like with all these sisters dating white guys,' and the women say 'the men are so sexist, you're hapa, you're a product of this.'" Rather than identifying or taking sides with only Asian or white, Fulbeck identifies with both.

NEW MASCULINE MULTIRACIALITY

Masculine displays of "softness" and "sensitivity" have recently been touted as a "New Masculinity" (Hondagneu-Sotelo & Messner, 1994).[3] Most comedians identifying as mixed descent describe themselves as being more sensitive, having feminine sides, open-minded, and nonhomophobic. Several multiracially identified female comedians I interviewed also regard multiracial men to be generally more sensitive and open-minded than single-race-identified men. According to one female comedian, "Multiracial male comics I know tend to be much less masculine, and express a more feminine and sensitive outlook. There are some people that think they are gay even if they're not—they play up a much more humble way. You hear of angry white male comics, but not angry multiracial male comics. White male comics are often adversarial towards women. For multiracial men, there's more of 'this is what I am, let me explain.' They are more on the subtle side, more on the loving side, not like 'oh, you're the other.' They see women as also minorities, relate to women better, not having a male racial bent to humor, like the way some black males have a stereotypical way of expressing masculinity."

Andrew Kennedy, an immigrant from Columbia of Columbian and English descent, refers to his feminine side:

> I am very in touch with my feminine side. I'm married, my brother is gay. I don't have gay tendencies but I'm very in tune with what it's like to be a woman. I can be emotional and cry when I want to as an actor, so I let myself be carried away in the movies when it is meant to be. Then it is over and I can shut it off or turn it on at will. I'm not a violent person, I don't yell at all." (personal communication, Dec. 18, 2000)

Kennedy believes being multiethnic is conducive to an open-mindedness and identifying with the underdog:

Rather than making judgmental assumptions, it's like having some kind of hinge that allows you to open up and let different objects and things in rather than only one type, shape, or size. I always liked the underdog, I will always choose or think of the other view and I'll take that side and try to show people a different side. I look for reasons that aren't all bad or all their fault: Rather than saying "that bum should get a job!" I'll say "you just don't know the situation they're in unless you walk in their shoes." (personal communication, Dec. 18, 2000)

Kennedy believes a multicultural outlook is helpful as a comedian because humor is often based on being able to see things from different and less-heard perspectives.

Although Teina Manu wants people to get their minds off of his race, he tells audiences, "'I'm half Samoan' to get their minds off it because they might be whispering 'oh, he looks Mexican.'" Rather than focusing on his ethnicity, he'd rather think of himself and present himself as "a regular single guy." Manu believes "as a mixed man, I'm more at ease, not worried. I don't have to blow up like Texan men do." "I touch women's issues, but not in a sensitive John Grey *Men are From Mars, Women are From Venus* way." Taking a more direct and uncensored approach, Manu jokes that women shouldn't feel bad if they have stretch marks: "Just pretend they're tiger stripes, which are really cool and sexy" (personal communication, Dec. 19, 2000).

Some comedy agents want him to identify only as Samoan to create an ethnic niche for himself.

Agents were pushing the Samoan part. They want me to say I like big women with stretch marks because I'm Samoan, do the dances, or if I had a joke where I talked to a guy in a store, they'd tell me to make the other guy Samoan. (personal communication, Dec. 19, 2000)

Men can joke about their "feminine" sides. Aaron Kayder, who is Palestinian and Mormon, identifies with Arab women: "Arab women don't have it good, they can't get money, can't get educated—pretty much I'm more like an Arab woman" (live performance, The Comedy Store, Los Angeles, Dec. 13, 2000). Mark Fernandez, who describes himself as half white and half Filipino, jokes "I don't like fighting. I feel like an Etch A Sketch. One of my buddies said, 'Your problem is you think like a woman.' So I didn't speak to him for three weeks" (live performance Hallembeck's, Los Angeles, Dec. 12, 2000).

Being nonhomophobic allows comedians to perform material that could raise questions about their sexual orientations if interpreted literally. De-emphasizing conflicts between cultures, Chatman jokes, "It's not about growing up with two different cultures. It's about growing up with two parents who force their child to dress up as a girl. Just kidding, they didn't have to force me, I did it on my own."

Gregory Carey, of black and white descent, plays on the sexual exotification of mixed-race men in narrating how a tourist he slept with in Jamaica helped him immigrate to New York.

I came to America, only to find she has a husband and she wants me to sleep with him and her at the same time. There's a lot of things I would do to stay in this country but I have to put my foot down and clear that up right away! It turned out I wound up sleeping with her on Monday and Wednesday, and him on Tuesday and Thursday, and I'll tell ya, Tuesday and Thursday was a real pain in the ass! (live performance, Aku Aku, Boston, May, 1994)

Although multiracial masculinity can be approached in holistic terms, comedians often ascribe different masculine styles to their heritages.

Juxtaposing Masculinities

Many comedians juxtapose their heritages according to different styles of masculinity.

Many multiracial male comedians depict their non-European sides as more emotionally expressive, sensitive, and multicultural than their European American or white parts, which they characterize as reserved, nonemotive, and insensitive toward others.

Culture Clash's "Bowl of Beings" casts Vinnie, "history's first Chicano," in a gendered conflict between his European father "Don Colon" [Columbus] and Native American mother "America the Beautiful." Don Colon kills America and tells Vinnie, "Maybe it's best that you forget your Indian past . . . now act like a man and bury your Mama America." Vinnie refuses and asserts Chicano independence: "One day my people will populate this so-called New World . . . Yes, yes. Your time has come, Don Colon. I am the Nuevo Hombre [new man], a product of both worlds" (Montoya, Salinas, & Siguenza, 1998, p. 72).

In Rick Najera's "A Quiet Love" (1997), Rick jokingly juxtaposes his heritages "I'm light-skinned, my sister's dark. I have a lot of Spanish blood, but my sister's got all the Indian blood. I know that because when we were young, I stole her gold and made her build me beautiful Spanish missions in my back yard" (p. 145). In Najera's (1997) "The Pain of the Macho," Professor Steve Sanchez critically compares macho styles to point out an imbalance in how men of each group are portrayed: "The difference between and Anglo macho and a Latino macho is that Anglo machos usually attack in large groups after U.N. approval. Latino machos attack whenever they damn well please, especially after a World Cup Soccer game" (p. 29). Sanchez traces macho to Spain: "The beginning of the macho can be traced back to Spain, *Ethpana*. Repeat after me, *Ethpana*. They have a lisp. That is why they overcompensate: they have to prove themselves" (p. 30).

Reflecting on his experiences living in both Japan and the United States, Teja Arboleda (personal communication, June 1, 2001) discusses Japanese culture as more accepting of men expressing sensitivity. For example, "It is okay for men to cry in public or display touching and closeness to other men in public. In contrast, such behaviors in American society are regarded to be signs of weakness and of being homosexual." "In Japan, men are encouraged to cry and be sensitive. In the U.S. men are raised primarily as independent, strong and macho. Therefore, humor based on male sensitivity was not feasible or even acceptable in the U.S. until recently." Arboleda believes macho culture compromises his sense of self. Drawing on multiple ethnicities provides the freedom to draw from different styles of masculinity.

Mixed Advantages

A major advantage in identifying with multiple groups rather than only one is that it gives greater license to joke about more groups, particularly in times of political correctness. Arboleda explains, "I can basically satirize and make fun of many different backgrounds because of my many heritages. Japan, China, the Philippines, Africa, America, Germany—I am those peoples and places so I have the right to make fun of them."

Some multiracial comedians observe they are perceived as less threatening than if they were monoracial. As Manu, son of a Samoan father and white mother, explained, "A big part of being mixed as a male is you're not as threatening as if you're only one race. It's like you're accepted everywhere because they see something in you they identify with." Manu observes, "Women prefer mixed guys" and "as mixed becomes more popular, and as you see more mixed people in fashion and movies some men secretly wish they were mixed too."

Ahmed Ahmed, who was born of Middle Eastern descent in Cairo, Egypt, and grew up in Riverside and Los Angeles, jokes about blacks accepting him because they think he's mulatto.

They always think I'm mixed, like I'm mulatto, half black and half white. Do I look mulatto? Black folks and I always get along well. Black guys are like "yo, I know the boy's got cream in his coffee, what's your name fool?" "Oh, you Egyptian, that's cool, that means we related, we both from the motherland, you O.G." (live performance, The Comedy Store, Los Angeles, Dec. 13, 2000)

Kennedy believes identifying with multiple races increases his options for expressing masculinity: "Every race has different ways of expressing masculinity. Asians are shy versus Latino or black. If you're of multiple races, then you can play two or more different racial styles of masculinity." Drawing on multiple racial heritages provides more masculine and racial styles to perform.

Some multiracial comedians think of themselves as multiethnic heroes on a mission to overcome racial boundaries, misconceptions, and inequalities.

In "The Adventures of Ethnic Man," Arboleda narrates how his multiethnic heritage and experiences give him an open-mindedness able to transcend rigid conceptions and boundaries. He explains that his father's father is Filipino Chinese, his father's mother is African American/Native American, his mother's father is Danish, and his mother's mother is German, and he was born in Brooklyn, New York. However, he grew up in Japan "and that's why they call me Ethnic Man!" "Yes it's Ethnic Man. He can leap from race to race in a single bound. It's Ethnic Man. Not quite Black as Black, not quite White as White, sort of brown, sort of in-between, but he's never ever green!" (live performance, World Trade Center, Boston, Nov. 2, 1993).

Many mixed comedians consider themselves to be multiethnic ambassadors on a mission for the betterment of humanity. Manu explains,

Being mixed it's our duty to extend humanity. I've been in both your camps and this is what you're doing wrong. When you're mixed, it's like we're the next generation of human beings. We're all these, so we don't exclude, we're more open-minded.

Guillermo Gomez-Pena, a self-described Latino "Border Warrior" of Spanish, Indian, German, and British blood, celebrates mixedness as a site for creating new identities: "We assume a multiple repertoire of identities. We have transitional identities in the making. We are developing new cultures. Jokingly, we have talked about imaginary identities that make more sense than the ones we are offered as possibilities" (quoted in Fusco, 1995, p. 154). Gomez-Pena (1996) envisions a multicentric hybrid borderless future with "incredible mixtures beyond science fiction: cholo-punks, pachuco krishnas, Irish concheros, buto rappers, cyber Aztecs, Gringofarians, Hopi rockers, y demas . . . jumping borders with ease, jumping borders with pleasure, amen, hey man." (pp. 2-3). Multiracial masculinity can be configured in unlimited ways.

CONCLUSION

Multiracial comedians imaginatively expand our conceptions of multiraciality and masculinity beyond those we have historically been offered by the dominant culture. They humorously reveal raciality and maleness to be socially constructed, changing, and situational rather than inherent, rigid, and homogenous. Creatively using multiplistic identities, worldviews, and wits as vehicles for addressing conflicts between groups, they open possibilities for a more pluralistic and inclusive humanity.

NOTES

1. Freda Scot Giles writes in "From Melodrama to the Movies: The Tragic Mulatto as a Type Character" (1995): "Even as a joke an image of black male sexual potency would prove too threatening." (p. 64).

2. In the late 19th century, the solution to the Indian "problem" went through the stages of extermination, containment on reservations, and then cultural assimilation. "Kill the Indian, save the man" was a slogan used by Captain Richard Pratt, who created the 19th-century Indian boarding school system to force Indians to become culturally white.

3. Hondagneu-Sotelo and Messner problematize the dichotomy between "new masculinity" displays among privileged men and proud expressions of power among lower-class men of color as classist and racist because it overlooks such men's structural positions of privilege over women and certain groups of men.

REFERENCES

Bogle, D. (1996). *Toms, coons, mulattoes, mammies, & bucks*. New York: Continuum.

Connel, R. (1995). *Masculinities*. Berkeley: University of California Press.

Davies, C. (1990). *Ethnic humor around the world: A comparative analysis*. Bloomington: Indiana University Press.

Day, D. (Ed.). (1921). *The autobiography of Will Rogers*. New York: Lancer Books.

Fulbeck, K. (2001). *Paper bullets: A fictional autobiography*. Seattle: University of Washington Press.

Fusco, C. (1995). *English is broken here: Notes on cultural fusion in the Americas*. New York: The New Press.

Giles, F. S. (1995). From melodrama to the movies: The tragic mulatto as a type character. In N. Zack (Ed.), *American mixed race: The culture of microdiversity*. Lanham, MD: Rowman & Littlefield.

Gomez-Pena, G. (1996). *The new world border: Prophecies, poems, and loqueras for the end of the century*. San Francisco: City Lights.

Haskins, J. (1984). *Richard Pryor: A man and his madness*. New York: Beaufort Books.

Hasu-Houston, V. (1997). To the colonizer goes the spoils: Amerasian progeny in Vietnam War films and owning up to the gaze. *Amerasia Journal, 23*(1), 69-86.

Hernandez, G. E. (1991). *Chicano satire: A study in literary culture*. Austin: University of Texas Press.

Hondagneu-Sotelo, P., & Messner, M. A. (1994). Gender displays and men's power: The "new man" and the Mexican immigrant man. In H. Brod & M. Kaufman (Eds.), *Theorizing masculinities* (pp. 200-218). Thousand Oaks, CA: Sage.

Kimmel, M. (1994). Masculinity as homophobia: Fear, shame, and silence in the construction of gender identity. In H. Brod & M. Kaufman (Eds.), *Theorizing masculinities* (pp. 119-141). Thousand Oaks, CA: Sage.

Leschin, L., Molina, A., Najera, R., & Franco, C. (1996). *Latins anonymous*. Houston, TX: Arte Publico Press.

Montoya, R., Salinas, R., & Siguenza, H. (1998). *Culture clash: Life, death, and revolutionary comedy*. New York: Theatre Communications Group.

Najera, R. (Ed.) (1997). A quiet love. In *The pain of the macho and other plays* (pp. 53-92). Houston, TX: Arte Publico Press.

O'Brien, P. J. (1935). *Will Rogers: Ambassador of good will, prince of wit and wisdom*. Chicago: John Winston.

Pryor, R. (1995). *Pryor convictions and other life sentences*. New York: Pantheon.

Purdie, S. (1992). *Comedy: The mastery of discourse*. Toronto, Ontario, Canada: Toronto University Press.

Rogin, M. (1996). *Blackface, white noise: Jewish immigrants in the Hollywood melting pot*. Berkeley: University of California Press.

Scheick, W. J. (1979). *The half-blood: A cultural symbol in 19th century America*. Lexington: University of Kentucky Press.

Spickard, P. (1989). *Mixed blood: Intermarriage and ethnic identity in twentieth-century America*. Madison: University of Wisconsin Press.

PART V

SPECIAL TOPICS

CHAPTER 17

Gang Affiliation and Self-Esteem
The Effects of a Mixed-Heritage Identity

PATRICIA O'DONNELL BRUMMETT
LORETTA I. WINTERS

California State University, Northridge

PREVALENCE OF GANGS AND GANG CRIME

According to the National Youth Gang Survey, in 1998 there were approximately 28,700 gangs in the United States with 780,200 active gang members (U.S. Department of Justice, 2000). In California in 1998, 22% of all homicides were gang related, and more homicide victims aged 5 through 17 died as a result of gang- or drug-related activities than from any other circumstance known (California Department of Justice, 1998). The Los Angeles Police Department (LAPD) estimates that in the city of Los Angeles in April 2001 there were 407 gangs with 56,471 active gang members.[1] Furthermore, these gang members are thought to be responsible for 260 homicides and 526 attempted homicides from January 2000 through October 2000.

Clearly, gangs represent a large subculture of youth and young adults in the United States, specifically in California and more specifically in Los Angeles. As is done in Los Angeles, gangs are often categorized by their race or ethnicity. The LAPD estimates, for example, that there are 204 Hispanic gangs, 107 Crip gangs (typically African American; here, the police are referring to "sets" or smaller groups within the larger Crip gang), 43 Blood gangs (also typically African American; again, the reference is to sets within the larger Blood gang), 32 Asian gangs, 16 Stoner gangs (typically white), and 5 (other) white gangs. Although some racial or ethnic mixing within gangs occurs, by and large gangs represent groups of the same racial or ethnic background. The violence perpetrated by gangs is also typically intraracial.

The notion of racial or ethnic identity has been explored by many researchers in relation to gang membership as it has been in other areas; however, mixed heritage is not considered in law enforcement's or others' categorizations of gangs.

NEED FOR THE STUDY

Thus far, no research has looked at the relationship between mixed heritage and gang affiliation. In fact, very little research looks at racial/ethnic identity and gang affiliation or mixed heritage, gang affiliation, and self-esteem. This research will add to the growing racial/ethnic identity literature, mixed-heritage or multiracial identity literature, gang literature, and the delinquency/self-esteem debate, and will suggest future direction for similar studies.

LITERATURE REVIEW

Mixed Heritage and Multiracial Identity Literature

Before looking at the literature on mental health and mixed-heritage or multiracial identity, a discussion of the history of mixed race or mixed heritage is useful. Although designations were historically constructed to indicate mixtures of various socially designated groups of people with European Americans, the emphasis continued to focus on the black/white distinction. The early 20th-century literature on multiracial identity reflects the rule of hypodescent (commonly known as the "one-drop rule"), which reinforces white superiority and black inferiority. The field of eugenics was the discipline most focused on multiracial identity during the late 1890s and through the 1940s (Kahn & Denmon, 1997), subordinating social and environmental factors to supposed biological ones. Edward B. Reuter, Robert E. Park, and Everett V. Stonequist were instrumental in

laying the groundwork for early beliefs in the marginality of multiracial people arising from the incompatibility of the two different worlds from which their parents came as well as the imposition of the one-drop rule.[2]

Some positive aspects of being multiracial were apparent in the earlier literature (advantages of insight into two worlds), but the negative aspects of the "marginal man" were generally emphasized. Rather than the conclusion of marginality being drawn from rigorous empirical work, early studies reflected the biases of the researchers (Kahn & Denmon, 1997). Support provided for the assumed pathology of mixed-raced people and their parents was in the form of crime rates and the divorce rates of their parents (Kahn & Denmon, 1997). Root (1992) makes a distinction between the "old" research (pre-1967) and "new" research (post-1967). She criticizes the old research as "largely not useful today because of the profound influences of antimiscegenist attitudes on the hypotheses and on the interpretations of findings" (p. 181). These attitudes no doubt have some origins in the marginal-man literature.

Ethnicity became an important element in counseling during the 1970s, and as people of color were compared with whites, oppressed groups became a concern in the literature (Reynolds & Pope, 1991). Eric Erickson's (1959, 1968) work provided the framework for much scholarly work on identity, and he did include discussions of race and ethnicity, but he based his observations on a monoracial social designation and a linear identity development model. The development of ethnic identity scales and assimilation scales in the 1970s (Kahn & Denmon, 1997) and racial-ethnic identity developmental models in the 1980s (Reynolds & Pope, 1991) came about. Studies with more methodological rigor between the early 1980s and mid 1990s revealed the volatile nature of ethnic identity and within-group variability resulting from fluctuating environments (Kahn & Denmon, 1997). Conflict between two worlds continued to be a theme, especially in clinical studies; however, some more positive aspects of a multiracial identity began to reveal themselves in the empirical literature during the early 1980s. This was a time when research began to indicate the benefits of a multiracial experience. Research in the late 1980s and early 1990s also revealed the possibility of multiracial identity to be "a normal process of human development" (Kahn & Denmon, 1997, p. 128).

Contemporary literature in the 1990s continues to identify a number of problems that are common to multiracial persons. Many of these problems can be linked to one's racial identity. Winn and Priest (1993) argue that without the achievement of a positive racial identity a likelihood of negative psychological consequences exists. When individual perceptions or persuasions of family and friends at the microlevel and the one-drop rule or political loyalties at the macrolevel dictate how multiracial people are to identify and these pressures are contrary to the desires to identify with the ethnicity of both parents, multiracial individuals are bound to experience difficulties. Kerwin, Ponterotto, Jackson, and Harris (1993) found parents to claim not having a label for their biracial children to be a core problem in identity formation. They also point out that many potential problems have been suggested about biracial children in the literature, among them "cultural and racial identification issues, lowered self-esteem, difficulties in dealing with conflicting cultural demands, and feeling marginal in two cultures" (p. 221). Other predicted problems include anxiety, insecurity, guilt, anger, and depression alongside identity conflicts (Stephan, 1992). Clinical studies tend to emphasize low self-esteem, divided family loyalties, and parental rejection (Gibbs & Hines, 1992).

Arguing a common experience and sometimes even for recognition as a separate race or ethnicity for multiracial people dominates a segment of followers of the multiracial movement. A history of the legacy of marginality, including a lack of a mechanism to acknowledge a unique social position on governmental forms, and the self-esteem issues that accompany the forced choice resulting from the one-drop rule are some experiences that multiracial people share. In addition to the one-drop rule operating from the outside, an internal dilemma exists. Brown (1990) states that

> in the case of the biracial person, information concerning status and identity is received from two primary and valued cultural groups. In order to resolve this cognitive dissonance, there is a strong drive to stabilize and identify with either one group or the other. (p. 330)

He describes the marginal experience that arises from the pressure to choose.

> Cultural assimilation into one or the other ethno-cultural groups presents a serious dilemma for biracial persons because it means sacrificing one or the other of their cultural frames of reference. Consequently, the struggle for biracial persons is related to adequately adjusting to and functioning within mainstream society without sacrificing the integrity of one's personal identity. (p. 327)

A number of multiracial respondents in Mass's (1992) study reported that the way they saw themselves was not always consistent with the way others treated them. Multiracial children also experience racism from two groups and have to deal with two different parenting styles and beliefs (Cauce, Hiraga, Mason, Aguilar, Ordonez, & Gonzales, 1992).

The results of the studies conducted in the last decade on nonclinical samples of multiracial people are mixed with respect to mental health and self-esteem issues. This is not surprising because numerous methodological problems with studying this population exist (Root, 1992), and interracial families resist being studied (Herring, 1995). However, some common themes do emerge. Some difficulties that have been revealed in studies of multiracial people include feelings of shame, emotional isolation (Bowles, 1993), depression (Bowles, 1993; Brown, 1990), identity confusion (Brown, 1990; Winn & Priest, 1993), and low self-esteem (Bowles, 1993). In addition, these children have not been prepared for the realities of prejudice and racism and receive negative responses from both white society and members of a parent's nonwhite culture (Winn & Priest, 1993).

Many studies find multiracial children to be similar to monoracial children in a variety of ways. Cauce et al. (1992) found no greater difficulties for multiracial adolescents on any "qualitative aspects of family and peer relations" (p. 219) or in terms of "life stress, behavioral problems, psychological distress, competence or self-worth" (p. 220). Kerwin et al. (1993) found that marginality did not describe the biracial participants in their study. Neither were multiracial people found to be different from monoracial people as far as self-esteem (Hall, 1992; Mass, 1992), self-perceptions (Field, 1996), psychological adjustment (R. Johnson, 1992; Mass, 1992), or self-concept (Mass, 1992).

Contrary to a marginal-man thesis, multiracial people can exhibit mental health and adjustment. Gibbs and Hines (1992) found that most of their subjects feel comfortable with a biracial identity, and some studies actually reveal benefits for multiracial children. More recent works like Wehrly and Kenny (1999) emphasize the strengths of multiracial families. Stephan (1992) argues that bilingual children are more cognitively flexible and less dogmatic compared with monolinguals and

possess more favorable intergroup attitudes, and that a wider exposure to varied cultures contributes to better adjustment for minority group members. Her study revealed a sample of multiracial college students to be less ethnocentric than monoracial college students and to have more informal voluntary contact with single-heritage groups than single-heritage groups have with each other. Cauce et al. (1992) suggest that biracial children may have a wider circle of peers from which to select friends and that the friends of biracial children hold more positive values than monoracial children. Hall (1992) reports the benefits of adopting positive qualities from two heritages and greater understanding and empathy for people of other cultures and races.

When problems that are connected to the racial identity of mixed-race children do emerge, interracial couples may respond to these difficulties by denying race and color, by encouraging racial and ethnic identity according to phenotype, or by promoting a biracial identity, and the children endure these consequences (Herring, 1995). The context with which understanding of race comes to be at any given time or in any given place may be more important to whether multiracial people exhibit mental health or pathology than the actual designation of multiracial itself.

McRoy and Freeman (1986) argue that in the context of the arenas of school, home, and community, mixed-race children receive messages, positive or negative, about the racial groups of their parents. They point out that children learn "who they are," which is closely related to "the values of who they are" (p. 165). D. Johnson (1992) also emphasizes the importance of child, family, and community. Minority group members gain positive images of who they are from group membership. This membership buffers the negative images individuals may receive about their racial status from society in general. When a child has parents who are each a member of a different racial group, especially when one parent belongs to a minority group and the other to the majority group, confusion may arise. McRoy and Freeman (1986) describe how adolescence, when one's peer group is very influential and may contribute to self-perception of a given individual, can be a particularly difficult time for black/white biracial children. They expound:

> In adolescence, particularly, ideas and perceptions are shaped by peer standards. According to Logan, the black adolescent begins to identify with a sense of "peoplehood" and begins to question the relevancy of using the white norm for self-measurement. If a mixed-race adolescent is rejected by peers on the basis of racial background or is unable to discuss racial identity with peers or parents, this transition period can become even more difficult. For children to view their mixed-racial background positively, the family must nurture both parts of the background by providing the child with both black and white role models and by exposing the child to black as well as white peers in the community and in school. In this process, the child is able to acquire more realistic attitudes and perceptions about his or her racial background. Mixed-race adolescents who are unable to reconcile their mixed cultural background into a personal and socially acceptable coalescence will not resolve this developmental stage. Thus, the individual may exhibit neurotic behavior. (p. 166)

For McRoy and Freeman (1986), then, an important aspect of whether multiracial children will exhibit mental health problems or not is whether or not parents will encourage a multiracial identity, one that is not historically encouraged in American society because of the influence of the one-drop rule and political loyalties. More recent research emphasizes that integrating all aspects of one's racial heritage is healthy (Fong, Spickard, & Ewalt, 1995; Jacobs, 1992; Wardle, 1996), and many

biracial youth are learning about both of their parents' cultures (Winn & Priest, 1993) and claiming both sides of their ethnic heritage (Bowles, 1993). In addition, Brown (1990) argues that it is "more appropriate to assess biracial persons on the basis of their dual frames of reference rather than try to stereotype or miscategorize them" (p. 335). Bowles (1993) found that when a number of young women in therapy were able to accept their "bi-racial selves, in each instance self-esteem soared and anxiety levels lessened considerably" (p. 420). Herring (1995) believes that encouraging biracial youth to explore both heritages will contribute to a positive self-esteem. Kerwin et al. (1993) concluded that adolescents who discussed racial matters frequently with their families and openly with others tended to use interracial labels to describe themselves and to perceive themselves as members of two groups. Gibbs and Hines (1992) also found that an open and warm relationship with parents was common to respondents possessing a healthy biracial identity. Mass's (1992) study also indicates the potential for parents to either buffer the negative aspects that society presents to multiracial children or create problems themselves through their own prejudices. Mass (1992) and Pinderhughes (1995) also emphasize the importance of support and acceptance from grandparents, other relatives, friends, and community members. Their participants had parents who agreed to consider their children biracial as opposed to monoracial and reported no alienation from their extended families. A multiracial environment also facilitates identity development for multiracial children (Gibbs & Hines, 1992; Jacobs, 1992; R. Johnson, 1992; Mass, 1992; Pinderhughes, 1995).

Multiracial children make sense out of their dual heritage by using names for themselves that capture their unique status. Even when their parents do not supply these names

(Jacobs, 1992) or when a black identity is encouraged by parents (Gibbs & Hines, 1992), they construct such terms. Other research indicates that a monoracial orientation for some biracial youth is not always problematic. Field (1996) found that biracial adolescents who possessed a "reference group orientation" that indicated comfort with the African American group, regardless of whether they possessed an African American or bicultural orientation, had more positive self-concepts than those who chose a European American reference group orientation, who also tended to express negative feelings about their African American heritage. Field concludes that minority communities because of a history of prejudice and discrimination are more equipped to teach coping skills and "offer youths standards of beauty, emotional expressiveness, interpersonal distance, degree of extraversion, and comfort with physical intimacy that is often quite different from the white norm" (p. 225). She also asserts that these are standards in which affirmation may be found. It appears that a connection to the African American community is important for black/white biracial adolescents regardless of whether they also possess a European American orientation. Relevant here is the study by Cauce et al. (1992), who found no differences in the healthy functioning of biracial adolescents from others and cautioned that these results should not be generalized to multiracial adolescents who consider themselves white or are ashamed of their minority status.

In spite of the struggles that surround multiracial people, various behaviors that arise and are sometimes considered to be dysfunctional or deviant might be part of the normal process of developing a healthy biracial identity. For instance, "movement back and forth across color lines" can be viewed as a creative strategy rather than dysfunction (Thornton, 1996, p. 108). Comparing the identity development of multiracial people with Erickson's linear monoracial model may result in false-negative assumptions because he does not account for the complex nature of developing a multiracial identity.[3] Stephan (1992) points out that ethnic identity, in general, "has been shown to be both subjective and unstable" (p. 51). Identity also tends to be situational (Root, 1990; Stephan, 1992) or change according to life changes, and people with the same biological make-up can have different identities or identities may develop when no biological or social heritage is evident (Stephan, 1992). For multiracial individuals, the subjective and unstable nature of identity is of greater concern. For instance, temporarily distancing oneself from one parent and his/her heritage is considered by Jacobs (1992) to be a necessary part of the identity development of multiracial people. Gibbs and Hines (1992) call choosing a monoracial identity for mixed-race people a strategy, whereas Hall (1992) calls it a stage. Kich (1992) identifies "an initial awareness of differentness and dissonance between self-perceptions and others' perceptions of them" to be the first stage in "the development and continuing resolution of their biracial identity" (p. 305). Winn and Priest (1993) found that the responses of the adolescents they interviewed suggests that "racial identification/clarification is a developmental process that continues at least through adolescence as opposed to one that is completed by nine years of age (p. 33). Further, a nonlinear identity model capturing a complex process may be natural rather than problematic for multiracial people (Kich, 1992; Root, 1990). Empirical studies show the development of identity for multiracial people to be unique (Gibbs & Hines, 1992).

Most of the research supporting the hypothesis that multiracial adolescents will have lower self-esteem than monoracial adolescents comes from clinical populations. This sample can be considered "clinical" in that many adolescents confined to probation camps suffer from mental health problems. Huizinga and Jakob-Chein (1998) found that "delinquents of any kind have a higher prevalence of psychological problems than do nondelinquent youth" (p. 53). Furthermore, they found that "roughly one third of the serious or serious violent offenders display high levels of each psychological problem" (p. 53). Delinquency itself has, more and more, been classified as a mental health problem, such as through the *Diagnostic and Statistical Manual of Mental Disorders* (fourth edition; APA, 1994) categories of "intermittent explosive disorder," "conduct disorder," "oppositional defiant disorder," and "antisocial personality disorder." We argue, therefore, that this particular sample can be considered a clinical sample of youth.

Delinquency and Self-Esteem

Although little research has been done on the relationship between "gang affiliation" and self-esteem, a large amount exists examining the relationship between "delinquency" and self-esteem. This literature shows very mixed results. Whereas a number of studies show no significant effect between delinquency and self-esteem (e.g., Jang & Thornberry, 1998; McCarthy & Hoge, 1984), others do find some relationship between the two. These studies are discussed herein.

Stager, Chassin, and David (1983) found, among mentally retarded educable youths, that deviant social labeling was related to low self-esteem if the youth believed the label was negative and that the label was similar to himself or herself. Similarly, Chassin and Stager (1984) found, among adjudicated male delinquents, that adolescents who were labeled delinquent and who viewed the delinquent label negatively and personally relevant had lowered global and role-specific self-esteem. The suggestion here is that

the labeling comes first, thus lowering the self-esteem.

Other research suggests that low self-esteem precedes delinquency. For example, Owens (1994) in analyzing the 1974 Youth in Transition data, found that a sense of self-worth combined with high global self-esteem, high positive self-worth, or low self-deprecation reduced delinquent behavior, but delinquency had almost no impact on self-worth. Other research suggests a correlation between self-esteem and delinquency without attesting to time ordering. For example, Forest and Tambor (2000) found that male youths incarcerated in juvenile facilities had lower self-esteem compared with those in school.

With regard to gangs and self-esteem, the results are similarly mixed. Horowitz and Schwartz (1974) found that gang violence arises when there are threats to a gang member's self-esteem. Arthur (1989) found that gangs give members a sense of security and, therefore, self-esteem that is lacking in their lives. More specifically, Wang (1994) found that among 11th- and 12th-grade Caucasian males, nongang members had higher positive self-esteem than did gang members. However, the same relationship was not found for African American males.

In considering "gender" and self-esteem among gang members, Esbensen and Deschenes (1999), in a nationally representative sample of youth analyzed for the Gang Resistance Education and Training program, discovered that females had lower self-esteem overall than did males. They also found that self-identified gang members reported lower levels of self-esteem than did nongang members. Furthermore, they found that girls with high self-esteem were less likely to join gangs, whereas boys with high self-esteem were more likely to join gangs. In a later study, Esbensen and Deschenes (1999), also using a nationally representative sample, found that for four of six measures of self-esteem gang girls report lower levels of self-esteem than do gang boys. This is not surprising because girls in general tend to have lower levels of self-esteem than do their male counterparts.

Although the results are mixed, there is significant support for a hypothesis that gang members will have lower levels of self-esteem than will nongang members. Furthermore, Esbensen's and Deschenes's studies lend support for the hypothesis that girl gang members will have lower self-esteem than boy gang members. Because multiracial identity has been linked to self-esteem and because adolescence is a time when identity issues become prevalent, particularly when one begins to date,[4] an examination of the self-esteem of multiracial adolescents is important. According to Overmier (1990), biracial youth are confronted with integrating the identifications with parents from different racial backgrounds while "simultaneously negotiating their own social status in a peer group" (p. 159). Unfortunately, adolescent peers are not very flexible in the expectations of those they include. Kerwin et al. (1993) discuss the adolescent subculture and its intolerance of differences. This is potentially problematic for multiracial children because their struggle for acceptance frequently occurs in school or community environments (Kich, 1992). Their research indicated that adolescents tend to group according to race and conjectured that biracial adolescents may be pressured to choose sides" (Kerwin et al., 1993, p. 230).

If adolescents are not tolerant of multiracial identities and have expectations of group loyalties, and if gang membership tends to have a race factor, mixed-heritage gang members in this study may be influenced by the one-drop rule regardless of the origin of its influence and not encouraged to embrace a multiracial identity. A socioeconomic factor may be operating as well because low socioeconomic status (SES) is associated with a single heritage identity, whereas a high SES is associated with a mixed-heritage identity (Rockquemore, 1998). If a multiracial identity is associated with mental health and high self-esteem as the aforementioned literature indicates, then mixed-heritage gang members under pressure to identify with a single heritage may be expected to have problems beyond those normally experienced by single-heritage gang members. If this were the case, then mixed-heritage gang members would be expected to have lower levels of self-esteem than gang members who are single heritage. On the other hand, if mixed-heritage adolescents find acceptance and refuge in a gang that organizes according to minority group status, this may not be the case.

Some identity issues for children belonging to gangs echo those prevalent among some multiracial children. According to Vigil and Yun (1996), "many gang members have failed to form conventional attachment bonds, the first and probably most important element of social control" (p. 153). Furthermore, "socioeconomic factors (such as poverty, economic dislocation, divorce and single-parent households, and racism) placed severe stresses on many household units, so that family life is regularly unstable and often involves the child being pushed into the streets" (p. 153). Coming from a higher SES, intact home contributes to a positive identity for multiracial children (Gibbs & Hines, 1992); therefore, an absence of these elements might be found among biracial gang members as well. The youth rebels against the parents or primary caretakers and instead gravitates and adapts to the role models of the street subculture.

Culture change is a particularly predominant disruption in the lives of ethnic street youth, whose experiences of culture shock and adaptation can lead to a phase of ethnic identity ambivalence and confusion. . . . Caught between cultures, they encountered confusion and ambiguity in reconciling their transitional identity with the traditional cultural identity of their parents. (Vigil & Yun, 1996, p. 154)

The common element here is racism and being caught between two cultures, whether they be subcultures in the United States or across nations. It appears that both monoracial and multiracial children may struggle with some sort of dual-identity issues and the racism that society affords children whose heritage places them at lower rungs of the social ladder. This study attempts to examine both single- and mixed-heritage adolescents to tease out any differences or similarities that may emerge in their self-perceptions.

METHODOLOGY

Study Funding

This study was funded in part by California Legislative Bill AB2650 (Cardenas-D). Bill AB2650 was passed in August 1998 allocating funding to the California State University system to evaluate Communities in Schools of San Fernando Valley (CIS-SFV). In November 1999, California State University, Northridge (CSUN) received funding from the CSU system to conduct the evaluation. As part of that evaluation, youth in seven probation camps in the county of Los Angeles were surveyed. This chapter uses data from that particular survey.

Court Order

CSUN received a court order from the Superior Court of the State of California for the County of Los Angeles on June 30, 1999 allowing researchers access to the minors in probation camps and juvenile halls for the purpose of distributing a survey containing a test of self-esteem.

Probability Versus Nonprobability Sampling

The original intention of the data collection was to evaluate the CIS-SFV project. Therefore, the three probation camps where CIS-SFV offered programs were included in the study. In addition, three similar camps within Los Angeles were chosen for comparison. The only female probation camp within Los Angeles was also included in the study because CIS-SFV does provide programs for that camp. This first stage of sampling was nonprobability in nature. However, seven of 19 camps (36.8%) within Los Angeles were included in the study and are fairly representative of all camps within Los Angeles County.

The second stage of sampling occurred within each camp. For each of the seven camps the entire population of the camp was targeted. The probation camps operate at a maximum capacity of 110 juveniles. However, often camps are not operating at their maximum. Additionally, youth may be away from the camp for various reasons, including training, work, or poor health. Youth were surveyed within the classroom setting of the camp because all youth within the camps are required to attend school. All students within the classroom were surveyed. Classroom populations ranged from 55% to 98% of maximum camp capacity.[5] Although nonprobability in nature, our sample of 623 of a possible 770 youths (80.9%) should give us a sample representative of the youth within these seven probation camps.

Sample Description

The sample used in this analysis includes only those individuals for whom age was available and between 13 and 19. Because we are interested in the development of self-esteem during adolescence, only teenagers were included in the sample (9 youth were excluded because they were younger than 13 or older than 19; 53 youth were excluded because they did not answer the age question). The final sample consists of 561 youth and includes 10.9% (61) females from the only female camp in Los Angeles County. The remaining 89.1% (500) are males. With regard to race/ethnicity, 23.9% identify themselves as African Americans, 2.9% as Asians, 6.9% as Caucasians, 59.9% as Latinos, and 6.4% as "others."[6] Thirty-five youth identified their race/ethnicity as other. About 13% (*n* = 72) of the sample is "mixed heritage" (determined by asking mother's race/ethnicity and father's race/ethnicity). Furthermore, 93.1% of the sample is nonwhite, and 6.9% is white. The average age of the sample is 16.4 years. This sample is comparable to overall Los Angeles County Probation Camp demographics from 1998. In October 1998, 2,110 youths were detained within Los Angeles County Probation Camps. Roughly 92% were males, and 7.6% were females. With regard to race/ethnicity, 26.8% of youths identified themselves as African Americans, 1.4% as Asians, 7.3% as Caucasians, 61.8% as Latinos and 2.8% as others. About 81% of the 2,110 youth in Los Angeles County Probation Camps in October 1998 were aged 15 to 17. No measure for mixed heritage was available.

MEASURES

Variables Used in the Study

One variable of major interest in this study is self-esteem. For this research, self-esteem was measured using Battle's Culture-Free Self-Esteem Inventory (SEI). The SEI was created in part to assess self-esteem in a way that is not culturally biased. The scale consists of 40 questions. The General, Social, and Personal subscales were used in this study. The advantage of this self-esteem test is that multiple levels of self-esteem can be assessed in relation to gang affiliation and mixed heritage in a way that is meant to be applicable to all cultures.

The General subscale consists of 16 questions (scored on a scale ranging from 0–16): Are you happy most of the time? Can you do most things as well as others? Do you like being a male/female? Are you usually successful when you attempt important tasks or assignments? Do you feel you are as important as most people? Would you change many things about yourself if you could? Are you lacking in self-confidence? Do you often feel that you are no good at all? Is it difficult for you to express your views or feelings? Do you often feel ashamed of yourself? Are other people generally more successful than you are? Would you like to be as happy as others appear to be? Are you a failure? Is it hard for you to meet new people? Are you as happy as most people? Are you definitely lacking in initiative?

The Social subscale consists of the following eight questions (scored on a scale ranging from 0–8): Do you have only a few friends? Do you spend most of your free time alone? Do most people you know like you? Are you as intelligent as most people? Do many people dislike you? Are you as strong and healthy as most people? Do people like your ideas? Do most people respect your views?

The Personal subscale consists of the following eight questions (scored on a scale ranging from 0–8): Are you easily depressed? Are you as nice looking as most people? Are you usually tense or anxious? Are your feelings easily hurt? Do you feel uneasy much of the time without knowing why? Are you often upset about something? Are you more sensitive than most people? Do you worry a lot?

The three subscales were used as dependent variables. Additionally, the subscales were used as independent variables in predicting gang affiliation. Because the data are cross-sectional, temporal ordering cannot be determined. It is difficult to determine whether (a) self-esteem affects gang membership, (b) gang membership affects self-esteem, or (c) something else is going on. Therefore, both self-esteem and gang membership were considered as dependent and independent variables.

Two other variables of major consideration in this study were gang affiliation and mixed heritage. Gang affiliation was determined by asking respondents whether they consider themselves to be gang members. Surveys were anonymous, thus decreasing perceived consequences for identifying as a gang member. Research suggests that self-identified gang affiliation is often a better measure of gang membership than law enforcement (or in this case probation department) criteria.[7] Of the 561 respondents, 46.4% identified themselves as gang members.

Mixed heritage was determined by asking respondents their mothers' and fathers' race/ethnicity. As previously mentioned, categories for the race/ethnicity variable included African American, Asian, Caucasian, Latino, and Other. Using parents' racial/ethnic categories is an effective measure of mixed heritage because youth may not self-identify as mixed heritage but instead identify as one or the other of their parents' races/ethnicities. Therefore, those who responded with different races/ethnicities for their parents, 13.3% of the sample, were classified as mixed heritage.

Several other variables were used in the analysis. Sex (male vs. female) is an important variable, especially considering Esbensen's and Deschenes's studies comparing self-esteem among gang and nongang boys and girls. In this study, only 10.9% of the sample are girls. Only one probation camp in Los Angeles County, Camp Scott, houses females. The remaining camps are for boys. Although the sample is heavily male, there are a significant number of females, from the only female probation camp in Los Angeles County, so that preliminary comparisons and generalizations may be made.

Two other variables included in the study were age and number of times arrested. In predicting gang membership as well as self-esteem, these variables can have an impact. The average age of respondents was 16.4 years. The average number of times respondents reported having been arrested was 5.93.

Reliability and Validity

According to Battle, the test-retest reliability correlation for the overall self-esteem scale (from all 40 variables) is .81. The alpha (kr 20) analysis conducted for internal consistency of the subscales is as follows: General, a = .78; Social, a = .57; Personal, a = .72. No validity data are available on Battle's original self esteem test.

ANALYSIS AND DISCUSSION

Descriptive Statistics

Of those respondents who identify their parents as belonging to two different racial/ethnic groups, 17.6% ($n = 13$) identify as African American, 1.4% ($n = 1$) as Asian, 9.5% ($n = 7$) as Caucasian, 47.3% ($n = 35$) as Latino/a, 1.4% ($n = 1$) as Hawaiian, and 1.4% ($n = 1$) as American Indian. One respondent whose mother was Caucasian and whose father was African American scribbled under the Other category. This may indicate the frustration resulting from racial/ethnic categories not allowing expression for those who embrace a mixed-heritage identity. About 5% ($n = 4$) of adolescents with parents of different race/ethnic groups did not answer the question on race/ethnicity for themselves. Roughly 15% ($n = 11$) identify with a mixed heritage.

The mean score for the General self-esteem subscale is 9.73 ($N = 436$, $SD = 3.22$); for the

Social self-esteem subscale, 5.62 ($N = 459$, $SD = 1.73$); and for the Personal self-esteem subscale, 3.89 ($N = 468$, $SD = 2.05$). For gang membership, 46.4% of respondents in this study identify themselves as gang members ($N = 534$, $SD = .499$). Of the 561 respondents, 13.3% are categorized as mixed heritage ($N = 540$, $SD = .340$). Only 10.9% ($N = 561$, $SD = 312$) of the sample are girls. The average age of respondents is 16.4 years ($N = 561$, $SD = 1.29$). The average number of times respondents reported having been arrested is 5.93 ($N = 494$, $SD = 7.14$).

Bivariate Analysis

When comparing the mixed-heritage adolescents with single-heritage adolescents, very similar average ages ($Ms = 16.47$ and 16.44; $SDs = 1.39$ and 1.26, respectively) were found. Mixed-heritage and single-heritage adolescents also have very similar self-esteem scores (General: $Ms = 9.63$ and 9.74, $SDs = 3.24$ and 3.2; Social: $Ms = 5.76$ and 5.61, $SDs = 1.52$ and 1.75; Personal: $Ms = 3.97$ and 3.87, $SDs = 2.08$ and 2.02; all respectively). Mixed-heritage adolescents have a slightly higher number of arrests ($M = 6.8$, $SD = 10.946$) compared with single-heritage adolescents ($M = 5.82$, $SD = 6.51$).

These findings show that within a clinical population mixed-heritage adolescents are similar to single-heritage adolescents. These results do not indicate additional self-esteem problems from mixed heritage, but instead may reflect what both the single-heritage and mixed-heritage adolescents have in common; they are recipients of racism and are caught between two cultures. This adds to the literature that uses nonclinical samples and found mixed-heritage youths and adults to be similar with respect to mental health issues.

To determine the effects of both race/ethnicity (minority group memberships versus majority group membership) and heritage (mixed heritage vs. single heritage), we compared self-esteem scores for majority-group single-heritage youth, minority-group single-heritage youth, and minority-group mixed-heritage youth (no mixed-heritage youth in the sample identified as white/Caucasian). For general self-esteem, majority-group single-heritage youth scored an average of 10.65 ($SD = 3.64$), minority-group single-heritage youth an average of 9.66 ($SD = 3.18$); and minority-group mixed-heritage youth an average of 9.63 ($SD = 3.24$). Using analysis of variance (ANOVA), it was determined that these differences were not statistically significant. For personal self-esteem, majority-group single-heritage youth scored an average of 5.17 ($SD = 2.30$), minority-group single-heritage youth an average of 3.76 ($SD = 1.97$), and minority-group mixed-heritage youth an average of 3.97 ($SD = 2.08$). Using ANOVA, it was determined that these differences were statistically significant ($p < .001$). Finally, for social self-esteem, majority-group single-heritage youth scored an average of 6.21 ($SD = 1.70$), minority-group single-heritage youth an average of 5.56 ($SD = 1.75$), and minority-group mixed-heritage youth an average of 5.76 ($SD = 1.72$). ANOVA determined that there were no significant differences between these scores.

These results suggest that mixed-heritage youth match closely the minority-group single-heritage youth at least in terms of self-esteem. The self-esteem scores of the minority-group single-heritage youth and the nonwhite mixed-heritage youth are very similar, and both differ from their majority-group counterparts. Majority-group status yields higher self-esteem and minority-group status lower self-esteem (regardless of whether one is a single-heritage or mixed-heritage youth). This finding supports the one-drop rule, especially for this clinical sample. However, mixed-heritage youth overall do not differ from single-heritage youth when comparing self-esteem scores. This is likely because most single-heritage youth (93.1%) are minority group members.

Interestingly, a greater proportion of the girls in this clinical sample (31%) than boys (11.2%) are of mixed heritage (this relationship between sex and single- vs. mixed-race heritage is statistically significant, Pearson's Chi-Square = 17.62 (df = 1, N = 520, p = .096). Further, 96.6% of the girls are minority group members, and 3.4% are majority group members. For boys, 92.6% are minority group members, and 7.4% are majority group members. As noted, mixed-heritage youth in this sample seem to match closely with their minority-group single-heritage counterparts. Although several of the mixed-heritage youth have a majority-group parent, none identified with the majority group. The fact that this sample has so many more mixed-heritage girls than boys and more minority-group girls than boys suggests that minority status or mixed-heritage status may have more of an impact on girls' lives than on boys' lives. Minority status appears to be a detriment for women in the criminal justice system. Chesney-Lind (1997) suggests, for example, that "the most recent women's 'crime wave' appears to be a cultural attempt to reframe the problems of racism and sexism in society" (p. 57). Prior research has also suggested that minority status for women is more detrimental for criminal justice processing than it is for men. Chesney-Lind and Shelden (1998) state, "For girls of color, particularly African American girls, bootstrapping may be the response to their acting out, but for white girls a different approach is taken: 'transinstitutionalization' into the world of private institutions and placements" (p. 162). Whereas white girls may be treated with "chivalry" in crime processing, women of color are often treated more harshly. It appears that the impact of being female and minority applies also for mixed-heritage women.

Mixed-heritage adolescents are also less likely to be gang members (36.6%) than nongang members (63.4%), whereas single-heritage adolescents are only slightly more likely to be gang members (52.8%) compared with nongang members (47.2%). This relationship approaches statistical significance, Pearson's Chi-Square = 2.77 (df = 1, N = 520, p = .096). This finding may have something to do with the racial homogeneity found within gangs. Mixed-heritage youths may not feel as comfortable in this kind of environment. This inference may have some bearing because mixed-heritage adolescents who identify with the other category and specify more than one heritage for race/ethnicity (n = 11) are less likely to belong to gangs (n = 8 compared with 2 respondents who do not belong to a gang; 1 did not answer the question on gang membership).

Table 17.1 displays the correlation matrix for the variables used in the analysis. Not surprisingly, the self-esteem variables are highly correlated with one another but not so high as to preclude including them as independent variables within the same equation. In addition, males have significantly higher personal self-esteem than do females, although there is no significant difference between males and females for general or social self-esteem. This finding supports Esbensen's and Deschenes's studies that female gang members, in this case female delinquents in general, have lower self-esteem than do their male counterparts (in this case, personal self-esteem). Interestingly, gang members have lower general and personal self-esteem than do nongang members; however, there is no significant difference between gang and nongang members' social self-esteem, although it is close to statistical significance. This finding adds to the mixed literature on delinquency, gang membership, and self-esteem, with some preliminary support for Wang's (1994) and Esbensen's and Deschenes's (1998) conclusions. Mixed

Table 17.1 Correlations for Variables Used in the Analysis

Variable	General S.E.	Personal S.E.	Social S.E.	Mixed Heritage	Gang Affiliate	Male	Age	No. Arrests
Gen. S.E.	1.00							
	.							
	n = 436							
Per. S.E.	.647	1.00						
	p = .000	.						
	n = 408	n = 468						
Soc. S.E.	.475	.274	1.00					
	p = .000	p = .000	.					
	n = 402	n = 420	n = 459					
Mixed heritage	−.012	.016	.029	1.00				
	p = .804	p = .728	p = .536	.				
	n = 420	n = 451	n = 445	n = 540				
Gang Af.	−.162	−.109	−.083	−.073	1.00			
	p = .001	p = .021	p = .083	p = .096	.			
	n = 422	n = 451	n = 440	n = 520	n = 534			
Male	.075	.111	.059	−.181	.096	1.00		
	p = .116	p = .016	p = .207	p = .000	p = .027	.		
	n = 436	n = 468	n = 459	n = 540	n = 534	n = 561		
Age	.094	.060	.132	.006	.025	.122	1.00	
	p = .050	p = .193	p = .005	p = .897	p = .565	p = .004	.	
	n = 436	n = 468	n = 459	n = 540	n = 534	n = 561	n = 561	
No. arrests	−.118	−.002	−.077	.045	.155	.081	−.029	1.00
	p = .020	p = .971	p = .122	p = .328	p = .001	p = .073	p = .521	.
	n = 388	n = 419	n = 408	n = 480	n = 479	n = 494	n = 494	n = 494

heritage is not significantly correlated with general, personal, or social self-esteem. This result supports the literature that monoracial or single-heritage people do not differ from mixed-heritage or multiracial people on self-esteem; however, instead of this finding resulting from nonclinical samples, it was found in a clinical sample. In addition, the older the adolescent, the higher the general and social self-esteem, indicating that age alone will take care of some self-esteem problems. This is consistent with working through identity issues. Finally, the greater the number of arrests, the lower the general self-esteem. This finding may reflect Stager et al's (1983) finding that deviant social labeling is associated with low self-esteem. A greater number of arrests may increasingly lead to a negative label.

Multivariate Analysis

To further examine the relationship among self-esteem, gang affiliation, and mixed heritage, OLS and logistic regressions were performed. Because the literature is not clear as to whether self-esteem precedes gang affiliation or vice versa, both variables were considered as dependent variables in different models. Logistic regression was run for gang affiliation because this variable is a dichotomous dependent variable.[8] OLS regression was run for the self-esteem variables because they are continuous dependent variables.

Table 17.2 displays the results of the first model, the logistic regression of mixed heritage, general social self-esteem, social

Table 17.2 Logistic Regression for Self-Esteem (S.E.) and Select Variables on Gang Affiliation

Variable	β	SE	p
Mixed heritage	−.155	.376	.681
General S.E.	−.084	.051	.101
Social S.E.	.001	.079	.992
Personal S.E.	−.050	.077	.511
Male	.354	.393	.367
Age	.088	.095	.354
No. arrests	.063	.022	.004
Constant	−1.380	1.538	.370

self-esteem, personal self-esteem, sex, age, and number of arrests on gang affiliation.

Controlling for sex, age, and number of arrests in the model, none of the self-esteem variables are significant predictors of gang affiliation, although general self-esteem did approach significance ($p = .101$). Additionally, mixed heritage is not significant in predicting gang membership in this model. In fact, only number of arrests is a significant predictor of gang affiliation. This finding contradicts that of other researchers who have found self-esteem a significant predictor of gang membership. It appears that this relationship may be a spurious one because number of arrests is related to both general self-esteem and gang membership, and these relationships are statistically significant. Sex is also related to both personal self-esteem and gang membership. Perhaps because this entire sample is "delinquent," significance is more difficult to obtain. Most research focuses on gang members versus nongang members in the high school environment, with the assumption that the nongang members, by and large, are not delinquent (or so labeled). It is interesting to find the relationship between number of arrests and gang membership among this sample of detained delinquents. Even among delinquents, gang members are more "seriously" delinquent at least with regard to getting caught.

The second multivariate analysis includes three models, one each for social, personal, and general self-esteem. This was done to determine whether different variables predicted the different types of self-esteem. Table 17.3 shows results of OLS regression of gang affiliation, mixed heritage, sex, age, and number of arrests on social self-esteem. Table 17.4 displays results of OLS regression of gang affiliation, mixed heritage, sex, age, and number of arrests on personal self-esteem. Finally, Table 17.5 shows results of OLS regression of gang affiliation, mixed heritage, sex, age, and number of arrests on general self-esteem.

For all three models, only gang membership and age are significant predictors of the various types of self-esteem. Nongang members and older juveniles have higher self-esteem. This finding, then, confirms prior research suggesting a relationship between gang membership and lower self-esteem. Gang membership is related to general self-esteem and number of arrests at the bivariate level, and the relationship between number of arrests and general self-esteem is not statistically significant at the multivariate level. It appears, then, that the relationship between general self-esteem and number of arrests is likely spurious. Mixed heritage is not a significant predictor of any type of self-esteem, although it approaches significance for social self-esteem ($p = .122$). Again, this finding supports the research that

Table 17.3 Ordinary Least Squares Regression for Select Variables on Social Self-Esteem

Variable	β	SE	p
Mixed heritage	.415	.268	.122
Gang affiliate	−.298	.177	.092
Male	.393	.295	.184
Age	.147	.070	.037
No. arrests	−.001	.012	.238
Constant	3.04	1.14	.008

Table 17.4 Ordinary Least Squares Regression for Select Variables on Personal Self-Esteem

Variable	β	SE	p
Mixed heritage	.008	.308	.783
Gang affiliate	−.595	.203	.004
Male	.535	.329	.105
Age	.168	.080	.036
No. arrests	.000	.013	.655
Constant	.813	1.30	.533

Table 17.5 Ordinary Least Squares Regression for Select Variables on General Self-Esteem

Variable	β	SE	p
Mixed heritage	−.139	.518	.789
Gang affiliate	−1.130	.340	.001
Male	.584	.542	.282
Age	.221	.133	.097
No. arrests	−.004	.025	.103
Constant	6.228	2.16	.004

single-heritage or monoracial identity and mixed-heritage or multiracial identity do not determine self-esteem.

CONCLUSIONS

A smaller number of incarcerated mixed-heritage adolescents identify with a mixed race/ethnicity than those who identify with a single heritage. Also, among mixed-heritage adolescents who identify with a single heritage, all identify with a minority group. Because a mixed-race identity has been connected with mental health, it is not surprising to find a lack of a strong presence of a mixed-heritage identity among this clinical group. It is also more than likely that SES has some bearing on this finding. Children from higher SES may be able to afford to assert their desired identities more easily than those from lower SES. Mixed-race people involved in the multiracial movement tend to be more advantaged than the average incarcerated adolescent.

One interesting finding of this research is that a higher percentage of incarcerated females are mixed heritage than are males. This raises some interesting questions about the effects of mixed heritage for males versus females. Because this is an incarcerated sample, it may be that the effects or interpretations of mixed heritage are more negative for females than for males at least during adolescence. Clearly, more research is needed in this area.

Another interesting finding was that mixed-heritage adolescents were less likely to be gang members than were single-heritage adolescents. Perhaps the racial composition of gangs (e.g., black gangs, Hispanic gangs) makes gangs a more difficult subculture in which mixed-heritage youth may find "family" or "protection" than it is for their single-heritage counterparts. The role of number of arrests and gang membership and their relationships to self-esteem are not clear because of the possibilities of spurious relationships and issues of time order.

Also interesting is the fact that mixed-heritage youth did not statistically differ from their single-heritage counterparts with regard to self-esteem scores. However, a closer look at majority versus minority status makes it clear that the mixed-heritage youth in this sample identify as minority group members (not one having identified with the majority group). Compared with the majority group, both single- and mixed-heritage minority youth had lower self-esteem scores. One policy implication of this finding is that programs to enhance self-esteem should be adopted by the probation camps. Programs that are especially racially and culturally sensitive would be ideal with this "captive" audience.

Temporal ordering is problematic when using cross-sectional data. Few studies of gangs use longitudinal data, especially in determining causal ordering of self-esteem and joining a gang. It is, therefore, difficult to determine whether the gang increases or decreases a youth's self-esteem after joining. A reasonable temporal interpretation of the data from this and other studies would be that marginalized youth have lower

self-esteem to begin with. They join the gang to find a place of belonging, family, and importance. However, the longer they are in the gang, the more ostracized they become from society, being labeled a "gang member" with all of the concomitant negative connotations. The longer they remain in the gang, the more separate they become from conventional societal institutions: school, perhaps their families, the mall, the park. The gang youth watch their friends die, predict they themselves will not survive much beyond their early 20s, cannot find jobs, and are getting arrested. These factors likely have a negative impact on their self-esteem. One variable missing from this area of research on gangs and self-esteem is length of time in the gang. This variable would be helpful, even for cross-sectional data, in determining how gang tenure impacts self-esteem. Although we have no measure of length of time in a gang, we do have a proxy: number of arrests. The longer the youth is in a gang, the more arrests she or he is likely to have. Number of arrests is negatively correlated with self-esteem. Further research is needed to test this relationship in more detail.

It was argued earlier that the context with which understanding of race comes to be is more important than the actual designation of mixed heritage. Special circumstances surround the arena in which adolescents define themselves and make choices to participate in delinquent behavior, including gang membership. A more in-depth study of the context of the school, home, and community of mixed-heritage, incarcerated teenagers and how it impacts identity selection and delinquent behavior is warranted. Because monoracial identification is also a stage for mixed-heritage people, it may be that these adolescents are not stuck in a single-heritage identity. More longitudinal studies with a qualitative analysis on clinical populations might address this issue.

NOTES

1. Web site address: www.lapdonline.org.

2. See Reuter (1918, 1934), Park (1928, 1931), and Stonequist (1937) for more information.

3. See D. Johnson (1992), Williams (1992), and Daniel (1996) for studies that capture the complexity of identity for mixed-race people.

4. Pinderhughes (1995) describes how a teenager from an affluent suburban neighborhood once doing well, with friends and achieving success at school, found that her girlfriends became distant and the boys at school would not date her. It was suggested that she date the students of color who were bused in.

5. Unfortunately, the specific percentage for each camp is not available.

6. These categories were recommended by an advisory board to reflect the racial/ethnic categories of the Los Angeles Probation Department's report on probation camp demographics.

7. For example, Winfree, Fuller, Vigil, and Mays (1992), in comparing self-identification with a more restrictive definition of gang membership, found a self-reported definition to be more inclusive. Criteria often used in more restrictive definitions include style of dress, friends, and other variables that are questionable in their ability to predict gang membership.

8. The use of OLS for a dichotomous dependent variable leads to problems of inefficient coefficients because of heteroscedasticity, non-normal error distribution, and bias resulting from specification error (Achen, 1982).

REFERENCES

Achen, C. H. (1982). *Interpreting and using regression.* Newbury Park, CA: Sage.

American Psychiatric Association. (1994). *Diagnostic and statistical manual of mental disorders* (4th ed.). Washington, DC: Author.

Arthur, R. F. (1989). How to help gangs win the self-esteem battle. *The School Administrator, 46*(5), 8-20.

Bowles, D. D. (1993). Bi-racial identity: Children born to African-American and white couples. *Clinical Social Work Journal, 21,* 417-428.

Brown, P. M. (1990). Biracial identity and social marginality. *Child and Adolescent Social Work, 7,* 319-337.

California Department of Justice. (1998). *Homicide in California 1998.* Sacramento: Attorney General's Office, Division of Criminal Justice Information Services.

Cauce, A. M., Hiraga, Y., Mason, C., Aguilar, T., Ordonez N., & Gonzales, N. (1992). Between a rock and a hard place: Social adjustment of biracial youth. In M. P. P. Root (Ed.), *Racially mixed people in America* (pp. 207-222). Newbury Park, CA: Sage.

Chassin, L., & Stager, S. F. (1984). Determinants of self-esteem among incarcerated delinquents. *Social Psychology Quarterly, 47,* 382-390.

Chesney-Lind, M. (1997). *The female offender: Girls, women, and crime.* Thousand Oaks, CA: Sage.

Chesney-Lind, M., & Shelden, R. G. (1998). *Girls, delinquency, and juvenile justice* (2nd ed.). Belmont, CA: West/Wadsworth/ITP.

Daniel, G. R. (1996). Black and white identity in the new millennium: Unsevering the ties that bind. In M. P. P. Root (Ed.), *The multiracial experience* (pp. 211-226). Thousand Oaks, CA: Sage.

Erickson, H. (1959). Identity and the life cycle. *Psychological Issues,1,* 18-64.

Erickson, H. (1968). *Identity, youth and crisis.* New York: W.W. Norton.

Esbensen, F.-A., & Deschenes, E. P. (1998). A multisite examination of youth gang membership: Does gender matter? *Criminology, 36*(4), 799-827.

Esbensen, F.-A., & Deschenes, E. P. (1999). Differences between gang girls and gang boys. *Youth & Society, 31*(1), 27-53.

Field, L. D. (1996). Piecing together the puzzle: Self-concept and group identity in biracial black/white youth. In M. P. P. Root (Ed.), *The multiracial experience* (pp. 211-226). Thousand Oaks, CA: Sage.

Fong, R., Spickard, P. R., & Ewalt, P. L. (1995). A multiracial reality: Issues for social work. *Social Work, 40,* 725-728.

Forest, C., & Tambor, E. (2000). The health profile of incarcerated male youths. *Pediatrics, 105*(1), 286-291.

Gibbs, J. T., & Hines, A. M. (1992). Negotiating ethnic identity: Issues for black-white biracial adolescents. In M. P. P. Root (Ed.), *Racially mixed people in America* (pp. 223-238). Newbury Park, CA: Sage.

Hall, C. C. I. (1992). Please choose one: Ethnic identity choices for biracial individuals. In M. P. P. Root (Ed.), *Racially mixed people in America* (pp. 250-264). Newbury Park, CA: Sage.

Herring, R. D. (1995). Developing biracial ethnic identity: A review of the increasing dilemma. *Journal of Multicultural Counseling and Development, 23,* 29-38.

Horowitz, R., & Schwartz, G. (1974). Honor, normative ambiguity and gang violence. *American Sociological Review, 39,* 238-251.

Huizinga, D., & Jakob-Chein, C. (1998). The contemporaneous co-occurrence of serious and violent juvenile offending and other problem behaviors. In R. Loeber & D. P. Farrington (Eds.), *Serious & violent juvenile offenders: Risk factors and successful interventions* (pp. 47-67). Thousand Oaks, CA: Sage.

Jacobs, J. H. (1992). Identity development in biracial children. In M. P. P. Root (Ed.), *Racially mixed people in America* (pp. 190-206). Newbury Park, CA: Sage.

Jang, S. J., & Thornberry, T. P. (1998). Self-esteem, delinquent peers, and delinquency: A test of the self-enhancement thesis. *American Sociological Review, 63,* 586-598.

Johnson, D. J. (1992). Developmental pathways: Toward an ecological theoretical formulation of race identity. In M. P. P. Root (Ed.), *Racially mixed people in America* (pp. 37-49). Newbury Park, CA: Sage.

Johnson, R. C. (1992). Offspring of cross-race and cross-ethnic marriages in Hawaii. In M. P. P. Root (Ed.), *Racially mixed people in America* (pp. 238-249). Newbury Park, CA: Sage.

Kahn, J. S., & Denmon, J. (1997). An examination of social science literature pertaining to multiracial identity: A historical perspective. *Journal of Multicultural Social Work, 6*(1/2), 117-138.

Kerwin, C., Ponterotto, J. G., Jackson, B. L., & Harris, A. (1993). Racial identity in biracial children: A qualitative investigation. *Journal of Counseling Psychology, 40,* 221-231.

Kich, G. K. (1992). The developmental process of asserting a biracial, bicultural identity. In M. P. P. Root (Ed.), *Racially mixed people in America* (pp. 304-317). Newbury Park, CA: Sage.

Mass, A. I. (1992). Interracial Japanese Americans: The best of both worlds or the end of the Japanese American community? In M. P. P. Root (Ed.), *Racially mixed people in America* (pp. 265-279). Newbury Park, CA: Sage.

McCarthy, J., & Hoge, D. R. (1984). The dynamics of self-esteem and delinquency. *American Journal of Sociology, 90,* 396-410.

McRoy, R. G., & Freeman, E. (1986). Racial-identity issues among mixed-race children. *Social Work in Education, 8,* 164-174.

Overmier, K. (1990). Biracial adolescents: Areas of conflict in identity formation. *Journal of Applied Social Sciences, 14,* 157-177.

Owens, T. (1994). Two dimensions of self-esteem: Reciprocal Effects of positive self-worth and self-deprecation on adolescent problems. *American Sociological Review, 59,* 391-407.

Park, R. E. (1928). Human migration and the marginal man. *American Journal of Sociology, 6,* 881-893.

Park, R. E. (1931). Mentality of racial hybrids. *American Journal of Sociology, 36,* 534-551.

Pinderhughes, E. (1995). Biracial identity-asset or handicap? In H. W. Harris, H. C. Blue, & E. E. H. Griffith (Eds.), *Racial and ethnic identity* (pp. 73-93). New York: Routledge.

Reuter. E. B. (1918). *The mulatto in the United States: Including a study of the role of mixed-blood races throughout the world.* Boston: Badger.

Reuter, E. B. (Ed.). (1934). *Race and culture contacts* (1ˢᵗ edition). London: McGraw-Hill.

Reuter, E. B. (1937). *The marginal man: A study in personality and culture conflict.* New York: Russell & Russell.

Reynolds, A. L., & Pope, R. L. (1991). Complexities of diversity: Exploring multiple oppressions. *Journal of Counseling and Development, 70,* 174-180.

Rockquemore, K. A. (1998). Between black and white: Exploring the biracial experience. *Race and Society, 1*(2), 197-212.

Root, M. P. P. (1990). Resolving "other" status: Identity development of biracial individuals. In L. Brown & M. P. P. Root (Ed.), *Complexity and diversity in feminist theory and therapy* (pp. 185-205). New York: Haworth.

Root, M. P. P. (1992). Back to the drawing board: Methodological issues in research on multiracial people. In M. P. P. Root (Ed.), *Racially mixed people in America* (pp. 181-189). Newbury Park, CA: Sage.

Stager, S. F., Chassin, L., & David, R. (1983). Determinants of self-esteem among labeled adolescents. *Social Psychology Quarterly, 46,* 3-10.

Stephan, C. W. (1992). Mixed-heritage individuals: Ethnic identity and trait characteristics. In M. P. P. Root (Ed.), *Racially mixed people in America* (pp. 50-63). Newbury Park, CA: Sage.

Stonequist, E. U. (1937). *The marginal man: A study in personality and culture conflict,* New York: Russell and Russell.

Thornton, M. C. (1996). Hidden agendas, identity theories, and multiracial people. In M. P. P. Root (Ed.), *The multiracial experience* (pp. 211-226). Thousand Oaks, CA: Sage.

U.S. Department of Justice. (2000). *1998 National Youth Gang Survey.* Washington, DC: Office of Justice Programs.

Vigil, J. D., & Yun, S. C. (1996). Southern California gangs: Comparative ethnicity and social control. In C. R. Huff (Ed.), *Gangs in America* (2nd ed., pp. 139-156). Thousand Oaks, CA: Sage.

Wang, A. Y. (1994). Pride and prejudice in high school gang members. *Adolescence, 29*(114), 279-291.

Wardle, F. (1996). Multicultural education. In M. P. P. Root (Ed.), *The multiracial experience* (pp. 380-391). Thousand Oaks, CA: Sage.

Wehrly, B., Kenney, K. R., & Kenney, M. E. (1999). *Counseling multiracial families.* Thousand Oaks, CA: Sage.

Williams, T. K. (1992). Prism lives: Identity binational Amerasians. In M. P. P. Root (Ed.), *Racially mixed people in America* (pp. 280-303). Newbury Park, CA: Sage.

Winfree, L. T., Jr., Fuller, K., Vigil, T., & Mays, G. L. (1992). The definition and measurement of 'gang status': Policy implications for juvenile justice. *Juvenile & Family Court Journal, 43*(1), 19-38.

Winn, N. N., & Priest, R. (1993). Counseling biracial children: A forgotten component of multicultural counseling. *Family Therapy, 20,* 29-36.

CHAPTER 18

Black/White Interracial Couples and the Beliefs That Help Them to Bridge the Racial Divide

KRISTYAN M. KOURI

California State University, Northridge

This chapter examines the belief systems that serve to guide the behavior of 20 black/white interracial couples living in Los Angeles. While a variety of factors, taken together, influence interracial marriage, I examine one particular piece of this puzzle: the effect of American ideologies of equality. I argue that a person's whole-hearted adaptation of these cultural frameworks of equality play a strong role in a couple's decision to marry.

Although marriage between black and white individuals remains relatively rare, interracial marriage has slowly continued to rise. Whereas in 1990 there were only 211,000 black/white interracial marriages, in 1998 the number rose to 330,000, an increase of 56%. Still 330,000 is a very small number when compared with the 55 million married couples living in the United States (U.S. Census Bureau, 1999).

The social forces that serve to hinder black/white interracial marriage are rooted deeply in America's past. For most of the colonial and national periods, America instituted a set of laws that served to thwart interracial marriages, making marriages between blacks and whites against the law. The civil rights struggle, however, ultimately forced the American government to curtail the discriminatory laws that mandated segregation and prohibited miscegenation. It also induced the government to institute programs such as affirmative action, which brought some blacks and whites together in situations of relative equality.

AUTHOR'S NOTE: In addition to editors Herman DeBose and Loretta Winters, I would like to thank James Allen, Merry Ovnick, and Barrie Thorne for reading earlier drafts of this chapter.

Even though the U.S. Supreme Court overturned the laws that prevented interracial marriage in 1967 (*Loving v. Commonwealth of Virginia*), social barriers that limit the kinds of interactions that lead to marriage between blacks and whites remain strong. In the contemporary United States, a general uneasiness continues to exist between the two groups, an uneasiness that is a direct result of slavery and the all-encompassing discriminatory practices that existed thereafter. So while the social changes brought about by the civil rights struggle inevitably led to some interracial unions, the desegregation of schools and the workplace has failed to ameliorate the plethora of social constraints that continue to keep blacks and whites apart. Blacks and whites may work together in the office or sit beside each other in the classroom, but they fail to socialize during off-hours. This general apprehensiveness severely limits the kind of friendship formation that precedes marriage.

Because those black and white individuals who do choose to marry must overcome a complex set of social forces that hinder black/white unions, it is no wonder that that marriage rates between black and white individuals remain so low. Interracial couples are, therefore, made up of people who were somehow able to transcend those persistent and powerful cultural barricades. This makes their life stories especially important because they provide us with examples of individuals who were able to surmount the social barriers that keep blacks and whites apart. Their ability to overcome the kinds of thinking that impedes interracial marriage may indeed provide us with clues for bringing together groups of people who have endured long-standing conflicts.

LITERATURE REVIEW

The existing research on black/white interracial marriage suggests that a number of factors contribute to this phenomenon. Social historian Paul Spickard (1989) believes that cultural imagery plays a role in the formation of interracial unions. When it comes to black/white interracial marriage, for example, he points to the fact that there are three times as many black male/white female combinations as that of black female/white male combinations. Drawing from a comparative historical method of data collection and analysis, Spickard asserts that these gender differences are largely the result of the cultural meanings associated with black and white women and men.

For example, Spickard writes that black males have a tendency to see white women as "prettier," "nicer," and more "pliable" than their black counterparts. Conversely, black women, who were perpetually exploited by white men during slavery and after emancipation, continue to view white men with suspicion. In addition, black women tend to find black men far more physically and culturally appealing. As well, white men, Spickard argues, are apt to find black women unattractive because they fail to measure up to the Anglocentric standards of American beauty and because they are thought to be dominant, overbearing, and disagreeable.

Whereas Spickard's historical research is drawn from secondary sources, other researchers have made use of empirical data collection methods. In 1978 Earnest Porterfield interviewed 44 black/white couples living in Illinois, Ohio, Alabama, and Mississippi. He discovered that most of his respondents met in integrated settings, shared common interests, and chose to marry as a result of love and overall compatibility. Porterfield concluded that the desegregation of American institutions such as the schools and the workplace provided those black and white individuals with relatively equal social standing the opportunity to become acquainted with each other. As a result, some of them ultimately chose to marry. I came to this same conclusion in my earlier study of 29 interracial couples living in the Los Angeles area (Kouri & Lasswell, 1993).

Rosenblatt, Karis, and Powell (1995) conducted a study drawn from the interviews of black/white interracial couples living in the Minneapolis/St. Paul area and they present their research in the book, *Multiracial Couples: Black and White Voices*. Although these social scientists uncovered some of the same patterns that are presented in this chapter they admittedly provide their readers with little theoretical interpretation of their findings. Their work is thus intended to present stories of interracial couples from their own points of view.

In doing so Rosenblatt et al. illustrate the ways in which their respondents dealt with the ever-present racism and discrimination that overshadowed thier lives. With this in mind, they examined their respondents' decisions to marry, relationships with families of origin, and their interactions with the community at large. These investigators report that the vast majority of their Minneapolis informants were able to overcome any difficulties associated with their marriage and families and were thus able to lead satisfying and productive lives.

However, McNamara, Tempenis, and Walton (1999), in their text *Crossing the Line: Interracial Couples in the South,* do not come to these same positive conclusions. The researchers discovered that it was common for interracial couples living in the northern region of South Carolina to be faced with extreme opposition from both their families and the community, so much so that the couples were driven to isolation. Drawing from the work of Irving Goffman (1963), the authors argue that this social withdrawal was the strategy used to manage the stigmas they incurred on entering into a black/white interracial marriage.

Why did so many of their respondents meet with such persistent family opposition?

McNamara et al. argue that the parents of their informants, both black and white, had little meaningful contact with groups of people unlike themselves. They support their argument with a detailed discussion of Gordon Allport's (1955) contact theory, specifically addressing the kinds of social interactions that would lead to a reduction in prejudice.

Whatever the thrust of the analysis, it is obvious that some type of contact must occur before an interracial marriage can take place, because people must meet before they marry. Allport (1955) delineated a number of factors that he believed would work together with contact to reduce racial tensions. He asserted that the individuals involved must first be of equal social standing and must then be in situations that allow ample opportunity for communication. In this way, people would learn that the common stereotypes associated with blacks and whites were patently false.

Still, the relationship between contact and improved relations between blacks and whites is rather tricky, because as Forbes (1997) has shown, increased interaction does not necessarily lead to improved relations. Forbes (1997) reviewed a plethora of studies that examine school integration and change in attitudes among black and white students who were believed to be on equal social footing and who were in close enough proximity to engage in meaningful conversation. The findings were inconclusive; sometimes there was a slight reduction of prejudice, sometimes there was no change, and other times there was an actual increase in prejudicial attitudes. In addition, Forbes notes that when people are surveyed in large cities, the fewer the minorities the lower the prejudicial attitudes. Likewise, the greater the percentage of minorities living in a given community leads to an increase in prejudiced points of view. Because one would presume that the more blacks and whites living in close proximity the greater is the chance for contact, it would seem that contact actually exacerbated racial hostilities.

Qualitative studies that examine the interactions between blacks and whites in housing projects or residential areas, however, do find support for contact theory (Forbes, 1997). When blacks and whites in close residential proximity interact on a regular basis, friendships do occur and prejudicial attitudes decrease.

Correspondingly, my research, which is also a small-scale qualitative study, also confirms Allport's hypothesis. The interviews show that contact does lead to at least some friendships between blacks and whites, friendships that ultimately led to marriage. The individuals I interviewed were indeed people of equal social standing who found themselves in places where they could communicate. In addition, most of them believed that contact with black and white individuals played a part in their decision to enter into an interracial marriage.

There is, however, more to this picture than just mere contact. What struck me about my informants was their sincere belief that blacks and whites are similar rather than different and equal rather than inferior. Thus, the whole-hearted adaptation of an ideology that stresses equality or mitigates difference works with contact to bring about interracial marriage. It is this finding that clearly adds to what we know about the inception of interracial marriage, and thus it is this finding that I focus on here.

METHOD

After interviewing 29 black/white interracial couples in an earlier study, I had a number of questions that warranted further exploration. As a result, I decided to conduct another, more focused research project on this same topic. In this second study, I interviewed 20 black/white interracial couples: 10 included black women married to white men and 10 included white women married to black men. The types of research question that elicited the responses presented here were as follows: "It is common knowledge that black/white interracial marriages are less than common. What is it about you that allowed you to enter into a relationship that is considered taboo by much of our society?" or "Did your parents ever talk to you about interracial marriage while you were growing up?"

All of the couples were interviewed together in their homes. The women and men, who had all been legally married for a period ranging from 3 and 24 years, had at least one black/white multiracial child. Our conversations, which ranged in length from 1 to 3 hr, were tape-recorded and later transcribed.

I found all of my respondents through a snowball sampling procedure, because interracial couples are relatively rare and thus hard to find. Because this sample is small in number and not random, these findings cannot be generalized to all interracial couples living in the United States. Nevertheless, these rich conversational data are far from meaningless for they do provide insight into what life might be like for interracial couples living in the United States.

I attempted to interview women and men of middle-class status as inferred from income, education, and occupation. However, in the end, I obtained a sample of people who could be loosely placed into upper-middle-, middle-, and lower-middle-class socioeconomic status categories.

The vast majority of these women and men were in their late 30s and 40s. The black women were between the ages of 38 and 45 years of age; the white men between the ages of 38 and 49 years; the white women between 26 and 46 years of age; and the black men between 28 and 49 years of age.

Only one couple, a black husband and white wife, were still in their 20s.

In analyzing the transcribed interviews, I used the Glaser and Strauss (1967) method of constant comparison as well as the universal semantics method outlined by James Spradley (1979). Because universal semantic relationships exist in all human languages (Spradley, 1979), categories of thought derived from these semantic relationships can, therefore, be used to uncover a respondent's own way of thinking. In this way, the researcher can elicit a pure observation rather than one riddled with the researcher's bias. One such semantic relationship, for example, entails strict inclusion: X is a kind of Y or, for example, "Sally is a particular kind of person." Another semantic relationship involves rationale: X is a reason for doing Y or, for example, "This is the reason why I chose to marry my spouse." I then made lists of all of the semantic relationships I could find. One such list included all of the different reasons why the couples thought they were able to transcend rules of endogamy, or X is the reason I was able to do Y. Afterward, I attempted to make theoretical sense of the entire category.

Glaser and Strauss (1967) argue that when social scientists limit their analysis to the verification of preexisting theories, they often are in danger of forcing their data to fit within the confines of a preconceived framework. Drawing from these ideas, I attempted to develop fresh theoretical interpretations of the data, working inductively rather than deductively and weaving formal theories into the analysis when appropriate.

FINDINGS

A number of themes emerged from my intensive interviews that correspond to what other researchers have discovered about black/white interracial marriage. In accordance with earlier work (Kouri & Lasswell, 1993; Porterfield, 1978), my second set of respondents often met in integrated or partially integrated settings. Nine of the couples met at work, two met in high school, three met in college, two met at church, one met at a gym, another met at a party, and another at a dance. The vast majority of my respondents stated they married a "person" rather than an individual who was either black or white. When I asked them what attracted them to each other, their responses were made up of phrases such as "He was a good person," "We were both interested in our children, " "We wanted the same things out of life," and "I knew we could build something together." Some respondents did, however, allude to the cultural images and/or notions of difference associated with blacks and whites that Spickard (1989) believes have a strong impact on interracial marriage rates. This finding emerged when the respondents talked about their initial meetings with their future spouse. For example, a number of the black women I spoke with first reacted to their future white husbands with skepticism and disdain. However, in accordance with Allport (1955), after these women became acquainted with their future husbands and began to see them as individuals rather than as a caricature or cultural stereotype, their feelings began to change. Tina, a black woman, put it this way:

> Well, we found out, to my surprise, that we had things in common and that we shared the same values. Well, I thought that maybe we wouldn't because I had prejudices too, that because we were different ethnicities we wouldn't have a whole lot to share. I liked his qualities and respect and commitment and sincerity; those sorts of things were very important. He's worked all of his life in an integrated setting.

Similarly, Laura met her white husband while working in an educational enrichment program for black youth:

You asked what I like about him? Once I got to know him I did. When I first met him the first thing I thought is 'What is this white dude doing in the center?' I met so many young white males and females who were sort of disassociating themselves from their own culture and sort of embedding themselves in black culture and wanting to be black. And after I was in the program for about four months, I realized he was very sincere, that he was not trying to be black. He was who he was [and] he genuinely liked being there. And the kids, he genuinely liked doing car washes with them.

Maureen was one of the few people who were either able or willing to articulate the cultural meanings they assigned to white people. However, the serious conversations she held with the white man who would one day become her husband helped her to broaden her perspective.

I was surprised; it was real scary. Basically, it was after I sat down and talked with [my husband], because I was no different than a lot of people . . . a lot of the myths were there. When I talk about the myths—'cause I remember this real well—when [my husband] shared with me his background and his life and what had happened with him, [it] was so similar to mine. When you came in a predominantly black area—how can I explain it—you are kind of taught and you hear whites are so much better off than blacks. I guess it was things I heard of as a kid. My thoughts were like white people lived in Beverly Hills. They didn't understand where we came from as blacks. That's what I thought. And I remember the first time we had a conversation and he shared with me his childhood and the things he did and the troubles he had and the things he'd gotten into. I was like real shocked. This doesn't happen to white people. I remember thinking that.

Although these were some the most pronounced indicators of racial stereotypes, it does not mean that the rest of my respondents

failed to hold such views or that cultural images play little role in interracial marriage. It may instead demonstrate a general reluctance to voice socially unacceptable thoughts and feelings. However, as Allport (1955) predicted, when the black women found themselves in situations where they could converse with white men, they were able to find common ground. In doing so, the women were able to transcend the stereotypic beliefs that might have otherwise impeded the newfound friendships that eventually led to marriage.

People also come into contact with each other when they live in integrated neighborhoods and attend integrated schools. Tony, a white husband who first met his future wife in high school, believed that his social setting played a major role in his decision to marry a black woman.

The big point is that the school we went to was like a model of integration, although unintentionally I'm sure. I know it had an influence on me as part of being color-blind because Asians were dating white people. Everybody was really just people. Everybody's got equal problems, kids of all different races . . . it was just never a big thing where you were looking down on anybody. That's how I can put my finger on it.

Ellen, a white woman, shared a similar story:

I lived in a city on the East Coast in the '60s that was a model town for integration. It was a model program that was started in my school system. . . . In junior high I was part of a group of kids where we all hung out together. There was just blacks and whites and we all hung out together. So my thinking was that there wasn't anything wrong with it.

Her husband, Gary, was also patently aware of his experiences with school integration, school segregation, and the friendships he formed.

When I went to school in New Mexico in first and second grades, I was the only [black kid]. There were only three black males in the whole school. So the girlfriends I had, even when I was in first grade, were of other races. Then when I came back to Texas, there was segregation and all my girlfriends were black. Then when I went to high school in Texas during integration, my girlfriends were black, but there were girls that liked me . . . who were black and Spanish. . . . I was an athlete, but I didn't go with them because I knew what Texas was like. Then I went to UCLA and my girlfriends became everything else again.

In several cases, my respondents reported that they came from one of a few white families living in a black neighborhood or one of a few black families living in a white neighborhood. If they were white they were quite comfortable around blacks and black culture, and if they were black they were quite comfortable around whites and white culture. David, a white man who grew up in a predominately black housing project and had many black close friends, explained how he developed a special affinity for black women:

I had no preference but I was growing up I was always attracted more to the black young ladies. And when a new girl would move into the neighborhood, and say she was pretty, all the little boys would say "Woo, look at Cheryl. She sure is fine," and I'd say "Woo, yeah, she sure is."

This example clearly describes how a person's peers can help to shape their notions of beauty. If he had grown up in another milieu, he may have constructed his definition of physical attractiveness in an entirely different manner.

Growing up in a predominantly black neighborhood also helped David to acquire a love for black culture, a love that also led to his interracial marriage:

Why did I want to marry a black woman? I found more love in black people as a whole. Now there might have been some this and that's or nit picking about little prejudices, or words that they said, but there was no power behind those words. I found more love in the black community that I grew up in than any other area besides my home. 'Cause my home had a lot of love.

This same pattern also occurred with black children who grew up in white localities. Pat, a black woman who grew up in a predominantly white neighborhood, became quite comfortable with whites:

All the kids I played with were white so I always felt very comfortable around Caucasians. And I went to school and I majored in psych and in a lot of my classes I was the only Afro-American person in there and it was fine with me.

Whatever the situation, my respondents described their experiences with integration in a favorable light, and they were able to form strong and solid friendships with both their black and white peers. The fact that their experiences were framed in a positive manner is a particularly important part of this analysis because many integrated neighborhoods and schools in the United States are often fraught with severe racial tensions.

The ability to form childhood friendships with black and white children, however, may not have been the result of contact alone. Living one's life in an integrated setting and having positive interactions with people from varying racial backgrounds appear to work in tandem with another striking pattern I discovered while interviewing black/white interracial couples in Los Angeles. My respondents exhibited the whole-hearted belief that all people are equal, a belief often instilled in them as children.

PARENTAL TEACHINGS

Parental teachings played an important role in my respondents' developing worldviews. The vast majority of my informants had parents who did not fill their heads with thoughts of hatred toward particular groups of people. Michael, a black man, believed that if his parents had presented him with racist points of view, his belief system might be considerably different:

If I heard my parents, my father, talking about those niggers and those kikes I'd grow up with the same attitude.

One group of respondents described their mothers and fathers as liberal nonracist individuals who made it clear to them that all people were equal regardless of their religious, racial, or ethnic backgrounds. Laura, a white woman, had liberal parents who practiced what they preached:

My parents . . . I feel their views are very liberal. . . . My dad's best friend is black and I grew up knowing him my whole life. I mean every Sunday he was at our house. It wasn't like I never knew him. I always knew black people.

Ann, a black woman, had this to say about her parental teachings:

My parents always taught me that you don't judge a person by the color or how they look but you judge people by the way they are as people, and that you shouldn't allow yourself to be judged that way. I don't recall whether my mother said this or not . . . my father was such a strong force in the family. My father said it doesn't make any difference who you bring home.

Rosenblatt et al. (1995) noted this pattern as well, reporting that a number of their respondents living in Minnesota had notions of tolerance instilled in them as children.

Another group of informants had parents who never mentioned the concept of race at all and, as a result, never developed negative views toward different groups of people. Tony, a white husband who met his future wife in high school, put it this way:

[My parents taught me] whatever Beaver Cleaver's parents conveyed to him. Pretty much don't steal and lie and cheat, the golden rule sort of thing. Everybody's equal, but, on the other hand, it wasn't like "Gee, that Martin Luther King's really great." It was more like the Beaver's family, where there were no controversies about that sort of thing.

In accordance with Rosenblatt et al.'s (1995) Minneapolis sample, a third group of my respondents reported that their mothers and fathers sent out mixed signals. As Ellen, a white woman, recalls:

It was more like double messages . . . I mean because they didn't espouse hateful epitaphs against other groups. Let's say they made remarks against other groups that weren't like them, the way somebody dressed or the way somebody's hair was or something like that. It was like an uncomfortableness with difference. . . . My father had two businesses and some of his employees were black. He was their boss and he treated everybody who was his employee fairly.

Although many of my black and white respondents were never forbidden to marry a person of another race, not all of their parents were pleased when they brought home their partners. It appears that these parents were often unaware of their own personal prejudices. Ellen, a white woman, described her particular situation:

I didn't know [my parents had a problem with interracial romances] until this person wanted to go out with me that they were so adamant against it—not being the right thing. What if you end up getting married and having children, it's just not done.

A few of the interviewees who were presented with conflicting views, however, did learn that marriage outside of one's race was not desirable, but the messages conveyed were often fraught with contradictions. One example comes from Jon, a black man who grew up in the South and whose mother feared he would be killed if he became involved with white women.

> My mom's not prejudiced at all. My mom's not prejudice because she's a very loving person. She's a very strong practicing Christian. Christ is her life. [But] my mother was always afraid that I was going to get killed. She begged me not to be involved with white people at all. She warned me, begged me, pleaded.

However, Jon's mother enrolled him in white neighborhood schools because the schools housed in black neighborhoods were deemed inferior, hence providing Jon with very confusing instructions. How might he refrain from involving himself with white people when he spent a good part of his day with white classmates and teachers?

Penny, a white woman, was also presented with a conflicting set of beliefs:

> My mom thought of herself as a liberal. My mother always felt that everybody was equal, and that everybody had a right to do whatever they saw fit. She didn't want her kids marrying out of their race and their religion. I don't know if she ever told us that. Maybe it was just assumed. We always had help in the house, and—I don't know—she would treat people as if everyone was equal.

Jeanette's family held a similar point of view.

I know my family was racist. I think their explanation was "Oh, we don't have anything against colored people and we know that they're just as good as we are, but don't mix with them."

When my respondents were presented with ideologies riddled with ambivalence however, they managed to internalize the "all people are equal" part of the message leaving the separatist part of the message behind.

Marcia, a black woman raised in a segregated black neighborhood, had parents who said little about race and never even mentioned interracial marriage. She did, however, remember her father make the following comment, which led her to believe that he felt at least some antipathy toward whites.

> You only need two white people in your life: Jesus Christ and one other.

Even if parents made small derogatory racial remarks or presented their children with conflicting points of view, one factor became strikingly clear: None of my interviewees were the children of white supremacists or black nationalists. While growing up, fewer than 25% of my respondents came from homes where they were overtly forbidden to marry a person of another race.

This stands in sharp contrast to what many parents tell their children in the United States and throughout the world for a vast majority of the world's cultures practice some form of endogamy. Social scientists have long demonstrated how different groups of people exclude other groups of individuals from the marriage pool, deeming them unsuitable for marriage. Gypsies in the United States and Europe, for example, see any person outside of their group as polluted and unpure. In these cultures, economic transactions are the only interactions permitted to occur between gypsies and nongypsies. A romantic dalliance with a nongypsy is seen as a serious offense that will result in formal exclusion from the group (Fonseca, 1995; Sway, 1988). Likewise, the primary justification for segregation between blacks and whites was the prevention of interracial mating. Because blacks were seen as genetically inferior, whites believed that rampant intermixing would taint their genetically superior blood (Myrdal, 1944).

Mary Waters (1990) uncovered American rules for endogamy while studying the ways in which white Americans construct their ethnic identities. During discussions with her informants, she discovered that the majority of her respondents had parents who stated that marriage to a person outside of their racial group was patently unacceptable or, as Waters puts it, "marriage across racial barriers was not the subject of subtle clues or indirect messages" (p. 105).

Other studies, however, suggest that attitudes toward interracial marriage are changing. A recent *New York Times* article found that 63% of white Americans say they approve of interracial marriage (Correspondents of the *New York Times,* 2001). However, this broadbased question does not ask the respondents if they were more comfortable with certain combinations of interracial couples rather than others or whether they themselves would consider interracial marriage. It is my hunch that these responses reflect a general belief rather than something the respondents would want for themselves or for their own children. If people truly held such liberal attitudes, the rate of black/white interracial marriage would be presumably higher.

In fact, when surveys clearly specify interracial marriage between blacks and whites the approval rate is much lower. For example, a 1991 Gallup Poll focusing on people's opinions regarding black/white interracial marriage found that 48% approved, 42% disapproved, and 10% didn't know (Correspondents of the *New York Times,* 2001).

Current research, moreover, suggest that whites are still uncomfortable with the idea of having close contacts with blacks. Schuman, Steeh, Bobo, and Krysan (1997) report that a majority of whites believe that blacks should be treated with the same kind of respect that they have always enjoyed. Yet these same people said they had no desire to live next door to a black family. Furthermore, Ellis Cose (1993) found that professional blacks who work with professional whites are often inundated with insults and indignities. Many of the black professionals he interviewed reported that their white coworkers treated them as though they were thugs, criminals, or drug addicts.

As a result of these continual assaults, it is no wonder that black people may be opposed to interracial marriage as well. Although the *New York Times* poll found that 79% of respondents approve of interracial marriage, there is also evidence to the contrary. Blacks have always been wary of whites as a result of the abuse they endured at the hands of whites throughout the Antebellum and postslavery years (Myrdal, 1944). These historical acts of exploitation lay the groundwork for the trends in black/white interracial marriage we see today.

Contemporary black women, for example, appear to be especially apprehensive of white men because of the rape and sexual coercion inflicted on them by white men for much of American history. In times of slavery, black mothers and fathers taught their daughters to resist the attacks of their white slave masters. Fathers risked their lives to protect their wives and daughters from the unwanted attentions of white men. A few black women did seek sexual liaisons with white slave masters, usually in the hope of securing special privileges. However, most slave communities held these women in scorn (Giddings, 1984). Even after emancipation, illicit relations between black women and white men were seen as disgraceful (Myrdal, 1944).

Author bell hooks (1981) believes that the fear of being subjugated by white men or the fear of being scorned by their families and community prevents black women from forming romantic attachments with white men who may genuinely care for them. She elucidates a double standard often found in black communities. It is far easier for a black man to have a relationship with a white woman than for a black woman to form a loving bond with a white man. It is also common for black men who are involved with white women to frown on the same kind of relationship between a black woman and a white man.

Beverly Tatum (1999) has also observed ambivalence toward interracial romance among both blacks and whites who engage in a social process she calls "the birthday party effect." While studying children in racially mixed communities, she found that children's birthday parties were made up of youngsters whose racial and ethnic backgrounds clearly reflected the diversity in the community. However, when these children reached puberty, parents became especially fearful of interracial romance. As a result, older children's parties were often composed of a racially unified set of kids.

So despite these broad changes in public opinion, interracial couples must still overcome a complex set of derogatory meanings that blacks assign to whites and that whites assign to blacks. To achieve this goal, they often develop an alternative set of cultural understandings to refute those that already exist. The informants who adapted ideologies put forth during the civil rights movement provide another example of how this process works.

A CHANGING CULTURAL MILIEU

C. Wright Mills (1959) asserted that one must examine the interplay between individual motivation and the historical time period in which that individual exists to truly understand human behavior. Likewise, the ebb and flow of interracial marriage is also the result of individual motivation and historical context. All of my informants live in a time when beliefs about the natural equality of black and white individuals are pronounced in ways they had not been seen before the civil rights movement of the 1950s and 1960s.

Of course, strong beliefs about the equality of all people have always played a prominent role in the American cultural scene. Gunnar Myrdal (1944) wrote that the American value system is composed of notions of liberty, equality, justice, fair opportunity, and the Christian ideals of human brotherhood. Myrdal called these ideals "the American creed." He asserted that this strong moral force was incorporated into the Declaration of Independence, the American Constitution, and the Bill of Rights, and that aspects of this American creed were woven into every American institution. He writes,

All means of intellectual communication are utilized to stamp [the American Creed] into everybody's mind. The schools teach them, the churches preach them. The courts pronounce their judicial decisions in their terms. They permeate editorials with a pattern of idealism so ingrained that the writers could scarcely free themselves from it even if they tried. (p. 3)

Yet Myrdal (1944) was keenly aware of the contradiction between the American creed and the actual behavior of white American citizens toward black American citizens, a contradiction he addressed in his classic *The American Dilemma*. When it came to the "negro situation," he concluded, Americans failed to measure up to their own set of standards.

By the end of World War II, however, the American collective consciousness began to change. Arthur Schlesinger, Jr. (1991) writes that "Hitler's fascism forced Americans to look hard at their own racial assumptions . . . challenged the consciousness of the majority, and raised the consciousness of minorities (p. 45). Discontented blacks began to develop an intensified group consciousness (Myrdal, 1944). Philosophies of racial/ethnic equality were also brought to light, expanded on, and disseminated by the likes of the charismatic Martin Luther King, Jr., who saw the integration of blacks and whites as a social ideal (Zinn, 1989). This principle was illustrated in an emblem depicting two shaking hands: one black, the other white.

Evidence of these beliefs of unity emerged within the popular culture as well. Ideologies of equality found their way into the lyrics of pop songs played on radio stations in the late 1960s and 1970s that contained words such as "the color of your skin don't matter to me, as long as we can live in harmony. Why can't we be friends?" (Alan, Brown, Dickerson, et al., 1975).

The message came through loud and clear, and a more inclusive way of thinking began to take hold among an increasing number of Americans. It is no accident that the expansion of this ideology coincided with the Civil Rights Act of 1964 and the *Loving v. Commonwealth of Virginia* 1967 Supreme Court decision, because philosophies of racial unity and equality guided the struggles that led to these landmark victories.

The civil rights movement had a massive impact on the beliefs and behaviors of six of the white men whom I interviewed, a finding that Rosenblatt et al. (1995) found among some of their Minneapolis informants as well. Philip, a white husband, was keenly aware of how the zeitgeist of the civil rights era shaped his beliefs and behaviors.

> I worked when I was 18, 19, 20, integrating pools, integrating restaurants, integrating schools. When I was 17, I think the first thing I did was help the miners in Kentucky [who] had been on strike for three years and were starving to death in the winter and I helped the food drive. It was the time that the country was changing and it was clear to me the rules weren't fair.

Civil rights teachings led Steven, a white husband who was raised in the segregated South, to broaden his perspective.

> Well, you just decide if you really like somebody enough, that's not one of the things they you want to allow yourself to be limited by—this sort of bi-racial world. I certainly made a conscious decision to let things evolve. [I liked her] certainly better than other girls I'd gone out with. [I developed] a broader perspective. And I read a lot of things that [my parents] never would read. And this was during the civil rights movement, so talk about race and racism and segregation and racial violence was very much in the air. It was very hard to read about that or watch that stuff on television without realizing how wrong it was, the racism and the segregation that I grew up with. It was very hard to go along with. That was a movement that had tremendous influence on a lot of people.

Because of his experiences during the civil rights movement, Dave developed an alternative set of views, and he did not allow beliefs about the sanctity of segregation to prevent him from forming a relationship with a black woman he truly admired.

Thomas learned about the importance of racial equality from his parents, teachers, church, and the spirit of the civil rights movement. Then, to his great surprise, his mother and father objected to him dating a black woman he met in college. He responded to his parents with the following:

> And I had to remind them that I was both a child of the '60s and that I was also their child; that they had instilled certain values. The Vatican II, the openness, the interest in

the cause of the underdog, the interest in liberalism with a small L. For example, there were two Ethiopian students [who] lived with us for two years. [They taught me] that the situation generating the civil rights protest was an immoral situation in the South, [and] that the riots that began to occur in the northern cities had some justified causes.

RELIGIOUS TEACHINGS

Thomas was not the only respondent to incorporate religious teachings into his worldview. There were a number of individuals whose beliefs were visibly drawn from their religious teachings, a pattern that Rosenblatt et al. (1995) found among their Minneapolis informants as well. Michael, a black man, explained:

The teaching I got was basically in church. I went to church a lot when I was young. So what teaching I got talked about love for mankind. We never discussed about blacks and white and yellow people. Which is kind of funny I used to think that, and that's the real world and they should have discussed that.

Michael was never taught to fear white people. Instead of being told that whites were dangerous, he was taught to love all mankind.

In contemplating marriage to a white man, Marcia turned to her faith for guidance.

When he asked me about marriage, all these things ran through my mind like, first of all he's asking me to marry him, he's white, what is my father going to think and all of this kind of stuff. There was this one particular guy [who] was kind of nice. He was black, but the black guy . . . he didn't ask me to marry him. And here I'm believing in God and I'm saying, "Wait a minute. What's going on?" So when [my husband asked me to marry him] I called up the guy,

we had become really good friends, and I told him [my husband] had asked me to marry him and why hadn't he? "What's the deal, you're around all of the time, I know there must be an interest."

And he said, "You know what happens, that when I ask the lord about you I never get an answer." I said, "Fine." [A white man's] asking me to marry him, so based upon that I'm a believer in God and what you learn believing in God is you walk by faith and not by sight. And that's exactly what I did.

Marcia went on to explain how her religious convictions helped her to grapple with the belief that "white people think they are superior to black people."

When I was a little girl, [we had to sit] in the back of the movie house and we used to throw things down at the white people. I didn't know what I was doing but my brothers were older so I just did what they did. I never heard my mother and father when I was young saying anything about white or black. So I believe what I felt in regards to white people was my own thing—that as you start hearing that they think that they're superior to you, you have a kind of attitude kind of thing . . . a "Why do they think they're better than me" kind of thing. But after you grow up and you learn what the real problems are . . . Not just they, people in general. In the Bible it doesn't even talk about black and white. The only thing it talks about is either you're Jew or you're gentile. So if you're not Jew, you're gentile . . . period. That what God looks at you as. He doesn't look at you as black and white.

In this situation religious doctrine is used to mitigate a common assumption that blacks make about whites.

These kinds of religious interpretations are typical of many black church doctrines that use Christian teachings to challenge beliefs about racial inferiority and the sanctity of racial separation. For example, civil rights leader Martin Luther King, Jr., drew from Bible passages that stressed Christ's love for all mankind to justify the civil rights struggle (Cone, 1986).

Religious ideology, however, can have the exact opposite effect. Gordon Allport (1955) argued that religious doctrines are often intertwined with "subcultural and national groups so that religious divisions march hand in hand with ethnic and national divisions. When religious distinctions are made to do double duty, the grounds of prejudice are laid" (p. 446). Linda Brent, a former slave who captured her slave years in her book *Incidents in the Live of a Slave Girl* (1861/1973), devoted an entire chapter to this very theme. Whenever a slave insurrection occurred, she wrote, the Episcopal white slave masters would attempt to provide the slaves with an extra dose of religious instruction. They would gather the slaves together and force them to read Bible verses that advised them to be obedient to their masters as you are obedient unto Christ.

A modern-day example of how religious doctrine can be used for racist purposes comes from Cude and Dean (1998), who report that a number of state legislators in South Carolina are publicly opposed to interracial marriage. The legislators claim that their convictions are not rooted in prejudice but rather the Bible. For instance, Representative Lanny Little John asserts that God created the races and God set them apart. People who engage in interracial marriage, therefore, have a general disregard for the will of God. So some Americans continue to interpret Christian teachings in ways that actually widens the gulf that exists between blacks and whites.

While religious doctrine can be used to validate the subjugation of one group over another, some individuals, Allport (1955) believed, "take its universalistic teaching as an authentic guide to conduct" (p. 455). My informants did indeed use their religious beliefs as a moral guide that enabled them to overcome powerful ideological strains of thought that drive blacks and whites apart.

IDEOLOGIES OF EQUALITY WITH UNIDENTIFIED ROOTS

Another group of respondents who believed in the inherent equality of all people did not feel that their beliefs were rooted in their parental upbringings or their social milieus. Instead, they thought that their worldviews were something they had developed on their own. This is not surprising because it is common for people to think that their behaviors are the result of their own individual motivations, and they are often completely unaware of how environmental forces shape their lives (Bellah, Madsen, Sullivan, Swindler, & Tipton, 1985). For example, Penny, a white woman whose mother described herself as a liberal while denouncing marriages between people of different racial and religious groups, had the following recollection:

I remember myself when I was in kindergarten and I was asked to paint murals and I painted one black person, one white person, one black person, one white person. And I thought at the time, I had no idea what I was doing. I was five years old. But obviously I perceived something. And they were all the same to me.

Jeanette, the white woman who learned that she should not mix with blacks despite the fact that blacks and whites were inherently equal, came to this same conclusion.

I have an open mind and a kind heart, and I love people. I don't care what race or what they are as long as they aren't harmful. I just don't have a prejudice against people. It was not bred in me. It was not trained.

I was taught not to hate but [nothing else.] And everything I did hear about race, other than ours, was negative—Jews whatever.

Although these women believed that their principles stemmed from their own innate characteristics, their cultural environments had to have influenced them to a certain extent. Both of these women grew up during the 1960s and 1970s, a time when themes of racial integration and racial equality were especially pronounced, and their value systems were at least partially rooted in our American creed, an ideology that is passed on to all Americans in one form or another.

IDEOLOGIES OF EQUALITY AND OTHER VARIABLES

Human beings are driven to behave in certain ways for a variety of reasons, some of which include hunger, aggression, love, and the quest for wealth and power. However, Max Weber argued that powerful "ideas" also induce humans to act (Giddens, 1971), and it appears that "ideas" also help pave the way for black/white interracial marriage. Ideologies of equality refute cultural assumptions that state that certain groups of people are evil, inferior, different, or impure by asserting that humans share important commonalties that make them all the same. If people are looked on as equal rather than inferior, similar rather than different, they have a greater chance of being seen as a friend or a potential marriage partner. Hence, when the majority of my respondents found themselves in situations in which they came into contact with people from different racial backgrounds as students or colleagues, they did not say to themselves, "This is the kind of person I should stay away from." They instead thought of the person in question as not only equal but ultimately like themselves. If they experienced an initial apprehension, they

drew from cultural frameworks that promote racial equality and racial inclusiveness to justify their newfound romance.

I want to stress, however, that interracial couples are not acting solely on their egalitarian principles, because their decision to marry certainly involved love and the need for companionship. In addition, structural factors, such as the relative desegregation of American institutions, certainly play an important role. These women and men never would have married had they not come in contact as equals in integrated or semi- integrated places, such as school and work, had the laws that supported racial segregation and discrimination survived. Hence, there is not one factor but rather many factors that, taken together, give rise to interracial marriage. This chapter serves to demonstrate that the incorporation of a philosophy that mitigates difference and stresses equality and racial inclusiveness as an important part of this puzzle as well.

BELIEFS VERSUS ACTUAL BEHAVIOR

There is one final point I want to make about this argument. After reading this chapter, a person might ask: If the ideologies of equality are such an integral part of the American collective conscious, why is there so much racial tension and why aren't there more black/white interracial marriages? I respond to this question by stating that American culture continues to possess many competing and contradicting ideologies that are shared by large numbers of people, and these philosophies may frown on interracial marriage. It is apparent that many individuals continue to adhere to an ideology of racism and separatism. As Myrdal (1944) pointed out more than a half century ago, Americans may accept ideologies of equality in theory but fail to implement them in practice.

While it is clear that there are many more black/white interracial marriages than ever before and that ideologies of equality have expanded to include people of color, racist thoughts and behaviors have not been obliterated. Blacks continue to be harassed on the streets with insults and hate stares. They fail to be served in restaurants, and they are often victims of consumer racism (Feagin, 1991). Furthermore, although the majority of respondents surveyed in a *New York Times* poll believed that race relations were relatively good, these same Americans reported that "they did not live, work or worship with those of other races" (Correspondents of the *New York Times,* 2001, p. 368). Hence, blatant racist beliefs and a general ambivalence toward racial integration serve to fuel an underlying "separate but equal" mentality.

Despite the complex relations that exist between blacks and whites, my respondents managed to bridge a wide gulf that exists for most Americans using ideologies of equality to help them along. Not only did they hold such beliefs, but they acted on their principles as well. It is here that my respondents may be different from the norm, because if the majority of Americans wholly acted on the beliefs that promote the natural equality of all humans, there would be much less racial tension and much more social interaction between blacks and whites.

REFERENCES

Allen, P., Brown, H., Dickerson, B., et al. (1975). *Why can't we be friends.* Los Angeles: TMC Music, Inc./Far Out Music, Avenue Records.

Allport, W. G. (1955). *The nature of prejudice.* Reading, MA: Addison-Wesley.

Bellah, R., Madsen, R., Sullivan, W., Swindler, A., & Tipton, S. (1985). *Habits of the heart: Individualism and commitment in American life.* Berkeley: University of California Press.

Brent, L. (1973). *Incidents in the life of a slave girl.* New York: Harcourt Brace. (Original work published 1861)

Cone, J. H. (1986). *A black theology of liberation.* New York: Orbis Books.

Correspondents of the *New York Times.* (2001). *How race is lived in America: Pulling together, pulling apart.* New York: Times Books.

Cose, E. (1993). *The rage of a privileged class.* New York: Harper Perennial.

Cude, D., & Dean, S. E. (1998, February 7). Many support wiping out mixed race marriage ban. In *Spartanburg Herald Journal,* p. 1.

Feagin, R. F. (1991). The continuing significance of race: Antiblack discrimination in public places. *American Sociological Review, 56,* 101-116.

Fonseca, I. (1995). *Bury me standing: The gypsies and their journey.* New York: Vintage Books.

Forbes, H. D. (1997). *Ethnic conflict: Commerce, culture, and the contact hypothesis.* New Haven, CT: Yale University Press.

Giddens, A. (1971). *Capitalism & modern social theory: An analysis of the writings of Marx, Durkheim, and Max Weber.* Cambridge, UK: Cambridge University Press.

Giddings, P. (1984). *When and where I enter: The impact of black women on race and sex in America.* New York: Free Press.

Glaser, B., & Strauss, A. (1967). *The discovery of grounded theory: Strategies for qualitative research.* Chicago: Aldine.

Goffman, E. (1963). *Stigma: Notes on the management of spoiled identity.* Englewood Cliffs, NJ: Prentice Hall.

hooks, b. (1981). *Ain't I a woman? Black women and feminism.* Boston: South End Press.

Kouri, K. M., & Lasswell, M. (1993). Black-white marriages: Social change and intergenerational mobility. *Marriage & Family Review, 19*(3/4), 241-255.

Loving v. Commonwealth of Virginia, 338, U.S. 1. (1967).

McNamara, R. P., Tempenis, M., & Walton, B. (1999). *Crossing the line: Interracial couples in the south.* Westport, CT: Praeger.

Mills, C. W. (1959). *The sociological imagination.* New York: Oxford University Press.

Myrdal, G. (1944). *An American dilemma.* New York: Harper & Row.

Porterfield, E. (1978). *Black and white mixed marriages.* Chicago: Nelson-Hall.

Rosenblatt, P., Karis, T. A., & Powell, R. D. (1995). *Multiracial couples: Black and white voices.* Thousand Oaks, CA: Sage.

Schlesinger, A. M., Jr. (1991). *The disuniting of America: Reflections on a multicultural society.* New York: W. W. Norton.

Schuman, H., Steeh, C., Bobo, L., & Krysan, M. (1997). *Racial attitudes in the United States.* Cambridge, MA: Harvard University Press.

Spickard, P. R. (1989). *Mixed blood: Intermarriage and ethnic identity in twentieth-century America.* Madison: University of Wisconsin Press.

Spradley, J. P. (1979). *The ethnographic interview.* New York: Holt, Rinehart, & Winston.

Sway, M. (1988). *Familiar strangers: Gypsy life in America.* Urbana: University of Illinois Press.

Tatum, B. D. (1999). *Why are all the black kids sitting together in the cafeteria? And other conversations about race.* New York: Basic Books.

U.S. Census Bureau. (1999). *Interracial married couples: 1960 to present.* Retrieved August 12, 2002, from http://www.census.gov/population/socdemo/ms-la/tabms-3.txt

Waters, M. C. (1990). *Ethnic options: Choosing identities in America.* Berkeley: University of California Press.

Zinn, H. (1989). *The twentieth century: A people's history.* New York: Harper Perennial.

Epilogue
The Multiracial Movement

HARMONY AND DISCORD

Loretta I. Winters

The U.S. government has been aware of multiracial people and responded to their unique racial status in a variety of ways depending on what slice of history one cuts (Morning, Chapter 3). When examining the positions of the contributors to this volume, three models appear: the multiracial movement (MM) model, the counter multiracial movement (CMM) model, and the ethnic movement (EM) model. The first model focuses on the individual level, at which multiracial people want to embrace all of their ethnic heritages, comfortably and without justification. Maria Root's (1996) bill of rights for racially mixed people expresses a human rights or civil rights framework.

I have the right
    not to justify my existence in this world
    not to keep the races separate within me
    not to be responsible for people's
    discomfort with my physical ambiguity
    not to justify my ethnic legitimacy

I have the right
    to identify myself differently than
    strangers expect me to identify
    to identify myself differently than how
    my parents identify me

    to identify myself differently than my
    brothers and sisters
    to identify myself differently in different
    situations

I have the right
    to create a vocabulary to communicate
    about being multiracial
    to change my identity over my
    lifetime—and more than once
    to have loyalties and identify with more
    than one group of people
    to freely choose whom I befriend and
    love (p. 7)

By framing what some consider a personal problem, the dilemma of mixed-race/ethnic people has been recast in a social problem's framework (DaCosta, Chapter 4), in particular a human rights or Civil Rights issue (Williams, Chapter 5). Examining the mission of prominent multiracial organizations (Brown and Douglass, Chapter 7) reveals both the individual needs and desires of some multiracial people as well as efforts toward breaking down institutional racism through education and influencing the way the public views race through the categories supplied by the U.S. Census Bureau. The MM model reflects the philosophies of political activists such as Nancy Brown and Ramona Douglass (Chapter 7) and trailblazers such as Maria P. P. Root (Root, 1992, 1996; Chapter 1), who laid the foundations for contemporary discussions of mixed-race or multiracial identity. Her statement about the increasing numbers of multiracial people "transforming the 'face' of the United States" (Root, 1992, p. 3) influenced the selection of the title of the book. Other spokespersons for the MM model include G. Reginald Daniel (Chapter 13), Paul Spickard (Chapter 14), and Teresa Williams-León (Chapter 9), who have made significant contributions in this area.

Activists have pushed for changing the racial/ethnic categories on government forms but have not always agreed on how that expansion should manifest itself. Spencer (Chapter 6) discusses the two main proposals that made their way to the Census 2000 debate as either a "stand-alone multiracial category" or a "multiracial header with racial sublistings" as alternatives to the "mark all that apply" format. Root (1996, p. xxv) suggests a third proposal because the "race question confounds race and ethnicity." She suggests reducing the race question to either multiracial or monoracial. She then asks, "Could we not move on to the ethnicity and ancestry questions?" This alternative has yet to be adequately articulated or well publicized.

Heated debate about Census categories occurs among participants of the multiracial movement; however, one thing remains clear. Classifying groups through the socially constructed concept of race has justified the history of prejudice and discrimination against people of color as well as the conflict and confusion claimed to be inherent in multiracial children. Root (1992,) makes a contribution here:

> Accomplishing the synthesis of different heritages into a dynamic whole requires

that the ordinal nature of hierarchical notions about race to which we have been socialized must be replaced by both simpler models (such as naming without rank ordering, or nominal categorization) and more complex models (such as ecological and multidimensional models for understanding social order and human behavior). (p. 344)

She further points out that the contributors to her anthology "believe that if it is possible for a single person to accomplish this synthesis for her- or himself, it might be very possible for us to accomplish it as a society" (p. 344).

An alternative position to the MM model is reflected in the CMM model. Some members of minority communities believe that proliferating the current list of racial categories will only impede the dissolution of the harmful construct of race. The CMM model is illustrated in the work of Mary Thierry Texeira (Chapter 2) and Rainier Spencer (Chapter 6). Although supporters of this model believe in the elimination of the concept of race altogether, they continue to support monoracial categories for reasons of protecting the political solidarity of minority groups and ensuring civil rights compliance.

Texeira compares the multiracial designations of today with historical categories used to divide people of color. The historical categories support the myth that light-skinned people of color were superior to darker-skinned people of color and, therefore, entitled to privileges that other people of color were not. Acknowledgment of any difference of light-skinned people of color was not to break down racist notions or end white supremacy but to use and manipulate light-skinned people of color to perpetuate the illusion of white supremacy. That is, light-skinned people of color were only slightly different from darker people of color but not at the same time equal in any way to whites. Texeira points out that "it is difficult to say with any degree of certainty how much their appearance [fair-skinned blacks] helped them succeed in white society, but it undoubtedly did not hurt them." The extent to which light-skinned blacks may or may not have been afforded certain privileges is less important than the belief itself of hierarchy within the African American community.

Herein lies the fear among some that multiracial people in the United States will gain further advantage by forming another group of light-skinned people of color who, for a few crumbs of the American pie, will forfeit their darker-skinned relatives. Some contemporary mixed-race people may indeed have varying degrees of feelings of superiority to darker-skinned peoples and may have received more benefits of affirmative action policies than their darker-skinned contemporaries, because some people in positions of power (usually whites) see them as more desirable than people of darker color. No doubt, a large number of African Americans and members of other racial/ethnic minority groups believe that the force behind the multiracial movement today will create a new era of light-skinned privilege and the manipulation of light-skinned people of color. Daniel (Chapter 13), although very supportive of the multiracial movement, adds to the caveats of caution by pointing out that "the new multiracial identity's radical potential as a racial project should not be underestimated any more than its reactionary potential should be overestimated."

Various supporters and critics of the multiracial movement do not agree on how to eliminate institutional racism as well as prejudice and discrimination. Both groups believe that unraveling the last thread of the social construction of race will support that goal, but they disagree on how and when this should be done.

Both the MM and CMM models continue to support the social construction of race—the former by proliferating the categories by adding a multiracial dimension and the latter by entrenching the monoracial categories and the rule of hypodescent in the process. Supporters of both models are concerned with accuracy in counting. Supporters of both models fear that the Census 2000 data will create a group that further divides minority communities. Both philosophical positions are concerned that the data collected by Census 2000 may be tabulated in a way to compromise civil rights compliance monitoring.

The MM model supports multiracial identity, and the CMM model supports minority group identity. Herein lies the real difference between the two models. The MM model links the private sphere with the public sphere at the same time, the CMM model separates the private sphere from the public sphere. Neither Spencer (1999) nor Texeira (Chapter 2) have a problem with people of multiple heritages professing a multiracial identity in private, but they argue that this private matter should have no bearing on the process that will thwart the use of the concept of race as a means of classifying people in America. Instead, they feel that making a private matter public interferes with the institutional monitoring of civil rights.

Spencer (1999) criticizes some of the literature on mixed race for conflating race and culture. Root (1992) identifies how the confusion of race and ethnicity plays a role in cultural identification. Listing factors that have prevented the empowerment of multiracial persons in the form of self-naming, Root's fifth factor states that "race and ethnicity have been confused such that many multiracial people may identify monoculturally, as in the case of many Latinos, American Indians, and African Americans" (p. 8).

Before elaborating on the EM model, a historical discussion of evolution of the concepts of race and ethnicity is warranted. Cornell and Hartman (1998) point out that "for several centuries, scholars of one stripe or another from various countries tried to specify the number of races in the world" (p. 21). They quote Gossett to demonstrate this point.

> Linnaeus had found four human races; Blumenbach had five; Cuvier had three; John Hunter had seven; Burke had sixty-three; Pickering has eleven; Virey had two "species," each containing three races; Haeckel had thirty-six; Huxley had four; Topinard had nineteen under three headings; Desmoulins had sixteen "species"; Deniker had seventeen races and thirty types. (Cornell & Hartman, 1998, p. 82)

Regardless of which attributes of race one may address, they are not connected to any consistent set of physical or genetic variation according to most modern analyses.

Distinguishing between race and ethnicity and providing workable definitions at this juncture is important. Lay people view race and ethnicity as the same concept. Modern scholars dismiss race as having any biological reality and expose it for the social construction it is while recognizing the reality of racism (Root, Chapter 1; Texeira, Chapter 2). Some scholars perceive race as a subset of ethnicity and vice versa. In 1948 Cox provided a social science definition of race (Feagin & Feagin, 1999): "Any people who are distinguished, or who consider themselves distinguished, in social relations with other people, by their physical characteristics." Van den Berghe provided a similar definition of racial group (Feagin & Feagin, 1999): "Human group that defines itself and/or is defined by other groups as different from other groups by virtue of innate and immutable physical characteristics." Feagin and Feagin (1999) went a step further in defining a racial group in the context of how membership is perceived by others. They defined a racial group as "a social group that persons inside or outside the group have decided is important to single out as inferior or superior, typically on the basis of real or alleged physical characteristics subjectively selected" (p. 8).

Race is intrinsically linked to identity because phenotype, according to American society, is such a determining factor in one's identity, even when culture and life experience may be counterintuitive to the conclusions that phenotype may bring. The concept of race proposes that physical characteristics are an essential component of this type of categorization. Doob (1999, p. 262) separates race and ethnicity altogether and defines race as a "classification of people into categories falsely claimed to be derived from a distinct set of biological traits." Doob (1999) defines ethnicity as a "classification of people into a particular category with distinct cultural or national qualities" (p. 261).

Cornell and Hartman (1998) depict race and ethnicity as distinct but overlapping constructs. They claim that race and ethnicity "potentially involve two different processes of identity construction" (p. xiii). Using a constructionist approach, Cornell and Hartman focus on how ethnic and racial identities are asserted or assigned and emphasize the fluidity of this process. Although they acknowledge that economic, political, and other social forces have a major influence on identity formation, they also point out that, once established, identities exert their own influences.

The EM model would eliminate race in favor of ethnicity. The work of Baird-Olson on American Indians (Chapter 11), Edles on Hawaiians (Chapter 12), and Velazco y Trianosky on Hispanics (Chapter 10) provides evidence of this model. Edles shows how for the multiracial population in Hawai'i the ethnic definition of being local or not takes precedence in interpersonal relations and identity over race. The term local, defined by a group of students at the University of Hawai'i, Manoa emphasizes first culture (the spirit of aloha) and second ethnicity (being from Hawai'i). It also has an implicit racial and social class dimension. Even when haoles have been born in Hawai'i and consider themselves local (local haoles), they are not truly accepted as local by other working class Native Hawaiians. This results from the hesitation to include members of a dominant group that would appropriate what they did not earn. Instead of labor and land, culture. Thus, although ethnicity is emphasized in the use of the word local, the internalized oppression essentialist notions of race still appear, however small. Baird-Olson discusses the problems that have arisen when the colonizer's racialized criterion of blood quantum has been used to determine group inclusion instead of traditional criteria of inclusion: family lineage, marriage, and adoption/naturalization. Resurrecting traditional inclusion would reduce divisions within Indian communities that results in exclusion of its members and further erosion of self-determination. Velazco y Trianosky speaks of including all members with a common ethnicity regardless of racial perceptions. He sees assimilation as reinforcing bipolar (black and white) essentialist notions of the nature of people. He believes that Latino(a)s must acknowledge all the people who have contributed to the "morphing" Latino culture (black and white) or the group we think of as Latino in the United States. This group embodies mixed race and may transcend bipolar notions by embracing all of its members without "becoming white" (assimilation). Resisting assimilation and mass-commercialized American culture by allowing the creativity that comes when one allows an emotional connection to all family (and with it the culture) is the key to breaking down the

essentialist notions of race that are reflected in the assimilation paradigm.

Desire to be included in an ethnic group may be dependent on rewards (psychological or financial) as well as political forces. Although individual factors may be present and imply individual choice, they ultimately can be linked to structural factors. Structural factors reflect the power arrangements of society. Because European Americans have more power, status, and privilege, they have more freedom to identify both themselves and others than do people of color. Panethnicity, whereby a general ethnicity is applied to a variety of cultural groups with phenotypic groupings in common to varying degrees, is typically coerced. However, voluntary allegiance to the superimposed group may occur for political gain. One individual may be included in a single racial group or more than one racial group depending on who is making the determination. The very notion of multiraciality challenges the hegemonic categorization of race. Multiraciality categorization, a classification that mirrors an "ideology of equality" (Kouri, Chapter 18), attempts to break down the coerced group membership in favor of an individually determined identity. Multiracial people who have dealt with any prejudices of their parents or extended families and their own internalized oppression increasingly are refusing to deny any attributes they receive from any parent. The Tiger Woods of the world, who refuse to elevate any ethnic heritage and to allow the ignorance of others define them, challenge the foundations of the concept of race. They are role models for other multiracial people who fear breaking the chains of the "one-drop rule" or who are successfully passing as white but are not totally comfortable with the dishonesty that comes with burying a part of self.

The time to set differences aside and stand on common ground has come. Interracial couples love beyond socially constructed differences and raise children who insist on the equality of all sides of their heritages while challenging those who want to dismiss their white side by rules of hypodescent or dismiss their darker side to enjoy any crumbs of the American pie. It is time to acknowledge, no embrace, what the new mixed-race generation has to offer: equality and harmony over inequality and discord. Now, "can't we all just get along?"

Many multiracial people, once resolving the turmoil imposed on them by racialization, desire to own all of their relatives, not only those who create political solidarity for people of color. In including all of their relatives, they break down the hierarchy apparent in the social construction of race. The age of multiracial people has ushered in a new generation that wants to fully embrace all heritages. They are struggling to deconstruct the hierarchy according to race and instead support qualitative assumptions of categorization over quantitative assumptions of categorization. They are seemingly very dark-skinned African Americans acknowledging white blood and seemingly white people who acknowledging darker blood like the family of Sally Hemings, who was the concubine of our third president (Daniel, Chapter 13). Tracing and giving credence to all of our heritages while stressing similarities and denying any inherent disabilities will further the deconstruction of race more quickly than being overly concerned with political loyalties to one minority group and thereby reinforcing differences.

Three models have been proposed as paths to the demise of racialization in American society. The MM model and the CMM model perspectives are not ready to throw out the concept of race yet. Historical definitions of race and multirace have reinforced the rule of hypodescent and the privileged position of European Americans (Morning, Chapter 3). The concept of race clearly divides the ethnic

minority communities in the United States and supports new forms of racialization in multicultural groups (DeBose and Winters, Chapter 8; Williams-León, Chapter 9; Velazco y Trianosky, Chapter 10; Baird-Olson, Chapter 11). Racialization also contributes to and reinforces sexism both in advertisement (Streeter, Chapter 15) and gang membership (Brummett and Winters, Chapter 17) and even extends to the choice of topics by biracial comics (Price, Chapter 16). A number of ethnic minority group members are concerned that the multiracial movement will erode civil rights monitoring. Reality is that the contemporary, conservative, political backlash to the civil rights achievements has already eroded civil rights monitoring in education and employment as well as in other social institutions, and the current political climate suggests that this erosion will not be remedied in the near future. Others believe that embracing multiraciality will result in diminishing service to minority communities. Spickard's study of prominent multiracial figures in history (Chapter 14) does not confirm this fear. The ethnic identity model promotes nonracialized group definitions of membership and discards race as a viable construct. The ethnic model currently operating in Hawaii clearly interacts with race but only in response to the hierarchical arrangements structured in American society and beyond stemming from the rule hypodescent. Eliminating the ideology of white supremacy is key to an emerging egalitarian typology according to ethnicity.

Given the reality of vertical pluralism in the United States and beyond (Daniel, Chapter 13), more attention needs to be given to ensuring equity. The unique legal and historical sovereign status of American Indians provides an avenue of escape from racialized membership not available to other ethnic minority groups in the United States. Thus, other groups need to continue to explore other forms of nonracialized group definitions. More attention needs to be given to how the multiracial literature addresses the conflation of race and ethnicity. More attention needs to be given to how both the private and public spheres may contribute to the breakdown of perceived quantitative differences according to race in favor of qualitative differences according to ethnicity. Spickard (Chapter 14) cautions against individualism and self-concern in the multiracial movement and more so in Whiteness studies and at the expense of group needs, particularly communities of color. Making the connection between the micro and the macro is important here. Maria Root's ecological model shows the complexity that accompanies a discussion of multiraciality that goes beyond the individual level (Chapter 1). Daniel's discussion of vertical (inegalitarian) and horizontal (egalitarian) pluralism (Chapter 13; Daniel, 2002), Dacosta's description of how the personal problem of multiracial identity becomes a social problem (Chapter 4), Williams' demonstration that the multiracial movement was initiated by the civil rights movement (Chapter 5) also provide a framework for understanding how the micro and the macro are linked. More attention needs to be given to dismantling the one-drop rule. This discussion appears regardless of which minority group one belongs to (DeBose & Winters, Chapter 8; Williams-Leon, Chapter 9; Velazco Y Trianosky, Chapter 10; Baird-Olsen, Chapter 11). Introducing multiraciality into how the state defines race and ethnicity (Census 2000) and into the curriculum at all educational levels (Daniel, 2002) will assist in debunking the myth of the one-drop rule. The work of Maria Root (1992, 1996) and Naomi Zack (1993, 1995, 1998) among others has been useful at the college level. As individuals increasingly confront their own hierarchically arranged notion of race, America will decreasingly be a race-centered society. The third model begins to suggest deeper and broader conceptual and political alternatives to civil rights monitoring, cultural sensitivity training, conflict mediation, and hate crime legislation.

REFERENCES

Cornell, S., & Hartman, D. (1998). *Ethnicity and race: Making identities in a changing world*. Thousand Oaks, CA: Pine Forge.

Daniel, G. R. (2002). *More than black?: Multiracial identity and the new racial order*. Philadelphia, PA: Temple University Press.

Doob, C. B. (1999). *Racism: An American cauldron* (3rd ed.). New York: Longman.

Feagin, J. R., & Feagin, C. B. (1999). *Racial and ethnic relations* (6th ed.). Upper Saddle River, NJ: Prentice Hall.

Root, M. P. P. (Ed.). (1992). *Racially mixed people in America*. Newbury Park, CA: Sage.

Root, M. P. P. (Ed.). (1996). *The multiracial experience: Racial borders as the new frontier* (pp. 277-290). Thousand Oaks, CA: Sage.

Spencer, R. (1999). *Spurious issues: Race and multiracial identity politics in the United States*. Boulder, CO: Westview Press.

Zack, N. (1993). *Race and mixed race*. Philadelphia, PA: Temple University.

Zack, N. (1995). *American mixed race: the culture of microdiversity*. Lanham, MD: Rowman & Littlefield.

Zack, N. (1998). *Thinking about race*. Belmont, CA: Wadsworth.

Author Index

Payne, R. J., 89
Pearlman, L. A., 9
Penn, W. S., 34, 290
Peters, K. M., 213
Phoenix, A., 290
Pinderhughes, E., 339, 342, 352
Piper, A., 178, 313, 320
Polednak, A. P., 120
Pollard, A. B. III, 26
Pollard, K. M., 48, 60
Ponterotto, J. G., 145, 146, 148, 337, 338, 339, 342
Pope, R. L., 138, 139, 336
Porterfield, E., 356, 359
Povich, M., 280
Powell, L. C., 290
Powell, R. D., 357, 362, 366, 367
Priest, R., 338, 339, 340
Prucha, F. P., 50, 51, 52, 62
Pryor, R., 324-325
Purdie, S., 324

Ragaza, A., 162
Ramirez, D., 89
Ramirez, M., III., 9, 11
Ramirez, R., 212
Ramphele, M., 276
Reddy, M., 290
Reichmann, R., 261, 262, 263
Reuter, E. B., 24, 54, 336, 352
Reynolds, A. L., 138, 139, 336
Rich, A., 180
Robinson, E., 57, 62
Robinson, L. S., 266
Rockquemore, K. A., 57, 294, 342
Rodriguez, C. E., 6, 15, 56
Rodriguez, N. M., 290
Rodriguez, R., 182, 183, 184, 190
Roediger, D., 290, 291, 292
Rogin, M., 324
Rohrer, J., 236, 239, 240, 242, 243, 244
Romero, J., 212
Root, M. P. P., 6, 7, 8, 11, 13, 14, 15, 16, 17, 27, 57, 72, 79, 81, 82, 95, 112, 121, 144, 158, 159, 161, 165, 224, 226, 290, 313, 320, 336, 338, 340, 373, 374, 375
Rosa, J., 235, 236
Rosen, H., 49
Rosenblatt, P., 357, 362, 366, 367
Russell, K., 24, 25
Russell-Wood, A. J. R., 256, 257, 258

Sahlins, M., 230, 242
Salinas, R., 329
Salins, P., 135, 136, 138, 151
Sandefur, G. D., 197
Sanjek, R., 6, 62
Sato, J. T., 8
Saxton, A., 290

Scales-Trent, J., 290, 313, 320
Schaefer, R. T., 30
Scheick, W. J., 325
Schemo, D. J., 292, 294, 296
Schlesinger, A. M., Jr., 365
Schmitt, E., 100
Schoen, R., 147
Schultze, C., 61
Schultze, G., 90
Schuman, H., 61, 364
Schwartz, G., 341
Schwarz, B., 176
Scibetta, B. S., 162, 163
Secord, P. F., 8, 13
Senna, D., 4, 290, 293, 305
Shelden, R. G., 347
Shell, R., 269, 270
Shinagawa, L. H., 159
Shirley, D., 164
Shukert, E. B., 162, 163
Siguenza, H., 329
Sikes, M. P., 278
Silva, N., 262 do V., 262
Simmons, M., 262
Skidmore, T. A., 256, 258, 259, 260, 261, 262, 263, 266
Skrentny, J. P., 76
Smedley, A., 51, 52, 62
Smelser, N. J., 61
Smith, A. S., xii
Smith, B., 313
Smith, R. A., 61
Smith, R. C., 92
Smith, S. K., 203
Smith, S. M., 303, 317
Snipp, C. M., 56, 62, 197
Sobel, M., 251
Sollors, W., 29, 41, 290
Solomos, J., 23
Song, M., 290
Sparks, A., 273, 274, 275, 276
Spencer, J. M., 33, 69, 159, 161, 162, 163, 168, 290, 292, 294
Spencer, R., 24, 28, 29, 30, 106, 195, 197, 213, 290, 292, 294, 374, 375
Spicer, P., 206
Spickard, P., 6, 48, 170, 234, 250, 251, 252, 253, 290, 291, 292, 295, 296, 297, 308, 318, 324, 339, 356, 359, 374
Spickard, P. R.,
Spivak, G. C., 266
Spohn, C., 31
Spradley, J. P., 359
Springwood, C. F., 201, 202
Sprott, J. E., 206
Stager, S. F., 341, 348
Starr, P., 86
Staub, E., 9

Subject Index

About the Editors

Herman L. DeBose is Associate Professor at California State University, Northridge in the Sociology Department. He has a BS in sociology from North Carolina Agriculture and Technical State University, a master's of social work from University of Southern California, and a PhD in social welfare from University of California, Los Angeles. His research interest focuses on multiracial identity, HIV/AIDS, juvenile delinquency, and community policing. This research has afforded him the opportunity to make at least 25 presentations at national, regional, and local professional conferences and meetings covering a wide range of topics. It has also led to publications and contributions to a report on *Working to End Gang Violence,* submitted to the California State University Chancellor's Office.

Loretta I. Winters is Associate Professor of Sociology at California State University, Northridge (CSUN). She also served as Coordinator of the American Indian Studies Program at CSUN August 1999 through July 2001. She received her PhD in sociology from University of California, Riverside. Her research interests include multiracial identity, teen pregnancy, and natural disasters. She recently published "Disasters" (with Harvey E. Rich) in *California's Social Problems* (2nd ed., 2002). Other publications include a book review of the work edited by Ahenakew, Freda, and H. C. Wolfart, *Our Grandmothers' Lives as Told in Their Own Words,* in the *American Indian Culture and Research Journal* (1994); "Dear Christopher" in Darryl Wilson and Barry Joyce's *Dear Christopher: Letters to Christopher Columbus by Contemporary Native Americans* (1992); and (with Herman DeBose) chapters in *Human Geography of African American* (1999); and *Foundations of African American Education* (1998). She is enrolled as Mississauga with Indian and Northern Affairs in Canada and is also of Polish American descent.

About the Contributors

Karren Baird-Olson is Assistant Professor of Sociology and Coordinator of the American Indian Studies program at California State University, Northridge. She earned her BS from Montana State University, Bozeman; her MA from the University of Montana, Missoula; and her PhD from the University of New Mexico, Albuquerque. She is of Wyandot descent and in 1958 she married into the Nakota Nation of the Fort Peck Assiniboine and Sioux Reservation (Montana). Her publications include articles on American Indian women's spirituality, victimization, and leadership and First Peoples and crime.

Nancy G. Brown, MN, CNS, is a clinical nurse specialist in mental health, having received her BS in nursing from Boston University and her MS in Psychiatric Nursing/Community Consultation from University of California, Los Angeles. She is a first-generation American, born in New York City and raised in New Jersey, and is of German-Jewish heritage. She currently works as a psychotherapist with the Kaiser Department of Psychiatry in West Los Angeles. Nancy has been a partner in an interracial marriage since 1977 and has two multiracial daughters. This was a major impetus for her cofounding of Multiracial Americans of Southern California (MASC), a nonprofit organization, in 1987. She served as president for 7 years and continues to serve on the board of directors. Nancy was also an affiliate representative for MASC at the annual AMEA meetings for many years. She has held the position of western regional vice president since 1994. She was elected president of AMEA in May 2001.

G. Reginald Daniel, PhD, is Assistant Professor in the Department of Sociology at University of California, Santa Barbara. He teaches courses exploring comparative race and ethnic relations. Since 1989 he has taught Betwixt and Between, one of the first and longest-standing courses in the United States to deal with multiracial identity. He authored "Passers and Pluralists: Subverting the Racial Divide" and "Beyond Black and White: The New Multiracial Consciousness," both chapters in *Racially Mixed People in America* (1992). Daniel's *More Than Black? Multiracial Identity* *and the New Racial Order* (2001) is a culmination of much of his thinking on this topic. In addition, Daniel has received a great deal of media attention and participated as a panelist at various conferences on the topic of multiracial identity. He is a member of the advisory board of Association of MultiEthnic Americans and a former advisory board member of Project RACE (Reclassify All Children Equally). Daniel's own multiracial identity includes African, Native American, Irish, East Indian, French, English, and possibly German-Jewish origins.

Laura Desfor Edles is Assistant Professor of Sociology at California State University, Northridge. Her primary interests are in culture, theory, politics, and race/ethnicity. She is the author of two books, *Symbol and Ritual in the New Spain: The Transition to Democracy After Franco* (1998) and *Cultural Sociology in Practice* (2002), as well as various articles on culture, social movements, and social theory.

Ramona E. Douglass has been a civil rights activist for nearly three decades. As a multiracial adult of Italian, Native American/Lakota, and mixed African American heritage, she has been a part of the multiracial movement in America since its inception. She was a pioneer in supporting freedom of choice in politics as a founding member of the National Alliance Against Racist and Political Repression and as an outspoken participant with Angela Davis's Political Defense Committee in the early 1970s. As a U.S. Department of Commerce federal appointee to the 2000 Census Advisory Committee in Washington, D.C., since 1995 she has consistently represented multiracial community interests before Congress, the national media, and the Executive Office of the President. She has been a part of the Association of MultiEthnic Americans (AMEA) board of directors since its inception in 1988, serving in the capacities of vice president (1988–1994), president (1994–1999), and currently director of media and public relations. She has also had a successful 26-year career in medical sales and marketing and is now a senior sales manager and corporate trainer for a medical manufacturing company in the San Fernando Valley. She has BS degree in geology and chemistry from Colorado State University and an AMS certification in medical sales.

Kristyan M. Kouri is an Instructor in the Departments of Sociology and Women's Studies at California State University, Northridge, where she has received numerous awards in recognition of her excellence in teaching and mentoring. She holds a BA in behavioral science from California State Polytechnic University, Pomona and a PhD in sociology from the University of Southern California. Her studies of black-white interracial families have garnered dozens of speaking invitations, and her findings have been published in both the scholarly and popular press.

Kimberly McClain DaCosta is Assistant Professor of Afro-American Studies and Social Studies at Harvard University. She received her PhD in sociology from the University of California, Berkeley in 2000.

Ann Morning is a PhD candidate in sociology at Princeton University. She specializes in racial classification in demography and has been invited to present her research at the meetings of the American Sociological Association, National Association for Ethnic Studies, and Population Association of America. Her publications include "The Multiple-Race Population of the United States: Issues and Estimates" (with Joshua Goldstein) in *Proceedings of the National Academy of Sciences*; "The Racial Self-Identification of South Asians in the United States" in *Journal of Ethnic and Migration Studies*, and "Who is Multiracial? Definitions and Decisions" in *Sociological Imagination*.

Patricia O'Donnell Brummett is Associate Professor of Sociology and Criminology at California State University, Northridge. She received her PhD in sociology from the University of Notre Dame. O'Donnell Brummett has published two articles on employee assistance program referrals in *Employee Assistance Quarterly*. In addition, she has been the co-principal investigator of a grant stemming from California Bill AB-2650 (Cardenas-D), which evaluated the Communities in Schools of San Fernando Valley gang prevention and intervention programs. She also authored and served as a researcher for a grant from the federal Department of Education to investigate the linkages between drugs and alcohol and violence at California State University, Northridge. Her research interests include gangs, community policing, drug and alcohol use among college students, women and crime, and employee assistance programs.

Darby Li Po Price is a lecturer at the University of California at Santa Cruz, and has taught at DePaul University, Vassar College, the University of California at both Berkeley and Davis, and the Encampment for Citizenship. He completed his PhD at the University of California, Berkeley, in Ethnic Studies. Price has published essays in *Amerasia Journal, American Indian Culture and Research Journal, Critical Mass*, and many anthologies.

Maria P. P. Root, PhD, a psychologist in Seattle, Washington, has researched and published extensively on the topic of multiracial identity development and related topics such as minority mental health, gender, and trauma. She has edited and authored six books, two of which are award winning: *Racially Mixed People in America* (1992) and *The Multiracial Experience: Racial Borders as the New Frontier* (1996). Her most recent book is *Love's Revolution: Racial Intermarriage* (2001). She has received several career contribution and research awards from the Washington State Psychological Association, American Psychological Association, Asian American Psychological Association, American Family Therapy Academy, and Filipino American National Historical Society. She is president of the Washington State Psychological Association.

Rainier Spencer is Associate Dean of the College of Liberal Arts and Director of Afro-American Studies at the University of Nevada, Las Vegas. He is the author of *Spurious Issues: Race and Multiracial Identity Politics in the United States* (1999), as well as several book chapters and journal articles on multiracial identity. His research focuses on interrogating the ways that biological race is reified in the ideology of the multiracial identity movement in the United States.

Paul Spickard is Professor of History at the University of California, Santa Barbara. He holds degrees from Harvard University and University of California, Berkeley and has taught at 10 universities in the United States, Asia, and the Pacific. He is the author and editor of many articles and 10 books, including *Mixed Blood: Intermarriage and Ethnic Identity in 20th-Century America* (1989), *Japanese Americans (1996), and Uncompleted Independence: Racial Thinking in the United States* (with G. Reginald Daniel, forthcoming).

Caroline A. Streeter received her PhD in Ethnic Studies from the University of California, Berkeley. Her dissertation concerned representations of the "mulatta" in post-civil rights era American literature, film, and popular culture. From 2000 to 2002 she held a Postdoctoral Fellowship at the Center for Cultural Studies at the University of California, Santa Cruz. In fall 2002, she joined the Department of English and the Center for African American Studies at the University of California, Los Angeles, as an Assistant Professor.

Mary Thierry Texeira is Associate Professor at California State University, San Bernadino, and teaches classes that explore gender, race, class, criminal, justice, and critical thinking. She holds a PhD in Sociology from the University of California, Riverside. Her research focuses on the complexities, contradictions, ambiguities, and consequences of race, racialization, and racial designation in the United States. She has published articles and reviews on racial profiling in the criminal justice system, symbolic legislation, women in prison, racial taxonomy, teaching about race in the classroom, and preparing African Americans for a college career. She is also a wife, mother, grandmother, voracious reader, and power walker.

Gregory Velazco y Trianosky is Professor of Philosophy and Chicano/a Studies at California State University, Northridge. He is the son of a Ukrainian father and a Puerto Rican mother. He earned his AB from Georgetown University in 1974 and his PhD in philosophy from the University of Michigan in 1980. He was the first in his family to graduate from college. He has taught at many universities, including the University of North Carolina at Chapel Hill and the University of Michigan in Ann Arbor and in Flint. His work on moral character has been internationally published and reprinted. His current research is divided between work on a subversive reinterpretation of our concept of race and a study of the altruistic virtues.

Kim M. Williams is Assistant Professor of Public Policy at the Kennedy School of Government, Harvard University, and specializes in race-ethnic politics and political movements. She has received fellowships and awards from the Ford Foundation, Dartmouth College, Horowitz Foundation for Social Policy, Center for Advanced Study in the Behavioral Sciences at Stanford University, Mathematical Policy Research Inc., and American Political Science Association. She received her BA from the University of California at Berkeley and her PhD from Cornell University. She is currently finishing a book, *Ironies of the Post-Civil Rights Era: The U.S. Multiracial Movement*, and has contributed to a number of edited volumes.

Teresa Williams-León is Associate Professor and Associate Chair of the Asian American Studies Department at California State University, Northridge. She received her BA from the University of Hawai'i in Japanese and MAs in Asian American studies and sociology and a PhD in sociology from University of California, Los Angeles (UCLA). Dr. Williams-León has taught courses on multiracial/multiethnic identity at UCLA; University of California, Santa Barbara; Santa Monica College; and California State University, Northridge. She has written numerous articles and book chapters on multiracial identity, including *Prism Lives/Emerging Voices of Multiracial Asians*, an annotated bibliography on mixed-race Asian Americans (compiled with Steven Masami Ropp and Curtiss Takada Rooks); a special issue of the *Amerasia Journal* entitled "No Passing Zone: Artistic and Discursive Writings by and About Asian-Descent Multiracials" (coedited with Velina Hasu Houston); and *The Sum of Our Parts: Mixed Heritage Asian Americans*, a social scientific anthology (coedited with Cynthia L. Nakashima). She is the recipient of the 2002 Hapa Issues Forum 10th Anniversary Gala Academic Contribution Prism Award.